TAKING SIDES

Clashing Views in

Lifespan Development

SECOND EDITION

TAKING SIDES

Clashing Views in
Lifespan Development
SECOND EDITION

Selected, Edited, and with Introductions by

Andrew M. Guest
University of Portland

Higher Education

Boston   Burr Ridge, IL   Dubuque, IA   New York   San Francisco   St. Louis
Bangkok   Bogotá   Caracas   Kuala Lumpur   Lisbon   London   Madrid   Mexico City
Milan   Montreal   New Delhi   Santiago   Seoul   Singapore   Sydney   Taipei   Toronto

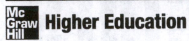

Higher Education

TAKING SIDES: CLASHING VIEWS IN LIFESPAN DEVELOPMENT, SECOND EDITION

Published by McGraw-Hill, a business unit of The McGraw-Hill Companies, Inc., 1221 Avenue of the Americas, New York, NY 10020. Copyright © 2009 by The McGraw-Hill Companies, Inc. All rights reserved. Previous edition(s) 1999–2007. No part of this publication may be reproduced or distributed in any form or by any means, or stored in a database or retrieval system, without the prior written consent of The McGraw-Hill Companies, Inc., including, but not limited to, in any network or other electronic storage or transmission, or broadcast for distance learning.

Some ancillaries, including electronic and print components, may not be available to customers outside the United States.

Taking Sides® is a registered trademark of the McGraw-Hill Companies, Inc.
Taking Sides is published by the **Contemporary Learning Series** group within the McGraw-Hill Higher Education division.

2 3 4 5 6 7 8 9 0 DOC/DOC 0 9

MHID: 0-07-351528-0
ISBN: 978-0-07-351528-1
ISSN: 1559-2642

Managing Editor: *Larry Loeppke*
Production Manager: *Faye Schilling*
Senior Developmental Editor: *Jill Peter*
Editorial Assistant: *Nancy Meissner*
Production Service Assistant: *Rita Hingtgen*
Permissions Coordinator: *Lori Church*
Senior Marketing Manager: *Julie Keck*
Marketing Communications Specialist: *Mary Klein*
Marketing Coordinator: *Alice Link*
Project Manager: *Jane Mohr*
Design Specialist: *Tara McDermott*
Senior Administrative Assistant: *DeAnna Dausener*
Cover Graphics: *Kristine Jubeck*

Compositor: Hurix Systems Private Limited
Cover Image: Digital Archive Japan/PunchStock

www.mhhe.com

Preface

We all have a vested stake in the study of lifespan development because we are all experts in the ages and stages of our own lives. Yet our experiences, and our understandings of those experiences, vary dramatically from person to person. Where some of us are sure that our childhood interactions with our parents shaped everything about the way we function in the world, others are convinced that we are living out a biologically or genetically determined destiny. While many people see childhood as a period of risks and challenges, others appreciate the joy and opportunity of being young. Where we often focus on adulthood as defined by careers and family, we also recognize that well-being in adulthood depends upon abstract qualities such as happiness and success. In one sense, these types of contrasts show how the study of lifespan development is inherently controversial. The purpose of this book is to make that controversy useful by providing educated and intelligent perspectives on issues that are important to everyone's life, not to mention being important to academic study of the lifespan.

This second edition of *Taking Sides: Clashing Views on Controversial Issues in Lifespan Development* presents 20 issues that challenge students and scholars to think deeply about issues confronted throughout the ages and stages of our lives. Each issue is framed by a question about what, why, or how we develop, and each question is addressed from two distinct perspectives presenting different views. These 40 views represent high quality contemporary work by scholars and experts. Each of the 20 issues also has an introduction with an explanation of how and why it is important for the larger study of lifespan development, and a postscript providing challenge questions to elaborate on the issue along with suggestions for further reading.

The materials and ideas dealt with in this book derive from diverse fields of study including psychology, sociology, biology, cognitive science, gerontology, and pediatrics. In fact, one appealing aspect of studying lifespan development is that it is an interdisciplinary subject focused on answering interesting questions. Thus, while the materials provided with each issue allow an understanding of what experts in diverse subjects think, the challenge for readers is to use the evidence and opinions to answer the questions for themselves. The book explains, for example, why understanding how much our development depends upon our parents is important, but it is up to readers to take that explanation and the available evidence to establish their own educated position.

Although the perspectives presented in this book represent educated thinking on these issues, the reason the issues are controversial is because that thinking is still evolving. Researchers are always developing new techniques for studying human development, individuals are always adapting to the different challenges faced at each stage of life, and societies are always changing the way they treat children, adults, and the elderly. Likewise, readers of this book, as experts in their own lifespan development, will have valuable experiences and perspectives that complement those discussed in the book. In the end, what is most important is to have a point of view on these issues that is educated and informed—sometimes that point of view will match earlier beliefs, other times it will represent a dramatic change. In all cases, however, the most valuable understandings derive from using controversy as an opportunity to think through the challenges of our lives.

A word to the instructor   An *Instructor's Resource Guide with Test Questions* (multiple-choice and essay) is available through the publisher for the instructor using Taking Sides in the classroom. A general guidebook, *Using Taking Sides in the Classroom,* which discusses methods and techniques for integrating the pro-con approach into any classroom setting, is also available. An online version of *Using Taking Sides in the Classroom* and a correspondence service for Taking Sides adopters can be found at http://www.mhcls.com/usingts/.

Taking Sides: Clashing Views in Lifespan Development is only one title in the Taking Sides series. If you are interested in seeing the table of contents for any of the other titles, please visit the Taking Sides Web site at http://www.mhcls.com/takingsides/.

Acknowledgments   I greatly appreciate the opportunities for learning about the lifespan provided by my former teachers and colleagues at the University of Chicago's Committee on Human Development and by my current students at the University of Portland (who allowed me the opportunity to draft all the material with an intelligent and critical audience). Beyond those groups, I owe the most thanks to Sara Guest for her support and understanding.

Contents In Brief

Contents

Victoria Rideout, Elizabeth Hamel, and the Kaiser Family Foundation find that television and electronic media allow families to cope with busy schedules and are of value to parents of infants. Psychologists Daniel Anderson and Tiffany Pempek, instead focus on infant learning. In their review of available literature, they concur with the American Academy of Pediatrics in recommending that infants should have no exposure to television.

UNIT 3   EARLY CHILDHOOD AND MIDDLE CHILDHOOD   137

In a review of research on media exposure and childhood obesity the Kaiser Family Foundation concludes that exposure to advertising, more than inactivity, best explains the increasing rates of childhood obesity. In contrast, the Federal Trade Commission Bureau of Economics Staff specifically evaluated television advertising to children and found that increasing rates of childhood obesity do not correspond with increasing exposure to food advertising.

The U.S. Department of Health and Human Services argues that preschool programs can help young children most by emphasizing academic and cognitive skills. Professors C. Cybele Raver and Edward F. Zigler argue that overemphasizing academic and cognitive skills at the expense of social, emotional, and physical well-being is a mistake dependent on misguided efforts to make the entire educational system focused on concrete assessment.

UNIT 5   YOUTH AND EARLY ADULTHOOD   267

UNIT 6   MIDDLE ADULTHOOD   303

Sociologist Andrew J. Cherlin suggests that the institution of marriage is losing its preeminence and may become just one of many relationship options for couples. Frank Furstenberg, on the other hand, proposes that the institution of marriage will persist with appropriate government policies and support to families.

The American Psychological Association's research concluded that all of the evidence suggests that lesbian and gay couples are as equally competent to parent as heterosexual couples. In contrast, Timothy Dailey asserts that homosexual relationships are less stable than heterosexual marriages and thus are less able to provide a stable two-parent home for children.

Psychologist and author David Myers asserts that religion is an antidote to the discontent many adults feel despite incredible relative material wealth. Professor of psychology Julia Juola Exline asserts that research suggesting religion to be a pure good for adult development neglects to account for the fact that it can also be a source of significant sadness, stress, and confusion.

With a drastically increasing population of the elderly, professors of medicine John W. Rowe and Robert L. Kahn suggest that a unified model of healthy aging is necessary to guide work with the elderly. Martha B. Holstein and Meredith Minkler, professors of religion and public health, respectively, counter that a unified model of successful aging is based on particular values and assumptions that may not be fair to marginalized populations.

Although mental exercises designed to maintain mental functioning in old age have become quite popular, psychologist Timothy Salthouse asserts that there is little convincing evidence to support that appealing idea. Carmi Schooler, a researcher at the National Institute of Mental Health, counters that although the loss of mental functioning with age is not fully understood there is good reason to believe that more activity can delay cognitive decline.

Philosopher Richard T. Hull claims that allowing physician-assisted suicide will appropriately give control over dying to patients and families rather than medical professionals. Ethicist Margaret Somerville instead asserts that allowing euthanasia oversimplifies the complex issues at the end of life, and allows people to ignore the imperative of providing appropriate care.

Correlation Guide

The *Taking Sides* series presents current issues in a debate-style format designed to stimulate student interest and develop critical thinking skills. Each issue is thoughtfully framed with an issue summary, an issue introduction with points and counterpoints, and challenge questions. The pro and con essays—selected for their liveliness and substance—represent the arguments of leading scholars and commentators in their fields.

Taking Sides: Clashing Views in Lifespan Development, 2/e is an easy-to-use reader that presents issues on important topics such as *childhood obesity, self-esteem,* and *successful aging.* For more information on *Taking Sides* and other *McGraw-Hill Contemporary Learning Series* titles, visit www.mhcls.com.

This convenient guide matches the issues in **Taking Sides: Lifespan Development, 2/e** with the corresponding chapters in two of our best-selling McGraw-Hill Lifespan Development textbooks by Santrock.

Taking Sides: Lifespan Development, 2/e	A Topical Approach to Life-Span Development, 4/e by Santrock	Essentials of Life-Span Development, 1/e by Santrock
Issue 1: Does the Cultural Environment Influence Lifespan Development More Than Our Genes?	**Chapter 2:** Biological Beginnings	**Chapter 4:** Socioemotional Development in Infancy
Issue 2: Are Peers More Important than Parents During the Process of Development?	**Chapter 15:** Peers and the Sociocultural World	**Chapter 10:** Socioemotional Development in Adolescence
Issue 3: Do Significant Innate Differences Influence the Career Success of Males and Females?	**Chapter 12:** Gender and Sexuality	
Issue 4: Does Prenatal Exposure to Drugs Such as Cocaine Create "Crack Babies" With Special Developmental Concerns?	**Chapter 2:** Biological Beginnings	**Chapter 2:** Biological Beginnings
Issue 5: Is There a "Myth of the First Three Years?"		**Chapter 5:** Physical and Cognitive Development in Early Childhood
Issue 6: Are There Good Reasons to Allow Infants to Consume Electronic Media, Such as Television?	**Chapter 15:** Peers and the Sociocultural World	**Chapter 6:** Socioemotional Development in Early Childhood
Issue 7: Is Advertising Responsible for Childhood Obesity?	**Chapter 4:** Health	

Taking Sides: Lifespan Development, 2/e	A Topical Approach to Life-Span Development, 4/e by Santrock	Essentials of Life-Span Development, 1/e by Santrock
Issue 8: Does Emphasizing Academic Skills Help At-Risk Preschool Children?	**Chapter 16:** Schools, Achievement, and Work	**Chapter 5:** Physical and Cognitive Development in Early Childhood
Issue 9: Is Attention Deficit Disorder (ADD/ADHD) a Legitimate Medical Condition That Affects Childhood Behavior?	**Chapter 16:** Schools, Achievement, and Work	**Chapter 7:** Physical and Cognitive Development in Middle and Late Childhood
Issue 10: Are Efforts to Improve Self-Esteem Misguided?	**Chapter 11:** The Self, Identity, and Personality	**Chapter 8:** Socioemotional Development in Middle and Late Childhood
Issue 11: Should Contemporary Adolescents Be Engaged in More Structured Activities?		
Issue 12: Does Violent Media Cause Teenage Aggression?	**Chapter 13:** Moral Development, Values, and Religion **Chapter 15:** Peers and the Sociocultural World	**Chapter 6:** Socioemotional Development in Early Childhood
Issue 13: Are Contemporary Young Adults More Selfish than Previous Generations?		
Issue 14: Are College Graduates Unprepared for Adulthood and the World of Work?	**Chapter 16:** Schools, Achievement, and Work	**Chapter 11:** Physical and Cognitive Development in Early Adulthood
Issue 15: Is the Institution of Marriage at Risk?	**Chapter 14:** Families, Lifestyles, and Parenting	**Chapter 12:** Socioemotional Development in Early Adulthood
Issue 16: Can Lesbian and Gay Couples Be Appropriate Parents for Children?	**Chapter 14:** Families, Lifestyles, and Parenting	**Chapter 6:** Socioemotional Development in Early Childhood
Issue 17: Is Religion a Pure Good in Facilitating Well-Being During Adulthood?	**Chapter 13:** Moral Development, Values and Religion	**Chapter 13:** Physical and Cognitive Development in Middle Adulthood
Issue 18: Can We Universally Define "Successful Aging"?	**Chapter 15:** Peers and the Sociocultural World	**Chapter 16:** Socioemotional Development in Late Adulthood
Issue 19: Are Brain Exercises Unhelpful in Preventing Cognitive Decline in Old Age?	**Chapter 7:** Information Processing	**Chapter 15:** Physical and Cognitive Development in Late Adulthood
Issue 20: Should the Terminally Ill Be Able to Have Physicians Help Them Die?	**Chapter 17:** Death, Dying, and Grieving	**Chapter 17:** Death, Dying, and Grieving

Introduction

Thinking about Change

The study of lifespan development centers on a question of great intuitive interest: Do people ever really change? Can an introverted child who is full of worry become a confident and composed adult? Might an apathetic student go on to become successful in the world of work? Do relationships with those we care about inevitably shift across the years?

These types of questions weighed heavily on my mind many years ago when I was a 17-year-old preparing to leave the only home I had ever known to attend college. On the night I was leaving, I rode to the airport with my father, a well-educated and thoughtful man. We were rushing so that I could board an overnight flight from the West Coast to the East Coast, bringing with me all my worldly possessions in two suitcases. As with so many adolescents going off to college, I was both excited and overwhelmed by possibilities. My imagination flowed with ideas about who and what I might become, and most of those ideas centered on a hope that I could change for the better. I loved the idea of self-improvement; I was devoted to developing into a "better person." As I talked with my father, expressing my hopes in anxious tones, he listened calmly. Finally, when we arrived at the gate and it was time for me to board my plane, my father looked at me casually and said: "You know, in my experience, people don't really change." I was stunned.

From his perspective as a mature adult, using the wisdom accumulated through his life, my father told me that while people might change the things they do, the places they live, the details of their daily routine, they do not change who they are in deep and substantive ways. With youthful idealism, I firmly disagreed. I felt deeply that people could change across the lifespan, so much so that understanding aspects of that change became my life's work. Now, as a developmental psychologist, I've studied, read, and investigated many aspects of how people do and don't change. And in looking back I have to admit that in ways my father was right: in certain ways people don't change. But the story is much more complicated and wonderful than that. And that story is told through the study of lifespan development: the study of patterns in human thought, feelings, and behavior in relation to particular ages, with general attention to change over time.

The study of lifespan development makes clear that even the continuities in life, the things that do not change, take place in shifting contexts: changing social environments, changing physical capacities, changing psychological perspectives. As such, I've come to appreciate, and be fascinated by, the necessary interaction of change and continuity in people through their lives—how can people be both the same and different? That question involves inherent contradictions and inherent controversy, which suggests that the study of lifespan development is particularly well-suited to the nature of this book: it advances by taking conflicting perspectives on complex and important issues regarding change and continuity through life.

History of the Study of Lifespan Development

Historically the question of how people do (or do not) change through their lives has evoked opposing perspectives. Many ancient societies assumed that people were created with a pre-determined character that was destined through some supernatural power. Yet those beliefs were tempered by the realization that what people experience matters. Parents, societies, and philosophers have long negotiated between an assumption that people have an inherent developmental destiny, and the knowledge that what happens to people in the social world can alter that destiny.

While these positions have an extensive history, in academic circles they are most commonly identified with 17th and 18th century European philosophers Jean-Jacques Rousseau and John Locke. Rousseau suggested that infants were "noble savages" born with an inherent nature that is only corrupted by society. Locke, in contrast, is known for the famous claim that people come into the world as a *tabula rasa*, or blank slate, to be shaped entirely by experience. In a recent book about the history of child rearing advice in America, Ann Hulbert argues this opposition plays itself out in many subsequent historical epochs: one group argues that people have potent natural dispositions guiding development with a strong hand, while another group asserts that people develop entirely through social experiences. The recurring nature of this opposition shows one way in which those who are concerned with lifespan development have always been "taking sides."

Taking a scientific, rather than philosophical or parental, approach to understanding development has only become a widespread endeavor in recent centuries. In fact, the idea of childhood as a distinct lifespan stage, rather than as just adulthood in miniature, may be a relatively recent invention. In a famous and controversial book titled *Centuries of Childhood*, French historian Philippe Aries argued that Western societies only began treating children as different from adults in the 15th and 16th centuries, and such treatment did not become commonplace until the 19th and 20th centuries. This theory has generated strong reactions, with many scholars responding to say that childhood has always been associated with distinct characteristics. Nevertheless, the idea that contemporary perspectives on childhood are historically exceptional has much support: the transition to worlds of adulthood with work and responsibility happens later than ever. Partially as a result, we now take for granted that people advance through different stages of life. Further, scholars and scientists from diverse fields of study recognize that the lifespan needs to be understood within the context of those stages.

So what are the stages? That question turns out to be more complicated than many people expect. While we are always talking about "children," or "youth," or "middle-age," or the "elderly" the characteristics of such stages are not entirely distinct. Much of how we understand these stages depends upon earlier schemes.

Perhaps the most famous such scheme was presented by Sigmund Freud. In the late 19th century Freud provoked and dismayed Western society by proposing that unconscious experiences in very early childhood, often of a sexual nature, formed personality throughout the rest of the lifespan. Freud further asserted that the formative experiences cohered around different foci at different ages: infants were concerned with oral gratification—being able to suck and bite, toddlers with anal functions and toilet training, young children with phallic organs—learning about gender roles, and teenagers with genital functions—experiencing puberty and a blossoming sexuality. For Freud, the way a person negotiated those foci influenced them for the rest of their lives. While there is a general consensus that Freud placed far too much emphasis on sexuality as the axis of all development, his theory contributed much. We now take for granted that early experiences shape later life, and we recognize that those experiences occur in a stagewise progression.

While Freud focused on personality development, another influential scientist working in the early and middle part of the 20th century turned scholarly attention to stages of cognitive development: the Swiss psychologist Jean Piaget virtually founded modern developmental psychology through his recognition that the way children think progresses in orderly patterns. Piaget based his provocative insight on rigorous observations suggesting that children's cognitive functioning (the way they think) develops naturally through a series of detached steps. In a way, Piaget provided enduring support for stage models, suggesting that children's thinking is not just less sophisticated than that of adults—it is qualitatively different. Thus, when children make assumptions about toy dolls being alive, or about objects only existing when they can see them, they are not making "errors" but instead are demonstrating patterns of thought that meaningfully represent their age. Piaget's work is still the standard for much research in child development, though some of his specific claims have become controversial. As such, several issues in this book explicitly reference the work and legacy of Piaget.

A third giant in the history of the study of lifespan development was a student of Freud's named Erik Erikson. In the middle part of the 20th century Erikson took Freud's basic insights about personality, built on the increasing popularity of stage models for the lifespan, and outlined an influential framework for understanding lifespan development—a framework that guides the organization of this book. Erikson's model of the lifespan had two major advantages over previous models. First, in contrast to Freud, Erikson reduced the emphasis on sexuality, focusing on psychosocial challenges rather than psychosexual stages. Second, in contrast to both Freud and Piaget, Erikson asserted that developmental stages continue throughout life, rather than ending after adolescence.

Though this now seems somewhat obvious—of course adults continue to develop—for much of the 20th century scholars paid little attention to anything other than child development. The implicit assumption was that the lifespan included a period of rapid growth during childhood, a period of decline at the end of life, and was largely at stasis in the many years of adulthood. In recent decades, however, scholars have recognized that a great deal of patterned development and change occurs during the long years of adulthood.

Finally, Erik Erikson was influential because he recognized the "biopsychosocial" nature of lifespan development. While biology, psychology, and society are often studied separately, biological factors (such as physical health, sexual maturation, and genetic predispositions) interact with psychological factors (such as personality, attitudes, and cognitive appraisals), which interact with social factors (such as schools, peer networks, the media, and cultural meaning systems) to craft our individual lives. Some of the issues addressed in this book involve all three of these types of influences, while some emphasize one or the other. Overall, however, the collection of issues as a whole represents diverse and interacting influences.

Modern advances in technology and research methods allow us to study biological, psychological, and sociological influences on the lifespan with increasing depth and accuracy. But the contemporary issues covered in this book still rely upon some fundamental insights from history, and as such are organized by an idea shared by all the major scholars of lifespan development: different ages associate with meaningfully different patterns of thought and behavior. Beyond that shared idea, however, no stage model proposed by any one leading scholar is perfect: the nature and definition of the stages remains controversial. Perhaps the only thing about stages of the lifespan that we can say with certainty is that they are only as meaningful as the society in which they are used. Thus, it is important to consider the stages of lifespan in their own historical and cultural context.

Stages of the Lifespan in Context

Representations of the lifespan as a series of stages exist across centuries and across cultural traditions. These representations are interesting to consider both for their diversity and for their similarity. There is something universal about patterns of development, but there are also tremendous local differences in how those patterns look.

From an Eastern tradition, stages are represented in a parable about how Confucius, who lived between 551–479 BC, reflected on his life:

> At 15 I set my heart upon learning.
> At 30 I had planted my feet firmly upon the ground.
> At 40 I no longer suffered from perplexities.
> At 50 I knew what were the biddings of heaven.
> At 60 I heard them with docile ear.
> At 70 I could follow the dictates of my own heart; for what I desired no longer overstepped the boundaries of right.

From classic Western literature, Shakespeare articulated the lifespan in his play "As You Like It" as different ages of man:

> At first the infant, Mewling and puking in the nurse's arms.
> And then the whining school-boy, with his satchel
> And shining morning face, creeping like snail
> Unwillingly to school.

And then the lover,
Sighing like furnace, with a woeful ballad
Made to his mistress' eyebrow.
Then a soldier,
Full of strange oaths and bearded like the pard,
Jealous in honour, sudden and quick in quarrel,
Seeking the bubble reputation
Even in the cannon's mouth.
And then the justice,
In fair round belly with good capon lined,
With eyes severe and beard of formal cut,
Full of wise saws and modern instances;
And so he plays his part.
The sixth age shifts
Into the lean and slipper'd pantaloon,
With spectacles on nose and pouch on side,
His youthful hose, well saved, a world too wide
For his shrunk shank; and his big manly voice,
Turning again toward childish treble, pipes
And whistles in his sound.
Last scene of all,
That ends this strange eventful history,
Is second Childishness and mere oblivion,
Sans teeth, sans eyes, sans taste, sans everything.

One of the great books of religion, "The Sayings of the Fathers" in the *Talmud* set out the lifespan as marked by specific ages:

5 years is the age for reading;
10 for Mishnah (the laws);
13 for the Commandments (moral reasoning);
15 for Gemara (Talmudic discussions—abstract reasoning);
18 for Hupa (wedding canopy);
20 for seeking a livelihood;
30 for attaining full strength;
40 for understanding;
50 for giving counsel;
60 for becoming an elder;
70 for white hair;
80 for Gevurah (new, special strength of age);
90 for being bent under the weight of the years;
100 for being as if already dead and passed away from the world

And finally in modern society, beyond academia, we represent the lifespan in advertising and different consumer choices—as in advertisements for Farmers' Insurance suggesting that the stages of the lifespan focus on:

Buying a Car,
Buying a Home,
Getting Married,

Having a Baby,
Beginning Driver,
Sending a Child to College,
Starting a Business,
Planning your Retirement.

Regardless of the source or the historical period, most people find something that resonates in all of these representations. Yet history also teaches us that stages are not universal; in fact, the lifespan could easily be represented simply as one continuous stage. There are, however, several reasons that dividing the lifespan into multiple stages proves useful. For one thing, the lifespan is extraordinarily complex, and categorizing information into smaller groups helps make it feel more manageable and less daunting. Likewise, learning about ordered change that seems consistent across different people and groups helps to make sense of what is fundamental in development. If, for example, we find that the teen years are tumultuous and stressful in all societies then we can reasonably suspect that there is something fundamental about development during that age.

As it turns out, in the case of adolescence, many components of development vary significantly in different societies—adolescence is not tumultuous for all teens around the world, and thus it seems that the "storm and stress" of adolescence is at least partially a social and cultural construction. In fact, even the definition of stages is not as simple as it might first appear. Adolescence, for example, was not considered a major stage of the lifespan until the end of the 19th century, when the broadening of educational opportunities created a longer transition between childhood and adulthood. In contemporary Western society some scholars have proposed that the continuing expansion of higher education and longer transition to independent adulthood has created another "new stage" of something like "emerging adulthood." In some senses, then, the very nature of the stages in the lifespan is controversial.

Even placing the term "lifespan" in front of the word "development" generates disagreement. The notion of a lifespan suggests a progressive and constrained period of time that some scholars feel unfairly minimizes the disjointed and social nature of development. Thus, some people prefer the term "life-course" as more accurately representing the twists and turns of development that necessarily occurs in a social world. Still others prefer the term "life-cycle" as more accurately representing the sequential process that brings people through a full circle of growth and decline.

Ultimately, despite viable alternatives, this book is organized into seven parts. The first part covers general issues in the study of lifespan development and the other six parts invoke a basic set of lifespan stages: prenatal and infancy, early and middle childhood, adolescence, youth and early adulthood, middle adulthood, and later adulthood. The issues discussed in relation to these stages can, however, equally be considered topically. Though there are multiple ways of topically organizing the issues in this book, several possible examples include:

- Focusing on the topic of cognitive development and intellectual ability by combining Issue 3 (regarding the cognitive abilities of men and women), Issue 8 (regarding the types of abilities necessary to help at-risk preschool children), and Issue 19 (regarding brain exercises and cognitive decline in old age).

- Focusing on physical health and development by combining Issue 7 (regarding childhood obesity), Issue 11 (regarding the importance of structured activities for adolescents), and Issue 18 (regarding the definition of "successful aging").
- Focusing on parenting by combining Issue 2 (regarding the relative influence of parents and peers upon development), Issue 4 (regarding prenatal drug use), Issue 6 (regarding whether infants should be exposed to electronic media), and Issue 16 (regarding sexual orientation and parenting).

Fundamental Questions

Regardless of how the issues are organized, several questions underlie the topics in this book. First is a question that runs across the social sciences, but that is particularly relevant to thinking about development: the question of nature or nurture? Is lifespan development more a product of natural and biological dispositions, or is development the result of nurturing experiences in the world? This question has become particularly contentious with the advent of modern technology that allows researchers to map genetic codes and produce detailed images of mental activity. It is clear that human thought, feeling, and behavior all originate in a biological organ: the brain. Yet scientists are actively debating what aspect of the brain activity that guides such thought, feeling, and behavior comes from biological programs and what comes from learned concepts. It is obvious that we are products of both nature and nurture, but the necessary balance for lifespan development is the subject of tremendous controversy. This question is implicit in most of the issues in this book, while being explicitly addressed in Issue 1 (regarding the relative influence of culture and genes), Issue 5 (regarding the importance of external stimulation during the first three years), and Issue 9 (regarding the nature of Attention Deficit Disorder).

A second fundamental question relates to the role of culture. While cultural differences and diversity are genuine, it is not clear whether culture fundamentally alters patterns of development. Can we apply research about human development in a city in the United States to human development in rural India? Could we even apply research from urban cities to the rural United States? Could we apply knowledge equally to males and females? Implicit in many studies of lifespan development is the idea that there is a "best" pattern of development. But what if there is no one best pattern of development, only patterns of development that are more or less appropriate to different cultural settings and groups? Does that invalidate the effort of finding general principles of lifespan development? This question is fundamental to most of the issues in this book, being directly addressed in Issue 2 (regarding the influence of parents on development), Issue 10 (regarding the value of a social emphasis on self-esteem), Issue 13 (regarding generational changes in young adults), and Issue 15 (regarding general changes in the institution of marriage).

A third fundamental question fits best with the issue raised at the start of this introduction: do people really change? As noted earlier, development is a process of both continuity and change. Yet, the above models of stages in the lifespan suggest that each stage is a discrete entity. But are they? Where does one stage begin and another end? When teaching about the lifespan I often ask my traditionally college-aged undergraduate students whether they are adults—they usually are not entirely sure. They are kind of adults, kind of adolescents, kind of kids. So when do they become adults? Do they just wake up one day and there they are? Of course not; becoming an adult is a slow and gradual process. Further, the very idea that what happens to us as children has a direct impact on how we turn out in later life suggests a continuous process of development. If it were not, we wouldn't care so much about the quality of schools, parenting, and programs for children.

Yet when we step back we can all acknowledge that there are clear differences between children and adults, and between younger adults and older adults. Those differences are not just physical; there are differences in the way people think, and the contexts in which they live their lives. The question of whether it is best to conceptualize the lifespan as one continuous process, or as a series of discrete stages, is particularly important in our increasingly specialized society where products, services, and interactions are guided by understandings of people at specific ages. The question also influences numerous scholarly debates, and as such it orients several of the issues in this book including Issue 5 (regarding the developmental importance of infancy), Issue 8 (regarding academic skills for at-risk preschool children), and Issue 14 (regarding the preparation of college graduates for adulthood).

The Uses of Controversy

The fundamental questions for the study of lifespan development continuously manifest themselves in different and specific topical controversies. While this process can be occasionally confusing and frustrating to those who want to know the "right" answers about development, controversy is how our knowledge of the lifespan advances. Over time, controversies spark knowledge and ideas that are central to all of our lives. There are several prominent historical examples of how this works.

One example comes from the start of the lifespan: what happens to newborn babies? Prior to advances in medical technology during the 20th century, an extraordinarily high number of babies died before reaching their first birthday (sadly, this is still the case in many parts of the developing world—but that is a slightly different issue). When the germ theory of disease became prominent, doctors and scientists realized that inadequate hygiene and unnecessary exposure to germs caused many infant deaths. In a well-intentioned effort to keep babies safe and healthy, many hospitals started keeping babies in sterile conditions separate from human contact. Over time, such efforts were extended to children born to mothers who were considered deviant, such as those convicted of crimes. The logic in all these cases was that of contagion: certain types of human contact were too risky for vulnerable infants.

Fortunately, this logic was controversial, and researchers studying the earliest stages of life began to challenge the new scientifically based practices. Studies of children removed at birth from their mothers demonstrated remarkable physical, social, and psychological deficits. Researchers began to hypothesize that something about human contact, and forming an attachment bond, was virtually essential to healthy human development. For many years controversy raged; with one side suggesting that infants needed to be kept safely away from excessive contact, and the other suggesting that human contact was exactly what made infants safe. Eventually the evidence became overwhelming in favor of the latter position; the debate promoted scholarship demonstrating irrefutably that babies have an innate need for attachment, contact, and simple touch. Without any controversy we would not possess that essential knowledge.

In a more contemporary example, recent decades have brought increasing attention to the role of self-esteem in lifespan development. Due to a confluence of historical and social conditions, the idea that feeling good about one's self is a foundation for healthy development became received wisdom in the 1970s and 1980s. Numerous social service agencies, schools, activity programs, and therapists made promoting self-esteem the centerpiece of efforts to facilitate healthy development. While self-esteem is still extremely popular—as it is indeed nice to feel good about one's self—scholars have generated controversy by raising important questions about the evidence for self-esteem as a cure for social and personal ills. Despite massive research attention, the evidence that self-esteem alone provides a direct foundation for healthy development is sorely lacking. Though a virtual industry of self-esteem promoters has resisted the challenge, the controversy continues to have important implications for schools, counselors, parents, and programs. The question of whether there is still a role for promoting self-esteem as part of healthy development is still at play (and as such is included as Issue 10 in this book) but the controversy has generated a much more nuanced and realistic perspective on how and why feeling good about one's self might matter.

In both of these examples, and in most of the issues discussed in this book, controversy provides useful knowledge when scholars and individuals combine a genuine interest in facilitating healthy lifespan development with a concern for tangible evidence. In the case of infant attachment and touch, both sides cared about healthy babies and both sides deeply believed their side was right. In the case of self-esteem and positive development, both sides care about reducing social ills and both sides believe in what they are doing. Ultimately, however, resolving these issues, and resolving other controversies in social science, requires intelligent interpretations of evidence that go beyond taken-for-granted beliefs.

Our taken-for-granted beliefs are strong and pervasive, partially because many of the issue questions in this book relate to issues people confront in their daily lives; we are all experienced in our own process of development. As such, when considering these questions it is natural to have instinctive reactions and beliefs. The material in this book will, however, be most useful when readers get beyond initial beliefs to carefully consider the points and the evidence. In fact, when I teach about these issues I do not allow my students to make statements that start with "I believe . . . " or "In my opinion . . . " While I value the importance of students' beliefs and opinions, the controversies that we study must be evaluated primarily in regard to available evidence. Evidence is the foundation of scientific understanding, even though it may contradict deeply held beliefs. But much educational value lies in the space between evidence and beliefs: I hope that both my students, and those who read this book, are able to learn what scholars know and apply that knowledge to form educated positions on issues of great importance in contemporary society.

Conclusion

Ultimately, focusing on evidence and carefully considering intelligent positions from all viewpoints is how I have dealt with the challenge posed by my father when I was starting my own college experience: concluding that people do indeed change. While my own approach has focused on developmental psychology, the evidence and intelligent positions in this book come from diverse sources because the study of lifespan development takes many perspectives. A partial list of the academic disciplines that both contribute to and draw from the study of lifespan development might include: psychology, sociology, anthropology, education, social work, biology, history, cognitive science, geriatrics, and pediatrics. Thus, the readings and positions in this book represent quality work from many fields. Clear and quality thinking about controversial issues is not limited to any particular academic approach.

As you consider the issues in this book, reflecting on the questions raised in this introduction may facilitate your own clear and quality thinking. Ask yourself, for example, about how each issue relates to what you know or imagine from your own experience regarding each stage of the lifespan? Ask yourself how much nature and nurture play a role in influencing the different developmental issues? Ask yourself about the social and policy implications of taking specific positions on each issue. And keep in mind that vexing question raised by so many people starting to learn about lifespan development: Do people really change?

Engaging with these issues has certainly helped me change: I've become a better scholar of lifespan development, and my hope is that readers will have a similar experience. I'd like for readers to experience some small level of change in their own development by earnestly confronting the different sides of these controversial issues. By keeping in mind the history of the field, the useful but historically particular nature of defining lifespan stages, the fundamental questions underlying most controversies, and the value of controversy for advancing knowledge, readers should indeed be able to experience change firsthand.

Internet References . . .

This Web site provides academic resources and links related to developmental psychology.

> http://www.psy.pdx.edu/PsiCafe/Areas/
> Developmental/

The American Psychological Association is a general resource for many of the issues most pertinent to developmental psychology and lifespan development.

> http://www.apa.org/

This provides an overview of the debate on whether nature or nurture, culture or genes, is more influential in lifespan development.

> http://en.wikipedia.org/wiki/Nature_versus_nurture

The American Academy of Pediatrics is a professional organization focused on the health of children. Their Web site provides featured articles, books, and other reference materials on children's health topics.

> http://www.aap.org/

This Web site provides extensive links related to the controversial argument that parents do not matter as much in development as most people think.

> http://home.att.net/~xchar/tna/

Future of Children is a digital journal, providing an example of developmental research aimed at promoting effective policies and programs for families and children.

> http://www.futureofchildren.org/

General Issues in the Study of Lifespan Development

Although this book organizes development into a series of stages, several issues central to understanding the lifespan are not exclusive to one particular age. These issues relate to larger questions about the nature of development: what forces and characteristics shape us into the people we become? The issues in this section deal with this larger question, and provide a foundation for thinking about specific stages, by directly addressing the role of culture, genes, parents, and sex/gender in shaping the thoughts, feelings, behaviors, and experiences that make us human.

- Does the Cultural Environment Influence Lifespan Development More than Our Genes?

- Are Peers More Important than Parents during the Process of Development?

- Do Significant Innate Differences Influence the Career Success of Males and Females?

ISSUE 1

Does the Cultural Environment Influence Lifespan Development More than Our Genes?

YES: Paul Ehrlich and Marcus Feldman, from "Genes and Cultures: What Creates Our Behavioral Phenome?" *Current Anthropology* (February 2003)

NO: Gary Marcus, from "Making the Mind: Why We've Misunderstood the Nature-Nurture Debate," *Boston Review* (December 2003/ January 2004)

ISSUE SUMMARY

YES: Stanford University professors of biology Paul Ehrlich and Marcus Feldman argue that human behavior exhibits such complexity that genetic programs simply can't explain the way people develop.

NO: Psychologist and researcher Gary Marcus asserts that research clearly demonstrates how a relatively small number of genes influence our environmental learning by "cascading" to determine the paths of our behavioral development.

Perhaps the most central question in the study of lifespan development is whether nature or nurture exerts more influence on our developing thoughts, feelings, and behavior. Even in daily life, we regularly wonder about people—do they act that way because of things in their experience (nurture), or is it just the way they were born (nature)? This debate takes many different forms, and it underlies many of the important topics of study within lifespan development.

Most reasonable people agree that both nature and nurture, both genes and culture, shape development. Thus, the debate is mostly about the relative influence of each: does nature overwhelm nurture, or does nurture trump nature. Historically, the pendulum of popular opinion has tended to swing back and forth between trusting nature or emphasizing nurture.

In recent years, with advanced technology and research methods, the pendulum seems to have swung in favor of nature. With the ability to identify individual genes and image activity in the brain, scientists have made regular claims about how diverse aspects of behavior and development—everything from political affiliation to sexual behavior—are controlled by innate biology.

In the first of the following selections, however, renowned biologists Paul Ehrlich and Marcus Feldman argue that biological determinism, the idea that evolved predispositions determine behavior beyond the influence of the environment, does not make biological sense. Drawing from the recent mapping of the human genome, they claim there are simply too few genes and too much variation in human development. They take particular aim at claims that gender differences are biological, which has been an important part of this debate because gender differences often seem to persist despite diverse environments. Ehrlich and Feldman, however, claim that in looking at the grand scheme of history the clear variations in behavior patterns belie a biological explanation.

In contrast, New York University professor of psychology Gary Marcus claims that the dominant influence of genes on development has only become more clear in recent research. While acknowledging that genes and the environment always interact, Marcus draws on extensive research with animals demonstrating that small genetic manipulations have dramatic influences on behavior. He also responds to the claim that there are not enough genes to control complex behaviors by insisting that relationships between genes and behavior don't have to be one to one. Genes often interact, or "cascade," in various patterns that account for a massive number of developmental outcomes.

POINT

- There are simply too few genes to explain all of the complexity in human development.

- While gender differences are frequently cited as having a genetic base, there is actually significant historical variation in what is considered "normal" behavior for each gender.

- Focusing on the genetic causes of behavior and development has led to horrible social policies such as those of the Nazis during World War II.

COUNTERPOINT

- Genes do not influence behavior individually, but rather through nearly infinite combinations.

- Small genetic differences in animals create large differences in behavior patterns.

- While our brains are "plastic" in the sense of changing through development, those changes are constrained by genetic limits.

YES

**Paul Ehrlich and
Marcus Feldman**

Genes and Cultures: What Creates Our Behavioral Phenome?

The recent publication of the first draft of the human genome has brought to public attention the relationship between two concepts, genotype and phenotype—a relationship that had previously been discussed largely by academics. The genotype of an organism is encoded in the DNA that is held in chromosomes and other structures inside its cells. The phenotype is what we are able to observe about that organism's biochemistry, physiology, morphology, and behaviors. We will use the term "phenome" to circumscribe a set of phenotypes whose properties and variability we wish to study. Our focus will be on that part of the human phenome that is defined by behaviors and especially on the behavioral phenome's connection with the human genome.

Our understanding of human behavioral traits has evolved; explanations of the control of those traits offered 50 years ago differ from those most common today. In prewar decades genetic determinism—the idea that genes are destiny—had enormous influence on public policy in many countries: on American immigration and racial policies, Swedish sterilization programs, and, of course, Nazi laws on racial purity. Much of this public policy was built on support from biological, medical, and social scientists, but after Hitler's genocidal policies it was no longer politically correct to focus on putative hereditary differences. The fading of genetic determinism was an understandable reaction to Nazism and related racial, sexual, and religious prejudices which had long been prevalent in the United States and elsewhere. Thus, after World War II, it became the norm in American academia to consider all of human behavior as originating in the environment—in the way people were raised and the social contexts in which they lived.

Gradually, though, beginning in the 1960s, books like Robert Ardrey's *Territorial Imperative* and Desmond Morris's *The Naked Ape* began proposing explanations for human behaviors that were biologically reductionist and essentially genetic. Their extreme hereditarian bias may have been stimulated by the rapid progress at that time in understanding of the role of DNA, which spurred interest in genetics in both scientists and the public. But perhaps no publication had broader effect in reestablishing genetic credibility in the behavioral sciences than Arthur Jensen's article "How Much Can We Boost IQ?" Although roundly criticized by quantitative geneticists and shown to be based

From *Current Anthropology*, vol. 44, no. 1, February 2003, pp. 87–89, 92–95. Copyright © 2003 by University of Chicago Press. Reprinted by permission.

on the fraudulent data of Sir Cyril Burt, Jensen's work established a tradition that attempts to allocate to genetics a considerable portion of the variation in such human behaviors as for whom we vote, how religious we are, how likely we are to take risks, and, of course, measured IQ and school performance. This tradition is alive and well today.

Within the normal range of human phenotypic variation, including commonly occurring diseases, the role of genetics remains a matter of controversy even as more is revealed about variation at the level of DNA. Here we would like to reexamine the issue of genetics and human behavior in light of the enormous interest in the Human Genome Project, the expansion of behavioral genetics as described above, and the recent proliferation of books emphasizing the genetic programming of every behavior from rape to the learning of grammar. The philosopher Helena Cronin and her coeditor, Oliver Curry, tell us in the introduction to Yale University Press's "Darwinism Today" series that "Darwinian ideas . . . are setting today's intellectual agenda." In the *New York Times*, Nicholas Wade has written that human genes contain the "behavioral instructions" for "instincts to slaughter or show mercy, the contexts for love and hatred, the taste for obedience or rebellion—they are the determinants of human nature."

Genes, Cultures, and Behavior

It is incontrovertible that human beings are a product of evolution, but with respect to behavior that evolutionary process involves chance, natural selection, and, especially in the case of human beings, transmission and alteration of a body of extragenetic information called "culture." Cultural evolution, a process very different from genetic evolution by natural selection, has played a central role in producing our behaviors.

This is not to say that genes are uninvolved in human behavior. *Every* aspect of a person's phenome is a product of interaction between genome and environment. An obvious example of genetic involvement in the behavioral phenome is the degree to which most people use vision to orient themselves—in doing everything from hitting a baseball to selecting new clothes for their children. This is because we have evolved genetically to be "sight animals"—our dominant perceptual system is vision, with hearing coming in second. Had we, like dogs, evolved more sophisticated chemical detection, we might behave very differently in response to the toxic chemicals in our environment. The information in our DNA required to produce the basic morphology and physiology that make sight so important to us has clearly been molded by natural selection. And the physical increase in human brain size, which certainly involved a response to natural selection (although the precise environmental factors causing this selection remain something of a mystery, has allowed us to evolve language, a high level of tool use, the ability to plan for the future, and a wide range of other behaviors not seen in other animals.

Thus at the very least, genetic evolution both biased our ability to perceive the world and gave us the capacity to develop a vast culture. But the long-running nature-versus-nurture debate is not about sight versus smell. It is about the degree to which differences in today's human behavioral patterns from person to person, group to group, and society to society are influenced by genetic differences, that is, are traceable to differences in human genetic endowments. Do men "naturally" want to mate with as many women as possible while women "naturally" want to be more cautious in choosing their copulatory partners? Is there a "gay gene"? Are human beings "innately" aggressive? Are differences in educational achievement or income "caused" by differences in genes? And are people of all groups genetically programmed to be selfish? A critical social issue to keep in mind throughout our discussion is what the response of our society would be if we knew the answer to these questions. Two related schools of thought take the view that genetic evolution explains much of the human behavioral phenome; they are known as evolutionary psychology and behavioral genetics.

Evolutionary Psychology

Evolutionary psychology claims that many human behaviors became universally fixed as a result of natural selection acting during the environment of evolutionary adaptation, essentially the Pleistocene. A shortcoming of this argument, as emphasized by the anthropologist Robert Foley (1995–96), lies in the nonexistence of such an environment. Our ancestors lived in a wide diversity of habitats, and the impacts of the many environmental changes (e.g., glaciations) over the past million years differed geographically among their varied surroundings. Evolutionary psychologists also postulate that natural selection produced modules ("complex structures that are functionally organized for processing information") in the brain that "tell" us such things as which individuals are likely to cheat, which mates are likely to give us the best or most offspring, and how to form the best coalitions. These brain "modules," which are assumed to be biological entities fixed in humans by evolution, also have other names often bestowed on them by the same writers, such as "computational machines," "decision-making algorithms," "specialized systems," "inference engines," and "reasoning mechanisms." The research claims of evolutionary psychology have been heavily criticized by, among others, colleagues in psychology.

Those critics are correct. There is a general tendency for evolutionary psychologists vastly to overestimate how much of human behavior is primarily traceable to biological universals that are reflected in our genes. One reason for this overestimation is the ease with which a little evolutionary story can be invented to explain almost any observed pattern of behavior. For example, it seems logical that natural selection would result in the coding of a fear of snakes and spiders into our DNA, as the evolutionary psychologist Steven Pinker thinks. But while Pinker may have genes that make him fear snakes, as the evolutionist Jared Diamond points out, such genes are clearly lacking in New Guinea natives. As Diamond says, "If there is any single place in the world where we might expect an innate fear of snakes among native peoples, it would be in New Guinea, where one-third or more of the snake species are poisonous, and certain non-poisonous constrictor snakes are sufficiently big to be dangerous." Yet there is no sign of innate fear of snakes or spiders among the indigenous people, and children regularly "capture large spiders, singe off the legs and hairs, and eat the bodies. The people there laugh at the idea of an inborn phobia about snakes, and account for the fear in Europeans as a result of their stupidity in being unable to distinguish which snakes might be dangerous." Furthermore, there is reason to believe that fear of snakes in other primates is largely learned as well.

Another example is the set of predictions advanced by Bruce Ellis about the mating behavior that would be found in a previously unknown culture. The first five characteristics that "the average woman in this culture will seek . . . in her ideal mate," he predicts, are:

1. He will be dependable, emotionally stable and mature, and kind/considerate toward her.
2. He will be generous. He may communicate a spirit of caring through a willingness to share time and whatever commodities are valued in this culture with the woman in question.
3. He will be ambitious and perceived by the woman in question as clever or intelligent.
4. He will be genuinely interested in the woman in question, and she in him. He may express his interest through displays of concern for her well-being.
5. He will have a strong social presence and be well liked and respected by others. He will possess a strong sense of efficacy, confidence, and self-respect.

Evolutionary theory does not support such predictions, even if an "average woman" could be defined. First of all, it would be no small developmental trick genetically to program detailed, different, and *independent* reproductive strategies into modules in male and female brains. Those brains, after all are minor variants of the same incredibly complex structures, and, furthermore, the degree to which they are organized into modules is far from clear. If the women in the unknown culture actually chose mates meeting Ellis's criteria, a quite sufficient alternative evolutionary explanation would be that women (simultaneously with men) have evolved big brains, are not stupid, and respond to the norms of their cultures. Scientifically, the notion that the detailed attributes of desirable mates must be engraved in our genetic makeup is without basis, especially in light of the enormous cultural differences in sexual preferences.

For any culture, Ellis's evolutionary arguments would require that in past populations of women there were DNA-based differences that made some more likely to choose in those ways and others more likely to seek mates with other characteristics. And those that chose as Ellis predicts would have to have borne and raised more children that survived to reproduce than those with other preferences. Might, for example, a woman who married a stingy male who kept her barefoot and pregnant out-reproduce the wife of a generous and considerate mate? That is the way genetic evolution changes the characteristics of populations over time: by some genetic variants' out-reproducing others.

When that happens, we say that natural selection has occurred. But, unfortunately, there are no data that speak to whether there is (or was) genetic variation in human mate preferences—variation in, say, ability to evaluate specifically whether a potential mate is "ambitious"—upon which selection could be based. And there are no data for any population showing that women who seek those characteristics in their sexual partners are more successful reproductively—are represented by more children in the subsequent generation—than women who seek husbands with other characteristics. Ellis is simply confusing the preferences of women he knows in his society with evolutionary fitness. . . .

What Does Determine the Behavioral Phenome?

Geneticists know that a large portion of the behavioral phenome must be programmed into the brain by factors in the environment, including the internal environment in which the fetus develops and, most important, the cultural environment in which human beings spend their entire lives. Behavioral scientists know, for instance, that many dramatic personality differences *must* be traced to environmental influences. Perhaps the most important reason to doubt that genetic variation accounts for a substantial portion of observed differences in human behavior is simply that we lack an extensive enough hereditary apparatus to do the job—that we have a "gene shortage." To what extent could genes control the production of these differences?

It is important to remember that behaviors are the results of charge changes that occur in our network of neurons, the specialized cells that make up our nervous system. Behaviors are ultimately under some degree of control in the brain. Neuron networks are the locus of the memories that are also important to our behavior. That genes can control some general patterns is unquestioned; they are obviously involved in the construction of our brains. They might therefore also build in the potential for experience to affect a large part of the details involved in the neural circuitry. But they cannot be controlling our individual behavioral choices.

Human beings have only three times as many genes as have fruit flies (many of those genes appear to be duplicates of those in the flies, and the biochemistry of fly nerve cells seems quite close to ours). But in addition to having sex and eating (what flies mostly do) we get married, establish charities, build hydrogen bombs, commit genocide, compose sonatas, and publish books on evolution. It is a little hard to credit all this to the determining action of those few additional genes. Those genes are, however, likely to have contributed to the increased brain size and complexity that support the vast cultural superstructure created by the interaction of our neurons and their environments. They may also contribute to the wonderful flexibility and plasticity of human behavior—the very attributes that make our behavior less rather than more genetically determined. But to understand the development of and variation in specific human behaviors such as creating charities and cheesecakes, we must invoke culture, its evolution, and its potential interaction with biology.

It might be argued that since a relative handful of genes can control our basic body plan—one's height depends on millions of the body's cells' being stacked precisely—a handful could also determine our behavioral phenome. Genes initiate a process of development that might be analogized with the way a mountain stream entering a floodplain can initiate the development of a complex delta. Why, then, couldn't just a few genes have evolved to program millions of our behaviors? In theory they might have, but in that case human behavior would be very stereotyped. Consider the problem of evolving human behavioral flexibility under such circumstances of genetic determination. Changing just one behavioral pattern—say, making women more desirous of mating with affluent men—would be somewhat analogous to changing the course of one distributary (branch in the delta) without altering the braided pattern of the rest of the delta. It would be difficult to do by just changing the flow of the mountain stream (equivalent to changing the genes) but easily accomplished by throwing big rocks in the distributary (changing the environment).

This partial analogy seems particularly apt in that it is apparently difficult for evolution to accomplish just one thing at a time. There are two principal reasons for this. The first is the complexity of interactions among alleles and phenotypic traits, especially pleiotropy and epistasis. Because there are relatively so few of them, most genes must be involved in more than one process (pleiotropy). Then if a mutation leads to better functioning of one process, it may not be selected for because the change might degrade the functioning of another process. And changes in one gene can modify the influence of another in very complex ways (epistasis). Second, because they are physically coupled to other genes on the same chromosome, the fates of genes are not independent. Selection that increases the frequency of one allele in a population will often, because of linkage, necessarily increase the frequency of another. Selection favoring a gene that made one prefer tall mates might also result in the increase of a nearby gene that produced greater susceptibility to a childhood cancer.

The Mysteries of Environmental Control

Behavioral scientists are still, unhappily, generally unable to determine the key environmental factors that influence the behavioral phenome. For instance, in the case of the Dionne quintuplets, quite subtle environmental differences—perhaps initiated by different positions in the womb or chance interactions among young quints, their parents, and their observers—clearly led to substantially different behavioral and health outcomes in five children with identical genomes. As their story shows, we really know very little about what environmental factors can modify behavior. For example, some virtually undetectable differences in environments may be greatly amplified as developing individuals change their own environments and those of their siblings. Equally, subtle and undetected environmental factors may put individuals with the same genetic endowments on similar life courses even if they are reared apart, perhaps explaining anecdotes about the similarities of some reunited identical twins.

We also know too little about the routes through which genes may influence behavior, where again changes may be behaviorally amplified. Suppose that a study shows that identical twins, separated at birth, nonetheless show a high correlation of personality type—both members of twin pairs tend to be either introverted or extraverted. This is interpreted as a high heritability of introversion and extraversion. What really is heavily influenced by genetics, however, could be height, and tall people in that society (as in many societies) may be better treated by their peers and thus more likely to become extraverted. Genes in this case will clearly be involved in personality type but by such an indirect route as to make talk of "genes for introversion or extraversion" essentially meaningless.

And, of course, scientists *do* know that what appears to be "genetic" is often simply a function of the environment. An example suggested by the philosopher Elliott Sober illustrates this. In England before the 18th century, evolutionary psychologists (had there been any) would have assumed that males had a genetic proclivity for knitting. The knitting gene would have been assumed to reside on the Y chromosome. But by the 19th century, evolutionary psychologists would have claimed that women had that genetic proclivity, with the knitting gene on the X chromosome. With historical perspective, we can see that the change was purely culture-driven, not due to a genetic change. As it did with knitting, the environment, especially the cultural environment, seems to do a good job of fine-tuning our behavior. A major challenge for science today is to elucidate how that fine-tuning occurs.

Would Selection Generally Favor Genetic Control of Behavior?

Would we be better off if we had more than enough genes to play a controlling role in every one of our choices and actions and those genes could operate independently? Probably not. One could imagine a Hobbesian battle in which genes would compete with each other to improve the performance of the reproducing individuals that possessed them—genes for caution being favored in one environment one day and genes for impulsiveness in another environment the next ("Look before you leap," "He who hesitates is lost"). It is difficult to imagine how *any* organism could make the grade evolutionarily if its behavior were completely genetically determined and interactions between its genes and its environments did not exist. Even single-celled organisms respond to changes in their surroundings. Without substantial environmental inputs, evolution would not occur and life could not exist.

Biological evolution has avoided that problem by allowing our behavior to be deeply influenced by the environments in which genes operate. In normal human environments, genes are heavily involved in creating a basic brain with an enormous capacity for learning—taking in information from the environment and incorporating that information into the brain's structure. It is learning that proceeds after birth as an infant's brain uses inputs such as patterns of light from the eyes to wire up the brain so that it can see, patterns of sound that wire up the brain so that it can speak one or more languages, and so on. As the brain scientist John Allman put it, "the brain is unique among the organs of the body in requiring a great deal of feedback from experience to develop its full capacities." And the situation is not so different for height. There aren't enough genes to control a child's growth rate from day to day—adding cells rapidly in favorable (e.g., food-rich) situations and slowly or not at all under starvation. And there aren't enough genes to govern the growth of each column of cells, some to regulate those in each column on the right side of the spine, some for each in the left. Instead, all growth patterns depend on environmental feedback. . . .

Conclusions

What the recent evidence from the Human Genome Project tells us is that the interaction between genes, between the separate components of genes, and between controlling elements of these separate components must be much more complex than we ever realized. Simple additive models of gene action or of the relationship between genes and environments must be revised. They have formed the basis for our interpretation of phenotype-genotype relationships for 84 years, ever since R. A. Fisher's famous paper that for the first time related Mendelian genes to measurable phenotypes. New models and paradigms are needed to go from the genome to the phenome in any quantitative way. The simplistic approach of behavioral genetics cannot do the job. We must dig deeper into the environmental and especially cultural factors that contribute to the phenome. The ascendancy of molecular biology has, unintentionally, militated against progress in studies of cultural evolution.

Theories of culture and its evolution in the 20th century, from Boas's insistence on the particularity of cultural identities to the debates between material and cultural determinism described by Sahlins, were proudly nonquantitative. Recent discussions on the ideational or symbolic nature of the subjects of cultural evolution, while critical of attempts to construct dynamical models of cultural evolution based on individual-to-individual cultural transmission, nevertheless acknowledge the centrality of cultural evolution to human behavioral analysis. Thus, although the quantitative paradigms used in behavioral genetics do not inform evolutionary analysis, this does not mean that we cannot or should not take an evolutionary approach to the understanding and modification of human behavior. Genetically evolved features such as the dominance of our visual sense should always be kept in mind, but an evolutionary approach to changing behavior in our species must primarily focus on *cultural* evolution. In the last 40,000 years or so, the scale of that cultural evolution has produced a volume of information that dwarfs what is coded into our genes. Just consider what is now stored in human memories, libraries, photographs, films, video tapes, the Worldwide Web, blueprints, and computer data banks—in addition to what is inherent in other artifacts and human-made structures. Although there have been preliminary investigations by Cavalli-Sforza and Feldman and Boyd and Richerson, scientists have barely begun to investigate the basic processes by which that body of information changes (or remains constant for long periods)—a task that social scientists have been taking up piecemeal and largely qualitatively for a very long time. Developing a unified quantitative theory of cultural change is one of the great challenges for evolutionary and social science in the 21st century.

Identifying the basic mechanisms by which our culture evolves will be difficult; the most recent attempts using a "meme" approach appear to be a dead end. Learning how to influence that evolution is likely to be more difficult still and fraught with pitfalls. No sensible geneticist envisions a eugenic future in which people are selected to show certain behavioral traits, and most thinking people are aware of the ethical (if not technical and social) problems of trying to change our behavior by altering our genetic endowments. Society has long been mucking around in cultural evolution, despite warnings of the potential abuses of doing so. Nazi eugenic policies and Soviet, Cambodian, Chinese, and other social engineering experiments stand as monuments to the ethical dangers that must be guarded against when trying systematically to alter either genetic or cultural evolution.

Nevertheless, we are today all involved in carrying out or (with our taxes) supporting experiments designed to change behavior. This is attested to by the advertising business, Head Start programs, and the existence of institutions such as Sing Sing Prison and Stanford University. The data used by evolutionary psychologists to infer the biological antecedents of human behavior, while not telling us anything about genetic evolution, may actually be helpful in improving our grasp of cultural evolution. What seems clear today, however, is that evolutionary psychology and behavioral genetics are promoting a vast overemphasis on the part played by genetic factors (and a serious underestimation of the role of cultural evolution) in shaping our behavioral phenomes.

Gary Marcus  **NO**

Making the Mind: Why We've Misunderstood the Nature-Nurture Debate

What do our minds owe to our nature, and what to our nurture? The question has long been vexed, in no small part because until recently we knew relatively little about the nature of nature—how genes work and what they bring to the biological structures that underlie the mind. But now, 50 years after the discovery of the molecular structure of DNA, we are for the first time in a position to understand directly DNA's contribution to the mind. And the story is vastly different from—and vastly more interesting than—anything we had anticipated.

The emerging picture of nature's role in the formation of the mind is at odds with a conventional view, recently summarized by Louis Menand. According to Menand, "every aspect of life has a biological foundation in exactly the same sense, which is that unless it was biologically possible it wouldn't exist. After that, it's up for grabs." More particularly, some scholars have taken recent research on genes and on the brain as suggesting a profoundly limited role for nature in the formation of the mind.

Their position rests on two arguments, what Stanford anthropologist Paul Ehrlich dubbed a "gene shortage" and widespread, well-documented findings of "brain plasticity." According to the gene shortage argument, genes can't be very important to the birth of the mind because the genome contains only about 30,000 genes, simply too few to account even for the brain's complexity—with its billions of cells and tens of billions of connections between neurons—much less the mind's. "Given that ratio," Ehrlich suggested, "it would be quite a trick for genes typically to control more than the most general aspects of human behavior."

According to the brain plasticity argument, genes can't be terribly important because the developing brain is so flexible. For instance, whereas adults who lose their left hemisphere are likely to lose permanently much of their ability to talk, a child who loses a left hemisphere may very well recover the ability to speak, even in the absence of a left hemisphere. Such flexibility is pervasive, down to the level of individual cells. Rather than being fixed in their fates the instant they are born, newly formed brain cells—neurons—can sometimes shift their function, depending on their context. A cell that would ordinarily help to give us a sense of touch can (in the right circumstances) be recruited into the visual system and accept signals from the eye. With that high level of brain plasticity, some imagine that genes are left on the sidelines, as scarcely relevant onlookers.

All of this is, I think, a mistake. It is certainly true that the number of genes is tiny in comparison to the number of neurons, and that the developing brain is highly plastic. Nevertheless, nature—in the form of genes—has an enormous impact on the developing brain and mind. The general outlines of how genes build the brain are finally becoming clear, and we are also starting to see how, in forming the brain, genes make room for the environment's essential role. While vast amounts of work remain to be done, it is becoming equally clear that understanding the coordination of nature and nurture will require letting go of some long-held beliefs.

How to Build a Brain

In the nine-month dash from conception to birth—the flurry of dividing, specializing, and migrating cells that scientists call embryogenesis—organs such as the heart and kidney unfold in a series of ever more mature stages. In contrast to a 17th century theory known as preformationism, the organs of the body cannot be found preformed in miniature in a fertilized egg; at the moment of conception there is neither a tiny heart nor a tiny brain. Instead, the fertilized egg contains information: the three billion nucleotides of DNA that make up the human genome. That information, copied into the nucleus of every newly formed cell, guides the gradual but powerful process of successive approximation that shapes each of the body's organs. The heart, for example, begins as a simple sheet of cell that gradually folds over to form a tube; the tube sprouts bulges, the bulges sprout further bulges, and every day the growing heart looks a bit more like an adult heart.

Even before the dawn of the modern genetic era, biologists understood that something similar was happening in the development of the brain—that the organ of thought and language was formed in much the same way as the rest of the body. The brain, too, develops in the first instance from a simple sheet of cells that gradually curls up into a tube that sprouts bulges, which over time differentiate into ever more complex shapes. Yet 2,000 years of thinking of the mind as independent from the body kept people from appreciating the significance of this seemingly obvious point.

The notion that the brain is drastically different from other physical systems has a long tradition; it can be seen as a modernized version of the ancient belief that the mind and body are wholly separate—but it is untenable. The brain is a physical system. Although the brain's function is different from that of other organs, the brain's capabilities, like those of other organs, emerge from its physical properties. We now know that strokes and gunshot wounds can interfere with language by destroying parts of the brain, and that Prozac and Ritalin can influence mood by altering the flow of neurotransmitters. The fundamental components of the brain—the neurons and the synapses that connect them—can be understood as physical systems, with chemical and electrical properties that follow from their composition.

Yet even as late as the 1990s, latter-day dualists might have thought that the brain developed by different principles. There were, of course, many hints that genes must be important for the brain: identical twins resemble each other more than nonidentical twins in personality as well as in physique; mental disorders such as schizophrenia and depression run in families and are shared even by twins reared apart; and animal breeders know that shaping the bodies of animals often leads to correlated changes in behavior. All of these observations provided clues of genetic effects on the brain.

But such clues are achingly indirect, and it was easy enough to pay them little heed. Even in the mid-1990s, despite all the discoveries that had been made in molecular biology, hardly anything specific was known about how the brain formed. By the end of that decade, however, revolutions in the methodology of molecular biology—techniques for studying and manipulating genes—were beginning to enter the study of the brain. Now, just a few years later, it has become clear that to an enormous extent the brain really is sculpted by the same processes as the rest of the body, not just at the macroscopic level (i.e., as a product of successive approximation) but also at the microscopic level, in terms of the mechanics of how genes are switched on and off, and even in terms of which genes are involved; a huge number of the genes that participate in the development of the brain play important (and often closely related) roles in the rest of the body. . . .

The . . . power of genes holds even for the most unusual yet most characteristic parts of neurons: the long axons that carry signals away from the cell, the tree-like dendrites that allow neurons to receive signals from other nerve cells, and the trillions of synapses that serve as connections between them. What your brain does is largely a function of how those synaptic connections are set up—alter those connections, and you alter the mind—and how they are set up is no small part a function of the genome. In the laboratory, mutant flies and mice with aberrant brain wiring have trouble with everything from motor control (one mutant mouse is named "reeler" for its almost drunken gait) to vision. And in humans, faulty brain wiring contributes to disorders such as schizophrenia and autism.

Proper neural wiring depends on the behavior of individual axons and dendrites. And this behavior once again depends on the content of the genome. For example, much of what axons do is governed by special wiggly, almost hand-like protuberances at the end of each axon known as growth cones. Growth cones (and the axonal wiring they trail behind them) are like little animals that swerve back and forth, maneuvering around obstacles, extending and retracting feelers known as filopodia (the "fingers" of a growth cone) as the cone hunts around in search of its destination—say in the auditory cortex. Rather than simply being launched like projectiles that blindly and helplessly follow whatever route they first set out on, growth cones constantly compensate and adjust, taking in new information as they find their way to their targets.

Growth cones don't just head in a particular direction and hope for the best. They "know" what they are looking for and can make new plans even if experimentally induced obstacles get in their way. In their efforts to find their destinations, growth cones use every trick they can, from "short-range" cues emanating from the surface of nearby cells to long-distance cues that broadcast their signals from millimeters away—miles and miles in the geography of an axon. For example, some proteins appear to serve as "radio beacons" that can diffuse across great distances and serve as guides to distant growth cones—provided that they are tuned to the right station. Which stations a growth cone picks up—and whether it finds a particular signal attractive or repellent—depends on the protein receptors it has on its surface, in turn a function of which genes are expressed within.

Researchers are now in a position where they can begin to understand and even manipulate those genes. In 2000, a team of researchers at the Salk Institute in San Diego took a group of thoracic (chest) motor neurons that normally extend their axons into several different places, such as axial muscles (midline muscles that play a role in posture), intercostal muscles (the muscles between the ribs), and sympathetic neurons (which, among other things, participate in the fast energy mobilization for fight-or-flight responses), and by changing their genetic labels persuaded virtually the entire group of thoracic neurons to abandon their usual targets in favor of the axial muscles. (The few exceptions were a tiny number that apparently couldn't fit into the newly crowded axial destinations and had to find other targets.)

What this all boils down to, from the perspective of psychology, is an astonishingly powerful system for wiring the mind. Instead of vaguely telling axons and dendrites to send and accept signals from their neighbors, thereby leaving all of the burden of mind development to experience, nature in effect lays down the cable: it supplies the brain's wires—axons and dendrites—with elaborate tools for finding their way on their own. Rather than waiting for experience, brains can use the complex menagerie of genes and proteins to create a rich, intricate starting point for the brain and mind.

The sheer overlap between the cellular and molecular processes by which the brain is built and the processes by which the rest of the body is built has meant that new techniques designed for the study of the one can often be readily imported into the study of the other. New techniques in staining, for instance, by which biologists trace the movements and fates of individual cells, can often be brought to bear on the study of the brain as soon as they are developed; even more important, new techniques for altering the genomes of experimental animals can often be almost immediately applied to studies of brain development. Our collective understanding of biology is growing by leaps and bounds because sauce for the goose is so often sauce for the gander.

Nature and Nurture Redux

This seemingly simple idea—that what's good enough for the body is good enough for the brain—has important implications for how we understand the roles of nature and nurture in the development of the mind and brain.

Beyond the Blueprint

Since the early 1960s biologists have realized that genes are neither blueprints nor dictators; instead, as I will explain in a moment, genes are better seen as *providers of opportunity*. Yet because the brain has for so long been treated as separate from the body, the notion of genes as sources of options rather than purveyors of commands has yet to really enter into our understanding of the origins of human psychology.

Biologists have long understood that all genes have two functions. First, they serve as templates for building particular proteins. The insulin gene provides a template for insulin, the hemoglobin genes give templates for building hemoglobin, and so forth. Second, each gene contains what is called a regulatory sequence, a set of conditions that guide whether or not that gene's template gets converted into protein. Although every cell contains a complete copy of the genome, most of the genes in any given cell are silent. Your lung cells, for example, contain the recipe for insulin but they don't produce any, because in those cells the insulin gene is switched off (or "repressed"); each protein is produced only in the cells in which the relevant gene is switched on. So individual genes are like lines in a computer program. Each gene has an IF and a THEN, a precondition (IF) and an action (THEN). And here is one of the most important places where the environment can enter: the IFs of genes are responsive to the environment of the cells in which they are contained. Rather than being static entities that decide the fate of each cell in advance, genes—because of the regulatory sequence—are dynamic and can guide a cell in different ways at different times, depending on the balance of molecules in their environment.

This basic logic—which was worked out in the early 1960s by two French biologists, François Jacob and Jacques Monod, in a series of painstaking studies of the diet of a simple bacterium—applies as much to humans as to bacteria, and as much for the brain as for any other part of the body. Monod and Jacob aimed to understand how *E. coli* bacteria could switch almost instantaneously from a diet of glucose (its favorite) to a diet of lactose (an emergency backup food). What they found was that this abrupt change in diet was accomplished by a process that switched genes on and off. To metabolize lactose, the bacterium needed to build a certain set of protein-based enzymes that for simplicity I'll refer to collectively as lactase, the product of a cluster of lactase genes. Every *E. coli* had those lactase genes lying in wait, but they were only expressed—switched on—when a bit of lactose could bind (attach to) a certain spot of DNA that lay near them, and this in turn could happen only if there was no glucose around to get in the way. In essence, the simple bacterium had an IF-THEN—if lactose and not glucose, then build lactase—that is very much of a piece with the billions of IF-THENs that run the world's computer software.

The essential point is that genes are IFs rather than MUSTs. So even a single environmental cue can radically reshape the course of development. In the African butterfly *Bicyclus anynana*, for example, high temperature during development (associated with the rainy season in its native tropical climate) leads the butterfly to become brightly colored; low temperature (associated with a dry fall) leads the butterfly to become a dull brown. The growing butterfly doesn't learn (in the course of its development) how to blend in better—it will do the same thing in a lab where the temperature varies and the foliage is constant; instead it is genetically programmed to develop in two different ways in two different environments.

The lesson of the last five years of research in developmental neuroscience is that IF-THENs are as crucial and omnipresent in brain development as they are elsewhere. To take one recently worked out example: rats, mice, and other rodents devote a particular region of the cerebral cortex known as barrel fields to the problem of analyzing the stimulation of their whiskers. The exact placement of those barrel fields appears to be driven by a gene or set of genes whose IF region is responsive to the quantity of a particular molecule, Fibroblast Growth Factor 8 (FGF8). By altering the distribution of that molecule, researchers were able to alter barrel development: increasing the concentration of FGF8 led to mice with barrel fields that were unusually far forward, while decreasing the concentration led to mice with barrel fields that were unusually far back. In essence, the quantity of FGF8 serves as a beacon, guiding growing cells to their fate by driving the regulatory IFs of the many genes that are presumably involved in barrel-field formation.

Other IF-THENs contribute to the function of the brain throughout life, e.g., supervising the control of neurotransmitters and participating . . . in the process of laying down memory traces. Because each gene has an IF, every aspect of the brain's development is in principle linked to some aspect of the environment; chemicals such as alcohol that are ingested during pregnancy have such enormous effects because they fool the IFs that regulate genes that guide cells into dividing too much or too little, into moving too far or not far enough, and so forth. The brain is the product of the actions of its component cells, and those actions are the products of the genes they contain within, each cell guided by 30,000 IFs paired with 30,000 THENs—as many possibilities as there are genes. (More, really, because many genes have multiple IFs, and genes can and often do work in combination.)

From Genes to Behavior

Whether we speak of the brain or other parts of the body, changes in even a single gene—leading to either a new IF or a new THEN—can have great consequences. Just as a single alteration to the hemoglobin gene can lead to a predisposition for sickle-cell anemia, a single change to the genes involved in the brain can lead to a language impairment or mental retardation.

And at least in animals, small differences within genomes can lead to significant differences in behavior. A Toronto team, for example, recently used genetic techniques to investigate—and ultimately modify—the foraging habits of *C. elegans* worms. Some *elegans* prefer to forage in groups, others are loners, and the Toronto group was able to tie these behavioral differences to differences in a single amino acid in the protein template (THEN) region of a particular gene known as npr-1; worms with the amino acid valine in the critical spot are "social" whereas worms with phenylalanine are loners. Armed with that knowledge and modern genetic engineering techniques, the team was able to switch a strain of loner *C. elegans* worms into social worms by altering that one gene.

Another team of researchers, at Emory University, has shown that changing the regulatory IF region of a single gene can also have a significant effect on social behavior. Building on an observation that differences in sociability in different species of voles correlated with how many vasopressin receptors they had, they transferred the regulatory IF region of sociable prairie voles' vasopressin receptor genes into the genome of a less sociable species, the mouse—and in so doing created mutant mice, more social than normal, with more vasopressin receptors. With other small genetic modifications, researchers have created strains of anxious, fearful mice, mice that progressively increase alcohol consumption under stress, mice that lack the nurturing instinct, and even mice that groom themselves constantly, pulling and tugging on their own hair to the point of baldness. Each of those studies demonstrates how behavior can be significantly changed when even a single gene is altered.

Still, complex biological structures—whether we speak of hearts or kidneys or brains—are the product of the concerted actions and interactions of many genes, not just one. A mutation in a single gene known as FOXP2 can interfere with the ability of a child to learn language; an alteration in the vasopressin gene can alter a rodent's sociability—but this doesn't mean that FOXP2 is solely responsible for language or that vasopressin is the only gene a rat needs in order to be sociable. Although individual genes can have powerful effects, no trait is the consequence of any single gene. There can no more be a single gene for language, or for the propensity for talking about the weather, than there can be for the left ventricle of a human heart. Even a single brain cell—or a single heart cell—is the product of many genes working together.

The mapping between genes and behavior is made even more complex by the fact that few if any neural circuits operate entirely autonomously. Except perhaps in the case of reflexes, most behaviors are the product of multiple interacting systems. In a complex animal like a mammal or a bird, virtually every action depends on a coming together of systems for perception, attention, motivation, and so forth. Whether or not a pigeon pecks a lever to get a pellet depends on whether it is hungry, whether it is tired, whether there is anything else more interesting around, and so forth. Furthermore, even within a single system, genes rarely participate directly "on-line," in part because they are just too slow. Genes do seem to play an active, major role in "off-line" processing, such as consolidation of long-term memory—which can even happen during sleep—but when it comes to rapid on-line decision-making, genes, which work on a time scale of seconds or minutes, turn over the reins to neurons, which act on a scale of hundredths of a second. The chief contribution of genes comes in advance, in laying down and adjusting neural circuitry, not in the moment-by-moment running of the nervous system. Genes build neural structures—not behavior.

In the assembly of the brain, as in the assembly of other organs, one of the most important ideas is that of a cascade, one gene influencing another, which influences another, which influences another, and so on. Rather than acting in absolute isolation, most genes act as parts of elaborate networks in which the expression of one gene is a precondition for the expression of the next. The THEN of one gene can satisfy the IF of another and thus induce it to turn on. Regulatory proteins are proteins (themselves the product of genes) that control the expression of other genes and thus tie the whole genetic system together. A single regulatory gene at the top of a complex network can indirectly launch a cascade of hundreds or thousands of other genes leading to, for example, the development of an eye or a limb.

In the words of Swiss biologist Walter Gehring, such genes can serve as "master control genes" and exert enormous power on a growing system. PAX6, for example, is a regulatory protein that plays a role in eye development, and Gehring has shown that artificially activating it in the right spot on a fruit fly's antenna can lead to an extra eye, right there on the antenna—thus, a simple regulatory gene leads directly and indirectly to the expression of approximately 2,500 other genes. What is true for the fly's eye is also true for its brain—and also for the human brain: by compounding and coordinating their effects, genes can exert enormous influence on biological structure.

From a Tiny Number of Genes to a Complex Brain

The cascades in turn help us to make sense of the alleged gene shortage, the idea that the discrepancy between the number of genes and the number of neurons might somehow minimize the importance of genes when it comes to constructing brain or behavior.

Reflection on the relation between brain and body immediately vitiates the gene shortage argument: if 30,000 genes weren't enough to have significant influence on the 20 billion cells in the brain, they surely wouldn't have much impact on the trillions that are found in the body as a whole. The confusion, once again, can be traced to the mistaken idea of genome as blueprint, to the misguided expectation of a one-to-one mapping from individual genes to individual neurons; in reality, genomes describe processes for building things rather than pictures of finished products: better to think of the genome as a compression scheme than a blueprint.

Computer scientists use compression schemes when they want to store and transmit information efficiently. All compression schemes rely in one way or another on ferreting out redundancy. For instance, programs that use the GIF format look for patterns of repeated pixels (the colored dots of which digital images are made). If a whole series of pixels are of exactly the same color, the software that creates GIF files will assign a code that represents the color of those pixels, followed by a number to indicate how many pixels in a row are of the same color. Instead of having to list every blue pixel individually, the GIF format saves space by storing only two numbers: the code for blue and the number of repeated blue pixels. When you "open" a GIF file, the computer converts those codes back into the appropriate strings of identical bits; in the meantime, the computer has saved a considerable amount of memory. Computer scientists have devised dozens of different compression schemes, from JPEGs for photographs to MP3s for music, each designed to exploit a different kind of redundancy. The general procedure is always the same: some end product is converted into a compact description of how to reconstruct that end product; a "decompressor" reconstructs the desired end product from that compact description.

Biology doesn't know in advance what the end product will be; there's no StuffIt Compressor to convert a human being into a genome. But the genome is very much akin to a compression scheme, a terrifically efficient description of how to build something of great complexity—perhaps more efficient than anything yet developed in the labs of computer scientists (never mind the complexities of the brain—there are trillions of cells in the rest of the body, and they are all supervised by the same 30,000-gene genome). And although nature has no counterpart to a program that stuffs a picture into a compressed encoding, it does offer a counterpart to the program that performs decompression: the cell. Genome in, organism out. Through the logic of gene expression, cells are self-regulating factories that translate genomes into biological structure.

Cascades are at the heart of this process of decompression, because the regulatory proteins that are at the top of genetic cascades serve as shorthand that can be used over and over again, like the subroutine of a software engineer. For example, the genome of a centipede probably doesn't specify separate sets of hundreds or thousands of genes for each of the centipede's legs; instead, it appears that the leg-building "subroutine"—a cascade of perhaps hundreds or thousands of genes—gets invoked many times, once for each new pair of legs. Something similar lies behind the construction of a vertebrate's ribs. And within the last few years it has become clear that the embryonic brain relies on the same sort of genetic recycling, using the same repeated motifs—such as sets of parallel connections known as topographic maps—over and over again, to supervise the development of thousands or even millions of neurons with each use of a given genetic subroutine. There's no gene shortage, because every cascade represents the shorthand for a different reuseable subroutine, a different way of creating more from less.

From Prewiring to Rewiring

In the final analysis, I think the most important question about the biological roots of the mind may not be the question that has preoccupied my colleagues and myself for a number of years—the extent to which genes prewire the brain—but a different question that until recently had never been seriously raised: the extent to which (and ways in which) genes make it possible for experience to *rewire* the brain. Efforts to address the nature-nurture question typically falter because of the false assumption that the two—prewiring and rewiring—are competing ideas. "Anti-nativists"—critics of the view that we might be born with significant mental structure prior to experience—often attempt to downplay the significance of genes by making what I earlier called "the argument from plasticity": they point to the brain's resilience to damage and its ability to modify itself in response to experience. Nativists sometimes seem to think that their position rests on downplaying (or demonstrating limits on) plasticity.

In reality, plasticity and innateness are almost logically separate. Innateness is about the extent to which the brain is prewired, plasticity about the extent to which it can be rewired. Some organisms may be good at one but not the other: chimpanzees, for example, may have intricate innate wiring yet, in comparison to humans, relatively few mechanisms for rewiring their brains. Other organisms may be lousy at both: *C. elegans* worms have limited initial structure, and relatively little in the way of techniques for rewiring their nervous system on the basis of experience. And some organisms, such as humans, are well-endowed in both respects, with enormously intricate initial architecture and fantastically powerful and flexible means for rewiring in the face of experience. . . .

CHALLENGE QUESTIONS

Does the Cultural Environment Influence Lifespan Development More than Our Genes?

- Does it make sense that the human brain would be programmed in different ways for men and women, who do, on average, show clear developmental differences?
- Do studies that show identical twins to be more alike than fraternal (nonidentical) twins provide convincing evidence of genetic dominance? Why or why not?
- Applying Darwinian principles to explain psychological aspects of behavior and development has become increasingly popular in recent years, often phrased as "evolutionary psychology." Does that popularity suggest the applications are correct, or could there be other reasons for the popularity of this approach?
- Marcus suggests that understanding genetic influences on development requires appreciating the complexity of how genes work. Is it possible that that complexity will make it too difficult to analyze?
- Much of the evidence for this debate comes from nonhuman animal research. How much can we learn about the nature and nurture of human development from experiments on other species?

Suggested Readings

S. Ceci and W. Williams, *The Nature-Nurture Debate: The Essential Readings* (Blackwell Publishers, 1999)

S. Johnson, "Sociobiology and You," *The Nation* (November 18, 2002)

G. Marcus, *The Birth of the Mind: How a Tiny Number of Genes Creates the Complexity of Human Thought* (Basic Books, 2004)

L. Menand, "What Comes Naturally," *The New Yorker* (November 25, 2002)

S. Pinker, *The Blank Slate* (Viking Adult, 2002)

S. Pinker, "Why Nature and Nurture Won't Go Away," *Daedalus* (Fall 2004)

M. Ridley, *Nature via Nurture* (Harper Collins, 2003)

ISSUE 2

Are Peers More Important than Parents during the Process of Development?

YES: **Judith Rich Harris**, from "How to Succeed in Childhood," *Wilson Quarterly* (Winter 1991)

NO: **Howard Gardner**, from "Do Parents Count?" *New York Times Book Review* (November 5, 1998)

ISSUE SUMMARY

YES: Developmental psychology writer Judith Rich Harris presents a strong and provocative argument suggesting that parents do not influence child development to any significant degree, while peers and social groups have a primary influence.

NO: Harvard psychologist Howard Gardner reviews Harris's work and suggests her argument is overstated and misleading—parents do matter.

If you ask people about their personal development—why did you turn out the way you have—most will tell you about their parents. In contrast, when you ask researchers and scholars about the role of parents in personal development their answer tends to be a little more complicated. Many years of research have focused on estimating and understanding the influence of parenting, but the results have not been as clear as you might expect.

In fact, many scholars now feel the influence of parental "socialization" (the forming of behavior and personality by parenting behaviors) may be much less than most people think. It may be that parents are simply an easy target for child rearing "experts" because most parents want to make sure they are doing the best for their children. Instead of only focusing on parents, however, researchers are devoting significant attention to at least two alternative explanations for what influences lifespan development. One explanation is based on increased attention to biological and genetic influences on behavior, finding high levels of significance for our inherited predispositions. The other explanation is based on the role of culture and society, beyond individual parents, that shapes norms and expectations for children.

That being the case, perhaps it was inevitable that someone would turn the tables on all of the parenting experts by drawing on developmental research to suggest that parents may not really matter much at all. That person turned out to be Judith Rich Harris, who had been writing textbooks about developmental psychology for years before realizing that there was very little evidence for all of the emphasis on the influence of parents in development. She eventually turned this realization into a provocative and award-winning article for psychologists and a controversial book for a popular audience. Her basic argument, stated simply as "parents don't matter nearly as much as we think, and peers matter a lot more," went against both popular wisdom and academic trends. Harris's work instigated a flurry of debate.

One of the prominent psychologists to respond was Howard Gardner, most well known for his influential theory of multiple intelligences. While appreciating Harris's ability to challenge conventional wisdom, Gardner asserts that she significantly overstates her case by massaging data. Gardner is relatively certain that parents do matter, and that the problem with research is simply that personality and character are too difficult to measure. He suggests that the lack of evidence for parents' direct influence derives from an over-reliance on crude surveys, which creates an impression of development that is not true to its complex nature.

POINT

- Most research finds a very modest correlation between parenting behaviors and developmental outcomes.

- The idea that parents matter is really a cultural myth based on invalid aspects of Freudian theory.

- Children do not want to be like their parents and other adults; children want to be like other children.

- Much of what we assume to be parenting effects is actually based on parents sharing genetic material with their children.

COUNTERPOINT

- Harris is selective in what evidence she attends to; there is more evidence than she acknowledges suggesting that parents do matter.

- While Harris claims that our ideas about how parents matter is a cultural myth, she assumes that what happens to children in American society is a true representation of development everywhere.

- It is a disservice to children to assume that they do not take direction from parents, who do most of the explicit care-giving for children.

- Most research on the influence of parents relies on methods that are too crude and general to pick up the nuances of personality development.

How to Succeed in Childhood

Every day, tell your children that you love them. Hug them at least once every 24 hours. Never hit them. If they do something wrong, don't say, "You're bad!" Say, "What you did was bad." No, wait—even that might be too harsh. Say, instead, "What you did made me unhappy."

The people who are in the business of giving out this sort of advice are very angry at me, and with good reason. I'm the author of *The Nurture Assumption*—the book that allegedly claims that "parents don't matter." Though that's not what the book actually says, the advice givers are nonetheless justified in their anger. I don't pull punches, and I'm not impressed by their air of benevolent omniscience. Their advice is based not on scientific evidence but on prevailing cultural myths.

The advice isn't wrong; it's just ineffective. Whether parents do or don't follow it has no measurable effect on how their children turn out. There is a great deal of evidence that the differences in how parents rear their children are not responsible for the differences among the children. I've reviewed this evidence in my book; I will not do it again here.

Let me, however, bring one thing to your attention: the advice given to parents in the early part of this century was almost the mirror image of the advice that is given today. In the early part of this century, parents were not warned against damaging their children's self-esteem; they were warned against "spoiling" them. Too much attention and affection were thought to be bad for kids. In those days, spanking was considered not just the parents' right but their duty.

Partly as a result of the major retoolings in the advice industry, child-rearing styles have changed drastically over the course of this century. Although abusive parents have always existed, run-of-the-mill parents—the large majority of the population—administer more hugs and fewer spankings than they used to.

Now ask yourself this: Are children turning out better? Are they happier and better adjusted than they were in the earlier part of the century? Less aggressive? Less anxious? Nicer?

⋅⊙⋅

It was Sigmund Freud who gave us the idea that parents are the be-all and end-all of the child's world. According to Freudian theory, children learn right

From *Wilson Quarterly*, Winter 1991, pp. 30–37. Copyright © 1991 by Judith Rich Harris. Reprinted by permission.

from wrong—that is, they learn to behave in ways their parents and their society deem acceptable—by identifying with their parents. In the calm after the storm of the oedipal crisis, or the reduced-for-quick-sale female version of the oedipal crisis, the child supposedly identifies with the parent of the same sex.

Freud's name is no longer heard much in academic departments of psychology, but the theory that children learn how to behave by identifying with their parents is still accepted. Every textbook in developmental psychology (including, I confess, the one I co-authored) has its obligatory photo of a father shaving and a little boy pretending to shave. Little boys imitate their fathers, little girls imitate their mothers, and, according to the theory, that's how children learn to be grownups. It takes them a while, of course, to perfect the act.

It's a theory that could have been thought up only by a grownup. From the child's point of view, it makes no sense at all. What happens when children try to behave like grownups is that, more often than not, it gets them into trouble. Consider this story, told by Selma Fraiberg, a child psychologist whose book, *The Magic Years* was popular in the 1960s:

> Thirty-month-old Julia finds herself alone in the kitchen while her mother is on the telephone. A bowl of eggs is on the table. An urge is experienced by Julia to make scrambled eggs. . . . When Julia's mother returns to the kitchen, she finds her daughter cheerfully plopping eggs on the linoleum and scolding herself sharply for each plop, "NoNoNo. Mustn't dood it! NoNoNo. Mustn't dood it!"

Fraiberg attributed Julia's lapse to the fact that she had not yet acquired a superego, presumably because she had not yet identified with her mother. But look at what was Julia doing when her mother came back and caught her egg-handed: she was imitating her mother! And yet Mother was not pleased.

❦

Children cannot learn how to behave appropriately by imitating their parents. Parents do all sorts of things that children are not allowed to do—I don't have to list them, do I?—and many of them look like fun to people who are not allowed to do them. Such prohibitions are found not only in our own society but everywhere, and involve not only activities such as making scrambled eggs but patterns of social behavior as well. Around the world, children who behave too much like grownups are considered impertinent.

Sure, children sometimes pretend to be adults. They also pretend to be horses and monsters and babies, but that doesn't mean they aspire to be horses or monsters or babies. Freud jumped to the wrong conclusions, and so did several generations of developmental psychologists. A child's goal is not to become an adult; a child's goal is to be a successful child.

What does it take to be a successful child? The child's first job is to learn how to get along with her parents and siblings and to do the things that are expected of her at home. This is a very important job—no question about it.

But it is only the first of the child's jobs, and in the long run it is over-shadowed in importance by the child's second job: to learn how to get along with the members of her own generation and to do the things that are expected of her outside the home.

Almost every psychologist, Freudian or not, believes that what the child learns (or doesn't learn) in job 1 helps her to succeed (or fail) in job 2. But this belief is based on an obsolete idea of how the child's mind works, and there is good evidence that it is wrong.

Consider the experiments of developmental psychologist Carolyn Rovee-Collier. A young baby lies on its back in a crib. A mobile with dangling doo-dads hangs overhead. A ribbon runs from the baby's right ankle to the mobile in such a way that whenever the baby kicks its right leg, the doodads jiggle. Babies are delighted to discover that they can make something happen; they quickly learn how to make the mobile move. Two weeks later, if you show them the mobile again, they will immediately start kicking that right leg.

But only if you haven't changed anything. If the doodads hanging from the mobile are blue instead of red, or if the liner surrounding the crib has a pattern of squares instead of circles, or if the crib is placed in a different room, they will gape at the mobile cluelessly, as if they've never seen such a thing in their lives.

⦿

It's not that they're stupid. Babies enter the world with a mind designed for learning and they start using it right away. But the learning device comes with a warning label: what you learn in one situation might not work in another. Babies do not assume that what they learned about the mobile with the red doodads will work for the mobile with the blue doodads. They do not assume that what worked in the bedroom will work in the den. And they do not assume that what worked with their mother will work with their father or the babysitter or their jealous big sister or the kids at the daycare center.

Fortunately, the child's mind is equipped with plenty of storage capacity. As the cognitive scientist Steven Pinker put it in his foreword to my book, "Relationships with parents, with siblings, with peers, and with strangers could not be more different, and the trillion-synapse human brain is hardly short of the computational power it would take to keep each one in a separate mental account."

That's exactly what the child does: keeps each one in a separate mental account. Studies have shown that a baby with a depressed mother behaves in a subdued fashion in the presence of its mother, but behaves normally with a caregiver who is not depressed. A toddler taught by his mother to play elaborate fantasy games does not play these games when he's with his playmates—he and his playmates devise their own games. A preschooler who has perfected the delicate art of getting along with a bossy older sibling is no more likely than a first-born to allow her peers in nursery school to dominate her. A school-age child who says she hates her younger brother—they fight like cats and dogs, their mother complains—is as likely as any other child to have warm and serene peer relationships. Most telling, the child who follows the rules at home, even when no one is watching, may lie or cheat in the schoolroom or on the playground, and vice versa.

Children learn separately how to behave at home and how to behave outside the home, and parents can influence only the way they behave at home. Children behave differently in different social settings because different behaviors are required. Displays of emotion that are acceptable at home are not acceptable outside the home. A clever remark that would be rewarded with a laugh at home will land a child in the principal's office at school. Parents are often surprised to discover that the child they see at home is not the child the teacher sees. I imagine teachers get tired of hearing parents exclaim, "Really? Are you sure you're talking about *my* child?"

The compartmentalized world of childhood is vividly illustrated by the child of immigrant parents. When immigrants settle in a neighborhood of native-born Americans, their children become bicultural, at least for a while. At home they practice their parents' culture and language, outside the home they adopt the culture and language of their peers. But though their two worlds are separate, they are not equal. Little by little, the outside world takes precedence: the children adopt the language and culture of their peers and bring that language and culture home. Their parents go on addressing them in Russian or Korean or Portuguese, but the children reply in English. What the children of immigrants end up with is not a compromise, not a blend. They end up, pure and simple, with the language and culture of their peers. The only aspects of their parents' culture they retain are things that are carried out at home, such as cooking.

<hr />

Late-20th-century native-born Americans of European descent are as ethnocentric as the members of any other culture. They think there is only one way to raise children—the way they do it. But that is not the way children are reared in the kinds of cultures studied by anthropologists and ethologists. The German ethologist Irenäus Eibl-Eibesfeldt has described what childhood is like in the hunter-gatherer and tribal societies he spent many years observing.

In traditional cultures, the baby is coddled for two or three years—carried about by its mother and nursed whenever it whimpers. Then, when the next baby comes along, the child is sent off to play in the local play group, usually in the care of an older sibling. In his 1989 book *Human Ethology,* Eibl-Eibesfeldt describes how children are socialized in these societies:

> Three-year-old children are able to join in a play group, and it is in such play groups that children are truly raised. The older ones explain the rules of play and will admonish those who do not adhere to them, such as by taking something away from another or otherwise being aggressive. Thus the child's socialization occurs mainly within the play group. . . . By playing together in the children's group the members learn what aggravates others and which rules they must obey. This occurs in most cultures in which people live in small communities.

Once their tenure in their mothers' arms has ended, children in traditional cultures become members of a group. This is the way human children
were designed to be reared. They were designed by evolution to become
members of a group, because that's the way our ancestors lived for millions of
years. Throughout the evolution of our species, the individual's survival
depended upon the survival of his or her group, and the one who became a valued member of that group had an edge over the one who was merely tolerated.

❦

Human groups started out small: in a hunter-gatherer band, everyone knows
everyone else and most are blood relatives. But once agriculture began to
provide our ancestors with a more or less dependable supply of food, groups
got bigger. Eventually they became large enough that not everyone in them
knew everyone else. As long ago as 1500 B.C. they were sometimes that large.
There is a story in the Old Testament about a conversation Joshua had with a
stranger, shortly before the Battle of Jericho. They met outside the walls of the
beleaguered town, and Joshua's first question to the stranger was, "Are you for
us or for our adversaries?"

Are you one of *us* or one of *them*? The group had become an idea, a
concept, and the concept was defined as much by what you weren't as by what
you were. And the answer to the question could be a matter of life or death.
When the walls came tumbling down, Joshua and his troops killed every man,
woman, and child in Jericho. Even in Joshua's time, genocide was not a
novelty: fighting between groups, and wholesale slaughter of the losers, had
been going on for ages. According to the evolutionary biologist Jared
Diamond, it is "part of our human and prehuman heritage."

Are you one of *us* or one of *them*? It was the question African Americans
asked of Colin Powell. It was the question deaf people asked of a Miss America
who couldn't hear very well but who preferred to communicate in a spoken
language. I once saw a six-year-old go up to a 14-year-old and ask him, "Are
you a kid or a grownup?"

The human mind likes to categorize. It is not deterred by the fact that
nature often fails to arrange things in convenient clumps but instead provides
a continuum. We have no difficulty splitting up continua. Night and day are
as different as, well, night and day, even though you can't tell where one
leaves off and the other begins. The mind constructs categories for people—male
or female, kid or grownup, white or black, deaf or hearing—and does not hesitate
to draw the lines, even if it's sometimes hard to decide whether a particular
individual goes on one side or the other.

Babies only a few months old can categorize. By the time they reach their
first birthday, they are capable of dividing up the members of their social
world into categories based on age and sex: they distinguish between men and
women, between adults and children. A preference for the members of their
own social category also shows up early. One-year-olds are wary of strange
adults but are attracted to other children, even ones they've never met before.
By the age of two, children are beginning to show a preference for members

of their own sex. This preference grows steadily stronger over the next few years. School-age girls and boys will play together in places where there aren't many children, but when they have a choice of playmates, they tend to form all-girl and all-boy groups. This is true the world around.

✸

The brain we won in the evolutionary lottery gave us the ability to categorize, and we use that skill on people as well as things. Our long evolutionary history of fighting with other groups predisposes us to identify with one social category, to like our own category best, and to feel wary of (or hostile toward) members of other categories. The emotions and motivations that were originally applied to real physical groups are now applied to groups that are only concepts: "Americans" or "Democrats" or "the class of 2001." You don't have to like the other members of your group in order to consider yourself one of them; you don't even have to know who they are. The British social psychologist Henri Tajfel asked his subjects—a bunch of Bristol schoolboys—to estimate the number of dots flashed on a screen. Then half the boys were privately told that they were "overestimators," the others that they were "underestimators." That was all it took to make them favor their own group. They didn't even know which of their schoolmates were in their group and which were in the other.

✸

The most famous experiment in social psychology is the Robber's Cave study. Muzafer Sherif and his colleagues started with 22 eleven-year-old boys, carefully selected to be as alike as possible, and divided them into two equal groups. The groups—the "Rattlers" and the "Eagles"—were separately transported to the Robber's Cave summer camp in a wilderness area of Oklahoma. For a while, neither group knew of the other's existence. But the first time the Rattlers heard the Eagles playing in the distance, they reacted with hostility. They wanted to "run them off." When the boys were brought together in games arranged by researchers disguised as camp counselors, push quickly came to shove. Before long, the two groups were raiding each other's cabins and filling socks with stones in preparation for retaliatory raids.

When people are divided (or divide themselves) into two groups, hostility is one common result. The other, which happens more reliably though it is less well known, is called the "group contrast effect." The mere division into two groups tends to make each group see the other as different from itself in an unfavorable way, and that makes its members *want* to be different from the other group. The result is that any pre-existing differences between the groups tend to widen, and if there aren't any differences to begin with, the members create them. Groups develop contrasting norms, contrasting images of themselves.

In the Robber's Cave study, it happened very quickly. Within a few days of their first encounter, the Eagles had decided that the Rattlers used too many "cuss-words" and resolved to give up cussing; they began to say a prayer before every game. The Rattlers, who saw themselves as tough and manly, continued to favor scatology over eschatology. If an Eagle turned an ankle or skinned a knee, it was all right for him to cry. A Rattler who sustained a similar injury might cuss a bit, but he would bear up stoically.

⋅⊶⦿⊷⋅

The idea for group socialization theory came to me while I was reading an article on juvenile delinquency. The article reported that breaking the law is highly common among adolescents, even among those who were well behaved as children and who are destined to turn into law-abiding adults. This unendearing foible was attributed to the frustration teenagers experience at not being adults: they are longing for the power and privilege of adulthood.

"Wait a minute," I thought. "That's not right. If teenagers really wanted to be adults, they wouldn't be spraying graffiti on overpasses or swiping nail polish from drugstores. If they really wanted to emulate adults they would be doing boring adult things, like sorting the laundry or figuring out their taxes. Teenagers aren't trying to be like adults; they are trying to *contrast* themselves with adults! They are showing their loyalty to their own group and their disdain for adults' rules!"

I don't know what put the idea into my head; at the time, I didn't know beans about social psychology. It took eight months of reading to fill the gaps in my education. What I learned in those eight months was that there is a lot of good evidence to back up my hunch, and that it applies not only to teenagers but to young children as well.

Sociologist William Corsaro has spent many years observing nursery school children in the United States and Italy. Here is his description of four-year-olds in an Italian *scuola materna*, a government-sponsored nursery school:

> In the process of resisting adult rules, the children develop a sense of community and a group identity. [I would have put it the other way around: I think group identity leads to the resistance.] The children's resistance to adult rules can be seen as a routine because it is a daily occurrence in the nursery school and is produced in a style that is easily recognizable to members of the peer culture. Such activity is often highly exaggerated (for instance, making faces behind the teacher's back or running around) or is prefaced by "calls for the attention" of other children (such as, "look what I got" in reference to possession of a forbidden object, or "look what I'm doing" to call attention to a restricted activity).

Group contrast effects show up most clearly when "groupness"—Henri Tajfel's term—is salient. Children see adults as serious and sedentary, so when the social categories *kids* and *grownups* are salient—as they might be, for instance, when the teacher is being particularly bossy—the children become sillier and more active. They demonstrate their fealty to their own age group by making faces and running around.

This has nothing to do with whether they like their teachers personally. You can like people even if they're members of a different group and even if you don't much like that group—a conflict of interests summed up in the saying, "Some of my best friends are Jews." When groupness is salient, even young children contrast themselves with adults and collude with each other in defying them. And yet some of their best friends are grownups.

❧

Learning how to behave properly is complicated, because proper behavior depends on which social category you're in. In every society, the rules of behavior depend on whether you're a grownup or a kid, a female or a male, a prince or a peon. Children first have to figure out the social categories that are relevant in their society, and then decide which category they belong in, then tailor their behavior to the other members of their category.

That brief description seems to imply that socialization makes children more alike, and so it does, in some ways. But groups also work to create or exaggerate differences among their members—differences in personality. Even identical twins reared in the same home do not have identical personalities. When groupness is not salient—when there is no other group around to serve as a foil—a group tends to fall apart into individuals, and differences among them emerge or increase. In boys' groups, for example, there is usually a dominance hierarchy, or "pecking order." I have found evidence that dominant boys develop different personalities from those at the bottom of the ladder.

Groups also typecast their members, pinning labels on them—joker, nerd, brain—that can have lifelong repercussions. And children find out about themselves by comparing themselves with their group mates. They come to think well or poorly of themselves by judging how they compare with the other members of their own group. It doesn't matter if they don't measure up to the standards of another group. A third-grade boy can think of himself as smart if he knows more than most of his fellow third-graders. He doesn't have to know more than a fourth-grader.

❧

According to my theory, the culture acts upon children not through their parents but through the peer group. Children's groups have their own cultures, loosely based on the adult culture. They can pick and choose from the adult culture, and it's impossible to predict what they'll include. Anything that's common to the majority of the kids in the group may be incorporated into the children's culture, whether they learned it from their parents or from the television set. If most of the children learned to say "please" and "thank you" at home, they will probably continue to do so when they're with their peers. The child whose parents failed to teach her that custom will pick it up from the other children: it will be transmitted to her, via the peer group, from the parents of her peers. Similarly, if most of the children watch a particular TV show, the behaviors and attitudes depicted in the show may be incorporated into the norms of their group. The child whose parents do not permit him to watch that show will nonetheless be exposed to those behaviors and attitudes. They are transmitted to him via the peer group.

Thus, even though individual parents may have no lasting effects on their children's behavior, the larger culture does have an effect. Child-rearing practices common to most of the people in a culture, such as teaching children to say "please" and "thank you," can have an effect. And the media can have an effect.

In the hunter-gatherer or tribal society, there was no privacy: everybody knew what everybody else was doing. Nowadays children can't ordinarily watch their neighbors making love, having babies, fighting, and dying, but they can watch these things happening on the television screen. Television has become their window on society, their village square. They take what they see on the screen to be an indication of what life is like—what life is supposed to be—and they incorporate it into their children's cultures.

❧

One of my goals in writing *The Nurture Assumption* was to lighten some of the burdens of modern parenthood. Back in the 1940s, when I was young, the parents of a troublesome child—my parents, for instance—got sympathy, not blame. Nowadays parents are likely to be held culpable for anything that goes wrong with their child, even if they've done their best. The evidence I've assembled in my book indicates that there is a limit to what parents can do: how their child turns out is largely out of their hands. Their major contribution occurs at the moment of conception. This doesn't mean it's mostly genetic; it means that the environment that shapes the child's personality and social behavior is outside the home.

I am not advocating irresponsibility. Parents are in charge of how their children behave at home. They can decide where their children will grow up and, at least in the early years, who their peers will be. They are the chief determiners of whether their children's life at home will be happy or miserable, and they have a moral obligation to keep it from being miserable. My theory does not grant people the license to treat children in a cruel or negligent way.

Although individual parents have little power to influence the culture of children's peer groups, larger numbers of parents acting together have a great deal of power, and so does the society as a whole. Through the prevailing methods of child rearing it fosters, and through influences—especially the media—that act directly on peer-group norms and values, a society shapes the adults of the future. Are we shaping them the way we ought to?

Do Parents Count?

1.

We all want to know how and why we got to be who we are. Parents have a special interest in answering the "how" and "why" questions with respect to their own children. In addressing the mysteries of human growth, traditional societies have invoked God, the gods, the fates, with luck sometimes thrown in. Shakespeare called our attention to the struggle between "nature and nurture."

In our own time the natural sciences and the social sciences have been supplying a bewildering variety of answers. Those with biological leanings look to heredity—the gene complexes of each parent and the ways in which their melded sets of genes express themselves in the offspring. The traits and capacities of the biological parents are seen as in large part determining the characteristics of offspring. Those with a psychological or sociological perspective point to the factors beyond the child's physiology. Psychoanalysts emphasize the pivotal role of parents, and especially the young child's relationship to his or her mother. Behaviorists look at the contingencies of reward and punishment in the child's experience; the character of the child depends on the qualities that are "reinforced," with those in control of reinforcement in early life having an especially significant influence.

Recently, three new candidates have been proposed to explain "socialization"—i.e., how children grow up within a society and absorb its norms. Impressed and alarmed by the powers of new means of communication, particularly television, students of culture like Marie Winn and Neil Postman have described a generation raised by the electronic media. The historian of science Frank Sulloway has brought new attention to the once discounted factor of "birth order": on his account, first-borns embrace the status quo, while later-borns are far more likely to support scientific, political, or religious revolutions. And now, in a much publicized new work, Judith Rich Harris suggests that all of these authorities have got it wrong. On her account, the most potent "socializers" are the child's peers, with parents having little or no effect.

Harris's work has many things going for it. For a start, she has an arresting hypothesis, one that should strike especially responsive chords in adults who feel they are inadequately involved in the formation of the post-baby boom Generation X and the generations to come. She has an appealing personal story. Kicked out of graduate school in psychology in the early 1960s and a victim of a lupus-like disease, she has hitherto led the life of a semi-invalid, making her living coauthoring textbooks in psychology. One day in 1994, after reading a scholarly article about juvenile delinquency, she was struck by the idea that the role of peers in socialization had largely been ignored while the influence of parents had been much overestimated. She succeeded in publishing a theoretical statement of her view in *Psychological Review*, the most prestigious journal of psychological theory. She soon gained recognition among scholars and, in a delicious irony, won a prestigious award named after George Miller, the very professor who had signed her letter of expulsion from Harvard almost four decades ago. Harris's book is well-written, toughly argued, filled with telling anecdotes and biting wit. It has endorsements from some of the most prestigious names in the field. Already it has been widely—and mostly favorably—reported on and reviewed in the popular press.

However, in my view, Harris's thesis is overstated, misleading, and potentially harmful. Overstated in the sense that she highlights evidence consistent with her thesis and understates evidence that undermines it. Misleading because she treats as "natural" and "universal" what, in my view, is really a characterization of contemporary American culture (and those societies influenced by America). Potentially harmful in that it may, if inadvertently, discourage parents from promoting their own beliefs and values, and from becoming models of behavior, at a time when such values and models should be clearly and continually conveyed to children.

2.

Harris begins by outlining familiar positions in psychology. On her account, Freud's view of the Oedipal period is quaint and unsupported, while the behaviorists have been widely discredited, both by the cognitivists (who put the mind back into psychology) and the biologists (who reminded us that we are as much a product of our genes as of our experiences). She then turns her keen critical skills to an attack on the branch of empirical psychology that attempts to document important contributions of parents to their children's personality and character. (Harris uses both terms.)

For over half a century, psychologists and anthropologists have observed parents and children in different settings; they have filled out checklists in which they record predominant kinds of behavior and action, and they have administered questionnaires to the parents and children themselves. These researchers, according to Harris, began with the "nurture assumption"; they presupposed that the most important force in the child's environment is the child's parents and then collected evidence to support that assumption. Moreover, while scholars themselves are often guarded in their conclusions, some "pop" psychologists have no inhibitions whatever. They stress the role of parents over all other forces, thus making parents feel guilty if they fail (according to their own criteria), and full of pride when they succeed.

As Harris shrewdly points out, there are two problems with the nurture assumption. First, when viewed with a critical eye, the empirical evidence about parental influences on their children is weak, and often equivocal. After hundreds of studies, many with individually suggestive findings, it is still difficult to pinpoint the strong effects that parents have on their children. Even the effects of the most extreme experiences—divorce, adoption, and abuse—prove elusive to capture. Harris cites Eleanor Maccoby, one of the leading researchers in the field, who concluded that "in a study of nearly four hundred families, few connections were found between parental child-rearing practices (as reported by parents in detailed interviews) and independent assessments of children's personality characteristics—so few, indeed, that virtually nothing was published relating the two sets of data.

The second problem with the nurture assumption is potentially more devastating. Harris draws heavily on recent results from behavioral genetics to argue that, even in those cases where children resemble their parents, the presence and actions of parents have little to do with that resemblance. The argument she makes from behavioral genetics runs as follows. Studies of siblings, fraternal twins, identical twins reared together, and identical twins reared apart all point to the same conclusion: about half of one's intellect and personality results from one's genes. That is, in any group of people drawn from a particular "population" (e.g., middle-class white youngsters living in the United States), about one half of the variations in an observed trait (for instance, IQ or aggressiveness) is owing to one's parents' genetic contribution. The other half is, of course, the result of one's environment.

For those who assume that the behavior of parents and the models they offer make up a major part of the child's environment, the results of studies in behavioral genetics are surprising. According to those studies, when we examine any population of children and try to account for the nongenetic variations among them, we find that remarkably few variations can be attributed to their "shared environment"—i.e., when parents treat all of their children the same way, for example, being equally punitive to each child.

In fact, according to the behavioral geneticists, nearly all of the variation is due to what is called the "nonshared environment"—i.e., the variety of other influences, including instances where children are treated differently by the parents (e.g., a brother is punished more than his sister, or differently). In the case of any particular child, we simply do not know with any accuracy what makes up the nonshared environment. We can guess that it consists of siblings, printed matter, radio and television, other adults, school, luck, accident, the different (as opposed to the common or "shared") ways in which each parent responds to each child, and—if Judith Rich Harris is correct—most especially, a child's peers.

⋅◀◉▶⋅

So much for Harris's demolition of the importance of parents—except genetically—to the behavior and psyche of the child. Harris adduces evidence from a wide variety of sources, moreover, to stress the important contribution of peers. She goes back to the studies of nonhuman primates to indicate the importance of peer groups in child-rearing—pointing out that monkeys can be successfully reared by peers alone but not by their mothers alone. (It's not known whether this would be true in "higher" primates.) She cites observations of children in different cultures who play together as much and as early as possible, and routinely gang up on the adults (teachers, parents, masters). She searches in the experimental literature for cases where peers exert an appreciable influence upon one another—for example, adolescents who have the same friends turn out to resemble one another. And she places great emphasis on the human tendency to form groups—and particularly "in-groups" with which one strongly identifies.

Harris also provides many telling anecdotes from her own experiences, and from the press and television, about how adults are ignored and peers admired. British boys who rarely see their parents successfully absorb social values at boarding school. Secretary of Labor Robert Reich quit the Cabinet to be with his sons in Cambridge and found that they would rather hang out "in the Square." Touchingly she indicates how she and her husband tried to deal with their wayward adopted daughter but finally realized that the peers had more influence. No such problems existed with their biological daughter, who simply followed her biological destiny; the model provided by her parents was no more than an unnecessary bonus.

Harris describes recurrent situations where youngsters overlook the evident models of their parents in favor of those provided by peers. Deaf children of speaking parents ignore their parents' attempts to teach them to read lips and instead begin to invent gestural signs to communicate with other deaf children and seek opportunities to learn formal signing. The hearing children of deaf parents, Harris points out, learn to speak normally in the absence of a parental model. Analogously, children raised by parents with foreign accents soon begin to speak like their peers, without an accent; like the deaf children, they ignore the models at home and turn, as if magnetized, to the most available set of peers. Arguments like these convince Harris, and apparently many readers (both lay and professional), that young human beings are wired to attend to people of similar age, rather than to those large and obvious authority figures who give them birth and early shelter.

3.

Harris has collected an impressive set of examples and findings to fortify a position that is indeed novel in empirical investigations of "human socialization." I have sought to do justice to her arguments, though I cannot convey her passion, her missionary sense of having seen the light. Yet I do not find her "peer hypothesis" convincing, partly because I read the literature on the subject differently. My deeper reservations come from my belief that Harris has misconstrued the problem of socialization and, in doing so, has put forth a position that harbors its own dangers.

When we consider the empirical part of Harris's argument, we find it is indeed true that the research on parent-child socialization is not what we would hope for. However, this says less about parents and children and more about the state of psychological research, particularly with reference to "softer variables" such as affection and ambition. While psychologists have made genuine progress in the study of visual perception and measurable progress in the study of cognition, we do not really know what to look for or how to measure human personality traits, individual emotions, and motivations, let alone character.

Consider, as an example, the categories that the respondents must use when they describe themselves or others on the Personal Attributes Questionnaire, a test used to obtain data about a person's self-esteem and gender-linked traits. Drawing on a list reminiscent of the Boy Scout oath, those who answer the questionnaire are asked whether they would describe themselves as Gentle, Helpful, Active, Competitive, and Worldly. These terms are not easy to define and people are certainly prone to apply them favorably to their own case. Or consider the list of acts from which observers can choose to characterize children from different cultures—Offers Help, Acts Sociably, Assaults Sociably, Seeks Dominance. Even if we could agree on what kinds of physical behavior merit these labels, we don't know with any confidence what these acts mean to children, adolescents, and adults in diverse cultures—let alone to the observers from a distant university. What does a raised fist or a frown mean to a three-year-old or to the thirty-year-old who observes it? The same question could be asked about a wink or an imitated curtsy. We are not measuring chemical bonds or electrical voltage in such cases. We are seeking to quantify the most subtle human characteristics—the sentiments described so finely by Henry James. And therefore it is not surprising when studies—whether by empirical psychologists or behavioral geneticists—do not yield strong results.

I do not want to elevate psychoanalytic theory or practice over other kinds of inquiry, but at least the Freudians were grappling with the deeper aspects of human character and personality—our urgent longings, our innermost fears and anxieties, our wrenching conflicts. We might perhaps find evidence for these complex feelings—and their putative causes—through long narratives, or projective testing (where the subjects respond to ambiguous photographs or inkblots), or by analyzing a series of sessions on the couch. We won't reach them through questionnaires or checklists; yet Harris relies on many studies that use them.

As social scientists we have been frustrated by our own clumsy efforts to understand personality and character, and even relatively measurable skills, like intelligence or the capacity for problem-solving. And perhaps that is why so many talented psychologists—including the ones quoted on the jacket of *The Nurture Assumption*—have become drawn to evolutionary psychology and behavioral genetics. Here, at last, is the chance to put psychology and social science (and even squishy inquiries into personality, temperament, and character) on what seems a "real" scientific footing. Physics envy has been replaced by biological bias.

But things are not as clear-cut in the biobehavioral world as outsiders may imagine. Because of the possibility of controlled experiments, sociobiology has made genuine progress in explaining the social life of insects; but its account of human behavior remains controversial. The speculations of evolutionary psychology are just that; as commentators such as Stephen Jay Gould and Steve Jones have pointed out . . . , it is difficult to know how to disprove a hypothesis in evolutionary psychology. (For example, what evidence can help us decide whether genes, or humans, are really selfish, or really altruistic, or really both?—in which case we are back where we started.)

⋘◈⋙

And what of behavioral genetics? Certainly the opportunity to study twins who have been separated early in life gives us an additional advantage in understanding the heritability of various traits. And Judith Harris rightly calls attention to two enigmas: the fact that identical twins reared apart are almost as alike as those that are reared together; and the fact that identical twins still turn out to be quite different from one another.

But this subject is also dogged by difficulties. We cannot really do experiments in human behavioral genetics; we have to wait until events happen (as when twins are separated early in life) and then study the effects retrospectively. But this approach leaves too many puzzles unaddressed. First of all, for at least nine crucial months, the twins share the same environment—the womb of the birth mother—and we still know very little about the shared chemical and other effects of gestation on their neurological systems. Then, too, they may or may not have been separated right at birth. (And under what extraordinary circumstances does such separation occur?) They may or may not have been raised for a while by family members. The children are not randomly placed; in nearly all cases, they are raised within the same culture and very often in the same community, with similar social settings. Also, infants who look the same and behave the same are likely to elicit similar responses from adults, while those who are raised in the same house may try all the harder to distinguish themselves from one another. Or they may not.

When you add together the uncertainties (and I have only suggested a few of them here) of human behavioral genetics, and the imprecision of the measures used to describe personality and character, it is no wonder that we find little reliable evidence of parental influence. It would be reassuring if we did—but it is not surprising that we do not.

Which brings me to the alternative picture that Harris attempts to construct. She argues that "peers" are the real instrument of socialization. She may be right; but she does not have the evidence to show this. Her assertions depend almost entirely on what she thinks could one day be shown. Indeed, I find it extremely telling that she relies very heavily on the arguments about language—language-learning among the deaf, and the loss of foreign accents. Neither of these has to do with personality, character, or temperament, her supposed topics. In the case of accents, I assume that we are dealing with an unconscious (and presumably innate) process in which the growing child generalizes from his encounters with many of the adults and children he meets outside the home and through television, the movies, and other media. In the case of deafness, the enormous difference between child and parents forces youngsters to make use of resources outside the home—ranging from adult teachers to television and other visual media.

Indeed, despite some imaginative suggestions by Harris, it is very difficult to envision how one could test her hypothesis. For, after all, who are peers? Do they include siblings? Are they the children in the neighborhood? The children in class? The children in after-school activities or in Sunday school? The children on television? In the movies? At some remote spot on the Internet? Who decides? What happens when peers change because the family moves, or one child switches schools, or leaves (or is kicked out of) one group and then enters another? Most important, who selects peers? At least with parents, we researchers stand on fairly firm ground; and with siblings as well. But for all Ms. Harris's anecdotes, when it comes to peers, we're afloat.

Undoubtedly, psychological researchers inspired by Harris's book will seek evidence bearing on her thesis. We will learn from these studies; and some of us who have taken skeptical positions in this debate may have to acknowledge influences we hadn't sufficiently recognized. Meanwhile, I want to suggest an entirely different approach to the problem, one that might be called "the culture assumption."

4.

What is socialization about? It is about becoming a certain kind of person— gaining specific knowledge, skills, manners, attitudes, and habits. Animals have little culture; human beings revel in it. Yet what is striking in Harris's book is that the words "disciplines," "civilization," and "culture" (in the sense of civilization) are largely absent from the text and from her thinking. Socialization is reduced to having, or not having, certain personality traits—traits that are measured by rather coarsely conceived and applied tests.

The work of the much-maligned Freud remains the best point of departure for a treatment of these issues. In his *Civilization and Its Discontents*, Freud defined culture: "the sum of the achievements and institutions which differentiate our lives from those of our animal forebears, namely that of protecting humanity against nature and of regulating the relations of human beings among themselves." He concentrates particularly on "the one feature of culture which characterizes it better than any other, and that is the value that it sets upon the higher mental activities—intellectual, scientific, and aesthetic achievement." And he speculates that culture (or civilization) rests upon the human superego—the sense of guilt—which develops (or fails to develop) during the child's early interactions with his parents. Guilt keeps us from murdering our fellow citizens; guilt prompts us to delay gratification, to sublimate our primordial passions in favor of loftier pursuits.

Whether one examines the least developed preliterate culture or the most advanced technological society, the question remains the same: What structures and practices will enable children to assume their places in that culture and ultimately aid in transmitting it to the generations to come?

Children will have some say in this process, and it is to Harris's credit (and that of the authorities whom she cites) that she has called attention to this fact. But children are not born just into a family or into a peer group. They are born into an entire culture, whose assumptions begin when the parents say, happily or with a twinge of regret, "It's a girl," and continues to exert its influence in nearly every interaction and experience until the funerary rites, burial, cremation, or ascent to heaven takes place.

Earlier, I referred to Eleanor Maccoby's pessimistic conclusions about documenting parental influence, and I mentioned some of the studies of it that both Maccoby and Harris seem to have had in mind. But let me reconsider the most ambitious of these studies in a different light. In the 1950s and 1960s, John Whiting, Beatrice Whiting, and their colleagues studied childrearing in six cultures, ranging from a small New England town to agricultural settings in Kenya, India, Mexico, the Philippines, and Okinawa. What emerges from that study is that childrearing practices are distinctly different around the globe: different in treatment of infants, in parental sleeping patterns, in how children do chores, in their helping or not helping in rearing younger siblings, in initiation rites, in ways of handling aggression, and in dozens of other variables. So differently are children reared in these cultures that no one would confuse an adult New Englander with an adult Gusii of Kenya or an adult Taira of Okinawa—whether in their knowledge, skills, manners, habits, personality, or temperament.

For the social scientist, the analytic problem is to find the source of these differences. Parents behave differently in these cultures, but so do siblings, peers, other adults, and even visiting anthropologists. And of course the adult roles, natural resources, technology, and means of communication (primitive or modern) differ as well. In all probability, each of these factors makes its contribution to the child's "personality and character." But how to tell them apart? Harris chooses to minimize these other factors and zooms in on the peers, but her confident choice is not justified.

5.

Harris takes little note of a crucial fact: all but a few of the studies that she reviews, including several of the most influential behavioral genetic ones, were carried out in the United States. The United States is not a country without culture; it has many subcultures and a more general "national" culture as well. Harris and most of the authorities that she cites are not studying child-rearing in general; indeed, they are studying child-rearing largely in the white, middle-class United States during the last half-century.

From the time of Alexis de Tocqueville's visit to the United States in the early 1830s, observers have noted the relative importance in this country of peers, friends, or fellow workers of the same age, the members of one's own community. Tocqueville commented, "In America the family, in the Roman and aristocratic signification of the word, does not exist. All that remains are a few vestiges in the first years of childhood. . . ." As a sociologist might put it, America is a more horizontal, "peer-oriented" society than most others, and particularly more so than most traditional societies.

When empirical social science began in this country, these unusual cultural patterns were noted as well. Studying the America of the 1940s, the sociologist David Riesman and his coauthors called attention to the decline of tradition-centered and "inner-directed" families, where the parental models were powerful; and to the concomitant rise of the "other-directed families" that made up "the Lonely Crowd." In this increasingly common family constellation, much socialization occurred at the behest of the peer group, whether for adults or for children. Riesman wrote, "The American peer group, too, cannot be matched for power throughout the middle-class world."

Examining the America of the 1950s and 1960s, the psychologist Urie Bronfrenbrenner noted that children spend more time with peers than with parents and reached the same conclusion: "Whether in comparison to other contemporary cultures, or to itself over time, American society emerges as one that gives decreasing prominence to the family as a socializing agency. . . . We are coming to live in a society that is exaggerated not only by race and class, but also by age." Thus not only has the peer group had an important part in American society from the first; but in recent decades this trend has accelerated.

But there are many possible peer groups. To which ones are children drawn and why? Here I believe (and Harris concedes this) that parents have a decisive role—by the friendships they encourage or discourage, by the schools they select or avoid, by the after-school activities they encourage and summer camps they approve of, parents contribute substantially to the choice of possible peer groups. I would go one step further. Children themselves select—and are selected for—various peer groups according to parental predilections. The work of the social psychologist Mihaly Csikszentmihalyi on "talented teens" strongly suggests that the values exhibited at home—integrity vs. dishonesty, hard work vs. laziness, artistic interests vs. philistinism—imprint themselves on children and in turn serve as major determinants of the peer groups to which children are attracted and, not incidentally, the ones where they are welcomed or spurned.

6.

It seems that in every passing decade—perhaps in every passing selection of fall books—we are told of a new approach to bringing up children or of a new, villainous influence on family life. Certainly, we do not have the feeling of a steady scientific march toward truth. It is more as if we are on a roller-coaster, with each new hypothesis tending to invalidate the previous one.

Still, it would be defeatist simply to embrace the opposite perspective, to declare that each of the various factors—mother, father, grandparents, same-sex siblings, different-sex peers, television, etc.—is important and be done with it. As a scientific community, we can do better than this. To do so, we should be undertaking two activities.

First, even as we welcome the clarifications provided by evolution and genetics, we cannot lose sight of the different cultural settings in which research is carried out and the different meanings attached to seemingly similar traits and actions. Parents and peers have different meanings in Japan, Brazil, and the United States; what we learn from the Whitings, and from much other sociological and anthropological research, is that these "independent variables" cannot simply be equated in designing research or in interpreting findings. In fact, a father may be treated more like a sibling in one society, and an older sibling more like a father in another; parents may encourage children to associate with peers in one culture and to steer clear of them in another and, in yet another, to combat their influence in every way they can.

Second, even as we discover genes or gene clusters that appear to influence important social or psychological variables, we must not assume that we have "solved" the problem of socialization. We still don't know the physical mechanisms by which genes actually affect the brain and cause people to make one choice or another. What triggers (or fails to trigger) genes will vary across cultural settings; and how their expression is understood will also vary. Young men, for example, may have a proclivity to imitate other young men of similar size and power, but that proclivity can be manipulated, depending upon whom the child is exposed to and which rewards and punishments are contingent upon imitation or non-imitation.

Each of the numerous influences on a child's personality I have mentioned can surely have an effect, but the effect will vary among different children, families, and cultures. As science progresses, we may someday be able to predict the relative importance of each across these different factors. My reading of the research suggests that, on the average, parents and peers will turn out to have complementary roles: parents are more important when it comes to education, discipline, responsibility, orderliness, charitableness, and ways of interacting with authority figures. Peers are more important for learning cooperation, for finding the road to popularity, for inventing styles of interaction among people of the same age. Youngsters may find their peers more interesting, but they will look to their parents when contemplating their own futures.

Parental attitudes and efforts will determine to a significant extent how a child resolves the conflicting messages of the home and the wider community as well as the kind of parent the child one day becomes. I would give much weight to the hundreds of studies pointing toward parental influence and to the folk wisdom accumulated by hundreds of societies over thousands of years. And I would, accordingly, be skeptical of a perspective, such as Ms. Harris's, that relies too heavily on heritability statistics and manages to reanalyze numerous studies and practices so that they all somehow point to the peer group.

⚬⚬⚬

To gain attention, an author often states a finding or hypothesis very strongly. (I've been guilty of this myself.) In Harris's case, this has led to a belittling of the roles of parents in childrearing and to a stronger endorsement of the role of peers than the current data allow. I do not question Harris's motives but I do question her judgment, which might have been better guided by the old medical oath "first, do no harm."

It is all to the good if parents do not become crushed with anxiety when they have problems with their children or when their children turn out differently than they would like. Guilt is not always productive. But to suggest, with little foundation, that parents are not important in socialization borders on the irresponsible. Perhaps, on the average, those of us who are parents are not particularly successful in encouraging the personality traits we would hope to see in our children, whether because we do not know how to get their attention, or because they are "primed" to pay attention to their peers and we are not aware of how long and how hard we must work to counter these proclivities.

But children would not—could not—grow to be members of a civilized culture if they were simply left to the examples of their peers. Indeed, parents are especially important when children's peers set strong and destructive examples. In the absence of credible parents and other adults, most children will not be able to deal effectively with life. A social science—or a layman's guide—that largely left out parents after birth would be absurd. So would a society.

Whether on the scene, or behind the scenes, parents have jointly created the institutions that train and inspire children: apprenticeships, schools, works of art and literature, religious classes, playing fields, and even forms of resistance and rebellion. These institutions, and the adults who run them, sustain civilization and provide the disciplines—however fragile they may seem—that keep our societies from reverting to barbarism.

Sad to say, these most important parts of life—which make life satisfying and fascinating—are largely absent from *The Nurture Assumption*. They are absent as well from most of the work emanating from the biotropic pole of contemporary social science. Until their importance is realized, and the biological and cultural perspectives are somehow deeply integrated with one another, scientific claims about children and family life are bound to remain barren.

CHALLENGE QUESTIONS

Are Peers More Important than Parents during the Process of Development?

- While most people automatically assume parents are the most significant influence on lifespan development, what is the tangible evidence?
- Harris never finished her PhD in developmental psychology, causing some scholars to criticize her for lacking proper academic credentials. Should that matter for her argument?
- Gardner claims that current research methods do not really give a full picture of how complex people are. Will psychology ever be able to fully describe personality and the outcomes of development in ways that are true to who we become?
- Most people concerned with lifespan development would acknowledge that many factors influence how we turn out—parents, genes, peers, the media, schools, and more. Why is it worth the effort to try and understand which of those influences matter the most and in what ways?

Suggested Readings

N. Barber, *Why Parents Matter: Parental Investment and Child Outcomes* (Greenwood Publishing Group, 2000)

W. A. Collins, E. E. Maccoby, L. Steinberg, E. M. Hetherington, and M. H. Bornstein, "Contemporary Research on Parenting: The Case for Nature and Nurture," *American Psychologist* (February 2002)

J. Rich Harris, *The Nurture Assumption: Why Children Turn Out the Way They Do* (The Free Press, 1998)

J. Rich Harris, *No Two Alike: Human Nature and Human Individuality* (W. W. Norton, 2006)

J. Rich Harris and J. Kagan, "Slate Dialogues: E-mail Debates of Newsworthy Topics—The Nature of Nurture: Parents or Peers?" available at http://slate.msn.com/id/5853/ (November 1998)

M. Spett, "Is It True That Parenting Has No Influence on Children's Adult Personalities?" *NJ-ACT Newsletter* (March 1999)

D. L. Vandell and J. R. Harris, "Genes, Parents, and Peers: An Invited Exchange of Views," *Developmental Psychology* (November 2000)

W. Williams, "Do Parents Matter? Scholars Need to Explain What Research Really Shows," *The Chronicle of Higher Education* (December 11, 1998)

ISSUE 3

Do Significant Innate Differences Influence the Career Success of Males and Females?

YES: Steven Pinker, from "The Science of Gender and Science: Pinker vs. Spelke, A Debate," *Edge: The Third Culture* (May 2005)

NO: Elizabeth Spelke, from "The Science of Gender and Science: Pinker vs. Spelke, A Debate," *Edge: The Third Culture* (May 2005)

ISSUE SUMMARY

YES: After the Harvard president controversially suggested innate gender differences may play a role in men's disproportionate representation in science careers, cognitive psychologist Steven Pinker suggested that research does find clear innate differences between men and women in some basic cognitive abilities relevant to success.

NO: Harvard psychologist Elizabeth Spelke draws on research into cognitive development to suggest that the major reasons for any differences in career success lie in social, rather than genetic, forces.

In 2004, the then-president of Harvard University Lawrence Summers stirred an energetic controversy about the origin of differences between males and females in fields such as science and math. He provocatively suggested that one of the reasons (and, it is important to note, Summers clearly identified other social forces as influential) for the differences could be innate mental capacity. Immediately after making the comments a prominent woman scientist attending the talk left the room appalled by the suggestion, and a popular uproar ensued. The comments clearly touched a nerve in a society extremely conscious of group differences in opportunity, resources, and success. The comments also spoke directly to research and scholarship addressing the development of gender differences through the lifespan.

In recent social science research and writing it has been common to suggest that evolution designed the male and female brain for slightly different adaptive tasks. Steven Pinker, contextualizing Summers's remarks in relation to such research, has been a prominent proponent of the idea that our minds have clear innate predispositions. As one of the most prodigious academic psychologists of recent decades, Pinker argues forcefully that the idea that the mind is originally a "blank slate" is highly improbable. He reviews a variety of different types of well-established gender differences and the likelihood that those differences originate with innate predispositions, referring to extensive research showing that cognitive development in areas as diverse as motivation and spatial reasoning does, on average, vary by gender.

Despite the familiarity of this argument to social science researchers, it seems a general audience displays a much more emotional response. De-contextualized, it seems Summers was simply claiming women are less able than men. We all know too many personal examples of women's achievement to believe this to be the case.

And, in fact, as Elizabeth Spelke observes in arguing against innate gender differences, the tendency to attribute male and female differences in cognitive abilities to innate biological capacities is a major part of the problem. Even though a great deal of research on infancy and early development shows significant similarities between boys and girls in basic cognitive skills, people persist in expecting differences. Spelke acknowledges that innate predispositions matter, and that gender matters, but asserts firmly that any differences in career success are much easier to explain by looking at social influences.

POINT	COUNTERPOINT
• The evidence for gender differences in cognitive abilities is too obvious to ignore.	• There is also evidence suggesting that infants come into the world with relatively equal cognitive abilities.
• Just because it is morally right to promote opportunities for women, does not mean it is empirically true that there are no innate differences.	• By focusing on gender differences we implicitly, and often unintentionally, perpetuate the social forces that lead to inequality.
• There are clear average differences (with lots of individual variation) between men and women in priorities regarding status, in the desire to work with people, in risk taking, in certain visual-spatial skills, in mathematical reasoning, and in representation at extreme ends of ability.	• Men and women may have average differences, but neither gender has a comprehensive advantage in all of the skills relevant to career success.
• Men are more variable in their abilities, so there are more who are very smart but also more who are very dumb.	• When people are at the extremes of ability, gender discrimination does not matter as much as for more average people.
• Many sex differences are universal, are present very early in life, and generally seem to not be influenced by culture.	• Gender differences in abilities are more likely to be caused by social, rather than biological, forces.

YES

Steven Pinker

The Science of Gender and Science: Pinker Vs. Spelke, A Debate

For those of you who just arrived from Mars, there has been a certain amount of discussion here at Harvard on a particular datum, namely the under-representation of women among tenure-track faculty in elite universities in physical science, math, and engineering.

As with many issues in psychology, there are three broad ways to explain this phenomenon. One can imagine an extreme "nature" position: that males but not females have the talents and temperaments necessary for science. Needless to say, only a madman could take that view. The extreme nature position has no serious proponents.

There is an extreme "nurture" position: that males and females are biologically indistinguishable, and all relevant sex differences are products of socialization and bias.

Then there are various intermediate positions: that the difference is explainable by some combination of biological differences in average temperaments and talents interacting with socialization and bias.

Liz [Elizabeth Spelke] has embraced the extreme nurture position. There is an irony here, because in most discussions in cognitive science she and I are put in the same camp, namely the "innatists," when it comes to explaining the mind. But in this case Liz has said that there is "not a shred of evidence" for the biological factor, that "the evidence against there being an advantage for males in intrinsic aptitude is so overwhelming that it is hard for me to see how one can make a case at this point on the other side," and that "it seems to me as conclusive as any finding I know of in science."

Well we certainly aren't seeing the stereotypical gender difference in *confidence* here! Now, I'm a controversial guy. I've taken many controversial positions over the years, and, as a member of *Homo sapiens,* I think I am right on all of them. But I don't think that in any of them I would say there is "not a shred of evidence" for the other side, even if I think that the evidence *favors* one side. I would not say that the other side "can't even make a case" for their position, even if I think that their case is not *as good as* the one I favor. And as for saying that a position is "as conclusive as any finding in science"—well, we're talking about social science here! This statement would imply that the extreme nurture position on gender differences is more conclusive than, say the evidence that the sun is at the center of the solar system, for the laws of thermodynamics, for the theory of evolution, for plate tectonics, and so on.

These are extreme statements—especially in light of the fact that an enormous amount of research, summarized in these and many other literature reviews, in fact points to a very different conclusion. I'll quote from one of them, a book called *Sex Differences in Cognitive Ability* by Diane Halpern. She is a respected psychologist, recently elected as president of the American Psychological Association, and someone with no theoretical axe to grind. She does not subscribe to any particular theory, and has been a critic, for example, of evolutionary psychology. And here what she wrote in the preface to her book:

> "At the time I started writing this book it seemed clear to me that any between sex differences in thinking abilities were due to socialization practices, artifacts, and mistakes in the research. After reviewing a pile of journal articles that stood several feet high, and numerous books and book chapters that dwarfed the stack of journal articles, I changed my mind. The literature on sex differences in cognitive abilities is filled with inconsistent findings, contradictory theories, and emotional claims that are unsupported by the research. Yet despite all the noise in the data, clear and consistent messages could be heard. There are real and in some cases sizable sex differences with respect to some cognitive abilities. Socialization practices are undoubtedly important, but there is also good evidence that biological sex differences play a role in establishing and maintaining cognitive sex differences, a conclusion I wasn't prepared to make when I began reviewing the relevant literature."

This captures my assessment perfectly.

Again for the benefit of the Martians in this room: This isn't just any old issue in empirical psychology. There are obvious political colorings to it, and I want to begin with a confession of my own politics. I am a feminist. I believe that women have been oppressed, discriminated against, and harassed for thousands of years. I believe that the two waves of the feminist movement in the 20th century are among the proudest achievements of our species, and I am proud to have lived through one of them, including the effort to increase the representation of women in the sciences.

But it is crucial to distinguish the *moral* proposition that people should not be discriminated against on account of their sex—which I take to be the core of feminism—and the *empirical* claim that males and females are biologically indistinguishable. They are not the same thing. Indeed, distinguishing them is essential to protecting the core of feminism. Anyone who takes an honest interest in science has to be prepared for the facts on a given issue to come out either way. And that makes it essential that we not hold the ideals of feminism hostage to the latest findings from the lab or field. Otherwise, if the findings come out as showing a sex difference, one would either have to say, "I guess sex discrimination wasn't so bad after all," or else furiously suppress or distort the findings so as to preserve the ideal. The truth cannot be sexist. Whatever the facts turn out to be, they should not be taken to compromise the core of feminism.

Why study sex differences? Believe me, being the Bobby Riggs of cognitive science is not my idea of a good time. So should I care about them, especially since they are not the focus of my own research?

First, differences between the sexes are part of the human condition. We all have a mother and a father. Most of us are attracted to members of the opposite sex, and the rest of us notice the difference from those who do. And we can't help but notice the sex of our children, friends, and our colleagues, in every aspect of life.

Also, the topic of possible sex differences is of great scientific interest. Sex is a fundamental problem in biology, and sexual reproduction and sex differences go back a billion years. There's an interesting theory, which I won't have time to explain, which predicts that there should be an overall equal investment of organisms in their sons and daughters; neither sex is predicted to be superior or inferior across the board. There is also an elegant theory, namely Bob Trivers' theory of differential parental investment, which makes highly specific predictions about when you should expect sex differences and what they should look like.

The nature and source of sex differences are also of practical importance. Most of us agree that there are aspects of the world, including gender disparities, that we want to change. But if we want to *change* the world we must first *understand* it, and that includes understanding the sources of sex differences.

Let's get back to the datum to be explained. In many ways this is an *exotic* phenomenon. It involves biologically unprepared talents and temperaments: evolution certainly did not shape any part of the mind to do the work of a professor of mechanical engineering at MIT, for example. The datum has nothing to do with basic cognitive processes, or with those we use in our everyday lives, in school, or even in most college courses, where indeed there are few sex differences.

Also, we are talking about extremes of achievement. Most women are not qualified to be math professors at Harvard because most *men* aren't qualified to be math professors at Harvard. These are extremes in the population.

And we're talking about a subset of fields. Women are not underrepresented to nearly the same extent in all academic fields, and certainly not in all prestigious professions. . . .

. . . Let me begin the substance of my presentation by connecting the political issue with the scientific one. Economists who study patterns of discrimination have long argued (generally to no avail) that there is a crucial conceptual difference between *difference* and *discrimination*. A departure from a 50–50 sex ratio in any profession does not, by itself, imply that we are seeing discrimination, unless the interests and aptitudes of the two groups are equated. Let me illustrate the point with an example, involving myself.

I work in a scientific field—the study of language acquisition in children—that is in fact dominated by women. Seventy-five percent of the members the main professional association are female, as are a majority of the keynote speakers at our main conference. I'm here to tell you that it's not because men like me have been discriminated against. I decided to study language development, as opposed to, say, mechanical engineering, for many reasons. The goal of designing a better automobile transmission does not turn me on as much as the goal of figuring out how kids acquire language. And I don't think I'd be as good at designing a transmission as I am in studying child language.

Now, all we need to do to explain sex differences without invoking the discrimination or invidious sexist comparisons is to suppose that whatever traits *I* have that predispose *me* to choose (say) child language over (say) mechanical engineering are not exactly equally distributed statistically among men and women. For those of you out there—of either gender—who also are not mechanical engineers, you should understand what I'm talking about.

Okay, so what *are* the similarities and differences between the sexes? There certainly are many similarities. Men and women show no differences in general intelligence or *g*—on average, they are exactly the same, right on the money. Also, when it comes to the basic categories of cognition—how we negotiate the world and live our lives; our concept of objects, of numbers, of people, of living things, and so on—there are no differences.

Indeed, in cases where there *are* differences, there are as many instances in which women do slightly better than men as ones in which men do slightly better than women. For example, men are better at throwing, but women are more dexterous. Men are better at mentally rotating shapes; women are better at visual memory. Men are better at mathematical problem-solving; women are better at mathematical calculation. And so on.

But there are at least six differences that are relevant to the datum. we have been discussing. The literature on these differences is so enormous that I can only touch on a fraction of it. I'll restrict my discussion to a few examples in which there are enormous data sets, or there are meta-analyses that boil down a literature.

The first difference, long noted by economists studying employment practices, is that men and women differ in what they state are their priorities in life. To sum it up: men, on average, are more likely to chase status at the expense of their families; women give a more balanced weighting. Once again: Think statistics! The finding is not that women value family and don't value status. It is not that men value status and don't value family. Nor does the finding imply that every last woman has the asymmetry that women show on average or that every last man has the asymmetry that men show on average. But in large data sets, on average, an asymmetry what you find.

Just one example. In a famous long-term study of mathematically precocious youth, 1,975 youngsters were selected in 7th grade for being in the top 1% of ability in mathematics, and then followed up for more than two decades. These men and women are certainly equally talented. And if anyone has ever been encouraged in math and science, these kids were. Both genders: they are equal in their levels of achievement, and they report being equally satisfied with the course of their lives. Nonetheless there are statistical differences in what they say is important to them. There are some things in life that the females rated higher than males, such as the ability to have a part-time career for a limited time in one's life; living close to parents and relatives; having a meaningful spiritual life; and having strong friendships. And there are some things in life that the males rated higher than the females. They include having lots of money; inventing or creating something; having a full-time career; and being successful in one's line of work. It's worth noting that studies of highly successful people find that single-mindedness and competitiveness are recurring traits in geniuses (of both sexes).

Here is one other figure from this data set. As you might expect, this sample has a lot of people who like to work Herculean hours. Many people in this group say they would like to work 50, 60, even 70 hours a week. But there are also slight differences. At each one of these high numbers of hours there are slightly more men than women who want to work that much. That is, more men than women don't care about whether they have a life.

Second, interest in people versus things and abstract rule systems. There is a *staggering* amount of data on this trait, because there is an entire field that studies people's vocational interests. I bet most of the people in this room have taken a vocational interest test at some point in their lives. And this field has documented that there are consistent differences in the kinds of activities that appeal to men and women in their ideal jobs. I'll just discuss one of them: the desire to work with people versus things. There is an enormous average difference between women and men in this dimension, about one standard deviation.

And this difference in interests will tend to cause people to gravitate in slightly different directions in their choice of career. The occupation that fits best with the "people" end of the continuum is "director of a community services organization." The occupations that fit best with the "things" end are physicist, chemist, mathematician, computer programmer, and biologist.

We see this consequence not only in the choice of whether to go into science, but also in the choice which branch of science the two sexes tend to go into. Needless to say, from 1970 to 2002 there was a huge increase in the percentage of university degrees awarded to women. But the percentage still differs dramatically across fields. Among the Ph.Ds awarded in 2001, for example, in education 65% of the doctorates went to women; in the social sciences, 54%; in the life sciences, 47%; in the physical sciences, 26%; in engineering, 17%. This is completely predictable from the difference in interests between people and living things, on the one hand, and inanimate objects, on the other. And the pattern is pretty much the same in 1980 and 2001, despite the change in absolute numbers.

Third, risk. Men are by far the more reckless sex. In a large meta-analysis involving 150 studies and 100,000 participants, in 14 out of 16 categories of risk-taking, men were over-represented. The two sexes were equally represented in the other two categories, one of which was smoking, for obvious reasons. And two of the largest sex differences were in "intellectual risk taking" and "participation in a risky experiment." We see this sex difference in everyday life, in particular, in the following category: the Darwin Awards, "commemorating those individuals who ensure the long-term survival of our species by removing themselves from the gene pool in a sublimely idiotic fashion." Virtually all—perhaps all—of the winners are men.

Fourth, three-dimensional mental transformations: the ability to determine whether the drawings in each of these pairs the same 3-dimensional shape. Again I'll appeal to a meta-analysis, this one containing 286 data sets and 100,000 subjects. The authors conclude, "we have specified a number of tests that show highly significant sex differences that are stable across age, at least after puberty, and have not decreased in recent years." Now, as I mentioned, for some kinds of spatial ability, the advantage goes to women, but in "mental rotation, "spatial perception," and "spatial visualization" the advantage goes to men.

Now, does this have any relevance to scientific achievement? We don't know for sure, but there's some reason to think that it does. In psychometric studies, three-dimensional spatial visualization is correlated with mathematical problem-solving. And mental manipulation of objects in three dimensions figures prominently in the memoirs and introspections of most creative physicists and chemists, including Faraday, Maxwell, Tesla, Kéekulé, and Lawrence, all of whom claim to have hit upon their discoveries by dynamic visual imagery and only later set them down in equations. A typical introspection is the following: "The cyclical entities which seem to serve as elements in my thought are certain signs and more or less clear images which can be voluntarily reproduced and combined. This combinatory play seems to be the essential feature in productive thought before there is any connection with logical construction in words or other kinds of signs." The quote comes from this fairly well-known physicist.

Fifth, mathematical reasoning. Girls and women get better school grades in mathematics and pretty much everything else these days. And women are better at mathematical calculation. But consistently, men score better on mathematical word problems and on tests of mathematical reasoning, at least statistically. Again, here is a meta analysis, with 254 data sets and 3 million subjects. It shows no significant difference in childhood; this is a difference that emerges around puberty, like many secondary sexual characteristics. But there are sizable differences in adolescence and adulthood, especially in high-end samples. Here is an example of the average SAT mathematical scores, showing a 40-point difference in favor of men that's pretty much consistent from 1972 to 1997. In the Study of Mathematically Precocious Youth (in which 7th graders were given the SAT, which of course ordinarily is administered only to older, college-bound kids), the ratio of those scoring over 700 is 2.8 to 1 male to female. (Admittedly, and interestingly, that's down from 25 years ago, when the ratio was 13-to-1, and perhaps we can discuss some of the reasons.) At the 760 cutoff, the ratio nowadays is 7 males to 1 female.

Now why is there a discrepancy with grades? Do SATs and other tests of mathematical reasoning aptitude underpredict grades, or do grades overpredict high-end aptitude? At the Radical Forum Liz was completely explicit in which side she takes, saying that "the tests are no good," unquote. But if the tests are really so useless, why does every major graduate program in science still use them—including the very departments at Harvard and MIT in which Liz and I have selected our own graduate students.

I think the reason is that school grades are affected by homework and by the ability to solve the kinds of problems that have already been presented in lecture and textbooks. Whereas the aptitude tests are designed to test the application of mathematical knowledge to unfamiliar problems. And this, of course, is closer to the way that math is used in actually *doing* math and science.

Indeed, contrary to Liz, and the popular opinion of many intellectuals, the tests are *surprisingly* good. There is an enormous amount of data on the predictive power of the SAT. For example, people in science careers overwhelmingly scored in 90th percentile in the SAT or GRE math test. And the tests predict earnings, occupational choice, doctoral degrees, the prestige of one's degree, the probability of having a tenure-track position, and the number of patents. Moreover this predictive power is the same for men and for women. As for why there is that underprediction of grades—a slight underprediction, one-tenth of a standard deviation—the Educational Testing Service did a study on that phenomenon, and were able to explain the mystery by a combination of the choice of major, which differs between the sexes, and the greater conscientiousness of women.

Finally there's a sex difference in variability. It's crucial here to look at the right samples. Estimates of variance depend highly on the tails of the distribution, which by definition contain smaller numbers of people. Since people at the tails of the distribution in many surveys are likely to be weeded out for various reasons, it's important to have large representative samples from national populations. In this regard the gold standard is the *Science* paper by Novell and Hedges, which reported six large stratified probability samples. They found that in 35 out of 37 tests, including all of the tests in math, space, and science, the male variance was greater than the female variance. . . .

Now the fact that these six gender differences exist does not mean that they are innate. This of course is a much more difficult issue to resolve. A necessary preamble to this discussion is that nature and nurture are not alternatives; it is possible that the explanation for a given sex difference involves some of each. The only issue is whether the contribution of biology is greater than zero. I think that there are ten kinds of evidence that the contribution of biology *is* greater than zero, though of course it is nowhere near 100 percent.

First, there are many biological mechanisms by which a sex difference *could* occur. There are large differences between males and females in levels of sex hormones, especially prenatally, in the first six months of life, and in adolescence. There are receptors for hormones all over the brain, including the cerebral cortex. There are many small differences in men's and women's brains, including the overall size of the brain (even correcting for body size), the density of cortical neurons, the degree of cortical asymmetry, the size of hypothalamic nuclei, and several others.

Second, many of the major sex differences—certainly some of them, maybe all of them, are universal. The idea that there are cultures out there somewhere in which everything is the reverse of here turns out to be an academic legend. In his survey of the anthropological literature called *Human Universals,* the anthropologist Donald Brown points out that in all cultures men and women are seen as having different natures; that there is a greater involvement of women in direct child care; more competitiveness in various measures for men than for women; and a greater spatial range traveled by men compared to by women.

In personality, we have a cross-national survey (if not a true cross-cultural one) in Feingold's meta-analysis, which noted that gender differences in personality are consistent across ages, years of data collection, educational levels, and nations. When it comes to spatial manipulation and mathematical reasoning, we have fewer relevant data, and we honestly don't have true cross-cultural surveys, but we do have cross-national surveys. David Geary and Catherine Desoto found the expected sex difference in mental rotation in ten European countries and in Ghana, Turkey, and China. Similarly, Diane Halpern, analyzing results from ten countries, said that "the majority of the findings show amazing cross-cultural consistency when comparing males and females on cognitive tests."

Third, stability over time. Surveys of life interests and personality have shown little or no change in the two generations that have come of age since the second wave of feminism. There is also, famously, *resistance* to change in communities that, for various ideological reasons, were dedicated to stamping out sex differences, and found they were unable to do so. These include the Israeli kibbutz, various American Utopian communes a century ago, and contemporary androgynous academic couples.

In tests of mental rotation, the meta-analysis by Voyer et al found no change over time. In mathematical reasoning there has been a decline in the size of the difference, although it has certainly not disappeared.

Fourth, many sex differences can be seen in other mammals. It would be an amazing coincidence if these differences just happened to be replicated in the arbitrary choices made by human cultures at the dawn of time. There are large differences between males and females in many mammals in aggression, in investment in offspring, in play aggression play versus play parenting, and in the range size, which predicts a species' sex differences in spatial ability (such as in solving mazes), at least in polygynous species, which is how the human species is classified. Many primate species even show a sex difference in their interest in physical objects versus conspecifics, a difference seen their patterns of juvenile play. Among baby vervet monkeys, the males even prefer to play with trucks and the females with other kinds of toys!

Fifth, many of these differences emerge in early childhood. It is said that there is a technical term for people who believe that little boys and little girls are born indistinguishable and are molded into their natures by parental socialization. The term is "childless."

Some sex differences seem to emerge even in the first week of life. Girls respond more to sounds of distress, and girls make more eye contact than boys. And in a study that I know Liz disputes and that I hope we'll talk about, newborn boys were shown to be more interested in looking at a physical object than a face, whereas newborn girls were shown to be more interested in looking at a face than a physical object.

A bit later in development there are vast and robust differences between boys and girls, seen all over the world. Boys far more often than girls engage in rough-and-tumble play, which involves aggression, physical activity, and competition. Girls spend a lot more often in cooperative play. Girls engage much more often in play parenting. And yes, boys the world over turn anything into a vehicle or a weapon, and girls turn anything into a doll. There are sex differences in intuitive psychology, that is, how well children can read one another's minds. For instance, several large studies show that girls are better than boys in solving the "false belief task," and in interpreting the mental states of characters in stories.

Sixth, genetic boys brought up as girls. In a famous 1970s incident called the John/Joan case, one member of a pair of identical twin boys lost his penis in a botched circumcision (I was relieved to learn that this was not done by a moyl, but by a bumbling surgeon). Following advice from the leading gender expert of the time, the parents agreed to have the boy castrated, given female-specific hormones, and brought up as a girl. All this was hidden from him throughout his childhood.

When I was an undergraduate the case was taught to me as proof of how gender roles are socially acquired. But it turned out that the facts had been suppressed. When "Joan" and her family were interviewed years later, it turned out that from the youngest ages he exhibited boy-typical patterns of aggression and rough-and-tumble play, rejected girl-typical activities, and showed a greater interest in things than in people. At age 14, suffering from depression, his father finally told him the truth. He underwent further surgery, married a woman, adopted two children, and got a job in a slaughterhouse.

This is not just a unique instance. In a condition called cloacal exstrophy, genetic boys are sometimes born without normal male genitalia. When they are castrated and brought up as girls, in 25 out of 25 documented instances they have felt that they were boys trapped in girls' bodies, and showed male-specific patterns of behavior such as rough-and-tumble play.

Seventh, a lack of differential treatment by parents and teachers. These conclusions come as a shock to many people. One comes from Lytton and Romnev's meta-analysis of sex-specific socialization involving 172 studies and 28,000 children, in which they looked both at parents' reports and at direct observations of how parents treat their sons and daughters—and found few or no differences among contemporary Americans. In particular, there was no difference in the categories "Encouraging Achievement" and "Encouraging Achievement in Mathematics."

There is a widespread myth that teachers (who of course are disproportionately female) are dupes who perpetuate gender inequities by failing to call on girls in class, and who otherwise having low expectations of girls' performance. In fact Jussim and Eccles, in a study of 100 teachers and 1,800 students, concluded that teachers seemed to be basing their perceptions of students on those students' actual performances and motivation.

Eighth, studies of prenatal sex hormones: the mechanism that makes boys boys and girls girls in the first place. There is evidence, admittedly squishy in parts, that differences in prenatal hormones make a difference in later thought and behavior even within a given sex. In the condition called congenital adrenal hyperplasia, girls in utero are subjected to an increased dose of androgens, which is neutralized postnatally. But when they grow up they have male-typical toy preferences—trucks and guns—compared to other girls, male-typical play patterns, more competitiveness, less cooperativeness, and male-typical occupational preferences. However, research on their spatial abilities is inconclusive, and I cannot honestly say that there are replicable demonstrations that CAH women have male-typical patterns of spatial cognition.

Similarly, variations in fetal testosterone, studied in various ways, show that fetal testosterone has a nonmonotic relationship to reduced eye contact and face perception at 12 months, to reduced vocabulary at 18 months, to reduced social skills and greater narrowness of interest at 48 months, and to enhanced mental rotation abilities in the school-age years.

Ninth, circulating sex hormones. . . . Though it's possible that all claims of the effects of hormones on cognition will turn out to be bogus, I suspect something will be salvaged from this somewhat contradictory literature. There are, in any case, many studies showing that testosterone levels in the low-normal male range are associated with better abilities in spatial manipulation. And in a variety of studies in which estrogens are compared or manipulated, there is evidence, admittedly disputed, for statistical changes in the strengths and weaknesses in women's cognition during the menstrual cycle, possibly a counterpart to the changes in men's abilities during their daily and seasonal cycles of testosterone.

My last kind of evidence: imprinted X chromosomes. In the past fifteen years an entirely separate genetic system capable of implementing sex differences has been discovered. In the phenomenon called genetic imprinting, studied by David Haig and others, a chromosome such as the X chromosome can be altered depending on whether it was passed on from one's mother or from one's father. This makes a difference in the condition called Turner syndrome, in which a child has just one X chromosome, but can get it either from her mother or her father. When she inherits an X that is specific to girls, on average she has a better vocabulary and better social skills, and is better at reading emotions, at reading body language, and at reading faces.

A remark on stereotypes, and then I'll finish.

Are these stereotypes? Yes, many of them are (although, I must add, not all of them—for example, women's superiority in spatial memory and mathematical calculation). There seems to be a widespread assumption that if a sex difference conforms to a stereotype, the difference must have been *caused* by the stereotype, via differential expectations for boys and for girls. But of course the causal arrow could go in either direction: stereotypes might *reflect* differences rather than cause them. In fact there's an enormous literature in cognitive psychology which says that people can be good intuitive statisticians when forming categories and that their prototypes for conceptual categories track the statistics of the natural world pretty well. For example, there is a stereotype that basketball players are taller on average than jockeys. But that does not mean that basketball players grow tall, and jockeys shrink, because we expect them to have certain heights! Likewise, Alice Eagly and Jussim and Eccles have shown that most of people's gender stereotypes are in fact pretty accurate. Indeed the error people make is in the direction of *under*predicting sex differences.

To sum up: I think there is more than "a shred of evidence" for sex differences that are relevant to statistical gender disparities in elite hard science departments. There are reliable average difference in life priorities, in an interest in people versus things, in risk-seeking, in spatial transformations, in mathematical reasoning, and in variability in these traits. And there are ten kinds of evidence that these differences are not *completely* explained by socialization and bias, although they surely are in part.

A concluding remark. None of this provides grounds for ignoring the biases and barriers that do keep women out of science, as long as we keep in mind the distinction between *fairness* on the one hand and *sameness* on the other. And I will give the final word to Gloria Steinem: "there are very few jobs that actually require a penis or a vagina, and all the other jobs should be open to both sexes."

Elizabeth Spelke

The Science of Gender and Science: Pinker Vs. Spelke, A Debate

I want to start by talking about the points of agreement between Steve and me, and as he suggested, there are many. If we got away from the topic of sex and science, we'd be hard pressed to find issues that we disagree on. Here are a few of the points of agreement that are particularly relevant to the discussions of the last few months.

First, we agree that both our society in general and our university in particular will be healthiest if all opinions can be put on the table and debated on their merits. We also agree that claims concerning sex differences are empirical, they should be evaluated by evidence, and we'll all be happier and live longer if we can undertake that evaluation as dispassionately and rationally as possible. We agree that the mind is not a blank slate; in fact one of the deepest things that Steve and I agree on is that there is such a thing as human nature, and it is a fascinating and exhilarating experience to study it. And finally, I think we agree that the role of scientists in society is rather modest. Scientists find things out. The much more difficult questions of how to use that information, live our lives, and structure our societies are not questions that science can answer. Those are questions that everybody must consider.

So where do we disagree?

We disagree on the answer to the question, why in the world are women scarce as hens' teeth on Harvard's mathematics faculty and other similar institutions? In the current debate, two classes of factors have been said to account for this difference. In one class are social forces, including overt and covert discrimination and social influences that lead men and women to develop different skills and different priorities. In the other class are genetic differences that predispose men and women to have different capacities and to want different things.

In his book, *The Blank Slate,* and again today, Steve argued that social forces are over-rated as causes of gender differences. Intrinsic differences in aptitude are a larger factor, and intrinsic differences in motives are the biggest factor of all. Most of the examples that Steve gave concerned what he takes to be biologically based differences in motives.

My own view is different. I think the big forces causing this gap are social factors. There are no differences in overall intrinsic aptitude for science and mathematics between women and men. Notice that I am not saying the genders are indistinguishable, that men and women are alike in every way, or even that men and women have identical cognitive profiles. I'm saying that when you add up all the things that men are good at, and all the things that women are good at, there is no overall advantage for men that would put them at the top of the fields of math and science.

On the issue of motives, I think we're not in a position to know whether the different things that men and women often say they want stem only from social forces, or in part from intrinsic sex differences. I don't think we can know that now.

I want to start with the issue that's clearly the biggest source of debate between Steve and me: the issue of differences in intrinsic aptitude. This is the only issue that my own work and professional knowledge bear on. Then I will turn to the social forces, as a lay person as it were, because I think they are exerting the biggest effects. Finally, I'll consider the question of intrinsic motives, which I hope we'll come back to in our discussion.

Over the last months, we've heard three arguments that men have greater cognitive aptitude for science. The first argument is that from birth, boys are interested in objects and mechanics, and girls are interested in people and emotions. The predisposition to figure out the mechanics of the world sets boys on a path that makes them more likely to become scientists or mathematicians. The second argument assumes, as Galileo told us, that science is conducted in the language of mathematics. On the second claim, males are intrinsically better at mathematical reasoning, including spatial reasoning. The third argument is that men show greater variability than women, and as a result there are more men at the extreme upper end of the ability distribution from which scientists and mathematicians are drawn. Let me take these claims one by one.

The first claim, as Steve said, is gaining new currency from the work of Simon Baron-Cohen. It's an old idea, presented with some new language. Baron-Cohen says that males are innately predisposed to learn about objects and mechanical relationships, and this sets them on a path to becoming what he calls "systematizers." Females, on the other hand, are innately predisposed to learn about people and their emotions, and this puts them on a path to becoming "empathizers." Since systematizing is at the heart of math and science, boys are more apt to develop the knowledge and skills that lead to math and science.

To anyone as old as I am who has been following the literature on sex differences, this may seem like a surprising claim. The classic reference on the nature and development of sex differences is a book by Eleanor Maccoby and Carol Jacklin that came out in the 1970s. They reviewed evidence for all sorts of sex differences, across large numbers of studies, but they also concluded that certain ideas about differences between the genders were myths. At the top of their list of myths was the idea that males are primarily interested in objects and females are primarily interested in people. They reviewed an enormous literature, in which babies were presented with objects and people to see if they were more interested in one than the other. They concluded that there were no sex differences in these interests.

Nevertheless, this conclusion was made in the early 70s. At that time, we didn't know much about babies' understanding of objects and people, or how their understanding grows. Since Baron-Cohen's claims concern differential predispositions to learn about different kinds of things, you could argue that the claims hadn't been tested in Maccoby and Jacklin's time. What does research now show?

. . . From birth, babies perceive objects. They know where one object ends and the next one begins. They can't see objects as well as we can, but as they grow their object perception becomes richer and more differentiated.

Babies also start with rudimentary abilities to represent that an object continues to exist when it's out of view, and they hold onto those representations longer, and over more complicated kinds of changes, as they grow. Babies make basic inferences about object motion: inferences like, the force with which an object is hit determines the speed with which it moves. These inferences undergo regular developmental changes over the infancy period.

In each of these cases, there is systematic developmental change, and there's variability. Because of this variability, we can compare the abilities of male infants to females. Do we see sex differences? The research gives a clear answer to this question: We don't.

Male and female infants are equally interested in objects. Male and female infants make the same inferences about object motion, at the same time in development. They learn the same things about object mechanics at the same time.

Across large numbers of studies, occasionally a study will favor one sex over the other. For example, girls learn that the force with which something is hit influences the distance it moves a month earlier than boys do. But these differences are small and scattered. For the most part, we see high convergence across the sexes. Common paths of learning continue through the preschool years, as kids start manipulating objects to see if they can get a rectangular block into a circular hole. If you look at the rates at which boys and girls figure these things out, you don't find any differences. We see equal developmental paths.

I think this research supports an important conclusion. In discussions of sex differences, we need to ask what's common across the two sexes. One thing that's common is infants don't divide up the labor of understanding the world, with males focusing on mechanics and females focusing on emotions. Male and female infants are both interested in objects and in people, and they learn about both. The conclusions that Maccoby and Jacklin drew in the early 1970s are well supported by research since that time.

Let me turn to the second claim. People may have equal abilities to develop intuitive understanding of the physical world, but formal math and science don't build on these intuitions. Scientists use mathematics to come up with new characterizations of the world and new principles to explain its functioning. Maybe males have an edge in scientific reasoning because of their greater talent for mathematics.

As Steve said, formal mathematics is not something we have evolved to do; it's a recent accomplishment. Animals don't do formal math or science, and neither did humans back in the Pleistocene. If there is a biological basis for our mathematical reasoning abilities, it must depend on systems that evolved for other purposes, but that we've been able to harness for the new purpose of representing and manipulating numbers and geometry.

Research from the intersecting fields of cognitive neuroscience, neuropsychology, cognitive psychology, and cognitive development provide evidence for five "core systems" at the foundations of mathematical reasoning. The first is a system for representing small exact numbers of objects—the difference between *one*, *two*, and *three*. This system emerges in human infants at about five months of age, and it continues to be present in adults. The second is a system for discriminating large, approximate numerical magnitudes—the difference between a set of about ten things and a set of about 20 things. That system also emerges early in infancy, at four or five months, and continues to be present and functional in adults.

The third system is probably the first uniquely human foundation for numerical abilities: the system of natural number concepts that we construct as children when we learn verbal counting. That construction takes place between about the ages of two and a half and four years. The last two systems are first seen in children when they navigate. One system represents the geometry of the surrounding layout. The other system represents landmark objects.

All five systems have been studied quite extensively in large numbers of male and female infants. We can ask, are there sex differences in the development of any of these systems at the foundations of mathematical thinking? Again, the answer is no. . . .

These findings and others support two important points. First, indeed there is a biological foundation to mathematical and scientific reasoning. We are endowed with core knowledge systems that emerge prior to any formal instruction and that serve as a basis for mathematical thinking. Second, these systems develop equally in males and females. Ten years ago, the evolutionary psychologist and sex difference researcher, David Geary, reviewed the literature that was available at that time. He concluded that there were no sex differences in "primary abilities" underlying mathematics. What we've learned in the last ten years continues to support that conclusion.

Sex differences do emerge at older ages. Because they emerge later in childhood, it's hard to tease apart their biological and social sources. But before we attempt that task, let's ask what the differences are.

I think the following is a fair statement, both of the cognitive differences that Steve described and of others. When people are presented with a complex task that can be solved through multiple different strategies, males and females sometimes differ in the strategy that they prefer.

For example, if a task can only be solved by representing the geometry of the layout, we do not see a difference between men and women. But if the task can be accomplished either by representing geometry or by representing individual landmarks, girls tend to rely on the landmarks, and boys on the geometry. To take another example, when you compare the shapes of two objects of different orientations, there are two different strategies you can use. You can attempt a holistic rotation of one of the objects into registration with the other, or you can do point-by-point featural comparisons of the two objects. Men are more likely to do the first; women are more likely to do the second.

Finally, the mathematical word problems on the SAT-M very often allow multiple solutions. Both item analyses and studies of high school students engaged in the act of solving such problems suggest that when students have the choice of solving a problem by plugging in a formula or by doing Ven diagram-like spatial reasoning, girls tend to do the first and boys tend to do the second.

Because of these differences, males and females sometimes show differing cognitive profiles on timed tests. When you have to solve problems fast, some strategies will be faster than others. Thus, females perform better at some verbal, mathematical and spatial tasks, and males perform better at other verbal, mathematical, and spatial tasks. This pattern of differing profiles is not well captured by the generalization, often bandied about in the popular press, that women are "verbal" and men are "spatial." There doesn't seem to be any more evidence for that than there was for the idea that women are people-oriented and men are object-oriented. Rather the differences are more subtle.

Does one of these two profiles foster better learning of math than the other? In particular, is the male profile better suited to high-level mathematical reasoning?

At this point, we face a question that's been much discussed in the literature on mathematics education and mathematical testing. The question is, by what yardstick can we decide whether men or women are better at math?

Some people suggest that we look at performance on the SAT-M, the quantitative portion of the Scholastic Assessment Test. But this suggestion raises a problem of circularity. The SAT test is composed of many different types of items. Some of those items are solved better by females. Some are solved better by males. The people who make the test have to decide, how many items of each type to include? Depending on how they answer that question, they can create a test that makes women look like better mathematicians, or a test that makes men look like better mathematicians. What's the right solution?

Books are devoted to this question, with much debate, but there seems to be a consensus on one point: The only way to come up with a test that's fair is to develop an independent understanding of what mathematical aptitude is and how it's distributed between men and women. But in that case, we can't use performance on the SAT to give us that understanding. We've got to get that understanding in some other way. So how are we going to get it?

A second strategy is to look at job outcomes. Maybe the people who are better at mathematics are those who pursue more mathematically intensive careers. But this strategy raises two problems. First, which mathematically intensive jobs should we choose? If we choose engineering, we will conclude that men are better at math because more men become engineers. If we choose accounting, we will think that women are better at math because more women become accountants: 57% of current accountants are women. So which job are we going to pick, to decide who has more mathematical talent?

These two examples suggest a deeper problem with job outcomes as a measure of mathematical talent. Surely you've got to be good at math to land a mathematically intensive job, but talent in mathematics is only one of the factors influencing career choice. It can't be our gold standard for mathematical ability.

So what can be? I suggest the following experiment. We should take a large number of male students and a large number of female students who have equal educational backgrounds, and present them with the kinds of tasks that real mathematicians face. We should give them new mathematical material that they have not yet mastered, and allow them to learn it over an extended period of time: the kind of time scale that real mathematicians work on. We should ask, how well do the students master this material? The good news is, this experiment is done all the time. It's called high school and college.

Here's the outcome. In high school, girls and boys now take equally many math classes, including the most advanced ones, and girls get better grades. In college, women earn almost half of the bachelor's degrees in mathematics, and men and women get equal grades. Here I respectfully disagree with one thing that Steve said: men and women get equal grades, even when you only compare people within a single institution and a single math class. Equating for classes, men and women get equal grades.

The outcome of this large-scale experiment gives us every reason to conclude that men and women have equal talent for mathematics. Here, I too would like to quote Diane Halpern. Halpern reviews much evidence for sex differences, but she concludes, "differences are not deficiencies." Men and women have equal aptitude for mathematics. Yes, there are sex differences, but they don't add up to an overall advantage for one sex over the other.

Let me turn to the third claim, that men show greater variability, either in general or in quantitative abilities in particular, and so there are more men at the upper end of the ability distribution. I can go quickly here, because Steve has already talked about the work of Camilla Benbow and Julian Stanley, focusing on mathematically precocious youth who are screened at the age of 13, put in intensive accelerated programs, and then followed up to see what they achieve in mathematics and other fields.

As Steve said, students were screened at age 13 by the SAT, and there were many more boys than girls who scored at the highest levels on the SAT-M. In the 1980s, the disparity was almost 13 to 1. It is now substantially lower, but there still are more boys among the very small subset of people from this large, talented sample who scored at the very upper end. Based on these data, Benbow and Stanley concluded that there are more boys than girls in the pool from which future mathematicians will be drawn. But notice the problem with this conclusion: It's based entirely on the SAT-M. This test, and the disparity it revealed, are in need of an explanation, a firmer yardstick for assessing and understanding gender differences in this talented population.

Fortunately, Benbow, Stanley and Lubinski have collected much more data on these mathematically talented boys and girls: not just the ones with top scores on one timed test, but rather the larger sample of girls and boys who were accelerated and followed over time. Let's look at some of the key things that they found.

First, they looked at college performance by the talented sample. They found that the males and females took equally demanding math classes and majored in math in equal numbers. More girls majored in biology and more boys in physics and engineering, but equal numbers of girls and boys majored in math. And they got equal grades. The SAT-M not only under-predicts the performance of college women in general, it also under-predicted the college performance of women in the talented sample. These women and men have been shown to be equally talented by the most meaningful measure we have: their ability to assimilate new, challenging material in demanding mathematics classes at top-flight institutions. By that measure, the study does not find any difference between highly talented girls and boys.

So, what's causing the gender imbalance on faculties of math and science? Not differences in intrinsic aptitude. Let's turn to the social factors that I think are much more important. Because I'm venturing outside my own area of work, and because time is short, I won't review all of the social factors producing differential success of men and women. I will talk about just one effect: how gender stereotypes influence the ways in which males and females are perceived.

Let me start with studies of parents' perceptions of their own children. Steve said that parents report that they treat their children equally. They treat their boys and girls alike, and they encourage them to equal extents, for they want both their sons and their daughters to succeed. This is no doubt true. But how are parents perceiving their kids?

Some studies have interviewed parents just after the birth of their child, at the point where the first question that 80% of parents ask—is it a boy or a girl?—has been answered. Parents of boys describe their babies as stronger, heartier, and bigger than parents of girls. The investigators also looked at the babies' medical records and asked whether there really were differences between the boys and girls in weight, strength, or coordination. The boys and girls were indistinguishable in these respects, but the parents' descriptions were different.

At 12 months of age, girls and boys show equal abilities to walk, crawl, or clamber. But before one study, Karen Adolph, an investigator of infants' locomotor development, asked parents to predict how well their child would do on a set of crawling tasks: Would the child be able to crawl down a sloping ramp? Parents of sons were more confident that their child would make it down the ramp than parents of daughters. When Adolph tested the infants on the ramp, there was no difference whatever between the sons and daughters, but there was a difference in the parents' predictions.

My third example, moving up in age, comes from the studies of Jackie Eccles. She asked parents of boys and girls in sixth grade, how talented do you think your child is in mathematics? Parents of sons were more likely to judge that their sons had talent than parents of daughters. A panoply of objective measures, including math grades in school, performance on standardized tests, teachers' evaluations, and children's expressed interest in math, revealed no differences between the girls and boys. Still, there was a difference in parents' perception of their child's intangible talent. Other studies have shown a similar effect for science.

There's clearly a mismatch between what parents perceive in their kids and what objective measures reveal. But is it possible that the parents are seeing something that the objective measures are missing? Maybe the boy getting B's in his math class really is a mathematical genius, and his mom or dad has sensed that. To eliminate that possibility, we need to present observers with the very same baby, or child, or Ph.D. candidate, and manipulate their belief about the person's gender. Then we can ask whether their belief influences their perception.

It's hard to do these studies, but there are examples, and I will describe a few of them. A bunch of studies take the following form: you show a group of parents, or college undergraduates, video-clips of babies that they don't know personally. For half of them you give the baby a male name, and for the other half you give the baby a female name. (Male and female babies don't look very different.) The observers watch the baby and then are asked a series of questions: What is the baby doing? What is the baby feeling? How would you rate the baby on a dimension like strong-to-weak, or more intelligent to less intelligent? There are two important findings.

First, when babies do something unambiguous, reports are not affected by the baby's gender. If the baby clearly smiles, everybody says the baby is smiling or happy. Perception of children is not pure hallucination. Second, children often do things that are ambiguous, and parents face questions whose answers aren't easily readable off their child's overt behavior. In those cases, you see some interesting gender labeling effects. For example, in one study a child on a video-clip was playing with a jack-in-the-box. It suddenly popped up, and the child was startled and jumped backward. When people were asked, what's the child feeling, those who were given a female label said, "she's afraid." But the ones given a male label said, "he's angry." Same child, same reaction, different interpretation.

In other studies, children with male names were more likely to be rated as strong, intelligent, and active; those with female names were more likely to be rated as little, soft, and so forth.

I think these perceptions matter. You, as a parent, may be completely committed to treating your male and female children equally. But no sane parents would treat a fearful child the same way they treat an angry child. If knowledge of a child's gender affects adults' perception of that child, then male and female children are going to elicit different reactions from the world, different patterns of encouragement. These perceptions matter, even in parents who are committed to treating sons and daughters alike.

I will give you one last version of a gender-labeling study. This one hits particularly close to home. The subjects in the study were people like Steve and me: professors of psychology, who were sent some vitas to evaluate as applicants for a tenure track position. Two different vitas were used in the study. One was a vita of a walk-on-water candidate, best candidate you've ever seen, you would die to have this person on your faculty. The other vita was a middling, average vita among successful candidates. For half the professors, the name on the vita was male, for the other half the name was female. People were asked a series of questions: What do you think about this candidate's research productivity? What do you think about his or her teaching experience? And finally, Would you hire this candidate at your university?

For the walk-on-water candidate, there was no effect of gender labeling on these judgments. I think this finding supports Steve's view that we're dealing with little overt discrimination at universities. It's not as if professors see a female name on a vita and think, I don't want her. When the vita's great, everybody says great, let's hire.

What about the average successful vita, though: that is to say, the kind of vita that professors most often must evaluate? In that case, there were differences. The male was rated as having higher research productivity. These psychologists, Steve's and my colleagues, looked at the same number of publications and thought, "good productivity" when the name was male, and "less good productivity" when the name was female. Same thing for teaching experience. The very same list of courses was seen as good teaching experience when the name was male, and less good teaching experience when the name was female. In answer to the question would they hire the candidate, 70% said yes for the male, 45% for the female. If the decision were made by majority rule, the male would get hired and the female would not.

A couple other interesting things came out of this study. The effects were every bit as strong among the female respondents as among the male respondents. Men are not the culprits here. There were effects at the tenure level as well. At the tenure level, professors evaluated a very strong candidate, and almost everyone said this looked like a good case for tenure. But people were invited to express their reservations, and they came up with some very reasonable doubts. For example, "This person looks very strong, but before I agree to give her tenure I would need to know, was this her own work or the work of her adviser?" Now that's a perfectly reasonable question to ask. But what ought to give us pause is that those kinds of reservations were expressed *four times more often* when the name was female than when the name was male.

So there's a pervasive difference in perceptions, and I think the difference matters. Scientists' perception of the quality of a candidate will influence the likelihood that the candidate will get a fellowship, a job, resources, or a promotion. A pattern of biased evaluation therefore will occur even in people who are absolutely committed to gender equity. . . .

From the moment of birth to the moment of tenure, throughout this great developmental progression, there are unintentional but pervasive and important differences in the ways that males and females are perceived and evaluated.

I have to emphasize that perceptions are not everything. When cases are unambiguous, you don't see these effects. What's more, cognitive development is robust: boys and girls show equal capacities and achievements in educational settings, including in science and mathematics, despite the very different ways in which boys and girls are perceived and evaluated. I think it's really great news that males and females develop along common paths and gain common sets of abilities. The equal performance of males and females, despite their unequal treatment, strongly suggests that mathematical and scientific reasoning has a biological foundation, and this foundation is shared by males and females.

Finally, you do not create someone who feels like a girl or boy simply by perceiving them as male or female. That's the lesson that comes from the studies of people of one sex who are raised as the opposite sex. Biological sex differences are real and important. Sex is not a cultural construction that's imposed on people.

But the question on the table is not, Are there biological sex differences? The question is, Why are there fewer women mathematicians and scientists? The patterns of bias that I described provide four interconnected answers to that question. First, and most obviously, biased perceptions produce discrimination: When a group of equally qualified men and women are evaluated for jobs, more of the men will get those jobs if they are perceived to be more qualified. Second, if people are rational, more men than women will put themselves forward into the academic competition, because men will see that they've got a better chance for success. Academic jobs will be more attractive to men because they face better odds, will get more resources, and so forth.

Third, biased perceptions earlier in life may well deter some female students from even attempting a career in science or mathematics. If your parents feel that you don't have as much natural talent as someone else whose objective abilities are no better than yours, that may discourage you, as Eccles's work shows. Finally, there's likely to be a snowball effect. All of us have an easier time imagining ourselves in careers where there are other people like us. If the first three effects perpetuate a situation where there are few female scientists and mathematicians, young girls will be less likely to see math and science as a possible life.

So by my personal scorecard, these are the major factors. Let me end, though, by asking, could Steve also be partly right? Could biological differences in motives—motivational patterns that evolved in the Pleistocene but that apply to us today—propel more men than women towards careers in mathematics and science?

My feeling is that where we stand now, we cannot evaluate this claim. It may be true, but as long as the forces of discrimination and biased perceptions affect people so pervasively, we'll never know. I think the only way we can find out is to do one more experiment. We should allow all of the evidence that men and women have equal cognitive capacity, to permeate through society. We should allow people to evaluate children in relation to their actual capacities, rather than one's sense of what their capacities ought to be, given their gender. Then we can see, as those boys and girls grow up, whether different inner voices pull them in different directions. I don't know what the findings of that experiment will be. But I do hope that some future generation of children gets to find out.

CHALLENGE QUESTIONS

Do Significant Innate Differences Influence the Career Success of Males and Females?

- Do you agree with Pinker that part of the challenge with thinking about this issue in a reasonable way comes from the social taboo against suggesting that any differences might be innate rather than learned? Why or why not?
- Both authors agree that there are some average differences that might favor men, while others might favor women. Which of these differences seem most important for career success and other outcomes of lifespan development?
- Spelke notes that we as a society tend to focus on gender from the moment children are born, when the first question is usually "boy or girl?" Given our interest in gender, is it possible to completely remove ideas about innate differences?
- Although there are still differences in career patterns for men and women, these differences have shifted greatly during recent decades. How do you think each side would explain these shifts?

Suggested Readings

B. Barres, "Does Gender Matter?" *Nature* (July 13, 2006)

L. Brizendine, *The Female Brain* (Broadway, 2006)

A. Fausto-Sterling, "Beyond Differences: A Biologist's Perspective," *Journal of Social Issues* (vol. 53, no. 2, 1997)

D. Geary, "Evolution and Developmental Sex Differences," *Current Directions in Psychological Science* (August 4, 1999)

S. Glazer, "Gender and Learning: Are There Innate Differences Between the Sexes?" *The CQ Researcher* (May 20, 2005)

C. Leaper, "The Social Construction and Socialization of Gender During Development," *Toward a Feminist Developmental Psychology* (Routledge, 2000)

R. Monastersky, "Women and Science: The Debate Goes On," *The Chronicle of Higher Education* (March 4, 2005)

A. Ripley, N. Mustafa, D. van Dyk, and U. Plon, "Who Says a Woman Can't be Einstein?" *Time* (March 7, 2005)

Internet References . . .

This Web site provides information and resources related to pregnancy and prenatal development.

http://www.babycenter.com/

This educational site provides a wide range of information about prenatal development.

http://www.pregnancy.org/

This Web site is an extensive reference for checking the influence of various substances on a fetus during pregnancy.

http://www.safefetus.com

This site provides links to various resources related to physical, cognitive, language, and social development in infants.

http://www.mhhe.com/socscience/devel/common/infant.htm

Part of a larger site for pediatricians, this site provides information about healthy infant development.

http://www.keepkidshealthy.com/infant/
infantdevelopment.html

This site has extensive links to information about many aspects of child development.

http://www.childdevelopmentinfo.com/

This site provides a good overview of the work of Jean Piaget, who started the discussion of infant symbolic representation.

http://www.ship.edu/~cgboeree/genpsypiaget.html

The James S. McDonnell Foundation funds research related to brain development, and is headed by the author of *The Myth of the First Three Years*.

http://www.jsmf.org/

Zero to Three is a non-profit organization working to facilitate healthy development, and their Web site contains information and resources focused on infants and their families.

http://www.zerotothree.org/

Prenatal Development and Infancy

*O*ur most rapid and astonishing physical changes occur during the approximately nine months prior to birth and during the first years of postnatal life. These are unique years in development because of our complete dependence on others. Being without language, a concept of self, and other complex capacities, it is easy to imagine these initial stages as a simple matter of accommodating needs and wants. There is, however, an increasing awareness that there is more to our earliest development than initially meets the eye. This section considers three issues dealing with ways that our experiences during prenatal development and infancy provide a foundation for all of the complexity that follows.

- Does Prenatal Exposure to Drugs Such as Cocaine Create "Crack Babies" with Special Developmental Concerns?

- Is There a "Myth of the First Three Years"?

- Are There Good Reasons to Allow Infants to Consume Electronic Media, Such as Television?

ISSUE 4

Does Prenatal Exposure to Drugs Such as Cocaine Create "Crack Babies" with Special Developmental Concerns?

YES: Sherri McCarthy and Thomas Franklin Waters, from "A Crack Kid Grows Up: A Clinical Case Report," *Journal of Offender Rehabilitation* (vol. 37, 2003)

NO: Mariah Blake, from "The Damage Done: Crack Babies Talk Back," *Columbia Journalism Review* (September/October, 2004)

ISSUE SUMMARY

YES: Sherri McCarthy and Thomas F. Waters, educational psychology and criminal justice professors at Northern Arizona University, review the research on "crack babies" suggesting a link between prenatal cocaine exposure and serious physical, socioemotional, and cognitive effects requiring special care and attention.

NO: Journalist and editor Mariah Blake contends that the idea of "crack babies" with special needs is more a media creation than a medical fact.

Most people are familiar enough with the idea of "crack babies" to be somewhat surprised to learn that there is a scientific controversy about the validity of that label. While no scientist would ever endorse using crack cocaine, or any illicit drug, during pregnancy, many scientists have raised questions about whether research evidence warrants the powerfully negative stigma of labeling babies as "crack babies."

Any external agent that causes malformation of organs and tissue during prenatal development is called a teratogen. Common teratogens include alcohol, tobacco, and narcotics. Fetal exposure to these drugs, most often through use by the mother, has varying degrees of detrimental influence on prenatal development. While the generally negative influence of exposure to teratogens is clear and accepted, the controversy comes with regard to the relative influence of particular quantities and types of exposure. For example, how much alcohol is necessary to produce clear negative effects?

Because crack cocaine is illegal it is associated with a much more negative social taboo than alcohol or cigarettes. Yet research concerning prenatal development suggests that, aside from social appropriateness, the actual biological effects of alcohol and cigarette smoking are at least as harmful to a fetus as the biological effects of narcotics such as cocaine. In fact, according to ratings by the FDA, a drug like aspirin has more established negative biological effects on a fetus than cocaine. These biological effects, however, cannot necessarily be removed from their social context—the direct effects of drug use are almost always compounded by other health and parenting behaviors of a mother and father. A great deal of research on cocaine exposure in utero suggests that any prenatal effects are at least compounded by problems that may exist in the postnatal environment.

With regard to evidence, note that while McCarthy and Waters focus on the negative outcomes of "crack kids" by citing a variety of research studies, they also note that some of the research results are contradictory and few are firmly established. They also point out that the effects of crack specifically are difficult to disentangle from other potential developmental influences either prenatal (such as alcohol or tobacco exposure) or postnatal (such as malnutrition or lack of parental warmth). Yet, using a case study to illustrate their argument, they feel that a category of "crack kids" is still warranted.

In contrast, Blake suggests that the inability of research to disentangle the effects of crack from other developmental influences provides strong evidence that the category of "crack babies" is based on moralistic stereo-types and the tendency of the media to want to craft good stories regardless of science. In fact, she explains, the original fear of an epidemic of "crack babies" was based on the media exaggerating the results of a very limited research study, using a small sample, that has since been brought into question. She also notes examples of children who were exposed to cocaine in utero, but suffered more from the label than from an inherent biological deficiency.

POINT	COUNTERPOINT
• Research studies indicate negative outcomes from prenatal exposure to crack.	• The research on the effects of prenatal exposure to crack are easy to misinterpret.
• When pregnant women use drugs such as crack it is likely that they might engage in other problematic behaviors.	• Larger social problems that are problematic for raising healthy children are often ignored due to focus on biological problems associated with the label "crack babies".
• It seems plausible that increasing rates of ADD and ADHD among school children could be linked to prenatal exposure to drugs.	• Many children who were exposed to crack during fetal development are actually high functioning and healthy.
• Because this has been a politically loaded issue, it is possible that "crack kids" from white, middle class families may have been ignored.	• The label of "crack babies" creates stereotypes and expectations that cause more problems than they solve.

YES

Sherri McCarthy and Thomas Franklin Waters

A Crack Kid Grows Up: A Clinical Case Report

"**C**rack baby" is a term commonly utilized in the U.S. to describe infants born to mothers who ingested rock cocaine while pregnant. Early research, often exaggerated or misrepresented by the popular media, heightened social concern to epidemic proportions resulting in a moral crusade to "save" infants from the addicted caregivers. A public fervor to prosecute and jail mothers who abused drugs during pregnancy developed, along with a despair that public education would be destroyed when these babies entered school. Biogenics, class politics and stereotypes of the "evil mother" shadowed the debates. The fervor has now faded, replaced by more thoughtful but often contradictory or confounded research on the developmental effects of in utero exposure to cocaine.

In 1987, it was estimated that as many as 375,000 infants born in the U.S. each year had been exposed to crack cocaine by maternal use. Although many consider this estimate high, and there are probably no reliable national estimates of prenatal cocaine exposure, there are doubtless many adolescents and young adults today who were exposed to rock cocaine during gestation. Little information is available on how these maturing "crack kids" fare as they enter the passage to adulthood. It is our purpose to offer some insight into this passage. . . .

Background Research

Physical Effects

Women who abuse cocaine during pregnancy may experience a variety of complications, including spontaneous abortions, stillbirths, ruptured placentas and premature delivery. Because cocaine crosses the blood/brain barrier after passing through the placenta during pregnancy, it also potentially effects the developing fetal brain as well as other organs and tissues. Since the fetal liver is not fully developed and cannot quickly eliminate the drug, it also has a far longer half-life in a fetus than in an adult. Documented consequences of exposure include impaired fetal growth, low birth weight and small head circumference. Respiratory and urinary tract difficulties also

From *Journal of Offender Rehabilitation*, vol. 37, 2003, pp. 201–207, 210–216. Copyright © 2003 by Haworth Press. Reprinted by permission.

appear more common among cocaine-exposed infants. Some studies also report birth defects of the kidneys, arms and heart; however, these studies may not have accounted for synergistic effects of other teratogens used during pregnancy, such as alcohol. Cocaine also appears to be linked to the likelihood of Sudden Infant Death Syndrome (SIDS), although this relationship is uncertain due to the difficulty of separating out the multiple effects of poverty, cigarette smoking, alcohol use, poor nutrition and inadequate prenatal care from cocaine use. Thus, studies do not agree regarding the increase of incidence of SIDS and other health problems among cocaine-exposed infants and are often difficult to interpret due to other risks present such as use of other teratogens and poor prenatal care. Regardless, there appears to be sufficient evidence to assume that "crack babies" are likely to be less healthy than other infants. Some researchers have claimed that difficulties seem to disappear as early as three years of age and others have noted that nutrition and environment after birth may account for either continued poor health or improvement. However, if crack exposure during infancy does have long-term effects on physical health, "crack kids" may be less healthy, overall, than their non-exposed peers during adolescence and early adulthood and may require more frequent medical care.

Socioemotional Effects

Because cocaine is a powerful central nervous system stimulant with lasting neurobehavioral effects, it can potentially retard social and emotional development. Mayes notes that potential manifestations include excessive crying, heightened reactivity to light and touch, delays in language development and lower intelligence. It has been difficult to demonstrate long-term behavioral, cognitive and language problems in children who were exposed prenatally to cocaine. Because prenatal cocaine exposure was not widely recognized or researched until the mid-1980s, the study of neurological impairment related to use has a brief history and continued study is necessary to confirm or refute general clinical impressions. Documented clinical impressions of crack-exposed infants include sleep dysfunction, irregularities in response to stimuli, excessive crying and fussiness. Most studies suggest these infants are more easily aroused but others have found cocaine-exposed infants to be more difficult to stimulate. Lester suggests this can be accounted for by the fact that the easily aroused infants are experiencing the effects of recent maternal cocaine use while the others are displaying the effect of chronic use on infant growth and development.

Studies employing tools such as the Brazelton Neonatal Behavioral Assessment Scale (NBAS) or the Bayley Scales of Infant Development (BSID) have mixed results. Dow-Edwards found that newborns exposed to crack had decreased interactive skills, short attention spans, comparatively depressed performance in psychomotor development and oversensitivity to stimulation, coping with stimulus by either frantic wails or sleep. Bateman reported brief tremors for the first 24 hours after birth. Mayes, Bornstein, Chawarska and Granger found evidence that visual information processing demonstrated increased arousal to stimuli which may exceed optimal levels for sustaining attention or processing information. Chasnoff, Griffith, Macgregor, Dirkes and Burns found that cocaine-exposed infants demonstrated poorer state regulation, orientation and motor performance than controls and presented more abnormal reflexes. Richardson, Hamel, Goldschmidt and Day, in a carefully controlled study, found maternal cocaine use was significantly related to poorer autonomic stability, poorer motor maturity and tone and increased abnormal reflexes 2 days after birth. They suggest that infants exposed to cocaine may be more vulnerable to the stress of birth and exhibit a delayed recovery from that stress. Mentis and Lundgren suggest that explicit conclusions are difficult to reach from this data because measures used may not be sufficiently sensitive to identify other potential problems which may not manifest until later stages of development.

In a study of toddlers who had been exposed to crack cocaine while in utero, Howard, Beckwith, Rodning and Kropenske found that, compared to controls, subjects were emotionally and socially underdeveloped and had difficulty learning. Drug-exposed children did not show strong feelings of pleasure, anger or distress and appeared to be less purposeful and organized when playing. They also appeared unattached to their primary caregivers. During infancy, development of empathy is fostered by the affective relationship that develops between infant and caregiver. Later, empathy develops when caregivers provide opportunities for children to experience a variety of emotions and encourage them to attend to the emotional experiences of others. Lack of attachment combined with poor attention span may make it difficult for "crack kids" to develop empathy. Similarly, avoidant or ambivalent attachment appears to foster an external locus of control. Individuals with highly external loci of control assume that they have no control over their own actions or circumstances. From the perspective of these individuals, fate or destiny, those in power or other criteria determine the outcome of events. They do not see their own behavior or effort as having any effect on the events in their lives.

Implications of this research for later development of "crack kids" suggests lack of empathy and a highly external locus of control as defined by Rotter may be common characteristics as they mature. The current profile for Attention Deficit Hyperactivity Disorder (ADHD), a condition which has been increasingly common in recent years, also sounds strikingly consistent with this early research on "crack babies." Leichtman notes that parent/child attachment, internal representation of the world, empathy, self-soothing, self-regulation, self-esteem, values and competencies, learning and organizational strategies, social skills, responsibility and problem-solving are all difficulties encountered in a child with ADHD personality development. Martinez and Bournival note that ADHD children exhibit low cortical arousal as infants. Rapoport and Castellanos found evidence that ADHD children had significantly smaller right frontal brain regions and right striatum than controls. These findings seem consistent with the physiological and neurological data gathered on crack-exposed newborns and suggest that ADD or ADHD may be yet another manifestation of in utero crack exposure as children mature.

This is not to suggest that ADD or ADHD is indicative of maternal cocaine use, as a variety of other factors may also contribute to the condition. However, one precursor to the condition may, indeed, be exposure to teratogens in utero, making it far more likely that "crack kids" will suffer from this condition than others.

Cognitive Effects

An ADD or ADHD profile markedly effects learning, cognition and educational success. Other cognitive developmental influences of cocaine exposure include delays in the acquisition of language skills, literacy and memory. In a study of 35 crack-exposed infants and 35 matched controls, van Baar and Graaff concluded that drug-exposed children tended to score lower on all general intelligence and language measures than controls and were functioning at a lower cognitive level as preschoolers. Similar studies by Mentis and Lundgren and Nulman provided similar results. However, cognitive assessments using general cognitive, verbal performance, quantitative and memory scales given by Hawley, Halle, Drasin and Thomas did not reveal significant differences between drug-exposed and non-drug-exposed children. Barone studied 26 cocaine-exposed children from 1 to 7 years of age who were placed in stable foster homes. She reported there were some noticeable delays but, overall, literacy patterns were developing in a manner similar to non-exposed children. It appears adverse cognitive effects may be mediated to some degree by a stable home environment and exacerbated by an unstable environment. Mayes suggested that a number of neurobehavioral differences between crack-exposed and non-exposed infants may disappear by 6 months of age, noting that the plasticity of the brain, combined with adequate caretaking, may compensate for some or all of the neurological insult. Zuckerman concurs. However, it seems to be evident that prenatal cocaine exposure does effect neurological functioning and is manifested by inappropriate response to stimulus, attentional impairments, language difficulties and learning problems. Such data suggests that difficulty in school, difficulty holding jobs and relatively low verbal intelligence scores may be characteristic of "crack kids" during adolescence and early adulthood.

Summary

No comparative studies of adolescents and young adults who were exposed to crack cocaine in utero are presently available. Based on the data gathered on cocaine-exposed infants and children, however, several likely characteristics can be extrapolated. Adolescents and young adults exhibiting several of these characteristics may have difficulty completing their schooling, holding jobs and functioning in society. Homelessness and incarceration may be likely potential outcomes for many members of this cohort unless intensive early intervention is continued throughout adolescence and early adulthood. Given the characteristics likely to present themselves during adolescence and early adulthood such as a strong desire to "fit in" with peers, low impulse control, low self-esteem and poor self-monitoring ability, prison is a likely future outcome for this group, but not necessarily a useful one. The case study presented here supports this conclusion.

Methodology

Subject

The subject of this case study is a young American male of Scottish and German heritage. He was born in January 1979, in southern California. His father was a college-educated U.S. Naval officer; his mother had also attended college but, according to interview data gathered from the subject, the subject's father and his maternal grandmother, his mother was addicted to crack cocaine and smoked it regularly throughout her pregnancy. Despite this, the subject was delivered normally, only two weeks prior to full term. He was healthy and weighed approximately 6.5 lbs. at birth. He is currently 6′ 3″ tall, slim and muscular.

At the age of 2, he reportedly ingested a rock of crack cocaine from his mother's "stash" and was hospitalized for several days. His parents subsequently divorced, ostensibly because of his mother's addiction. His father remarried and acquired custody when the subject was 4 years of age. The subject attended elementary school at a Department of Defense school in Japan, where his father was stationed. He was retained in second grade. He next attended middle school in the Washington, D.C., area, where he was diagnosed as ADHD. He moved to a small city in the southwestern U.S. in early adolescence where he remained until being sent to prison at the age of 21.

The subject was unable to finish high school, but obtained a G.E.D. at the age of 20. He reports being close to his stepmother who "tried hard to be a Mom but had problems of her own." He has two half-brothers, over ten years younger than he is. He reports that he enjoys spending time with them and says he "loves my brothers really a lot—kids are so cool!" He viewed his childhood as normal, although he reports his father was "very strict, had a lot of rules and got mad at me a lot." He reports still admiring and loving his father and reports that "I understand why he doesn't like me. I wish I hadn't disappointed him so much but I guess I just can't help it." The subject has had no contact with his birth mother (now dead) for the last eighteen years. His stepmother died of a heroin overdose when he was 17 years of age. His father kicked him out of the house on his eighteenth birthday, telling him it was "time he became a man." He was homeless and lived on the street for approximately one month before being invited to participate in this study. He and his father had no contact for approximately one year after that time. They now have a limited but civil relationship. He reported to his probation officer on one occasion that "I think I need a lot of counseling because of all that stuff, but as long as I have my friends, I'll be okay."

The subject reported his long-range goals at the time the study began as "I want to get a job I like, maybe doing something with science where I can take things apart and mix chemicals or in a hospital . . . and to marry and have a family." . . .

Physical Effects

As noted earlier, it may be expected that early physical and neurological stress imposed by cocaine exposure can impair health. The subject's diagnosis as ADHD may well be related to early exposure. In addition, compared to other young adults with similar lifestyles, he appeared far more prone to colds, pneumonia, accidents and infections, and made frequent visits to medical facilities for these conditions. Early evidence of respiratory and urinary difficulty and of poor motor coordination appears, in this case, to be long lasting. He reported, on several occasions "I get sick a lot," and "I have a lot of accidents and I'd like to play sports but I've never been very good at running or catching things."

The subject appears to have a rapid metabolism. He consumes large quantities of food, yet remains lean and reports being constantly hungry. His preferences are for healthy food. Fruits, vegetables, juices and pasta were preferred menu choices. He sleeps comparatively little, having difficulty sleeping at night and generally remaining awake until 2 or 3 a.m. He was generally awake by 7 a.m. each morning during the years observed and occasionally took short afternoon naps. Sleep dysfunction, apparently, also was a lasting effect of inutero exposure in this case. It should be noted, however, that the subject did not view his health or his sleep patterns as problematic or different from others.

Socioemotional Effects

The subject exhibited delays in social development. He gravitated toward peers who were much younger, chronologically. In fact, he often reported viewing the first author's son, nearly four years his junior, as "like a big brother to me." That son also noted that the subject "sure seems a lot younger than me." The subject seemed to relate best to friends between the ages of 11 and 14 (early adolescence) even at the age of 21. His preferred pastimes included music, video games, activities with large, mixed-sex peer groups, disassembling mechanical objects, creating strange chemical compounds to "kill bugs," and riding a bicycle. These behavior patterns are characteristic of early, not late, adolescence.

Observations indicated the subject was frequently preoccupied with justice and fairness and had a very literal view of the world and of good and evil. He perceived himself as evil. He demonstrated tremendous concern for and loyalty to friends and family and especially enjoyed participating in family meals and outings. He reported "macaroni and cheese with tomatoes is my favorite food because that's what my (step)mom used to make when things were going good and she was trying to be a mom." He also loved caring for and spending time with his younger brothers and considered his peer group "my best family." He often demonstrated sensitivity to others. He saw himself as a peaceloving flower child who "would only fight if I absolutely had to, because I think it is wrong." He did, however, report that he had, on occasion, needed to fight to establish himself in new neighborhoods or to "stand up for myself against gangs and stuff" and according to peer accounts, motor coordination aside, he was a good "street-fighter" who was "safe to be around 'cuz gang kids leave us alone if he's there." He liked "taking care of his friends and of people that are good to me." He reported that "playing music is the best thing in the world for me. It really helps me cope and calms me down." He always appeared relatively calm, demonstrating either good emotional control or relatively flat effect. He displayed a ready smile, good sense of humor, interesting perspective on many issues and generally sunny disposition.

He often noted that "I really want to get married and have a family and take good care of them." During the course of the study, he had only one serious romantic relationship. It lasted for approximately six months before the girl, four years younger than he and equally troubled, albeit for different reasons, broke it off. He reported "I'll still always love her and take care of her." She later became a teen, unwed mother (the father was a friend of the subject's, now also in prison). The subject remained helpful and supportive, often caring for her child, trying to "cheer her up" and in other ways supporting her. He still writes to her frequently from prison. Although she has yet to return a letter, he states "she's the only one for me." He is almost chivalrous in his general treatment of women.

The subject demonstrates strong contradictory urges "to fit in and earn respect" and to "stand out and be really unique." This is not inconsistent with early adolescent development. In his peer group, he is more a follower than a leader in activities even though he associates with younger peers.

He admittedly "is really a stoner and need my pot." He also frequently used hallucinogens and drank alcohol. He is adamantly opposed to any other illegal drug use, however. "I've seen what that stuff does to people—no way! If one of my friends was doing meth or smoking crack, I'd take it away and flush it or even turn them in."

Based on the data collected, he did not seem to demonstrate major problems with attachment. He attributed many events to "luck" or "karma," demonstrating a more external locus of control, but often accepted responsibility for his actions. He did not seem particularly aggressive, violent, antisocial or insensitive, although cruelty to animals was observed on more than one occasion. Other destructive tendencies noted were a penchant for "killing bugs" and a habit of disassembling mechanical objects.

Cognitive Effects

Disorganization was apparent. Care for personal property was chaotic; the subject consistently forgot even such simple tasks as closing doors and turning out lights, although he responded well to a structured behavior-management program using social praise and token reinforcement. He seemed to respond well to highly structured situations and short, specific orders but had difficulty with complex directions. Although friendly, he was not highly verbal and, although he had a unique way of expressing his feelings, he often had difficulty doing so. He had been retained in elementary school and was a "fifth-year senior" in high school when he was first displaced from his home.

Due to several events (described in Outcomes, below) he was unable to finish high school, although he was very motivated to do so. His teachers reported that "he tries really hard," "he likes and needs a lot of attention," and "he can learn; in fact he's pretty good at science compared to some kids, but he has a hard time studying and doing homework."

He was persistent with his studies, and seemed almost oblivious to his difficulties. "Oh, don't worry, I can help you with your homework," he eagerly told a friend who was complaining about his Freshman Algebra class on one occasion. "I've already taken that class 3 times, so I know the stuff really good by now!" Standardized testing done during his senior year of high school indicated he was reading at approximately a ninth-grade level and his math skills were at approximately the eighth-grade level. He scored at approximately the 25th percentile, overall, compared to his chronological peers. He was eventually able to pass the exam for a General Education Diploma (G.E.D.) after approximately six months of tutoring and preparation.

Vocational and Life Skills Implications

The subject had difficulty functioning in the workplace. He maintained a job at a fast-food restaurant for approximately one month. He was fired, according to his supervisor, "because of constant illness and because he seemed to get flustered when things got busy. During rush hours, he couldn't count change correctly if he was at the cash register and he couldn't produce food quickly enough when he was in the kitchen. He did okay during training or when things were slow. He was a nice kid and he tried really hard, but it just didn't work out." He next worked as a taxi driver but, after two accidents in his first week of work, was again dismissed. He worked on construction sights, first mixing concrete. "He was so clumsy," reported his supervisor. "He tripped over things and spilled things all the time. He was a hazard on the worksite and probably cost us $1000.00 in broken equipment and wasted supplies." He also apprenticed briefly as a drywall finisher. "I could train him if I had enough time," reported his supervisor. "He had a good eye and he had the height, strength and speed necessary. He needed a lot of direction, though." The job he held the longest was in a warehouse, loading crates of fertilizer and other chemicals for delivery. He eventually quit because "being around all that stuff all the time was making me sick. My skin stung and I couldn't breathe." Currently, in prison, he is employed cleaning bathrooms. "I think I'm pretty good at it, but it doesn't pay very well," he reported in a letter to a friend.

He was always willing to help with household tasks, especially when structured chore lists and operant behavior management strategies were used. He was best at simple tasks, however, and needed constant direction and step-by-step instructions to complete assigned chores. His attention deficits were noticeable; even when playing music, which he loved, it was rare for him to be able to finish a song without stopping in the middle. His memory for events, however, seemed good. He often demonstrated novel, creative problem-solving skills, especially in social situations and enjoyed disassembling various household items and reassembling the parts together into "new machines." . . .

Present Outcomes

When the subject was 16, he was involved in a break-in. According to his own report and the report of several peers, his involvement was not intentional. "It was one of those times when his Dad had kicked him out of the house because he forgot to feed the dog or something," reported one source. "It was kinda late and he was tired and didn't have anywhere to go and he ran into this kid who said 'Hey, come with me, I have a place.' He was supposedly watching these people's trailer for them or something. He went and there was a big party going on. He pretty much just slept on the couch. But they really trashed the place while he was asleep and the cops came and when they got there it was just him and a couple of little kids that they caught inside 'cuz everybody else ran out the back. He got blamed for it 'cuz he was the oldest and the whole thing was on film, too. His Dad said to the cops he probably did it 'cuz he was no good."

The subject was not charged with the crime until after his eighteenth birthday. Despite the fact that it had occurred nearly two years earlier, he was tried as an adult. He was arrested and locked up until his trial less than a month from his projected high school graduation date. His absences from school made it impossible for him to finish his educational goal. Undaunted, he reported "jail wasn't that bad," and began studying for his G.E.D. As a result of his trial, he was sentenced to intensive probation and required to pay over $60,000.00 in restitution over the course of his life. After serving over two-and-one-half years on probation successfully, he was issued a violation by a newly assigned probation officer when a urine screen tested positive for marijuana use. He was sentenced to 5 years in prison, where he currently resides. His initial response was characteristically sunny and concrete—"You know what they say; if you're gonna do the crime than you gotta do the time." He advises his friends in letters from jail to "stay out of trouble; you don't want to go the route I've gone. Stupidity is why I'm here. I rebelled against the system and look where I'm at. I have learned from my mistakes." His letters have remained generally upbeat; he has access to a guitar and has formed a band with other inmates. He reports that they may have a CD made soon. He reads frequently, is happy that he has a job cleaning toilets and is "making lots of new friends."

Other indicators in letters, however, suggest that these "new friends," combined with his high influenceability and the desire to fit in documented elsewhere, may be part of a process that obliterates any chance for a normal, prosocial life for this young man when he is released. He is learning how to make "homemade acid" and getting tattoos. He is learning "I have to fight to stand up for myself." His formerly sunny disposition is being replaced by bouts with depression. "I feel so alone, confined to my own hell," he writes in a letter to a friend. "I'm left to rot in my own depressions and hatreds of life, locked in a closet. I sit here and do the same shit everyday. My young life has grown old. I wish I could take a step forward into the good side. Sometimes I want to die and be free from my terrors and fears, but one thing keeps me here alive and that is the thought of being able to be with you and all the others I care about that also care for me again some day."

Discussion

Social Implications

There may be a strong underlying relationship between the current plethora of ADD- and ADHD-diagnosed students in American public schools and maternal drug use that bears further investigation. It is worth noting that the subject described here was not in any way reminiscent of the "crack kids" portrayed in the media. He was not Black or Hispanic. He was not born to a single, uneducated mother in the inner city and was not raised in poverty. Overall, despite obvious deficits, he experienced good parenting in a stable, structured home throughout most of his childhood. He had adequate nutrition, good medical care and education.

This case supports the hypothesis that much of the early "crack data" was politically motivated, reflecting racial bias, gender bias and classism. There are undoubtedly many other cases like this young man—crack kids born to white, middle and upper class homes who were missed in all of the early hype when data was collected primarily in treatment centers and public health facilities. A large cohort of "hidden" cases may exist, suggesting estimates should be higher, rather than lower, for incidence of maternal drug use.

It is also worth noting that many characteristics noted in "crack babies" seemed to have lasting effects on this subject. Developmental delays, poor health and coordination and cognitive deficits seemed lasting. On the other hand, the more labile emotional traits such as failure to attach, inability to bond, aggressiveness and lack of control were lacking. Perhaps this suggests that a nurturing environment more easily ameliorates social outcomes than physical and cognitive outcomes. As Zuckerman and Frank note, intervention focused on parenting is well worth pursuing and very effective.

Lasting physical and cognitive outcomes may be problematic for the social welfare system, especially as homelessness may be a particular problem for this group. Additional vocational counseling and jobs skills training may be needed to help this generation of "crack babies" as they enter adulthood. These services should perhaps also be coordinated with criminal justice organizations, where many of this group may find themselves. . . .

The Damage Done:
Crack Babies Talk Back

Antwaun Garcia was a shy boy whose tattered clothes reeked of cat piss. Everyone knew his father peddled drugs and his mother smoked rock, so they called him a "crack baby."

It started in fourth grade when his teacher asked him to read aloud. Antwaun stammered, then went silent. "He can't read because he's a crack baby," jeered a classmate. In the cafeteria that day no one would sit near him. The kids pointed and chanted, "crack baby, crack baby." Antwaun sat sipping his milk and staring down at his tray. After that, the taunting never stopped. Unable to take it, Antwaun quit school and started hanging out at a local drug dealer's apartment, where at age nine he learned to cut cocaine and scoop it into little glass vials. *"Crack baby,"* he says. "Those two words almost cost me my education."

Antwaun finally returned to school and began learning to read a year later, after he was plucked from his parents' home and placed in foster care. Now twenty, he's studying journalism at LaGuardia Community College in New York City and writing for *Represent*, a magazine for and by foster children. In a recent special issue he and other young writers, many of them born to crack addicts, took aim at a media myth built on wobbly, outdated science: crack babies. Their words are helping expose the myth and the damage it has done.

Crack hit the streets in 1984, and by 1987 the press had run more than 1,000 stories about it, many focusing on the plight of so-called crack babies. The handwringing over these children started in September 1985, when the media got hold of Dr. Ira Chasnoff's *New England Journal of Medicine* article suggesting that prenatal cocaine exposure could have a devastating effect on infants. Only twenty-three cocaine-using women participated in the study, and Chasnoff warned in the report that more research was needed. But the media paid no heed. Within days of the first story, CBS News found a social worker who claimed that an eighteen-month-old crack-exposed baby she was treating would grow up to have "an IQ of perhaps fifty" and be "barely able to dress herself."

Soon, images of the crack epidemic's "tiniest victims"—scrawny, trembling infants—were flooding television screens. Stories about their bleak future abounded. One psychologist told *The New York Times* that crack was "interfering with the central core of what it is to be human." Charles Krauthammer, a columnist for the *The Washington Post*, wrote that crack babies were doomed to "a life of certain suffering, of probable deviance, of permanent inferiority." The public braced for the day when this "biological underclass" would cripple our schools, fill our jails, and drain our social programs.

But the day never came. Crack babies, it turns out, were a media myth, not a medical reality. This is not to say that crack is harmless. Infants exposed to cocaine in the womb, including the crystallized version known as crack, weigh an average of 200 grams below normal at birth, according to a massive, ongoing National Institutes of Health study. "For a healthy, ten-pound Gerber baby this is no big deal," explains Barry Lester, the principal investigator. But it can make things worse for small, sickly infants.

Lester has also found that the IQs of cocaine-exposed seven-year-olds are four and a half points lower on average, and some researchers have documented other subtle problems. Perhaps more damaging than being exposed to cocaine itself is growing up with addicts, who are often incapable of providing a stable, nurturing home. But so-called crack babies are by no means ruined. Most fare far better, in fact, than children whose mothers drink heavily while pregnant.

Nevertheless, in the midst of the drug-war hysteria, crack babies became an emblem of the havoc drugs wreak and a pretext for draconian drug laws. Hospitals began secretly testing pregnant women for cocaine, and jailing them or taking their children. Tens of thousands of kids were swept into foster care, where many languish to this day.

Represent magazine was founded at the height of the crack epidemic to give voice to the swelling ranks of children trapped in the foster-care system. Its editors knew that many of their writers were born to addicts. But it wasn't until late last year, when a handful expressed interest in writing about how crack ravaged their families, that the picture snapped into focus. "I remember hearing about crack babies and how they were doomed," says editor Kendra Hurley. "I suddenly realized these were those kids."

Hurley and her co-editor, Nora McCarthy, had worked with many of the writers for years, and had nudged and coddled most through the process of writing about agonizing personal experiences. But nothing compared to the shame their young scribes expressed when discussing their mothers' crack use. Even the most talented believed it had left them "slow," "retarded," or "damaged." The editors decided to publish a special crack issue to help break the stigma and asked the writers to appear on the cover, under the headline 'CRACK BABIES'—ALL GROWN UP. Initially, only Antwaun agreed. He eventually convinced three others to join him. "I said, 'Why shouldn't we stand up and show our faces?" he recalls. "We rose above the labels. I wanted to reach other kids who had been labeled and let them know it doesn't mean you can't succeed."

❧◈❧

As it happens, when the crack issue went to press, a group of doctors and scientists was already lobbying *The New York Times* to drop terms like "crack baby" from its pages. The group included the majority of American researchers investigating the effects of prenatal cocaine exposure or drug addiction. They were spurred to action by the paper's coverage of a New Jersey couple found to be starving their four foster children in late 2003. For years the couple had explained the children's stunted growth to neighbors and friends by saying, among other things, that they were "crack babies." The *Times* not only failed to inform readers that crack babies don't exist, but reinforced the myth by reporting, without attribution, that "the youngest [of the children] was born a crack baby."

Assistant Managing Editor Allan Siegal refused to meet with the researchers, saying via e-mail that the paper simply couldn't open a dialogue with all the "advocacy groups who wish to influence terminology." After some haggling, he did agree to publish a short letter to the editor from the researchers. While the paper hasn't used "crack baby" in the last several months, it has referred to babies being "addicted" to crack, which, as the researchers told the editors, is scientifically inaccurate, since babies cannot be born addicted to cocaine.

The researchers later circulated a more general letter urging all media to drop the term "crack baby." But the phrase continues to turn up. Of the more than 100 news stories that have used it in the last year, some thirty were published after the letter was distributed in late February.

Represent's writers made a more resounding splash. National Public Radio and AP both featured them in stories on crack's legacy. Inspired by their words, the columnist E.R. Shipp called on New York *Daily News* readers to consider the damage the crack-baby myth has done. A July *Newsday* op-ed made a similar plea, and also urged readers to avoid rushing to judgment on the growing number of babies being born to mothers who use methamphetamines.

Still, a number of recent "meth baby" stories echo the early crack-baby coverage. A July AP article cautioned, for instance, that an "epidemic" of meth-exposed children in Iowa is stunting infants' growth, damaging their brains, and leaving them predisposed to delinquency. In May, one Fox News station warned that meth babies "could make the crack baby look like a walk in the nursery." Research is stacking up against such claims. But, then, scientific evidence isn't always enough to kill a good story.

CHALLENGE QUESTIONS

Does Prenatal Exposure to Drugs Such as Cocaine Create "Crack Babies" with Special Developmental Concerns?

- Why is the label "crack baby" so persistant in popular culture? Even though alcohol, nicotine, or aspirin can be equally harmful, why do we not talk about "aspirin babies" or "cigarette babies"?
- How likely does it seem that a good postnatal environment could make up for significant exposure to teratogens, such as crack cocaine, in a bad prenatal environment?
- Should people interested in lifespan development focus more on the ability of a healthy postnatal environment to allow for normal development, or should they focus on the fact that a crack cocaine epidemic in the 1980s created a large number of babies challenged by an environment that started with prenatal crack exposure?
- Even if being exposed to drugs in utero does not absolutely determine a negative outcome of development, is it still a significant enough developmental influence to warrant a labeled category? What is the developmental influence of a label?
- The articles on both sides use provocative case studies to make their point. Taking for granted that most people do want the best for their children, how can we ensure that children experience healthy development?

Suggested Readings

L. Berger and J. Waldfogel, "Prenatal Cocaine Exposure: Long-Run Effects and Policy Implications," *Social Science Review* (March 2000)

W. Chavkin, "Cocaine and Pregnancy—Time to Look at the Evidence," *Journal of the American Medical Association* (March 28, 2001)

D. Frank, M. Augustyn, W. Grant Knight, T. Pell, and B. Zuckerman, "Growth, Development, and Behavior in Early Childhood Following Prenatal Cocaine Exposure," *Journal of the American Medical Association* (March 28, 2001)

K. Greider, "What About the "Drug Babies"? Crackpot Ideas", *Mother Jones* (July/August 1995)

S. Hans, "Studies of Prenatal Exposure to Drugs Focusing on Prenatal Care of Children," *Neurotoxicology and Teratology* (2002)

J. Harvey, "Cocaine Effects on the Developing Brain: Current Status," *Neuroscience and Biobehavioral Reviews* (2004)

J. Jackson, "The Myth of the 'Crack Baby'," *Extra! The Magazine of FAIR* (September/October 1998)

B. Lester, "Is Day Care Worse Than Cocaine?" *Brown University News Service* (2001)

B. Lester, "No Simple Answer to 'Crack Baby' Debate," *Alcoholism & Drug Abuse Weekly* (September 20, 2004)

B. Lester and L. LaGasse, "Cocaine Exposure and Children: The Meaning of Subtle Effects," *Science* (October 23, 1998)

L. Marcellus, "Critical Social and Medical Constructions of Perinatal Substance Misuse: Truth in the Making," *Journal of Family Nursing* (November 2003)

D. Messinger and B. Lester, "Prenatal Substance Exposure and Human Development," *Human Development in the 21st Century* (Council on Human Development, February 12, 2005)

L. Singer, R. Arendt, S. Minnes, K. Farkas, A. Salvator, H. Kirchner, and R. Kleigman, "Cognitive and Motor Outcomes of Cocaine-Exposed Infants," *Journal of the American Medical Association* (April 17, 2002)

T. Van Beveren, B. Little, and M. Spence, "Effects of Prenatal Cocaine Exposure and Postnatal Environment on Child Development," *American Journal of Human Biology* (2000)

B. Zuckerman, D. Frank, and L. Mayes, "Cocaine-Exposed Infants and Developmental Outcomes," *Journal of the American Medical Association* (April 17, 2002)

ISSUE 5

Is There a "Myth of the First Three Years"?

YES: Gwen J. Broude, from "Scatterbrained Child Rearing," *Reason* (December 2000)

NO: Zero to Three: National Center for Infants, Toddlers and Families, from "Zero to Three: Response to *The Myth of the First Three Years*," `http://www.zerotothree.org/no-myth.html`

ISSUE SUMMARY

YES: Gwen J. Broude, who teaches developmental psychology and cognitive science at Vassar College, reviews, supports, and augments John Bruer's idea that a "myth of the first three years" has falsely used neuroscience to claim that infancy is the only critical developmental period.

NO: Zero to Three, a national organization devoted to promoting healthy infant development, contradicts Bruer's idea by asserting that a great deal of diverse research supports the idea that the first three years are critical to development and success in adulthood.

Advances in technology and research methods have allowed developmental scientists to establish that there is a massive amount of complex brain activity going on during the infant years. In fact, the explosion of changing neuronal and synaptic activity (neurons being brain cells and synapses being the connections between brain cells) during infancy may be unmatched at any other point in the lifespan. After infancy it seems that much of brain development and cognitive functioning depends upon synaptic pruning—the process of shaping and organizing the way brain cells communicate with each other. The implications of these basic findings, however, are subject to much controversy.

The key question, given all the brain change during infancy, is whether that means infants need special attention and expertly enriched environments. One strain of popular wisdom suggests yes; many parents feel extremely anxious about the need to provide careful attention and stimulation to ensure that their infants develop well—buying videos, games, music, and toys that claim to be specially designed for proper brain stimulation. Most developmental scientists would agree that this extreme anxiety is unnecessary—infants for generations and across cultures have developed successfully in natural environments without scientific intervention. But does that mean that we are wrong to consider the first three years of life as special? Does that create a harmful "myth of the first three years"?

Gwen J. Broude writes that, indeed, the first three years are only crucially important to sensationalist journalism, misguided child advocates, and misinformed anxious parents. In discussing ideas from a well-publicized book titled *The Myth of the First Three Years* by John T. Bruer, Broude substantiates the idea that misinterpretations of neuroscience and developmental ideas, such as critical periods, have created the mistaken impression that infancy is a developmental stage that requires extra attention to brain development. For Broude the problem is not that we fail to provide enough attention and stimulation to infants, but that we fail to appreciate the amazing ability of a brain to develop in its own time in its own normal environment.

In contrast, Zero to Three, a national parenting organization, fears that the real danger lies in promoting the idea that the importance of the first three years is a "myth." They acknowledge that some findings related to cognitive development have been misinterpreted, but assert strongly that the first three years of life are a distinct and crucial developmental period. Thus, from this perspective, while the direct influence of brain stimulation may be overplayed by some sources, the first three years provide an essential foundation for whatever development will occur later in life.

POINT

- Neuroscience has been misinterpreted such that many parents think the more stimulation the better—something not evident in research.

- People often fail to appreciate the amazing abilities of the brain to develop within any reasonably normal circumstance.

- Most cognitive development proceeds normally, at its own pace, based on having the types of experiences most infants have every day.

- The brain is far more "plastic" than we used to think, and the idea that most learning takes place only during the first three years is obviously wrong.

COUNTERPOINT

- While some neuroscience has been misinterpreted, that does not mean infancy is any less critical.

- People need to learn about the importance of appropriate care and environments during infancy.

- While cognitive development may proceed normally at its own pace, socioemotional development depends upon healthy interactions with fully engaged caregivers.

- Although the brain and the child continue to develop throughout life, the first three years provide a critical foundation for everything that comes later.

YES

Gwen J. Broude

Scatterbrained Child Rearing

When it comes to raising children, there is no such thing as too much good advice. So when accounts of neuroscientific advances in our understanding of child development began to appear in the popular press a couple of years ago, it sure sounded like good news. Parents could now raise their children in line with the hard facts about the relationship between human growth and brain development.

Don't rejoice just yet. . . . Education expert John T. Bruer warn(s) us not to believe what we have been hearing about the new neuroscience of child rearing. [He points] out that the media's version of brain-based child development bears little resemblance to the real thing. Even worse, those same wrong-headed theories have landed on the desks of policy makers. The result, as Bruer describe(s) in grim detail, is policy initiatives that can be very dangerous to children.

The mangled accounts of brain science that Bruer . . . want[s] to debunk begin with the assumption that brain development is crucial to child development. So far, so good. It is the more detailed claims, or "myths," as Bruer calls them, about the relationship between brain maturation and a child's maturation that can lead to trouble. *The Myth of the First Three Years* focuses on three such myths, which will doubtless sound familiar to most readers—though most Americans would probably consider them rock-solid facts about how the brain works. Although Bruer is not himself a neuroscientist, his discussion of where and how popular brain science has gone wrong accurately reflects the current neuroscientific literature.

Bruer's three myths are that learning is limited to "windows of opportunity," or critical periods; that these windows of opportunity occur only as long as there is a significant growth of connections, or synapses, between brain cells; and that children require enriched environments for optimal learning to take place during these windows of opportunity. As there is substantial evidence of an explosion in synaptic connections during the first three years of a child's life, the conclusion from popular neuroscience is that development is basically over by the end of the third birthday.

Many recent public policy initiatives have been based on the "vital first three years" vision of brain development. For instance, the frantic push toward universal preschool from the Clinton administration follows logically from that vision, as does the loony notion from Georgia Gov. Zell Miller that state legislators should distribute CDs of classical music to newborns to give them an intellectual head start. This notion causes many parents to believe that the early experiences of their children will seal their fates forever, and to worry that a single parenting mistake will doom their youngsters for life. Bruer argues that all those ideas are based on fantasy.

The myth that learning is limited to the first years of life is based on the finding that the density of connections among brain cells increases very rapidly during the second and third years of life. After that, the number of connections begins to stabilize or to actually decrease. This is a correct description of brain maturation. But as Bruer explains, it's not correct to assume that the brain is gaining connections during the first years of life because children are cramming their skulls with learning.

The "Mythmakers" of popular neuroscience, as Bruer calls them, suppose that brain growth means that learning is happening, and that the subsequent decrease in synaptic density must mean that learning is no longer happening. While that sounds logical, no neuroscientist believes this is an accurate description of the relationship between brain maturation and development. Indeed, it would be more nearly correct to posit the opposite relationship between children's learning and what the brain is doing.

The consensus among neuroscientists is that the explosion of connections among neurons that we see in early life merely sets the stage for the acquisition of knowledge. It is as if nature is preparing the canvas on which the world subsequently paints. The decrease, or pruning, of connections is what seems to coincide with actual learning. Ironically, then, the brain is most prepared to begin learning at just the point when popular brain science says it is too late for learning to take place. After the synaptic explosion happens, children become newly capable of learning things that they could not learn before.

The idea that there are critical periods is similarly wrongheaded as a general theory of how children develop. There are certain skills that are most easily learned early in life—for instance, seeing or talking. But as Bruer points out, we are dealing here with abilities that all normal human beings acquire. Psychologists call these "experience-expectant traits" to underscore the plain fact that the kinds of experience required for their proper development are so basic that virtually no child can help but be exposed to them. It is as if the neurophysiology underlying the trait "expects" to meet up with the needed experience. And indeed, the number of children who are not exposed to language, or light, is vanishingly small. Experience-expectant traits, Bruer observes, are acquired "easily, automatically, and unconsciously."

Not all traits are experience-expectant. My brain did not expect to meet up with algebra in the environment. Nor did it expect to encounter writing. Or the piano. But the skills of math or reading or playing music are just the sorts of skills for which there are no critical periods. They are experience-dependent traits that can be learned at any point in life. These, ironically, are also the very sorts of skills on which popular versions of brain science focus when they warn us about critical periods. Children in our culture do tend to learn particular skills, such as reading or adding, at predictable ages. But "we should not confuse this kind of learning with the existence of critical periods for those skills," Bruer writes. "What is culturally normal is not biologically determined."

Bruer also debunks the idea that enriched environments are required for optimal development. This notion originates from a misunderstanding of decades-old rat studies in which the learning of rats placed in a so-called enriched environment was superior to that of rats placed in less enriched environments. From this we are to conclude that human children should be exposed to as much stimulation as possible. This is in spite of the fact that the rats in the original experiment were adults and that their enriched environments were still deprived in comparison with what any rat would experience in the wild.

Bruer assures us that all kids need for normal development is exposure to very basic experiences, like ambient light to see, a language to hear, gravity with which to interact, and so on. Thus, his advice is that parents should make sure that their children's sensory systems are in good working order—not too tough a challenge.

Indeed, there is good reason to believe that children can't make use of all the enrichment we offer them, as they tend to develop according to their own timetables regardless of our ambitions. Try to correct the grammar of a young child who is not ready to learn the lesson. Janie comes home bursting with excitement. "My teacher brought a rabbit to school and I holded it," she gushes. "You held the rabbit?" you say. "Yes, I holded it." "Did you say you held it tightly?" you ask. "No, I holded it loosely," she responds. Janie will learn about irregular verbs on her schedule, not on yours.

Contrary to the almost blatant idiocy of the "first three years" myth—clearly, most useful human learning happens long after age 3—brains are always changing, which is another way of saying that people are always learning, regardless of their age. The greatest surprises from the laboratories of neuroscientists come in the form of evidence that the brain is far more plastic than we used to think. Since the 1980s neuroscientists have demonstrated that adult brains are extremely malleable, so much so that areas of the adult primate brain originally responsible for one function can change jobs. For instance, adult primate brain cells once receiving input from the animal's arm will subsequently reorganize to receive input from the chin and jaw if connections from the arm to the brain are interrupted. If adult brains seem stable, that's only because their experiences have been stable.

This isn't just of interest to academic neuropsychologists. Bruer's Myth-makers have a message that can hurt kids: that we should try to cram all of life's lessons into the first three years of development and then call it quits. This would clearly be fatal to any child's development, as anyone familiar with how brains—or children—actually function will plainly see. If we followed the advice implied by this version of brain development, we would be trying to teach children at exactly the time in their lives when their brains are not yet ready to learn and then stop teaching them at precisely the time that their brains do become ready. Bruer tells us that public policy is in fact heading in this direction. For instance, state legislatures are already considering bills that would decrease or eliminate support for later child interventions to invest those funds in birth-to-3 programs in the belief that this is the only time during which brains are capable of learning.

. . . As Bruer tells us, children respond to the environment at their own pace. Some psychologists have begun to suggest that this allows youngsters to fine-tune basic competencies before taking up the challenge of developing more sophisticated ones. We see this self-pacing in the way that children naturally regulate the amount of stimulation to which they will respond. Babies turn their heads away if you try to get in their faces. When there is too much going on around them, infants will go to sleep on you. Basically, children tune out stimulation for which they are not ready.

. . . Bruer's robust child [is] illustrated in his example from rural Guatemala, where children spend the first 18 months of life in circumstances that we would call severely deprived. Nevertheless, these kids perform at the same cognitive level as middle-class American children by the time they reach adolescence. Neuroscientist Steve Peterson, quoted by Bruer, captures the meaning of this anecdote when he observes that "development really wants to happen. It takes very impoverished environments to interfere with development because the biological system has evolved so that the environment alone stimulates development." How does this translate into advice for parents? "Don't raise your children in a closet, starve them, or hit them in the head with a frying pan."

. . . *The Myth of the First Three Years* is a fine rebuttal to the claim that children are fragile and a vindication for those of us who have always suspected that we were still capable of growing and learning even though we were well past 3 years old.

 **NO**

Zero to Three: Response to *The Myth of the First Three Years*

*T*he *Myth of the First Three Years,* by John Bruer, is an attempt to redress some popular misconceptions about the importance to brain development of a child's earliest experiences. The book is an extension of "Education and the Brain: A Bridge Too Far," a scholarly article by Bruer that appeared in the November 1997 issue of *Educational Researcher.* Bruer, who is president of the James S. McDonnell Foundation, which awards $18 million annually for biomedical, educational, and international projects, has no formal training in either neuroscience or child development. But his "Bridge Too Far" article provided an astute examination of the ways in which recent findings in neuroscience have been blown out of proportion and used to imply that we know how to increase the neural connections in a child's brain and ultimately, the child's intelligence. Take the so-called "Mozart effect," for example, the notion that playing classical music, especially Mozart, will boost a child's IQ. This idea was popularized in the press and capitalized on by entrepreneurs selling Mozart CDs for babies and parents, but it has no clear foundation in science.

However, in *The Myth of the First Three Years,* a book written for a popular, mass audience, Bruer crosses his own bridge and then burns it, taking his correct observation that the neuroscience of early childhood is, in a sense, in its own infancy, and leaping to the extreme conclusion that what happens to a child in the early years is of little consequence to subsequent intellectual development. He also suggests that intervening in the lives of very young children at risk for poor outcomes in school and adulthood will have little or no effect. Nothing could be further from the truth.

We are particularly concerned that readers will come away from this book confused about what babies need and what parents can do to encourage development, and that policymakers will see Bruer's argument as an excuse to ignore the growing interest and demand for policies and services that support babies, toddlers, and their families.

The Myth of Boosting Baby's Brain

Zero to three agrees with some of Bruer's assertions. He is right that science has just begun to sort out how the trillions of nerve cells in a child's brain are organized during the first three years of life to allow a child to learn to talk, read, and reason. The application of these new and exciting findings has sometimes been exaggerated, particularly by the media, or used inappropriately to make claims about what parents, educators, and policymakers should or should not be doing.

Much of the confusion centers on the notion that the first three years are a "critical period," defined as a window of opportunity for laying down circuits in a child's brain or learning a particular set of skills that closes irrevocably after a set amount of time. What we know from early research is that critical periods exist in children only for some very basic capacities, such as vision, and to a lesser extent for learning language. For example, it has been well-documented that young children can learn a second language much more easily—and often with better pronunciation and grammar—than can adolescents or adults.

We agree with Bruer that a child's brain is not even close to being completely wired when the third candle on the birthday cake has been blown out. In fact, brain research suggests the opposite conclusion: Important parts of the brain are not fully developed until well past puberty, and the brain, unlike any other organ, changes throughout life. The human brain is capable of learning and laying down new circuitry until old age. But this does not mean that the first three years are unimportant.

Why the Early Years Are So Important

While scientists have so far only confirmed a few "critical periods" in the development of the human brain, there is no doubt that the first three years of life are critical to the growth of intelligence and to later success in adulthood. We know from rigorous psychological and sociological research, and from compelling clinical experience, that early childhood is a time when infants and toddlers acquire many of the motivations and skills needed to become productive, happy adults. Curiously, Bruer turns a blind eye to the immense and crucial social and emotional development that begins during a child's first three years, which provides a foundation for continued later intellectual development. *The importance of the first three years is no myth, and parents and policymakers must not be misled by Bruer's book.*

Following are a few examples that underscore why and how a child's intellectual development rests on social and emotional skills learned in the early years:

1. Development of Trust

Every person needs to learn to trust other human beings in order to function successfully in society. It is crucial that this sense of trust begins to grow during the earliest years. While it is certainly possible to learn this later, it becomes much more difficult the older a child gets. Years of living in an interpersonal environment that is unresponsive, untrustworthy, or unreliable is difficult to undo in later relationships.

Trust grows in infancy in the everyday, ordinary interactions between the child and the significant caregivers. A baby learns to trust through the routine experiences of being fed when she is hungry, and held when she is upset or frightened. The child learns that her needs will be met, that she matters, that someone will comfort her, feed her, and keep her warm and safe. She feels good about herself and about others.

Children whose basic needs are not met in infancy and early childhood often lack that sense of trust, and have difficulty learning to believe in themselves or in others. We know this from a multitude of scientific studies, including the research of Alan Sroufe and Byron Egeland, at the University of Minnesota. In a long-term study that followed infants through toddlerhood and into adulthood, Sroufe and his colleagues found that when children were reared within relationships they could count on, they had fewer behavior problems in school, had more confidence, and were emotionally more capable of positive social relationships.

2. Development of Self-Control

From the time a child begins to walk, we can see the progress she is making in mastering an important skill: self-control. Babies do not come into the world knowing that nobody likes it when they bite and hit, or grab toys and food from them; they need help from adults to understand that these impulses are not socially acceptable. John Gottman, of the University of Washington, among others, has demonstrated that children who get no help monitoring or regulating their behavior during the early years, especially before the age of three, have a greater chance of being anxious, frightened, impulsive, and behaviorally disorganized when they reach school. Further, these children are more likely to rely on more violent or other intimidating means to resolve conflicts than their peers who have successfully begun the long process of learning self-control.

3. The Source of Motivation

Another pillar of intellectual development and success in school is motivation. Infants and toddlers develop this through day-to-day interactions with responsive caregivers. Responding to the needs of the child is a powerful process that builds confidence and an inner sense of curiosity. This motivates the child to learn and has direct effects on success in school. The more confident a child is, the more likely she is to take on new challenges with enthusiasm.

The Emotional Foundations of Learning

Trust, self-control, and motivation form the bedrock of a child's intellectual development. Intelligence and achievement in school do not depend solely on a young child's fund of factual knowledge, ability to read or recite the alphabet, or familiarity with numbers or colors. Rather, in addition to such knowledge and skills, success rests on children, of whatever background, coming to school curious, confident, and aware of what behavior is expected. Successful children are comfortable seeking assistance, able to get along with others, and interested in using their knowledge and experience to master new challenges.

Bruer is right that there is no magic bullet for making kids smart. *But by erroneously focusing exclusively on intellectual achievement, he fails to recognize that all aspects of development affect one another, and that children cannot learn or display their intelligence as well if they have not developed emotionally and socially.* The task for parents and other caregivers who want their children to succeed in school is not to force development. Rather, it is to try to ensure that the moment-to-moment events of daily life give babies and toddlers the sense of security, encouragement, and confidence that are the foundation of emotional health. It is this that will ultimately allow them to learn at home, in school and throughout life.

Dangers of the Book

We are concerned that readers will draw the wrong conclusions. Many **parents** are likely to be confused by Bruer's message, which contradicts what they may know instinctively about the importance of the first three years. The book may let other parents off the hook—particularly those parents who aren't willing or able to devote the time and attention that is needed to provide a nurturing environment for babies and toddlers.

Moreover, some parents will be offended by Bruer's assertion that "mothers who behave in acceptable American middle-class fashion tend to have securely attached children. The challenge is to get more non-complying, mostly minority and disadvantaged, mothers to act in this way." We know that there are plenty of poor, minority parents doing a marvelous job of raising their children in securely attached relationships. Whether by design or accident, Bruer stigmatizes minority racial and ethnic groups by defining them as the exception to the rule. And just what is "acceptable American middle-class" parenting? We know of no such thing as a homogeneous approach to parenting and attachment.

Policymakers may come away from Bruer's book with the misconception that efforts to help young children are a waste of money and time. Indeed, it appears that this may be Bruer's intent. For example, he attacks the very modest funding provided for such programs as Early Head Start, a desperately needed initiative that is a drop in the bucket relative to other government programs. Early Head Start was conceived on the basis of ample evidence for the value of early intervention—evidence that was gathered long before the hoopla began over neuroscience, but that Bruer conveniently omits from his book.

Pioneering work done in the 1970s by Sally Provence, at the Child Study Center at Yale University provides just one example. Over a period of several years, Provence studied two groups of families with young children who were at risk for poor outcomes in school and adulthood. One group was offered free medical care and high quality day care, which included help in learning to be more responsive parents. The other group received no assistance. Provence found that when the children of both groups reached school age, those who received help missed far less school than the others, were able to learn and retain information more easily, and were more motivated. Their families had fewer children and the births were spaced farther apart.

Efforts to help all children achieve the basic skills of trust, motivation, and self-control needed for later intellectual and emotional development should not be aimed at creating super-babies, or giving anxious parents one more thing to worry about, or overambitious parents one more reason to push their children. Our aim should be to ensure that all children reach school age with a solid foundation for learning and relating to others, and that all parents know what they can do to help their children develop. In the last decade, the United States has made important progress in recognizing the needs of young children. Businesses have made efforts to create family-friendly policies. Government has made efforts to provide services to families. Parents are increasingly interested in how best to encourage and prepare their children. Taking to heart many of the negative messages of The Myth of the First Three Years *can only set back those efforts. Our nation's youngest citizens deserve better.*

CHALLENGE QUESTIONS

Is There a "Myth of the First Three Years"?

- While some parents recognize that more extreme levels of stimulation are not necessary for healthy development, they feel that extra stimulation can do no harm. How would you respond to that feeling? Are there ways in which too much stimulation during infancy could be harmful?
- Both readings are addressing the provocative argument made by John T. Bruer in his book *The Myth of the First Three Years*. Why do you think this book was so divisive to those interested in lifespan development?
- Broude points out ways that our scientific understanding of early brain development is easily misinterpreted by a culture interested in "building better brains." Why might this be a cultural belief that is not universally shared?
- Zero to Three asserts that infancy is a special and distinct period in lifespan development. Beyond brain development, why is this the case and what really differentiates the changes of infancy from changes at other stages?
- Some developmental scientists think that the term "critical period" is a misleading term, and that a term such as "sensitive period" may be more appropriate. What difference might various labels make to how we understand infancy?

Suggested Readings

J. Bruer, "Education and the Brain: A Bridge Too Far," *Educational Researcher* (November 1997)

J. Bruer, *The Myth of the First Three Years: A New Understanding of Early Brain Development and Lifelong Learning* (Free Press, 1999)

L. Eliot, *What's Going on in There?* (Bantam Books, 2000)

S. Gerhardt, *Why Love Matters: How Affection Shapes a Baby's Brain* (Brunner-Routledge, 2004)

H. Guldberg, "The Myth of 'Infant Determinism'," www.spiked-online.com (October 2004)

K. Hirsh-Pasek and R. M. Golinkoff with D. Eyer, *Einstein Never Used Flash Cards* (Rodale, 2003)

ISSUE 6

Are There Good Reasons to Allow Infants to Consume Electronic Media, Such as Television?

YES: Victoria Rideout, Elizabeth Hamel, and the Kaiser Family Foundation, from "The Media Family: Electronic Media in the Lives of Infants, Toddlers, Preschoolers and Their Parents," A Report from the Kaiser Family Foundation (May 2006)

NO: Daniel R. Anderson and Tiffany A. Pempek, from "Television and Very Young Children," *American Behavioral Scientist* (January 2005)

ISSUE SUMMARY

YES: Victoria Rideout, Elizabeth Hamel, and the Kaiser Family Foundation find that television and electronic media allow families to cope with busy schedules and are of value to parents of infants.

NO: Psychologists Daniel Anderson and Tiffany Pempek, instead focus on infant learning. In their review of available literature they concur with the American Academy of Pediatrics in recommending that infants should have no exposure to television.

In this technology age most people at all stages of the lifespan consume massive amounts of electronic media. For better or worse, the media and market forces tend to move faster than scientific efforts to understand the impact of that consumption. This fact is particularly evident in the contemporary controversy regarding electronic media and infancy. Despite a 1999 policy statement from the American Academy of Pediatricians recommending against any exposure to electronic screens during infancy, there is a growing market of media specifically targeting very young children.

So what is the impact of this media on infants and the young mind during a time of life when so much change and development is taking place? The short answer is that no one is entirely sure. Parents and media companies hope that the impact might be positive—it seems logically possible that well-designed media could be a positive and educational influence on a developing mind.

103

Or, at the very least, some would argue that electronic media could do no harm. Right? Actually, many scholars are concerned that exposure to electronic media at very young ages may in fact have a negative impact on developing capacities for language, attention, and other crucial cognitive skills. As such, groups such as the *Campaign for a Commercial Free Childhood* have been vociferous in their opposition to electronic media marketed toward infants. At the heart of both sides is the core question for infant development: what is the healthiest environment for the development of a young child?

From the perspective of many parents, the healthiest environment is one in which electronic media provides a safe and easy forum for engagement. As Victoria Rideout, Elizabeth Hamel, and the Kaiser Family Foundation explain in their effort to understand the role of electronic media in contemporary families, many parents rely on electronic media to help create just such an environment. In surveys and interviews with diverse groups of parents it becomes clear that parents are aware that certain types of electronic media can be problematic for infants but that there may be a thoughtful and healthy way to use other media formats to manage the challenges of raising children in contemporary society. They suggest that exposing children to electronic media is simply a reality of modern life, and that is not necessarily a bad thing.

Psychologists Daniel R. Anderson and Tiffany A. Pempek, on the other hand, focus their attention specifically on the developing child. Based on their review of evidence, the influence of electronic media on infants seems almost entirely negative. Rather than just being a harmless distraction, Anderson and Pempek draw on research suggesting that exposure to electronic media may actually associate with deficits in critical developmental capacities such as language and attention.

POINT

- Electronic media is a way that parents can manage the increasing demands on their time.

- The educational value of media for infants and young children has improved.

- The research is not very up to date—the marketplace for infant media has moved faster than the science.

- Children may pick up things they would otherwise not be exposed to (such as different languages and types of people).

COUNTERPOINT

- Infants may actually be watching less TV now than they were a decade ago, so parents are becoming more cautious.

- The preliminary research finds that TV is not a good way to educate infants.

- Infants learn less from television than from actual life experiences.

- Electronic media may actually cause cognitive problems such as language and attention deficits.

YES

Victoria Rideout, Elizabeth Hamel, and Kaiser Family Foundation

The Media Family

Introduction

Today's parents live in a world where media are an ever-changing but increasingly important part of their family's lives, including even their very youngest children. Baby videos designed for one-month-olds, computer games for 9-month-olds, and TV shows for one-year-olds are becoming commonplace. An increasing number of TV shows, videos, websites, software programs, video games, and interactive TV toys are designed specifically for babies, toddlers, and preschoolers.

One thing that hasn't changed is that parents have a tough job—in fact, maybe tougher, often with both husband and wife working and juggling complex schedules, and with a growing number of single parents. In this environment, parents often turn to media as an important tool to help them manage their household and keep their kids entertained.

And for many parents, media are much more than entertainment: from teaching children letters and numbers, to introducing them to foreign languages or how to work with computers, many parents find the educational value of media incredibly helpful.

> "My daughter is learning a lot from the different shows she watches. She's so into it. I think it's important."
>
> [Mother of a 1–3 year-old, Irvine, California]

At the same time, there is growing controversy about media use among very young children, with pediatricians recommending no screen media for babies under two, and limited screen time after that. Most child development experts believe that the stimuli children receive and the activities they engage in during the first few years of life are critical not only for their physical well-being but also for their social, emotional, and cognitive development.

But scientific research about the impact of media use on babies and toddlers has not kept pace with the marketplace. As a result, very little is known for sure about what is good and bad when it comes to media exposure in early childhood.

On the positive side of the ledger, research does indicate that well-designed educational programs, such as *Sesame Street,* can help 4- and 5-year-olds read

From *The Media Family: Electronic Media in the Lives of Infants, Toddlers, Preschoolers and Their Parents,* May 2006, pp. 4–7, 14–17, 21–23, 26, 32–33. Copyright © 2006 by The Henry J. Kaiser Family Foundation. Reprinted by permission.

and count and that children that age also benefit from pro-social messages on TV that teach them about kindness and sharing. On the other hand, studies have also found that exposure to television violence can increase the risk of children behaving aggressively and that media use in early childhood may be related to attentional problems later in life. And while the producers of early childhood media believe their products can help children learn even at the earliest ages, other experts worry that time spent with media may detract from time children spend interacting with their parents, engaging in physical activity, using their imaginations, or exploring the world around them.

One thing this study makes clear is that for many families, media use has become part of the fabric of daily life. Parents use TV or DVDs as a "safe" activity their kids can enjoy while the grownups get dressed for work, make a meal, or do the household chores. Working parents who worry that they don't have enough time to teach their kids the basics feel relieved that educational TV shows, videos, and computer games are helping their kids count and learn the alphabet and even say a word or two in Spanish. When children are grouchy, or hyper, or fighting with their siblings, moms and dads use TV as a tool to help change their mood, calm them down, or separate squabbling brothers and sisters. Media are also used in enforcing discipline, with a TV in the bedroom or a handheld video game player offered as a powerful reward or enticement for good behavior. Everyday activities, such as eating a meal or going to sleep, are often done with television as a companion. And media are used to facilitate moments of transition in daily life: waking up slowly while groggily watching a couple of cartoons on mom and dad's bed, or calming down to a favorite video before bedtime.

> "Media makes my life easier. We're all happier. He isn't throwing tantrums. I can get some work done."
>
> [Mother of a 4–6 year-old, Irvine, California]

Many parents of young children are quite enthusiastic about the role media plays in their lives and the impact it has on their kids. They are grateful for what they see as higher quality, more educational choices than when they were young, and for the wider variety of options they now have available. They see their children learning from TV and imitating the positive behaviors modeled on many shows. But it appears that the primary reason many parents choose to bring media into their children's lives is not because of the educational benefits it offers kids, but because of the practical benefits it offers parents: uninterrupted time for chores, some peace and quiet, or even just an opportunity to watch their own favorite shows.

At the same time, many parents feel an underlying guilt about their children's media use: primarily a sense that they should be spending more time with their kids and that they shouldn't be feeling so relieved at not having to be responsible for teaching their children their ABCs. Some express a suspicion that they may have set in motion something they soon won't be able to control: that today's good-natured educational shows will lead to tomorrow's sassy cartoons, and to next year's violent video games. And others also bemoan the fundamental changes they see from their own childhoods when they were more likely to play outside or to use their imaginations to make up their own play activities indoors.

> "It makes life easier now, but in the long run, when they're older and starting to run into all these problems, I think I'll wish I wouldn't have let them do it when they were five."

> [Mother of a 4–6 year-old in Columbus, Ohio]

Parents' beliefs about media—and their own media habits—are strongly related to how much time their children spend with media, the patterns of their children's use, and the types of content their children are exposed to. Two- and four-year-olds watching *CSI* and *ER* with their moms don't seem to be as rare as one might think. Parents who are big TV fans and hate the interruptions from their little ones are more likely to get a TV for their child's bedroom. Dads who play a lot of video games use that activity as a way to bond with their sons. And parents who think TV mostly hurts children's learning are more likely to limit their children's viewing and less likely to leave the TV on during the day. In short, children's media use is as much or more about parents as it is about children.

This report presents the results of a national study to document how much time infants, toddlers, and preschoolers are spending with media, what types of media they're using, and what role media are playing in their environments. The study has two parts: a nationally representative telephone survey of parents about their children's media use; and a series of focus groups with parents, for a more in-depth discussion of issues raised in the survey. All statistical findings in this report are from the national survey; all quotes are from the focus groups.

The study concerns children ages 6 months to 6 years old. It focuses primarily on the role of electronic screen media in young people's lives, including television, videos or DVDs, computers, and video games. Occasional references to "children 6 years and under" or "children six and under" are made as shorthand and refer to children ages 6 months to 6 years old. References to children "under two" refer to children 6–23 months old. . . .

One thing this study makes clear is that even the youngest children in our society have a substantial amount of experience with electronic media. Perhaps not surprisingly, almost all children ages 6 months to 6 years old have watched television (94%) and videos or DVDs (87%). But use of "new" media among this age group also abounds. More than four in ten (43%) have used a computer, about three in ten (29%) have played console video games, and just under one in five (18%) have played handheld video games.

In a typical day, 83% of children ages 6 months to 6 years use some form of screen media, including 75% who watch television, 32% who watch videos or DVDs[1],16% who use a computer, and 11 % who play either console or handheld video games. The percent of children who watch TV in a typical day is somewhat smaller than the share who spend any time reading or being read to (83%) and listening to music (82%).

Figure 1

In a Typical Day, Percent of Children 6 and Under Who . . .

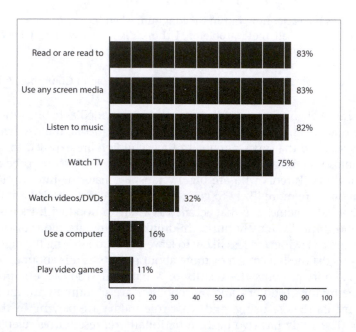

Note: Screen media includes TV, videos/DVDs, video games, or computers.

Kids who watch television and those who watch videos or DVDs spend an average of about one and a quarter hours on each (1:19 for TV and 1:18 for videos/DVDs), while those who play video games and use computers spend an average of just under an hour on each (0:55 for video games and 0:50 for computers). On the whole, the 83% of children who use screen media in a typical day spend an average of just under 2 hours (1:57) doing so. . . .

> "For our little guy, TV time is all of us on the couch together. The cat comes and sits with us. We'll talk about what's going on. If it's *Blues Clues*, we'll answer back. We only do 20 minutes a night."

> [Mother of a 1–3 year-old, Irvine, California]

Parents' Attitudes about Children's Media Use

Why Parents Want Their Kids to Use Media

Focus groups indicate that many parents are encouraging their children to spend time with media because they think it's good for their kids, and because it gives them a chance to get things done without their children underfoot.

Indeed, in focus groups parents speak about "getting" their kids to watch certain videos or TV shows, or about DVDs being better than TV because they're longer and afford a longer chunk of time in which to get things done.

> "They wake up and get to watch TV while I shower and get dressed. It keeps them in my sight line."

> [Mother of a 4–6 year-old, Denver, Colorado]

Many parents speak of the numerous demands on their time and of their strong need to keep their kids occupied while they get chores done. As a mom from Denver said about her 1–3 year-old, "If he is watching TV, I can get other things done. I don't have to constantly watch him." Some parents spoke about the fact that they simply can't let their kids play outdoors unsupervised. Others pointed out how much trouble their children could cause inside the house if they are left unmonitored: "If the TV isn't on, he's putting the 'Orange Glo' all over my daughter's bedspread. That makes more work for me."

> "He's a good little boy. He won't bother anything. He won't get into stuff. He's glued to the TV."

> [Mother of a 4–6 year-old from Columbus, Ohio]

Many parents also talked about how important it is for them to have "me" time, which often means getting their kids set up with a TV show or a DVD. The mother of a 4–6 year-old from the Denver area pointed out that: "Being an adult is hard. There are times when my interacting with my children is best served by me having an opportunity to allow them to do something alone so I can regroup. When I got laid off a couple of weeks ago, I didn't know it was coming. I got blindsided. I couldn't have interacted with my children that night. I couldn't have done it. 'Let's watch *Finding Nemo*, kids. Here are some chicken strips, here are sippy cups—I'll see you in about an hour and a half'."

The Educational Value of Television

In the national survey, parents are fairly evenly split on whether, in general, TV mostly helps (38%) or mostly hurts (31%) children's learning (22% say it doesn't have much effect either way). But in focus groups, many parents cited "learning" as one of the positive things about television, and indicated that they thought their children were learning from TV. Several mothers mentioned being surprised by their children saying a word in Spanish or being able to count. The mother of a 4–6 year-old from Denver said, "My daughter started saying something to me in Spanish—I don't know a word of Spanish. [TV is] definitely educational." Another Denver-area mom said, "My 2-year-old can count to 10. I haven't really practiced that much with her. She did it. Where else would she have possibly learned it?"

"Out of the blue one day my son counted to five in Spanish. I knew immediately that he got that from *Dora.*"

[Mother of a 1–3 year-old, Columbus, Ohio]

Mothers are also enthusiastic about the different experiences children are exposed to through television and videos. "[My son] has developed a passion about the ocean and angler fish because of Nemo," said one Denver mom. "He fell in love with that character. That door wouldn't have even been open if it wasn't for *Finding Nemo.*" Another Denver mother said her 4–6 year-old son was "always telling me what is right and wrong from the things he sees on TV. It has opened doors in being able to talk to him." Several mothers mentioned the "diversity" TV brings their young children. As one mom from Columbus said, "I think they are exposed to a little bit more diversity. I think that it's good for them to be comfortable with that. . . . to know that it's okay for everyone to be different."

"My daughter knows . . . her letters from *Sesame Street.* I haven't had to work with her on them at all."

[Mother of a 1–3 year-old, Columbus, Ohio]

"It shows them a world that they aren't familiar with. We live in the suburbs. She watches *Dora* and learns a little bit of Spanish."

[Mother of a 4–6 year-old, Columbus, Ohio]

Some parents feel they need media to help them with their child's education. As one mother from Irvine, California, said, "I think they (media) are in a way necessary. So much more is expected of kids these days. . . . When you go to kindergarten now, you can't just go and play with toys. You have to know how to write your name and spell. It's all about what you know." Most parents seemed to think their children would learn what they needed to know just fine without media, but they would be under a lot more pressure to do the teaching themselves. As the mother of a 1–3 year-old from Denver said, "I don't think it's important to use it as a learning tool, but for me to use it to keep them occupied."

The national survey indicates that there is a relationship between parents' attitudes about the educational value of television and how much time their children spend watching TV. Children whose parents think TV mostly *hurts* learning are *less likely* to watch than those whose parents say it mostly helps or doesn't have much effect one way or the other. For example, 48% of children whose parents say TV mostly hurts learning watch every day, compared to 76% of those whose parents believe TV mostly helps children's learning. Likewise, children whose parents say TV mostly hurts learning spend an average of 27 minutes less per day watching than children whose parents think TV mostly helps.

Table 1

Relationship of Parental Attitudes to Children's Media Use

Child's Media Use	Parent Attitude Towards TV		
	Mostly helps	No effect	Mostly hurts
Percent who watch TV on typical day	84%‡~	75%~	64%
Mean hours watching TV for kids who watched	1:27~	1:16	1:12
Mean hours watching TV for all kids	1:12‡~	0:57~	0:45
Percent who watch TV daily	76%~	71 %~	48%

‡Significantly higher than "No effect."; ~Significantly higher than "Mostly hurts."

It is not possible to tell from this survey whether parents who think TV hurts learning are more likely to restrict their children's viewing, or whether parents whose children spend more time watching TV develop a higher opinion of television's role in learning, or whether some other factor is influencing this relationship.

> "I just don't have time to sit on the computer with him to try and teach him all this other stuff. . . . I'm not going to put him on it if I have to teach him how to use the mouse or something else. . . . I am like—play it at your dad's and break *his* computer."
>
> [Mother of a 1–3 year-old, Denver, Colorado]

Educational Value of Computers

When it comes to using computers, most parents think this activity helps rather than hurts learning (69% vs. 8%, with 15% saying it doesn't have much effect).

Many parents feel that since their children are going to have to use computers later in life, getting familiar with them at an early age is a benefit in and of itself, regardless of what they're doing on the computer. One mother from Irvine said, "Anything they are doing on the computer I think is learning." Another mom from Columbus said, "I think they get more skills from the computer. Our world is so computer-oriented. I certainly didn't know how to use a computer when I was 3. . . . If I had a choice of the computer or TV, I would definitely choose the computer."

> "They'll survive without the video games and TV. . . . I don't think they'll survive without the computer. When they're older, they aren't going to have a cashier to check them out at Kroger."
>
> [Mother of a 4–6 year-old, Columbus, Ohio]

Other focus group mothers pointed to certain features of the computer that they found beneficial, such as interactivity or the parent being able to control the content through specific software. The mother of a young child from Irvine said, "The computer is far more interactive than TV. His mind is more active when he is using the computer. It's more of an analysis and figuring things out." A Denver-area mom (of a 4–6 year-old) said, "I think you have more control over the computer. If they're watching TV, you don't know what the lesson is going to be. With the computer you can put in specific software or go to a specific website."

> "I don't spend nearly as much time with my son as I need to. He has learned huge amounts through the video and computer games that we have. . . . I'm very grateful for the computer games. My kid learned his colors and letters from the computer. It's been very beneficial to us."
>
> [Mother of a 1–3 year-old, Irvine, California]

Another mother from Denver (of a 1–3 year-old) described one of the CD-ROMs she and her daughter enjoy using: "They have a 5-a-day vegetable game. My daughter doesn't like to eat, so we show her all the different foods that are good for her. We make things on the computer, and then we will go downstairs and make them to eat. She seems to eat better after we play the food game."

Despite the advantages some focus group mothers pointed to, many others expressed a lot of concerns about having their kids use the family computer. There was a sense that most of what children can learn from a computer they can also learn from TV or videos—without as much parental oversight and without as much risk to expensive equipment. As one mom from Irvine said, "If they're on the Internet, I have to be right there with them. That can be annoying because I don't always have the time to sit there while my 3- and 6-year-old go on the Internet. It isn't that fun for me to watch the same *Dora* clip 20,000 times. I would rather do other things." Some pointed to the safety of the Nickelodeon TV channel over the Nick Jr. website: one mom said, "If I leave my son on Nick Jr. for just a minute, he will click on every possible ad or whatever, and there will be a thousand things open," while another noted, "If they're watching Nickelodeon, you know they aren't going to have any porn sites popping up."

Educational Value of Video Games

According to the national survey, most parents think playing video games hurts rather than helps learning (49% vs. 17%, with 22% saying not much effect). In the focus groups, parents didn't indicate having as much experience using educational video games as they did with TV, computers, or videos and DVDs. One mother of a 4–6 year-old from Columbus did have experience with an educational video game: "My daughter and I played a Mickey Mouse (video) game where you had to . . . move the cursor around to find different things. If you find the remote, you can go back to the TV, and it will show a clip. It's like thinking."

Figure 2

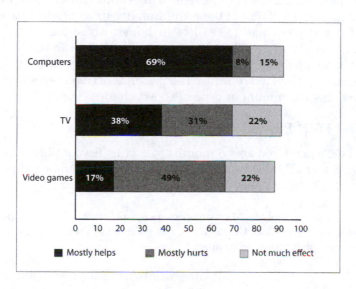

Percent of Parents Who Say Each Medium Mostly Helps or Hurts Children's Learning:

Focus group parents also felt that video games tended to be more violent, especially those for the older kids. Some worried about the types of games young children see their older siblings play: "My older kids play . . . a lot of the violent stuff. They let [my younger son] play one time, and the poor child was traumatized. . . . He couldn't even sleep that night. He kept telling us about it all night."

Many parents noted that their younger children tried to mimic either their dads or their older siblings by playing with game controllers, but just got frustrated because they couldn't do it properly.

Conversations with Pediatricians

Relatively few parents (15%) say that their pediatrician has ever discussed their child's media use with them. Parents with higher income and more formal education are more likely to say their pediatrician has discussed this with them (for example, 22% of college graduates, vs. 11% of those with a high school education or less). There is no indication from these data that children whose parents have discussed media use with their pediatrician are less likely to watch TV or that the household media environment is different for these children than for those whose parents haven't had those discussions. Even the youngest children are growing up in homes where media are an integral part of the environment—with multiple TVs, VCRs, computers, and video game players in the home; TVs left on much of the time (many with large screens and surround sound), whether anyone is watching or not; TVs in children's bedrooms; and portable DVD players and handheld video game players ready for children on the go.

Television

Nearly all children ages 6 months to 6 years (99%) live in a home with at least one television. Eighty-four percent live in a home with two or more televisions, and nearly a quarter (24%) live in homes with four or more TVs.

A large majority (80%) of these children live in homes that have cable or satellite TV, and about half (53%) live in homes where the largest TV is 30 inches or larger (25% have TVs 40 inches or larger). Four in ten (40%) have a television with surround sound, and two in ten (20%) have TiVo or some other type of digital video recorder. The presence ofTiVo in the home was not related to either the amount or type of shows children watched.

VCRs and DVD Players

Nearly all (93%) children ages 6 months to 6 years have a VCR or DVD player in the home, and a third (33%) have a portable DVD player. In addition, nearly one in five (18%) have a television or DVD player in their car.

> "While my daughter has her princess movie in, my son can be upstairs playing his *Blues Clues* CD-ROM. . . . It gives them their own space and their own quality time to be apart."
>
> [Mother of a 1–3 year-old, Denver, Colorado]

Video Games

Half (50%) of children 6 years and under have a console video game player in the home, and nearly three in ten (28%) have a handheld video game player. Children ages 4–6 are more likely than children ages 0–3 to live in homes with a console video game player (54% vs. 46%), and with a handheld video game player (34% vs. 22%).

> "I told my kids we weren't going to get an Xbox. . . . because we have the computer. To me it's just one more thing that I would have to fight over with them. I'm big on entertaining yourself—go play. Don't just sit here vegetating."
>
> [Mother of a 1–3 year-old, Columbus, Ohio]

Computers

More than three-quarters (78%) of children 6 years and under live in a household with a computer, and about three in ten (29%) live in a household with two or more computers. Nearly seven in ten (69%) have Internet access in the household, including 42% who have high-speed Internet access (26% have dial-up access). . . .

Calming Children Down or Pumping Them Up

Just over half (53%) of parents say that TV tends to calm their child down, while only about one in six (17%) say that TV gets their child excited. The rest

Figure 3

Percent of Children Age 6 and Under Who Live in a Home with . . .

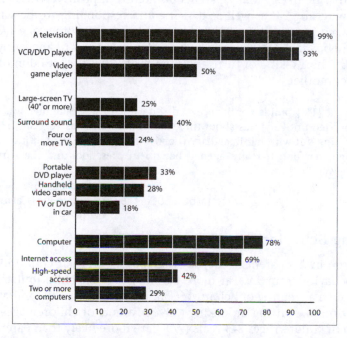

A television	99%
VCR/DVD player	93%
Video game player	50%
Large-screen TV (40" or more)	25%
Surround sound	40%
Four or more TVs	24%
Portable DVD player	33%
Handheld video game	28%
TV or DVD in car	18%
Computer	78%
Internet access	69%
High-speed access	42%
Two or more computers	29%

of parents either say: TV calms and excites their child equally (9%); it depends on what the child is watching (8%) or on the child's mood or time of day (3%); or they don't know (10%). Television's effect on children does not vary reliably with the child's age or gender. Children who watch mostly entertainment shows are more likely to be calmed by TV than are those who watch mostly educational shows (72% vs. 50%).

> "When he watched the *Buzz Lightyear of Star Command* video from the library, he was a monster child. The very next week I got *Teletubbies,* and it was completely opposite. He was very mellow."
>
> [Mother of a 1–3 year-old, Columbus, Ohio]

In focus groups, parents describe a range of responses their children have to TV. A number of parents talked about how TV can calm their children down. The mother of a 4-6 year-old from Irvine said, "My son is really hyper. That's a time when I can get him to actually calm down and watch a little TV. . . . He will slow down and that helps change his mood. . . . It's much better for him and for me."

> "She plays along with what she's watching most of the time. She's dancing. She's not being a couch potato . . ."
>
> [Mother of a 4–6 year-old, Columbus, Ohio]

But another mother, from Columbus, said, "My 2-year-old is so rambunctious you cannot turn your back for a second. With TV I notice that his temperament changes. He gets more wild and hyper when he is watching the stuff that he likes." Many parents pointed to a positive energy their kids get from watching TV as well as dancing and responding to the screen. "My kids will stand in front of the TV and hop and clap," a mother of a 1–3 year-old from Columbus said. Others describe kids who "zone out"or appear hypnotized by the TV. "The TV kind of turns their brain off, that's what I don't like," said one Denver mother.

> "I think [TV] builds confidence and self-esteem. My daughter was very introverted until she was about three and a half. She was very shy. . . . By her acting out with her imaginary friends on the TV or *Dora*, it just really brought her out. It really opened her up in preschool and she is really doing well."
>
> [Mother of a 4–6 year-old, Irvine, California]

Imitating Behavior from TV

Nearly seven in ten parents (68%) say they have seen their child imitate some type of behavior from TV. Far more parents say their child imitates positive behavior, such as sharing or helping (66%), than say their child imitates aggressive behavior, like hitting or kicking (23%). Parents of children ages 4–6 years (83%) and of children ages 2–3 years (77%) are more likely than parents of children under 2 years (27%) to say their child imitates any type of behavior.

> "She was going around kissing everyone with her mouth open. She wanted to be like Ariel and Eric."(From Disney's *The Little Mermaid*.)
>
> [Mother of a 1–3 year-old, Columbus, Ohio]

Boys in both age ranges (2–3 and 4–6) are more likely than girls to imitate aggressive behavior (nearly half—45%—of parents of boys ages 4–6 say their child imitates aggressive behavior). Children who primarily watch kids' educational programming are more likely than those who primarily watch kids' entertainment shows to imitate positive behavior (76% vs. 59%).

> "My daughter just sits in the beanbag chair watching TV. If it's something that she's really into, she just sits there with her mouth hanging open."
>
> [Mother of a 4–6 year-old, Columbus, Ohio]

Response to Commercials

In focus groups, when asked to list the positives and negatives of TV for their children, many parents mentioned commercials as a negative. But when asked how many commercials their children were exposed to in a typical day,

Table 2

Imitating Positive or Aggressive Behavior from TV

	Ages			Ages		
	2–3 Years			4–6 Years		
Percent whose parents say they . . .	All	Boys	Girls	All	Boys	Girls
Imitate positive behavior	75%	75%	75%	80%	79%	82%
Imitate aggressive behavior	24%	31%[†]	17%	33%[*]	45%[†]	21%
Imitate neither	23%[^]	20%	25%	17%	17%	17%

[*]Significantly higher than ages 2–3; [^]Significantly higher than ages 4–6; [†]Significantly higher than girls in this age range.

most parents seemed at a loss to guess, and estimates ranged from 5 to 100. Many parents indicated that their children liked commercials and were influenced by them. "She pays attention to the commercials more than the shows," said the mother of one 1–3 year-old from Columbus. "That's what gets her attention." Several talked about their children memorizing things from commercials. A Denver mom (of a 4–6 year-old) said, "My kids are—'I want that, I want that, I want that'. They commit things to memory for months." But one mother said she thought the commercials just went right past her kids: "I don't think they watch them. . . . I don't think they're paying attention."

> "I want this, I want that, I want chocolate cereal."

> [Mother of a 1–3 year-old, Denver, Colorado]

At the same time, a couple of parents mentioned that ads give them gift ideas, and they're grateful for them. The mother of one 1–3 year-old girl from Columbus said, "My daughter's birthday is next week. She saw a commercial for a Strawberry Shortcake doll toy. She said she wanted it for her birthday. If she hadn't seen the commercial, she wouldn't have known about it. I was glad that I was in the room and she could tell me that."

> "I would be at a total loss if it wasn't for commercials at Christmas time. I wouldn't know what to get my kids. They know what they like when they see it on TV."

> [Mother of a 4–6 year-old, Denver, Colorado]

Among parents whose children watch TV at least several times a month, the vast majority (83%) say their child watches mostly shows specifically for kids around his or her age (2% say the child watches mostly shows for all ages, including adults; and 13% say the child watches both types of shows about equally). More parents say their child watches mostly educational shows

Figure 4

Percent of Children Who Watch . . .

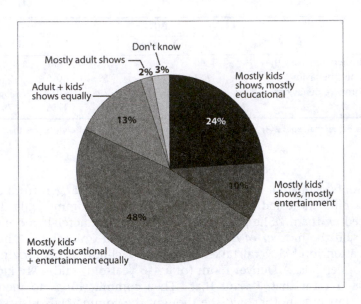

Note: Among those who watch TV at least several times a month.

(24%) than say their child watches mostly entertainment shows (10%), but a plurality (48%) say their child watches both types of shows about equally.

> "A show can seem fine one minute, and in the next minute Tom pulls a gun on Jerry."
>
> [Mother of a 4–6 year-old, Denver, Colorado]

In focus groups, a number of parents indicated that their young children watch mature content and that both the child and the parent seem fine with that. For example, the mother of one 4-year-old from Denver said, "*The Punisher,* my son loves that movie. He's more mature." Another said she "goes by her child's personality" in deciding what he can or can't watch. "Not a lot of people would be comfortable with a 4-year-old watching medical shows where they show people coming in and bleeding and crying," she said. "Obviously it is a tragedy. But he really loves the human body." Another mom from Irvine said, "I try not to really shelter my daughter. . . . She's two. She wants to watch *Jurassic Park.* . . . There's a dinosaur [that] ate a guy—that's what dinosaurs do—they eat people and animals. She understands that. She doesn't getfreaked about it. She even watched *Chuckie* the other day. She thought it was funny."

"I've found that my kids are usually about a year ahead of what the games or movies say. My son is two so I look at ones for 3–4 year-olds. I always pick one that is above their level to help them learn."

[Mother of a 1–3 year-old, Denver, Colorado]

Many parents in focus groups say they are guided by brands in choosing what their kids can or can't watch. One Denver mom said that children's TV shows are "all pretty much educational now. They help teach the kids how to help each other and how to love one another. Everything on Nick is like that." Another had a similar feeling about PBS: "I like my kids to watch PBS because it's more of a learning thing instead of the cartoons. I have no problem with them watching PBS for two hours straight. They have all those good learning shows." But one mother of a 4–6 year-old from Columbus said she made a mistake thinking she could go by the brand alone: "I thought you could trust Cartoon Network because of the name. I just recently paid attention to what he was watching and saw it. I said, 'What the *heck!'* I couldn't believe it."

"Because of the rules that I have set forth he doesn't ask to watch things that he can't watch."

[Mother of a 4–6 year-old, Denver, Colorado]

A number of parents in focus groups talked about the influence of their older siblings on what their younger kids see on TV or videos. The mother of one 1–3 year-old from Denver told about a time when her young son watched the movie *Alien vs. Predator:* "He liked it. . . . When I saw it I couldn't believe my older son let him watch it. I thought he would be up all night, but it didn't bother him at all." . . .

Children Under Age Two

Many experts consider the first two years of life especially critical for children's development and are particularly interested in monitoring media use patterns during this period. For example, the American Academy of Pediatrics has recommended no screen media use at all for children under two.

In fact, this study indicates that children under age 2 have quite different media habits than children 2 years and older, although it also indicates that they live media-rich lives. Almost all babies 6–23 months old have listened to music (98%), or been read to (94%). Nearly eight in ten (79%) have watched TV, and two-thirds (65%) have watched videos or DVDs. Only a very few have ever used a computer (5%) or played any kind of video game (3%).

More than four in ten (43%) children this age watch TV *every* day, while another 17% watch several times a week. Nearly one in five (18%) watch videos or DVDs every day, while another 26% watch at least several times a week. In a typical day, 61% of children this age watch TV, a video, or a DVD, for an average of one hour and nineteen minutes. Most parents say they are in the same room with their child while they're watching TV either all or most of the time (88% of those whose children this age watch TV in a typical day).

Around four in ten children under two can turn on the TV by themselves (38%) and change channels with the remote (40%). Almost one in five (19%) have a TV in their bedroom. A quarter (26%) of parents report that their children this age have already imitated a positive behavior from a TV show, like sharing or helping. Among the 63% of children this age who watch at least several times a month or more, 35% watch mostly kids' educational shows, 40% watch a mix of kids' educational and entertainment shows, and 19% watch a mix of programming for both children and adults.

In addition to watching their own shows, babies this age are also exposed to "background" television. A third (33%) live in homes where the TV is on most or all of the time, whether anyone is watching or not. Seventy percent of parents with children under two say they watch their own TV shows in a typical day, for an average of an hour and forty-three minutes, including 32% who say their child was in the room with them all or most of the time, 17% who say half or less of the time, and 20% who say none of the time.

More than half (58%) of children under two are read to every day, with another 25% being read to several times a week. In any given day, 77% are read to, for an average of 44 minutes. . . .

Figure 5

Percent of Children Under Age Two Who Watch TV . . .

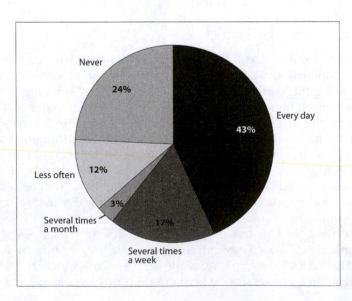

Summary and Conclusions

The Role of Parents

In the public debate about children and media, people on all sides of the issue often end up pointing to the role of parents in monitoring their children's media use, encouraging them to push the "off" button. This study provides important documentation of just how powerful a role parents have in shaping their children's media habits. A third of children live in homes where parents simply leave the TV on most of the day, whether anyone is watching or not—and, not surprisingly, those children end up watching significantly more than other kids do. Many parents spend a fair amount of time watching TV or on the computer themselves, and again, children of those parents also spend more time watching a screen each day. And a third of children 6 years and under have been allowed to have a TV in their bedroom—mostly to avoid conflicts with parents'or other family members' viewing—and again, those children spend more time watching TV.

Why Parents Are Drawn to Media

Many parents find media a tremendous benefit in parenting and can't imagine how they'd get through the day without it (especially TV, videos, and DVDs). Media allow parents a chance to get their chores done, quiet their kids down, or just have some "me" time, knowing that their kids are "safe"—not playing outside, and less likely to be making trouble around the house. Multiple TV sets, DVD players, and computers help solve sibling quarrels and also let parents get their own screen time uninterrupted. While fewer than four in ten (38%) parents say they think TV mostly helps children's learning, parents are relieved that they can make use of media in these ways with less guilt, because of what they see as real advances in the educational quality of media content.

The Educational Value of Children's Television

While parents in the survey seem pretty evenly split on whether TV in general is mostly helpful (38%) or harmful (31%) to children's learning, in the focus groups almost all parents pointed to "learning" as one of the big positives of TV for their kids, and many made comments about observing their children learning things from TV shows. In general, parents in the focus groups seemed well satisfied with the quality of programming available to their kids. Most felt their children would learn just as well *without* TV, but didn't want the extra burden that that would place on them as parents. The reigning sentiment seemed to be that there is simply no way they can live their lives and get everything done without TV and videos, and that the educational content and positive lessons in much of the programming lessens their guilt at not spending more time with their kids. And while parents in the survey indicate that they think the computer is more educational than is TV, the focus groups revealed that many parents greatly prefer TV or videos because they require less supervision (and because they're worried about their kids hurting the computer).

A Big Role for Media

Media, especially television, are clearly playing a key role in children's lives, starting at an early age. In a typical day, more than eight in ten (83%) children ages 6 months to 6 years old use screen media, averaging about two hours each (1:57). As mentioned above, a third live in homes where the TV is left on most or all of the time, whether anyone is watching or not, and a similar proportion (30%) have the TV on during most or all of their meals. Homes with multiple TV sets and portable media allow kids to watch in the privacy of their rooms, or when they're on the go—a third (33%) have a portable DVD player, and a third (33%) have a TV in their bedroom. About one in eight (12%) are put to bed with the TV on at least half the time.

Less Time with TV and DVDs

While there haven't been any major changes in children's daily media habits since a similar survey was conducted in 2003—they aren't more likely to use computers or video games, or less likely to watch TV—when children *do* watch TV or videos, they are spending less time doing so (10 minutes less watching TV, and 7 minutes less watching videos or DVDs). It's possible that this change follows on the slight—but statistically significant—drop in the proportion of parents nationally who say they leave the TV on all or most of time (from 37% to 32%) or who say they usually eat meals in front of the TV (from 35% to 30%). It is also possible that the shift comes from a greater number of parents thinking TV mostly *hurts* children's learning (up from 27% to 31%). However, it is also possible that it is an artifact of a shift in the time of year the survey was conducted, from April and May to September, October, and November. Slight decreases in time spent with computers and playing video games were not statistically significant. We will continue to track these data over time.

American Academy of Pediatrics Recommendations

A substantial number of children are using media in excess of the amounts recommended by the American Academy of Pediatrics (AAP). In a typical day, nearly two-thirds (61%) of babies under two years old use screen media, and 43% of children this age watch TV *every* day (the AAP recommends no screen time for babies under two). And while the AAP recommends no more than 1–2 hours per day of screen media for children two and older, in a typical day 41% of 2–3 year-olds and 43% of 4–6 year-olds use screen media for 2 hours or more. Few parents report having spoken with their doctor about their child's media use. . . .

Electronic media have clearly become a central focus of many young children's lives, a key component in family routines such as working up, eating, relaxing, and falling asleep. Not only do children—starting when they are just babies—spend hours a day using media, but they are also learning to use the media by themselves, often watching their own TVs, DVD players or hand-held devices, many times in the privacy of their own rooms. As much as media have become a part of the fabric of family life, they are often consumed separately, used as much or more to keep the peace than to bring family members together.

It is hoped that the data in this report will be used to help families assess their own media habits; to spur the development of media products that are beneficial to children and families; to inform policy debates about public broadcasting, digital media, and children's commercial exposure; and to provide the data to help inform future research about the impact of various media on young children. To date, there has been very little research about the impact of media on the youngest children, especially those 2 years and under. Given how much a part of children's lives these media are, it seems important to explore in greater depth the impact media may be having on their development.

Note

1. The percent of parents who report that their children watched videos or DVDs may be an underestimate due to the way the question was worded. The question read "Did your child spend anytime watching videos or DVDs, including while riding in the car?" In a previous survey, the question was asked without the phrase "including while riding in a car," and a far greater proportion of parents reported that their children had watched videos or DVDs (46%, compared to 32% in the current survey). Many respondents in the current survey may have misunderstood the question and answered "yes" *only* if their child watched videos or DVDs while riding in the car.

**Daniel R. Anderson
and Tiffany A. Pempek**

 **NO**

Television and Very Young Children

The American Academy of Pediatrics (AAP) has recommended that children younger than 24 months of age not be exposed to electronic screens. Practically speaking, *electronic screens* refers to television, although toddlers may increasingly become exposed to computers as software and interfaces are developed for them. At the time this recommendation was made, very little was known about toddlers' exposure to screens, use of screens, or the impact on them. Much of the recommendation was based on the known or presumed harmful effects of television on older children. The recommendation was thus highly conservative, pending new research. Because the recommendation was made, a number of research groups have begun to investigate television and very young children. This article summarizes and reviews that research, along with some older studies that have received little attention in this context. We subsequently revisit the AAP recommendation and make suggestions for future investigations.

Our review is organized in part on a distinction made by Anderson and Evans. In that largely speculative article, a contrast was made between *foreground* and *background* television. Foreground television is programming to which very young children overtly attend in a sustained manner. Ordinarily, foreground television consists of programming that is designed for young children and is presumably at least partially comprehensible to them. Background television consists of programming to which very young children pay little overt attention. Such programming is generally not produced for children and would be largely incomprehensible to them. The distinction between foreground and background television is relevant because foreground television could in principle be educational for very young children and have a positive impact in addition to or instead of the presumed negative impact. Such a possibility was not considered by the AAP. On the other hand, it is hard to imagine that background television could have a positive impact if it has an impact at all. In the remainder of this article, we examine research on very young children's exposure and attention to television, learning from foreground television, the effects of background television on behavior, and what is known about television's impact on development. We conclude with a discussion of areas for future research.

From *American Behavioral Scientist*, Vol. 48, No. 5, 2005, pp. 505–508, 512–513, 515–519. Copyright © 2005 by Sage Publications. Reprinted by permission of Sage Publications via the Copyright Clearance Center References omitted.

Exposure

Because the national television rating services do not report results on children younger than 2 years of age, there are relatively few studies of very young children's exposure to television. Exposure to television, of course, consists of the total of foreground and background TV. The few studies that attempt to assess exposure do not distinguish between foreground and background TV but instead, ask parents how much television their children "watch" during some period of time, such as a typical day or week. It is not clear how parents interpret this question. They may include times the children are present with a TV set in use but not paying overt attention, or they may answer according to their estimate of the amount of television to which the children do apparently pay attention. This is highly relevant to estimates of exposure because at home, very young children initially pay little attention to most television programs but extend their attention to increasingly diverse content as they mature. Consequently the amount of television that is in the foreground increases with development.

Christakis, Zimmerman, DiGiuseppe, and McCarty reanalyzed data collected for a national longitudinal study during the 1980s. Parents were asked how much television their children watched during typical weekdays and weekends. Children aged 1½ years watched an average 2.2 hours a day, whereas children aged 3½ years watched 3.6 hours a day. The variability in the parent estimates from this study is enormous. About 42% of the 1½-year-olds watched no television (the modal viewing time), whereas a few parents described their children as watching upwards of 18 hours a day. Among the 3½-year-olds, in contrast, only about 10% were described as watching no television, and the modal viewing time shifted to about 2 hours a day. Certain and Kahn analyzed data from later cohorts of the same study as surveyed in the early and mid-1990s. They reported that of infants 0 to 11 months of age, 83% were reported as watching no TV, whereas among 12- to 23-month-olds, 52% watched no TV and 27% watched 1 to 2 hours a day, with the remainder watching greater amounts. Of children from 24 to 35 months of age, 21% watched no TV, 38% watched 1 to 2 hours a day, and the remainder watched greater amounts. It is important to note that average figures given for very young children's viewing times combine large percentages of children who do not watch any TV with substantial percentages of children who do watch. In that sense, the averages are quite misleading. In our view, all these numbers should be taken with a grain of salt insofar as it is likely that some parents included background television in their estimates, whereas others did not.

The introduction of baby videos such as the *Baby Einstein* series and TV series such as *Teletubbies* in the 1990s substantially increased the amount of foreground television available to very young children. To our knowledge, only two studies estimate very young children's exposure to television since these media have become well established. Picrroutsakos, Hanna, Self, Lewis, and Brewer surveyed 100 parents on the amount of time that children aged 2 and younger are exposed to and attend to television and videos. In this study, parents of 100 infants, ranging in age from 2½ to 24 months, were asked to complete a diary tracking the infants' TV exposure. On average, parents reported that their infants were exposed to about 120 minutes of TV per day, 50% of which was infant and toddler programming, 40% adult programming, and 9% preteen programming. In addition, parents reported that the child attended to about 60 minutes of TV per day, or about half of their total exposure time.

The Kaiser Family Foundation commissioned a national survey of parents of children aged 6 months to 6 years. With the permission of Vicky Rideout of the Kaiser Family Foundation, we examined reported viewing for children in the survey who were younger than 1 year of age and 1, 2, and 3 years of age. The percentages of children who did not watch TV on a typical day were 48%, 40%, 29%, and 21% for each age group, respectively. The corresponding percentages for videotapes and DVDs were 70%, 53%, 47%, and 49%. For those who did watch TV, the average daily times spent watching were 1 hour 8 minutes, 1 hour 26 minutes, 1 hour 35 minutes, and 1 hour 29 minutes, respectively. The average daily times spent with videotapes or DVDs for those who watched them were 1 hour 16 minutes, 1 hour 27 minutes, 1 hour 39 minutes, and 1 hour 29 minutes, respectively. It is interesting to compare the numbers with those reported by parents surveyed in the early 1990s. For children younger than 1 year of age, the nonviewers dropped from 83% to 48% 10 years later; for 1-year-olds, the nonviewers dropped from 52% to 40%. It is clear that a much larger percentage of babies are watching TV and videos now. However, times spent viewing TV and videos have actually decreased if the numbers reported by Christakis et al. are used as a baseline against which to compare the recent data. We expected that with the advent of baby videos and TV series, parents would have reported more, not less, time spent viewing TV.

If the above numbers primarily represent foreground television viewing (but we do not really know), what can we say about exposure to background television? American homes have a television set in use about 6 hours a day, on the average, and Rideout et al. reported that 40% of parents with young children characterized a TV as being on "most" or "all" of the time. In addition, Pierroutsakos et al. estimated that about half of exposure is to TV not made for young children. We have not been able find more specific numbers, but presumably, a large percentage of America's very young children are exposed to many hours of background television as their parents or other older family members watch their programs or as the TV is simply left on all day with no one watching. . . . As we will argue below, foreground and background television are likely to have distinctly different impacts and should be clearly distinguished in future research with very young children.

Comprehension and Learning

Even if very young children are sensitive to the comprehensibility of TV programs, it is another question as to whether they can or do learn anything from them. The totality of results thus far suggests that very young children learn less from television than from equivalent real-life experiences. We refer to this as the *video deficit.*

One line of experiments focuses on imitation. In the typical experiment, a child is shown either a live or video version of an experimenter engaged in demonstrating the functioning of a puppet. The demonstrated functions could be simple one-step operations, such as removing a mitten; or they could be more complicated operations, such as removing a mitten, shaking it to demonstrate a bell inside the mitten, and then removing the bell. Even after a 24-hour delay, 12- to 15-month-olds have little difficulty imitating the live demonstrations, but they are quite poor at imitating the video demonstrations, showing some success only with the one-step demonstrations. When this procedure was extended to children as old as 30 months, the imitations were still poorer when based on video. Only when children received six repetitions of the video did imitation performance become as good as a single live demonstration. Of considerable interest, Muentener et al. found imitation from video with six repetitions in infants as young as 6 months of age. Note that the above experiments compared live demonstrations with video that was as comparable to the live demonstrations as possible. If standard techniques of television production (editing, zoom shots, sound effects) are applied to the demonstrations, then performance does improve.

A second line of research uses variations on an object retrieval task. Children are shown a toy being hidden in an adjacent room and then are asked to go into that room and retrieve the toy. In the typical study, one group watches through a window as the toy is being hidden and another group watches the hiding event on video. If they saw the hiding event while watching through a window, 24-month-olds correctly retrieved the toy without searching multiple locations. If they saw the hiding event on TV, however, their performance was very poor. On either task, 3-year-olds did well; 2½-year-olds did well with video in one study and at an intermediate level in another. It is not known why 2-year-olds do so poorly when the hiding information is presented by video. The problem is not due to the three-dimensional nature of the search task, as was hypothesized by Schmitt and Anderson. Evans, Crawley, and Anderson found the video deficit even when the search space was a 2-dimensional felt board. The problem is also not due to the visual nature of the task. In their second experiment, Evans, Crawley, et al. simply told the children where the toy was hidden. If a real person told where the toy was hidden the children successfully retrieved it. If the same person, via closed-circuit TV, told where the toy was hidden, the children were not able to retrieve it.

Difficulty with the video toy retrieval problem experienced by 2-year-olds is not a consequence of absorbing no information from TV whatsoever. Their performance was substantially better on the first than later search trials, indicating that they did remember something from TV at least on the first trial. Once they had the experience of actually finding the toy in a particular location in the room, however, that experience appears to have overwhelmed any information provided by television. After the first trial, the children would generally search for the toy where it had been hidden the previous trial (known as the perseverative error). In light of the findings that this problem did not exist if they viewed through a window (or were told by a real person) where the toy was hidden, it appears that they found something deeply unconvincing about information provided by TV as a basis for guiding their behavior.

It is interesting that if 2-year-olds are given extensive experience with closed-circuit video, frequently seeing themselves live on TV during a 2-week period, they are then able to perform correctly on the toy retrieval task. This indicates that by 24 months, the video deficit may be overcome by relevant experience, suggesting that the video deficit is not necessarily a consequence of fundamental and biologically based cognitive immaturity.

A third line of research is concerned with language learning. Children 2 years and older can clearly learn vocabulary from television. Nevertheless, when comparisons are made between video and equivalent live conditions in children younger than 2½ years, the results suggest a video deficit. Grela, Lin, and Krcmar tried to teach object labels either live, in an equivalent video, or in a version of *Teletubbies* that used the labels. They found better learning in the live as compared to video conditions. Learning from video by children near their 2nd birthday was substantially better than that by younger children.

Infants are able to perceive many phonetic contrasts that are not found in their native language; this ability is lost by about 12 months of age if infants are not exposed to other languages. Kuhl, Tsao, and Liu exposed American infants to contrasts found in Mandarin. One group of infants was exposed to live speakers of Mandarin for about 5 hours during 12 sessions between 9 and 10 months of age. Other groups were exposed to equivalent audiovisual or audio-only DVDs. The infants exposed to live speakers did not experience the loss of ability to perceive Mandarin contrasts. Infants exposed to the DVD stimuli, however, showed the same loss as infants exposed to no Mandarin at all. Again, this research indicates a profound video (and audio) deficit.

Finally, one experiment represents a fourth line of research. Mumme and Fernald were interested in whether infants could learn emotional responses from video. They exposed 10- and 12-month-old infants to videos in which an actress was portrayed as looking at a novel object with a positive facial expression and talking about the object with a positive tone of voice. The actress looked at other objects fearfully and with a fearful tone of voice. Subsequently, the infants were presented with the objects. The main result was that 12-month-olds avoided the "fearful" object but did not show increased approach behavior to the positive object. The 10-month-olds showed no avoidance of the fearful object or increased approach to the positive object. Thus, only in one of the four conditions did infants show emotional learning from video.

Although the experimental studies are still few, they are remarkably consistent in indicating a video deficit for children 24 months and younger. Although there is some learning indicated by some of the studies, the learning is dramatically less than that found for equivalent live displays. . . .

Impact of Television

Thus far, the research indicates that there is growing use of television by very young children, and that they pay attention to programs made for them.

Children are sensitive to comprehensibility as young as 18 months of age, but there is a video deficit in learning from television insofar as learning is substantially less from video compared to equivalent live displays. In addition, background television disrupts play and interactions with parents. With these findings in mind, we now consider the small literature on the impact of television on very young children.

Language

In a case study reviewed by Naigles and Mayeux, Sachs, Bard, and Johnson analyzed the speech of a 3-year-old boy with deaf parents whose only exposure to spoken English was via television. Although this boy had clearly acquired vocabulary, his grammar was seriously dysfunctional, suggesting that he had acquired little if any grammar from exposure to television. Although the boy had acquired vocabulary, it is not known how much, if any, was acquired before the age of 2 years.

Although not the primary goal, a study by Nelson assesses the impact of foreground television in a larger investigation of language development during the 2nd year of life. Nelson found that the amount of time children watched television (primarily *Sesame Street*, as reported by mothers) was negatively associated with several measures of language development, such as the rate at which children acquired words, and developmental markers, such as the age when 50 words had been acquired.

Recently, Linebarger and Walker analyzed vocabulary and expressive language in 30-month-olds in relation to TV viewing logs kept by parents starting at 6 months of age. Unlike other studies, this one analyzes outcome in relation to the particular programs to which the children were exposed. Programs associated with enhanced language growth were *Dora the Explorer, Blue's Clues, Dragon Tales, Arthur,* and *Clifford*. Programs associated with reduced language growth were *Sesame Street* and *Teletubbies. Barney and Friends* was associated with reduced vocabulary but increased expressive language. Total viewing, including adult programming, was associated with reduced vocabulary but slightly increased expressed language. This is provocative research indicating that early television viewing may have both positive and negative impacts on language development, depending on content. Alternatively, the associations may be due to selection effects with slower language learners being drawn to different programs than faster language learners.

It is interesting to note that two studies find negative associations of language development and viewing *Sesame Street* younger than the age of 2 years. This stands in contrast to consistent findings of increased language development associated with viewing of *Sesame Street* by older children. The producers of *Sesame Street* have always considered their target audience to be children 2 years and older. It may be that by being too advanced for children younger than 2, the program actually hinders rather than helps language development in such young children.

Symptoms of Attention Disorders

In a reanalysis of data collected in a longitudinal study during the 1980s, Christakis et al. examined the associations between early TV viewing and later symptoms of attention disorders. Time spent TV viewing (without reference to content) was assessed from parent estimates when the children were 1½ and 3½ years of age. Symptoms of attention disorders were assessed at age 7 years from five questions asked of the parents. For example, the parent was asked if the child had trouble concentrating, with the possible answers being never, some of the time, or all of the time. The researchers considered a symptom as being present if the parent answered sometimes or all of the time to the question. The symptoms were summed so that a child would receive a score from 0 to 5. Children in the upper 10% of the resulting distribution were considered as having symptoms of attention disorders. After statistically controlling for a large array of parent, child, and home factors, the researchers reported a small positive association (an odds ratio of 1.09) between viewing at age 1½ years and having symptoms of attention disorders. They repeated the analysis for 3½-year-old viewing and found the same small association. Not taking advantage of the longitudinal nature of the data, they did not control for 1½-year-old viewing to assess the 3½-year-old association or the reverse. It would have been very useful to know whether the 3½-year-old viewing accounted for variance additional to that accounted by 1½-year-old viewing or whether the association is established by 1½ years and does not change thereafter. It should also be noted that the viewing data were collected in the 1980s when there were no TV programs directed at children younger than 2. As with any correlational study, the Christakis et al. findings are open to alternative interpretations. Although it is possible that early TV viewing causes later symptoms of attention disorders, it is also possible that children with attention disorders are selectively drawn to early TV viewing. It could also be that the children, who may be hyperactive, are more likely to calm down when with TV; their parents may therefore encourage TV viewing. This latter interpretation is consistent with findings reported by Pierroutsakos et al. that 70% of parents say their infant is less fussy when watching TV, and 55% say their infant becomes more focused when watching TV.

Cognitive Development

In a series of studies, Wachs examined the effects of background noise and household chaos on development of infants and toddlers. He identified background television as an important component of background noise. He reported that background noise is associated with poorer cognitive development.

Carew conducted a longitudinal study of the impact of six "intellectual sources" on spatial and language skills related to intelligence. These skills were assessed by means of items taken from standardized tests. The six sources varied to the extent that the child was active in constructing his or her own experience, ranging from active construction during solitary play to shared construction during interactions with others and finally, to passive construction during television viewing. Participants were 23 children who were observed in their homes at several points between the ages of 12 and 33 months. Associations were consistent with the hypothesis that television had a negative impact on cognitive development during the first 2 years of life. However, from about 24 months and older, the impact of television became positive and the associations were stronger. The Carew study did not distinguish between types of content to which the children were exposed, but given the era, the foreground programs were most likely *Sesame Street, Mister Rogers' Neighborhood, Captain Kangaroo,* and *Romper Room School.*

A study by von Stauffenberg and Campbell assesses the relationship between TV viewing and quality of child care in a subsample from a larger study by the National Institute of Child Health and Human Development in which participants were families with children born in 1991. Data were collected when the children were approximately 36 months of age. Results indicate that children who were cared for in their own homes watched the most TV, those in family day care watched an intermediate amount, and those in day care centers watched the least. In addition, greater TV viewing was associated with poorer cognitive outcomes for children cared for in their homes by a nonmaternal caregiver but not for those in family day care or day care centers. It should be noted that this study does not differentiate between foreground and background television exposure. It may be that children in more formal day care settings were presented with programming designed for them, whereas those at home were exposed to both foreground and background television.

Summary and Conclusions

When we have talked to parents about the effects of TV on very young children, the most common questions focus on violent or scary content. We are not aware of any studies that examine the consequences of exposure to these types of content. Although there is some evidence that very young children can learn emotional responses from TV, most of the research focuses on cognitive issues.

The research indicates that very young children are much more likely to watch TV than they did in the past. Given that children watch, it is unclear whether time spent viewing has changed. They pay attention to video that is made for them, and their patterns of attention are remarkably similar to those of older children and adults. They are sensitive to the sequential and linguistic comprehensibility of video at least as young as 18 months of age. That said, the evidence so far indicates a video deficit when it comes to learning. There is less learning from a video display as compared to an equivalent live display. This is not to say that no learning occurs. With sufficient repetition, learning from video can match learning from a live display. With respect to impact, one study finds positive associations of vocabulary growth with viewing particular children's TV programs and negative associations with other programs. Other studies find negative associations of viewing before age 2 with language, cognitive, and attentional development. Associations become positive after age 2 when educational programs are viewed. Background adult television is a disruptive influence both on children's play and on parent-child interactions.

At the time of this writing, the AAP guideline, adopted without the guidance of almost any relevant research, appears to have been prescient. With the exception of the Linebarger and Walker findings, there is very little evidence that children younger than 2 learn anything useful from television. The evidence indicates that learning from television by very young children is poor and that exposure to television is associated with relatively poor outcomes. For example, two studies find that viewing of *Sesame Street* by children younger than 2 is associated with poorer language development, notwithstanding that research with older children finds valuable learning and long-term positive outcomes.

With the caveat that the total amount of research is still small, it appears that for children younger than 2 years of age, television has a different impact than it does for older children. Not yet addressed are the reasons why. One possibility is that television, although substantially iconic in its representation, is nevertheless a symbolic medium. For example, when we see a shot of a building followed by a cut to an interior room shot, we infer that the room is inside of the building. This inference is based on experience with the medium so that we understand that the juxtaposition of shots symbolizes the containment relationship between the room and the building. Children younger than 2, on the other hand, have been widely characterized as functioning in a sensorimotor manner with symbolic understanding quite limited. It may be that television in its present form is difficult for children younger than 2 to comprehend, even though they are, to some extent, sensitive to the canonical order of shots in a program such as *Teletubbies*. There are, of course, other possibilities than a lack of symbolic awareness, including immature perceptual, linguistic, attentional, and other cognitive skills. Whatever the case, by about age 2½ years, understanding of television appears to improve significantly, and the evidence for a positive impact of educational television is clear.

What is also clear is that additional research is needed. First, it is important to try to understand the reasons why there is so little apparent learning from video. A useful line of research would be to experimentally develop videos for very young children that are designed to maximize learning of a specified type, for example vocabulary. With systematic experimentation, it might be possible to develop far more effective educational videos than currently exist. After all, with substantial repetition, Barr et al. have shown that infants as young as 6 months of age can show imitation learning from video. Such research may help clarify the problems with video while at the same time providing guidelines for educationally successful video production. Second, it is important to begin to assess the impact of new video technologies as they are entering American homes. We found substantial disruptive effects of background TV using a 19-inch standard National Television Standards Committee monaural TV set. Many American homes are acquiring "home theaters" incorporating large-format high-definition screens with surround sound. It seems likely that the disruptive effects of background TV will only be magnified. On the other hand, as foreground television, it is possible that these new technologies will enhance learning.

Finally, and most important, prospective longitudinal studies and intervention experiments should be undertaken. Such experiments should, among other things, compare the AAP recommended "best practice" of no exposure to screens with current standard exposure to television. Although we have hints that television may be having a negative impact on children younger than 2 years old, the evidence is still weak and open to alternative explanations. As a society, we are engaged in a vast and uncontrolled experiment with our infants and toddlers, plunging them into home environments that are saturated with electronic media. We should try to understand what we are doing and what are the consequences.

CHALLENGE QUESTIONS

Are There Good Reasons to Allow Infants to Consume Electronic Media, Such as Television?

- Both sides in this controversy agree that more research needs to be done to fully understand the impact of electronic media on infants. What types of research would be most convincing to you? What are the key questions that we really need to understand?
- If you were talking to the parents of an infant, what would you say? Do the potential benefits of electronic media outweigh the potential risks?
- Rideout, Hamel, and the Kaiser Family Foundation rely entirely on parents' perspectives, without contrasting those to what research finds. Is this a case of parents know best, or do parents' perspectives need to be contrasted with scientific research?
- Anderson and Pempek do not consider the usefulness of electronic media in allowing parents to manage family life. Does that matter? Is it possible that by making parenting a more manageable task, electronic media may actually create a more healthy general environment for infants even if causing some immediate cognitive deficits?

Suggested Readings

American Academy of Pediatrics, "Media Education," *Pediatrics* (August 1999)

D. Anderson and M. Evans, "Peril and Potential of Media for Infants and Toddlers," *Zero to Three* (2001)

D. Christakis, F. Zimmerman, D. DiGiuseppe, and C. McCarty, "Early Television Exposure and Subsequent Attentional Problems in Children," *Pediatrics* (April 2004)

S. Fisch and R. Truglio (Eds.), *"G" is for "Growing": Thirty Years of Research on Children and Sesame Street* (Lawrence Erlbaum, 2001)

J. Golin, "Breaking Free from Baby TV," Mothering.com (July 2006)

A. Poussaint, S. Linn, and J. Golin, "Zero to Three and Sesame Beginnings: The Consequences of Selling Out Babies." *CommonDreams* (April 19, 2006)

E. Wartella, A. Caplovitz, and J. Lee, "From Baby Einstein to Leapfrog, From Doom to Sims, From Instant Messaging to Internet Chat Rooms: Public Interest in the Role of Interactive Media in Children's

Lives." *Society for Research in Child Development Social Policy Report* (2004)

Zero to Three, "Statement from Zero to Three on Partnership with Sesame Workshop on *Sesame Beginnings* DVDs," `http:// www.sesameworkshop.org/aboutus/pressroom/presskits/ sbpress/zero.php`

Internet References . . .

This site provides links and information about parenting, with a particular emphasis on early childhood.

http://www.kidsource.com

This is the official site for the National Association for the Education of Young Children, an organization focused on preschool and other forms of early childhood education.

http://www.naeyc.org/

The Association for Childhood Education International (ACEI) is a group focused on the optimal education and development of children.

http://www.acei.org/

This site is a resource for teacher and parents. It focuses on activities and curriculum for early childhood.

http://www.earlychildhood.com/

The character and education partnership is a coalition trying to promote character education as a way of shaping children to be good citizens.

http://www.character.org/

This group produces publications focused on successful child development.

http://www.partnershipforlearning.org/

This is the official site for the Attention Deficit Disorder Association, which is one of the largest international clearinghouses of information about ADD/ADHD.

http://www.add.org/

Information about childhood obesity from the Mayo Clinic health center can be found here.

http://www.mayoclinic.com/health/
childhood-obesity/DS00698

Early Childhood and Middle Childhood

*E*arly childhood (sometimes referred to as toddlerhood) generally encompasses the years between 2 and 6, while middle childhood generally refers to early school years prior to puberty. These ages comprise a gradual transition into the physical, social, and psychological ways of being that orient any lifespan. As such, scholars of development take particular interest in trying to ensure that these ways of being are healthy, hoping to give all children the chance to succeed in an increasingly complex world. The issues in this section focus on three topics that underlie healthy physical, social, and psychological development: our bodies, our schools, and our mental health.

- Is Advertising Responsible for Childhood Obesity?
- Does Emphasizing Academic Skills Help At-Risk Preschool Children?
- Is Attention Deficit Disorder (ADD/ADHD) a Legitimate Medical Condition That Affects Childhood Behavior?

ISSUE 7

Is Advertising Responsible for Childhood Obesity?

YES: The Kaiser Family Foundation, from "The Role of Media in Childhood Obesity," *Issue Brief* (February 2004)

NO: The Federal Trade Commission Bureau of Economics Staff, from "Children's Exposure to Television Advertising in 1977 and 2004: Information for the Obesity Debate," *Federal Trade Commission Bureau of Economics Staff Report* (June 1, 2007)

ISSUE SUMMARY

YES: In a review of research on media exposure and childhood obesity the Kaiser Family Foundation concludes that exposure to advertising, more than inactivity, best explains the increasing rates of childhood obesity.

NO: In contrast, the Federal Trade Commission Bureau of Economics Staff specifically evaluated television advertising to children and found that increasing rates of childhood obesity do not correspond with increasing exposure to food advertising.

Groups from the World Health Organization to the United States Centers for Disease Control have spent considerable effort in recent years warning us about an "epidemic" of obesity. According to the Kaiser Family Foundation report, since 1980 the proportion of overweight children in the United States has doubled, and for adolescents it has tripled. They estimate that 20% of 2–5-year-olds and 30% of 6–19-year-olds are at least "at risk" for being significantly overweight. Although the epidemic is certainly not limited to children, children are a primary focus of scholarly investigation because they represent the future of our public health.

The developmental norms that are relevant to obesity are a complex mix of biological, psychological, and social factors. From a biological perspective, there does seem to be a genetic component to obesity—but that component depends heavily upon an interaction with environmental factors. For example, children today are simply less physically active than in the past and thus are more prone to put on weight. From a psychological perspective, it is clear that attitudes toward both physical activity and food contribute significantly to obesity and other weight issues. As such, much attention is devoted to facilitating the development of healthy attitudes toward food and exercise. That attention, however, is only part of broader social influences that shape eating and exercise patterns. The availability and popularity of fast food, for example, is a relatively new social phenomenon that is a part of most childhoods.

While there is not one clear culprit in the childhood obesity epidemic, the influence of advertising and electronic media is a popular target for blame because it relates in various ways to the biological, psychological, and social issues at hand. The popularity of advertising and media may lead children to be less physically active because the attitudes toward food and physical activity are often guided by advertising, and the social world is saturated with a commercial and somewhat sedentary food culture.

In their report, the Kaiser Family Foundation presents data suggesting that advertising and electronic media do indeed play a significant role in the obesity epidemic. They note that media consumption correlates with being overweight, and that food advertising commonly encourages children to make unhealthy diet choices. Thus, while the Kaiser Family Foundation acknowledges that other factors play a significant role in childhood obesity, their data seem to suggest that advertising plays an important role and should be regulated.

The United States Government's Federal Trade Commission, on the other hand, in an analysis of food-related advertising on television, finds no reason to assume it plays any causal role in childhood obesity. They think that the usual estimates about children's exposure to food marketing are too high, and find that advertising exposure has not really gone up significantly during the last 30 years. Yet, this 30-year period is exactly when the obesity epidemic came into being. The Federal Trade Commission notes that regulating food advertising to children has the potential to merely exacerbate the problem since children would be likely to see much more advertising for sedentary activities and entertainments.

POINT	COUNTERPOINT
• The exposure of children to food advertising is likely one of several factors contributing to increased rates of obesity.	• The estimates of the amount of ads children view are likely significantly too high.
• Children who consume more electronic media generally are more likely to be overweight.	• Most ads that children see are for nonfood products.
• Food advertising tends to encourage children toward unwise food choices.	• Children in 2004 saw fewer ads than children in 1977, thus the rise in obesity has not corresponded with a rise in advertising.
• Limiting advertising directed at children could help to reduce obesity.	• Restricting food advertising might just lead to more ads for other products that contribute to obesity.

YES

The Role of Media in Childhood Obesity

Introduction

In recent years, health of officials have become increasingly alarmed by the rapid increase in obesity among American children. According to the Centers for Disease Control and Prevention (CDC), since 1980 the proportion of over-weight children ages 6–11 has more than doubled, and the rate for adolescents has tripled. Today about 10% of 2- to 5-year-olds and 15% of 6- to 19-year-olds are overweight. Taking into consideration the proportion who are "at risk" of being overweight, the current percentages double to 20% for children ages 2–5 and 30% for kids ages 6–19. Among children of color, the rates are even higher: 4 in 10 Mexican American and African American youth ages 6–19 are considered overweight or at risk of being overweight.

According to the American Academy of Pediatrics, the increase in child-hood obesity represents an "unprecedented burden" on children's health. Medical complications common in overweight children include hypertension, type 2 diabetes, respiratory ailments, orthopedic problems, trouble sleeping, and depression. The Surgeon General has predicted that preventable morbid-ity and mortality associated with obesity may exceed those associated with cigarette smoking. Given that an estimated 80% of overweight adolescents continue to be obese in adulthood, the implications of childhood obesity on the nation's health—and on health care costs—are huge. Indeed, the American Academy of Pediatrics has called the potential costs associated with childhood obesity "staggering."

In an effort to seek the causes of this disturbing trend, experts have pointed to a range of important potential contributors to the rise in child-hood obesity that are unrelated to media: a reduction in physical education classes and after-school athletic programs, an increase in the availability of sodas and snacks in public schools, the growth in the number of fast-food outlets across the country, the trend toward "super-sizing" food portions in restaurants, and the increasing number of highly processed high-calorie and high-fat grocery products.

The purpose of this issue brief is to explore one other potential contribu-tor to the rising rates of childhood obesity: children's use of media.

From *Issue Brief #7030*, February 2004. Copyright © 2004 by The Henry J. Kaiser Family Foundation. This information was reprinted with permission from the Henry J. Kaiser Family Foundation. The Kaiser Family Foundation, based in Menlo Park, California, is a nonprofit, independent national health care philanthropy and is not associated with Kaiser Permanente or Kaiser Industries.

Figure 1

Proportion of Overweight Children in the United States

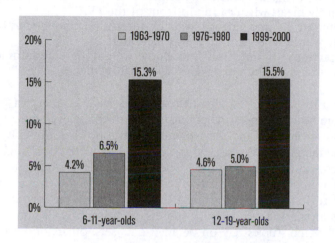

Source: Centers for Disease Control and Prevention, National Center for Health Statistics, Health, United States, 2009, Table 69.

During the same period in which childhood obesity has increased so dramatically, there has also been an explosion in media targeted to children: TV shows and videos, specialized cable networks, video games, computer activities and Internet Web sites. Children today spend an average of five-and-a-half hours a day using media, the equivalent of a full time job, and more time than they spend doing anything else besides sleeping. Even the very youngest children, preschoolers ages six and under, spend as much time with screen media (TV, videos, video games and computers) as they do playing outside. Much of the media targeted to children is laden with elaborate advertising campaigns, many of which promote foods such as candy, soda, and snacks. Indeed, it is estimated that the typical child sees about 40,000 ads a year on TV alone.

For the first time, this report pulls together the best available research, going behind the headlines to explore the realities of what researchers do and do not know about the role media plays in childhood obesity. In addition, the report lays out media-related policy options that have been proposed to help address childhood obesity, and outlines ways media could play a positive role in helping to address this important public health problem.

Pediatricians, child development experts, and media researchers have theorized that media may contribute to childhood obesity in one or more of the following ways:

- The time children spend using media displaces time they could spend in physical activities;
- The food advertisements children are exposed to on TV influence them to make unhealthy food choices;

- The cross-promotions between food products and popular TV and movie characters are encouraging children to buy and eat more high-calorie foods;
- Children snack excessively while using media, and they eat less healthy meals when eating in front of the TV;
- Watching TV and videos lowers children's metabolic rates below what they would be even if they were sleeping;
- Depictions of nutrition and body weight in entertainment media encourage children to develop less healthy diets.

The research to date has examined these issues from a variety of perspectives ranging from health sciences and public health, to child development and family relations, to advertising and mass communications. These investigations have been methodologically diverse, and the results have often been mixed. As with any research, caution must be used when comparing the outcomes of studies because of variations in the methods and measures used. For example, some studies are regional, while others use large, nationally representative samples. Some focus on specific demographic subsets, such as 6th-grade girls, while others are broader. Some studies rely on detailed data sets, others on fairly simplistic measures. For example, television use may be measured through self-reports, parental reports, or detailed diaries. Likewise, body fat may be assessed through multiple clinical measures or by self-reports of height and weight.

The following section of this report reviews the major research that has been conducted on the key issues concerning media and childhood obesity, and summarizes the major findings.

Defining Childhood Obesity

The phrases "obese," "overweight," and "at risk for being overweight" are commonly used in the public health community. With regard to children, the terms "obese" and "overweight" are generally used interchangeably in the medical literature. The Body Mass Index (BMI), which measures the ratio of weight to height, is a standard tool used to define these terms. BMI definitions for children and adolescents are age- and gender-specific in order to accommodate growth patterns. The Centers for Disease Control and Prevention (CDC) classify children as "overweight" if they are above the 95th percentile for their age and sex, and "at risk of being overweight" if they are between the 85th and 95th percentile.

Research on Media and Childhood Obesity

Do major studies find a relationship between childhood obesity and the time children spend using media?   The first major evidence that children's media consumption may be related to their body weight came in a 1985 article by William Dietz and Stephen Gortmaker in the journal *Pediatrics*, and it was dramatic. An analysis of data from a large national study of more than 13,000 children, the National Health Examination Survey (NHES), found significant associations between the amount of time children spent watching television and the prevalence of obesity. The authors concluded that, among 12- to 17-year-olds, the prevalence of obesity increased by 2% for each additional hour of television viewed, even after controlling for other variables such as prior obesity, race, and socio-economic status. Indeed, according to the authors, "only prior obesity had a larger independent effect than television on the prevalence of obesity." In a commentary published in 1993, the authors went on to note that another interpretation of their findings is that "29% of the cases of obesity could be prevented by reducing television viewing to 0 to 1 hours per week."

Since then, several more studies have found a statistically significant relationship between media use and rates of obesity, while others have found either a weak relationship or no relationship at all. In addition to the Dietz and Gortmaker study, other large-scale national studies have found a correlation between media use and body weight:

- Analysis of data from a nationally representative survey of more than 700 kids ages 10–15, conducted in the late 1980s, concluded that "the odds of being overweight were 4.6 times greater for youth watching more than 5 hours of television per day compared with those watching for 0–1 hours," even when controlling for prior overweight, maternal overweight, race, and socio-economic status. The authors concluded, "Estimates of attributable risk indicate that more [than] 60% of overweight incidence in this population can be linked to excess television viewing time."

- Data from the 1988–1994 waves of the National Health and Nutrition Examination Surveys (NHANES) were analyzed to explore the relationship between TV watching and obesity among 8- to 16-year-olds. The study concluded that "television watching was positively associated with obesity among girls, even after controlling for age, race/ethnicity, family income, weekly physical activity, and energy intake." The study did not find a correlation for boys.

- Another analysis of the 1988–1994 NHANES data found that among 8- to 16-year-olds, both boys and girls "who watched the most television had more body fat and greater BMIs than those who watched less than 2 hours a day."

- A study based on the CDC's 1999 Youth Risk Behavior Survey which sampled more than 12,000 high school students nationwide, found that watching television more than 2 hours a day was related to being overweight; these findings were consistent for the entire student population, controlling for race, ethnicity, and gender.

- A later study found a link between television viewing and obesity using a different methodology. The Framingham Children's Study was a longitudinal study in which slightly more than 100 children were enrolled as preschoolers and followed into early adolescence. In this study, published in 2003, the authors found that "television watching was an independent predictor of the change in the child's BMI" and other measures of body fatness. They noted that the effect of TV viewing was "only slightly attenuated" by controlling for factors such as the child's body-fat measures at the time they were enrolled in the study, and their parents' BMI or education. The authors concluded that "television watching is a risk factor for change in body fat, not simply reflective of more obese children tending to watch more television as a consequence of their obesity making it difficult to exercise."

Other studies—one from a nationally representative cross-sectional sample and the others from specific regions or communities—have not found a relationship between television viewing and childhood obesity:

- A recent analysis of data from a national study of more than 2,800 children ages 12 and under, which relied on detailed time-use diaries, found a "striking" lack of relationship between time spent watching television and children's weight status. On the other hand, this study did find a relationship between obesity and time spent playing video games, although that relationship was not linear: Children with higher weight played moderate amounts of games, while those with low weight played electronic games either very little or a lot.
- A 1993 study of 6th- and 7th-grade girls in Northern California found that over a two-year period "baseline hours of after-school television viewing was not significantly associated with either baseline or longitudinal change in BMI." The authors argued that their study "refutes previous suggestions that . . . television viewing is causally related to obesity."
- A study of nearly 200 preschoolers in Texas observed the children for several hours on each of four different days a year, over the course of three years, recording the amount of TV the children watched and their physical activities. This study found that although television watching was weakly negatively correlated with physical activity levels, it was not associated with body composition.

In evaluating this research, it is important to note that some of these studies are cross-sectional rather than longitudinal—that is, they take a specific point in time and look at whether TV viewing is associated with obesity. One problem with this approach is that while a study may indicate a relationship between TV viewing and being overweight, it does not prove that the TV viewing *caused* the increased weight. Controlling for other risk factors such as socio-economic status and parental body weight (as many studies do) can help clarify the results. Another problem with the cross-sectional approach is that the causal relationship could run in the opposite direction: that is, being obese may cause children to engage in more sedentary (and isolated) activities, including watching more television.

Longitudinal studies can help address the causality issue; however, the results of these studies have varied. As noted above, the two-year longitudinal study of adolescent girls in Northern California did not find a causal relationship between children's weight and the time they spent with media. On the other hand, the Framingham Children's Study, which tracked preschoolers through early adolescence, did find such a relationship. The authors of the latter study have theorized that the effects of media use on body weight may emerge slowly over time, and hence were not revealed in the two-year study in Northern California. It has also been argued that the lack of effect in that study may be due to factors specific to the sample of 6th- and 7th-grade girls in Northern California. Additionally, the study of 700 10- to 15-year-olds referenced above used height and weight data from 1986 and compared it to TV viewing and BMI measures in 1990. These authors concluded that "no evidence was found for a selective effect of overweight; i.e., children who were overweight in 1986 were unlikely to watch more television in 1990 than were children who were not overweight."

Others argue that the only way to truly demonstrate a causal relationship is through an experimental trial; for example, reduce TV viewing and see whether that affects children's weight when compared to a control group. Several interventions of this nature have been found to have a positive impact in reducing children's body weight.

Do experimental interventions that reduce children's media time result in weight loss?   Experimental trials are considered the best way of determining whether there is a causal relationship between television viewing and childhood obesity. Some experiments have incorporated reductions in media time as part of a more comprehensive program involving diet and increased physical activity as well. Another experiment used reduced media time as the only intervention, yet still found an impact on children's weight and body fatness.

- During the 1996–97 school year, Stanford University researchers conducted a randomized controlled trial in which they reduced the amount of time a group of about 100 3rd- and 4th-graders in Northern California spent with TV, videos, and video games. Two matched elementary schools were selected to participate, one of which served as the control group. The intervention involved a "turnoff" period of no screen time for 10 days followed by limiting TV time to 7 hours per week, as well as learning media literacy skills to teach selective viewing. At the end of a 6-month, 18-lesson classroom curriculum, students who received the intervention achieved statistically significant reductions in their television viewing and meals eaten in front of the TV set, as well as decreases in BMI, triceps skinfold thickness, waist circumference, and waist-to-hip ratio. While these changes were not accompanied by reduced high-fat food intake or increased physical activity, the findings do appear to demonstrate the feasibility of decreasing body weight by reducing time spent with screen media.
- Another school-based intervention found improved diet, increased physical activity, and decreased television time to be effective. The study, which measured prevalence, incidence, and remission of obesity among ethnically diverse middle-school boys and girls, involved a randomized controlled field trial with five intervention and five control schools. Classroom teachers in math, science, language arts, social studies, and physical education incorporated lessons within the existing curricula over two years. The lessons focused on decreasing television

viewing to 2 hours per day, increasing physical activity, reducing consumption of high-fat food, and increasing servings of fruits and vegetables. For each hour television viewing was reduced, the prevalence of
obesity was reduced among girls in the intervention schools compared
with the control schools; no similar effect was found for boys. The
program also resulted in an increase in girls' consumption of fruits
and vegetables.
- A family-based weight-control program found that decreasing sedentary
  behaviors (such as screen media use) is a viable alternative to increasing
  physical activity in treating childhood obesity. Families with obese children ages 8–12 were randomly assigned to one of four groups that
  included dietary and behavior change information, but differed in
  whether they tried to decrease sedentary activities or increase physical
  activity. Results indicated that significant decreases in percent of overweight and body fat were associated with decreasing sedentary behaviors
  such as watching TV or videos, or playing video or computer games.

These interventions indicate that reducing the time children spend with media
may indeed be an effective way to address childhood obesity. Researchers,
health professionals, and advocates have theorized several ways media may
contribute to childhood obesity. The following sections summarize some of the
major scientific studies in order to provide an understanding of media's potential
influence on the incidence of overweight among children and adolescents in the
United States.

**Does the time children spend using media displace time spent in more
physical activities?**   From toddlers to teens, American youth are spending a
substantial part of every day of their lives using media. But the time children
spend using media does not necessarily mean a decrease in time spent in
physical activities. Surprisingly, few studies have examined this relationship,
and results have been mixed. Some studies have found a weak but statistically
significant relationship between hours of television viewing and levels of
physical activity, while others have found no relationship between the two.

- A study of 6th- and 7th-grade adolescent girls in four Northern California
  middle schools found that the number of hours they spent watching
  TV after school was negatively associated with their level of physical
  activity; however, the relationship accounted for less than 1% of the
  variance and there was no connection with body weight.
- A study of a small sample of preschool children in Texas, conducted in
  a naturalistic setting, found a weak but statistically significant relationship between TV viewing and physical activity, although it did
  not find a relationship between viewing and body weight.
- A recent national telephone survey of parents of children ages 4–6
  found that children who spent more than two hours watching TV the
  previous day spent an average of a half-hour less playing outside that
  day than did other children their age.
- A review of data from the 1999 National Youth Risk Behavior Study,
  which includes a nationally representative sample of more than

15,000 high school students, found that among white female students only, time spent watching TV was associated with being sedentary.

- A survey of close to 2,000 9th-graders in Northern California found a weak but statistically significant relationship between TV viewing and physical activity for white males only.
- A study of national data from the 1988–1994 NHANES found no relationship between TV viewing and the number of bouts of vigorous physical activity, although it did find a statistically significant relationship between TV viewing and body weight.

While logic suggests that extensive television viewing is part of a more sedentary lifestyle, the evidence for this relationship has been surprisingly weak to date. In order for this relationship to be true, as one study noted, children who watch less TV would have to be choosing physically vigorous activities instead of TV, rather than some other relatively sedentary pastime such as reading books, talking on the phone, or playing board games.

Another possibility is that the act of watching TV itself actually reduces children's metabolic rate, contributing to weight gain. One study of 8- to 12-year-olds found that TV viewing decreased metabolic rates even more than resting or sleeping, but several other studies found no such effect.

The fact that most studies have failed to find a substantial relationship between the time children spend watching TV and the time they spend in physical activity may suggest that the *nature* of television viewing—that is, how children watch and what they watch—may be as or more important than the number of hours they watch.

Do the food ads children are exposed to on TV influence them to make unhealthy food choices?   Many researchers suspect that the food advertising children are exposed to through the media may contribute to unhealthy food choices and weight gain. Over the same period in which childhood obesity has increased so dramatically, research indicates that the number of ads children view has increased as well. In the late 1970s, researchers estimated that children viewed an average of about 20,000 TV commercials a year; in the late 80s, that estimate grew to more than 30,000 a year. As the number of cable channels exploded in the 1990s, opportunities to advertise directly to children expanded as well. The most recent estimates are that children now see an average of more than 40,000 TV ads a year.

The majority of ads targeted to children are for food: primarily candy (32% of all children's ads), cereal (31%), and fast food (9%). One study documented approximately 11 food commercials per hour during children's Saturday morning television programming, estimating that the average child viewer may be exposed to one food commercial every 5 minutes. According to another study, even the two minutes of daily advertising targeted to students in their classrooms through Channel One expose them to fast foods, candy, soft drinks, and snack chips in 7 out of 10 commercial breaks.

A review of the foods targeted to children in commercials on Saturday morning television indicates that the nutritional value has remained consistently low over the past quarter-century. Over the years, the most prevalent foods advertised have been breakfast cereals. Up until the 1990s, the next most-advertised products were foods high in sugar, such as cookies, candy, and other snacks. By the mid-1990s, canned desserts, frozen dinners, and fast foods over-took ads for snack foods. The data indicate that ads for these high-fat and high-sodium convenience foods have more than doubled since the 1980s. While studies vary as to the exact percentages, the same pattern emerges: a predomi-nance of ads for high-sugar cereals, fast food restaurants, and candy, and an absence of ads for fruit or vegetables.

The Effect of Food Advertising on Children

The vast majority of the studies about children's consumer behavior have been conducted by marketing research rms and have not been made publicly available. Clearly, the conclusion advertisers have drawn is that TV ads can influence children's purchases—and those of their families. Fast food outlets alone spend $3 billion in television ads targeted to children. Recent years have seen the development of marketing firms, newsletters, and ad agencies special-izing in the children's market. The New York Times has noted that "the court-ship of children is no surprise, since increasingly that is where the money is," and added that marketing executives anticipate that children under 12 will spend $35 billion of their own money and influence $200 billion in house-hold spending in 2004. The enthusiasm of marketers can be felt in the Febru-ray 2004 edition of Harris Interactive's "Trends and Tudes" newsletter, which notes that "This generation has become a huge consumer group that is worthy of attention from many businesses seeking to maximize their potential. Kids, teens and young adults spend significant amounts of their own money, and they influence the shopping behavior of their parents, their siblings, their rel-atives, and other adults in their lives."

Scientific studies that are available in the public realm back up these mar-keting industry assessments of the effectiveness of advertising directed at children. Studies have demonstrated that from a very young age, children influ-ence their parents' consumer behavior. As many parents can attest after a trip down the grocery aisle with their children, television viewing has also been found to impact children's attempts to influence their parents' purchases at the supermarket. For example, several studies have found that the amount of time children had spent watching TV was a significant predictor of how often they requested products at the grocery store, and that as many as three out of four requests were for products seen in TV ads. These studies have also found that children's supermarket requests do indeed have a fairly high rate of success.

One study found that among children as young as 3, the amount of weekly television viewing was significantly related to their caloric intake as well as their requests and parent purchases of specific foods they saw advertised on television. Another study manipulated advertising shown to 5- to 8-year-olds at summer camp, with some viewing ads for fruit and juice, and others ads for candy and Kool-Aid. This study found that children's food choices were signifi-cantly impacted by which ads they saw.

Experimental studies have demonstrated that even a brief exposure to food commercials can influence children's preferences. In one study, researchers designed a randomized controlled trial in which one group of 2- to 6-year-olds from a Head Start program saw a popular children's cartoon with embedded commercials, and the other group saw the same cartoon without commercials. Asked to identify their preferences from pairs of similar products, children who saw the commercials were significantly more likely to choose the advertised products. Preference differences between the treatment and control group were greatest for products that were advertised twice during the cartoon rather than only once.

Researchers are beginning to document a link between viewing television and children's consumption of fast foods and soda, a possible result of exposure to food advertising. A recent study found that students in grades 7–12 who frequently ate fast food tended to watch more television than other students. Another study found that middle-school children who watched more television tended to consume more soft drinks.

Other evidence of television's potential impact on children's dietary habits indicates a negative relationship between viewing television and consuming fruits and vegetables. The USDA's Dietary Guidelines recommend that youth eat three to five daily servings of fruits and vegetables, yet only 1 in 5 children meet the guideline, and one-quarter of the vegetables consumed reportedly are french fries. In a recent study, more than 500 middle school students from ethnically diverse backgrounds were studied over a 19-month period to determine whether daily television and video viewing predicted fruit and vegetable consumption. Using a linear regression analysis, researchers found that for each additional hour of television viewed per day, daily servings of fruits and vegetables decreased among adolescents. The researchers who conducted the study conclude that this relationship may be a result of television advertising.

Some researchers believe that TV ads may also contribute to children's misconceptions about the relative health benefits of certain foods. One of the earlier studies found that 70% of 6- to 8-year-olds believed that fast foods were more nutritious than home-cooked foods. Another study showed a group of 4th- and 5th-graders a series of paired food items and asked them to choose the healthier item from each pair (for example, corn flakes or frosted flakes). Children who watched more television were more likely to indicate that the less healthy food choice was the healthier one. These results replicated the results of an earlier study conducted with children of the same age.

Do cross-promotions between food products and popular TV and movie characters encourage children to buy and eat more high-calorie foods? Recent years have seen what appears to be a tremendous increase in the number of food products being marketed to children through cross-promotions with popular TV and movie characters. From SpongeBob Cheez-Its to Hulk pizzas and Scooby-Doo marshmallow cereals, today's grocery aisles are filled with scores of products using kids' favorite characters to sell them food. Fast food outlets also make frequent use of cross-promotions with children's media characters.

A recent article in the New York Times business section noted that "aiming at children through licensing is hardly new. What has changed is the scope and intensity of the blitz as today's youth become unwitting marketing targets at ever younger ages through more exposure to television, movies, videos and the Internet." One food industry executive was quoted as saying that licensing "is a way to . . . infuse the emotion and popularity of a current kids' hit into a product."

Some promotions involve toys based on media characters that are included in the food packages or offered in conjunction with fast food meals. McDonald's and Disney have an exclusive agreement under which Happy Meals include toys from top Disney movies. In the past, Happy Meals have reportedly also included toys based on the Teletubbies TV series, which is aimed at pre-verbal babies. Burger King has also featured Teletubbies tie-ins, along with Rugrats, Shrek, Pokemon and SpongeBob. More than a decade ago, researchers were finding that the typical "kid's meal" advertised to children consisted of a cheeseburger, french fries, soda, and a toy. One study found that about 1 in 6 (16.9%) food commercials aimed at children promise a free toy. In addition to the use of toys as an incentive in marketing food to children, many commercials use cartoon characters to sell products, which research has shown to be particularly effective in aiding children's slogan recall and ability to identify the product.

A recent example of the effectiveness of this technique is the growth in the dried fruit snack market. Almost half (45%) of fruit snacks had licensing agreements in 2003 compared to 10% in 1996. Sales have increased substantially every year since 1999: 5.6% in 2000, 8.7% in 2001, 3.2% in 2002, and 5.5% in 2003. Marketing experts attribute the sales growth to children's influence on their parents' purchasing decisions and parental beliefs that dried fruit snacks are healthier than other sweets. . . .

Reduce or regulate food ads targeted to children   For decades, policymakers, child advocates, pediatricians, and others have advocated for policy measures to protect children from advertising, including ads for unhealthy food. In light of the rapid increase in childhood obesity, food ads aimed at children have come under increasing scrutiny. Policy suggestions to reduce or regulate food advertising targeted to children take a wide array of forms, from voluntary action taken by media companies or the food industry to government regulation. [See box on next page.]

Most researchers agree that children do not understand commercials in the same way adults do. Most children under age 6 cannot distinguish between program content and commercials, and most children under age 8 do not understand that the purpose of advertising is to sell a product. Even children ages 8–10 who have the cognitive ability to understand the nature of advertising may not always discern the persuasive intent or understand the wording of a disclaimer. The American Academy of Pediatrics reviewed the publicly available research about children and advertising and concluded that "advertising directed toward children is inherently deceptive and exploits children under 8 years of age."

Children's advertising guidelines are currently regulated by the Federal Communications Commission (FCC), which requires compliance before renewing a station's license. One guideline requires that a clear distinction between program content and commercial messages be maintained by using separation devices known as "bumpers" to signal the beginning and end of a commercial break. Others prohibit ads with character endorsements from running during or immediately adjacent to that character's show. The Children's Television Act, passed by Congress in 1990, also mandates advertising limits during programming aired primarily for children under age 12 to 10.5 minutes per hour on weekends and 12 minutes per hour on weekdays.

Children's advertising is also subject to self-regulatory policies adopted under the Children's Advertising Review Unit (CARU). The Grocery Manufacturers Association has pointed out that CARU guidelines suggest that advertising should: not mislead children about the nutritional benefits of products; depict appropriate amounts of a product for the situation portrayed; depict food products "with a view toward development of good nutritional practices"; refrain from portraying snacks as substitutes for meals; and show mealtime products in the context of a balanced diet. The latter policy, for example, is illustrated in cereal ads that show a bowl of cereal with milk and juice, and a voice-over noting that cereal should be part of a balanced, healthy breakfast.

Among the Options That Have Been Suggested Are:

- A ban on any advertising to preschoolers
- A ban on advertising of "junk" food to very young children
- An FTC investigation into marketing of "junk" food to children
- A prohibition on food product placement in children's programming
- The provision of "equal time" for messages on nutrition or fitness, to counteract food ads in children's shows
- Parental "warnings" about the nutritional value of advertised foods
- A repeal of the tax deduction for company expenses associated with advertising "junk" food products to children
- A prohibition on food advertising in school-based TV programs such as Channel One
- Explicit announcement of food-related product placement deals in popular TV shows or movies seen by large numbers of children
- Eliminating or limiting cross-promotions between popular children's media characters and unhealthy food products
- Increasing the use of popular media characters and celebrities to promote healthy food alternatives

In December 2003, while on the campaign trail, Senator Joseph Lieberman called for a Federal Trade Commission (FTC) investigation into the marketing practices of companies that target unhealthy foods to children. Just recently a coalition of obesity experts, health professionals, and child advocates asked Sesame Workshop not to air sponsorship messages for McDonald's before or after "Sesame Street." In response, children's TV producers note that banning food advertising or underwriting would remove one of the most lucrative sources of funding for children's television, particularly given the lack of public funds available in this country for that purpose.

Several industrialized democracies have adopted policies designed to protect children from excessive marketing practices. Sweden, Norway, and Finland, for instance, do not permit commercial sponsorship of children's programs. Sweden also does not permit any television advertising directed to children under age 12. Belgium imposes restrictions on commercials five minutes before and after as well as during children's programming. The BBC decided to prohibit use of its cartoon characters in fast food ads, and England is pushing for stricter guidelines for advertising aimed at children. . . .

Conclusion

The rising rates of childhood obesity present one of the most significant public health challenges we face. While there are many factors that contribute to the problem, this review of the major studies indicates that children's use of media is an important piece of the puzzle. Fortunately, there are an array of options for policymakers, food companies, media companies and parents to consider that may help minimize any negative effect media may be having and maximize the positive role media can play in addressing the problem.

Most large national cross-sectional studies and several longitudinal studies indicate that children who spend more time with media are more likely to be overweight than children who don't. While several regional studies have come to different conclusions, experimental interventions clearly indicate that there is an opportunity to reduce children's body weight by curbing the time they spend with media.

Exactly *how* media may contribute to childhood obesity has not been conclusively documented. Contrary to common assumptions, most studies have found only limited evidence for the theory that the time children spend with media displaces time they would otherwise spend in more vigorous physical activities. There may be limitations to the measures used in these studies, and more research needs to be done in this area.

But in the absence of such research at this time, it appears likely that the main mechanism by which media use contributes to childhood obesity may well be through children's exposure to billions of dollars worth of food advertising and cross-promotional marketing year after year, starting at the very youngest ages, with children's favorite media characters often enlisted in the sales pitch. Research indicates that children's food choices—and parents' food purchases—are significantly impacted by the advertising they see. The number of ads children see on TV has doubled from 20,000 to 40,000 since the 1970s, and the majority of ads targeted to kids are for candy, cereal, and fast food.

More research, perhaps removing ads from children's media while not reducing their overall time spent with media, could help clarify this issue.

While the magnitude of the impact of media's effects on childhood obesity is not clear, the body of evidence indicates there is a role for media-related policies to play in a comprehensive effort to prevent and reduce childhood obesity. While this report does not endorse any specific policies, it does lay out a variety of possibilities for consideration, from reducing the time children spend with media, to reducing their exposure to food advertising, to increasing the number of media messages promoting fitness and sound nutrition.

Children's Exposure to TV Advertising in 1977 and 2004: *Information for the Obesity Debate*

Executive Summary

Obesity has become a major health concern in the U.S. and other countries as overweight and obesity rates have increased markedly since the early 1980s. The rise in children's obesity is a particular concern, because overweight children are more likely to become overweight adults, and because obese children are likely to suffer from associated medical problems earlier in life.

Food marketing is among the postulated contributors to the rise in obesity rates. Food marketing to children has come under particular scrutiny because children may be more susceptible to marketing and because early eating habits may persist. Some researchers report that children's exposure to television advertising has been increasing along with the rise in children's obesity rates.

This report presents a comprehensive analysis of the exposure of children, ages 2–11, to television advertising based on copyrighted Nielsen Monitor-Plus/ Nielsen Media Research audience data from the 2004 television programming season. The detailed data covers the individual advertisements shown during four weeks of national and local ad-supported programming and includes paid commercials, public service announcements, and promotions for television programming. These data are projected to annual estimates.

Thirty years ago similar assessments of children's television advertising were done for the Federal Trade Commission's 1978 Children's Advertising Rulemaking. Since these research reports were done before the rise in children's obesity, they provide a baseline to measure changes in children's exposure to television advertising.

Since the late 1970s, other marketing has likely changed and new forms of marketing have emerged, including Internet-based advertising techniques. This report does not cover these marketing activities, but the FTC is in the process of conducting another study to attempt to gauge the extent of all forms of marketing to children.[1]

Federal Trade Commission Bureau of Economics Staff Report, June 1, 2007, pp. ES-1–ES-9.

This report can also be used to measure future changes in children's exposure to television advertising as industry, parents, and children react to these health concerns.

Summary of Major Findings for 2004

Children's Exposure to Television Advertising   In 2004 we estimate that children ages 2–11 saw about 25,600 television advertisements. In this study, advertisements include paid ads, promotions for other programming, and public service announcements. Of these 25,600 ads, approximately 18,300 were paid ads and most of the remaining 7,300 ads were promotions for other programming. The average ad seen by children was about 25 seconds long. Thus, children saw about 10,700 minutes of TV advertising in 2004. For comparison, adults saw approximately 52,500 ads and 22,300 minutes of advertising.

Our estimates differ from other published estimates of children's exposure to television advertising; one widely cited estimate, that children see around 40,000 ads per year, is more than 50 percent higher than ours. Our estimates are based on very detailed data not available to most researchers. Most published estimates are based on aggregate estimates of the amount of time children watch television, combined with counts of ads aired per hour on selected samples of TV programming. This approach can be accurate as long as the component estimates are accurate representations of children's viewing habits. But our results indicate, for instance, that ad-supported television accounts for only 70 percent of children's TV viewing in 2004, and children get much of their advertising exposure from prime time and other nonchildren's programming. These and related issues must be reflected in the component estimates for such aggregate estimates to be accurate.

Amount of Time Children Spend Viewing Ad-Supported Television   We estimate that in 2004 children 2–11 watched about two and one-quarter hours of ad-supported television per day, for a total of 16 hours per week, about 70 percent of their total television viewing time, about 23 hours per week. Teens, ages 12–17, watched about two and one-half hours of ad-supported television daily. Adults watched nearly four and one-quarter hours daily, almost twice as much as children, and this accounts for most of adults' greater ad exposure.

When Children Are Exposed to Ads   We find considerable dispersion in when children accumulated their ad exposure. Saturday morning between 8 AM and noon was an important contributor to children's ad exposure, but was only 4.3 percent of the total. Sunday morning contributed 2.5 percent. Evenings between 8 PM and 12 AM contributed nearly 29 percent of children's total ad exposure. The time between 4 PM and 8 PM contributed another 26 percent of the total. Prime-time viewing peaked around 8 PM and was the primary time when ad exposure from broadcast programming exceeded that from cable programming. These patterns of ad exposure have important implications for studies that sample children's programming in an effort to produce broad

Figure 1

Exposure to TV Advertising

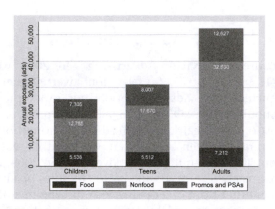

estimates of children's ad exposure, and they help to explain some of the differing results found in the research literature.

Children's Exposure to Food Advertising   Children 2–11 saw approximately 5,500 food ads in 2004, 22 percent of all ads viewed. The leading categories of food advertising seen by children include Restaurant and Fast Food (5.3 percent of total ad exposure); Cereal (3.9 percent; Highly Sugared Cereals are 85 percent of this category); Desserts and Sweets (3.5 percent); Snacks (1.9 percent); Sweetened Drinks (1.7 percent); Dairy (1.4 percent); and Prepared Entrees (0.9 percent). All other food categories combined are 3.1 percent of ad exposure.

We also group shows according to whether the children's share of the audience is at least 20 percent (family shows) or at least 50 percent (children's shows). Food advertising is a larger share of children's advertising exposure as child share increases—from 22 percent of ad exposures on all shows to 32 percent on children's shows. The proportion of children's ad exposure is higher on children's shows for all of the food categories listed above, except for Restaurant and Fast Food ads. Children get nearly 80 percent of their Cereal ad exposure on children's shows and about one-third of their Sweetened Drink and Restaurant and Fast Food advertising there. The other food categories are between these extremes.

Sedentary Entertainment Dominates Other Ads Seen by Children   Seventy-eight percent of the ads children saw in 2004 were for nonfood products. The top three nonfood product categories were Promotions for television programming (28 percent), Screen/Audio Entertainment (7.8 percent), and Games, Toys and Hobbies (7.5 percent). Together these three categories of sedentary entertainment products amounted to 43 percent of children's ad exposure, approximately double the number of food ads seen by children.

Children got approximately 85 percent of their Games, Toys and Hobbies ad exposure on children's shows, as well as 44 percent of their Screen/Audio

Entertainment exposure, and 33 percent of their Promotions exposure. Together these three categories constituted 85 percent of children's nonfood ad exposure from children's shows.

Children's TV Viewing Is Concentrated on Cable   Cable programming was a major source of children's television viewing and ad exposure in 2004. Sixty-one percent of children's ad exposure and 72 percent of their food ad exposure was from cable programming. For children's programming, the concentration was even higher; 96.5 percent of all children's ad exposure from children's shows and 97.6 percent of their food ad exposure from children's shows was from cable programming.

Changes in Children's Exposure to Advertising Between 1977 and 2004

Children's Exposure to Paid Advertising Has Fallen; Overall Ad Exposure Is Up   Studies from the FTC's Children's Advertising Rulemaking indicate that children 2–11 saw about 19,700 paid ads and 21,900 ads overall in 1977. When compared to our estimates of 18,300 paid ads and 25,600 ads in 2004, we find that children's exposure to paid advertising fell by about 7 percent and exposure to all advertising rose by about 17 percent since 1977. This difference reflects the substantial increase in children's exposure to promotional ads for television programming over this time period. Children saw approximately 2 percent fewer minutes of advertising and 19 percent fewer minutes of paid advertising in 2004 than in 1977. These reductions reflect the combined impact of the reduced amount of time children spend watching ad-supported television in 2004 compared to 1977 and ads that are shorter on average.

Children's Exposure to Food Advertising Has Not Risen   The 1977 studies do not give a complete estimate of children's exposure to food ads, but using other data from the period we find that food ad exposure has not risen and is likely to have fallen modestly. In our primary scenario, we estimate that children saw 6,100 food ads in 1977. This suggests that children saw about 9 percent fewer food ads in 2004 than in 1977.

In 1977 ads for Cereals and for Desserts and Sweets dominated children's food ad exposure, with the Restaurant and Fast Food and the Sweetened Drinks categories also among the top categories. As seen above, in 2004 these categories were still among the top categories of food ads children saw, though Cereals and Desserts and Sweets no longer dominated. Restaurant and Fast Food ads had an increased presence, and were joined by Snacks, Dairy and Prepared Entrees as substantial sources of children's food ad exposure. Thus, the mix of food ads seen by children in 2004 is somewhat more evenly spread across these food categories than in 1977.

Children's Exposure to Ads for Sedentary Entertainment Has Grown   The reduction in food advertisements seen by children has been more than compensated for by substantially increased Promotions for television programming

Figure 2

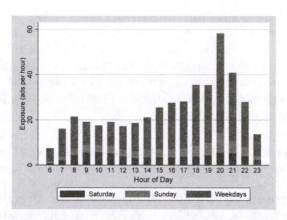

Time of Children's Exposure to Advertising

and increased advertising for Screen and Audio Entertainment. These two categories are both larger than any food category in 2004 and exceed Games, Toys and Hobbies, which had been the top nonfood category in 1977.

Children's Ad Exposure Is More Concentrated on Children's Cable Programming in 2004   Children get approximately half of their food advertising and about one-third of their total advertising exposure from programs in which children are at least 50 percent of the audience in 2004, compared to about one quarter in 1977. Ads for some food categories and for toys appear to be targeted to children.[2] Virtually all of this 2004 ad exposure on children's programming is from cable shows; in 1977, when cable programming was in its infancy, children's shows came from national broadcast and local sources.

Discussion of Empirical Findings and Obesity

Evidence on TV Advertising's Relation to Obesity   Many commentators have suggested that marketing to children may be a significant factor in the growth of obesity in U.S. children. This hypothesis is well beyond anything we could test formally with the television advertising data analyzed here. Nonetheless, our data can shed light on aspects of this hypothesized link.

First, our data do not support the view that children are exposed to more television food advertising today. Our best estimates indicate that children's exposure to food advertising on television has fallen by about 9 percent between 1977 and 2004. Children's exposure to all paid television advertising has fallen as well.

Second, our data do not support the view that children are seeing more advertising for low nutrition foods. In both years the advertised foods are concentrated in the snacking, breakfast, and restaurant product areas. While the foods advertised on children's programming in 2004 do not constitute a balanced diet, this was the case as well in 1977, before the rise in obesity.

Evidence Related to Ad Restrictions on Children's Programming Some have called for various restrictions on advertising to children, including a complete ban on advertising to younger children and further restrictions on the number of minutes of advertising on children's television programming. Others have called for self-regulation or legislation that would limit advertising on children's programming to foods that meet specified nutrition characteristics. Some industry members have proposed voluntary commitments along these lines. This report does not provide a basis to assess the likely effects of any of these approaches, or the substantial legal issues that would have to be addressed for regulation, but it does have several findings that relate to this discussion.

First, children today do get half of their food advertising from shows where children are at least 50 percent of the audience. Thus, changes to the mix of ads on children's shows could potentially have an effect on the mix and number of food advertisements that children see. This effect would be considerably larger than would have been the case in 1977, when programming was not as specialized and children did not get much of their advertising exposure from children's programs. That said, children also get half of their food advertising exposure from nonchildren's shows and food ads on those shows might increase if restrictions were placed on children's programming.

Second, our study does provide some insight on another issue that has received little attention in the public discussion: what type of advertising would likely replace the restricted food advertising, if it is replaced? The hope is that advertising for better food might increase. Beyond that, the best guidance on this question is found by looking at the other products currently advertised on children's programs, since these are the products most likely to increase their advertising if food advertising is reduced. Currently, advertisements for sedentary entertainment products outnumber food advertisements by two to one and constitute most of the other advertising on children's programming. Presumably these products would expand their advertising further, if food advertising is reduced. Whether such a shift in advertising seen by children would affect obesity in U.S. children—either positively or negatively—is an open question which has received little attention.

Finally, it is worth noting that a restriction on advertising on children's programming would not fall evenly on industry participants. In 2004 broadcast networks had very few programs where children were more than 50 percent of the audience. Successful children's programming is now largely on children's cable networks. In fact, over 97 percent of food advertisements children see on children's shows are from cable programming.

Final Notes

Our study is limited to advertising on television. Television is still the medium where food advertisers spend most of their advertising dollars. In 2004 approximately 75 percent of all food advertising spending on measured media was spent on television, down from 83 percent in 1977. Many producers are exploring other advertising media and methods as television audiences become more expensive to reach. This is true for advertising to children as well. Advergaming, child-oriented producer-sponsored websites, product placements and other tie-ins with movies and television programming are all part of the marketing landscape, and research to quantify these efforts is only beginning.[3]

This study was conducted to provide a comprehensive assessment of the amount and type of television advertising seen by children in 2004. It has been nearly 30 years since the last evaluation of children's television ad exposure using detailed viewing data. Advertising seen by children has received considerable attention in recent years as a possible contributor to rising obesity in American children, and as a possible vehicle to help reverse that trend. Hopefully, this report will provide useful information to guide discussion of the issues. The report also provides a baseline against which to measure future changes in children's exposure to television advertising as parents, firms and children react to obesity concerns.

Notes

1. **Federal Register** / Vol. 72, No. 74 / Wednesday, April 18, 2007 / Notices. See also Moore (2006) on advergaming.
2. See Gantz et al. (2007) for a recent content analysis of television advertising on children's and general interest programming. Neither this report nor Gantz et al. (2007) considers whether children may respond differently to the types of ads aired on children's programs.
3. The FTC is beginning a study to attempt to guage the extent of these other forms of marketting to children. **Federal Register** / Vol. 72, No. 74 / Wednesday, April 18, 2007 / Notices.

CHALLENGE QUESTIONS

Is Advertising Responsible for Childhood Obesity?

- Both sides acknowledge that advertising alone is not responsible for increasing rates of child obesity. Of the other factors, is it possible that some interact with the influence of the media to create weight problems?
- While the Federal Trade Commission focuses on direct food advertising, the Kaiser Family Foundation also considers the cross-marketing of food with media figures. What seems most likely to influence the eating choices of children?
- One of the arguments for limiting any advertising directed at children is that at young ages they have not yet developed the ability to take a critical perspective on information. Based on what you know about childhood as a developmental stage, how would you expect children to respond to advertising?
- The Federal Trade Commission offers a comparison of advertising between 1977 and 2004 partially because 1977 was before the rise in obesity. What other influences on children's health and diet choices may have differed significantly in 1977?

Suggested Readings

Dateline NBC Special Report: Food Fight, http://www.msnbc.msn.com/id/14349691/

C. Ebbeling, D. Pawlak, and D. Ludwig, "Childhood Obesity: Public-Health Crisis, Common Sense Cure," *The Lancet* (August 10, 2002)

M. Gard and J. Wright, *The Obesity Epidemic: Science, Morality and Ideology* (2005)

W. Gibbs, "Obesity: An Overblown Epidemic?" *Scientific American* (June 2005)

C. Hawkes, "Marketing Food to Children: Changes in the Global Regulatory Environment 2004–2006," (The World Health Organization)

J. Hersey and A. Jordan, "Reducing Children's TV Time to Reduce the Risk of Childhood Overweight: The Children's Media Use Study Highlights Report," Prepared for the Centers for Disease Control and Prevention Nutrition and Physical Activity Communication Team (2007)

Institute of Medicine, *Food Marketing to Children and Youth: Threat or Opportunity?* (2006)

J. Krishnamoorthy, C. Hart, and E. Jelalian, "The Epidemic of Childhood Obesity: Review of Research and Implications for Public Policy," *Society for Research in Child Development Social Policy Report* (2006)

D. Kulick and A. Meneley, *Fat: The Anthropology of an Obsession* (2005)

ISSUE 8

Does Emphasizing Academic Skills Help At-Risk Preschool Children?

YES: U.S. Department of Health and Human Services, from *Strengthening Head Start: What the Evidence Shows* (June 2003)

NO: C. Cybele Raver and Edward F. Zigler, from "Another Step Back? Assessing Readiness in Head Start," *Young Children* (January 2004)

ISSUE SUMMARY

YES: The U.S. Department of Health and Human Services argues that preschool programs can help young children most by emphasizing academic and cognitive skills.

NO: Professors C. Cybele Raver and Edward F. Zigler argue that overemphasizing academic and cognitive skills at the expense of social, emotional, and physical well-being is a mistake dependent on misguided efforts to make the entire educational system focused on concrete assessment.

A hallmark of early childhood is the start of educational experiences outside the home. For many children this means formal preschool. Many people take for granted that a quality preschool experience is essential to future success. You may have heard about exclusive preschools that are as competitive for admission as Ivy League colleges, and as expensive to match. On the other side of the spectrum, many children raised by families mired in poverty lack the opportunity for quality preschool. These children often start primary school behind their more well-off peers, and have difficulty breaking the cycle of poverty. As preschool became more common during the twentieth century, scholars of development became more aware that breaking the grip of poverty required early intervention.

The most famous and intensive North American effort to facilitate early childhood development for children from poor families is the Head Start program. Started in the 1960s as part of President Lyndon Johnson's "War on Poverty," Head Start was a collaborative effort between the government and scholars to provide an educational environment that would allow children living in poverty to succeed. One of the foundational ideas upon which Head Start was built is that early childhood development progresses as an integration of distinct components of children's well-being. Thus, rather than focusing exclusively on academic skills, Head Start has attempted to provide diverse services that attend to academic, social, emotional, cognitive, and physical aspects of development.

Longitudinal research following children years after Head Start has shown mixed results. Research on IQ, for example, shows that Head Start does provide an early bump in IQ scores that lasts several years. The positive impact, however, dissipates over time until Head Start children end up returning to IQ levels consistent with other poor individuals who did not experience Head Start. Other evidence, however, suggests that Head Start children are less likely to be held back later in school, less likely to be labeled with learning disabilities, and more likely to continue their education.

Both sides of this debate agree that Head Start has not done enough to eliminate the gaps between the success of children from poor and rich families. The controversy is about what needs to change. And this question ultimately gets at a fundamental issue in development: Can we separate out the different aspects of development or do they all work in integrated ways?

The U.S. Government's Department of Health and Human Services under the George W. Bush administration declares that to break the cycle of poverty the most important developmental aspect of early childhood is cognitive skills. They assert that Head Start needs to focus more on cognitive and academic skills such as pre-math and pre-literacy. The idea is to test these specific cognitive capacities and hold teachers and administrators accountable.

C. Cybele Raver and Edward F. Zigler point out that focusing exclusively on cognitive skills runs counter to the way most developmental scholars understand the importance of early childhood. These authors offer a convincing historical perspective, partially because Zigler was involved in the founding of Head Start. He notes that children from poor families do not simply have a cognitive disadvantage, but they have an integrated set of developmental needs.

POINT	COUNTERPOINT
• Head Start has not been successful enough in improving IQ and core cognitive abilities.	• Cognitive development cannot be separated out from social and emotional development.
• Skills, such as pre-literacy, will give children the best chance to succeed in school and escape poverty.	• Poverty is more complex than just doing well or poorly academically.
• The reason Head Start has failed is because it does not focus enough on academic skills.	• Head Start has not received sufficient resources, and is only part of the puzzle required to address poverty.
• Testing can ensure that children are learning the specific skills they need to succeed in school.	• Testing will serve to distract from inequalities such as access to resources and well-qualified teachers.

YES

Strengthening Head Start: What the Evidence Shows

Introduction

The period from birth through age 5 is a critical time for children to develop the physical, emotional, social, and cognitive skills they will need to be successful in school and the rest of their lives. Children from poor families, on average, enter school behind children from more privileged families. Targeting preschoolers in low-income families, the Head Start program was created in 1965 to promote school readiness to enable each child to develop to his or her fullest potential. Research shows that acquiring specific pre-reading, language, and social skills strongly predict future success in school.

As our knowledge about the importance of high quality early education has advanced dramatically since 1965, so have data on the outcomes for children and families served by Head Start. The knowledge and skill levels of low-income children are far below national averages upon entering the program. When the school readiness of the nation's poor children is assessed, it becomes clear that Head Start is not eliminating the gap in educational skills and knowledge needed for school. Head Start is not fully achieving its stated purpose of "promot[ing] school readiness by enhancing the social and cognitive development of low-income children." Head Start children show some progress in cognitive skills and social and emotional development. However, these low-income children continue to perform significantly below their more advantaged peers once they enter school in areas essential to school readiness, such as reading and mathematics.

States and the federal government fund a wide variety of programs that are either intended to enhance children's educational development or that could, with some adjustments, do a better job of preparing children for school. Head Start is one of many federal and state programs that together provide approximately $23 billion in funding for child-care and preschool education. Because these programs have developed independently, they are not easily coordinated to best serve the children and families who need them. In programs other than Head Start, states have the responsibility and the authority through planning, training, and the regulatory process to have a substantial impact on the type and quality of services provided, and are held

From U.S. Department of Health and Human Services, June 2003.

accountable for the delivery of high quality programs. However, Head Start funding goes directly from the federal level to local organizations, and thus states do not have the authority to integrate or align Head Start programs with other early childhood programs provided by the states.

The single most important goal of the Head Start reauthorization should be to improve Head Start and other preschool programs to ensure children are prepared to succeed in school. This paper describes the limited educational progress for children in Head Start and the problems resulting from a fragmented approach to early childhood programs and services. The paper also presents evidence from early childhood research and documents state efforts that have successfully addressed these problems. Finally, the paper explains the President's proposal for Head Start reauthorization, which builds on the evidence to strengthen the program and, through coordination, improve preschool programs in general to help ensure that children are prepared to succeed in school.

Children in Head Start Are Not Getting What They Need to Succeed in School

Certain knowledge, skills, and experiences are strong markers of school readiness. For example, we know that children who recognize their letters, who are read to at least three times a week, who recognize basic numbers and shapes, and who demonstrate an understanding of the mathematical concept of relative size as they entered kindergarten have significantly higher reading skills in the spring of first grade than children who do not have this background. In fact, the difference between children who do and do not have this knowledge upon entering kindergarten is approximately one year's worth of reading development at the end of first grade. This is true regardless of family income and race or ethnicity.

Head Start is a comprehensive early childhood development program designed to provide education, health, and social services to low-income children, ages 3 to 5, and their families. Last reauthorized in FY 1998, Head Start is scheduled for reauthorization in FY 2003. Federal grants to operate Head Start programs are awarded directly to the local organizations that implement the program, including public agencies, private non-profit and for-profit organizations, Indian Tribes, and school systems. Since it began in 1965, Head Start has enrolled over 20 million children.

However, while making some progress, Head Start is not doing enough to enhance the language, pre-reading, and pre-mathematics knowledge and skills that we know are important for school readiness. The knowledge and skill levels of young children entering Head Start are far below national averages. Children graduating from Head Start remain far behind the typical U.S. child. We know also that all disadvantaged children who need high quality early educational instruction are not in Head Start. Some are in pre-kindergarten programs, others are in child-care settings, and still others are at home with parents.

Most Children Enter and Leave Head Start with Below-Average Skill and Knowledge Levels

Currently, the primary source of information on outcomes for children and families served by Head Start comes from the Family and Child Experiences Survey (FACES). . . . These data are from the class of children who entered the program in 1997. The percentile scores show how Head Start children perform compared with the average performer. On a percentile scale, an average performer would be at the 50th percentile, meaning that half of children who take the test score above the average performer and half score below the 50% mark. Head Start children as a group fall far below the 50th percentile in all areas of achievement. Though children are making some progress, clearly few children perform as poorly as children who enter and leave the Head Start program. . . .

Both higher achieving and lower achieving Head Start children have low scores overall and show limited progress. Children who were in the upper 25% of their Head Start class when they entered Head Start in 1997 showed no gains on any measure of cognitive ability over the course of the Head Start program year, and actually experienced losses on some measures in comparison to national norms. Gains over the Head Start year were limited to children who were in the bottom 25% of their class. However, even these gains fell far short of bringing children to levels of skill necessary for school success. For example, children in the bottom 25% of their Head Start class left Head Start with language skill scores at the 5th percentile, meaning that only 5% of all children who take the test score lower than these Head Start children do. Findings for mathematics showed a similar pattern.

The more recent 2000 FACES data show modest improvement in results for children, but overall progress is still too limited. Children continue to lag behind national norms when they exit Head Start. Data from Head Start FACES 2000 shows that:

- The level of children's achievement in **letter-recognition** for the 2000 Head Start year is far below the majority of U.S. children who know all letters of the alphabet upon entering kindergarten, according to the Early Childhood Longitudinal Study of the Kindergarten class of 1998.
  Spanish-speaking children in Head Start did not gain at all in **letter recognition** skills in 2000.
- Although **writing** scores increased 2 points during the 2000 Head Start year, this was a drop from children who entered Head Start in 1997 who increased 3.8 points in writing during the 1997 Head Start year.
- Children entered Head Start in 2000 with scores at about the 16th percentile in **vocabulary**, or about 34 percentile points below the average. Children entering Head Start scored at about the 31st percentile in **letter recognition** and at about the 21st percentile in early **mathematics.**
- Children who entered Head Start in 2000 made progress in early **mathematics** during the Head Start year that was statistically significant; however the difference was small (from 87.9 to 89.0 on a scale

for which 100 is the average). [This] 1.2-point difference is not a substantial gain toward national averages. Moreover, this amount of progress was no greater than that found for children who attended Head Start from Fall to Spring in 1997.

- Children who entered the program in 2000 with overall lower levels of knowledge and skill showed larger gains during the program year compared to children who entered with higher levels of knowledge. However, they still lagged far behind national averages.
- Head Start children did not start kindergarten with the same social skill levels as their more socio-economically advantaged peers, and they continued to have more emotional and conduct problems.
- A follow-up study of children enrolled in Head Start in 1997 showed that children who attend Head Start make less progress than the average kindergartener. Thirty-four percent of Head Start children showed proficiency in knowing the ending sounds of words, 53% in knowing the beginning sounds of words, and 83% in letter recognition. Data from a nationally representative sample of all first-time kindergartners shows that fifty-two percent demonstrated proficiency in knowing the ending sounds of words, 72% in knowing the beginning sounds of words, and 94% in letter recognition.

. . . Head Start children have made some progress in some areas. A more detailed looks shows that:

- In 2000, the mean standard score for vocabulary increased 3.8 points, from 85.3 to 89.1 on a scale for which the average is 100. This result is similar to the data for 1997 that showed Head Start children scored about 85 at the beginning of the year and gained about 4 points by the end of the year.
- In 2000, the mean standard score for writing increased by 2 points, from 85.1 to 87.1.
- In 2000, children showed gains in book knowledge and print conventions (that is, they can show an adult the front of a storybook and open it to where the adult should start reading). This progress is statistically greater than for the 1997 Head Start year during which no progress was made in this area.
- In 2000, Spanish-speaking children in Head Start showed significant gains in English vocabulary skills without declines in their Spanish vocabulary.
- In 2000, children showed growth in social skills and reduction in hyperactive behavior during the Head Start year. Even children with the highest levels (scoring in the top quarter) of shy, aggressive, or hyperactive behavior showed significant reductions in these problem behaviors. Teachers rated children's classroom behavior as more cooperative at the end of the Head Start year than when children first entered the program.
- In 2000, children who received higher cooperative behavior ratings and lower problem behavior ratings from Head Start teachers scored better on cognitive assessments at the end of kindergarten, even after controlling for their scores on cognitive tests taken while in Head Start.

- Children who entered Head Start in 1997 showed significant gains in their social skills, such as following directions, joining in activities, and waiting turns in games, and gains in cooperative behaviors, according to ratings by teachers and parents. The quality of children's social relationships, including relating to peers and social problem solving, also improved.

Head Start program and teacher characteristics show some positive relationships to educational and social outcomes for children. Examples include:

- Teachers' educational credentials are linked to greater gains in early writing skills. Children taught by Head Start teachers with bachelors' degrees or associates' degrees showed gains toward national averages in an assessment of early writing skills, whereas children taught by teachers with lesser credentials merely held their own against national norms.
- Provision of preschool services for a longer period each day is linked to greater cognitive gains. Children in full-day classes in Head Start showed larger fall to spring gains in letter recognition and early writing skills than did children in part-day classes.

Head Start has other positive qualities:

- In 1997, the program received very high ratings of satisfaction from parents, and for the roughly 16% of children in Head Start with a suspected or diagnosed disability, 80% of parents reported that Head Start had helped them obtain special needs resources for the child.
- A follow up study of children who attended Head Start in 1997 showed that children were capable of making some progress during their kindergarten year in vocabulary, writing, and early mathematics, though performance remained significantly below national norms.

How do eligible children fare when they do not receive Head Start services? The FACES study is not designed to answer this question; there is no control group. Eligible children who do not receive services could be falling further behind or could be making gains similar to or greater than those for children in the program. The national Head Start Impact Study was launched in 2002 and is using a randomized design to answer this question. Additional experimental studies are being conducted to assess the effectiveness of specific quality improvement strategies.

A national study of Early Head Start, which is part of the Head Start program serving low-income pregnant women and children from birth through three, was recently conducted using a randomized experimental design. Results show that children receiving Early Head Start have scores that are statistically higher than their peers who did not receive Early Head Start on measures of cognitive, language, and social and emotional competency. Fewer Early Head Start children scored in the "at-risk" range of functioning in both language and cognitive functioning. However, Early Head Start children continue to perform below the national average.

In summary, there is more work to do. Despite the positive qualities of Head Start programs, children in Head Start are making only very modest progress in only some areas of knowledge and skill, and children in Head Start are leaving the program far behind their peers. More progress must be made and can be made to put Head Start children on par with others by the time they enter kindergarten.

Disadvantaged Children Lag Behind Throughout the School Years

Effective early childhood intervention is important because disadvantaged children are at great risk for poor educational outcomes throughout the school years. Data from the National Center for Education Statistics' (NCES) Early Childhood Longitudinal Study—Kindergarten Cohort (ECLS-K) and National Assessment of Educational Progress (NAEP) are reviewed below.

Children with Multiple Risks Suffer the Greatest Educational Disadvantage

Achievement differences in school are greatest for children who suffer the greatest disadvantage, in particular for children whose families have **multiple risk factors** or **receive welfare**. While many of the children we are trying to reach in early childhood are in Head Start and federal and state pre-kindergarten programs, others are in child-care and home-settings.

A key set of **risk factors** has been repeatedly associated with educational outcomes, such as low achievement test scores, grade repetition, suspension or expulsion, and dropping out of high school. These risk factors include: (a) having parents who have not completed high school, (b) coming from a low-income or welfare-dependent family, (c) living in a single-parent family, and (d) having parents who speak a language other than English in the home. Children who have one or more of these characteristics are more likely to be educationally disadvantaged or have difficulty in school.

These same risk factors are linked to achievement disparities in reading and mathematics skills at the point of kindergarten entry. Research emphasizes that achievement difficulties children experience in school "cannot be attributed solely to bad schools; many children are already behind when they open the classroom door."

- Children with **two or more risk factors** are about three times as likely as those with no risk factors to score in the bottom 25% in reading.
- Children from families with **3 or more risk factors** typically do not know their letters and cannot count to 20. Fifty-six percent could not identify letters of the alphabet compared with 25% in the no risk group. They are about one-third as likely to be able to associate letters with sounds at the end of words.
- Children with even **one risk factor** are twice as likely to have reading scores that fall into the lowest 25% of children studied compared to children with no risk factors. They are half as likely to be able to associate letters with sounds at the ends of words. Some children with one risk

factor have good reading scores, but far too few. They are half as likely to score in the top quartile as children with no risk factors (16% vs. 33%).

- In mathematics, 38% of the multiple risk group could count beyond 10 or make judgments of relative length compared with 68% in the no risk group. They were one-third as likely to be able to recognize 2-digit numerals or identify the ordinal position of an object in a series.
- Forty-four percent of children with multiple risk factors rarely paid attention, compared to 28% of children with no risk factors.

Children are at risk for poor educational outcomes when their families receive **welfare** (defined as receiving welfare or having received welfare in the past). These children were significantly less competent in reading, mathematics, and social skills compared to children who had never received welfare.

- In reading, children of welfare recipients are less likely to show pre-reading competencies that include letter recognition, recognition of beginning and ending sounds, and print familiarity. Forty-nine percent of these children scored in the lowest quartile, compared to 22% of children whose families were not welfare recipients.
- In mathematics, half of children whose families received welfare scored in the lowest quartile for mathematics, compared to 22% of children whose families had never received welfare. Twenty-three percent of children of welfare recipients scored in the top half for reading, compared to 53% of children whose families had never received welfare.
- Children from welfare families also are under-represented in the higher performing category: Fifty-three percent of children who had never received welfare scored in the top half for reading, compared to only 24% of children whose families were welfare recipients.
- Children of welfare recipients are also at risk for poor social skills. Kindergarten teachers rated these children as having more difficulty with forming friendships and interacting with peers compared to children whose families were not welfare recipients.

The Achievement Gap for Disadvantaged Children Widens During Kindergarten

Children who start behind are likely to stay behind and get further behind. Research shows that the achievement gap between advantaged and disadvantaged groups of children widens from Fall to Spring. Global reading and mathematics scores show gains for all children in reading and mathematics scores during the kindergarten year. But a closer look shows that achievement disparities between disadvantaged and more advantaged children depend on the particular knowledge and skills assessed.

By Spring, children from homes with at least one risk factor begin to close gaps in basic skills, such as recognizing letters, counting beyond 10, or comparing the size of objects. But because their more advantaged classmates move on to acquire more complex skills, these children are even further behind by Spring in reading and mathematics skills, such as reading words or solving simple addition and subtraction problems. Moreover, despite improvements in basic reading and mathematics skills during the kindergarten year, the disparity between advantaged and disadvantaged children was not eliminated.

The Achievement Gap Persists into Elementary and High School

Poor children eligible for the National School Lunch Program do not perform as well as more advantaged children who are ineligible for the program. Average scores for reading, mathematics and writing achievement are statistically lower for children who are eligible for the school lunch program compared to ineligible children. This achievement gap continues throughout the school years. . . .

Research Evidence Shows We Can Do Better in Helping Children Achieve

Research Has Identified What Children Need to Succeed in School

Before children can read, write or calculate, research shows that children must acquire foundational knowledge, skills, and behaviors that are stepping stones toward mastery of more advanced and complex skills.

Children Are Better Off If They Enter Kindergarten with Cognitive Resources

Children who bring certain knowledge and skills with them to kindergarten are likely to be at an advantage in classroom learning compared to their peers who do not possess these resources. A Department of Education report described the predictive power of having specific cognitive and health "resources" on children's reading and mathematics achievement. These resources included:

- possessing specific basic literacy knowledge and skills;
- being read to at least three times a week at kindergarten entry;
- being proficient in recognizing numbers and shapes at kindergarten entry;
- showing productive approaches to learning, such as an eagerness to learn, task persistence and ability to pay attention; and
- possessing good to excellent health.

Each of these was a key predictor of children's reading and mathematics achievement in the Spring of kindergarten and in first grade, even after controlling for children's race, ethnicity and poverty status. These data confirm that we must ensure that *all* children, regardless of background, are physically healthy *and* have the same basic literacy, mathematics, and cognitive experiences and skills needed to succeed in school.

Child Development Research Shows Which Areas of Competency to Target

Research experts and practitioners in fields relating to early childhood recommend that children make progress in each of the following areas to help ensure they are developing school readiness knowledge and skills.

- In the area of **pre-reading**, children should develop: phonological processing skills (hearing and playing with sounds in words, for example, through rhyming games), letter knowledge (knowing the names and sounds of letters), print awareness (knowing how to hold a book, that we read in English from left to right and usages of print), writing, and interest in and appreciation of books, reading, and writing.
- In the area of **language**, children should develop receptive and expressive vocabulary skills (ability to name things and use words to describe things and actions); narrative understanding (ability to understand and produce simple and complex stories, descriptions of events, and instructions); phonology (ability to distinguish and produce the different sounds of language); syntactic or grammatical knowledge (knowing how to put words together in order to communicate with meaning); and oral communication and conversational skills (knowing how to use words in appropriate contexts for a variety of purposes, such as knowing when and how to ask a teacher for more information, or understanding how to take turns in a conversation).
- Children should develop **pre-mathematics** knowledge and skills that include number concepts (recognizing written numerals, counting with an understanding of quantity, knowing quantitative relationships such as "more" and "less"), number operations (such as adding and subtracting); geometry concepts (such as recognizing shapes); space, patterns, and measurement concepts and skills (such as measuring length using their hands or measuring using conventional units such as inches).
- Children should develop **cognitive skills** that include the ability to plan and problem-solve, the ability to pay attention and persist on challenging tasks, intellectual curiosity and task engagement, and achievement motivation and mastery.
- Children need **social and emotional competencies** important for school success and a constructive learning environment. These include the ability to relate to teachers and peers in positive ways, the ability to manage feelings of anger, frustration and distress in age-appropriate ways, and the ability to inhibit negative behaviors with teachers and peers, for example, aggression, impulsiveness, noncompliance, and constant attention-seeking.

The Right Programs and Training Can Improve Children's School Readiness

Research, though limited, clearly demonstrates the value of providing comprehensive interventions with strong language and pre-academic components that develop the knowledge and skills necessary for kindergarten and the early grades and for closing the achievement gap. Though more research is needed, a few approaches that have been evaluated using rigorous designs show that comprehensive and language and literacy-rich early childhood programs can reduce achievement gaps for disadvantaged children. Here are highlights of major studies.

The Chicago Child-Parent Center (CPC) Program

This program for low-income minority children in high-poverty neighborhoods in innercity Chicago, funded in part by the Department of Education, includes half-day preschool for one or two years, full or part-day kindergarten, continuing support services in linked elementary schools, and a parent education program. The Chicago CPC program provides educational and health and nutrition services, such as hearing screening, speech therapy and nursing services, to children ages 3 to 9 years. The intervention emphasizes the acquisition of basic knowledge and skills in language arts and mathematics through relatively structured but diverse learning experiences. An intensive parent program includes volunteering in the classroom, attending school events and field trips, and completing high school. Teachers are required to have bachelor's degrees, are paid at the level of teachers in public school, and participate in regular staff development activities. Child-to-staff ratios are low (17:2).

A longitudinal study funded by the National Institutes of Health and other funders compared participant children to a non-experimental comparison group of children with similar demographics. Findings include:

Reading and mathematics achievement. At the end of the program in third grade, CPC graduates surpassed their comparison group counterparts by 4 to 6 points in reading and mathematics achievement, as measured by the Iowa Test of Basic Skills.

Preschool participation. One or two years of CPC preschool participation was associated with statistically significant advantages of 5.5 and 4.2 points in standard scores for reading achievements for ages 14 and 15. This corresponds to about a 4- to 5-month change. Likewise, preschool participation was significantly associated with a 4.4-point increase in standard scores in math achievement at age 14 and a 3.3-point advantage at age 15, above and beyond gender, environmental risk factors, and participation in follow-on interventions. This translates into a 3- to 4-month performance advantage over the comparison group. These effect sizes are considered moderate; however the effects persist up to 10 years after children leave the program, which is unique among early interventions and almost all social programs.

Follow-on participation. Because the early childhood program is linked to the kindergarten and elementary schools, children may participate in the program from 1 to 6 years. Each year of participation was associated with an increase of 1.3 to 1.6 points in the standard score for reading. Years in the follow-on intervention were significantly associated with reading achievement at ages 14 and 15 and went beyond that attributable to preschool participation. The most dramatic effect occurring after 4 years of intervention: Five or six years of participation resulted in the best performance, with children performing at or above the Chicago averages in reading and mathematics. (Even 6 years of participation, however, did not elevate the performance of the maximum intervention group to the national average.) A similar pattern occurred for mathematics achievement, though the size of the effect was smaller. The findings showed that the relationship between years of participation and school achievement is not strictly linear—greater advantages accrue as the length of the intervention increases.

Other outcomes.   Preschool participation was associated with lower rates of grade retention (23% vs. 38.4%) and special education placement (14.4% vs. 24.6%). Preschoolers who participated in the intervention spent an average of 0.7 years in special education compared with 1.4 years for non-participants. Children who participated in the preschool intervention for 1 or 2 years had a higher rate of high school completion (49.7% vs. 38.5%), more years of completed education (10.6 vs. 10.2), and lower rates of juvenile arrests (16.9% vs. 25.1%). Boys benefited from preschool participation more than girls, especially in reducing the school dropout rate.

Cost-benefit analyses.   With an average cost per child of $6,692 for 1.5 years of participation, the preschool program generates a total return to society at large of $47,759 per participant. These benefits are the result of participants' increased earnings capacity due to educational attainment, criminal justice system savings, reduced school remedial services, and averted tangible costs to crime victims. Benefits realized in each of these areas exceed the cost of just one year of the preschool program, which is $4,400. Overall, every dollar invested in the preschool program returns $7.14 in individual, educational, social welfare and socioeconomic benefits.

The Abecedarian Project

The Abecedarian Project was a carefully controlled study in which 57 infants from low-income families living in a small North Carolina town were randomly assigned to receive early intervention in a high quality child-care setting and 54 were in a non-treated control group. The treated children received full-time educational intervention in a high quality child-care setting from infancy through age five, which included cognitive development activities with a particular emphasis on language, and activities focusing on social and emotional development. Teachers were required to have bachelor's degrees and were paid at the level of teachers in public school.

Starting at age 18 months, and through follow-ups at ages 12 and 15, the treatment children had significantly higher scores on cognitive assessments. Treated children scored significantly higher on tests of reading and math from the primary grades through age 21 (though scores did not reach national averages).

At age 21, those in the treatment group were significantly more likely to still be in school and more likely to have attended a four-year college. Employment rates were higher for the treatment group than for the control group, although the trend was not statistically significant.

The Perry Preschool Study

This pioneering study begun in the 1960s was one of the first to identify lasting effects of high quality preschool programs on children's outcomes. One hundred twenty-three poor African American 3- and 4-year-olds were randomly assigned either to attend a high quality preschool program or to no preschool. The two groups began the study with equivalent IQ scores and socioeconomic status. Children attended 2½ hour classes and teachers conducted weekly 1.5-hour home-visits.

Results showed positive impacts on several intellectual and language tests prior to school entry and up to age 7, showing that the program enhanced children's school readiness. At age 14, participants outperformed non-participants on a school achievement test in reading, language, and mathematics. At age 19, participants' general literacy skills were better than non-participants. At age 27, participants had higher earnings and economic status, higher education and achievement levels in adolescence and young adulthood, as well as fewer arrests.

Benefit-cost analyses show that by the time participants were 27 years old, the program showed a sound economic investment, with significant savings from settlement costs for victims of crimes never committed, reduced justice system costs, increased taxes paid due to higher earnings, reduced need for special education services, and reduced welfare costs. . . .

Conclusions

Research shows that children in Head Start are falling behind and too often are not ready for school. In particular, those children who are the poorest and have the most risk factors do not enter kindergarten with the intellectual resources they need to succeed. Some of these children are being served by Head Start, but others are in state pre-kindergarten, child-care, and home-settings. From basic science on learning and development and from intervention studies we know a great deal about how to narrow the achievement gap for Head Start and other disadvantaged children before they enter kindergarten. Research tells us the knowledge and skills children need in language, pre-reading, and pre-mathematics, and the social and emotional competencies they must have to succeed in school. The President believes that the Head Start program must be strengthened and provide more emphasis on pre-reading, language, pre-mathematics and other cognitive skills, while continuing to promote children's health and social and emotional competence as part of school readiness. Research tells us that early childhood education implemented with qualified and well-trained teachers can make a significant and meaningful impact on the development of children's knowledge and skills, their achievement in school, and success in life. . . .

C. Cybele Raver and
Edward F. Zigler

 **NO**

Another Step Back? Assessing Readiness in Head Start

Since its founding in 1965, Head Start's goal has been to help children who live in poverty prepare for school. Over the last three and a half decades, Head Start has maintained a staunch commitment to the provision of genuinely comprehensive services. While impressive in its breadth, this wide range of services has made it difficult for researchers to benchmark children's progress in the program. One solution has been to rely on strictly cognitive measures as a means to assess the benefits of Head Start. We criticized this approach in an earlier paper entitled "Three Steps Forward, Two Steps Back." In that article, we pointed out that sole reliance on children's cognitive outcomes was neither in keeping with the goals of Head Start nor with many definitions of what it means to be ready to succeed in early elementary school.

Recently Head Start has been subjected to major policy changes at the federal administrative and legislative levels. In particular, the Bush Administration instituted a new set of accountability measures that will be used to test Head Start children twice a year on language, literacy, and pre-math skills. This policy is swiftly being put into place with full implementation plans announced in both April and June 2003. The assessment system, under the National Reporting System that is part of the current law but left to the Secretary to determine, has been controversial. The measures were quickly developed by Westat, Inc., and the national assessment process is now underway. This fall, all four- and five-year-old children in Head Start (who are eligible to enroll in kindergarten next year) will undergo the first of two annual assessments. This quick pace of change proceeded despite a letter to administrators signed by some 300 professionals questioning the psychometric properties of the measures.

The spring of 2003 was also the time Congress began work on reauthorizing Head Start's funding. The House version of the reauthorization bill (HR 2210) proposed substantial changes to the 38-year-old program. Most controversial was a plan to devolve Head Start to the states, but the bill also raised the issue of assessment. The bill (as introduced) emphasized children's knowledge and skills in the areas of language, literacy, and pre-math and deleted the current

From *Young Children*, January 2004, pp. 1–5. Copyright © 2004 by National Association for the Education of Young Children. Reprinted by permission.

law's references to children's social competence, emotional development, and cultural diversity. Why did the Bush Administration move so sharply away from Head Start's emphasis on school readiness in broadly defined terms, and toward a narrow emphasis on cognitive development as the critical factor in preparing for school?

⌘

Perhaps these moves are driven by well-meaning intentions on the part of policy makers to improve the educational chances of our nation's most disadvantaged young children. The evidence shows that while Head Start children make significant gains in preschool, they still score well below the national average on vocabulary, pre-reading, writing, and early math skills. Secretary of Health and Human Services Tommy Thompson argues that poor children deserve a better start to their educational trajectories. Lawmakers on both sides of the political spectrum began to focus the debate on what it means to close the achievement gap of Head Start children with their middle-class peers. However, their pathways to that goal were quite different, as were their expectations of closing that gap merely by adding a stronger focus on literacy and math skills.

On the face of it, there is some logic to the idea that if children are less knowledgeable regarding early academics like letters and numbers, strengthening these skills should help them when they begin school. And perhaps lawmakers were persuaded by a small number of studies that suggest that some programs (but not others) have shown limited short-term improvements in older children's educational achievement when "high-stakes" achievement tests are used to increase school monitoring and accountability. In our view, however, these intentions are misguided. As we will argue, the application of a strictly cognitive focus to assessments of school readiness runs counter to what the best developmental research tells us and what past policy experience has shown. A narrow focus on benchmarking Head Start's programmatic success on early cognitive gains to the exclusion of children's emotional and social development has been tried in the past and has backfired. In this article, we briefly review these past rounds of policy debate, and consider scientific evidence regarding what disadvantaged preschoolers need to be ready for school. We then offer three concrete policy recommendations for alternatives to the steps that are in the works for Head Start accountability.

What Does Past Policy Experience Tell Us?

This is not the first time that policy makers and research scientists have tried to peg evidence of Head Start's success to children's cognitive gains. During Head Start's early years, evaluators commonly found substantial gains in children's IQ scores after even brief periods of intervention. These gains were publicized as striking evidence that the programs worked. However, when the IQ benefits were found apparently to dissipate as children progressed through elementary school, intervention efforts were quickly deemed a failure not worthy of public support.

⚜

When Head Start and other early interventions failed to show permanent gains in children's cognitive scores (as assessed by IQ), policy makers had two choices: either to capitulate to the skeptical view that early intervention is not effective, or to question whether IQ gains were the appropriate metric to have used in the first place and whether the programs were improperly evaluated. Workers in a variety of disciplines eventually convinced policy makers that intelligence alone does not guarantee academic success—that even a very bright child will do poorly in school if he or she suffers physical health or emotional problems, has trouble staying motivated, or does not interact well with teachers or peers. Consequently, researchers, policy professionals, and practitioners in the field of early childhood education seemingly resolved this issue by establishing that Head Start must continue to encompass a broader mission of school readiness that includes physical and mental health, social and emotional needs, and academic skills. This emphasis on both cognitive and social-emotional development was validated by specific language in the 1998 Head Start reauthorization act. Further verifying policy makers' acceptance, data on children's social and emotional development (though in limited form) began to be collected in large-scale national surveys including the Family and Child Experiences Survey (FACES, Department of Health and Human Services), the Early Childhood Longitudinal Study (ECLS-K, Department of Education), and the Head Start National Impact Study (U.S. Department of Health and Human Services). Suddenly, however, the current administration decided to reverse course.

In part, we suspect that this reversal is due to consensus that there is an unacceptably large "achievement gap" between economically disadvantaged children and their more advantaged counterparts, and that it is our responsibility as a nation to do something to reduce that gap. Yet there is major disagreement regarding the best remedies to take. Similar to ongoing debate in educational research and policy, one view is that early interventions such as Head Start are not doing a good job teaching disadvantaged preschoolers. From an economic and partisan perspective, the argument is that Head Start programs (like public schools) are monopolies that are inefficient and have few incentives to improve because of the lack of competition. More strictly defined standards of child performance are seen as a way to impose accountability. Literacy and math skills can be tested, and test scores can yield information about school performance to consumers (e.g., parents, government funding agencies, etc.). The hope is that market-based systems will weed out bad performers and reward higher performers, that providers will strive to improve, and that children will benefit.

The opposing view, held by many early childhood educators and advocates, sees this emphasis on accountability as a way for fiscally conservative policy makers to avoid paying for the relatively expensive solutions that are needed to enact real gains in poor children's educational attainment. This group contends that high-quality early education and care can advance disadvantaged children's learning but that it is not cheap to provide. Advocates and educators in early childhood suggest that if policy makers really wanted to close the education gap, they would make the kind of fiscal investments that are needed to provide children with the things that we know work: comprehensive, full-day services with highly trained, well-paid staff, with fewer children in each classroom, and with more time and resources to devote to learning, literacy, and social and emotional development. They further argue that changes at the preschool level will not be enough. For Head Start children to maintain the gains they make in preschool, fiscal resources will be needed to improve the elementary schools they attend and—even more daunting—to alleviate home and community stressors that are likely to impede their future academic performance.

Our point is not to take one side of this debate or the other, but to suggest that a strictly cognitive approach to early education and assessment is likely to backfire, regardless of the position taken on best remedies for the "achievement gap" between affluent and poor preschoolers. For the sake of argument, let us consider the highly touted Texas prekindergarten program that Secretary of Health and Human Services Thompson uses as a model of success and as a purportedly strong contrast to Head Start. Using a nonexperimental research design (where investigators can inflate program effects by assigning better-performing schools to the treatment group), the evaluation of the program revealed moderate impacts on children's language scores for *less than half* of the participating sites. At best, this translates to modest success in narrowing the educational gap between low-income Texas preschoolers and their more affluent counterparts. But, even if we believe that the Texas program included the strongest of teaching efforts tied to the best curricular choices, it could just as easily be argued that the program did not meaningfully close the gap between poor and wealthier children. Using such narrow, cognitively oriented definitions of success, not only will programs be viewed as failures but poor children will be viewed as impervious to help.

To avoid this likely scenario, policy makers must understand that vocabulary, pre-reading, and pre-math tests only provide a rough approximation of where preschoolers stand in relation to their agemates, or where they stand relative to their own prior performance. But these tests do not capture the value of a program in supporting the multiple facets of development and learning that are undoubtedly taking place, both in those Texas classrooms and in Head Start classrooms across the country. For example, while IQ gains children make in preschool arguably fade out, graduates of quality intervention programs (including Head Start) are less likely to be retained in grade or placed in special education than similar children without good preschool experience. Clearly a wealth of learning experiences and benefits were accrued during intervention and carried through later schooling, but these were not tapped by cognitive measures. Thus a focus on cognitive outcomes without an understanding of the multiple processes that lead to school success runs the risk of disenfranchising children from learning, disenfranchising good teachers from teaching disadvantaged preschoolers, and disenfranchising voters from the view that investments in young children pay off.

What Does Early Educational Research Tell Us?

Policy makers must also understand that sole reliance on cognitively oriented measures is unsupported by the best scientific evidence we have about ways to support early learning. There is a bounty of scientific literature indicating that children's social and emotional skills are predictive of early achievement, with children's thinking skills *and* self-regulation likely to play important roles in early learning.

One might ask: What does self-regulation have to do with learning the basics such as preliteracy and early math? Children must be able to handle their emotions when sharing instructional materials, taking turns holding or choosing a book for story time, or getting in line. They must be able to focus their attention away from distracting sights and sounds outside the classroom window and toward the task at hand. They must be able to organize their activities and listen to and heed teachers' instructions. Emotionally supportive preschool classrooms foster children's motivation, their development of enthusiasm about school as a good place to be, and positive views of themselves as learners capable of tackling new problems and challenges. Children who are less distractible and more emotionally positive are viewed by teachers as more "teachable." In fact, a majority of teachers surveyed suggested that curiosity, enthusiasm, and ability to follow directions play a potent role in their judgment of children's "readiness" to learn.

Recent research in both areas of cognitive and emotional development has highlighted the ways in which children differ from each other in terms of "executive functioning" or "behavioral self-control." That is, while some children are good at planning, staying organized and focused when given a difficult task, and remaining attentive and calm in a classroom setting, other children have problems regulating their emotions and their attention. Decades of research suggest that (1) Children with emotional and behavioral difficulties are at greater risk for long-term academic problems, and (2) poverty-related stressors impose additional psychological strain on young children that may interfere with their ability to concentrate, pay attention, and control their feelings of sadness and frustration. Prevalence estimates suggest that between 7 percent and 25 percent of low-income children enrolled in early educational settings exhibit elevated behavioral problems. Children exposed to high levels of community and family violence also are more likely to be sad and withdrawn, with symptoms of inattentiveness and difficulty interacting prosocially with teachers and peers. In short, these problems are likely to have serious ramifications for learning. Low-income preschoolers' acquisition of preliteracy and other cognitive skills is likely to be *suppressed* unless the social and emotional domains of learning and development are recognized and supported.

In addition, research suggests that preschool-age children learn more and are more motivated when they are in emotionally supportive, "child-centered" classrooms, as compared to classrooms that emphasize drills, worksheets, seat-work, and "basic skills." In the recent U.S. Department of Health and Human Services report critiquing Head Start, the authors recognize the importance of teaching pre-academic content "without compromising social and emotional development." In the model Texas program that the report endorses, the evaluation included assessments of children's readiness in both cognitive and socioemotional domains. It is therefore baffling that some leaders want to eradicate social and emotional assessments from Head Start's planned evaluation efforts.

⟡

Plans to abandon assessment of children's social and emotional competencies in Head Start represent a grave loss of opportunity for social scientists and educators. With the emotional and behavioral data from the FACES and Head Start Impact Study, we can address questions of how changes in particular noncognitive domains are associated with changes in learning. Without the data that these assessments will provide, researchers will be unable to test the very hypotheses that may lead to teaching and curricula innovations. Finally, if measures of social and emotional development are struck from national evaluations, policy makers will be making a statement that these features are unrelated to learning and are therefore unimportant. A slew of developmental evidence, and a modicum of common sense, should tell them otherwise.

Cautions and Recommendations

What will the impact of national testing of Head Start's preschoolers be? We can imagine a range of scenarios that might result from the plan to use cognitively oriented tests to assess Head Start children. One benefit might be that training and technical assistance could be targeted to centers that need the help the most. On the other hand, classrooms in areas with high levels of community and family violence are likely to have children who are less able to weather the behavioral challenges involved in test-taking, so programs serving our nation's most vulnerable families will receive the greatest share of blame and the least amount of help for children's compromised performance. In short, we may repeat past policy mistakes, with Head Start and poor children blamed for their supposed educational failures rather than rewarded and supported for their successes in the face of substantial income and educational inequality. Without being able to predict the outcome, and without being able to forestall the implementation of cognitively oriented assessments, we offer a set of cautions and recommendations.

1. First, we remind readers that there is no single cognitive "magic bullet" to the problems of poverty or to the achievement gap between economically disadvantaged children and their more affluent classmates. Good curriculum and hard work on the part of teachers may partially remedy that gap, and programs, teachers, parents, and children themselves are to be lauded when such successes are achieved. Certainly, comprehensive services that address families' economic self-sufficiency, housing, health, and welfare are also needed, and we know that those services are expensive. If policy makers genuinely wish to see Head Start and low-income children succeed, they must match their interest in cognitive assessment with a substantially increased investment in families, programs, and teachers so that desired gains can be realized.

2. Second, we caution readers that there is not clear consensus of the predictive value of cognitive assessments in guaranteeing later school performance. School success likely rests on an integrated foundation, with physical health, cognitive features, and behavioral/emotional adjustment all playing key facilitative roles in children developing positive orientations toward learning. Children's beliefs in themselves as capable learners, their skills in working with teachers and peers in prosocial ways, their ability to stay focused and on task, and their capacity to maintain emotional and behavioral self-control may offer important advantages in learning. We will not know the relative importance of these abilities if we do not collect the data. Thus, we urge that the twin foci on both learning and socioemotional outcomes be maintained in all Head Start evaluation and research efforts.

3. Third, we recommend that current teacher-rated assessments of emotional and social development be continued. But we also recommend that better methods and measures be used to provide more direct assessments. The task is possible. Emotionally and behaviorally oriented direct assessments were developed and successfully implemented in the national evaluation of Early Head Start that included thousands of toddlers. Researchers have adequate empirical background on which to develop a comprehensive battery, through "consensus conference" on what measures provide most specificity and predictive validity on measurable change in children's emotional and behavioral adjustment. In short, researchers could standardize and validate a short set of age-appropriate measures that could be included in future years of Head Start assessments. Without such direct measurements, children's emotional and behavioral development will always be more vaguely defined and less vigorously measured than their cognitive development.

CHALLENGE QUESTIONS

Does Emphasizing Academic Skills Help At-Risk Preschool Children?

- Ultimately, identifying the developmental needs of children in poverty is the central issue for this controversy. What do young children in poverty-stricken communities need from schools and society in order to develop well?
- Raver and Zigler suggest that part of the academic problem with Head Start is simply not having enough qualified teachers and staff. Do you agree with their suspicion that the exclusive emphasis on cognitive skills and testing is more of a way to impose market values on preschool rather than really thinking about the developmental needs of children?
- While providing better access to early childhood education is a popular intervention against poverty, some people argue that it is not enough to solve inequality. What do young children need beyond quality education to ensure they have equal opportunities?
- Some people have suggested that the problem with Head Start is that it does not start early enough. From a developmental perspective, how effective would it be to put younger children in formal schooling?
- In addition to the larger developmental question about early intervention, this issue revolves around a question about the interaction of various developmental domains: the cognitive, the social, the emotional, the physical, and so on. Is development best facilitated by considering these diverse domains as they relate to each other?
- Is it reasonable to expect that simple intervention during early childhood will produce a lifetime of change?

Suggested Readings

S. Barnett and J. Huestedt, "Head Start's Lasting Benefits," *Infants & Young Children* (January–March 2005)

C. Bordignon and T. Lam, "The Early Assessment Conundrum: Lessons from the Past, Implications for the Future," *Psychology in the Schools* (September 2004)

R. Fewell, "Assessment of Young Children with Special Needs: Foundations for Tomorrow," *Topics in Early Childhood Special Education* (2000)

K. Kafer, "A Head Start for Poor Children?" *Backgrounder* (May 4, 2004)

S. Meisels, "Testing Culture Invades Lives of Young Children," *FairTest Examiner* (Spring 2005)

J. Neisworth and S. Bagnato, "The Case Against Intelligence Testing in Early Intervention," *Topics in Early Childhood Special Education* (Spring 1992)

J. Neisworth and S. Bagnato, "The MisMeasure of Young Children: The Authentic Assessment Alternative," *Infants and Young Children* (2004)

S. Olfman, "All Work and No Play: How Educational Reforms are Hurting Our Preschoolers," *Rethinking Schools Online* (Winter 2004/2005)

A. Papero, "Is Early, High-Quality Daycare an Asset for the Children of Low-Income, Depressed Mothers?," *Developmental Review* (2005)

R. Stahlman, "Standardized Tests: A Teacher's Perspective," *Childhood Education* (Summer 2005)

P. Williamson, E. Bondy, L. Langley, and D. Mayne, "Meeting the Challenge of High-Stakes Testing While Remaining Child-Centered," *Childhood Education* (Summer 2005)

ISSUE 9

Is Attention Deficit Disorder (ADD/ADHD) a Legitimate Medical Condition That Affects Childhood Behavior?

YES: Michael Fumento, from "Trick Question" *The New Republic* (February 2003)

NO: Rogers H. Wright, from "Attention Deficit Hyperactivity Disorder: What It Is and What It Is Not," in Rogers H. Wright and Nicholas A. Cummings, eds., *Destructive Trends in Mental Health: The Well-Intentioned Path to Harm* (Routledge, 2005)

ISSUE SUMMARY

YES: Science journalist and writer Michael Fumento suggests that despite the extensive political controversy, it is clear that ADHD is a legitimate medical condition disrupting childhood.

NO: Psychologist Rogers Wright argues that ADHD is a transitory condition and fad diagnosis rather than an enduring disease.

Middle childhood is often a period of changing behavior. As children move from primarily spending time with their parents and family to primarily spending time with peers and at school, they often establish new habits and attitudes. While most children adapt to the changes well, there are inevitably some children who struggle. In these cases, many children can be disruptive, hyperactive, and deviant. Their behavior is no longer just a family issue, but it is an issue for the school and community in which they interact. The controversial question, is whether extreme behavior constitutes a medical disorder requiring medication or a radical variation on normal childhood created by social forces.

Part of the controversy is due to the success of drugs such as Ritalin in modifying the behavior of children. Individuals who were previously out of control and unable to concentrate have used Ritalin and related drugs to control their attention and behavior. These drugs allowed parents to manage unruly children and schools to educate difficult students. Does applying a medical model and medication to extreme behavior prove that ADHD is a legitimate medical condition?

Ritalin, like any psychoactive drug, alters brain chemistry: our concentration, mood, attention, excitement, energy, and so on. As such, a drug that alters brain chemistry has the potential to both rectify disordered behavior and manage normal behavior. While some scholars argue that the efficacy of Ritalin and similar drugs proves the reality of ADHD, others argue that these drugs could have socially redeeming effects on anyone—including college students who have learned that Ritalin (and related drugs) will help their concentration and attention span.

Beyond the fact that Ritalin works to influence children's brains, statistics about ADHD serve to stir further controversy. First, ADHD is a relatively recent disorder—the diagnosis did not exist by that name until the last few decades. To some this suggests that ADHD is not an organic, or biological, disorder but an artifact of changing social norms. To others this demonstrates the advances made in medical science. Second, the overwhelming majority of cases of ADHD are diagnosed in North America. To some this suggests that ADHD reflects part of our culture that refuses to accept responsibility for the challenges of middle childhood. To others this shows the advanced progress of our system for managing children with serious problems. Third, ADHD is much more commonly diagnosed in boys than in girls. To some this means that ADHD is linked to male biology. To others this suggests that the tendency of boys to be more aggressive and assertive is more than contemporary parents and teachers can handle.

Michael Fumento asserts that any argument against the reality of ADHD is misguided. He points out that the efficacy of Ritalin in changing behavior should be considered positive, rather than negative. Children diagnosed with ADHD are different, and it is not just because of parenting. Ritalin helps them function effectively but it does not, contrary to popular opinion, create zombies.

Psychologist Rogers Wright, takes a clinical perspective and suggests that biomedical approaches to ADHD have gone too far. He notes that ADHD is an easy way to explain extreme behavior, but that medication can often do more harm than good. He also notes that behavioral interventions—efforts to systematically shape children's behavior through environmental changes—are a more effective primary option for dealing with disruptive children than medication.

POINT	COUNTERPOINT
• Mostly, the diagnosis of ADHD is based on clear and dramatic behavioral differences—similar to many other medical conditions.	• The frequency of diagnosing ADHD among children is a "fad" rather than a representation of a true medical condition.
• The behavioral problems that mark ADHD are extreme disruptions in functioning.	• ADHD is more of a "behavioral aberration" than a real disease, similar to Social Anxiety Disorder.
• The effectiveness of drugs such as Ritalin and the problems caused by ADHD clearly demonstrate that it is a neurological problem.	• There is a difference between being hyperactive and having a neurological disorder that originates in dysfunction.
• Medications often help children and families to have the opportunity for normal developmental experiences.	• Research suggests that behavioral interventions are more effective than medication—we are often too quick to medicate.

YES

Michael Fumento

Trick Question

It's both right-wing and vast, but it's not a conspiracy. Actually, it's more of an anti-conspiracy. The subject is Attention Deficit Disorder (ADD) and Attention Deficit Hyperactivity Disorder (ADHD), closely related ailments (henceforth referred to in this article simply as ADHD). Rush Limbaugh declares it "may all be a hoax." Francis Fukuyama devotes much of one chapter in his latest book, *Our Posthuman Future,* to attacking Ritalin, the top-selling drug used to treat ADHD. Columnist Thomas Sowell writes, "The motto used to be: 'Boys will be boys.' Today, the motto seems to be: 'Boys will be medicated.'" And Phyllis Schlafly explains, "The old excuse of 'my dog ate my homework' has been replaced by 'I got an ADHD diagnosis.'" A March 2002 article in *The Weekly Standard* summed up the conservative line on ADHD with this rhetorical question: "Are we really prepared to redefine childhood as an ailment, and medicate it until it goes away?"

Many conservative writers, myself included, have criticized the growing tendency to pathologize every undesirable behavior—especially where children are concerned. But, when it comes to ADHD, this skepticism is misplaced. As even a cursory examination of the existing literature or, for that matter, simply talking to the parents and teachers of children with ADHD reveals, the condition is real, and it is treatable. And, if you don't believe me, you can ask conservatives who've come face to face with it themselves.

Myth: ADHD Isn't a Real Disorder

The most common argument against ADHD on the right is also the simplest: It doesn't exist. Conservative columnist Jonah Goldberg thus reduces ADHD to "ants in the pants." Sowell equates it with "being bored and restless." Fukuyama protests, "No one has been able to identify a cause of ADD/ADHD. It is a pathology recognized only by its symptoms." And a conservative columnist approvingly quotes Thomas Armstrong, Ritalin opponent and author, when he declares, "ADD is a disorder that cannot be authoritatively identified in the same way as polio, heart disease or other legitimate illnesses."

The Armstrong and Fukuyama observations are as correct as they are worthless. "Half of all medical disorders are diagnosed without benefit of a lab procedure," notes Dr. Russell Barkley, professor of psychology at the College of

From *The New Republic*, Vol. 228, no. 4, February 3, 2003, pp. 18–21. Copyright © 2003 by New Republic. Reprinted by permission.

Health Professionals at the Medical University of South Carolina. "Where are the lab tests for headaches and multiple sclerosis and Alzheimer's?" he asks. "Such a standard would virtually eliminate all mental disorders."

Often the best diagnostic test for an ailment is how it responds to treatment. And, by that standard, it doesn't get much more real than ADHD. The beneficial effects of administering stimulants to treat the disorder were first reported in 1937. And today medication for the disorder is reported to be 75 to 90 percent successful. "In our trials it was close to ninety percent," says Dr. Judith Rapoport, director of the National Institute of Mental Health's Child Psychiatry Branch, who has published about 100 papers on ADHD. "This means there was a significant difference in the children's ability to function in the classroom or at home."

Additionally, epidemiological evidence indicates that ADHD has a powerful genetic component. University of Colorado researchers have found that a child whose identical twin has the disorder is between eleven and 18 times more likely to also have it than is a non-twin sibling. For these reasons, the American Psychiatric Association (APA), American Medical Association, American Academy of Pediatrics, American Academy of Child Adolescent Psychiatry, the surgeon general's office, and other major medical bodies all acknowledge ADHD as both real and treatable.

Myth: ADHD Is Part of a Feminist Conspiracy to Make Little Boys More Like Little Girls

Many conservatives observe that boys receive ADHD diagnoses in much higher numbers than girls and find in this evidence of a feminist conspiracy. (This, despite the fact that genetic diseases are often heavily weighted more toward one gender or the other.) Sowell refers to "a growing tendency to treat boyhood as a pathological condition that requires a new three R's—repression, re-education and Ritalin." Fukuyama claims Prozac is being used to give women "more of the alpha-male feeling," while Ritalin is making boys act more like girls. "Together, the two sexes are gently nudged toward that androgynous median personality . . . that is the current politically correct outcome in American society." George Will, while acknowledging that Ritalin can be helpful, nonetheless writes of the "androgyny agenda" of "drugging children because they are behaving like children, especially boy children." Anti-Ritalin conservatives frequently invoke Christina Hoff Sommers's best-selling 2000 book, *The War Against Boys*. You'd never know that the drug isn't mentioned in her book—or why.

"Originally I was going to have a chapter on it," Sommers tells me. "It seemed to fit the thesis." What stopped her was both her survey of the medical literature and her own empirical findings. Of one child she personally came to know she says, "He was utterly miserable, as was everybody around him. The drugs saved his life."

Myth: ADHD Is Part of the Public School System's Efforts to Warehouse Kids Rather Than to Discipline and Teach Them

"No doubt life is easier for teachers when everyone sits around quietly," writes Sowell. Use of ADHD drugs is "in the school's interest to deal with behavioral and discipline problems [because] it's so easy to use Ritalin to make kids compliant: to get them to sit down, shut up, and do what they're told," declares Schlafly. The word "zombies" to describe children under the effects of Ritalin is tossed around more than in a B-grade voodoo movie.

Kerri Houston, national field director for the American Conservative Union and the mother of two ADHD children on medication, agrees with much of the criticism of public schools. "But don't blame ADHD on crummy curricula and lazy teachers," she says. "If you've worked with these children, you know they have a serious neurological problem." In any case, Ritalin, when taken as prescribed, hardly stupefies children. To the extent the medicine works, it simply turns ADHD children into normal children. "ADHD is like having thirty televisions on at one time, and the medicine turns off twenty-nine so you can concentrate on the one," Houston describes. "This zombie stuff drives me nuts! My kids are both as lively and as fun as can be."

Myth: Parents Who Give Their Kids Anti-ADHD Drugs Are Merely Doping Up Problem Children

Limbaugh calls ADHD "the perfect way to explain the inattention, incompetence, and inability of adults to control their kids." Addressing parents directly, he lectures, "It helped you mask your own failings by doping up your children to calm them down."

Such charges blast the parents of ADHD kids into high orbit. That includes my Hudson Institute colleague (and fellow conservative) Mona Charen, the mother of an eleven-year-old with the disorder. "I have two non-ADHD children, so it's not a matter of parenting technique," says Charen. "People without such children have no idea what it's like. I can tell the difference between boyish high spirits and pathological hyperactivity. . . . These kids bounce off the walls. Their lives are chaos; their rooms are chaos. And nothing replaces the drugs."

Barkley and Rapoport say research backs her up. Randomized, controlled studies in both the United States and Sweden have tried combining medication with behavioral interventions and then dropped either one or the other. For those trying to go on without medicine, "the behavioral interventions maintained nothing," Barkley says. Rapoport concurs: "Unfortunately, behavior modification doesn't seem to help with ADHD." (Both doctors are quick to add that ADHD is often accompanied by other disorders that are treatable through behavior modification in tandem with medicine.)

Myth: Ritalin Is "Kiddie Cocaine"

One of the paradoxes of conservative attacks on Ritalin is that the drug is alternately accused of turning children into brain-dead zombies and of making them Mach-speed cocaine junkies. Indeed, Ritalin is widely disparaged as "kiddie cocaine." Writers who have sought to lump the two drugs together include Schlafly, talk-show host and columnist Armstrong Williams, and others whom I hesitate to name because of my long-standing personal relationships with them.

Mary Eberstadt wrote the "authoritative" Ritalin-cocaine piece for the April 1999 issue of *Policy Review*, then owned by the Heritage Foundation. The article, "Why Ritalin Rules," employs the word "cocaine" no fewer than twelve times. Eberstadt quotes from a 1995 Drug Enforcement Agency (DEA) background paper declaring methylphenidate, the active ingredient in Ritalin, "a central nervous system (CNS) stimulant [that] shares many of the pharmacological effects of amphetamine, methamphetamine, and cocaine." Further, it "produces behavioral, psychological, subjective, and reinforcing effects similar to those of d-amphetamine including increases in rating of euphoria, drug liking and activity, and decreases in sedation." Add to this the fact that the Controlled Substances Act lists it as a Schedule II drug, imposing on it the same tight prescription controls as morphine, and Ritalin starts to sound spooky indeed.

What Eberstadt fails to tell readers is that the DEA description concerns methylphenidate *abuse*. It's tautological to say abuse is harmful. According to the DEA, the drugs in question are comparable when "administered the same way at comparable does." But ADHD stimulants, when taken as prescribed, are neither administered in the same way as cocaine nor at comparable doses. "What really counts," says Barkley, "is the speed with which the drugs enter and clear the brain. With cocaine, because it's snorted, this happens tremendously quickly, giving users the characteristic addictive high." (Ever seen anyone pop a cocaine tablet?) Further, he says, "There's no evidence anywhere in literature of [Ritalin's] addictiveness when taken as prescribed." As to the Schedule II listing, again this is because of the potential for it to fall into the hands of abusers, not because of its effects on persons for whom it is prescribed. Ritalin and the other anti-ADHD drugs, says Barkley, "are the safest drugs in all of psychiatry." (And they may be getting even safer: A new medicine just released called Strattera represents the first true non-stimulant ADHD treatment.)

Indeed, a study just released in the journal *Pediatrics* found that children who take Ritalin or other stimulants to control ADHD cut their risk of future substance abuse by 50 percent compared with untreated ADHD children. The lead author speculated that "by treating ADHD you're reducing the demoralization that accompanies this disorder, and you're improving the academic functioning and well-being of adolescents and young adults during the critical times when substance abuse starts."

Myth: Ritalin Is Overprescribed Across the Country

Some call it "the Ritalin craze." In *The Weekly Standard,* Melana Zyla Vickers informs us that "Ritalin use has exploded," while Eberstadt writes that "Ritalin use more than doubled in the first half of the decade alone, [and] the number of schoolchildren taking the drug may now, by some estimates, be approaching the *4 million mark.*"

A report in the January 2003 issue of *Archives of Pediatrics and Adolescent Medicine* did find a large increase in the use of ADHD medicines from 1987 to 1996, an increase that doesn't appear to be slowing. Yet nobody thinks it's a problem that routine screening for high blood pressure has produced a big increase in the use of hypertension medicine. "Today, children suffering from ADHD are simply less likely to slip through the cracks," says Dr. Sally Satel, a psychiatrist, AEI fellow, and author of *PC, M.D.: How Political Correctness Is Corrupting Medicine.*

Satel agrees that some community studies, by the standards laid down in the APA's *Diagnostic and Statistical Manual of Mental Disorders (DSM),* indicate that ADHD may often be over-diagnosed. On the other hand, she says, additional evidence shows that in some communities ADHD is *under-*diagnosed and *under-*treated. "I'm quite concerned with children who need the medication and aren't getting it," she says.

There *are* tremendous disparities in the percentage of children taking ADHD drugs when comparing small geographical areas. Psychologist Gretchen LeFever, for example, has compared the number of prescriptions in mostly white Virginia Beach, Virginia, with other, more heavily African American areas in the southeastern part of the state. Conservatives have latched onto her higher numbers—20 percent of white fifth-grade boys in Virginia Beach are being treated for ADHD—as evidence that something is horribly wrong. But others, such as Barkley, worry about the lower numbers. According to LeFever's study, black children are only half as likely to get medication as white children. "Black people don't get the care of white people; children of well-off parents get far better care than those of poorer parents," says Barkley.

Myth: States Should Pass Laws That Restrict Schools from Recommending Ritalin

Conservative writers have expressed delight that several states, led by Connecticut, have passed or are considering laws ostensibly protecting students from schools that allegedly pass out Ritalin like candy. Representative Lenny Winkler, lead sponsor of the Connecticut measure, told *Reuters Health,* "If the diagnosis is made, and it's an appropriate diagnosis that Ritalin be used, that's fine. But I have also heard of many families approached by the school system [who are told] that their child cannot attend school if they're not put on Ritalin."

Two attorneys I interviewed who specialize in child-disability issues, including one from the liberal Bazelon Center for Mental Health Law in

Washington, D.C., acknowledge that school personnel have in some cases stepped over the line. But legislation can go too far in the other direction by declaring, as Connecticut's law does, that "any school personnel [shall be prohibited] from recommending the use of psychotropic drugs for any child." The law appears to offer an exemption by declaring, "The provisions of this section shall not prohibit *school medical staff* from recommending that a child be evaluated by an appropriate medical practitioner, or prohibit school personnel from consulting with such practitioner, with the consent of the parent or guardian of such child." [Emphasis added.] But of course many, if not most schools have perhaps one nurse on regular "staff." That nurse will have limited contact with children in the classroom situations where ADHD is likely to be most evident. And, given the wording of the statute, a teacher who believed a student was suffering from ADHD would arguably be prohibited from referring that student to the nurse. Such ambiguity is sure to have a chilling effect on any form of intervention or recommendation by school personnel. Moreover, 20-year special-education veteran Sandra Rief said in an interview with the National Education Association that "recommending medical intervention for a student's behavior could lead to personal liability issues." Teachers, in other words, could be forced to choose between what they think is best for the health of their students and the possible risk of losing not only their jobs but their personal assets as well.

"Certainly it's not within the purview of a school to say kids can't attend if they don't take drugs," says Houston. "On the other hand, certainly teachers should be able to advise parents as to problems and potential solutions. . . . [T]hey may see things parents don't. My own son is an angel at home but was a demon at school."

If the real worry is "take the medicine or take a hike" ultimatums, legislation can be narrowly tailored to prevent them; broad-based gag orders, such as Connecticut's, are a solution that's worse than the problem.

The Conservative Case for ADHD Drugs

There are kernels of truth to every conservative suspicion about ADHD. Who among us has not had lapses of attention? And isn't hyperactivity a normal condition of childhood when compared with deskbound adults? Certainly there are lazy teachers, warehousing schools, androgyny-pushing feminists, and far too many parents unwilling or unable to expend the time and effort to raise their children properly, even by their own standards. Where conservatives go wrong is in making ADHD a scapegoat for frustration over what we perceive as a breakdown in the order of society and family. In a column in *The Boston Herald,* Boston University Chancellor John Silber rails that Ritalin is "a classic example of a cheap fix: low-cost, simple and purely superficial."

Exactly. Like most headaches, ADHD is a neurological problem that can usually be successfully treated with a chemical. Those who recommend or prescribe ADHD medicines do not, as *The Weekly Standard* put it, see them as "discipline in pill-form." They see them as pills.

In fact, it can be argued that the use of those pills, far from being liable for or symptomatic of the Decline of the West, reflects and reinforces conservative values. For one thing, they increase personal responsibility by removing an excuse that children (and their parents) can fall back on to explain misbehavior and poor performance. "Too many psychologists and psychiatrists focus on allowing patients to justify to themselves their troubling behavior," says Satel. "But something like Ritalin actually encourages greater autonomy because you're treating a compulsion to behave in a certain way. Also, by treating ADHD, you remove an opportunity to explain away bad behavior."

Moreover, unlike liberals, who tend to downplay differences between the sexes, conservatives are inclined to believe that there are substantial physiological differences—differences such as boys' greater tendency to suffer ADHD. "Conservatives celebrate the physiological differences between boys and girls and eschew the radical-feminist notion that gender differences are created by societal pressures," says Houston regarding the fuss over the boy-girl disparity among ADHD diagnoses. "ADHD is no exception."

But, however compatible conservatism may be with taking ADHD seriously, the truth is that most conservatives remain skeptics. "I'm sure I would have been one of those smug conservatives saying it's a made-up disease," admits Charen, "if I hadn't found out the hard way." Here's hoping other conservatives find an easier route to accepting the truth.

Attention Deficit Hyperactivity Disorder: What It Is and What It Is Not

It is almost axiomatic in the mental health field that fads will occur in the "diagnosis" and treatment of various types of behavioral aberrations, some of which border on being mere discomforts. Although the same faddism exists to some degree in physical medicine, its appearance is not nearly as blatant, perhaps in part because physical medicine is more soundly grounded in the physical sciences than are diagnoses in the mental health field. These fads spill over into the general culture, where direct marketing often takes place. One has to spend only a brief period in front of a television set during prime time to discover ADHD (Attention Deficit Hyperactivity Disorder), SAD (Social Anxiety Disorder), or IBS (Irritable Bowl Syndrome). Even when purporting to be informational, these are more or less disguised commercials, inasmuch as they posit a cure that varies with the drug manufacturer sponsoring the television ad.

The other certainty is that these "diagnoses" will fall from usage as other fads emerge, as was the case a decade or so ago with the disappearance of a once-common designation for what is now sometimes called ADHD. That passing fad was known as minimal brain syndrome (MBS) and/or food disorder (ostensibly from red dye or other food additives). From this author's perspective, these fad "diagnoses" don't really exist. Other writers in this volume have commented on the slipperiness of these "diagnoses"—that is, the elevation of a symptom and/or its description to the level of a disorder or syndrome—and the concomitant tendency to overmedicate for these nonexistent maladies.

Children and ADHD

Certainly, there are deficiencies of attention and hyperactivity, but such behavioral aberrancies are most often indicative of a transitory state or condition within the organism. They are not in and of themselves indicative of a "disorder." Every parent has noticed, particularly with younger children, that toward the end of an especially exciting and fatiguing day children are literally "ricocheting off the walls." Although this behavior may in the broadest sense be classifiable as hyperactivity, it is generally pathognomonic of nothing more than excessive fatigue, for which the treatment of choice is a good night's sleep.

From *Destructive Trends in Mental Health: The Well Intentioned Path to Harm*, 2005, pp. 129–141. Copyright © 2005 by Taylor & Francis Books, Inc. Reprinted by permission.

Distractibility (attention deficit) is a frequent concomitant of excessive fatigue, particularly with children under five years of age, and can even be seen in adults if fatigue levels are extreme or if stress is prolonged. However, such "symptoms" in these contexts do not rise to the level of a treatable disorder.

Conversely, when distractibility and/or hyperactivity characterize the child's everyday (especially if accompanied by factors such as delayed development, learning difficulties, impaired motor skills, and impaired judgement), they may be indicative of either a neurological disorder or of developing emotional difficulties. However, after nearly fifty years of diagnosing and treating several thousand such problems, it is my considered judgement that the distractibility and hyperactivity seen in such children is not the same as the distractibility and hyperactivity in children currently diagnosed as having ADHD. Furthermore, the hyperactivity/distractibility seen in the non-ADHD children described above is qualitatively and quantitatively different, depending on whether it is caused by incipient emotional maldevelopment (functional; i.e., nonorganic) or whether it is due to neurological involvement.

It is also notable that most children whose distractibility and/or hyperactivity is occasioned by emotional distress do not show either the kind or degree of learning disability, delayed genetic development, poor judgement, and impaired motor skills that are seen in children whose "distractibility/hyperactivity" is occasioned by neurological involvement. Only in children with the severest forms of emotional disturbance does one see the kind of developmental delays and impaired behavioral controls that are more reflective of neurological involvement (or what was known as MBS until the ADHD fad took hold). Differentiating the child with actual neurological involvement from the child that has emotionally based distractibility is neither simple nor easy to do, especially if the behavioral (as opposed to neurological) involvement is severe.

A major and profound disservice occasioned by the current fad of elevating nonspecific symptoms such as anxiety and hyperactivity to the level of a syndrome or disorder and then diagnosing ADD/ADHD is that we lump together individuals with very different needs and very different problems. We then attempt to treat the problem(s) with a single entity, resulting in a one-pill-fits-all response. It is also unfortunately the case that many mental health providers (e.g., child psychiatrists, child psychologists, child social workers), as well as many general care practitioners (e.g., pediatricians and internists), are not competent to make such discriminations alone. Therefore, it follows that such practitioners are not trained and equipped to provide ongoing care, even when an appropriate diagnosis has been made.

To add to an already complicated situation, the symptom picture in children tends to change with time and maturation. Children with neurological involvement typically tend to improve spontaneously over time, so that the symptoms of distractibility and hyperactivity often represent diminished components in the clinical picture. Conversely, children whose distractibility and hyperactivity are emotionally determined typically have symptoms that tend to intensify or be accompanied/replaced by even more dramatic indices of emotional distress.

Management of Children Exhibiting "ADHD" According to Etiology

It is apparent that somewhat superfically similar presenting complaints (i.e., distractibility and hyperactivity) may reflect two very different causative factors, and that the successful treatment and management of the complaint should vary according to the underlying causation. Neurological damage can stem from a number of causative factors during pregnancy or the birth process, and a successful remedial program may require the combined knowledge of the child's pediatrician, a neuropsychologist specializing in the diagnosis and treatment of children, and a child neurologist. In these cases approptiate medication for the child is often very helpful.

Psychotherapy for the child (particularly younger children) is, in this writer's experience, largely a waste of time. On the other hand, remedial training in visual perception, motor activities, visual–motor integration, spatial relations, numerical skills, and reading and writing may be crucial in alleviating or at least diminishing the impact of symptoms. Deficits in these skills can be major contributors to the hyperactivity and distractibility so frequently identified with such children. Counseling and psychotherapeutic work with the parents is very important and should always be a part of an integrated therapeutic program. Such children need to be followed by an attending pediatrician, a child neurologist, a child neuropsychologist, and an educational therapist, bearing in mind that treatment needs change throughout the span of remediation. For example, medication levels and regimens may need to be adjusted, and training programs will constantly need to be revised or elaborated.

It is also noteworthy that so-called tranquilizing medication with these children typically produces an adverse effect. This writer remembers a situation that occurred early in his practice, a case he has used repeatedly to alert fledgling clinicians to the importance of a comprehensive initial evaluation and ongoing supervision in the development of neurologically involved children.

John, a two-and-a-half-year-old boy, was referred by his pediatrician for evaluation of extreme hyperactivity, distractibility, and mild developmental delay. The psychological evaluation elicited evidence of visual perceptual impairment in a context of impaired visual motor integration, a finding suggestive of an irritative focus in the parietal-occipital areas of the brain. This finding was later corroborated by a child neurologist, and John was placed on dilantin and Phenobarbital. A developmental training program was instituted, and the parents began participation in a group specifically designed for the parents of brain-injured children. Over the next couple of years, the patient's progress was excellent, and his development and learning difficulties were singularly diminished. The parents were comfortable with John's progress and with their ability to manage it, so they decided to have a long-wanted additional child. In the meantime, the father's work necessitated moving to another location, leading to a change of obstetrician and pediatrician.

The second pregnancy proceeded uneventfully and eventuated in the birth of a second boy. Shortly after the mother returned home with the new infant, John began to regress, exhibiting a number of prior symptoms such as hyperactivity and distractibility, as well as problems in behavioral control. The new pediatrician referred the family to a child psychiatrist, who promptly placed John on a tranquilizer. Shortly thereafter, John's academic performance began to deteriorate dramatically, and his school counseled the parents about the possibility that he had been promoted too rapidly and "could not handle work at this grade level."

At this point, the parents again contacted this writer, primarily out of concern for John's diminished academic performance. Because it had been more than two years since John had been formally evaluated, I advised the parents that another comprehensive evaluation was indicated. The parents agreed, and a full diagnostic battery was administered to John, the results of which were then compared to his prior performance. It immediately became apparent that he was not functioning at grade level, and that the overall level of his functioning had deteriorated dramatically.

In his initial evaluation, John's functional level had been in the Bright Normal range (i.e., overall IQ of 110 to 119), whereas his current functioning placed him at the Borderline Mentally Retarded level (IQ below 60). The history revealed nothing of significance other than the behavioral regression after the birth of the sibling and the introduction of the new medication. I advised the parents that I thought the child was being erroneously medicated, with consequent diminution of his intellectual efficiency, and that the supposition could be tested by asking the attending child psychiatrist to diminish John's medication to see if the child's performance improved.

The attending child psychiatrist was quite upset by the recommendations and the implications thereof and threatened to sue me for "practicing medicine without a license." I informed the physician that I was not practicing medicine but rather neuropsychology, along with deductive reasoning known as "common sense," which we could test by appropriately reducing John's dosage level for a month and then retesting him. Faced with the alternative of a legal action for slander or libel for having accused this neuropsychologist of a felony, the child psychiatrist agreed.

Upon retesting a month later, the child's performance level had returned to Bright Normal, and his academic performance and behavior in school had improved dramatically. By this time approximately six to eight months had elapsed since the birth of the sibling, and John had become accustomed to his new brother. All concerned agreed that the medication had not been helpful and that the child should continue for another three to six months without medication. Subsequent contact with the parents some six months later indicated that John was doing well at school. The parents were quite comfortable with the behavioral management skills they had learned, which enabled them to handle a child with an underlying neurological handicap.

As noted earlier, the marked distractibility and/or hyperactivity in children with neurological involvement tends to diminish through adolescence, especially after puberty, as do many of the other symptoms. As a consequence, these children present a very different clinical picture in adolescence and adulthood. Typically, they are characterized by impulsivity, at times poor judgement, and excessive fatigability. It is generally only under the circumstances of extreme fatigue (or other stress) that one will see fairly dramatic degreees of distractibility and hyperactivity. Thus an appropriate diagnosis leading to productive intervention is difficult to make.

Conversely, children who exhibit the symptoms of distractibility and hyperactivity on an emotional basis typically do not show the diminution of symptomatology with increasing age. In fact, the symptoms may intensify and/or be replaced by even more dramatic symptoms, especially during puberty and adolescence. It should also be emphasized that the kind of distractibility and hyperactivity exhibited by the emotionally disturbed youngster is very different in quality and quantity from that of a youngster whose hyperactivity and distracibility has a neurological basis. Unfortunately, it is also frequently the case that a youngster with a neurological handicap may have significant emotional problems overlaying the basic neurological problems, making diagnosis even more complicated. But the overriding problem confronting parents today is the misdiagnosis of emotionally-based symptoms that brings the recommendation of unwarranted medication.

In the largest study of its kind, Cummings and Wiggins retrospectively examined the records of 168,113 children and adolescents who had been referred and treated over a four-year period in a national behavioral health provider operating in thirty-nine states. Before beginning treatment, sixty-one percent of the males and twenty-three percent of the females were taking psychotropic medication for ADD/ADHD by a psychiatrist, a pediatrician, or a primary care physician. Most of them lived in a single parent home, and lacked an effective father figure or were subjected to negative and frequently abusive male role models. Behavioral interventions included a compassionate but firm male therapist and the introduction of positive male role models (e.g., fathers, Big Brothers, coaches, Sunday school teachers, etc.) into the child's life. Counseling focused on helping parents understand what constitutes the behavior of a normal boy.

After an average of nearly eleven treatments with the parent and approximately six with the child, the percentage of boys on medication was reduced from sixty-one percent to eleven percent, and the percentage of girls on medication went from twenty-three percent to two percent. These dramatic results occurred despite very strict requirements for discontinuing the medication, which seems to point to an alarming overdiagnosis and overmedication of ADD/ADHD and greater efficacy of behavioral interventions than is generally believed to be the case by the mental health community. . . .

Summary

When hyperactivity and/or distractibility is truly one of the presenting symptoms, it is indicative of a complex situation that warrants extensive and thoughtful evaluation, and, more often than not, complex and comprehensive treatment planning from the perspective of a variety of specialists.

In situations where the attention deficit and/or hyperactivity reflects problems in parenting, chemotherapeutic intervention for the child is likely to be, at best, no more than palliative and, at worse, may succeed in considerably complicating the situation. In this writer's experience, chemotherapeutic intervention for emotionally disturbed children is a last resort and of minimal value in addressing the overall problem. Psychotherapeutic intervention with the parents, which may or may not include the child, is more often than not the treatment of choice. This is a judgment that is best made only after exhaustive study by pediatrics, psychology, neurology, and perhaps, last of all, psychiatry, which so often seems all too eager to overmedicate (see chapter 6).

Where the presenting complaints of hyperactivity and distractibility are in a context of delayed development, excessive fatigability, learning deficits, and other such signs, the complexity of the diagnostic problem is substantially increased. In such circumstances, it is absolutely not in the child's best interest to limit the diagnostic evaluation to a single specialty. With the increasing evidence that neurological involvement can follow any number of prenatal and postnatal exposures, wise and caring parents will insist on a comprehensive evaluation by specialists in pediatrics, child neurology, and child neuropsychology. More often than not, if medication is indicated, it will be of a type quite different than what is used in the management of so-called ADHD.

Furthermore, treatment intervention and case management will likely involve skilled educational training of the specialized type developed for use with the brain-injured child. In the case of a friendly pediatrician, a concerned psychologist, or a caring child psychiatrist, any or all attempting unilaterally to diagnose and/or manage the treatment regimen, the concerned and caring parent is well advised to promptly seek additional opinions. . . .

CHALLENGE QUESTIONS

Is Attention Deficit Disorder (ADD/ADHD) a Legitimate Medical Condition That Affects Childhood Behavior?

- One piece of evidence commonly used to question the trend toward diagnosing ADHD for disruptive children is to note that the diagnosis occurs much more frequently in North America and among boys. If ADHD is a standard medical condition, how would you confront that evidence?
- There is no conclusive medical test for ADHD; instead it is diagnosed by the clinical judgment that sufficient criteria for the disorder are met. How might the lack of a clear diagnostic test influence this controversy?
- Are children who deviate from obedient and compliant behavioral expectations troubled or simply challenging? How much can parents, communities, teachers, and schools change the behavior of difficult children? Can people really change just by making enough effort?
- While drugs such as Ritalin do not always work, both authors would likely acknowledge that these drugs can produce dramatic behavioral changes in children. What seem to be the relative risks and benefits to using medication to modify childhood behavior?

Suggested Readings

American Academy of Pediatrics, "Clinical Practice Guideline: Treatment of the School-Aged Child with Attention-Deficit/Hyperactivity Disorder," *Pediatrics* (October 2001). Also at: www.aap.org/policy/s0120.html

"An Update on Attention Deficit Disorder," *Harvard Medical Health Letter* (May, 2004). Also at: http://www.health.harvard.edu/newsweek/An_update_on_attention_deficit_disorder.htm

R. A. Barkley, "Psychosocial Treatments for Attention-Deficit/Hyperactivity Disorder in Children," *Journal of Clinical Psychiatry* (vol. 63, suppl. 12, pp. 36–43, 2002).

A. Bowd, "'Curing' ADHD," *Skeptical Inquirer* (May/June 2006)

D. Cohen and J. Leo, "An Update on ADHD Neuroimaging Research," *The Journal of Mind and Behavior* (Spring 2004)

L. Diller, "Defusing the Explosive Child," *Salon* (August 18, 2001)

D. Matthews, *Attention Deficit Disorder Sourcebook* (Omnigraphics, 2002)

M. Olfson, et al., "National Trends in the Treatment of Attention Deficit Hyperactivity Disorder," *American Journal of Psychiatry* (June 2003)

B. Seitler, "On the Implications and Consequences of a Neurobiochemical Etiology of Attention Deficit Hyperactive Disorder (ADHD)," *Ethical Human Psychology and Psychiatry* (Fall/Winter 2006)

Internet References . . .

The National Association for Self-Esteem (NASE) is an organization promoting the value of self-esteem for society in general.

http://www.self-esteem-nase.org/

This page is an entry in a psychology oriented encyclopedia. It lays out some of the research controversy regarding the value of self-esteem.

http://www.enpsychlopedia.com/psypsych/Self-esteem

This Web site is sponsored by a center at New York University focused on mental health in childhood and adolescence.

http://aboutourkids.org/

This site is provided by the ANSWER (Adolescents Never Suicide When Everyone Responds) Network, which focuses on serious adolescent mental health issues.

http://www.teenanswer.org/

This site provides an overview of youth violence from the U.S. Centers for Disease Control.

http://www.cdc.gov/ncipc/factsheets/yvoverview.htm

The Society for Research on Adolescence provides information for academics, clinicians, and students.

http://www.s-r-a.org/

This site presents promising practices in afterschool programs, and is managed by the Academy for Educational Development's Center for Youth Development and Policy Research.

http://www.afterschool.org/

Adolescence

*A*dolescence is a distinctive stage in the lifespan because it is marked by a clear biological change: puberty. Developing adolescents cope with dramatic physical changes that often seem to combine a mature body with an immature mind. Further, because adolescence is associated with increasing independence and responsibility, adolescents seem both powerful and vulnerable. Society is compelled to provide adolescents care and opportunity, while simultaneously fearing that they will rebel. The issues in this section deal with the nature of success and failure in adolescence by asking three questions about what adolescents really need (and about what they could do without).

- Are Efforts to Improve Self-Esteem Misguided?
- Should Contemporary Adolescents Be Engaged in More Structured Activities?
- Does Violent Media Cause Teenage Aggression?

ISSUE 10

Are Efforts to Improve Self-Esteem Misguided?

YES: Roy F. Baumeister, Jennifer D. Compbell, Joachim I. Krueger, and Kathleen D. Vohs, from "Exploding the Self-Esteem Myth," *Scientific American* (January 2005)

NO: William B. Swann, Christine Chang-Schneider, and Katie Larsen McClarty, from "Do People's Self-Views Matter? Self-Concept and Self-Esteem in Everyday Life," *American Psychologist* (February–March 2007)

ISSUE SUMMARY

YES: Psychologist Roy Baumeister and colleagues found that despite its popularity, self-esteem contributes little of value to children and development.

NO: Psychologist William Swann and colleagues argue that substantive versions of self-esteem do facilitate positive developmental trajectories.

While promoting self-esteem as a benefit to many aspects of child and adolescent development has been a popular endeavor, years of accumulated research evidence has begun to raise important questions about the exact role feeling good about oneself plays in growing up.

Self-esteem has become such a popular concept in recent decades that many commentators have come to refer to the "self-esteem movement" as a prominent historical phenomenon. This movement took particular hold among parents and "experts" who proclaimed self-esteem to be the key concern for healthy development. The idea is to constantly praise and reinforce as a way of producing happy, eager, and productive youth. These attitudes were accompanied by a sense that problems and social ills were caused by low self-esteem and an absence of feeling worthy. This may have reached its apex in the 1980s when the California state legislature put together a commission using taxpayer dollars to promote self-esteem with the intention of facilitating the development of a generation of youth.

The California commission to promote self-esteem frequently has been cited, and mocked, by scholars who have collected evidence from years of self-esteem research. In general, the huge volume of research on self-esteem has found limited effects that *do not* match the popular claims of the self-esteem movement. Most researchers now agree that if self-esteem has a positive impact on development, it is more complicated than we usually assume. Among some academics, opinion has even gone to the opposite end of the spectrum, arguing that self-esteem has actually caused developmental problems by creating a generation of youth that have been indulged regardless of their achievements.

In response to this ongoing controversy, prominent social psychologist and self-esteem researcher Roy Baumeister and his colleagues engaged in an extensive evaluation of what research tells us about self-esteem. While their review deals with a variety of popular ideas about self-esteem (such as its role in mental health and interpersonal success) they note that ideas about the positive impact of self-esteem have been particularly influential in relation to adolescence, school, and achievement. Many teachers, parents, and administrators have taken for granted that high self-esteem produces achievement. Baumeister and colleagues find virtually no research support for this position, and assert that the relationship between achievement and self-esteem is much more a popular myth than an empirical reality.

Psychologists William Swann Jr., et al. argue that the pessimism about self-esteem has gone too far. In fact, they suggest, if you consider self-esteem in relation to multidimensional self-views then they think there is a lot of evidence to support the idea that self-esteem matters. Thus, from this perspective, the problem is not the quantity of efforts to promote self-esteem, but instead the problem is the quality.

POINT	COUNTERPOINT
• The value of self-esteem has been consistently overstated because it is something we want to believe can be a panacea.	• Although the value of self-esteem may have been overstated, people have been too quick to completely dismiss self-esteem as having any value.
• Self-esteem is difficult to study accurately because it biases how people report their own characteristics.	• Self-views, as cognitive constructions about who we are, do matter regardless of how accurate they may be.
• Research shows that having high self-esteem does not really predict any specific positive outcomes, such as school achievement.	• The research on self-esteem has been framed too narrowly—to predict specific achievements requires assessing specific self-views.
• Some people with high self-esteem may actually be dangerously narcissistic.	• There is a clear difference between true self-esteem and narcissistic efforts to protect the self.

YES

Roy F. Baumeister et al.

Exploding the Self-Esteem Myth

People intuitively recognize the importance of self-esteem to their psychological health, so it isn't particularly remarkable that most of us try to protect and enhance it in ourselves whenever possible. What *is* remarkable is that attention to self-esteem has become a communal concern, at least for Americans, who see a favorable opinion of oneself as the central psychological source from which all manner of positive outcomes spring. The corollary, that low self-esteem lies at the root of individual and thus societal problems and dysfunctions, has sustained an ambitious social agenda for decades. Indeed, campaigns to raise people's sense of self-worth abound.

Consider what transpired in California in the late 1980s. Prodded by State Assemblyman John Vasconcellos, Governor George Deukmejian set up a task force on self-esteem and personal and social responsibility. Vasconcellos argued that raising self-esteem in young people would reduce crime, teen pregnancy, drug abuse, school underachievement and pollution. At one point, he even expressed the hope that these efforts would one day help balance the state budget, a prospect predicated on the observation that people with high self-regard earn more than others and thus pay more in taxes. Along with its other activities, the task force assembled a team of scholars to survey the relevant literature. The results appeared in a 1989 volume entitled *The Social Importance of Self-Esteem* (University of California Press, 1989), which stated that "many, if not most, of the major problems plaguing society have roots in the low self-esteem of many of the people who make up society." In reality, the report contained little to support that assertion. The California task force disbanded in 1995, but a nonprofit organization called the National Association for Self-Esteem (NASE) has picked up its mantle. Vasconcellos, until recently a California state senator, is on the advisory board.

Was it reasonable for leaders in California to start fashioning therapies and social policies without supportive data? Perhaps, given that they had problems to address. But one can draw on many more studies now than was the case 15 years ago, enough to assess the value of self-esteem in several spheres. Regrettably, those who have been pursuing self-esteem-boosting programs, including the leaders of NASE, have not shown a desire to examine the new work, which is why the four of us recently came together under the aegis of the American Psychological Society to review the scientific literature.

In the Eye of the Beholder

Gauging the value of self-esteem requires, first of all, a sensible way to measure it. Most investigators just ask people what they think of themselves. Naturally enough, the answers are often colored by the common tendency to want to make oneself look good. Unfortunately, psychologists lack good methods to judge self-esteem.

Consider, for instance, research on the relation between self-esteem and physical attractiveness. Several studies have generally found clear positive links when people rate themselves on both properties. It seems plausible that physically attractive people would end up with high self-esteem because they are treated more favorably than unattractive ones—being more popular, more sought after, more valued by lovers and friends, and so forth. But it could just as well be that those who score highly on self-esteem scales by claiming to be wonderful people all around also boast of being physically attractive.

In 1995 Edward F. Diener and Brian Wolsic of the University of Illinois and Frank Fujita of Indiana University South Bend examined this possibility. They obtained self-esteem scores from a broad sample of the population and then photographed everybody, presenting these pictures to a panel of judges, who evaluated the subjects for attractiveness. Ratings based on full-length photographs showed no significant correlation with self-esteem. When the judges were shown pictures of just the participants' unadorned faces, the correlation between attractiveness and self-esteem was once again zero. In that same investigation, however, self-reported physical attractiveness was found to have a strong correlation with self-esteem. Clearly, those with high self-esteem are gorgeous in their own eyes but not necessarily to others.

This discrepancy should be sobering. What seemed at first to be a strong link between physical good looks and high self-esteem turned out to be nothing more than a pattern of consistency in how favorably people rate themselves. A parallel phenomenon affects those with low self-esteem, who are prone to floccinaucinihilipilification, a highfalutin word (among the longest in the Oxford English Dictionary) but one that we can't resist using here, it being defined as "the action or habit of estimating as worthless." That is, people with low self-esteem are not merely down on themselves; they are negative about everything.

This tendency has certainly distorted some assessments. For example, psychologists once thought that people with low self-esteem were especially prejudiced. But thoughtful scholars, such as Jennifer Crocker of the University of Michigan at Ann Arbor, questioned this conclusion. After all, if people rate themselves negatively, it is hard to label them as prejudiced for rating people not like themselves similarly. When one uses the difference between the subjects' assessments of their own group and their ratings of other groups as the yardstick for bias, the findings are reversed: people with *high* self-esteem appear to be more prejudiced. Floccinaucinihilipilification also raises the danger that those who describe themselves disparagingly may describe their lives similarly, thus furnishing the appearance that low self-esteem has unpleasant outcomes.

Given the often misleading nature of self-reports, we set up our review to emphasize objective measures wherever possible—a requirement that greatly reduced the number of relevant studies (from more than 15,000 to about 200). We were also mindful to avoid another fallacy: the assumption that a correlation between self-esteem and some desired behavior establishes causality. Indeed, the question of causality goes to the heart of the debate. If high self-esteem brings about certain positive outcomes, it may well be worth the effort and expense of trying to instill this feeling. But if the correlations mean simply that a positive self-image is a result of success or good behavior—which is certainly plausible—there is little to be gained by raising self-esteem alone. We began our two-year effort by reviewing studies relating self-esteem to academic performance.

School Daze

At the outset, we had every reason to hope that boosting self-esteem would be a potent tool for helping students. Logic suggests that having a good dollop of self-esteem would enhance striving and persistence in school, while making a student less likely to succumb to paralyzing feelings of incompetence or self-doubt. Modern studies have, however, cast doubt on the idea that higher self-esteem actually induces students to do better.

Such inferences about causality are possible when the subjects are examined at two different times, as was the case in 1986 when Sheila M. Pottebaum and her colleagues at the University of Iowa, tested more than 23,000 high school students, first in the 10th and again in the 12th grade. They found that self-esteem in 10th grade is only weakly predictive of academic achievement in 12th grade. Academic achievement in 10th grade correlates with self-esteem in 12th grade only trivially better. Such results, which are now available from multiple studies, certainly do not indicate that raising self-esteem offers students much benefit. Some findings even suggest that artificially boosting self-esteem may lower subsequent performance.

Even if raising self-esteem does not foster academic progress, might it serve some purpose later, say, on the job? Apparently not. Studies of possible links between workers' self-regard and job performance echo what has been found with schoolwork: the simple search for correlations yields some suggestive results, but these do not show whether a good self-image leads to occupational success, or vice versa. In any case, the link is not particularly strong.

The failure to contribute significantly at school or at the office would be easily offset if a heightened sense of self-worth helped someone to get along better with others. Having a good self-image might make someone more likable insofar as people prefer to associate with confident, positive individuals and generally avoid those who suffer from self-doubts and insecurities.

People who regard themselves highly generally state that they are popular and rate their friendships as being of superior quality to those described by people with low self-esteem, who report more negative interactions and less social support. But as Julia Bishop and Heidi M. Inderbitzen-Nolan of the University of Nebraska–Lincoln showed in 1995, these assertions do not reflect reality. The investigators asked 542 ninth-grade students to nominate their most-liked and least-liked peers, and the resulting rankings displayed no correlation whatsoever with self-esteem scores.

A few other methodologically sound studies have found that the same is true for adults. In one of these investigations, conducted in the late 1980s, Duane P. Buhrmester, now at the University of Texas at Dallas, and three colleagues reported that college students with high levels of self-regard claimed to be substantially better at initiating relationships, disclosing things about themselves, asserting themselves in response to objectionable behaviors by others, providing emotional support and even managing interpersonal conflicts. Their roommates' ratings, however, told a different story. For four of the five interpersonal skills surveyed, the correlation with self-esteem dropped to near zero. The only one that remained statistically significant was with the subjects' ability to initiate new social contacts and friendships. This does seem to be one sphere in which confidence indeed matters: people who think that they are desirable and attractive should be adept at striking up conversations with strangers, whereas those with low self-esteem presumably shy away from initiating such contacts, fearing rejection.

One can imagine that such differences might influence a person's love life, too. In 2002 Sandra L. Murray of the University at Buffalo found that people low in self-esteem tend to distrust their partners' expressions of love and support, acting as though they are constantly expecting rejection. Thus far, however, investigators have not produced evidence that such relationships are especially prone to dissolve. In fact, high self-esteem may be the bigger threat: as Caryl E. Rusbult of the University of Kentucky showed back in 1987, those who think highly of themselves are more likely than others to respond to problems by severing relations and seeking other partners.

Sex, Drugs, Rock 'n' Roll

How about teenagers? How does self-esteem, or the lack thereof, influence their love life, in particular their sexual activity? Investigators have examined this subject extensively. All in all, the results do not support the idea that low self-esteem predisposes young people to more or earlier sexual activity. If anything, those with high self-esteem are less inhibited, more willing to disregard risks and more prone to engage in sex. At the same time, bad sexual experiences and unwanted pregnancies appear to lower self-esteem.

If not sex, then how about alcohol or illicit drugs? Abuse of these substances is one of the most worrisome behaviors among young people, and many psychologists once believed that boosting self-esteem would prevent such problems. The thought was that people with low self-esteem turn to drinking or drugs for solace. The data, however, do not consistently show that low adolescent self-esteem causes or even correlates with the abuse of alcohol or other drugs. In particular, in a large-scale study in 2000, Rob McGee and Sheila M. Williams of the Dunedin School of Medicine at the University of Otago in New Zealand found no correlation between self-esteem measured between ages nine and 13 and drinking or drug use at age 15. Even when findings do show links between alcohol use and self-esteem, they are mixed and inconclusive. We did find, however, some evidence that low self-esteem contributes to illicit drug use. In particular, Judy A. Andrews and Susan C. Duncan of the Oregon Research Institute found in 1997 that declining levels of academic motivation (the main focus of their study) caused self-esteem to drop, which in turn led to marijuana use, although the connection was weak.

Interpretation of the findings on drinking and drug abuse is probably complicated by the fact that some people approach the experience out of curiosity or thrill seeking, whereas others may use it to cope with or escape from chronic unhappiness. The overall result is that no categorical statements can be made. The same is true for tobacco use, where our study-by-study review uncovered a preponderance of results that show no influence. The few positive findings we unearthed could conceivably reflect nothing more than self-report bias.

Another complication that also clouds these studies is that the category of people with high self-esteem contains individuals whose self-opinions differ in important ways. Yet in most analyses, people with a healthy sense of self-respect are, for example, lumped with those feigning higher self-esteem than they really feel or who are narcissistic. Not surprisingly, the results of such investigations may produce weak or contradictory findings.

Bully for You

For decades, psychologists believed that low self-esteem was an important cause of aggression. One of us (Baumeister) challenged that notion in 1996, when he reviewed assorted studies and concluded that perpetrators of aggression generally hold favorable and perhaps even inflated views of themselves.

Take the bullying that goes on among children, a common form of aggression. Dan Olweus of the University of Bergen was one of the first to dispute the notion that under their tough exteriors, bullies suffer from insecurities and self-doubts. Although Olweus did not measure self-esteem directly, he showed that bullies reported less anxiety and were more sure of themselves than other children. Apparently the same applies to violent adults.

After coming to the conclusion that high self-esteem does not lessen a tendency toward violence, that it does not deter adolescents from turning to alcohol, tobacco, drugs and sex, and that it fails to improve academic or job performance, we got a boost when we looked into how self-esteem relates to happiness. The consistent finding is that people with high self-esteem are significantly happier than others. They are also less likely to be depressed.

One especially compelling study was published in 1995, after Diener and his daughter Marissa, now a psychologist at the University of Utah, surveyed more than 13,000 college students, and high self-esteem emerged as the strongest factor in overall life satisfaction. In 2004 Sonja Lyubomirsky, Christopher Tkach and M. Robin DiMatteo of the University of California, Riverside, reported data from more than 600 adults ranging in age from 51 to 95. Once again, happiness and self-esteem proved to be closely tied. Before it is safe to conclude that high self-esteem leads to happiness, however, further research must address the shortcomings of the work that has been done so far.

First, causation needs to be established. It seems possible that high self-esteem brings about happiness, but no research has shown this outcome. The strong correlation between self-esteem and happiness is just that—a correlation. It is plausible that occupational, academic or interpersonal successes cause both happiness and high self-esteem and that corresponding failures cause both unhappiness and low self-esteem. It is even possible that happiness, in the sense of a temperament or disposition to feel good, induces high self-esteem.

Second, it must be recognized that happiness (and its opposite, depression) has been studied mainly by means of self-report, and the tendency of some people toward negativity may produce both their low opinions of themselves and unfavorable evaluations of other aspects of life. Yet it is not clear what could replace such assessments. An investigator would indeed be hard-pressed to demonstrate convincingly that a person was less (or more) happy than he or she supposed. Clearly, objective measures of happiness and depression are going to be difficult if not impossible to obtain, but that does not mean self-reports should be accepted uncritically.

What then should we do? Should parents, teachers and therapists seek to boost self-esteem wherever possible? In the course of our literature review, we found some indications that self-esteem is a helpful attribute. It improves persistence in the face of failure. And individuals with high self-esteem sometimes perform better in groups than do those with low self-esteem. Also, a poor self-image is a risk factor for certain eating disorders, especially bulimia—a connection one of us (Vohs) and her colleagues documented in 1999. Other effects are harder to demonstrate with objective evidence, although we are inclined to accept the subjective evidence that self-esteem goes hand in hand with happiness.

So we can certainly understand how an injection of self-esteem might be valuable to the individual. But imagine if a heightened sense of self-worth prompted some people to demand preferential treatment or to exploit their fellows. Such tendencies would entail considerable social costs. And we have found little to indicate that indiscriminately promoting self-esteem in today's children or adults, just for being themselves, offers society any compensatory benefits beyond the seductive pleasure it brings to those engaged in the exercise.

William B. Swann Jr., et al.

Do People's Self-Views Matter?
Self-Concept and Self-Esteem
in Everyday Life

For most of the past century, a deeply behavioristic field of psychology consigned theory and research on the self-concept and self-esteem to the backwaters of the discipline. Then, in the late 1970s, articles by Kuiper and Rogers, Markus, and others demonstrated that self-views had properties similar to schemas and beliefs—constructs that had recently been championed by cognitive psychologists. In so doing, these researchers legitimized the self-concept as a viable scientific construct. The result was a steep increase in research on the self during the 1980s.

At about the same time, an independent wave of enthusiasm within the lay community thrust the construct of self-esteem into the national limelight. On the basis of precious little evidence, the California Task Force to Promote Self-Esteem and Personal and Social Responsibility characterized self-esteem as a panacea whose cultivation would protect people from a host of ills, including welfare dependency, teenage pregnancy, dropping out of high school, and so on. Thousands of laypersons across America were smitten with the hope that in self-esteem they had found a modern-day Holy Grail.

No longer. With ample justification, members of the academic community pointed out that the extravagant claims of the self-esteem movement were nothing more than that. Yet, in very recent years, the pendulum has swung even further, both reflecting—and inspiring—deep doubts about the viability of the self-esteem construct. Several authors have questioned the utility of self-esteem in predicting important social outcomes, asserting that the effect sizes linking self-esteem to important outcome variables are small and inconsequential. Although some authors have championed more sophisticated strategies for using self-views to predict outcome variables of interest others have thrown up their hands, concluding that the evidentiary basis of self-esteem research is so fundamentally flawed that the entire enterprise should be reexamined. Recently, some of the original critics of self-esteem research have added that because self-esteem appears to be inconsequential, "efforts to boost people's self-esteem are of little value in fostering academic achievement or preventing undesirable behavior."

From *American Psychologist*, vol. 62, no. 2, March 2007, pp. 84–92. Copyright © 2007 by American Psychological Association. Reprinted by permission.

In this article, we place this recent wave of pessimism regarding the importance of self-views in theoretical and historical context. Drawing on past research on attitudes and traits, we propose that recent critiques of global self-esteem have framed the issue in an overly narrow manner and that a broader conceptualization that considers other types of self-views as well (i.e., self-concepts) is needed. With such a conceptualization in hand, we identify several strategies for increasing the predictive validity of self-views, including the use of additional predictor variables and the implementation of several time-tested methodological and psychometric principles. We conclude that our analysis supports a more optimistic assessment of the predictive validity of self-views that justifies theoretically based efforts to improve self-concepts and self-esteem.

Lessons from Three Decades of Psychological Science

. . . We propose that it is not enough for researchers interested in predicting socially important outcomes to focus exclusively on global self-esteem. Instead, researchers should also consider self-concepts and their metacognitive aspects.

To be sure, we are not the first to propose that predictive validity can be enhanced by measuring aspects of self-views other than global self-esteem. Why, then, have recent critics focused exclusively on the predictive utility of global self-esteem? One reason is that, until now, the extravagant claims of the California task force have defined the term of the debate. A second reason is that at least some critics have assumed that self-esteem is "affective" and self-concepts are merely "cognitive," with the implication being that if either of the two constructs would predict important outcomes, it would be self-esteem. Although common, such categorical distinctions between self-esteem and self-concepts have received virtually no empirical support. There is a good reason for this. Clearly, both self-esteem and self-concepts have cognitive as well as emotional elements: just as self-esteem is a cognition about the self (e.g., a belief about how worthwhile one is) as well as a feeling, so too are self-concepts emotional (e.g., people care enormously about personal attributes they deem important) as well as cognitive. From this vantage point, there is little basis for dismissing self-concepts as merely cognitive or for focusing on the predictive capacity of self-esteem at the expense of self-concepts.

We suggest that a more useful framework for assessing the predictive utility of self-views builds on treating self-esteem and self-concepts as members of a common self-view category. From this perspective, both self-esteem and self-concepts refer to thoughts and feelings about the self. People derive these self-views by observing the reactions others have toward them their own behavior, and the relative performances of others. Once formed, self-views give meaning to people's experiences, thereby enabling them to make sense of, and react appropriately to, such experiences. . . .

Specific combinations of certainty and importance can give rise to a metacognitive aspect of the self-view, an aspect that is associated with defensive and narcissistic reactions. Attitude researcher Gross and his colleagues for example, distinguished true certainty in beliefs from "compensatory confidence," with the latter actually reflecting a lack of certainty in the attitude. People with compensatory confidence about their self-views will theoretically be threatened by information that is inconsistent with self-views of which they are uncertain. These feelings of threat may be compounded when the self-view is important, as perceived importance and high goal commitment may trigger emotional reactivity in response to performance feedback. Thus, when people with self-views that are both low in certainty and high in importance encounter threats, an emotional, defensive lashing out may result. This idea is reminiscent of discussions of the narcissistic reactions that theoretically occur when people who are highly invested in uncertain, fragile self-views encounter challenges or threats. All of these perspectives clash sharply with recent efforts to equate the self-protective statements of narcissists with those of people with true high self-esteem. Indeed, we believe that conflating narcissism and true high self-esteem is profoundly problematic for the same reasons that it is problematic to mistake for a friend an enemy who is merely masquerading as a friend. . . .

Predictor–Criterion Relationships: Specificity Matching

A key insight gained by attitude and trait researchers was the specificity or specificity matching principle. This principle was designed to accommodate that fact that in naturally occurring settings, outcomes are typically caused by multiple factors, many of which may be rivals of the particular predictor variable the researcher is studying. To compensate for the influence of such rival predictors, the specificity matching principle holds that the specificity of predictors and criteria should be matched. When the predictor variable is relatively specific, then the impact of rival influences on the predictor–criterion relationship can be minimized by selecting an equally specific behavior (e.g., People's attitudes toward potato chips will predict how many chips they eat in a given year but not the total amount of food they consume that year). When the predictor variable is relatively general, the impact of rival influences can be averaged out by combining numerous behaviors (e.g., General predisposition to eat will predict how much food of all types that one consumes in a given year). In short, specific predictors should be used to predict specific behaviors and general predictors should be used to predict general behaviors. Specificity matching and related principles have received ample support in studies of both attitudes and traits.

Applied to research on the self, the specificity matching principle suggests that researchers interested in predicting relatively specific outcomes (e.g., math proficiency) should use a specific self-concept (e.g., self-perceived math ability) as a predictor rather than a global measure such as self-esteem. Similarly, researchers using global self-esteem as a predictor should focus on global outcome measures, such as several outcomes bundled together. From the perspective of the specificity matching principle, then, recent reviews of the self-esteem literature have violated that specificity matching principle by focusing on the capacity of global measures of self-esteem to predict specific outcomes (e.g., Does self-esteem predict grades in a math class?). It is thus not surprising that researchers have concluded that self-esteem does not predict much of anything.

To determine whether following the specificity matching principle would bolster estimates of the predictive validity of self-views, we examined two research traditions, each of which has approached specificity matching in a distinct way: specific self-views predicting specific behavior and global self-views predicting bundles of behaviors. We attempted to locate meta-analytic reviews that have the advantage of offering explicit criteria for determining which studies to include in a given pool of studies as well as statistical techniques for estimating the strength of relationships.

Specific self-views (academic self-concepts) predicting specific outcomes (academic performance).   In this social cognitive theory, Bandura defined perceptions of self-efficacy as "people's judgments of their capabilities to organize and execute courses of action required to attain designated types of performances." Theoretically, efficacy self-views influence the choices people make, the effort they expend, how long they persevere in the face of challenge, and the degree of anxiety or confidence they bring to the task at hand. Although these perceptions do not alter people's capabilities, they help determine what individuals do with the knowledge and skills they have. Efficacy self-views thus help explain why performances differ among people who have similar knowledge and skills. Consistent with the specificity notion, Bandura insisted that self-efficacy judgments should be specifically rather than globally assessed, must correspond directly to the criterion task, and must be measured as closely as possible in time to that task.

Several meta-analyses have now been conducted that have evaluated the ability of measures of self-efficacy to predict academic outcomes. In one particularly well-controlled analysis, Robbins et al. examined 109 prospective studies in which various psychosocial and study skill factors were used to predict college outcomes. The predictors were categorized into nine broad constructs, such as academic self-efficacy, achievement motivation, academic-related skills, and academic goals. Two college outcomes were targeted: performance, as measured by cumulative grade point average, and persistence, as measured by the length of time a student remained enrolled at an institution toward completion of a degree. Of all the studies analyzed, 18 studies ($N = 9,598$) met the inclusion criteria of academic self-efficacy predicting grade point average. Only academic self-efficacy and achievement motivation were strong predictors (ρs = .50 and .30, respectively, where ρ is the estimated true correlation between the predictor construct and the performance criterion, corrected for measurement error in both the predictor and criterion). An additional six studies ($N = 6,930$) met the inclusion criteria of academic self-efficacy predicting persistence. In this case, academic-related skills, academic self-efficacy, and academic goals were all strong predictors (ρs = .37, .36, and .34, respectively).

Other investigators have shown that as the specificity of the predictor and criterion variables increases, so too does the strength of the relationship between them. For example, in their meta-analysis of a large body of prospective studies, Hansford and Hattie found that relatively specific academic self-concepts offered better predictions of academic ability ($r = .42$) than did global self-esteem ($r = .22$). Similarly, Valentine et al. reported that predictor–outcome associations were stronger when the researchers assessed self-views specific to the academic domain and when measures of self-beliefs and achievement were matched according to subject area. Finally, in their review article, Marsh and Craven concluded that academic self-views predicted several types of academic outcomes, but global self-esteem did not. In one especially striking demonstration of this phenomenon, Marsh, Trautwein, Lüdtke, Köller, and Baumert reported that math self-concept was substantially related to math grades ($r = .71$), math standardized achievement test scores ($r = .59$), and selection of advanced math course ($r = .51$), but global self-esteem was not systematically related to academic self-concepts ($rs = -.03$ to .05). Such findings provide direct support for the notion that the specificity of predictor and criterion variables systematically determines the strength of the relationships observed between them.

The benefits of matching predictors and criterion is also supported by evidence that the predictive validity of self-esteem measures can be bolstered by breaking self-esteem into two components and matching each component with an appropriate criterion variable. Bosson and Swann used the distinction between self-liking and self-competence to bolster their ability to predict the feedback preferences of participants. They found that just as participants' feelings of self-liking (but not self-competence) predicted choice of feedback that confirmed their sense of self-liking, their feelings of self-competence (but not self-liking) predicted their choice of feedback that confirmed their sense of self-competence. This pattern emerged among people who had negative as well as positive self-views. Thus, in the spirit of the specificity matching principle, predictive validity was maximized insofar as predictors and outcomes referred to the same conceptual variable.

Global self-views (self-esteem) predicting bundled outcomes (various indices of adjustment).   Let us preface this section by acknowledging some important nuances in applying the specificity matching principle. One such nuance involves the proper identification of global outcomes. Consider the well-documented finding that low self-esteem predicts subsequent depression. At first glance, this finding may seem to violate that specificity matching principle, as it involves an instance in which a global predictor (self-esteem) is linked to a single criterion (depression). Nevertheless, in reality, clinically diagnosed depression actually represents a global behavior. That is, a diagnosis of clinical depression is typically based on detection of at least five symptoms, including, but not limited to, depressed or irritable mood, diminished interest in activities, insomnia or hypersomnia, fatigue or loss of energy, recurrent thoughts of death, and feelings of worthlessness. Much the same argument applies to most indices of psychological adjustment. In such instances, although a single variable may be used to describe the outcome measure, the fact that the outcome is a summary assessment based on multiple behavioral observations means that it should be considered a global outcome.

With this caveat in hand, we shall discuss a few investigations in which the researchers used measures of global self-esteem to predict global or bundled behaviors. One of the earliest studies that met this criterion was reported by Werner and Smith. These researchers focused on a sample of extremely impoverished youth in the Kauai Longitudinal Study. Self-esteem was assessed using interviews at age 18. When participants were 32 years old, the investigators collected a global measure of quality of adult adaptation. The findings indicate that the self-esteem ratings of teenagers significantly predicted their adaptation 14 years later ($r = .24$ for men, $r = .41$ for women).

More recently, a second team of researchers also reported that self-esteem significantly but weakly predicted specific outcomes and more strongly predicted global outcomes. The initial article reported that low self-esteem predicted externalizing problems two years later. This finding emerged whether they examined self-, teacher-, parent-, or interviewer-based measures of self-esteem and externalizing problems, and for participants from different nationalities (United States and New Zealand) and age groups (adolescents and college students). Moreover, this relation held when the investigators controlled for potential confounding variables such as supportive parenting, parent and peer relationships, socioeconomic status, and IQ. In a follow-up study that built on the methodological strengths of the earlier work, Trzesniewski et al. followed a group of adolescents for 11 years into adulthood. Even after controlling for numerous rival predictors of the outcome measures, the investigators found that self-esteem was a significant predictor of major depressive disorder, anxiety disorder, tobacco dependence, criminal convictions, school dropout, and money and work problems. Once again, these relations held whether the outcome measures were reports by the participants or observers.

Skeptics might point out that most of the effect sizes reported by Donnellan et al. and Trzesniewski et al. seemed small using conventional criteria. Additional findings, however, indicate that the predictive validity of self-esteem was bolstered when outcomes were aggregated. That is, when self-esteem was used to predict global outcomes, teenagers with low self-esteem ran an elevated risk for developing difficulties as adults. For example, among adults with five or more problems during adulthood, 63% had low self-esteem during adolescence and only 15% had high self-esteem during adolescence. Similarly, among problem-free adults, 50% had high self-esteem when they were adolescents and only 16% had low self-esteem during adolescence.

This evidence of the capacity of global self-esteem to predict global outcomes suggests that it may be limiting to frame questions regarding the predictive validity of self-concept and self-esteem in either–or terms as some scholars have. Rather, both types of self-views offer useful predictions as long as the criterion variables are defined at the appropriate level of specificity.

More generally, the findings reported by Donnellan et al. and Trzesniewski et al. are noteworthy in at least three more respects. First, the range and social significance of the outcomes predicted by self-esteem (e.g., depression, anxiety disorders, criminal convictions, school dropout, money and work problems, etc.) are impressive by any standard. Second, numerous potential confounding variables (e.g., depression, neuroticism) were appropriately controlled for, and objective outcome measures were examined. Third, the 11-year time lag between the measure of the predictor and criterion in Trzesniewski et al.'s study was substantial. The fact that self-esteem scores predicted outcomes over such a long period supports the idea that self-esteem can have enduring effects on people. As critics of past research on the predictive validity of self-esteem disparaged the lack of studies using objective measures, longitudinal designs, large representative samples, and appropriate controls to test the predictive utility of self-esteem indices, the methodological features of Donnellan et al. and Trzesniewski et al. counter critics who have claimed that measures of self-esteem predict outcome variables only because they happen to be correlated with variables that are causally related to these outcome variables. In short, although the Donnellan–Trzesniewski team's research was correlational, its methodological features help make the case that self-esteem exerted a causal impact on the outcome variables. . . .

Is It Worthwhile to Try to Improve Self-Views?

If self-views are meaningfully related to socially significant outcomes, does this mean that it makes sense to take steps to improve those self-views? We believe that it does. Furthermore, contrary to the critics of self-esteem research who "have not found evidence that boosting self-esteem (by therapeutic interventions or school programs) causes benefits," we have encountered evidence that programs designed to improve self-esteem improve standardized test scores, reduce school disciplinary reports, and reduce use of drugs and alcohol.

In acknowledging empirical support for the efficacy of programs designed to improve self-esteem, we must emphasize that such evidence should be treated cautiously because little is known about the precise mediators of these effects. Indeed, at this juncture, what is needed is careful, theory-driven research designed to specify how effective self-esteem programs work. Such mediational research is vitally important for two reason. First, of the effective programs of which we are aware, all are multifaceted schemes that include efforts to improve self-efficacy and interpersonal relationships as well as self-esteem. Because the effectiveness of the individual components (focus on changing self-views, modifying social skills, academic achievement, or other behaviors, etc.) of these programs is rarely, if ever, documented, it is quite possible that such programs include a mix of effective and ineffective strategies (or strategies that are effective for some people but ineffective for others). If so, the effectiveness of such programs could be enhanced still further by bolstering the effective components and eliminating the ineffective ones.

Identifying the effective components of such programs could also help silence critics by distinguishing treatments based on nonsense from those based on psychological principles. Consider the caricatures of self-esteem programs occasionally supplied by the media. Perhaps the best known example is satirist Al Franken's parody of self-esteem enhancement programs in which his character on *Saturday Night Live* (Stuart Smalley) gazed tentatively into the mirror, smiled, and then carefully recited, "I'm good enough, I'm smart enough, and gosh darn it, people like me". The newly esteemed Smalley then beamed triumphantly. This scenario was amusing because it was so obvious to everyone (except Stuart) that such affirmation procedures are hopelessly misguided.

Clearly, people cannot magically affirm their way into possessing high self-esteem. For this reason, any program organized around such affirmation procedures will (at best) produce positive self-images that are fanciful and ephemeral. Note, however, that although some self-esteem enhancement programs indeed are based on such simple-minded strategies, these Panglossian strategies are a far cry from the demonstrably effective ones reviewed in the recent literature. Instead of focusing exclusively on people's momentary self-esteem, the effective programs emphasize procedures that are also designed to alter the raw materials that are also designed to alter the raw materials that provide a basis for healthy, sustainable self-esteem. Ideally, these programs cultivate behaviors that produce self-views that are both realistic (i.e., based on objective evidence) and adaptive (i.e., emphasizing activities that are predictive of long-term adjustment in society). Therefore, the principles that underlie such programs make sound theoretical sense, and it is misleading and unfortunate to confuse them with programs that do not. Furthermore, these programs are effective; although the effect sizes are modest, they compare favorably with other types of interventions that are designed to change similar behaviors, self-reported personality functioning, and academic performance.

Skeptics could hypothetically object: "If the active ingredients in self-esteem change programs involve changing people's behaviors and life circumstances as well as their self-views, then perhaps improved self-esteem is an effect of such programs rather than a key ingredient in such programs. Indeed, calling these programs 'Self-esteem enhancement programs' is a misnomer because they do so much more than that."

We believe that it is legitimate to point out that although self-esteem enhancement is the overarching goal of such programs, the strategies through which this end is pursued often involve changing the behaviors and situations that feed into people's self-views rather than the self-views per se. That said, we also believe that it is misguided to underestimate the critically important role that changing self-views ultimately plays in such programs. Rather, just as it is not enough to change self-views only, so too is it not enough to change people's behaviors and life circumstances only.

Imagine, for example, a school boy who has a negative self-view that leads him to be hostile to his classmates. Thinking that a new environment might improve matters, the school counselor arranges to have the boy transferred to a new classroom in which the boy is unknown. Although the boy's new environment may be more benign initially, his self-view may inspire behaviors that quickly bring his classmates to see him just as negatively as he sees himself. And even if his classmates are slow to reciprocate the boy's hostile overtures, his negative self-views may nevertheless cause him to "see" their behaviors as more negative than they actually are. Moreover should he experience failure in this new setting, the research literature suggests that his negative self-views will hamper his coping ability. That is, research suggests that in the wake of failure experiences, people with negative self-views are more likely to suffer emotional trauma and impaired motivation than are people with positive self-views. For example, Greenberg et al. showed that whereas people whose self-views had been bolstered by personality feedback displayed relatively little anxiety in response to the threat of a shock, those whose self-views had not been bolstered suffered considerable anxiety. In these and other ways, negative self-views may sabotage people's ability to cope successfully with events in their lives. . . .

Summary and Conclusions

From this vantage point, people's self-views do matter, and the task of future researchers is to determine how, when, and with what consequences. This conclusion has direct implications for programs designed to change self-views. That is, given that people with negative self-views think and behave in ways that diminish their quality of life, it is incumbent on behavioral scientists to develop and refine strategies for improving these negative self-views.

CHALLENGE QUESTIONS

Are Efforts to Improve Self-Esteem Misguided?

- Both sides agree that opinions about self-esteem have involved a lot of misunderstandings. What seem to be the crucial misunderstandings about self-esteem, and how do those influence your response to the issue at hand?
- Why is self-esteem such a difficult issue to research? Why do you think so much research has been done on self-esteem, and yet it is still difficult to draw clear conclusions?
- Baumeister et al. suggest that self-esteem is more than just limited in its ability to help individuals, but rather it is something of a social problem. Do you think the other side would agree that self-esteem has social and cultural influence?
- Swann and colleagues suggest that when people talk about "self-esteem" they are really talking about things such as cognitive self-views and self-efficacy. Does that seem right? When you think about self-esteem, what does it mean to you?

Suggested Readings

R. F. Baumeister, "Should Schools Try to Boost Self-Esteem?" *American Educator* (Summer 1996)

R. Baumeister, J. Campbell, J. Krueger, and K. Vohs, "Exploding the Self-Esteem Myth," *Scientific American* (January 2005)

P. Bronson, "How Not to Talk to Your Kids: The Inverse Power of Praise," *New York Magazine* (February 9, 2007)

J. Crocker and L. Park, "The Costly Pursuit of Self-Esteem," *Psychological Bulletin* (2004)

M. Donnellan, K. Trzesniewski, R. Robins, T. Moffitt, and A. Caspi, "Low Self-Esteem Is Related to Aggression, Antisocial Behavior, and Delinquency," *Psychological Science* (April 2005)

D. DuBois and B. Flay, "The Healthy Pursuit of Self-Esteem: Comment on and Alternative to the Crocker and Park (2004) Formulation," *Psychological Bulletin* (2004)

D. L. DuBois and H. D. Tevendale, "Self-Esteem in Childhood and Adolescence: Vaccine or Epiphenonmenon?" *Applied & Preventative Psychology* (1999)

Carol S. Dweck, "Caution—Praise Can Be Dangerous," *American Educator* (Spring 1999)

A. Kohn, "Five Reasons to Stop Saying 'Good Job'," *Young Children* (September 2001)

D. Michaels, "The Trouble with Self-Esteem," *The New York Times Magazine* (February 3, 2002)

S. Rubin, "Self Esteem and Your Child," *Pull-Through Network News* http://www.pullthrough.org/ptnn8.html (accessed October 2005)

R. Sylvester, "The Neurobiology of Self-Esteem and Aggression," *Educational Leadership* (February 1997)

ISSUE 11

Should Contemporary Adolescents Be Engaged in More Structured Activities?

YES: Joseph L. Mahoney, Angel L. Harris, and Jacquelynne S. Eccles, from "Organized Activity Participation, Positive Youth Development, and the Over-Scheduling Hypothesis," *Social Policy Report* (August 2006)

NO: Alvin Rosenfeld, from "Comments on 'Organized Activity Participation, Positive Youth Development, and the Over-Scheduling Hypothesis'," http://www.hyper-parenting.com/

ISSUE SUMMARY

YES: Psychologist Joseph Mahoney and colleagues recognize the concern about "over-scheduling" but present research suggesting that the benefits to structured activities outweigh any costs.

NO: Child psychiatrist Alvin Rosenfeld asserts that all of the data suggest that most youth and adolescents need less structured activity and more balance.

Structured activities, including sports, music, academics, drama productions, and more, have become a standard part of many adolescent experiences. These activities, with their promise of a safe environment for enriching experiences, are popular with diverse constituencies from parents and educators to policymakers and scholars. From a developmental perspective, however, the phenomenon of a highly structured youth brings both opportunities and risks. While structured activities and youth organizations provide many rich opportunities for adolescents, structured time also has the potential to put stress on youth and families while taking away the joy and creativity that can come from free leisure.

Because of these two potential outcomes, the growing availability of structured activities has been accompanied by a growing concern that some children are over-scheduled. News outlets are reporting on youth and families that spend so much time with structured activities that the teens end up deprived of sleep and the families end up without any significant time together. Scholars have also been pointing out concerns in books such as *The Hurried Child* and *The Power of Play* by developmental psychologist David Elkind and *Unequal Childhoods* by sociologist Annette Lareau. This work describes fatigued and overwhelmed youth whom child psychiatrist Alvin Rosenfield and journalist Nicole Wise categorized in a 2000 book as *The Over-Scheduled Child*.

While the image of the over-scheduled child may seem familiar from the media, developmental psychologists Joseph Mahoney et al. realized that there was little direct research investigating broad issues related to the scheduling of today's youth. They thus compiled a review of new and existing research addressing specific issues related to structured activity participation, and empirically tested what they phrase "the over-scheduling hypothesis." In the selection, which is excerpted from their work, they find that overall, youth seem more likely to be under-scheduled than over-scheduled.

Mahoney and colleagues frame their work in relation to the emerging scholarly field of "positive youth development," which focuses on how to create environments for successful development. The general consensus is that structured activities are part of such environments, and few would disagree that activities can be a beneficial part of anyone's childhood years. But that does not necessarily mean the more the better.

Perhaps we are at a point where the quantity of structured activities has become too much of a good thing? This is the position articulated by child psychiatrist Alvin Rosenfeld in response to Mahoney and his colleagues. Rosenfeld thinks that Mahoney et al. have over-simplified the issue by comparing youth who participate in activities with youth who participate in no activities. Rosenfeld notes that structured activities are such a common part of growing up today that the children who do not participate at all are the exception. From Rosenfeld's perspective the important thing is to balance reasonable amounts of structured activity participation with free leisure and family life.

POINT

- Most children participate in activities because they enjoy them, and do not experience undue pressure.

- On average, American youth actually spend very little time directly participating in structured activities.

- There is a consistently positive relationship between activity participation and healthy developmental outcomes.

- By claiming that children are over-scheduled there may be an impetus to cut much-needed funding for positive youth development programs.

COUNTERPOINT

- The effects are not just on youth, but also on stressed parents and family life in general.

- The real goal is a balance of activities and free time. It is unreasonable to compare youth who are participating in no activities because the contemporary norm is to participate in some.

- Data suggest that moderation is best regarding structured activity participation, and there have been notable declines in family life during recent decades.

- Identifying over-scheduling does not seem to lead to cuts in funds for activity programs.

YES ⤹   Joseph L. Mahoney, Angel L. Harris, and Jacquelynne S. Eccles

Organized Activity Participation, Positive Youth Development, and the Over-Scheduling Hypothesis

School-aged children in the US and other Western nations average 40–50% of their waking hours in discretionary activities outside of school. There has been increasing awareness that how young people use this time has consequences for their development. As a result, research on the risks and benefits of a variety of after-school activities has been expanding rapidly and considerable attention has been devoted to school-age children's (ages 5–11) and adolescents' (ages 12–18) involvement in organized activities. Organized activities occur outside of the school day and are characterized by structure, adult-supervision, and an emphasis on skill-building. Common activities include school-based extracurricular activities (e.g., sports, clubs, and fine arts), after-school (i.e., programs, often targeted to youth between the ages 5–14, that provide participants with adult supervision during the afternoon hours while many parents are working and offer opportunities for academic assistance, recreation, and/or enrichment learning) and community-based programs and youth organizations (e.g., 4-H, Boys & Girls Clubs of America, and Girls, Inc). Organized activities can be contrasted with alternative ways that young people spend their discretionary time such as educational activities, household chores, watching television, playing games, hanging out, and employment.

Participation in organized activities is a common developmental experience for young people. For example, the 1999 National Survey of America's Families (NSAF) reported that 81% of 6- to 11-year-olds and 83% of 12- to 17-year-olds participated in one or more sports, lessons, or clubs during the past year. Approximately 7 million children are enrolled in after-school programs. Millions more participate in community-based programs and youth organizations such as 4-H, Boys & Girls Clubs of America, and Girls Inc. Moreover, national studies show that participation in some organized activities such as sports and before/after-school programs has increased significantly in recent years.

The growth of organized activities has resulted from several factors. First, there has been an expansion of local, state, and Federal expenditures to

From *Social Policy Report*, vol. XX, no. IV, 2006, pp. excerpts from 3–5, 14–15, 18–19, 21–22. Copyright © 2006 by Society for Research in Child Development. Reprinted by permission. Reference omitted.

support organized activities. A well–known example is the increase in Federal support for 21st-Century Community Learning Center grants that support after-school programs. This funding grew exponentially from $40 million in 1998 to $1 billion in 2002. Second, the historic rise in maternal employment has resulted in a gap between the school day of children and work day of their parents. This fact, coupled with research pointing to dangers for children who are unsupervised during the after-school hours, has called attention to orga-nized activities as a means to provide safety and supervision for children with working parents. Finally, on balance, the bulk of research on organized activi-ties has shown positive consequences of participation for academic, educa-tional, social, civic, and physical development.

In combination, these factors have increased awareness that organized activities represent a valuable resource for promoting positive youth develop-ment. This in evident in the out-of-school initiatives of major research intui-tions (e.g., Chapin Hall Center for Children, Harvard Family Research Project), granting institutions and foundations (e.g., C. S. Mott Foundation, W. T. Grant Foundation), advocacy and lobbying groups (e.g., Afterschool Alliance, Fight Crime Invest in Kids, National Institute on Out-of-School Time, National School-Aged Care Alliance), as well as the initiation of a bipar-tisan Congressional After-school Caucus in March 2005.

The Over-Scheduling Hypothesis

At the same time that initiatives to expand opportunities for organized activ-ity participation have been increasing, concern exists that some youth are participating in too many organized activities. Written and televised media reports and popular parenting books suggest that the lives of many young people are now replete with hurry, stress, and pressure brought on, in part, because of their involvement in too many organized activities. These articles maintain that an over-scheduling of organized activity participation may undermine family functioning and youth well-being.

With respect to organized activities, the over-scheduling hypothesis is based on three interrelated propositions. First, the motivation for participa-tion in organized activities is viewed as extrinsic. Youth are seen as taking part in a variety of activities because of the perceived pressure from parents or other adults to achieve and attain long-term educational and career goals (e.g., a college scholarship). Second, the time commitment required of children and parents to participate in organized activities is believed to be so extensive that traditional family activities—dinnertime, family outings, and even simple dis-cussions between parents and children—are sacrificed. Finally, owing to the assumed pressures from parents, coupled with the extensive time commit-ment and disruption of family functioning, youth devoting high amounts of time to organized activity participation are thought to be at risk for develop-ing adjustment problems and poor relationships with parents.

Although the basis for these propositions has been seldom anchored by empirical research, scientific evidence has been used to advance the notion that some youth (particularly middle class and affluent youth) are over-scheduled in some cases and that such over-scheduling can be detrimental to the optimal development of young people and their families. This evidence draws on qualitative studies of how organized activity participation affects family life and quantitative studies suggesting that perceived pressure from parents and other adults (e.g., coaches, teachers) may lead to poor adjustment particularly for affluent youth (i.e., families whose annual household earnings are at least twice as high the medium annual income for families in the US). As far as we know, the argument has not been directed to poor or working-class youth and there have been no studies of this issue focused on less advantaged populations.

Whether youth participate in organized activities depends, in part, on the behavior of their parents. Studies of children and adolescents suggest that they are more likely to become involved and to stay involved in organized activities when parents value and encourage their participation, provide the necessary material resources, and are participants themselves. However, a recent ethnographic study conducted with children (ages 9–10) from 12 diverse families suggests that organized activity schedules can determine the pace of life for all family members. The findings from Lareau's study show that the time budgeting and schedule commitments required of parents to support their children's activity participation can be challenging—particularly for working parents with several children. The qualitative accounts also suggest that participation in many organized activities can limit children's down time and constrain the nature parent-child interactions. While her study has been used to justify the inference that such scheduling might be problematic, Lareau did not actually investigate the children's well-being. Moreover, a systematic evaluation of how time spent in organized activities may affect discretionary time or parent-child interactions was not a goal of this study. Finally, although provocative, the findings are based on a small number of families and this raises concern about whether the results can be generalized beyond the study sample.

Quantitative studies suggesting possible risks for affluent adolescents have also been cited in support of the over-scheduling hypothesis. For example, in one of a few relevant studies, Luthar and her colleagues concluded, first, that adolescents (6th and 7th graders) from affluent homes can be at greater risk for substance use, depression, and anxiety as they enter adolescence than children living in less affluent homes, and, second, that excessive achievement pressures and isolation from parents may help to explain these associated risks. However, this research did not assess the association between time spent participating in organized activities and achievement pressures or adolescent adjustment. Accordingly, these studies neither intended to nor do they provide evidence that adolescents (affluent or otherwise) perceive pressure to participate in organized activities from their parents or are at-risk for adjustment problems as a result of their participation.

Our interest in conducting an evaluation of the scientific underpinnings of these propositions is twofold: First, these propositions suggest negative consequences resulting from too much organized activity participation. This has the potential to undermine recent efforts to support and expand opportunities for youth to participate in organized activities. Because policy decisions concerning children and families will be made with or without the use of scientific knowledge, this concern holds despite the limited evidence on which the over-scheduling hypothesis is based. Indeed, the response to findings from the national evaluation of 21st-Century Community Learning Centers show that substantial reductions in funding for organized activities can be proposed on the basis of a single study with controversial findings.

Second, despite research available to inform propositions of the over-scheduling hypothesis, the scientific community has been relatively silent on this issue. As the value and worth of psychological research depends increasingly on an appropriate and timely integration of science with policy, it is essential that the existing research informing this matter be communicated. To that end, one of our major goals is to evaluate the scientific basis of the over-scheduling hypothesis. Our second major goal is to evaluate the evidence for the alternative positive youth development perspective; namely, that participation in organized activities facilitates positive development and that more participation is associated with more positive development. . . .

Discussion

In this paper, we have explored two perspectives regarding the relation of organized activity participation and development: the positive youth development perspective and the over-scheduling perspective. On the one hand, advocates of positive youth development have argued that participation in organized activities facilitate optimal development and therefore policymakers should provide more opportunities for American youth to be involved in such activities. On the other hand, some writers have suggested that participating in organized activities has become excessive for some young people, owing, in part, to achievement pressures from parents and other adults. These authors maintain that external pressures, along with the activity-related time commitment, can contribute to poor psychosocial adjustment for youth and to undermine relationships with parents. If this is the case, then attention from scientists, practitioners, and policymakers are warranted. Our goal was to bring scientific evidence to bear on both of these perspectives.

The available research base provides far more support for the positive youth perspective than for the over-scheduling perspective. To begin, the belief that organized activity participation is often motivated by parental pressure to achieve or attain long-term educational and career goals is not supported by the limited available empirical data. Overwhelmingly, the primary reasons adolescents give for participating in organized activities are intrinsic and focus on the here and now. This holds for the few studies that sampled affluent and suburban youth with relatively high levels of involvement in organized activities. However, there is a paucity of information on whether the reasons for participation vary according to either the amount or type of organized activity participation, or the age and other demographic characteristics of the participants and their families. We need to know much more about the relation between the participants' and their parents' motivations, goals, values, and expectations and the choices children/adolescents make about their discretionary time, in general, and the amount of time they devote to various types of organized activities, more specifically.

On the basis of time alone, very few American youth devote enough time to organized activities to be classified as "over-scheduled." For example, youth in the PSID-CDS—the only nationally representative sample of American youth with time use data—averaged about 5 hours/week in organized activities on any given week during the school year; furthermore, roughly 40% of the PSID-CDS youth did not participate in any organized activities and those who did typically spent fewer than 10 hours/week doing so. Comparable estimates emerged in the other studies we reviewed. These findings suggest that organized activities do not dominate the vast majority of American youth's free time. Instead, the majority of their time is consumed by other leisure pursuits such as watching television, educational activities, playing games, hanging out, and personal care. In other words, given the considerable amount of discretion time typically available to young Americans, most appear able to balance their organized activity participation effectively with school-related tasks, family time, informal socializing with peers, and relaxing. Nevertheless, there was evidence in some of the studies reviewed as well as in the PSID-CDS analyses reported in this paper, of a subgroup of youth (3% of children and 6% of adolescents) who spend a very high amount of time (20 or more hours/week) participating in organized activities. Are these youth poorly adjusted as a result of their high levels of participation in organized activities? By and large the evidence suggests not. Like their slightly less involved peers, they appear to be functioning better than non-involved youth. We discuss this more later.

In general, youth who participate in organized activities score better on a variety of indicators of healthy development than youth who do not participate. For example, those PSID-CDS youth who participated in organized activities for fewer than 20 hours/week scored better than the youth who did not participate in any activities on all of the indicators of well-being. This finding was true for all of the studies we reviewed and is consistent with the evidence summarized by Eccles and Gootman in their 2002 report for the National Research Council and the Institute of Medicine on the Community Based Programs for Youth. Thus, reliable support for the benefits of participation in organized activities emerged across studies and these benefits, by and large, become stronger with increased participation. Although the scheduling of responsibilities surrounding organized activities can sometimes be challenging for families, the associated benefits of participation are apparent nonetheless.

What about those youth who participate a great deal? Once again the findings across studies provide very limited support for the hypothesis that too much participation can be harmful. Many of the existing studies find a linear increase in the psychological, social, and academic well-being of youth as the number of organized activities or weekly hours of participation increases. Other studies report a curvilinear trend such that the well-being of youth with very extreme levels of involvement may level off or decline somewhat; however, these studies do not provide evidence that even very high amounts participation confers risk. The findings regarding the well-being of the extreme 6% of PSID-CDS youth who participated in organized activities 20 or more hours/week are generally consistent with these other studies. Clearly, the White youth who participated for 20 or more hours/week were better off than those White youth who did not participate in any activities on all but one of the indicators assessed: They reported higher levels of self-esteem and psychological and emotional well-being; lower alcohol, marijuana, and cigarette use; and ate meals with their parents and engaged in discussion with them more frequently. The only potentially negative finding for these White youth was that shared activities with their parents occurred less frequently. The findings for PSID-CDS Black youth were less consistent. On the one hand, the Black youth who participated in organized activities for 20 or more hours/week had higher reading achievement; reported higher emotional well-being; lower alcohol, marijuana, and cigarette use; and ate meals together with their parents more frequently than their Black peers who did not participate in any organized activities. On the other hand, these Black youth also reported less frequent parent-adolescent discussions and lower self-esteem and psychological well-being than their Black peers who did not participate.

The reasons for few the negative findings from the PSID-CDS and other studies need to be investigated before policy implications can be drawn. They may or may not be indicators of a negative impact of over-scheduling on adolescent development. For example, in the PSID-CDS, the fact that older adolescents may spend somewhat less time with their parents is not necessarily an indication of problems. Instead it could reflect normative increases in autonomy among competent young people. Thus, more needs to be known about the causes and consequences of this association before drawing any conclusions about whether they imply a developmental risk in these adolescents' lives. Likewise, the finding by Luthar et al. that a very small group of early adolescent females from affluent families demonstrated high internalizing symptoms and poor school adjustment when they were both highly involved in academic activities and perceived their parents as critical and overly achievement-oriented requires additional study before conclusions concerning over-scheduling can be made. One possibility is that a high amount of activity participation is associated with adjustment problems primarily for youth who do not receive positive support from their parents. This is consistent with research showing that activity-related support and encouragement from parents plays an important role in youths' enrollment and continued participation in organized activities. Parent-adolescent relations may also help to explain why the PSID-CDS findings showed that a very high amount of organized activity participation was associated with lower self-esteem and psychological well-being for Black adolescents; these same youth also reported a low frequency of parent-adolescent discussions. However, other studies have found have found a positive, linear association between the amount of organized activity participation and self-esteem during adolescence. Thus, to understand better what underlies these associations, process-oriented longitudinal research is needed. Moreover, given the many associated benefits of participation for other areas of their adjustment, follow-up studies are required to assess whether these highly involved adolescents are at risk for poor adjustment in the long term.

Despite these few possible risks of very high levels of activity participation, we do not believe efforts to limit adolescents' participation in organized activities are warranted for several reasons. First, across all studies reviewed, those few youth with very high levels of organized activity participation did not show negative adjustment in most of the indicators assessed and they demonstrated significantly healthier functioning than non-participants on many indicators of well-being. Furthermore, there is evidence that greater amounts of participation are positively associated with civic engagement, high school graduation, and college attendance, and are negatively related to antisocial behaviors and criminal offending. Therefore, even if a causal relation exists between very high amounts of participation and some negative outcomes, it is not clear that the cumulative effect of limiting participation for this extreme subgroup would be positive or negative.

Second, none of the studies reviewed in this report focused on stability and change in the amount of organized activity participation over time. Therefore, they tell us nothing about whether the very high amounts of participation that characterizes a small subgroup of youth is stable or transient across adolescence. It is possible that some youth extend their time commitment in organized activities to a very high level for a limited time. During this time, certain indicators of well-being may decline somewhat. However, this does not imply that such youth maintain a very high level of participation across all of adolescence or that their long-term well-being is compromised as a result. To evaluate whether this is the cause, longitudinal data measuring adolescents' time use and well-being over time are required.

Third, the existing research concerning amount of organized activity participation and youth adjustment has only begun to examine whether findings vary according to individual characteristics or features of the activity context. For example, studies of high-risk youth show that a lack of organized activity participation predicts poor academic adjustment and high rates of obesity, school dropout, and crime. For these youth, even a very high amount of organized activity participation may be better than spending time in arrangements that lack adult supervision or do not provide opportunities to build competencies. Likewise, the consequences of high amounts of participation are certain to depend on the features of the activity considered. Participation in high-quality organized activities is likely to be associated with positive youth development across the full range of hours considered in this report. In contrast, participation in activities that are poorly designed is predictive of relatively poor adjustment. Thus, attention to person and program features is needed before making decisions concerning the small proportion of youth who demonstrate very high amounts of organized activity participation.

Fourth, attention to person and program features is also relevant when interpreting the somewhat small effect sizes reported in some studies reviewed in this report. For example, results from Marsh's study indicate that, across the multiple significant and positive outcomes, the well-being of youth who were highly involved in organized activities youth was, on average, .22 *SD* (range .05–.58) above that of youth who did not participate. Results from the PSID-CDS showed that the time spent in organized activities explained an average of 8.8% of variance in the adolescent outcomes considered. Because youth typically spend much less time in organized activities than in other contexts (e.g., school and family), the associated impact of participation in any one area of adjustment should ordinarily be modest. However, in regard to the positive youth development perspective, such effects sizes are reported consistently across a broad array of outcomes and, therefore, are large enough to be of practical importance. In addition, research suggests that the magnitude of activity-related benefits may be greatest for: 1) youth who show stable participation over time; 2) those at the highest risk for poor developmental outcomes; 3) when long-term indicators of well-being are considered; and 4) when the quality of the program is high. Thus, there are likely to be many youth for whom participating in organized activities has a very large and positive effect. Similarly, to the extent that some youth participate in low-quality organized activities, the average effect sizes reported may have been diminished. Given the positive associations identified in the PSID-CDS and the other studies reviewed, one conclusion that is possible is that we need to provide America's youth with more, rather than less, opportunities to participate in high-quality, organized activities.

Finally, we note some parallels between the findings connected to organized activity participation and those pertaining adolescent participation in the paid labor force. Both become normative developmental experiences during adolescence, show variability according the family earnings and race, are viewed as a source of preparation for adult roles and responsibilities, and call attention to a small proportion of youth with very high levels of involvement—the consequences of which appear mixed. In the youth employment literature, research on working conditions and quality, reasons that motivate long hours of work, and long-term follow-ups have helped to clarify the pros/cons of young people who work extended hours. These types of studies suggest next steps for research aimed at understanding better the consequences of very high amounts of organized activity participation.

Our overall conclusion is that there is scant support for the over-scheduling hypothesis and considerable support for the positive youth development perspective. As such, we recommend that recent efforts to expand opportunities for organized activity participation should stay the course. For the vast majority of young people, participation in organized activities is positively associated with indicators of well-being. Of greater concern than the over-scheduling of youth in organized activities is the fact that many youth do not participate at all. The well-being of youth who do not participate in organized activities is reliably less positive compared to youth who do participate.

Alvin Rosenfeld

"Organized Activity Participation, Positive Youth Development, and the Over-Scheduling Hypothesis," by Mahoney, Harris, and Eccles

Testing sociological hypotheses is difficult, so Mahoney, Harris, and Eccles should be commended for trying to approach a very complex child rearing question in a scientific fashion. Although these authors follow many well-accepted standards for empirical research, their study is based, in part, on an inaccurate account of Wise and my work and a questionable interpretation of their own data. The authors' conclusions are overly broad and their recommendations may misinform readers, persuading ambitious parents that over-scheduling their children is a scientifically validated way to raise emotionally well, academically successful children. In my opinion, that could have very unfortunate consequences.

Mahoney, Harris, and Eccles' paper contains serious shortcomings. I will name those I consider most important:

1. ***Mahoney, Harris, and Eccles misrepresent our work:*** Mahoney, Harris, and Eccles' paper tests "the overscheduling hypothesis," attributed in part to *The Over-Scheduled Child* (Griffin/St. Martin's, 2001) by Rosenfeld and Wise. Unfortunately, this "over-scheduling hypothesis" is a creation of their own that bears only scant resemblance to our work. For instance, Mahoney, Harris, and Eccles write that "the overscheduling hypothesis predicts that youth with very high amounts of organized activity participation will demonstrate poor adjustment relative to both those ***with little or no participation*** [italics added] and those with moderate amounts of participation." In their opinion, testing that contention will test the validity of what Wise, I, and others have said. Wise and I have never suggested that children do better if they participate in no activities nor have we posited that children who are in numerous organized activities do worse than ***those who do none***. In fact, we repeatedly call for balance in families, where activities, education, family time, and down time all get sufficient attention. We write that up to a point, enrichment activities can benefit children. When asked, we have

responded that young children who participate in no activities should be urged—even forced—to try some out. We also write that the contemporary pressure to fill every moment with activities can frazzle children *and parents*, diminish the amount of quiet time families spend together, make parents and children resentful and critical, and de-emphasize the importance of creativity and character development.

2. *After creating an inaccurate, simplistic version of Wise and my work and labeling it "the overscheduling hypothesis," the authors design a study—using existing time-use survey data collected for other purposes—to test it:* After grossly misrepresenting our work, Mahoney, Harris, and Eccles compare children who participate in many activities to those in a "no activity" group, arguing—erroneously—that we say the "no activity" group should be doing better. In addition to misrepresenting our position, this comparison is highly flawed. Likely, the "no activity" group is quite diverse; some percentage of it probably does no activities because they are drop-outs, acting out, have failed at school subjects and so are not allowed to participate, etc. Comparing these kids to almost any other group—other than perhaps to foster children and incarcerated youth—would prove the second group, however composed, to be doing better. Mahoney, Harris, and Eccles have selected a well-known marker of poor adjustment—as indicated by the children's partaking in no activities that are normative for their age—and used it as a normative comparison group. They then reverse cause and effect, saying that these children are doing less well because they are not in activities.

3. *Some of Mahoney, Harris, and Eccles' findings support our actual position:* What does Mahoney, Harris, and Eccles' data actually show? In some ways, rather than contradicting our ideas, it supports the position that we put forth, suggesting that balance is best. In published reports, Mahoney maintains that "the more activities they do, the better kids stack up on measures of educational achievement and psychological adjustment" (Newsweek). However, some of Mahoney, Harris, and Eccles' own data suggests the opposite: Black youth spending over 20 hours a week in organized activities had self-esteem lower even than those who participated in no organized activities and far lower than those who participate in a moderate number. Adolescents in 15 or more hours of scheduled activities drink more alcohol than those with 5–15 hours. White youth with 20 or more hours of organized activities report fewer shared activities with parents and doing fewer favorite activities with parents than did youth with 5–15 hours of activities. Black youth with more than 15 hours of organized activities reported fewer shared activities with parents than did those with 5–15 hours of activities; those with more than 20 hours of scheduled activities spent less time with parent-child favorite activities than did those with 10–20 hours of scheduled activities. Black youth with more than 20 hours of activities had fewer parent-adolescent discussions than did any other group, even those with no activities. Reading achievement for black youth doing over 15 hours of organized activities is significantly below those of adolescents doing 5–15 hours. Reading achievement

for white youths doing over 20 hours a week of organized activities is almost identical to those doing *no* organized activities and substantially below those doing moderate activity (though the authors' state that this did not reach statistical significance.) To us, this data seems to support our contention that a balanced number of activities is best rather than the idea that the more the better.

4. *The Mahoney, Harris, and Eccles study lacks observational data and does not include travel time:* The study analyzes data based on self-reports. As such, the data is subject to all the well known difficulties non-observational studies are prone to. It relies on time diaries asking people to put down everything they did in a 24 hour period. However, these diaries are written up to three days after a weekday set of activities and up to a week after a weekend day. It is highly questionable that a week after the events, people can accurately remember their activities and how much time they spent on each for an entire 24 hour period which may explain why Mahoney, Harris, and Eccles' study cannot account for how 13–14% of the time is spent. Furthermore, the study does not include travel time. Mahoney, Harris, and Eccles overlook the reality that many families have several children. A parent with three children each with three activities may spend four hours a day driving between activities. In our experience, this driving schedule creates substantial irritation, particularly among highly educated mothers; they love their kids but resent feeling they have become chauffeurs. It also leads to some siblings becoming "car potatoes."

5. *Mahoney, Harris, and Eccles approach the subject simply from the active child's perspective, discounting the effects on other family members:* The omission of travel time is part of Mahoney, Harris, and Eccles' general discounting of parental stress. Their study states, "although the scheduling of responsibilities surrounding organized activities can sometimes be challenging for families (Lareau, 2003), the associated benefits of participation are apparent nonetheless." It seems that they regard a child or adolescent seeming to be doing well by questionnaire report as a sufficient outcome marker. This runs diametrically against observational data, including our own clinical observations. Our books stress the importance of the whole family's needs being taken into account, *including the parents'.* Mahoney, Harris, and Eccles seem to contend that no matter how much the parents sacrifice and no matter how resentful they may feel, their kids do well in the long run if they have more activities. Much of the literature about over-scheduled children speaks of the ways the parents *feel* about leading stressed, overscheduled, and often frenzied lives. Mahoney, Harris, and Eccles do not take these into account.

In contrast, our books, and my talks since the book was published, speak of the need for parents to be sure that they are enjoying their lives because in my clinical experience parents who are satisfied with their situation—rather than feeling frenzied much of the time—have kids who do better. We repeatedly argue against one-size-fits-all solutions and speak of how in arriving at the number and types of activities that are suitable for the family as a whole, each family needs to balance the child's temperament and desires with the number of children in the family and the parents' abilities, capacity, needs, and schedules. We have said that some children—in our experience, often ambitious first born children—want to do everything and need to be reined in a bit. Other children are "couch potatoes" and need to be encouraged, even forced, to partake in organized activities.

6. *Mahoney, Harris, and Eccles discount a large body of data to the contrary and feel that results from their single, flawed study are sufficiently robust to conclude that the more scheduled activities children have, the better:* The conclusions Mahoney, Harris, and Eccles draw from this study seem to run contrary to what numerous experienced observers have noted. We will note just a few: Studies show that in just the past 20 years household conversations have become far less frequent and family dinners have declined 33%. Numerous observers have spoken of sleep deprivation among high achieving adolescents. This study does not even acknowledge that sleep deprivation may be a significant issue among over-scheduled children, nor does it note that as children's sports have become pro-fessionalized, orthopedic surgeons have reported an alarming increase of stress related sports and overuse injuries among 5–14 year olds. They ignore work that shows that homework among middles schoolers has grown dramatically and that some scholars feel that the high amount spent could actually harm children. They report but discount the findings, including their own, of higher levels of alcohol use among adolescents with many activities. We have noted that resumes are being shaped for what elite colleges supposedly expect; we and others have commented that community service no longer is a sign of a good heart but a box that must be checked. Speaking of over-scheduled youth, Harvard University's admissions director said that admitted freshman, and we paraphrase, look like the dazed survivors of a life long boot camp. MIT's admissions director has concurred. Parents and adolescents we speak to seem well aware of the pressure they are under. Mahoney, Harris, and Eccles acknowledge none of this as valid.

7. *Mahoney, Harris, and Eccles raise a concern that "the over-scheduling hypothesis," attributed in part to us, could lead to programs for the underprivileged being cut. In almost seven years since our book was first published, this has not happened even once:* Mahoney, Harris, and Eccles state, "These propositions [the "over-scheduling hypothesis"] suggest negative consequences resulting from too much organized activity participation. This has the potential to undermine recent efforts to support and expand opportunities for youth to participate in organized activities" (P 10 draft) particularly for the underprivileged.

A. We agree with the authors' contention that one of the cases in which activity-related benefits may be greatest is for "those at the highest risk for poor development," and when the program's quality is high (35). As a child advocate who has worked with— and written extensively about—indigent and high risk populations,

I am quite sensitive to the needs of people in these situations. Whenever Wise and I have been asked about underprivileged populations, we have said that they needed *more—not fewer—* organized activities.

B. Several months back, I wrote a letter to Dr. Mahoney after reading the final draft of this paper: "I would appreciate knowing where and when I—or my work—has been used *in any way* in opposition to these initiatives. In the almost seven years since our book was first published, *I have not once received a single contact or communication from any group or individual asking that my ideas, writings, or speeches be used as support for decreasing activity programs or funding* [italics added]. If such an attempt has ever occurred, I would be grateful if you could inform me of it." To date, I have not received a reply.

In summary, Mahoney, Harris, and Eccles take complex, nuanced ideas and try to make them one-dimensional caricatures. Our books have subtle ideas and a social commentary about the way American families are living their lives and the pressures they are responding to. To name just a few, our books speak of "hyper-parenting," a cultural pressure to involve children in increasing activities so that they turn out "winners" not "losers." We speak of how, from birth on, media play on parents' uncertainty, and how marketers use the idea that the more "enrichment" the better to sell unnecessary products to new parents. We note how individual families and children differ, how what benefits one may be counter-productive for another. Some families thrive on endless activities and sports while others prefer quiet down time. *We suggest that each individual family needs to assess what suits it; when activities are getting parents or the children frenetic, we suggest that they try cutting back 5–10%, hardly a notion that scheduled activities be eliminated.* We speak of needing down time to develop imagination, and of how focusing on activities and accomplishments often de-emphasizes relationships, character, and play which we consider critical to a good life. Our books have recommendations, such as trusting yourself, rather than relying on the experts who don't know you or your family. We suggest that parents do not rely on the most recent "scientific" study whose recommendations may change tomorrow. Mahoney, Harris, and Eccles take all this and create a one-dimensional "over-scheduling hypothesis" which attributes to us the idea that simply counting the number of activities a child participates in accurately and inversely reflects their mental health and life success.

We could discuss many other serious limitations in Mahoney, Harris, and Eccles' paper, but that would serve little purpose. As I wrote to Dr. Mahoney: "It is excellent that you are trying to do reliable, valid scientific work that criticizes my position and refutes my contentions. That keeps the academic process vigorous. If I turn out to have been mistaken, I will shamefacedly admit that I was in error. Nothing I see in my daily observation in our communities makes me think that I am. However, I would appreciate it if in trying to test a hypothesis you ascribe to me, you at the very least represent my positions accurately."

If competitive, affluent parents take to heart Dr. Mahoney's assertion that the more activities kids do the better—as they are wont to do with "expert, scientific" advice from a professor at an elite university—they may be following a path that leads them to more resentment, criticism of their children, and ultimately to damaging them. That would truly be a very unfortunate outcome.

CHALLENGE QUESTIONS

Should Contemporary Adolescents Be Engaged in More Structured Activities?

- Some commentators have noted that much of this issue seems to depend upon socioeconomic status—with wealthier children being at risk of having too much structured activity and children from other families being at risk of having too little. How do you think socioeconomic status may influence one's position on this controversial issue?
- Mahoney, Harris, and Eccles suggest that only a very small portion of youth participate in significant weekly hours of structured activities. Does that seem to be true among your friends and neighbors? Why or why not?
- What do you make of Rosenfeld's claim that structured activities influence the whole family, not just the involved youth? Why do you think Mahoney and colleagues did not test effects on family life more generally?
- If you were giving advice to parents about activity participation, what would you say? What does the research allow you to conclude?
- What might be the benefits of not having structured activities as part of adolescence? What might be the costs?

Suggested Readings

D. Brooks, "The Organization Kid," *The Atlantic Monthly* (April 2001)

D. Elkind, *The Power of Play* (Da Capo Books, 2007)

K. Ginsburg and the Committee on Communications and the Committee on Psychosocial Aspects of Child and Family Health, from "The Importance of Play in Promoting Healthy Child Development and Maintaining Strong Parent-Child Bonds," *Pediatrics* (January 2007)

R. Larson, "The Tip of an Iceberg?" *Society for Research in Child Development Social Policy Report* (2006)

S. Luthar, "Over-Scheduling Versus Other Stressors: Challenges of High Socioeconomic Status Families," *Society for Research in Child Development Social Policy Report* (2006)

J. Mahoney, R. Larson, and J. Eccles (Eds.), *Organized Activities as Contexts of Development: Extracurricular Activities, After-school and Community Programs* (Lawrence Erlbaum & Associates, 2005)

A. Rosenfeld and N. Wise, *The Over-scheduled Child: Avoiding the Hyperparenting Trap* (St. Martin's Griffin, 2000)

J. Roth, "Next Steps: Considering Patterns of Participation," *Society for Research in Child Development Social Policy Report* (2006)

ISSUE 12

Does Violent Media Cause Teenage Aggression?

YES: **Nancy Signorielli**, from *Violence in the Media: A Reference Handbook* ABC-CLIO (2005)

NO: **Jonathan L. Freedman**, from *Media Violence and Its Effect on Aggression: Assessing the Scientific Evidence* (University of Toronto Press, 2002)

ISSUE SUMMARY

YES: Professor of communication Nancy Signorielli uses research to support the popular assumption that media violence bears some responsibility for the acts of aggression that receive widespread publicity.

NO: Professor of psychology Jonathan L. Freedman argues that, despite many research efforts to demonstrate a link between media violence and teen aggression, the data does not support that case.

T he spate of dramatic violence perpetrated by aggressive youths in recent years, from Littleton, Colorado to Virginia Tech, has garnered much attention from society and scholars. It is not hard to find an intuitive link; violent teenagers often consume violent media and it is easy to assume the violence is connected. The killers in Littleton, for example, had a much publicized affinity for a violent video game titled "Doom" and they may have felt as though they were enacting a similar game on the horrific day in 1999 when they murdered 15 students and teachers in cold blood. But any social scientist knows that anecdotal evidence rarely proves a causal link. Is it possible that the association between violent media and violent acts is simply an association?

The controversial nature of this issue is compounded by the power of the media in contemporary society. When the Surgeon General of the United States commissioned a group of expert scholars to review youth violence for a 2000 report, a statement of connection between media violence and youth violence was submitted. For reasons unclear to the scholars, that section of the report was later omitted in favor of a more general statement regarding media violence that did not make any causal link to youth violence. While a modified version of the report with its original findings was later published by the American Psychological Society, the implication of the anecdote is that powerful interests do not want connections being made between the media and antisocial behavior.

In her review of violence in the media, Nancy Signorielli acknowledges that violent media does not dramatically influence all youth. Nevertheless, through systematic study she and her colleagues have found that we are exposed to extremely high quantities of violence in the media. Further, most research indicates a clear association between consuming violent media and engaging in aggressive behavior. Thus, on this side of the issue, the connection between media violence and aggressive behavior conforms to both common-sense and statistical evidence.

On the other hand, in Jonathan L. Freedman's review of the available literature he comes away unconvinced that there is a definitive link between the media and youth violence. He recognizes that massive amounts of attention have been devoted to researching the effects of media violence, and he knows that many scholars and scholarly groups have concluded the media causes youth violence. But Freedman does not believe that those two facts necessarily go together. In fact, he asserts, the easy intuitive assumption that media violence causes youth violence has provoked experts to draw conclusions that go well beyond the data. Freedman has done careful reviews of the psychological research about media violence, and he finds no conclusive evidence for a causal link to youth violence. He also notes that even the studies expert scholars usually rely upon often only address aggressive impulses and actions immediately after consuming violent media—potentially suggesting that any effects are only temporary.

POINT	COUNTERPOINT
• Violence in the media is hard to avoid—people see it every day.	• Because it is so easy to blame the media for aggression and violence, people ignore the lack of evidence.
• Negative consequences of violence are rarely presented by the media.	• Although contemporary youth may be exposed to more violence, rates of violent acts have been decreasing.
• Video game violence is increasing, and that may be affecting youth.	• More exposure to violent media has not universally correlated with more violent behavior.
• Although not all youth are affected, there are consistent positive relationships between exposure to media violence and aggressive behavior, desensitization to violence, and fear.	• Most research on the effects of violent media focuses on short-term outcomes, not general tendencies to become aggressive.

YES

Nancy Signorielli

What We Know about
Media Violence

A paradigm or model for understanding a phenomenon of mass communication, such as television violence, involves three areas. First, a study must be
made of the institutions of mass communication, including the people and
companies that create, produce, and distribute media messages, as well as
those government agencies involved in regulating the media. This area of
study provides information about the policies, practices, rules, and regulations regarding media. For example, congressional hearings, the passage of the
Telecommunications Act of 1996, lobbying by the National Association of
Broadcasters, and the growth of a few large, multinational communication
companies have all contributed, in some way, to today's climate of media violence. Second, the study of media content, especially what is on television,
tells us about the messages of violence that are seen by most adults and children. And, third, we must understand the effects of these mediated images of
violence on both adults and children. This chapter looks at parts two and
three of this model and focuses on what we currently know about the content
and effects of mediated violence, particularly in relation to television. The primary focus is on mediated violence in the United States, but where relevant,
comparisons are made on an international level.

Media Content

Violence on Television

Although some studies of television violence were conducted during the 1950s
and 1960s, most of the information about the amount of violence on television
in the United States comes from the long-term analysis of prime-time network
programs (1967 to 2002) conducted as part of the Cultural Indicators project
(CI) and the short-term analysis (1994–1995 to 1996–1997) of a more extensive
sample of network and cable channels by the National Television Violence
Study (NTVS). In the United Kingdom (U.K.), the understanding of television
violence comes from an analysis of samples of programs from 1994–1995 and
1995–1996 (Gunter, Harrison, and Wykes 2003). Knowledge about television
violence in other countries (Japan or the Netherlands, for example) comes from

a number of studies looking at violence in samples of programs taken at one point in time. Most of these studies, whether conducted in the United States or another country, focus specifically on physical violence because emotional violence is extremely difficult to define and isolate in a consistent and reliable way. . . .

Overall, the U.S. studies, particularly those conducted in the 1990s, show stability in the amount of violence on television—violence appears in roughly six out of ten programs in the United States. Consequently, whether viewers watch network broadcast channels or cable channels, it is relatively difficult to avoid violence. From an international perspective, countries that import considerable amounts of programming from the United States have levels of violence on television similar to those seen in the United States, whereas those who do not import many programs have lower levels of violence. Interestingly, except in Japan, domestic programs tend to be less violent than the imports. One of the reasons for the high level of violence in imported (typically U.S.) programs is that violence is a program stable that transcends language barriers—it is relatively easy to translate because the pictures are rather self-explanatory. Comedy, however, does not translate (travel) very easily because it is so dependent upon language. . . .

Violence in Video Games

During the past thirty years, video games have increased in popularity. The Kaiser Family Foundation reports that most homes with children now have a video game system (1999). Children start playing video games as early as age three and continue playing through high school, college, and beyond.[1] At all ages, boys play more than girls, and older children play more than younger children. There are particular concerns about the violence in video games and how it may influence players.

Video games have changed enormously from the 1970s, when *Pong* (an arcade, tennis-like, visual-motor activity) became a hit with young adults. Today, most children play real-time, first-person shooter (FPS) games in which the "players view the world through the eyes of the video game character that they control" (Espejo 2003, 6). Moreover, recent technology permits players to personalize game playing by scanning pictures of peers, teachers, or other people they know onto the images of the potential victims in the games (Funk 2002).

The potential effects (and theoretical perspectives) of video games on aggression are similar to those of television violence. Although a recent meta-analysis (Sherry 2001) found that the overall effect of video game playing on aggression is considerably smaller than the effects of television violence, there is cause for concern because children are the primary users of this medium and those who play video games become intentionally and actively involved in the action. Joseph Dominick (1984), for example, notes that playing video games is quite different from watching television because of the higher level of concentration and attention needed to play, which may give greater credibility to the images on the screen. Moreover, parents are even less likely to actively participate in video game playing and may be relatively unaware of the kinds of images seen in these games.

Although Derek Scott (1995) found that video game playing had no appreciable effect on aggression among university students, other studies have found that video game playing is associated with increased aggression and hostility (Bushman and Anderson 2002). A. Roland Irwin and Alan Gross (1995) found that second-grade children who played a martial arts game were more aggressive than children who played a motorcycle racing game. Game playing may also increase desensitization. Jeanne Funk (2002) found that game playing is related to exhibiting less empathy and more proviolence attitudes. For example, Mark Barnett and colleagues (1997), using a sample of fifteen- to nineteen-year-olds, found a negative relationship between preferences for violent video games and empathy. Nevertheless, the research also shows that children's preexisting traits, such as being empathic or aggressive, may have more influence on their behavior than short-term game playing. Funk (2002) also found that nine- to eleven-year-old children who played either violent or nonviolent games did not differ in aggressive and empathic responses, but those children who said their favorite game was aggressive were more aggressive than those who preferred nonviolent games and those who initially were more empathetic had higher empathy scores after playing. Funk concludes that although there may be some short-term negative effects of game playing, youngsters' preexisting characteristics (e.g., empathy) may be equally important in determining how they respond to game playing.

The long-term effects of video games cannot be studied in a laboratory setting because of the research model that looks at what happens over years of playing in many different types of situations—individually, with friends, with different types of games. Typically, studies rely on surveys that generate relational findings. Craig Anderson and Karen Dill (2000) found a relationship between measures of aggressiveness and preference for violent video games among a sample of college students and that those who spent more time playing had lower grade point averages than those who spent less time playing. Other studies have found relationships between stated preferences for violent games and psychopathology as measured by the Youth Self-Report, a measure of adolescent psychopathology (Funk 2002). . . .

How Media Violence Affects Us

There are numerous ways media violence affects us. Potter (2003) differentiates effects that are immediate or short-term from those that are long-term. Researchers, including John Murray (2003) and Potter (2003), further delineate three ways in which media violence may affect viewers: fostering aggression, becoming desensitized to violence, and becoming fearful. Each of these effects, in turn, may have both short- and long-term consequences.

Aggression and Aggressive Behavior

One of the biggest concerns about media violence is that exposure to violent images will result in aggression and aggressive behavior. There is a sizable body of research that supports this position. Although there is some disagreement with this statement, the number of researchers in this camp is rather small, and some have ties to the broadcast industry. The strength of the evidence led the American Psychological Association (1985) to conclude that one factor in the development of aggressive and/or antisocial behavior in children is a steady diet of real and/or mediated violence. Similarly, the 1982 report by the National Institute of Mental Health concluded that children and teens who watch violence on television tend to exhibit more aggressive behavior. The research evidence on which these conclusions were based comes from experimental studies, longitudinal studies, and meta-analyses (a particular type of analysis that simultaneously compares the statistical results from a large number of existing studies on the same topic).

Some of the earliest research on mediated violence was experimental in nature and found that filmed or televised (mediated) images affected behavior. Glenn Ellis and Francis Sekyra (1972) and O. Ivar Lovaas (1961) found that children exposed to media violence behaved aggressively shortly after seeing violence. Another study comparing violent and prosocial (positive messages) programs (Stein and Friedrich 1972) found that children who saw positive or prosocial programs (e.g., *Mister Roger's Neighborhood*) increased their helping behaviors, whereas those who saw violent images behaved more aggressively. Overall, numerous studies have found a causal relation between seeing violent portrayals and later aggressive behavior. L. Rowell Huesmann and Laurie Miller conclude: "In these well-controlled laboratory studies there can be no doubt that it is the children's observation of the scenes of violence that is *causing* the changes in behavior" (1994, 163).

Another strong line of evidence of long-term effects comes from studies conducted over several years (longitudinal studies), specifically the research of Leonard Eron and L. Rowell Huesmann. One study of young boys begun in the 1970s in New York state that was able to control for intelligence quotient (IQ), initial levels of aggressiveness, and social class found that the amount of violence seen on television at age eight was related to aggressiveness at age eighteen, as well as involvement in antisocial behavior (fights and spouse abuse) and criminal acts at age thirty (Huesmann and Miller 1994). Similar results were found in samples of youngsters in Chicago as well as children from other countries, including Finland, Poland, and Israel. These studies found that more aggressive children, compared to less aggressive children, watched more television, preferred programs that were more violent, and perceived mediated violence as closer to real life. The most recent study in this tradition (Huesmann, Moise-Titus, Podolski, and Eron 2003) found that watching violence, identification with same-sex aggressive characters, and a perception that television violence is realistic were related to adult aggression, regardless of how much aggression was exhibited as a child.

A particularly interesting and important longitudinal study (Joy, Kimball, and Zabrack, 1986) was conducted in the late 1970s in three communities in Canada as part of a larger study by Tannis MacBeth (formerly Williams). While vacationing in Canada, MacBeth visited an area in which a new and more powerful transmission tower was being built that would have a major impact on television reception in the area. One town located in the valley, Notel, would receive television for the first time. Unitel, a town about 50 miles away that had been receiving one television channel, would increase its reception by a second channel with the new transmitter. The third community, Multitel, was located close to the U.S. border and received numerous television channels originating both in Canada and the United States. The researchers gathered data relating to aggression, gender roles, and academic achievement both before and two years after the installation of the more powerful transmitter. The results showed that the children in Notel exhibited more aggressive behavior (both verbal and physical) after the introduction of television. Aggressive behavior increased for both boys and girls, for children of different ages, and for those who had different initial levels of aggressiveness. Interestingly, this comprehensive study also found that after the introduction of television, that children's gender role stereotyping increased and measures of academic success (e.g., reading levels) decreased (Williams 1986).

A recent cross-cultural study of twelve-year-old children (2,788 boys and 2,353 girls) from twenty-three different countries (funded by the United Nations Education, Scientific, and Cultural Organization, or UNESCO) found an interactive relationship between media violence and real violence such that "media can contribute to an aggressive culture" (Groebel 2001, 265). In short, these studies found that aggressive people, particularly those who live in more aggressive environments, use the media to confirm their attitudes and beliefs, which are then reinforced by media content. For example, the study found that one of the messages of aggressive content is that aggression is a good way to solve conflicts and that it is fun and provides status. Moreover, the study found that successful media figures, such as the Terminator (Arnold Schwarzenegger) and Rambo (Sylvester Stallone), had become cross-cultural heroes.

Another line of naturalistic research is the work of Brian Centerwall, MD (1989a; 1989b). Using an epidemiological approach, Centerwall examines relationships between the introduction of television in a society (e.g., the United States, Canada, and South Africa) and changes in homicide rates among the white population in these countries. In comparison with South Africa, where television was banned until 1975, Centerwall found that the white homicide rates in both the United States and Canada increased 90 percent between 1945 and 1975, whereas homicide rates for the white population in South Africa remained stable. These increases held despite the implementation of statistical controls for economic growth, urbanization, alcoholism, gun ownership, and so on. Moreover, in South Africa homicide rates in South Africa's white population increased by 56 percent between 1975, when television was introduced in the country, and 1983. Although most social scientists find Centerwall's research compelling, Elizabeth Perse (2001) notes that South Africa may not have been a good choice for comparison because it was a highly controlled and repressed society and had a higher homicide rate before the introduction of television. Moreover, Perse notes that Centerwall's method, a simple bivariate graphical analysis, does not dispel the possibility that the relationships may be due to a third, unmeasured, variable. Nevertheless, many find that these data are very compelling in that they show convincing, statistically significant increases in homicide rates of the white population over time.

Another solid base of evidence about the detrimental effects of media violence comes from a number of meta-analyses, a statistical technique that analyzes findings from a large number of studies about a particular topic. The first meta-analysis (Andison 1977) examined sixty-seven separate studies (experiments, surveys, longitudinal) conducted between 1956 and 1996 that examined over 30,000 participants. This analysis found strong support for a relationship between watching media violence and subsequent aggression. An analysis of samples of children, teens, and adults in 230 separate studies found a positive relationship between antisocial behavior (behaving aggressively, rule breaking, etc). and exposure to violent media in most of the studies (Hearold 1986). Similarly, Haejung Paik and George Comstock's (1994) meta-analysis of 217 studies found statistically significant and positive correlations between viewing and subsequent aggression in samples of adults, children, and teens. Meta-analyses thus show a solid and consistent base of evidence supporting the relationship between watching media violence and behaving aggressively.

Desensitization

A second major concern is that media violence may be related to increased desensitization; that is, viewers may become less sensitive to the violence they see and thus become willing to tolerate a more violent society (Murray 2003). Laboratory studies have shown that adults and children become callous and even punitive after watching violent images. Children in the third grade, for example, who either did not see mediated violence or were shown a short clip from a violent western, were then asked to monitor two younger children by listening to the noise of them playing through an intercom. As they listened to the children, it became apparent that their play had become physically aggressive (Drabman and Thomas 1974). The children who saw the violent episode took considerably longer to get adult help than those who did not see violence. Similarly, Daniel Linz, Edward Donnerstein, and Steven Penrod (1984) found that a group of college men who viewed violent "slasher" films for five consecutive days rated the films as less violent and degrading to women at the end of the week. Moreover, after watching these films and then watching a documentary about a trial for sexual assault, these young men were less sympathetic toward the rape victim than the group of young men who had not seen the slasher films. Similarly, Stacy Smith and Edward Donnerstein (1998) note that the more viewers see graphic media violence, the more they rate material they originally perceived as offensive or degrading as less offensive or degrading.

Desensitization is particularly a concern as the amount of viewing increases. Several studies have shown that those who watch more violent programming may become more desensitized. Victor Cline, Roger Croft, and Steven Courrier (1973) found that those who saw more graphic violent portrayals were more likely to become physiologically desensitized—in short, the images stopped having an impact. In some situations, however, desensitization may have positive outcomes. Repeated exposure to an initially frightening or threatening image or character (e.g., the Incredible Hulk, the Wizard of Oz) can reduce children's fears (Cantor and Wilson 1984). Humor also contributes to desensitization (Potter 1999). Emotional disturbed children (e.g., those with attention deficit hyperactivity disorder) are especially vulnerable to media violence and desensitization. Tom Grimes, Eric Vernberg, and Teresa Cathers (1997) found that after watching television violence, children with emotional problems (compared to a matched group of children without these disorders) showed less concern for the victims of violence and believed that the media violence they saw characters commit was justified.

Fear

Media violence may be related to fear, in both the short and long terms. Joanne Cantor (2002) has studied fright as both a physiological and emotional reaction and found that children may become fearful after seeing violent media images. These reactions typically do not last very long, but it is possible for some to last for several days, months, or even longer. For example, Kristen Harrison and Cantor (1999) found that nine out of ten college students said that they had an intense fear reaction to a media depiction that lasted for a long time. Some of the things that evoke fear responses include injuries and dangers as well as deformities and/or distortions, such as monsters or ghosts. Several factors are likely to induce fear or fright reactions. Viewers who identify and/or empathize with the target of violence are likely to feel more fearful. Similarly, viewers who think the violence could happen to them often become more fearful. Although these reactions may be immediate and short-lived, there may be some long-term consequences. For example, children may become scared while watching a movie or program and perhaps hide their eyes or scream and have nightmares. Fear, however, differs by age. Young children typically are more fearful of images that are fantastic, threatening, and just look scary; older, children, however, are more fearful of more realistic dangers, things that could possibly happen to them.

There is also evidence of a generalized fear effect—the result of long-term exposure to violent media. Cultivation theory posits a positive relationship between watching more television and being fearful and exhibiting the "mean world syndrome." Studies testing this theory show that those who watch more television believe that there are more people employed in law enforcement, exaggerate the numbers of people involved in violence in a given week, overestimate their own chances of being a victim of violence, are more likely to believe they need more protection, and believe that, in general, the world is a mean and scary place in that most people "cannot be trusted" and are "just looking out for themselves" (Gerbner et al. 2002, 52). Although there is some criticism of this approach (see Chapter 3), it is a position that takes into consideration the fact that the media are an ongoing facet of day-to-day life and that the influence of the media (cultivation) is "a continual, dynamic, ongoing process of interaction among messages, audiences, and contexts" (Gerbner et al. 2002, 49).

Cultivation, however, may be culturally determined. There is less evidence of fear-related cultivation effects in the United Kingdom. Mallory Wober (1978) reports no relationship between television viewing and notions of fear and violence. There are, however, several cultural differences that may explain the lack of relationship. First, as noted above, U.K. television is considerably less violent and U.S. imports make up only a small portion of available programming. Second, programming in the United Kingdom must follow the government's family viewing policy requirements. This policy ensures that programs with potentially objectionable content are scheduled later in the evening and that programs unsuitable for children cannot be shown before 9 PM. Moreover, in the United Kingdom televised films are given age-based ratings (Gunter, Harrison, and Wykes 2003). Similarly, in the Netherlands, Harry Bouwman (1984) found only weak associations between viewing and perceptions of violence, mistrust, and victimization. Even though the Netherlands imports a considerable amount of U.S. programming and Dutch and U.S. programming provides similar messages about violence, many viewers choose to watch programs that are more "informational" in nature.

Nevertheless, some cultures have shown cultivation effects. For example, students in Australia who watched more U.S. crime/adventure programs had higher scores on the "mean world" and "violence in society" indices (Pingree and Hawkins 1981). Other analyses have found evidence of the cultivation of conceptions of sex roles and political orientations as well as violence. For example, in South Korea, watching U.S. television was related, for women, to more liberal perspectives about gender roles and family values. Among the male students, however, seeing more U.S. programming was related to exhibiting greater protectiveness of Korean culture and more hostility toward the United States (Kang and Morgan 1988). Overall, the findings from numerous studies conducted in the cultivation tradition show that if televised images are less homogeneous and repetitive than those seen in the United States, the results of cultivation analyses are less consistent and predictable (Gerbner et al. 2002).

Who Will Be Influenced?

The research discussed in this section can be interpreted in three different ways: (1) that media violence is inconsequential and people, including children, are not affected by these images, particularly what they see on television (e.g., Fowless 1999); (2) that media violence will affect some people some of the time (Potter 2003); and (3) that media violence will always have a very negative impact (as believed, for example, by grassroots groups such as the National Coalition on Television Violence).

The evidence from numerous research studies indicates that the first and third interpretations are too extreme. The position that media violence is inconsequential has only a few supporters. For example, during the 1970s, when NBC was actively involved in a research program, Ronald Milavsky and others (1982) conducted a three-year longitudinal study (1970–1973) of 2,400 elementary school children and 800 teenage boys and reported no evidence of a relationship between television violence and aggressive behavior. A re-analysis of this data set, however, found a relationship between television violence and aggression (Turner, Hesse, and Peterson-Lewis 1986). Huesmann and Miller (1994) also interpret the NBC data as consistent with other research findings that support a relationship.

Similarly, the position that television violence always has a negative impact on people, particularly impressionable children, is also too extreme and again has very few supporters. The one group that has supported this outcome, the National Coalition on Television Violence . . . was founded in 1980 and has been active in both rating television programs for violence and assessing which companies advertise on the most violent programs. Although the lion's share of the research shows a relationship between viewing and behaving aggressively, media violence is only one of many potential causes of aggression and/or violence in people. For example, child abuse or living in an excessively violent neighborhood may also play a critical role in subsequent aggressive behavior. Consequently, it is unreasonable to say that television violence will always have negative effects on viewers.

The most reasonable argument to make in understanding the effects of violent media content is to say that not everyone is affected in the same way; indeed, the same person may respond to violence differently on different occasions. Violent media content may have large effects on a small number of adults and/or children or small effects on large numbers of viewers. The large, consistent body of literature points to a positive relationship between television violence and aggressive behavior. Moreover, even though findings may be modest in size, the relationship must be taken seriously because of the large numbers of children who watch television each day, largely unsupervised. Even though their aggressive behavior may not put society at risk, it still may have negative social and cognitive consequences, such as the alienation of their peers and teachers (Singer and Singer 1988).

There is, however, another potentially important consequence. Although many people are reluctant to admit that they or their children could be affected by media violence, they believe that others are affected. This perspective, called "third-person effects" (Davison 1983), is particularly illusionary because it allows people to believe that they (and their children) are immune from the effects of media, but their neighbors (and their children) are not. People tend to overestimate the media's effects on others while underestimating its effects on themselves. An example might be the person who claims not to pay attention to advertising and states that advertising does not influence his or her purchasing decisions, yet won't buy anything but brand-name products and typically wears brand-name clothing such as T-shirts from the Gap or Abercormbie and Fitch.

Potter (2003) believes that third-person effects constitutes one of the "myths of television violence" mentioned in the title of his book. This myth is troublesome because people do not understand how they may be affected by media violence. Although most people do not copy violent behavior they see in the media (and if they did with any regularity, the world would be extremely chaotic), that violence has numerous long-term effects, including physiological and/or emotional habituation and the cultivation of fear and the belief that the world is mean. Another of Potter's myths is that "children are especially vulnerable to the risks of negative exposure to media violence"

(2003, 67). Classifying this statement as a myth does not mean that children are not vulnerable, for indeed they may be particularly influenced by media violence. Rather, this myth underscores the third-person effects because it diminishes the fact that people of all age groups may be negatively influenced by media violence.

Finally, as cultivation theory postulates, the ultimate long-term effects of watching television violence may post threats for civil liberties and freedom. Cultivation studies have found that those who watch more television, compared to those who watch less, are more likely to overestimate their chances of being involved in violence, believe that fear of crime is an important personal problem, and assume that crime is rising. Those who spend more time watching television tend to believe that they are living in a mean and dangerous world and express feelings of alienation and gloom (Gerbner et al. 2002). Because violent images are almost impossible to avoid, those who watch more television may express sentiments of dependency and be willing to accept deceptively simple, strong, and hard-line political and religious postures, if these beliefs seem to promise to relieve existing insecurities and anxieties. From the perspective of cultivation theory, the overall long-term effects of television violence may be the ready acceptance of repressive political and social environments that could translate into a loss of personal liberties.

Note

1. Although recent surveys (Kaiser Family Foundation 1999; Annenberg Policy Research Center 2000) focused only on children ages eighteen and under, my personal experience (my college-age children, their friends, and students in my classes at the University of Delaware) indicates that video game playing does not end with graduation from high school and that earlier gender differences still prevail.

References

American Psychological Association, 1985. *Violence on Television*. Washington, DC: APA Board of Social and Ethical Responsibility for Psychology.

Anderson, C. A., and K. E. Dill. 2000. "Video Games and Aggressive Thoughts, Feelings, and Behavior in the Laboratory and in Life." *Journal of Personality and Social Psychology* 78: 772–790.

Anderson, F. S. 1977. "TV Violence and Viewer Aggression: A Cumulation of Study Results, 1956–1976." *Public Opinion Quarterly* 41: 314–331.

Barnett, M. A., G. D. Vitaglione, K. K. G. Harper, S. W. Quackenbush, L. A. Steadman, and B. S. Valdez. 1997. "Late Adolescents' Experiences with and Attitudes towards Videogames." *Journal of Applied Social Psychology* 27: 1316–1334.

Bushman, B. J, and C. A. Anderson. 2002. "Violent Video Games and Hostile Expectations: A Test of the General Aggression Model." *Personality and Social Psychology Bulletin* 28: 1679–1686.

Cantor, J. 2002. "Fright Reactions to Mass Media." In. J. Bryant and D. Zillmann, eds., *Media Effects: Advances in Theory and Research*, pp. 287–306. Mahwah, NJ: Lawrence Erlbaum Associates.

Cantor, J., and B. J. Wilson. 1984. "Modifying Fear Response to Mass Media in Preschool and Elementary School Children." *Journal of Broadcasting* 28: 431–443.

Center for Communication and Social Policy, University of California, Santa Barbara. *National Television Violence Study.* 1998. Vol. 3. Thousand Oaks, CA: Sage.

Centerwall, B. S. 1989a. "Exposure to Television as a Cause of Violence." In G. Comstock, ed., *Public Communication and Behavior,* pp. 1–58. Vol. 2, Orlando, FL: Academic.

——. 1989b. "Exposure to Television as a Risk Factor for Violence." *American Journal of Epidemiology* 129: 643–652.

Cline, V.B., R. G. Croft, and S. Courrier. 1973. "Desensitization of Children to Television Violence." *Journal of Personality and Social Psychology* 27: 260–265.

Davison, W. P. 1983. "The Third-Person Effect in Communication." *Public Opinion Quarterly* 47: 1–15.

Dominick, J. R. 1984. "Videogames, Television Violence, and Aggression in Teenagers." *Journal of Communication* 34: 136–147.

Drabman, R. S., and M. H. Thomas. 1974. "Does Media Violence Increase Children's Toleration of Real-Life Aggression?" *Developmental Psychology* 10: 418–421.

Ellis, G. T., and F. Sekyra III. 1972. "The Effect of Aggressive Cartoons on the Behavior of First Grade Children." *Journal of Psychology* 81: 7–43.

Espejo, R., ed. 2003. *Video Games.* San Diego: Greenhaven.

Fowles, J. 1999. *The Case for Television Violence.* Thousand Oaks, CA: Sage.

Funk, J. B. 2002. "Electronic Games." In V. C. Strausburger and B. J. Wilson, *Children, Adolescents, and the Media,* pp. 117–144. Thousand Oaks, CA: Sage.

Gerbner, G., L. Gross, M. Morgan, N. Signorielli, and J. Shanahan. 2002. "Growing Up with Television: The Cultivation Perspective." In J. Bryant and D. Zillmann, eds., *Media Effects: Advance in Theory and Research.* 2nd ed. Hillsdale, NJ: Lawrence Erlbaum Associates.

Grimes, T., E. Vernberg, and T. Cathers. 1997. "Emotionally Disturbed Children's Reactions to Violent Media Segments." *Journal of Health Communication* 2, no. 3: 157–168.

Groebel, J. 2001. Media Violence in Cross-Cultural Perspective." In D. G. Singer and J. L. Singer, eds., *Handbook of Children and the Media,* pp. 25–268. Thousand Oaks, CA: Sage.

Grossman, D., and G. DeGaetano. 1999. *Stop Teaching Our Kids to Kill: A Call to Action against TV, Movie and Video Game Violence.* New York: Crown.

Harrison, K. and J. Cantor. 1999. "Tales from the Screen: Enduring Fright Reactions to Scary Media." *Media Psychology* 1, no. 2: 97–116.

Hearold, S. 1986. "A Synthesis of 1043 Effects of Television on Social Behavior." In G. Comstock, ed., *Public Communications and Behavior,* pp. 65–133. Vol. 1. New York: Academic.

Huesmann, L. R., and L. S. Miller. 1994. "Long-Term Effects of Repeated Exposure to Media Violence in Childhood." In L. R. Huesmann, ed., *Aggressive Behavior: Current Perspectives,* pp. 153–186. New York: Plenum.

Huesmann, L. R., J. Moise-Titus, C. Podolski, and L. D. Eron. 2003. "Longitudinal Relations between Children's Exposure to TV Violence and Their Aggressive and Violent Behavior in Young Adulthood, 1977–1992." *Developmental Psychology* 39, no. 2: 201–221.

Irwin, A. R., and A. M. Gross. 1995. "Cognitive Tempo, Violent Video Games, and Aggressive Behavior in Young Boys." *Journal of Family Violence* 10: 337–350.

Joy, L. A., M. M. Kimball, and M. L. Zabrack. 1986. "Television and Children's Aggressive Behavior." In T. M. Williams. ed., *The Impact of Television: A Natural Experiment in Three Communities,* pp. 303–360. Orlando, FL: Academic.

Kaiser Family Foundation. 1999. *Kids and Media @ the New Millennium: A Comprehensive National Analysis of Children's Media Use.* Menlo Park, CA: Kaiser Family Foundation.

Kang, J. G., and M. Morgan. 1988. "Culture Clash: U.S. Television Programs in Korea." *Journalism Quarterly* 65, no. 2: 431–438.

Linz, D., E. Donnerstein, and S. Penrod. 1984. "The Effects of Multiple Exposures to Filmed Violence against Women." *Journal of Communication* 34, no. 3: 130–147.

Lovaas, O. I. 1961. "Effects of Exposure to Symbolic Aggression on Aggressive Behavior." *Child Development* 32: 37–44.

Milavsky, J. R., R. Kessler, H. Stipp, and W. S. Rubens. 1982. "Television and Aggression: Results of a Panel Study." In D. Pearl, L. Bouthilet, and J. Lazar, eds., *Television and Behavior: Ten Years of Scientific Progress and Implications for the 80s*, pp. 138–157. Vol. 2. Washington, DC: U.S. Government Printing Office.

Murray, J. P. 2003. "The Violent Face of Television: Research and Discussion." In E. L. Palmer and B. M. Young, eds., *The Faces of Televisual Media: Teaching, Violence, Selling to Children*. Mahwah, NJ: Lawrence Erlbaum Associates.

National Coalition of Television Violence (NCTV). No date. "Ten Common Myths about the V-Chap and the Facts." . . .

National Institute for Mental Health. 1982. *Television and Behavior: Ten years of Scientific Progress and Implications for the Eighties*. Vol. 1, *Summary Report*. Washington, DC: U.S. Government Printing Office.

Paik, H., and G. Comstock. 1994. "The Effects of Television Violence on Antisocial Behavior: A Meta-Analysis." *Communication Research* 21: 516–546.

Perse, E. 2001. *Media Effects and Society*. Mahwah, NJ: Lawrence Erlbaum Associates.

Pingree, S., and R. P. Hawkins. 1981. "U.S. Programs on Australian Television: The Cultivation Effect." *Journal of Communication* 31, no. 1: 97–105.

Potter, W. J. 1999. *On Media Violence*. Thousand Oaks, CA: Sage.

———. 2003. *The Eleven Myths of Media Violence*. Thousand Oaks, CA: Sage.

Scott, D. 1995. "The Effect of Video Games on Feelings of Aggression." *Journal of Psychology* 129: 121–132.

Sherry, J. L. 2001. "The Effects of Violent Video Games on Aggression: A Meta-Analysis." *Human Communication Research* 27: 409–431.

Singer, J. L., and D. G. Singer. 1988. "Some Hazards of Growing Up in a Television Environment: Children's Aggression and Restlessness." In S. Oskamp, ed., *Television as a Social Issue*, pp. 171–188. Newbury Park, CA: Sage.

Smith, S. L., and E. Donnerstein. 1998. "Harmful Effects of Exposure to Media Violence: Learning of Aggression, Emotional Desensitization, and Fear." In R. G. Geen and E. Donneerstein, eds., *Human Aggression: Theories, Research, and Implications for Social Policy*. San Diego: Academic.

Song, E., and J. E. Anderson. 2003. "Violence in Video Games May Harm Children." In R. Espejo, ed., *Video Games*, 9–17. San Diego, CA: Green-haven.

Stein, A. H., and L. K. Friedrich, with F. Vondracek. 1972. "Television Content and Young Children's Behavior. In J. P. Murray, E. A. Rubinstein, and G. A. Comstock, eds., *Television and Social Behavior*. Vol. 2, *Television and Social Learning*, pp. 202–317. Washington, DC: U.S. Government Printing Office.

Thomas, M. H., R. W. Horton, E. C. Lippincott, and R. S. Drabman. 1977. "Desensitization to Portrayals of Real-Life Aggression as a Function of Exposure to Television Violence." *Journal of Personality and Social Psychology* 35: 450–458.

Turner, C. W., B. W. Hesse, and S. Peterson-Lewis. 1986. "Naturalistic Studies of the Long-Term Effects of Television Violence." *Journal of Social Issues* 42: 51–73.

Williams, T. M., ed. 1986. *The Impact of Television: A Natural Experiment in Three Communities*. Orlando, FL: Academic.

Wober, M. 1978. "Televised Violence and Paranoid Perceptions: The View from Great Britain." *Public Opinion Quarterly* 42, no. 3: 315–321.

Jonathan L. Freedman

 **NO**

Villain or Scapegoat? Media Violence and Aggression

On 20 April 1999, at around 11:20 a.m. local time, two students wearing black trenchcoats walked into Columbine High School in Littleton, Colorado. Eric Harris, eighteen, and Dylan Klebold, seventeen, were armed with semiautomatic handguns, shotguns and explosives. They killed twelve students, one teacher, and then themselves.

On 1 December 1997, Michael Carneal killed three students at Heath High School in West Paducah, Kentucky.

On 30 April 1999 a fourteen-year-old Canadian boy walked into the W.R. Myers High School in Taber, a quiet farming community of 7,200 people two hours southeast of Calgary, Alberta. He shot and killed one seventeen-year-old student and seriously injured another eleventh-grade student.

It is difficult to imagine events more terrible than our young people deliberately killing each other. These horrifying incidents have caused almost everyone to wonder what has gone wrong with North American society. How can it be that in quiet, affluent communities in two of the richest countries on earth, children are taking guns to school and killing their classmates?

Many answers have been suggested. It was the parents' fault; it was Satanism and witchcraft; it was lack of religion in the schools and at home; it was moral breakdown; it was the availability of guns; it was the culture.

One answer proposed whenever events like this occur is that they are a result of exposure to media violence. Children who watch television and go to the movies see thousands of murders and countless other acts of violence. They see fistfights, martial arts battles, knifings, shootings, exploding cars, and bombs. These acts of violence are committed by heroes and villains, by good guys and bad guys. They are committed by live actors and animated figures; they appear in the best movies and TV programs as well as in the worst. It is almost impossible for children to avoid witnessing these violent acts time and time again. All of this has caused many people to ask whether watching violent television programs and movies causes people, especially children, to be more aggressive and to commit crimes.

Another reason some people worry about the effects of media violence is that television became available in the United States and Canada in the 1950s and violent crime increased dramatically in both countries between 1960 and 1990. Many people see a connection. They think that watching violence on

From *Media Violence and Aggression* by Jonathan L. Freedman, pp. 3–4, 7–16, 19–21. Copyright © 2002 by University of Toronto Press-Scholarly Div. Reprinted by permission.

television makes children more aggressive and causes them to grow into adults who are more likely to commit violent crimes. Brandon Centerwall, a psychiatrist and epidemiologist, has even suggested that the increase in violent crime during this period was due entirely to television. As he put it, 'if, hypothetically, television technology had never been developed, there would today be 10,000 fewer homicides each year in the United States, 70,000 fewer rapes, and 700,000 fewer injurious assaults.'

The belief that media violence is harmful is widespread. In a recent poll in the United States, 10 percent of people said that TV violence is the major cause of the increase in crime. This tendency to blame media violence has been fostered by some social scientists and whipped up by politicians and lobby groups. It has led politicians to propose bills restricting access to violent movies, banning violent television programs during certain hours, forcing television companies to rate every single program in terms of violence, and requiring that all television sets be fitted with V-chips to enable parents to block out programs they find offensive. We are told that all of this will reduce crime and make children better behaved, and that if we do not deal with media violence our society will continue to experience increased violence and crime.

Some people say they don't need science to know that watching violence makes children violent. To these people it is so clear, so self-evident, that we don't need to bother with research. They point to some horrible incidents to support this view.

On 14 October 1992 the headlines in many American papers read **boy lights fire that kills sister.** Two days earlier a television program had shown young boys setting fires. The very next day, Tommy Jones (not his real name) an eight-year-old boy, set a fire that burned down the trailer in which he and his family lived. His baby sister was trapped inside and burned to death. All over the United States, newspapers, television stations, and politicians concluded that Tommy must have seen the television program and gotten the idea of playing with matches and setting a fire. Surely this was a perfect example of why children should not be allowed to watch violent programs.

In February 1993 the whole world shuddered at an awful crime committed by two young boys in England. That month a small boy who was about to turn three was taken from a shopping mall in Liverpool by two ten-year-old boys. Jamie Bulger had walked away from his mother for only a second—long enough for Jon Venables to take his hand and lead him out of the mall with his friend Robert Thompson. They took Jamie on a walk of over two-and-a-half miles, along the way stopping every now and again to torture the poor little boy, who was crying constantly for his mommy. Finally they left his beaten small body on the tracks so that a train could run him over.

Jamie's frantic mother noticed almost at once that he was missing, and a massive search began. Jon and Robert were identified from surveillance tapes in the mall. At first they denied any knowledge of Jamie, but eventually they admitted everything and led police to the dead body. Although they confessed to taking Jamie, each accused the other of doing the torturing and killing. During the trial, Jon cried a lot and looked miserable, while Robert seemed unaffected. They were convicted and sentenced to long prison terms.

The trial judge had observed the boys for many days and heard all the testimony. At the sentencing he denounced them as inhuman monsters. He also said he was convinced that one of the causes of their crime was television violence. According to the judge, shortly before the crime the boys had watched a television program, involving kidnapping and murder. They had imitated this program and the result was Jamie's kidnapping, torture, and murder. It was, he said, one more case of the harmful effects of television violence.

People think they see the effects of media violence in their daily lives. Every day, parents and teachers watch children practising martial arts at home and in schoolyards. Pass by a playground and you will see martial arts in action—slashing arms, jumps, kicks, the works. A generation ago young boys almost never used karate kicks; now they all do. And this goes along with increased violence in our schools. Again, surely television violence has caused it.

The terrible crimes related to television programs, the increase in violent crime since the introduction of television, and the ordinary occurrences of fighting in imitation of television heroes have convinced many people that television violence causes aggression, violence and crime. It seems so obvious that there is no need to worry about the scientific evidence. Why should anyone care what the research shows?

Don't be so sure. Not so terribly long ago it was obvious that the world was flat, that the sun revolved around the earth, and that the longer women stayed in bed after childbirth the healthier they would be. Scientific research has proven all of these wrong. An awful lot of people also knew that men were smarter than women, that picking babies up when they cried would only encourage them to cry more in the future, and that rewarding kids for playing games would make them like the games more. Research has proven all of these wrong too. Perhaps it will do the same for beliefs about the effects of media violence—that is why so many people have done so much research to establish whether watching violent programs really does make children more aggressive.

Anecdotes are not always very reliable. Let's look at the examples I offered above. Consider the case of the fire that killed the little girl. At first glance there seems no question what happened. The newspapers all reported that the boy was a well-behaved child who had never been in trouble before. He happened to watch the TV program about setting fires, and he imitated what he saw. What more could one ask? Clearly, this was a simple case of TV causing a tragedy.

But it wasn't. As those reporters who looked into the incident more carefully found out, the truth was quite different from the early reports. First of all, little Tommy was not a very well-behaved boy. He had been playing with matches and setting fires for some time—long before the program was aired. No one had been killed or hurt in any of the fires before this, so they did not make the news, but they were set nonetheless. Second, and more important, the TV program in question was shown only on cable, not on the regular networks. *And Tommy's family did not have cable television.* In fact, no one in the trailer park had it, and no one he knew had it. *So there was no way he could have seen the show.* The tragic incident had nothing whatsoever to do with the television program that had been shown the day before. Rather than it being a case of television causing the tragedy, it was simply one more instance of children playing with fire and someone getting hurt.

Also consider the case of the two boys who killed Jamie Bulger. The judge announced in court that he was convinced that TV played a crucial role in the crime—that the boys had watched a program about kidnapping and had imitated it. Again, an obvious case of TV violence producing violence?

Yet the judge's belief had no basis in fact. The police made it absolutely clear that the boys had not watched the program in question, that they did not watch television much, and that there was no reason to believe that TV had anything to do with the crime. The last time children of this age had been found guilty of murder in England had been several hundred years earlier. It hadn't been due to television then, so why in the world would the judge think so this time? This was a horrific crime beyond human comprehension. We have no idea how they could have committed it, but there is not the slightest bit of evidence that it was caused by television.

Yes, the rate of violent crime increased after television was introduced. But there is no reason to think the two are in any way related. [Television] was also introduced to France, Germany, Italy, and Japan at around the same time as it came to the United States and Canada. Yet crime rates did not increase in these other countries. If television violence were causing the increase, surely it should have had the same effect elsewhere. We have to remember that the availability of television in the United States and Canada coincided with vast changes in our societies. Between 1960 and 1985—the period of the increase in crime—the divorce rate more than doubled, many more single parents and women began working outside the home, the use of illegal drugs increased, the gap between rich and poor grew, and because of the postwar baby boom, there was a sharp increase in the number of young males. Almost all of the experts, including police, criminologists, and sociologists, agree that these factors played a crucial role in the increase in crime, and no one seriously blames television for these changes in society. It is an accident, a coincidence, that television ownership increased during this same period. These important social changes are certainly some of the causes of the increase in crime; television ownership may be irrelevant.

Although it may seem as if youth violence is increasing, it is actually declining. In 1999 the rate of murder by white youths in California was at a record low, 65 per cent less than in 1970, and the rates for Black, Latino, and Asian youths were also low. According to FBI records, elementary-school students are much less likely to murder today than they were in the 1960s and 1970s. And, both Black and white children feel less menaced now by violence in their schools than twenty-five years ago. True, over the past seven years there has been an increase in incidents in school in which more than one person was killed. However, the number of children killed in schools in the United States and Canada has dropped during the same period, from a high of fifty-five in the 1992–93 school year to sixteen in 1998–99. This last year included one killing in Canada, which shocked a country not used to this kind of violence in its schools, but it is the only case of its kind in this decade.

Moreover, the rates for all violent crimes have been dropping steadily and dramatically since the early 1990s. The number of homicides in the big American cities has plunged to levels not seen since the early 70s, and the numbers for other violent crimes have been falling as well. This, at a time when movies and television shows are as violent as ever. Add to this the rising popularity of rap music, with its violent language and themes; and of video games, which are just as violent and just as popular. If violence in the media causes aggression, how can real-life violence and crime be dropping?

None of this proves that television violence plays no role in aggression and violence. The point is that stories about its effects are often false and that obvious effects may be explainable in other ways. People's intuitions and observations are sometimes wrong, and may be this time. That is why we have to rely on scientific research to answer the question whether exposure to media violence really makes children more aggressive. . . .

What about Pronouncements by Scientific Organizations?

The public has been told by panel after panel, organization after organization, that media violence causes aggression. A long list of prestigious scientific and medical organizations have said that the evidence is in and the question has been settled. The American Psychiatric Association and the Canadian Psychological Association have all weighed in on this matter. Recently, under some prodding by a congressional committee, the American Medical Association, the American Academy of Pediatrics, the American Psychological Association, and the American Academy of Child and Adolescent Psychiatry issued a joint statement. According to these groups, it is now proven that media violence causes aggression and probably causes crime. The pediatric group went so far as to urge that children under two should watch no television because it interferes with their normal development. The National Institute of Mental Health has published an extensive report on television in which it concludes that media violence causes aggression.

If all these respectable scientific organizations agree that media violence is harmful, surely it must be. Well, it isn't. Although they have all made unequivocal statements about the effects of media violence, it is almost certain that not one of these organizations conducted a thorough review of the research. They have surely not published or made available any such review. If they made these pronouncements without a scientific review, they are guilty of the worst kind of irresponsible behaviour. If they were in court as expert witnesses, they could be convicted of perjury. It is incredible that these organizations, which purport to be scientific, should act in this manner. Yet that seems to be the case.

Consider the policy statement from the American Academy of Pediatricians published in August 1999. It states: 'More than 1000 scientific studies and reviews conclude that significant exposure to media violence increases the risk of aggressive behavior in certain children and adolescents, desensitizes them to violence, and makes them believe that the world is a "meaner and scarier" place than it is.' Apparently not satisfied, in its November 2001 Policy Statement on Media Violence the AAP stated: 'More than 3500 research studies have examined the association between media violence and violent behavior [and] all but 18 have shown a positive relationship.' That sounds pretty impressive. After all, if over 3500 scientific studies reached this conclusion, who could doubt it? The only problem is that this is not true. There have not been over 3500 or even 1000 scientific studies on this topic. This vastly exaggerates the amount of work that has been done. That the pediatricians give such an inflated figure is only one indication that they do not know the research. Imagine the response if an organization of economists asserted that there were serious economic problems in over 150 American states. No one would bother asking for their statistics, since if they were so sloppy as to think there were that many states, who could possibly trust the rest of their statement? In the same way, since the pediatricians say that they are basing their statement on over 3500 scientific studies, it must be clear that they have not read the research because there are not anywhere near that many studies.

To make matters worse, the studies that do exist do not all reach the conclusion that media violence has any of the effects listed by the AAP. Indeed, . . . most of the studies show no ill effects of exposure to media violence. And there is virtually no research showing that media violence desensitizes people to violence. Why do these presumably well-meaning pediatricians make these unsupported and inaccurate statements? Who knows.

To cap it off, the policy goes on to 'urge parents to avoid television viewing for children under the age of 2 years.' It supports this extreme recommendation by saying that 'research on early brain development shows that babies and toddlers have a critical need for direct interactions with parents . . . for healthy brain growth and the development of appropriate social, emotional and cognitive skills.' I am not a neuroscientist and I have not reviewed the relevant research. However, an article in the *New York Times* quotes neuroscientists at Rockefeller University, the University of Minnesota, and the Washington University Medical School, as saying that there is no evidence to support the pediatricians' advice. 'There is no data like that at all,' according to Charles Nelson. The author of the *Times* article goes on to say that the person who wrote the pediatric academy's report agreed that there was no evidence but that they had 'extrapolated' from other data.

This is incredible. This organization is giving advice to medical doctors who deal directly with millions of American parents and children. And it is telling these doctors to urge their patients (i.e., the parents of their patients) to keep children under two away from television—not just limit their exposure but to keep them away from television entirely. Given the role that television plays in the lives of most families, following this advice would be a major undertaking. In the first place, it would be very difficult for the parents to manage it. Television keeps children occupied, stimulates them, entertains them, and educates them. Even if it did none of these things, imagine how difficult it would be for parents who like to watch television themselves or have older children who like to watch. Would they have to turn off the television whenever the under-two children are in the room? Or are they supposed to keep the young children out of the room with the television? Be serious.

Yet the pediatricians are supposed to tell parents that watching television will harm their children by preventing them from developing normally. This is quite a threat. Many parents will presumably take it to heart, worry about doing damage to their children, and try to follow the advice. This is not a matter of reducing fat intake a little or giving them enough milk—this is telling them to alter the social environment in their home, supposedly on the basis of hard, scary, scientific facts. Do *this* or your child will not grow up normally.

But there is no scientific evidence that television harms children under two—nothing at all to support this recommendation. It is junk science; pop psychology of the worst sort based on nothing but some vague extrapolations from research that is not cited and may not exist. This is truly irresponsible. Fortunately, I think we can trust most pediatricians to ignore this nonsensical policy and not give the advice; and if they do give it, we can probably trust most sensible parents to ignore it. . . .

CHALLENGE QUESTIONS

Does Violent Media Cause Teenage Aggression?

- When dealing with such a phenomenon, it is helpful to think about what qualifies as good evidence. Is the connection between the media and youth violence so logical and obvious that it becomes self-evident, or does it require definitive statistical evidence showing that there are not other factors more directly involved?
- The explosion of media options is a historically distinct characteristic of our times. What are the general implications of such a dramatic change for adolescent development?
- Freedman emphasizes the possibility that the media is simply an easy target to blame for acts of violence. Why might people want to blame the media, and does that tendency have its own developmental implications?
- If the media is not responsible for causing aggressive behavior in teens, then what is? What other aspects of adolescent development might contribute to extreme aggression?

Suggested Readings

C. Anderson, L. Berkowitz, E. Donnerstein, L. Huesmann, J. Johnson, D. Linz, N. Malamuth, and E. Wartella, "The Influence of Media Violence on Youth," *Psychological Science in the Public Interest* (December 2003)

B. Bushman and C. Anderson, "Media Violence and the American Public: Scientific Facts Versus Media Misinformation," *American Psychologist* (June/July 2001)

S. Ceci and R. Bjork, "Science, Politics, and Violence in the Media," *Psychological Science in the Public Interest* (December 2003)

M. Cieply, "After Virginia Tech, Testing Limits of Movie Violence," *The New York Times* (April 30, 2007)

M. Cutler, "Whodunit—the Media?" *Nation* (March 26, 2001)

J. Garbarino and E. deLara, "On the Anniversary of Columbine: Ten Lessons Learned and Forgotten," *Family Life Development Center, Cornell University* (2001). Available at http://www.news.cornell.edu/releases/April01/Columbine.lessons.html

D. Grossman, "We Are Training Our Kids to Kill," *The Saturday Evening Post* (September/October 1999)

G. Kleck, "There Are No Lessons to be Learned from Littleton," *Criminal Justice Ethics* (1999)

R. Long, "Hollywood, Littleton, and Us," *National Review* (July 26, 1999)

C. Olson, "Media Violence Research and Youth Violence Data: Why Do They Conflict?" *Academic Psychiatry* (2004)

J. Wenner, "Guns and Violence," *Rolling Stone* (June 10, 1999)

Internet References . . .

This is an academic's Web site about a lifespan stage between adolescence and adulthood.

> http://www.hs.ttu.edu/hd3317/emerging.htm

Jean Twenge's Web site discusses her book *Generation Me* and provides information about related research.

> http://www.generationme.org/

This site provides a list of useful references related to "emerging adulthood" by the originator of the concept, Jeffrey Jensen Arnett.

> http://www.jeffreyarnett.com/articles.htm

"The Future of Work" is an example of an organization looking at the changing nature of work, the workforce, and the workplace.

> http://thefutureofwork.net/

A page on the Web site of Dr. Mel Levine's "All Kinds of Minds" organization, this is a summary of his book about "work-life unreadiness."

> http://www.allkindsofminds.org/product/
> Summary_ReadyOrNot.aspx

This site is the homepage for an academic network studying changes in the transition to adulthood.

> http://www.transad.pop.upenn.edu/

Youth and Early Adulthood

*W*hile we often talk about "youth" in everyday conversation, it is an ill-defined concept as a stage of the lifespan. Generally, "youth" refers to a period when a person is developing the characteristics of adulthood but does not yet have adult responsibilities (such as a career and marriage) nor the full psychological sense of responsibility. In many contemporary societies this period of life seems longer and more intense because of increasing educational expectations, later average ages for starting a family, and more time allocated to self-exploration. Thus, youth and early adulthood are primarily times where people gradually make the transition to fully adult roles. That transition involves both psychological and practical challenges, two of which are dealt with in the issues covered in this section.

- Are Contemporary Young Adults More Selfish than Previous Generations?

- Are College Graduates Unprepared for Adulthood and the World of Work?

ISSUE 13

Are Contemporary Young Adults More Selfish than Previous Generations?

YES: Jean Twenge, from *Generation Me: Why Today's Young Americans Are More Confident, Assertive, Entitled—and More Miserable Than Ever Before* (Free Press, 2006)

NO: Jeffrey Jensen Arnett, from "Suffering, Selfish, Slackers? Myths and Reality About Emerging Adults," *Journal of Youth and Adolescence* (January 2007)

ISSUE SUMMARY

YES: Psychologist Jean Twenge asserts that contemporary young adults are perilously narcissistic.

NO: Jeffrey Jensen Arnett, a psychologist, counters that while contemporary young adults are self-focused they are not selfish.

Is there something different about today's young adults? Although this is a perennial question in many social and historical settings, psychologist Jeffrey Jensen Arnett thinks that young adults in contemporary society are so distinct that they merit their own new stage of lifespan development. He calls this stage "emerging adulthood" and argues that it is qualitatively different from the transitional period that has long characterized life between adolescence and full adulthood. With increasing educational demands, later ages for marriage, and more instability in work, Arnett thinks that post–high school life is now a distinct time of exploration in work, relationships, and the self. While exploring options related to work and relationships may be something of a necessary process, the prominence of self-exploration during one's twenties has raised more serious questions and concerns.

Although the United States and other Western nations have long emphasized the value of individual rights, there is a sense that the focus on individualism in contemporary society is new and extreme. Many emerging adults have come of age amidst a culture that emphasizes self-esteem and the idea that everyone is special. Self-reflection and self-awareness are now considered basic needs. We try to promote respect for differences and we emphasize the need for each person to find their own path. It has not always been that way. As psychologist Jean Twenge points out in the selection excerpted here, in the 1950s only 12% of teenagers agreed with the statement "I am an important person," but thirty years later 80% of teenagers considered themselves special.

Twenge thinks our contemporary emphasis on individualism has created more than just the new stage of emerging adulthood, it has created an entire group characterized by self-absorption: a group she calls "generation me." Scholars and popular commentators regularly invoke the concept of "generations" to describe groups characterized by particular sets of psychosocial characteristics that fit with different historical epochs. It is, for example, common to refer to the "World War II generation," the "baby boomers," and "generation X." While there are no clear and absolute boundaries between such generations, there is a sense that a distinct set of norms has guided the development of each group. Usually these norms are considered reasonable adaptations to the circumstances confronting people in a society. Twenge is concerned that this process has gone awry, and that today's emerging adults are, as stated by the subtitle of her book, "more confident, assertive, entitled—and more miserable than ever before."

Arnett, on the other hand, considers emerging adults to simply be making the reasonable adaptations to changing circumstances that most generations make. Although he recognizes concerns that emerging adults may be "suffering, selfish, slackers" he thinks that is a misinterpretation of the next generation of adults. Arnett sees their self-confidence as a sign of healthy psychological adjustment, their self-focus as a sign of purpose, and their many work transitions as a sign of changing economic demands. Ultimately, Arnett relies on the classic formulation of Erik Erikson to suggest that the seeming crisis of today's emerging adults is really just an extended period of identity exploration.

POINT	COUNTERPOINT
• The current generation of young adults came of age in a time when everything was about them.	• Although Twenge suggests it is a problem for emerging adults to be confident, it is actually a sign of well-being.
• There has been a generation shift, toward emphasizing independent self-fulfillment as the highest value.	• While emerging adults are optimistic about themselves, they are quite realistic about the world around them.
• According to survey comparisons, rates of narcissism among college students have risen to 66% in less than twenty years.	• College students are more likely than ever to engage in volunteer work.
• High rates of narcissism are a likely by-product of excessive efforts to raise self-esteem.	• Emerging adults are self-focused, but that is very different from being selfish.

An Army of One: *Me*

One day when my mother was driving me to school in 1986, Whitney Houston's hit song "The Greatest Love of All" was warbling out of the weak speakers of our Buick station wagon with wood trim. I asked my mother what she thought the song was about. "The greatest love of all—it has to be about children," she said.

My mother was sweet, but wrong. The song does say that children are the future (always good to begin with a strikingly original thought) and that we should teach them well. About world peace, maybe? Or great literature? Nope. Children should be educated about the beauty "inside," the song declares. We all need heroes, Whitney sings, but she never found "anyone to fulfill my needs," so she learned to depend on (wait for it) "me." The chorus then declares, "learning to love yourself is the greatest love of all."

This is a stunning reversal in attitude from previous generations. Back then, respect for others was more important than respect for yourself. The term "self-esteem" wasn't widely used until the late 1960s, and didn't become talk-show and dinner-table conversation until the 1980s. By the 1990s, it was everywhere.

Take, for example, the band Offspring's rockingly irreverent 1994 riff "Self-Esteem." The song describes a guy whose girlfriend "says she wants only me . . . Then I wonder why she sleeps with my friends." (Hmmm.) But he's blasé about it—it's OK, really, since he's "just a sucker with no self-esteem."

By the mid-1990s, Offspring could take it for granted that most people knew the term "self-esteem," and knew they were supposed to have it. They also knew how to diagnose themselves when they didn't have it. Offspring's ironic self-parody demonstrates a high level of understanding of the concept, the satire suggesting that this psychological self-examination is rote and can thus be performed with tongue planted firmly in cheek.

In the years since, attention to the topic of self-esteem has rapidly expanded. A search for "self-esteem" in the books section of amazon.com yielded 105,438 entries in July 2005 (sample titles: *The Self-Esteem Work-book, Breaking the Chain of Low Self-Esteem, Ten Days to Self-Esteem, 200 Ways to Raise a Girl's Self-Esteem*). Magazine articles on self-esteem are as common as e-mail spam for Viagra. *Ladies' Home Journal* told readers to "Learn to Love Yourself!" in March 2005, while *Parenting* offered "Proud to Be Me!" (apparently the exclamation point is required) in April, listing "5 simple ways to help your child love who he is." TV and radio talk shows would be immediately shut down by the FCC if "self-esteem" were on the list of banned words. The American Academy of Pediatrics guide to caring for babies and young children uses the word self-esteem ten times in the space of seven pages in the first chapter, and that doesn't even count the numerous mentions of self-respect, confidence, and belief in oneself.

How did self-esteem transform from an obscure academic term to a familiar phrase that pops up in everything from women's magazines to song lyrics to celebrity interviews? The story actually begins centuries ago, when humans barely had a concept of a self at all: your marriage was arranged, your profession determined by your parents, your actions dictated by strict religious standards. Slowly over the centuries, social strictures began to loosen and people started to make more choices for themselves. Eventually, we arrived at the modern concept of the individual as an autonomous, free person.

Then came the 1970s, when the ascendance of the self truly exploded into the American consciousness. In contrast to previous ethics of honor and duty, Baby Boomer ideals focused instead on meaning and self-fulfillment. In his 1976 bestseller, *Your Erroneous Zones*, Wayne Dyer suggests that the popular song "You Are the Sunshine of My Life" be retitled "I Am the Sunshine of My Life." Your love for yourself, he says, should be your "first love." The 1970 allegory, *Jonathan Livingston Seagull*, describes a bird bored with going "from shore to food and back again." Instead, he wants to enjoy flying, swooping through the air to follow "a higher meaning, a higher purpose for life," even though his actions get him exiled from his flock. The book, originally rejected by nearly every major publishing house, became a runaway bestseller as Americans came to agree with the idea that life should be fulfilling and focused on the needs of the self. The seagulls in the animated movie *Finding Nemo* were still on message almost twenty-five years later: all that comes out of their beaks is the word "Mine."

Boomers and Their "Journey" into the Self

But this book is not about Baby Boomers, and it's not about the 1970s. Because the Boomers dominate our culture so much, however, we have to understand them first so we can see how they differ from the younger Generation Me. Why aren't the Boomers—the Me Generation in the 1970s—the *real* Generation Me? It's about what you explore as a young adult versus what you're born to and take for granted.

For the Boomers, who grew up in the 1950s and 1960s, self-focus was a new concept, individualism an uncharted territory. In his 1981 book *New Rules: Searching for Self-Fulfillment in a World Turned Upside Down*, Daniel Yankelovich describes young Boomers struggling with new questions: How do you make decisions in a marriage with two equal partners? How do you focus on yourself when your parents don't even know what that means? The Boomers in the book sound like people driving around in circles in the dark, desperately searching for something. The world was so new that there were no road signs, no maps to point the way to this new fulfillment and individuality.

That's probably why many Boomers talk about the self using language full of abstraction, introspection, and "growth." New things call for this kind of meticulous thought, and require the idea that the process will take time. Thus Boomers talk about "my journey," "my need to keep growing," or "my unfulfilled potentials." Sixties activist Todd Gitlin called the Boomer quest the "voyage to the interior." Icky as they are to today's young people, these phrases drum with motion and time, portraying self-focus as a continuous project that keeps evolving as Boomers look around for true meaning. In a 1976 *New York Magazine* article, Tom Wolfe described the "new dream" as "remaking, remodeling, elevating and polishing one's very self . . . and observing, studying, and doting on it." Sixties radical Jerry Rubin wrote that he tried just about every fad of the 1970s (rolfing, est, yoga, sex therapy, finding his inner child); one of the chapters in his book *Growing (Up) at Thirty-Seven* is called "Searching for Myself."

Such introspection primarily surfaces today in the speech of New Agers, therapists who have read too much Maslow, and over-45 Boomers. When asked what's next in her life, Kim Basinger (born in 1953) replies, "Watching what the rest of my journey is going to be about." In answer to the same question, Sarah Ferguson, Duchess of York (born in 1959) says: "My coming to stay in America for a few months is like my blossoming into my true Sarah, into my true self. And I'm just coming to learn about her myself." Not all Boomers talk this way, of course, but enough do that it's an immediately recognizable generational tic. It's also a guaranteed way to get a young person to roll her eyes. She might also then tell you to lighten up.

Many authors, from William Strauss and Neil Howe in *Generations* to Steve Gillon in *Boomer Nation*, have noted that abstraction and spirituality are the primary hallmarks of the Boomer generation. Gillon describes Boomers as having a "moralistic style" and devotes a chapter to Boomers' "New Fundamentalism." Whether joining traditional churches or exploring meditation or yoga, Boomers have been fascinated with the spiritual for four decades.

Even Boomers who don't adopt New Age language seek higher meaning in the new religion of consumer products—thus the yuppie revolution. In *Bobos in Paradise*, David Brooks demonstrates that upper-class Boomers have poured their wealth into things like cooking equipment, which somehow feels more moral and meaningful than previous money sinks like jewelry or furs. Even food becomes "a barometer of virtue," Brooks says, as 1960s values are "selectively updated. . . . Gone are the sixties-era things that were fun and of interest to teenagers, like Free Love, and retained are all the things that might be of interest to middle-aged hypochondriacs, like whole grains."

The Boomers' interest in the abstract and spiritual shows up in many different sources. In 1973, 46% of Boomers said they "focused on internal cues." Only 26% of 1990s young people agreed. Thirty percent of Boomers said that "creativity comes from within," versus 18% of young people in the 1990s. Even stronger evidence comes from a national survey of more than 300,000 college freshmen. In 1967, a whopping 86% of incoming college students said that "developing a meaningful philosophy of life" was an essential life goal. Only 42% of GenMe freshmen in 2004 agreed, cutting the Boomer number in half. I'm definitely a member of my generation in this way; despite being an academic, I'm not sure I know what a "meaningful philosophy of life" even is. Jerry Rubin does—if you can understand him. "Instead of seeking with the expectation of finding, I experience my seeking as an end in itself," he writes. "I become one with my seeking, and merge with the moment." OK, Jerry. Let us know when you've reentered the Earth's atmosphere.

While up there, maybe Jerry met Aleta St. James, a 57-year-old woman who gave birth to twins in 2004. She explained her unusual actions by saying, "My whole world is about manifesting, so I decided to manifest children." It's not surprising that an enterprising GenMe member put together a list of books on amazon.com titled "Tired of Baby Boomer Self-Righteousness?"

Boomers display another unique and somewhat ironic trait: a strong emphasis on group meetings. Boomers followed in the footsteps of their community-minded elders—they just joined the Weathermen instead of the Elks Lodge. This is one of the many reasons why Boomers are not the true Generation Me—almost everything they did happened in groups: Vietnam protests, marches for feminism, consciousness raising, assertiveness training, discos, even seminars like est. Maybe it felt safer to explore the self within a group—perhaps it felt less radical. No one seemed to catch the irony that it might be difficult to find your own unique direction in a group of other people. Even Boomers' trends and sayings belied their reliance on groups: "Don't trust anyone over 30" groups people by age, as did the long hair many Boomer men adopted in the late 1960s and early 1970s to distinguish themselves from older folks. In a 1970 song, David Crosby says he decided not to cut his hair so he could "let my freak flag fly." If you've got a flag, you're probably a group. Boomers may have thought they invented individualism, but like any inventor, they were followed by those who truly perfected the art.

Boomers took only the first tentative steps in the direction of self-focus, rather than swallowing it whole at birth. Most Boomers never absorbed it at all and settled down early to marry and raise families. Those who adopted the ways of the self as young adults speak the language with an accent: the accent of abstraction and "journeys." They had to reinvent their way of thinking when already grown, and thus see self-focus as a "process." In his book, Rubin quotes a friend who says, "We are the first generation to reincarnate ourselves in our own lifetime."

The Matter-Of-Fact Self-Focus of Generation Me

Generation Me had no need to reincarnate ourselves; we were born into a world that already celebrated the individual. The self-focus that blossomed in the 1970s became mundane and commonplace over the next two decades, and GenMe accepts it like a fish accepts water. If Boomers were making their way in the uncharted world of the self, GenMe has printed step-by-step directions from Yahoo! Maps and most of the time we don't even need them, since the culture of the self is our hometown. We don't have to join groups or talk of journeys, because we're already there. We don't need to "polish" the self, as Wolfe said, because we take for granted that it's already shiny. We don't need to look inward; we already know what we will find. Since we were small children, we were taught to put ourselves first. That's just the way the world works—why dwell on it? Let's go to the mall.

GenMe's focus on the needs of the individual is not necessarily self-absorbed or isolationist; instead, it's a way of moving through the world beholden to few social rules and with the unshakable belief that you're important. It's also not the same as being "spoiled," which implies that we always get what we want; though this probably does describe some kids, it's not the essence of the trend (as I argue in Chapter 4, GenMe's expectations are so great and our reality so challenging that we will probably get less of what we want than any previous generation). We simply take it for granted that we should all feel good about ourselves, we are all special, and we all deserve to follow our dreams. GenMe is straightforward and unapologetic about our self-focus. In 2004's *Conquering Your Quarterlife Crisis*, Jason, 25, relates how he went through some tough times and decided he needed to change things in his life. His new motto was "Do what's best for Jason. I had to make *me* Happy; I had to do what was best for myself in every situation."

Our practical orientation toward the self sometimes leaves us with a distaste for Boomer abstraction. When a character in the 2004 novel *Something Borrowed* watched the 1980s show *thirtysomething* as a teen, she wished the Boomer characters would "stop pondering the meaning of life and start making grocery lists." The matter-of-fact attitude of GenMe appears in everyday language as well—a language that still includes the abstract concept of self, but uses it in a very simple way, perhaps because we learned the language as children. We speak the language of the self as our native tongue. So much of the "common sense" advice that's given these days includes some variation on "self":

- Worried about how to act in a social situation? "Just be yourself."
- What's the good thing about your alcoholism/drug addiction/murder conviction? "I learned a lot about myself."
- Concerned about your performance? "Believe in yourself." (Often followed by "and anything is possible.")
- Should you buy the new pair of shoes, or get the nose ring? "Yes, express yourself."
- Why should you leave the unfulfilling relationship/quit the boring job/tell off your mother-in-law? "You have to respect yourself."
- Trying to get rid of a bad habit? "Be honest with yourself."
- Confused about the best time to date or get married? "You have to love yourself before you can love someone else."
- Should you express your opinion? "Yes, stand up for yourself."

Americans use these phrases so often that we don't even notice them anymore. Dr. Phil, the ultimate in plainspoken, no-nonsense advice, uttered both "respect yourself" and "stop lying to yourself" within seconds of each other on a *Today* show segment on New Year's resolutions. One of his bestselling books is entitled *Self Matters*. We take these phrases and ideas so much for granted, it's as if we learned them in our sleep as children, like the perfectly conditioned citizens in Aldous Huxley's *Brave New World*.

These aphorisms don't seem absurd to us even when, sometimes, they are. We talk about self-improvement as if the self could be given better drywall or a new coat of paint. We read self-help books as if the self could receive tax-deductible donations. The *Self* even has its own magazine. Psychologist Martin Seligman says that the traditional self—responsible, hardworking, stern—has been replaced with the "California self," "a self that chooses, feels pleasure and pain, dictates action and even has things like esteem, efficacy, and confidence." Media outlets promote the self relentlessly; I was amazed at how often I heard the word "self" used in the popular media once I started looking for it. A careful study of news stories published or aired between 1980 and 1999 found a large increase in self-reference words (I, me, mine, and myself) and a marked decrease in collective words (humanity, country, or crowd).

The Self Across the Generations

Baby Boomers	Generation Me
Self-fulfillment	Fun
Journey, potentials, searching	Already there
Change the world	Follow your dreams
Protests and group sessions	Watching TV and surfing the Web
Abstraction	Practicality
Spirituality	Things
Philosophy of life	Feeling good about yourself

Young people have learned these self-lessons very well. In a letter to her fans in 2004, Britney Spears, 23, listed her priorities as "Myself, my husband, Kevin, and starting a family." If you had to read that twice to get my point, it's because we take it for granted that we should put ourselves first on our list of priorities—it would be blasphemy if you didn't (unless, of course, you have low self-esteem). Twenty-year-old Maria says her mother often reminds her to consider what other people will think. "It doesn't matter what other people think," Maria insists. "What really matters is how I perceive myself. The real person I need to please is myself."

Smart marketers have figured this out, too. In the late 1990s, Prudential replaced its longtime insurance slogan "Get a Piece of the Rock" with the nakedly individualistic "Be Your Own Rock." The United States Army, perhaps the last organization one might expect to focus on the individual instead of the group, has followed suit. Their standard slogan, adopted in 2001, is "An Army of One."

Changes in Self-Esteem: What the Data Say

The data I gathered on self-esteem over time mirror the social trends perfectly. My colleague Keith Campbell and I looked at the responses of 65,965 college students to the Rosenberg Self-Esteem Scale, the most popular measure of general self-esteem among adults. I held my breath when I analyzed these data for the first time, but I needn't have worried: the change was enormous. By the mid-1990s, the average GenMe college man had higher self-esteem than 86% of college men in 1968. The average mid-1990s college woman had higher self-esteem than 71% of Boomer college women. Between the 1960s and the 1990s, college students were increasingly likely to agree that "I take a positive attitude toward myself" and "On the whole, I am satisfied with myself." Other sources verify this trend. A 1997 survey of teens asked, "In general, how do you feel about yourself?" A stunning 93% answered "good." Of the remainder, 6% said they felt "not very good," and only 1% admitted they felt "bad" about themselves. Another survey found that 91% of teens described themselves as responsible, 74% as physically attractive, and 79% as "very intelligent."

Children's self-esteem scores tell a different but even more intriguing story. We examined the responses of 39,353 children, most ages 9 to 13, on the Coopersmith Self-Esteem Inventory, a scale written specifically for children. During the 1970s—when the nation's children shifted from the late Baby Boom to the early years of GenX—kids' self-esteem declined, probably because of societal instability. Rampant divorce, a wobbly economy, soaring crime rates, and swinging singles culture made the 1970s difficult time to be a kid. The average child in 1979 scored lower than 81% of kids in the mid-1960s. Over this time, children were less likely to agree with statements like "I'm pretty sure of myself" and "I m pretty happy" and more likely to agree that "things are all mixed up in my life." The individualism that was so enthralling for teenagers and adults in the 1970s didn't help kids—and, if their parents suddenly discovered self-fulfillment, it might have been hurt them.

But after 1980, when GenMe began to enter the samples, children's self-esteem took a sharp turn upward. More and more during the 1980s and 1990s, children were saying that they were happy with themselves. They agreed that "I'm easy to like" and "I always do the right thing." By the mid-1990s, children's self-esteem scores equaled, and often exceeded, children's scores in the markedly more stable Boomer years before 1970. The average kid in the mid-1990s—right in the heart of GenMe—had higher self-esteem than 73% of kids in 1979, one of the last pre-GenMe years. . . .

Changes in Narcissism

Narcissism is one of the few personality traits that psychologists agree is almost completely negative. Narcissists are overly focused on themselves and lack empathy for others, which means they cannot see another person's perspective. (Sound like the last clerk who served you?) They also feel entitled to special privileges and believe that they are superior to other people. As a result, narcissists are bad relationship partners and can be difficult to work with. Narcissists are also more likely to be hostile, feel anxious, compromise their health, and fight with friends and family. Unlike those merely high in self-esteem, narcissists admit that they don't feel close to other people.

All evidence suggests that narcissism is much more common in recent generations. In the early 1950s, only 12% of teens aged 14 to 16 agreed with the statement "I am an important person." By the late 1980s, an incredible 80%—almost seven times as many—claimed they were important. Psychologist Harrison Gough found consistent increases on narcissism items among college students quizzed between the 1960s and the 1990s. GenMe students were more likely to agree that "I would be willing to describe myself as a pretty 'strong' personality" and "I have often met people who were supposed to be experts who were no better than I." In other words, those other people don't know what they're talking about, so everyone should listen to me.

Definitive evidence for the rise in narcissism appeared in a recent study I conducted with Sara Konrath, Keith Campbell, Joshua Foster, and Brad Bushman. We examined responses to the Narcissistic Personality Inventory, the most popular and valid measure of narcissism. The scale features statements that might be funny if they hadn't been encouraged so strongly by our culture: "I think I am a special person," "I can live my life anyway I want to," and "If I ruled the world, it would be a better place." When I give this questionnaire in class, the discussion usually begins the same way: the first person to raise his hand will say, "Well, I scored high, and I think . . ." (Clearly the scale does its job well.) I then mention that the scale could be called "The Boyfriend Test," given the disastrous nature of many relationships with narcissists. Many young women eagerly take the scale home to their unwitting paramours.

These days, those boyfriends—and their girlfriends—are considerably more likely to be high in narcissism. My coauthors and I analyzed the responses of 15,234 American college students who completed the Narcissistic Personality Inventory between 1987 and 2006. The trend was extremely clear: younger generations were significantly more narcissistic. The average college student in 2006 scored higher in narcissism than 65% of students just nineteen years before in 1987. In other words, the number of college students high in narcissism rose to two-thirds in the space of less than twenty years.

This data shows that the generation William Strauss and Neil Howe call the "Millennials" is not as other-focused and group-oriented as their theory suggests. Strauss and Howe define this group as those born in 1982 and afterward, so college student samples were made up almost exclusively of Millennials by 2004. The data show that the 2004–2006 college students are the most narcissistic group of all—the most likely to agree that "I find it easy to manipulate people," "I expect a great deal from other people," and "I insist upon getting the respect that is due me." Far from being altruistic and focused on others, the Millennials are the most narcissistic generation in history.

Narcissism is the darker side of the focus on the self, and is often confused with self-esteem. Self-esteem is often based on solid relationships with others, whereas narcissism comes from believing that you are special and more important than other people. Many of the school programs designed to raise self-esteem probably raise narcissism instead. Lillian Katz, a professor of early childhood education at the University of Illinois, wrote an article titled "All About Me: Are We Developing Our Children's Self-Esteem or Their

Narcissism?" She writes, "Many of the practices advocated in pursuit of [high self-esteem] may instead inadvertently develop narcissism in the form of excessive preoccupation with oneself." Because the school programs emphasize being "special" rather than encouraging friendships, we may be training an army of little narcissists instead of raising kids' self-esteem.

Many young people also display entitlement, a facet of narcissism that involves believing that you deserve and are entitled to more than others. A scale that measures entitlement has items like "Things should go my way," "I demand the best because I'm worth it," and (my favorite) "If I were on the *Titanic*, I would deserve to be on the *first* lifeboat!" A 2005 Associated Press article printed in hundreds of news outlets labeled today's young people "The Entitlement Generation." In the article, employers complained that young employees expected too much too soon and had very high expectations for salary and promotions.

Teachers have seen this attitude for years now. One of my colleagues said his students acted as if grades were something they simply deserved to get no matter what. He joked that their attitude could be summed up by "Where's my A? I distinctly remember ordering an A from the catalog." Stout, the education professor, lists the student statements familiar to teachers everywhere: "I need a better grade," "I deserve an A on this paper," "I *never* get B's." Stout points out that the self-esteem movement places the student's feelings at the center, so "students learn that they do not need to respect their teachers or even earn their grades, so they begin to believe that they are entitled to grades, respect, or anything else . . . just for asking."

Unfortunately, narcissism can lead to outcomes far worse than grade grubbing. Several studies have found that narcissists lash out aggressively when they are insulted or rejected. Eric Harris and Dylan Klebold, the teenage gunmen at Columbine High School, made statements remarkably similar to items on the most popular narcissism questionnaire. On a videotape made before the shootings, Harris picked up a gun, made a shooting noise, and said "Isn't it fun to get the respect we're going to deserve?" (Chillingly similar to the narcissism item "I insist upon getting the respect that is due me.") Later, Harris said, "I could convince them that I'm going to climb Mount Everest, or I have a twin brother growing out of my back. I can make you believe anything" (virtually identical to the item "I can make anyone believe anything I want them to"). Harris and Klebold then debate which famous movie director will film their story. A few weeks after making the videotapes, Harris and Klebold killed thirteen people and then themselves.

Other examples abound. In a set of lab studies, narcissistic men felt less empathy for rape victims, reported more enjoyment when watching a rape scene in a movie, and were more punitive toward a woman who refused to read a sexually arousing passage out loud to them. Abusive husbands who threaten to kill their wives—and tragically sometimes do—are the ultimate narcissists. They see everyone and everything in terms of fulfilling their needs, and become very angry and aggressive when things don't go exactly their way. Many workplace shootings occur after an employee is fired and decides he'll "show" everyone how powerful he is.

The rise in narcissism has very deep roots. It's not just that we feel better about ourselves, but that we even think to ask the question. We fixate on self-esteem, and unthinkingly build narcissism, because we believe that the needs of individual are paramount. This will stay with us even if self-esteem programs end up in the dustbin of history. . . .

Jeffrey Jensen Arnett

Suffering, Selfish, Slackers? Myths and Reality about Emerging Adults

In this essay, I will examine some of the myths about emerging adulthood, the reasons for them, and the data that refute them. I have chosen three prominent myths that I have seen stated repeatedly in academic circles and/or popular media. The issues involving emerging adults are in some ways similar to and in some ways different from the issues that apply to adolescents. For emerging adults, three key myths concern their overall well-being, their "selfishness." And their alleged unwillingness to "grow up."

Are They Suffering? Well-being in Emerging Adulthood

One claim made frequently about emerging adults is that they are a miserable lot, wracked with anxiety and unhappiness, intimidated to the point of paralysis about their grim prospects for entering the adult world. According to this view, the years from age 18 to 25 are a dark and dreary period of the life course. Emerging adults are typically confused and glum, and overwhelmed by what the world seems to require from them.

Perhaps the best-known popular statement of this view is the book *Quarterlife Crisis*. This book was written by two emerging adult women, and there is much in it that is on target. They describe with accuracy and insight the ambivalence with which many emerging adults view their entry into adult responsibilities. There is truth, too, in their observation that the uncertainty and instability of the age period make it unsettling for many people. However, there is considerable hyperbole in their claim that the emerging adult years are a time of agony. They describe emerging adults as suffering from "overwhelming senses of helplessness and cluelessness of indecision and apprehension" and claim that it is common for them to experience "hopelessness" during this "often traumatic" age period. They describe the experience of a young woman who was "sobbing every other day, frantic with worry . . . doubting myself into a frenzy" as "hardly abnormal."

Although the term "quarterlife crisis" has entered the mainstream of popular culture, there is an older, better term for what the authors of that book

From *Journal of Youth and Adolescence*, vol. 36, January 2007, pp. excerpts from 23-8. Copyright © 2007 by Springer Journals (Kluwer Academic). Reprinted by permission. Reference omitted.

describe: Erikson's "identity crisis." Over a half century ago, Erikson observed that the primary challenge of adolescence is the identity crisis, in which young people face the challenge of evaluating their abilities, interests, and childhood influences, then using that knowledge to explore possible futures and eventually make enduring choices in love and work. What has changed since Erikson postulated the identity crisis is that it now takes place mainly in emerging adulthood, not adolescence. The first tentative steps toward an adult identity may take place in adolescence, but identity explorations become more prominent and serious in emerging adulthood. By and large, emerging adults respond to the challenges of identity development not by collapsing into a quivering mass of fear but by making their way gradually toward laying the foundations for an adult life in live and work, with some anxiety but without trauma.

It is not only in popular media that it has been asserted that the emerging adult years are a time of suffering. Some academics, too, have portrayed the late teens through the twenties as a period that is exceptionally difficult and unhappy. Many sociologists view the transition to adulthood in out time as full of terrors and trauma. The title of one book states it well: *Transitions to adulthood in a changing economy: No work, no family, no future?*

Some psychologists share this view. In the subtitle of one recent book, social psychologist Jean Twenge asserts that today's young people are "more confident, assertive, entitled—and more miserable than ever before." The evidence she presents for the first part of this thesis is quite persuasive in showing that today's emerging adults are more confident and assertive than in the past, and that they have high expectations for their lives ("entitled," as she puts it). However, the evidence for the claim that they are simultaneously "more miserable than ever before" is more questionable. She asserts that the incidence of major depression increased through the 20th century, but this is *lifetime* rate of major depression, not major depression in youth. She presents evidence from her meta-analysis showing that anxiety among college students has increased since the 1950s, but it has been widely documented that modern life feels more stressful to people of all ages, not just the young. She presents abundant evidence that young people face adult prospects of high housing prices, costly health care, and elusive child care—all of it true, but *non*e of it shown here or anywhere else to result in anxiety or depression among adolescents or emerging adults.

What does the evidence actually show about the well-being of emerging adults? In fact, the evidence shows emerging adults overall to be highly contented with themselves and their lives, and remarkably optimistic. In one national survey, 96% of 18–29 year-old Americans agreed with the statement "I am very certain that someday I will get to where I want to be in life." Overall well-being rises steadily from the late teens through the mid-twenties. The national Monitoring the Future surveys have followed American emerging adults longitudinally from their senior year in high school through their mid-twenties. Figure I shows the pattern from age 18 through 26, as average well-being rises with each year, reaching an average of over 4 on a 5-point scale by ages 25–26. A recent Canadian study shows a highly similar pattern of rising well-being, along with declining depressive affect. If the majority of emerging adults are miserable, they certainly are hiding it well.

This is not to portray emerging adulthood as entirely a time of pleasure-filled glory days, free of problems. Like every other period of life, emerging adulthood contains its distinctive developmental challenges and difficulties. As noted, there is validity to the "quarterlife crisis" insight that many emerging adults experience anxiety over the instability and identity challenges of their lives, even as they also celebrate their freedom and the wide range of possibilities before them. Their optimism frequently co-exists with an undercurrent of trepidation.

Furthermore, even as emerging adulthood is mostly in enjoyable for most people, there are some emerging adults who have particular difficulty handling the requirements of the age period. Emerging adulthood is exceptionally unstructured, the time of life when people are least likely to have their lives structured by social institutions. Children have their lives structured by their families and school, adults have their lives structured by family roles and work commitments. In contrast, emerging adults have mostly left their families of origin and not yet established new families, and they have not yet committed themselves to stable long-term work. Most of them thrive on this freedom, as indicated by their high levels of well-being, but some find it overwhelming. Schulenberg and Zarrett describe this paradox in detail. For most emerging adults, well-being increases, depressive affect decreases, and a wide variety of problems decrease. However, emerging adulthood is also a period when major depression spikes sharply. Thus the variance in mental health functioning expands during emerging adulthood, improving for most people even as it declines precipitously for a small proportion.

Even for emerging adults who are contented and optimistic about their lives, it is important to note that their contentment and optimism does not extend to the world around them. On the contrary, emerging adults are largely skeptical and even cynical about political and religious institutions, and they are less civically involved and more disengaged than older generations. They tend to have "high hopes in a grim world," believing that they will be able to create a good and satisfying life for themselves and those they love even as the world deteriorates around them. The failure to distinguish between their hopes for their own lives and their (limited) hopes for the world contributes to the myth that they are unhappy.

Are They Selfish? Or-Self-Focused?

Another myth about emerging adults is that they are selfish. In this view, the main reason emerging adults wait until at least their late twenties to enter enduring adult responsibilities is that they prefer to spend their time and money solely on themselves. They live a self-indulgent, materialistic lifestyle and care little about the world around them. This view is found in the United States, but it is perhaps especially prevalent in countries that are experiencing extremely low birth rates in recent decades, so low that their populations are expected to decline in the decades to come. In Japan, unmarried young people in their twenties and thirties are sometimes referred to with the derisive term "parasite singles."

Figure 1

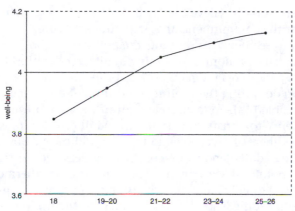

Trend in Well-being from Age 18 to 26

Source: Schulenberg and Zarrett (2006)

It does seem to be true that today's emerging adults are less interested than other recent generations in organized political activity. As Robert Putnam showed in *Bowling Alone*, today's American 18–29 year-olds report considerable less civic engagement than their parents or grandparents did when they were young, on a wide variety of items, from reading the newspaper daily to attending public meetings to serving as an officer in a local organization. However, the trend away from civic engagement has been occurring in American Society for over a half century and was not invented by today's emerging adults. Putnam observes that "Although X'ers [today's emerging adults] have often been blamed by their elders (especially the boomers) for the troubles of contemporary American society—especially the emphasis on materialism and individualism—the evidence I have already presented makes clear that this indictment is misplaced. The erosion of American social capital began before any X'er was born, so the X'ers cannot reasonably be blamed for these adverse treads. . . . The X Generation reflects in many respects a continuation of the generational course begun just after World War II."

More importantly, although traditional civic engagement among emerging adults is relatively low, they are more likely than ever before to engage in volunteer work. The proportion of college freshmen reporting that they had done volunteer work frequently or occasionally in the past year rose from 66% in 1989 to 82% in 2001. Over 8,000 persons a year serve in the Peace Corps and 70,000 a year serve in AmeriCorps, and the vast majority of the volunteers in both groups are emerging adults. These facts are difficult to square with the portrayal of emerging adults as selfish.

Perhaps the criticism of emerging adults as selfish stems in part from a misunderstanding of where they are developmentally. Most American emerging adults leave home by age 19, and for the next seven years (on average) they live with neither their family of origin nor a marriage partner. This makes emerging adulthood an exceptionally *self-focused* time of life, in the sense that it is a time of life when people have the most opportunity to focus on their self-development, including their educational and occupational preparation for adult life. Many emerging adults take advantage of their self-focused freedom to travel, to live somewhere they have always wanted to live, and to obtain experiences they believe they will not have the opportunity to obtain once they enter the commitments that structure adult life.

It is hard to see how this warrants the epithet "selfish." On the contrary, there is considerable wisdom in emerging adults' recognition that they are in a period of life that grants them exceptional freedom and that there are many things they can do during their self-focused time of emerging adulthood that will be inaccessible to them later. Nearly all of them plan eventually to make the commitments to others that structure adult life for most people, and three-fourths of them are married and have a child by age 30. Far from being selfish, emerging adults tend to be considerably less egocentric and better at seeing others' points of view than adolescents are. Furthermore, they view becoming less self-oriented and more considerate of others as an essential part of becoming fully adult. They reject selfishness in themselves and in others.

Are They Slackers? Do They Refuse to Grow Up?

There is little doubt that it takes longer to reach full adulthood today than it did in the past. This is verifiable demographically, in terms of traditional transitions such as finishing education, becoming financially independent from parents, marriage, and parenthood. It also seems confirmed subjectively by emerging adults' reports that during the 18–25 age period most of them feel not like adolescents and not like adults but somewhere in between, on the way to adulthood but not there yet. My proposal of the term emerging adulthood was predicated on the assertion that reaching adulthood takes so long today that it is necessary to recognize that a new period of the life course has developed in between the end of adolescence and the attainment of young adulthood.

Does this mean that emerging adults resist the responsibilities of adult life, preferring to perpetuate a child-like state of irresponsible play? This is the myth promulgated in popular culture, such the 2005 TIME magazine story that depicted an emerging adult man sitting in a sandbox and declared. "They Just Won't Grow Up." Physician and advice writer Mel Levine warns apocalyptically that "starting up into adulthood has never been more daunting than it is at present. . . . The end result is that many adolescents seek an extension of their high school and/or college years. They just don't want to pull away from their teens. . . . The effects on work-life readiness may be catastrophic." In the recent movie *Failure to Launch*, the main character, an emerging adult man, shows so little inclination to move along toward adult responsibilities that his parents hire an attractive young woman to lure him out of their household and into a responsible adult life.

One reason for these views is the speed of the social and demographic changes that have taken place in the lives of young people in recent decades.

For many of today's emerging adults, their parents and certainly their grand-parents remember that "in their day" reaching age 25 meant being well-settled in adult life, with a stable job expected to last for decades to come, a marriage, at least one child, and a mortgage. Many older adults look askance at today's unsettled emerging adults no where near to making such commitments, com-pare them to where they were themselves at that age, and find them wanting.

But does the delay in entering adult responsibilities mean that emerging adults are actively resisting the idea of becoming adult? This seems unfair in light of current economic realities. The economy in industrialized countries has changed dramatically in recent decades, away from a manufacturing base and toward valuing knowledge and information skills. Consequently, occupations increasingly require postsecondary education or training. More young Ameri-cans than ever—over 60%—obtain postsecondary education, not because they fear stable work but because they recognize that higher education is necessary in order to obtain the best jobs available in the information-based economy. For those who do not obtain higher education, many of them spend their twenties fruitlessly seeking a job that will enable them to support themselves adequately (much less support a joint household with a spouse and one or more children). With high-paying manufacturing jobs mostly gone to developing countries or eliminated by new technologies, the economic prospects of emerging adults who have not obtained higher education are grim during their twenties, and certainly do not lend themselves to the establishment of a stable adult life.

Still, emerging adults' slow, gradual entry into adult responsibilities can-not be explained entirely or even mostly by economic factors. Most emerging adults have feelings of ambivalence about adulthood that are unrelated to their economic situation. They regard adulthood as attractive in some ways, in the security and stability it seems to promise and the increased status it confers. However, they also regard adult responsibilities as a mixed blessing. It is satisfying to be able to stand on your own, make your own decisions, and run your own life, but at the same time, adult responsibilities are onerous—the daily grind of going to work, paying your own bills, washing your own clothes, making your own meals, and so on. Furthermore, to many emerging adults becoming an adult means the end of possibilities, the end of spontane-ity, the compromise of their dreams.

Is it true after all, then, that "they won't grow up"? Not in the sense that they wish to remain in a child-like state of self-indulgent play. On the con-trary, their views reflect a shrewd grasp of the realities of adult life. Are they not right to recognize that adulthood, whatever its rewards, involves con-straints and limitations that their lives during emerging adulthood do not have? At least, it seems evident that their ambivalence about adulthood is reasonable, and does not merit contempt or derision.

Few do, after all, fail to "launch." By age 30, for better or worse, three-fourths have entered marriage and parenthood, nearly all have entered stable employment, nearly all have become financially independent, and hardly any, live with their parents. Thus all the criticism and hand-wringing about their alleged refusal to grow up seems overblown.

CHALLENGE QUESTIONS

Are Contemporary Young Adults More Selfish than Previous Generations?

- Both Twenge and Arnett agree that today's emerging adults are a distinct group. In considering different generations, what characteristics seem most important as influences on development?
- Twenge thinks that high rates of narcissism among college students relate to a gradual shift toward more emphasis on the self and individualism. Are there other factors that might contribute to her findings?
- Do you agree with Arnett's contention that there is now a distinct stage between adolescence and full adulthood (which he terms "emerging adulthood")? Why or why not?
- Could there be advantages to both individuals and society from having emerging adulthood be a very self-focused period of life? What might be possible advantages?

Suggested Readings

J. Arnett, *Emerging Adulthood: The Winding Road From the Late Teens Through the Twenties* (Oxford University Press, 2004)

J. Arnett and J. Tanner (eds.), *Emerging Adults in America: Coming of Age in the 21st Century* (APA Books)

J. Côté, *Arrested Adulthood: The Changing Nature of Maturity and Identity in the Late Modern World* (New York University Press, 2000)

A. Robbins and A. Wilner, *Quarterlife Crisis: The Unique Challenges of Life in Your Twenties* (Tarcher, 2001)

J. Twenge and W. Campbell, "Isn't It Fun to Get the Respect that We're Going to Deserve?" Narcissism, Social Rejection, and Aggression," *Personality and Social Psychology Bulletin* (2003)

J. Foster, W. Campbell, and J. Twenge, "Individual Differences in Narcissism: Inflated Self-views across the Lifespan and around the World," *Journal of Research in Personality* (2003)

ISSUE 14

Are College Graduates Unprepared for Adulthood and the World of Work?

YES: Mel Levine, from "College Graduates Aren't Ready for the Real World," *The Chronicle of Higher Education* (February 18, 2005)

NO: Frank F. Furstenberg et al., from "Growing Up Is Harder to Do," *Contexts* (Summer 2004)

ISSUE SUMMARY

YES: Professor of pediatrics, author, and child-rearing expert Mel Levine argues that contemporary colleges are producing a generation of young adults who are psychologically "unready" for entering adulthood and the world of work.

NO: Sociologist Frank Furstenberg and colleagues assert that major social changes have extended the transition to adulthood, and college graduates are the group most apt to cope with these social changes.

There seems to be something attractive about idealizing previous generations. In each successive cohort there is a group of people who are convinced that the "youth today" just are not as able as those of previous decades. This concern often relates to one of the primary tasks of early adulthood—finding one's way in the world of work. One of the traditional markers of adulthood is settling into a career, and many young adults are very focused on finding a worthwhile job. In contemporary society, however, that task is more complicated than it once was because young adults often go through extensive educational training and a succession of different jobs.

Dr. Mel Levine thinks the current generation of youth, particularly recent college graduates, are unprepared and unready to be productive members of society. In researching a book, Levine undertook interviews with employers and young adults, and persistently found that college graduates were not ready for the world of work. He lays out a series of explanations for this problem—blaming colleges, parents, and the culture at large for allowing young adults to expect that fun and gratification should be easy and without rigorous dedication.

In contrast, Frank Furstenberg and his colleagues emphasize that young adulthood today cannot be understood outside of its historical context. In fact, they suggest, what is distinctive about the current generation of youth is that they face unprecedented expectations and challenges in making the transition to adulthood. Rather than being able to seamlessly move into career and family patterns that will provide stable lives, today's young adults face the expensive and challenging task of preparing themselves to enter a stunningly complex world. From Furstenberg et al.'s perspective, college graduates are the most able to take on that task.

There is no question that the nature of early adulthood and the expectations of college have changed. Just one century ago it was only elite youth that even graduated from high school. It wasn't until the 1920s that adolescents became more likely to attend high school than immediately transition to work, apprenticeships, or family responsibilities out of childhood. It wasn't until after World War II, when the GI bill paying college tuition for returning soldiers created a massive growth in the system of higher education, that college education became broadly accessible. Now, the proportion of youth who attend college is at an all-time high. Perhaps, then, it was inevitable that the role of college in creating tomorrow's adults would become controversial and essential to thinking about lifespan development.

Considering that, can we say that college graduates are reasonably well prepared for the challenges of the contemporary world of work? Or has the changing historical context accompanied reduced expectations and dysfunctional attitudes among those in early adulthood? If you are reading this as a college student, it will be important to not get defensive; note that neither author is talking about particular college students as individuals. Instead, both are concerned with what they consider to be dominant trends affecting college students as a group. The controversy is about the nature of those dominant trends. College students may ultimately be the perfect people to comment on the influences they experience in their social world.

POINT

- Employers consistently report that their young employees are not ready to earn their place, instead expecting everything to be easy.
- Young adults admit that they are not interested in hard work required at early points of a career.
- Colleges seem overly eager to coddle students, not preparing them for the challenges of the work world.
- Parents and the culture at large are now too indulgent, leading young adults to expect that they will always be treated as special.

COUNTERPOINT

- The demands of the contemporary workplace are higher than ever, and college graduates are the best prepared.
- More young adults than ever are going to college and getting higher levels of education.
- Colleges are more accessible now than in past generations, providing opportunities to more students.
- Having a stable family life in this age requires taking longer to establish one's self in the world of work.

YES

Mel Levine

College Graduates Aren't Ready for the Real World

We are witnessing a pandemic of What I call "worklife unreadiness," and colleges face a daunting challenge in immunizing students against it.

Swarms of start-up adults, mostly in their 20s, lack the traction needed to engage the work side of their lives. Some can't make up their minds where to go and what to do, while others find themselves stranded along a career trail about which they are grievously naïve and for which they lack broad preparation. Whether they spent their undergraduate or graduate years focused on a discrete pursuit—say, engineering, law, or medicine—or whether their college education was unbound from any stated career intentions, many are unprepared to choose an appropriate form of work and manage their first job experience.

In conducting interviews for my new book, *Ready or Not, Here Life Comes,* I heard repeatedly from employers that their current crop of novice employees appear unable to delay gratification and think long term. They have trouble starting at the bottom rung of a career ladder and handling the unexciting detail, the grunt work, and the political setbacks they have to bear. In fact, many contemporary college and graduate students fail to identify at all with the world of adults.

A variety of unforeseen hazards can cause an unsuccessful crossover from higher education to the workplace. Start-up adults may often not even sense that they are failing to show initiative or otherwise please their superiors. Some early-career pitfalls are unique to our times; some derive from the characteristics of individual students themselves; some are side effects of modern parenting; and others result from an educational system that has not kept pace with the era we live in. All have policy implications for higher-education leaders.

The problems start early. While many of today's young adults were growing up, their role models were each other. Kids today don't know or take an interest in grown-ups, apart from their parents, their teachers, and entertainers. That stands in contrast to previous generations, when young people "studied" and valued older people in the community.

Thus, a lot of contemporary college students are insatiable in their quest for social acceptance and close identification with an esteemed gaggle of

From *The Chronicle of Higher Education*, vol. 51, issue 24, February 18, 2005. Copyright © 2005 by Mel Levine. Reprinted by permission.

peers. The commercialization of adolescence has further fueled a desire to be "cool" and accepted and respected within a kid culture. Some young adults become the victims of their own popularity, experiencing surges and spasms of immense yet highly brittle ego inflation. But that bubble is likely to burst in early career life, when their supervisors are not all that impressed by how well they play shortstop, how they express their taste through their earrings, or the direction in which they orient the brim of their baseball caps.

Life in the dormitory or the fraternity or sorority house no doubt perpetuates and even intensifies that pattern of overreliance on peer approval. It may also serve to cultivate an overwhelming preoccupation with body image and sexual and chemical bodily excitation—at times to the detriment of intellectual development and reality-based reflection on the future. We live in a period of college education in which the body may be the mind's No.1 rival. While that tension has always existed, our culture stresses more than ever bodily perfection, self-marketing through appearance, and physical fitness over cognitive strength. Unbridled athletic fervor may reinforce such a somatically bent collegiate culture.

Meanwhile, many college students carry with them an extensive history of being overprogrammed by their parents and their middle schools and high schools—soccer practice Monday through Saturday, bassoon lessons on Tuesday evening, square dancing on Wednesday, kung fu on Saturday afternoon, on and on. That may make it hard for them to work independently, engage in original thought processes, and show initiative.

Other students were the golden girls and boys of their high schools—popular, attractive, athletic, and sometimes scholarly insofar as they were talented test takers. Yet many never had to engage in active analytic thinking, brainstorming, creative activity, or the defense of their opinions. In quite a few instances, their parents settled all their disputes with teachers, guided (or did) their homework, and filled out their college applications. As a result, such students may have trouble charting and navigating their own course in college and beyond.

Not uncommonly, start-up adults believe that everything they engage in is supposed to generate praise and fun, as opposed perhaps to being interesting or valuable. The quest for effusive verbal feedback has been a prime motivator throughout their lives, as they have sought approval from parents, teachers, and coaches. Unbridled and sometimes unearned praise may, in fact, fuel the pressure for grade inflation in college.

Similarly, students' favorite professors may well be those whose lectures are the funniest. But what if, eight years later, their bosses have no sense of humor, and their work pales in comparison to the visual and motor ecstasy of computer games and the instantaneous satisfaction of their social and sexual conquests? They might then find themselves mentally out of shape, lacking in the capacity for hard cognitive work, and unable to engage successfully in any extended mind toil that they don't feel like doing.

On top of that, some college students are afflicted with significant underlying developmental problems that have never been properly diagnosed and managed. Examples abound, including difficulties in processing language or communicating verbally (both speaking and writing), an inability to focus attention or reason, quantitatively, and a serious lack of problem-solving skills. We are currently encountering far more students with learning difficulties, for a multitude or reasons. Many young adults are growing up in a non-verbal culture that makes few, if any, demands on language skills, active information processing, pattern recognition, and original thinking.

The most common learning disorder among undergraduates is incomplete comprehension. Affected students have difficulty understanding concepts, terminology, issues, and procedures. Many of them succeeded admirably in high school through the exclusive use of rote memory and procedural mimicry (known in mathematics as the "extreme algorithmic approach"). So a student may have received an A in trigonometry by knowing how to manipulate cosines and tangents yet without really understanding what they represent. Such underlying deficiencies return to haunt start-up adults striving for success and recognition on the job. A young adult may be selling a product without fully understanding it, or preparing a legal brief without perceiving its ramifications.

Trouble handling the workload is an equally prevalent, and lingering, form of collegiate dysfunction that follows students into their careers. Some college students are abysmally disorganized and have serious trouble managing materials and time, prioritizing, and handling activities with multiple components that must be integrated—like writing a term paper, applying to graduate schools or prospective employers, and preparing for a final examination. Such difficulties can manifest themselves for the first time at any academic stage in a student's life, including during law, business, or medical school. The students who are burdened with them are vulnerable to dropping out, mental-health problems, and a drastic loss of motivation.

Certainly many students leave college well prepared and well informed for careers, and not every college is affected by such negative cultural forces. But work-life unreadiness is increasingly prevalent and merits the attention of faculty members and administrators. The deterrents that I have mentioned may or may not ignite implosions of grade-point averages, but they can become crippling influences in the work lives of young adults.

Although colleges can't be expected to suture all the gaps in the culture of kids, some changes merit consideration if students are to succeed after graduation. Too many start-up adults harbor serious discrepancies between what they would like to do and what they are truly capable of doing. Often they are interested in pursuits they are not good at or wired for. They opt for the wrong careers because they are unaware of their personal and intellectual strengths and weaknesses, as well as woefully uninformed about the specific job demands of their chosen trades. That combination is a time bomb set to detonate early in a career.

Therefore, colleges should re-examine the adequacy of their career-placement or career-advisory services. Those services should be able to interview students in depth, administer vocational-interest inventories, and make use of sophisticated neuropsychological tests to help floundering students formulate career aims that fit their particular skills and yield personal gratification.

Colleges can also lessen undergraduate naïveté through formal education. Within a core curriculum, perhaps offered by the psychology department, colleges should help students get to know themselves and to think
about the relationship between who they are and what they think they
might do with their lives. They should provide, and possibly require, courses
like "Career Studies," in which undergraduates analyze case studies and
biographies to explore the psychological and political nuances of beginning
a career.

Students need to anticipate the challenges and agonies of work life at the
bottom rungs of a tall and steep ladder. They should be taught generic career-
related skills—like how to collaborate, organize and manage projects, write
proposals, and decrypt unwritten and unspoken on-the-job expectations.
Colleges should also offer classes that cover topics like entrepreneurialism
and leadership. Further, students should also receive formal instruction,
including case studies, in the pros and cons of alternative career pathways
within their areas of concentration (e.g., medical practice versus health-care
administration, or teaching about real estate versus pursuing a money chase
in land investment).

To elucidate the specific learning problems of students who are not succeeding, colleges need to offer up-to-date diagnostic services. Those include
tests to pinpoint problems with memory, attention, concept formation, and
other key brain processes that will cause a career to implode whether or not a
student makes it through her undergraduate years.

Faculty members should change not only what they teach but *how* they
teach, to help students make a better transition to the adult world. They
should receive formal training in the latest research about brain development
and the learning processes that occur during late adolescence—including such
key areas as higher-language functioning, frontal-lobe performance (like planning, pacing, and self-monitoring), nonverbal thought processes, memory use,
and selective attention.

Professors also should base their pedagogy on some awareness of the
mechanisms underlying optimal learning and mastery of their subject matter.
Chemistry professors should understand and make use of the cognition of
chemistry mastery, while foreign-language instructors and those conducting
political-science seminars should be aware of the brain functions they are tap-
ping and strengthening through their coursework. Current students face complex decision-making and problem-solving career challenges, but many have
been groomed in high school to rely solely on rote memory—an entirely useless approach in a meaningful career.

At the same time, professors must have keen insight into the differences
in learning among the students who take their courses. They should seek to
offer alternative ways in which students can display their knowledge and
skills. They might discover, for instance, that their tests should de-emphasize
rote recall and the spewing out of knowledge without any interpretation on
the part of the student.

In short, faculty members must learn about teaching. It should not be
assumed that a learned person understands how people learn.

What's more, colleges should offer opportunities for scholarly research into the cognitive abilities, political strategies, and skills needed for career fulfillment in various fields. The study of success and failure should be thought of as a topic worthy of rigorous investigation at all higher-education institutions.

Finally, every college should also strive to promulgate a campus intellectual life that can hold its own against social, sexual, and athletics virtuosity. Varsity debating teams should receive vigorous alumni support and status, as should literary magazines, guest lectureships, concerts, and art exhibitions. Undergraduate institutions reveal themselves by what gets tacked up on campus bulletin boards—which often are notices of keg parties, fraternity and sorority rush events, and intramural schedules. Colleges can work to change that culture.

Our colleges open their doors to kids who have grown up in an era that infiltrates them with unfettered pleasure, heavy layers of overprotection, and heaps of questionably justified positive feedback. As a result, childhood and adolescence may become nearly impossible acts to follow.

Higher education has to avoid hitching itself to that pleasure-packed bandwagon. Otherwise, students will view the academic side of college as not much more than a credentialing process to put up with while they are having a ball for four years. Colleges must never cease to ask themselves, "What roles can and should these young adults play in the world of our times? And what must we do to prepare them?"

Frank F. Furstenberg, Jr., et al.

 **NO**

Growing Up Is Harder to Do

In the past several decades, a new life stage has emerged: early adulthood. No longer adolescents, but not yet ready to assume the full responsibilities of an adult, many young people are caught between needing to learn advanced job skills and depending on their family to support them during the transition.

In the years after World War II, Americans typically assumed the full responsibilities of adulthood by their late teens or early 20s. Most young men had completed school and were working full-time, and most young women were married and raising children. People who grew up in this era of growing affluence—many of today's grandparents—were economically self-sufficient and able to care for others by the time they had weathered adolescence. Today, adulthood no longer begins when adolescence ends. Ask someone in their early 20s whether they consider themselves to be an adult, and you might get a laugh, a quizzical look, a shrug of the shoulders, or a response like that of a 24-year-old Californian: "Maybe next year. When I'm 25."

Social scientists are beginning to recognize a new phase of life: early adulthood. Some features of this stage resemble coming of age during the late 19th and early 20th centuries, when youth lingered in a state of semi-autonomy, waiting until they were sufficiently well-off to marry, have children and establish an independent household. However, there are important differences in how young people today define and achieve adulthood from those of both the recent and the more distant past.

This new stage is not merely an extension of adolescence, as has been maintained in the mass media. Young adults are physically mature and often possess impressive intellectual, social and psychological skills. Nor are young people today reluctant to accept adult responsibilities. Instead, they are busy building up their educational credentials and practical skills in an ever more demanding labor market. Most are working or studying or both, and are developing romantic relationships. Yet, many have not become fully adult—traditionally defined as finishing school, landing a job with benefits, marrying and parenting—because they are not ready, or perhaps not permitted, to do so. For a growing number, this will not happen until their late 20s or even early 30s. In response, American society will have to revise upward the "normal" age of full adulthood, and develop ways to assist young people through the ever-lengthening transition.

Among the most privileged young adults—those who receive ample support from their parents—this is a time of unparalleled freedom from family responsibilities and an opportunity for self-exploration and development. For the less advantaged, early adulthood is a time of struggle to gain the skills and credentials required for a job that can support the family they wish to start (or perhaps have already started), and a struggle to feel in control of their lives. A 30-year-old single mother from Iowa laughed when asked whether she considered herself an adult: "I don't know if I'm an adult yet. I still don't feel quite grown up. Being an adult kind of sounds like having things, everything is kind of in a routine and on track, and I don't feel like I'm quite on track."

Changing Notions of Adulthood

Traditionally, the transition to adulthood involves establishing emotional and economic independence from parents or, as historian John Modell described it, "coming into one's own." The life events that make up the transition to adulthood are accompanied by a sense of commitment, purpose and identity. Although we lack systematic evidence on how adulthood was defined in the past, it appears that marriage and parenthood represented important benchmarks. Nineteenth-century American popular fiction, journalism, sermons and self-help guides rarely referred to finishing school or getting a job, and only occasionally to leaving home or starting one's own household as the critical turning point. On the other hand, they often referred to marriage, suggesting that marriage was considered, at least by middle-class writers, as the critical touchstone of reaching adulthood.

By the 1950s and 1960s, most Americans viewed family roles and adult responsibilities as nearly synonymous. In that era, most women married before they were 21 and had at least one child before they were 23. For men, having the means to marry and support a family was the defining characteristic of adulthood, while for women, merely getting married and becoming a mother conferred adult status. As Alice Rossi explained in 1968: "On the level of cultural values, men have no freedom of choice where work is concerned: they must work to secure their status as adult men. The equivalent for women has been maternity. There is considerable pressure upon the growing girl and young woman to consider maternity necessary for a woman's fulfillment as an individual and to secure her status as an adult."

Research conducted during the late 1950s and early 1960s demonstrated widespread antipathy in America toward people who remained unmarried and toward couples who were childless by choice. However, these views began to shift in the late 1960s, rendering the transition to adulthood more ambiguous. Psychologists Joseph Veroff, Elizabeth Douvan, and Richard Kulka found that more than half of Americans interviewed in 1957 viewed someone who did not want to get married as selfish, immature, peculiar or morally flawed. By 1976, fewer than one-third of a similar sample held such views. A 1962 study found that 85 percent of mothers believed that married couples should have children. Nearly 20 years later, just 40 percent of those women still agreed, and in 1993 only 1 in 5 of their daughters agreed. Arland Thornton and Linda Young-Demarco, who have studied attitudes toward family roles during the latter half of the 20th century, conclude that "Americans increasingly value freedom and equality in their personal and family lives while at the same time maintaining their commitment to the ideals of marriage, family, and children." While still personally committed to family, Americans increasingly tolerate alternative life choices.

To understand how Americans today define adulthood, we developed a set of questions for the 2002 General Social Survey (GSS), an opinion poll administered to a nationally representative sample of Americans every two years by the National Opinion Research Center. The survey asked nearly 1,400 Americans aged 18 and older how important each of the following traditional benchmarks was to being an adult: leaving home, finishing school, getting a full-time job, becoming financially independent from one's parents, being able to support a family, marrying and becoming a parent.

The definition of adulthood that emerges today does not necessarily include marriage and parenthood. [The] most important milestones are completing school, establishing an independent household and being employed full-time—concrete steps associated with the ability to support a family. Ninety-five percent of Americans surveyed consider education, employment, financial independence and the ability to support a family to be key steps on the path to adulthood. Nonetheless, almost half of GSS respondents do not believe that it is necessary to actually marry or to have children to be considered an adult. As a young mother from San Diego explained, having a child did not make her an adult; instead she began to feel like an adult when she realized that "all of us make mistakes, but you can fix them and if you keep yourself on track, everything will come out fine." Compared with their parents and grandparents, for whom marriage and parenthood were virtually a prerequisite for becoming an adult, young people today more often view these as life choices, not requirements.

The Lengthening Road to Adulthood

Not only are the defining characteristics of adulthood changing, so is the time it takes to achieve them. To map the changing transitions to adulthood, we also examined several national surveys that contain information on young adults both in this country and abroad. Using U.S. Census data collected as far back as 1900, we compared the lives of young adults over time. We also conducted about 500 in-depth interviews with young adults living in different parts of the United States, including many in recent immigrant groups.

Our findings, as well as the work of other scholars, confirm that it takes much longer to make the transition to adulthood today than decades ago, and arguably longer than it has at any time in America's history. [Based] on the 1960 and 2000 U.S. censuses, [there is a] large decline in the percentage of young adults who, by age 20 or 30, have completed all of the traditionally-defined major adult transitions (leaving home, finishing school, becoming financially independent, getting married and having a child). We define financial independence for both men and women as being in the labor force; however, because women in 1960 rarely combined work and motherhood, married full-time mothers are also counted as financially independent in both years. In 2000, just 46 percent of women and 31 percent of men aged 30 had completed all five transitions, compared with 77 percent of women and 65 percent of men at the same age in 1960.

Women—who have traditionally formed families at ages younger than men—show the most dramatic changes at early ages. Although almost 30 percent of 20-year-old women in 1960 had completed these transitions, just 6 percent had done so in 2000. Among 25-year-olds (not shown), the decrease is even more dramatic: 70 percent of 25-year-old women in 1960 had attained traditional adult status, in 2000 just 25 percent had done so. Yet, in 2000, even as they delayed traditional adulthood, 25-year-old women greatly increased their participation in the labor force to levels approaching those of 25-year old men. The corresponding declines for men in the attainment of traditional adult status are less striking but nonetheless significant. For both men and women, these changes can largely be explained by the increasing proportion who go to college and graduate school, and also by the postponement of marriage and childbearing.

If we use the more contemporary definition of adulthood. . . —one that excludes marriage and parenthood—then the contrasts are not as dramatic. In 2000, 70 percent of men aged 30 had left home, were financially independent, and had completed their schooling, just 12 points lower than was true of 30-year-old men in 1960. Nearly 75 percent of 30-year-old women in 2000 met this standard, compared to nearly 85 percent of women in 1960. Nonetheless, even these changes are historically substantial, and we are not even taking into account how many of these independent, working, highly educated young people still feel that they are not yet capable of supporting a family.

The reasons for this lengthening path to adulthood, John Modell has shown, range from shifting social policies to changing economic forces. The swift transition to adulthood typical after World War II was substantially assisted by the government. The GI Bill helped veterans return to school and subsidized the expansion of education. Similarly, government subsidies for affordable housing encouraged starting families earlier. At the same time, because Social Security was extended to cover more of the elderly, young people were no longer compelled to support their parents. The disappearance or reduction of such subsidies during the past few decades may help to explain the prolongation of adult transitions for some Americans. The growing cost of college and housing forces many youth into a state of semi-autonomy, accepting some support from their parents while they establish themselves economically. When a job ends or they need additional schooling or a relationship dissolves, they increasingly turn to their family for assistance. Thus, the sequencing of adult transitions has become increasingly complicated and more reversible.

However, the primary reason for a prolonged early adulthood is that it now takes much longer to secure a full-time job that pays enough to support a family. Economists Timothy Smeeding and Katherin Ross Phillips found in the mid-1990s that just 70 percent of American men aged 24 to 28 earned enough to support themselves, while fewer than half earned enough to support a family of three. Attaining a decent standard of living today usually requires a college education, if not a professional degree. To enter or remain in the middle class, it is almost imperative to make an educational commitment that spans at least the early 20s. Not only are more Americans attending college than ever before, it takes longer to complete a degree than in years past. Census data reveal that from 1960 to 2000, the percentage of Americans aged 20, 25, and 30 who were enrolled in school more than doubled. Unlike during the 1960s, these educational and work investments are now required of women as well as men. It is little wonder then that many young people linger in early adulthood, delaying marriage and parenthood until their late 20s and early 30s.

Those who do not linger are likely those who cannot afford to and, perhaps as a result, views on how long it takes to achieve adulthood differ markedly by social class. Less-educated and less-affluent respondents—those who did not attend college and those at the bottom one-third of the income ladder—have an earlier expected timetable for leaving home, completing school, obtaining full-time employment, marriage and parenthood. Around 40 percent of the less well-off in the GSS sample said that young adults should marry before they turn 25, and one-third said they should have children by this age. Far fewer of the better-off respondents pointed to the early 20s, and about one-third of them said that these events could be delayed until the 30s. These social class differences probably stem from the reality that young people with more limited means do not have the luxury of investing in school or experimenting with complex career paths.

New Demands on Families, Schools and Governments

The growing demands on young Americans to invest in the future have come at a time of curtailed government support, placing heavy demands on families. Growing inequality shapes very different futures for young Americans with more and less privileged parents.

Early adulthood is when people figure out what they want to do and how best to realize their goals. If they are lucky enough to have a family that can help out, they may proceed directly through college, travel or work for a few years, or perhaps participate in community service, and then enter graduate or professional school. However, relatively few Americans have this good fortune. Youth from less well-off families must shuttle back and forth between work and school or combine both while they gradually gain their credentials. In the meantime, they feel unprepared for marriage or parenting. If they do marry or parent during these years, they often find themselves trying to juggle too many responsibilities and unable to adequately invest in their future. Like the mother from Iowa, they do not feel "on track" or in control of their lives.

More than at any time in recent history, parents are being called on to provide financial assistance (either college tuition, living expenses or other assistance) to their young adult children. Robert Schoeni and Karen Ross conservatively estimate that nearly one-quarter of the entire cost of raising children is incurred after they reach 17. Nearly two-thirds of young adults in their early 20s receive economic support from parents, while about 40 percent still receive some assistance in their late 20s.

A century ago, it was the other way around: young adults typically helped their parents when they first went to work, if (as was common) they still lived with their parents. Now, many young adults continue to receive support from their parents even after they begin working. The exceptions seem to be in immigrant families; there, young people more often help support their parents. A 27-year-old Chinese American from New York explained why he continued to live with his parents despite wanting to move out, saying that his parents "want me [to stay] and they need me. Financially, they need me to take care of them, pay the bills, stuff like that, which is fine."

As young people and their families struggle with the new reality that it takes longer to attain adulthood, Americans must recognize weaknesses in the primary institutions that facilitate this transition—schools and the military. For the fortunate few who achieve bachelor's degrees and perhaps go on to professional or graduate training, residential colleges and universities seem well designed. They offer everything from housing to health care while training young adults. Likewise, the military provides a similar milieu for those from less-privileged families. However, only about one in four young adults attend primarily residential colleges or join the military after high school. The other three-quarters look to their families for room and board while they attend school and enter the job market. Many of these youth enter community colleges or local universities that provide much less in the way of services and support.

The least privileged come from families that cannot offer much assistance. This vulnerable population—consisting of 10 to 15 percent of young adults—may come out of the foster care system, graduate from special education programs, or exit jails and prisons. These youth typically lack job skills and need help to secure a foothold in society. Efforts to increase educational opportunities, establish school-to-career paths, and help students who cannot afford post-secondary education must be given higher priority, even in a time of budget constraints. The United States, once a world leader in providing higher education to its citizens, now lags behind several other nations in the proportion of the population that completes college.

Expanding military and alternative national service programs also can help provide a bridge from secondary school to higher education or the labor force by providing financial credit to those who serve their country. Such programs also offer health insurance to young adults, who are often cut off from insurance by arbitrary age limits. Finally, programs for the vulnerable populations of youth coming out of foster care, special education, and mental health services must not assume that young people are fully able to become economically independent at age 18 or even 21. The timetable of the 1950s is no longer applicable. It is high time for policy makers and legislators to address the realities of the longer and more demanding transition to adulthood.

CHALLENGE QUESTIONS

Are College Graduates Unprepared for Adulthood and the World of Work?

- Assuming that most people reading this are college students themselves, how do you feel about some of the strong claims made by Mel Levine? Are you and your peers disinterested in adults outside your immediate sphere of influence? Do you and your peers prioritize physical beauty and activity over qualities of mind? Are you and your peers thinking about and preparing for the world of work and adulthood?
- If you agree with Levine, then it is important to consider why? Do you agree with the factors he identifies: excessive praise during childhood, a culture saturated with short-term gratification, a failure of colleges to make their curriculum relevant to what is needed by both youth and society?
- If you don't agree with Levine, then it is important to consider why his perspective is prominent in our culture: Why is there a widespread perception that young people in college today are at risk of not making successful transitions to the world of work and to adulthood more generally?
- Furstenberg and colleagues note that expectations are higher than ever for young adults. Are there ways in which you think that the expectations on young adults are too high?

Suggested Readings

T. Apter, *The Myth of Maturity: What Teenagers Need from Parents to Become Adults* (W. W. Norton, 2001)

J. J. Arnett, *Emerging Adulthood: The Winding Road from the Late Teens Through the Twenties* (Oxford University Press, 2004)

J. E. Cote, *Arrested Adulthood: The Changing Nature of Maturity and Identity* (New York University Press, 2000)

Institute for Research on Higher Education, "Understanding Employers' Perceptions of College Graduates," *Change* (May/June 1998)

M. Levine, *Ready or Not, Here Life Comes* (Simon & Schuster, 2005)

R. A. Settersten, F. F. Furstenberg, and R. G. Rumbaut, *On the Frontier of Adulthood: Theory, Research, and Public Policy* (MacArthur Foundation Series) (University of Chicago Press, 2005)

J. Studley, "Are Liberal Arts Dead? Far From It." *Careers and Colleges* (September–October 2003)

Internet References . . .

This Web site provides information from Division 20 of the American Psychological Association, the division focused on adult development and aging.

> http://apadiv20.phhp.ufl.edu/apadiv20.htm

The Society for Research on Adult Development brings together researchers interested in positive adult development.

> http://www.adultdevelopment.org/

The Alternatives to Marriage Project advocates for diversity in adult relationships.

> http://www.unmarried.org/

The "Institute for American Values" promotes, among other things, marriage and traditional families.

> http://americanvalues.org/

This Web site provides access to an encyclopedia about the role of religion in society.

> http://hirr.hartsem.edu/ency/index.html

Information can be found here from the American Psychological Association about lesbian and gay parenting.

> http://www.apa.org/pi/parent.html

The site contains information and links, vetted by the Eliot-Pearson Department of Child Development at Tufts University, for information about parenting.

> http://www.cfw.tufts.edu/

Middle Adulthood

*I*n conventional terms, middle adulthood is often the most productive portion of the lifespan. During middle adulthood most people deeply engage with families, the world of work, and communities. As such, some versions of the lifespan present middle adulthood (generally conceptualized as being between the mid-30s and the mid-60s) as the peak of development. But middle adulthood also produces significant challenges and new expectations. This section focuses on the relationship between healthy development and three challenges and expectations confronted by most adults in contemporary society: marriage, parenting, and religion.

- Is the Institution of Marriage at Risk?
- Can Lesbian and Gay Couples Be Appropriate Parents for Children?
- Is Religion a Pure Good in Facilitating Well-Being during Adulthood?

ISSUE 15

Is the Institution of Marriage at Risk?

YES: Andrew J. Cherlin, from "The Deinstitutionalization of American Marriage" *Journal of Marriage and Family* (September 2004)

NO: Frank Furstenberg, from "Can Marriage Be Saved?" *Dissent Magazine* (Summer 2005)

ISSUE SUMMARY

YES: Sociologist Andrew J. Cherlin suggests that the institution of marriage is losing its preeminence and may become just one of many relationship options for couples.

NO: Frank Furstenberg, on the other hand, proposes that the institution of marriage will persist with appropriate government policies and support to families.

Marriage is one of the most significant markers of the adult lifespan. Both historically and cross-culturally, adulthood is often defined by getting married and starting a family. In contemporary society this norm is gradually changing. While there have always been a diversity of family types, the general expectation that a person will get married immediately upon becoming an adult has waned. It is much more likely for people to wait to get married, or to not get married at all. This trend has generated tremendous controversy among those interested in considering the relationship between marriage and lifespan development.

Some of the controversy derives from divorce rates that are astonishingly high. It is common to hear that half of all marriages in the United States end in divorce—though that figure is generally used more as a high-end estimate rather than the probability of any particular marriage working out. For example, by some estimates, college-educated people are half as likely to get a divorce than the less educated. Likewise, people who marry at a young age are significantly more likely to get divorced. While such statistics can be manipulated to serve varying agendas, it is true that divorce is a common outcome of contemporary marriage. And divorce is hard on people—it is hard on the people getting divorced, and it is hard on any children that may be involved. While the long-term impact of divorce is another controversial area of study, few people would argue divorce is a good outcome.

304

With the specter of divorce and all the other challenges to the institution of marriage, perhaps marriage will simply cease to be a central institution in contemporary society. This is the position taken by Johns Hopkins University sociologist Andrew J. Cherlin. In a broad analysis of trends in marriage, Cherlin finds a confluence of many factors that suggest the social norms surrounding marriage are irrevocably shifting. While Cherlin is wary of predicting anything with certainty because he realizes that future patterns for marriage are notoriously hard to foresee, he does persuasively illustrate trends toward an increasing diversity of relationship norms—from long-term cohabitation to same-sex marriage. Further, with the increasing social emphasis on emotional fulfillment and "expressive individualism" it may be unlikely for traditional marriage to persist as a normative part of adulthood.

Sociologist Frank Furstenberg, on the other hand, posits that marriage holds a peculiar and special place in contemporary society. While he acknowledges changing norms for marriage internationally and dramatic shifts in the United States from norms in the 1950s, he sees these more as evidence that the institution of marriage is always in flux. For Furstenberg, the key question now is how to best support marriage and he thinks the answer lies in adequately supporting children and families. Implicit in this argument is the idea that adults will marry as long as it makes sense within their circumstance. Thus, marriage is and will likely remain the norm for adulthood.

POINT

- The social norms surrounding marriage have significantly weakened during recent decades.

- Longstanding changes in gendered divisions of labor, along with childbearing outside of marriage, have served to dramatically shift relationship possibilities.

- The relatively new growth of cohabitation and same-sex marriage have provided additional impetus for deinstitutionalization.

- All of these changes are associated with broader changes in the relatively new emphasis on romantic love and the extreme emphasis on "expressive individualism."

COUNTERPOINT

- We cannot appropriately make comparisons with the 1950s and the baby boom generation, because that was a historical anomaly. The nuclear family, other than in the 1950s, has never really been central to society.

- Family systems are always in flux—it is not just a process of one directional change.

- If we as a society invest in children and make it realistic for all families to function well, marriage will continue to be a popular institution.

- Marriage norms are not really changing much among the educated middle-class, suggesting that there is no relationship between the institution of marriage and broad social trends.

YES

Andrew J. Cherlin

The Deinstitutionalization of American Marriage

This article argues that marriage has undergone a process of deinstitutionalization—a weakening of the social norms that define partners' behavior—over the past few decades. Examples are presented involving the increasing number and complexity of cohabiting unions and the emergence of same-sex marriage. Two transitions in the meaning of marriage that occurred in the United States during the 20th century have created the social context for deinstitutionalization. The first transition, noted by Ernest Burgess, was from the institutional marriage to the companionate marriage. The second transition was to the individualized marriage in which the emphasis on personal choice and self-development expanded. Although the practical importance of marriage has declined, its symbolic significance has remained high and may even have increased. It has become a marker of prestige and personal achievement. Examples of its symbolic significance are presented. The implications for the current state of marriage and its future direction are discussed.

A quarter century ago, in an article entitled "Remarriage as an Incomplete Institution" (Cherlin, 1978), I argued that American society lacked norms about the way that members of stepfamilies should act toward each other. Parents and children in first marriages, in contrast, could rely on well-established norms, such as when it is appropriate to discipline a child. I predicted that, over time, as remarriage after divorce became common, norms would begin to emerge concerning proper behavior in step-families—for example, what kind of relationship a stepfather should have with his stepchildren. In other words, I expected that remarriage would become institutionalized, that it would become more like first marriage. But just the opposite has happened. Remarriage has not become more like first marriage; rather, first marriage has become more like remarriage. Instead of the institutionalization of remarriage, what has occurred over the past few decades is the deinstitutionalization of marriage. Yes, remarriage is an incomplete institution, but now, so is first marriage—and for that matter, cohabitation.

By deinstitutionalization I mean the weakening of the social norms that define people's behavior in a social institution such as marriage. In times of social stability, the taken-for-granted nature of norms allows people to go about their lives without having to question their actions or the actions of others.

From *Journal of Marriage and Family*, vol. 66, September 2004, pp. 848–51, 853–861. Copyright © 2004 by National Council on Family Relations. Reprinted by permission of Blackwell Publishing, Ltd.

But when social change produces situations outside the reach of established norms, individuals can no longer rely on shared understandings of how to act. Rather, they must negotiate new ways of acting, a process that is a potential source of confict and opportunity. On the one hand, the development of new rules is likely to engender disagreement and tension among the relevant actors. On the other hand, the breakdown of the old rules of a gendered institution such as marriage could lead to the creation of a more egalitarian relationship between wives and husbands.

This perspective, I think, can help us understand the state of contemporary marriage. It may even assist in the risky business of predicting the future of marriage. To some extent, similar changes in marriage have occurred in the United States, Canada, and much of Europe, but the American situation may be distinctive. Consequently, although I include information about Canadian and European families, I focus mainly on the United States.

The Deinstitutionalization of Marriage

Even as I was writing my 1978 article, the changing division of labor in the home and the increase in childbearing outside marriage were undermining the institutionalized basis of marriage. The distinct roles of homemaker and breadwinner were fading as more married women entered the paid labor force. Looking into the future, I thought that perhaps an equitable division of household labor might become institutionalized. But what happened instead was the "stalled revolution," in Hochschild's (1989) well-known phrase. Men do somewhat more home work than they used to do, but there is wide variation, and each couple must work out their own arrangement without clear guidelines. In addition, when I wrote the article, 1 out of 6 births in the United States occurred outside marriage, already a much higher ratio than at midcentury (U.S. National Center for Health Statistics, 1982). Today, the comparable figure is 1 out of 3 (U.S. National Center for Health Statistics, 2003). The percentage is similar in Canada (Statistics Canada, 2003) and in the United Kingdom and Ireland (Kiernan, 2002). In the Nordic countries of Denmark, Iceland, Norway, and Sweden, the figure ranges from about 45% to about 65% (Kiernan). Marriage is no longer the nearly universal setting for childbearing that it was a half century ago.

Both of these developments—the changing division of labor in the home and the increase in childbearing outside marriage—were well under way when I wrote my 1978 article, as was a steep rise in divorce. Here I discuss two more recent changes in family life, both of which have contributed to the deinstitutionalization of marriage after the 1970s: the growth of cohabitation, which began in the 1970s but was not fully appreciated until it accelerated in the 1980s and 1990s, and same-sex marriage, which emerged as an issue in the 1990s and has come to the fore in the current decade.

The Growth of Cohabitation

In the 1970s, neither I nor most other American researchers foresaw the greatly increased role of cohabitation in the adult life course. We thought that, except among the poor, cohabitation would remain a short-term arrangement among childless young adults who would quickly break up or marry. But it has become a more prevalent and more complex phenomenon. For example, cohabitation has created an additional layer of complexity in stepfamilies. When I wrote my article, nearly all stepfamilies were formed by the remarriage of one or both spouses. Now, about one fourth of all stepfamilies in the United States, and one half of all stepfamilies in Canada, are formed by cohabitation rather than marriage (Bumpass, Raley, & Sweet, 1995; Statistics Canada, 2002). It is not uncommon, especially among the low-income population, for a woman to have a child outside marriage, end her relationship with that partner, and then begin cohabiting with a different partner. This new union is equivalent in structure to a step-family but does not involve marriage. Sometimes the couple later marries, and if neither has been married before, their union creates a first marriage with stepchildren. As a result, we now see an increasing number of stepfamilies that do not involve marriage, and an increasing number of first marriages that involve stepfamilies.

More generally, cohabitation is becoming accepted as an alternative to marriage. British demographer Kathleen Kiernan (2002) writes that the acceptance of cohabitation is occurring in stages in European nations, with some nations further along than others. In stage one, cohabitation is a fringe or avant garde phenomenon; in stage two, it is accepted as a testing ground for marriage; in stage three, it becomes acceptable as an alternative to marriage; and in stage four, it becomes indistinguishable from marriage. Sweden and Denmark, she argues, have made the transition to stage four; in contrast, Mediterranean countries such as Spain, Italy, and Greece remain in stage one. In the early 2000s, the United States appeared to be in transition from stage two to stage three (Smock & Gupta, 2002). A number of indicators suggested that the connection between cohabitation and marriage was weakening. The proportion of cohabiting unions that end in marriage within 3 years dropped from 60% in the 1970s to about 33% in the 1990s (Smock & Gupta), suggesting that fewer cohabiting unions were trial marriages (or that fewer trial marriages were succeeding). In fact, Manning and Smock (2003) reported that among 115 cohabiting working-class and lower middle-class adults who were interviewed in depth, none said that he or she was deciding between marriage and cohabitation at the start of the union. Moreover, only 36% of adults in the 2002 United States General Social Survey disagreed with the statement, "It is alright for a couple to live together without intending to get married" (Davis, Smith, & Marsden, 2003). And a growing share of births to unmarried women in the United States (about 40% in the 1990s) were to cohabiting couples (Bumpass & Lu, 2000). The comparable share was about 60% in Britain (Ermisch, 2001).

Canada appears to have entered stage three (Smock & Gupta, 2002). Sixty-nine percent of births to unmarried women were to cohabiting couples in 1997 and 1998 (Juby, Marcil-Gratton, & Le Bourdais, in press). Moreover, the national figures for Canada mask substantial provincial variation. In particular, the rise in cohabitation has been far greater in Quebec than elsewhere in Canada. In 1997 and 1998, 84% of unmarried women who gave birth in

Quebec were cohabiting (Juby, Marcil-Gratton, & Le Bourdais). And four out of five Quebeckers entering a first union did so by cohabiting rather than marrying (Le Bourdais & Juby, 2002). The greater acceptance of cohabitation in Quebec seems to have a cultural basis. Francophone Quebeckers have substantially higher likelihoods of cohabiting than do English-speaking Quebeckers or Canadians in the other English-speaking provinces (Statistics Canada, 1997). Céline Le Bourdais and Nicole Marcil-Gratton (1996) argue that Francophone Quebeckers draw upon a French, rather than Anglo-Saxon, model of family life. In fact, levels of cohabitation in Quebec are similar to levels in France, whereas levels in English-speaking Canada and in the United States are more similar to the lower levels in Great Britain (Kiernan, 2002).

To be sure, cohabitation is becoming more institutionalized. In the United States, states and municipalities are moving toward granting cohabiting couples some of the rights and responsibilities that married couples have. Canada has gone further: Under the Modernization of Benefits and Obligations Act of 2000, legal distinctions between married and unmarried same-sex and opposite-sex couples were eliminated for couples who have lived together for at least a year. Still, the Supreme Court of Canada ruled in 2002 that when cohabiting partners dissolve their unions, they do not have to divide their assets equally, nor can one partner be compelled to pay maintenance payments to the other, even when children are involved (*Nova Scotia [Attorney General] v. Walsh*, 2002). In France, unmarried couples may enter into Civil Solidarity Pacts, which give them most of the rights and responsibilities of married couples after the pact has existed for 3 years (Daley, 2000). Several other countries have instituted registered partnerships (Lyall, 2004).

The Emergence of Same-Sex Marriage

The most recent development in the deinstitutionalization of marriage is the movement to legalize same-sex marriage. It became a public issue in the United States in 1993, when the Hawaii Supreme Court ruled that a state law restricting marriage to opposite-sex couples violated the Hawaii state constitution (*Baehr v. Lewin*, 1993). Subsequently, Hawaii voters passed a state constitutional amendment barring same-sex marriage. In 1996, the United States Congress passed the Defense of Marriage Act, which allowed states to refuse to recognize same-sex marriages licensed in other states. The act's constitutionality has not been tested as of this writing because until recently, no state allowed same-sex marriages. However, in 2003, the Massachusetts Supreme Court struck down a state law limiting marriage to opposite-sex couples, and same-sex marriage became legal in May 2004 (although opponents may eventually succeed in prohibiting it through a state constitutional amendment). The issue has developed further in Canada: In the early 2000s, courts in British Columbia, Ontario, and Quebec ruled that laws restricting marriage to opposite-sex couples were discriminatory, and it appears likely that the federal government will legalize gay marriage throughout the nation. Although social conservatives in the United States are seeking a federal constitutional amendment, I think it is reasonable to assume that same-sex marriage will be allowed in at least some North American jurisdictions in the future. In Europe, same-sex marriage has been legalized in Belgium and The Netherlands.

Lesbian and gay couples who choose to marry must actively construct a marital world with almost no institutional support. Lesbians and gay men already use the term "family" to describe their close relationships, but they usually mean something different from the standard marriage-based family. Rather, they often refer to what sociologists have called a "family of choice": one that is formed largely through voluntary ties among individuals who are not biologically or legally related (Weeks, Heaphy, & Donovan, 2001; Weston, 1991). Now they face the task of integrating marriages into these larger networks of friends and kin. The partners will not even have the option of falling back on the gender-differentiated roles of heterosexual marriage. This is not to say that there will be no division of labor; one study of gay and lesbian couples found that in homes where one partner works longer hours and earns substantially more than the other partner, the one with the less demanding, lower paying job did more housework and more of the work of keeping in touch with family and friends. The author suggests that holding a demanding professional or managerial job may make it difficult for a person to invest fully in sharing the work at home, regardless of gender or sexual orientation (Carrington, 1999).

We might expect same-sex couples who have children, or who wish to have children through adoption or donor insemination, to be likely to avail themselves of the option of marriage. (According to the United States Census Bureau [2003b], 33% of women in same-sex partnerships and 22% of men in same-sex partnerships had children living with them in 2000.) Basic issues, such as who would care for the children, would have to be resolved family by family. The obligations of the partners to each other following a marital dissolution have also yet to be worked out. In these and many other ways, gay and lesbian couples who marry in the near future would need to create a marriage-centered kin network through discussion, negotiation, and experiment.

Two Transitions in the Meaning of Marriage

In a larger sense, all of these developments—the changing division of labor, childbearing outside of marriage, cohabitation, and gay marriage—are the result of long-term cultural and material trends that altered the meaning of marriage during the 20th century. The cultural trends included, first, an emphasis on emotional satisfaction and romantic love that intensified early in the century. Then, during the last few decades of the century, an ethic of expressive individualism—which Bellah, Marsden, Sullivan, Swidler, & Tipton (1985) describe as the belief that "each person has a unique core of feeling and intuition that should unfold or be expressed if individuality is to be realized" (p. 334)—became more important. On the material side, the trends include the decline of agricultural labor and the corresponding increase in wage labor; the decline in child and adult mortality; rising standards of living; and, in the last half of the 20th century, the movement of married women into the paid workforce.

These developments, along with historical events such as the Depression and World War II, produced two great changes in the meaning of marriage during the 20th century. Ernest Burgess famously labeled the first one as a transition "from an institution to a companionship" (Burgess & Locke, 1945). In describing the rise of the companionate marriage, Burgess was referring to the single-earner, breadwinner-homemaker marriage that flourished in the 1950s. Although husbands and wives in the companionate marriage usually adhered to a sharp division of labor, they were supposed to be each other's companions— friends, lovers— to an extent not imagined by the spouses in the institutional marriages of the previous era. The increasing focus on bonds of sentiment within nuclear families constituted an important but limited step in the individualization of family life. Much more so than in the 19th century, the emotional satisfaction of the spouses became an important criterion for marital success. However, through the 1950s, wives and husbands tended to derive satisfaction from their participation in a marriage-based nuclear family (Roussel, 1989). That is to say, they based their gratification on playing marital roles well: being good providers, good homemakers, and responsible parents. . . .

Sociological theorists of late modernity (or postmodernity) such as Anthony Giddens (1991, 1992) in Britain and Ulrich Beck and Elisabeth Beck-Gernsheim in Germany (1995, 2002) also have written about the growing individualization of personal life. Consistent with the idea of deinstitutionalization, they note the declining power of social norms and laws as regulating mechanisms for family life, and they stress the expanding role of personal choice. They argue that as traditional sources of identity such as class, religion, and community lose influence, one's intimate relationships become central to self-identity. Giddens (1991, 1992) writes of the emergence of the "pure relationship": an intimate partnership entered into for its own sake, which lasts only as long as both partners are satisfied with the rewards (mostly intimacy and love) that they get from it. It is in some ways the logical extension of the increasing individualism and the deinstitutionalization of marriage that occurred in the 20th century. The pure relationship is not tied to an institution such as marriage or to the desire to raise children. Rather, it is "free-floating," independent of social institutions or economic life. Unlike marriage, it is not regulated by law, and its members do not enjoy special legal rights. It exists primarily in the realms of emotion and self-identity.

Although the theorists of late modernity believe that the quest for intimacy is becoming the central focus of personal life, they do not predict that *marriage* will remain distinctive and important. Marriage, they claim, has become a choice rather than a necessity for adults who want intimacy, companionship, and children. According to Beck and Beck-Gernsheim (1995), we will see "a huge variety of ways of living together or apart which will continue to exist side by side" (pp. 141–142). Giddens (1992) even argues that marriage has already become "just one life-style among others" (p. 154), although people may not yet realize it because of institutional lag.

The Current Context of Marriage

Overall, research and writing on the changing meaning of marriage suggest that it is now situated in a very different context than in the past. This is true in at least two senses. First, individuals now experience a vast latitude for choice in their personal lives. More forms of marriage and more alternatives to marriage are socially acceptable. Moreover, one may fit marriage into one's life in many ways: One may first live with a partner, or sequentially with several partners, without an explicit consideration of whether a marriage will occur. One may have children with one's eventual spouse or with someone else before marrying. One may, in some jurisdictions, marry someone of the same gender and build a shared marital world with few guidelines to rely on. Within marriage, roles are more flexible and negotiable, although women still do more than their share of the household work and childrearing.

The second difference is in the nature of the rewards that people seek through marriage and other close relationships. Individuals aim for personal growth and deeper intimacy through more open communication and mutually shared disclosures about feelings with their partners. They may feel justified in insisting on changes in a relationship that no longer provides them with individualized rewards. In contrast, they are less likely than in the past to focus on the rewards to be found in fulfilling socially valued roles such as the good parent or the loyal and supportive spouse. The result of these changing contexts has been a deinstitutionalization of marriage, in which social norms about family and personal life count for less than they did during the heyday of the companionate marriage, and far less than during the period of the institutional marriage. Instead, personal choice and self-development loom large in people's construction of their marital careers.

Why Do People Still Marry?

There is a puzzle within the story of deinstitutionalization that needs solving. Although fewer Americans are marrying than during the peak years of marriage in the mid-20th century, most—nearly 90%, according to a recent estimate (Goldstein & Kenney, 2001)—will eventually marry. A survey of high school seniors conducted annually since 1976 shows no decline in the importance they attach to marriage. The percentage of young women who respond that they expect to marry has stayed constant at roughly 80% (and has increased from 71% to 78% for young men). The percentage who respond that "having a good marriage and family life" is extremely important has also remained constant, at about 80% for young women and 70% for young men (Thornton & Young-DeMarco, 2001). What is more, in the 1990s and early 2000s, a strong promarriage movement emerged among gay men and lesbians in the United States, who sought the right to marry with increasing success. Clearly, marriage remains important to many people in the United States. Consequently, I think the interesting question is not why so few people are marrying, but rather, why *so many* people are marrying, or planning to marry, or hoping to marry, when cohabitation and single parenthood are widely acceptable options. (This question may be less relevant in Canada and the many European nations where the estimated proportions of who will ever marry are lower.)

The Gains to Marriage

The dominant theoretical perspectives on marriage in the 20th century do not provide much guidance on the question of why marriage remains so popular. The structural functionalists in social anthropology and sociology in the early- to mid-20th century emphasized the role of marriage in ensuring that a child would have a link to the status of a man, a right to his protection, and a claim to inherit his property (Mair, 1971). But as the law began to recognize the rights of children born outside marriage, and as mothers acquired resources by working in the paid work force, these reasons for marriage become less important. . . .

From a rational choice perspective, then, what benefits might contemporary marriage offer that would lead cohabiting couples to marry rather than cohabit? I suggest that the major benefit is what we might call *enforceable trust* (Cherlin, 2000; Portes & Sensenbrenner, 1993). Marriage still requires a public commitment to a long-term, possibly lifelong relationship. This commitment is usually expressed in front of relatives, friends, and religious congregants. Cohabitation, in contrast, requires only a private commitment, which is easier to break. Therefore, marriage, more so than cohabitation, lowers the risk that one's partner will renege on agreements that have been made. In the language of economic theory, marriage lowers the transaction costs of enforcing agreements between the partners (Pollak, 1985). It allows individuals to invest in the partnership with less fear of abandonment. For instance, it allows the partners to invest financially in joint long-term purchases such as homes and automobiles. It allows caregivers to make relationship-specific investments (England & Farkas, 1986) in the couple's children—investments of time and effort that, unlike strengthening one's job skills, would not be easily portable to another intimate relationship.

Nevertheless, the difference in the amount of enforceable trust that marriage brings, compared with cohabitation, is eroding. Although relatives and friends will view a divorce with disappointment, they will accept it more readily than their counterparts would have two generations ago. As I noted, cohabiting couples are increasingly gaining the rights previously reserved to married couples. It seems likely that over time, the legal differences between cohabitation and marriage will become minimal in the United States, Canada, and many European countries. The advantage of marriage in enhancing trust will then depend on the force of public commitments, both secular and religious, by the partners. . . .

The Symbolic Significance of Marriage

What has happened is that although the practical importance of being married has declined, its symbolic importance has remained high, and may even have increased. Marriage is at once less dominant and more distinctive than it was. It has evolved from a marker of conformity to a marker of prestige. Marriage is a status one builds up to, often by living with a partner beforehand, by attaining steady employment or starting a career, by putting away some savings, and even by having children. Marriage's place in the life course used to come before those investments were made, but now it often comes afterward. It used to be the foundation of adult personal life; now it is sometimes the capstone. It is something to be achieved through one's own efforts rather than something to which one routinely accedes. . . .

How Young Adults in General See It

The changing meaning of marriage is not limited to the low-income population. Consider a nationally representative survey of 1,003 adults, ages 20–29, conducted in 2001 on attitudes toward marriage (Whitehead & Popenoe, 2001). A majority responded in ways suggestive of the view that marriage is a status that one builds up to. Sixty-two percent agreed with the statement, "Living together with someone before marriage is a good way to avoid an eventual divorce," and 82% agreed that "It is extremely important to you to be economically set before you get married." Moreover, most indicated a view of marriage as centered on intimacy and love more than on practical matters such as finances and children. Ninety-four percent of those who had never married agreed that "when you marry, you want your spouse to be your soul mate, first and foremost." In contrast, only 16% agreed that "the main purpose of marriage these days is to have children." And over 80% of the women agreed that it is more important "to have a husband who can communicate about his deepest feelings than to have a husband who makes a good living." The authors of the report conclude, "While marriage is losing much of its broad public and institutional character, it is gaining popularity as a Super-Relationship, an intensely private spiritualized union, combining sexual fidelity, romantic love, emotional intimacy, and togetherness" (p. 13). . . .

Alternative Futures

What do these developments suggest about the future of marriage? Social demographers usually predict a continuation of whatever is happening at the moment, and they are usually correct, but sometimes spectacularly wrong. For example, in the 1930s, every demographic expert in the United States confidently predicted a continuation of the low birth rates of the Depression. Not one forecast the baby boom that overtook them after World War II. No less a scholar than Kingsley Davis (1937) wrote that the future of the family as a social institution was in danger because people were not having enough children to replace themselves. Not a single 1950s or 1960s sociologist predicted the rise of cohabitation. Chastened by this unimpressive record, I will tentatively sketch some future directions.

The first alternative is the reinstitutionalization of marriage, a return to a status akin to its dominant position through the mid-20th century. This would entail a rise in the proportion who ever marry, a rise in the proportion of births born to married couples, and a decline in divorce. It would require a reversal of the individualistic orientation toward family and personal life that has been the major cultural force driving family change over the past several decades. It would probably also require a decrease in women's labor force partic-ipation and a return to more gender-typed family roles. I think this alternative is very unlikely—but then again, so was the baby boom.

The second alternative is a continuation of the current situation, in which marriage remains de-institutionalized but is common and distinctive. It is not just one type of family relationship among many; rather, it is the most presti-gious form. People generally desire to be married. But it is an individual choice, and individuals construct marriages through an increasingly long pro-cess that often includes cohabitation and childbearing beforehand. It still confers some of its traditional benefits, such as enforceable trust, but it is increasingly a mark of prestige, a display of distinction, an individualistic achievement, a part of what Beck and Beck-Gernsheim (2002) call the "do-it-yourself biography." In this scenario, the proportion of people who ever marry could fall further; in particular, we could see probabilities of marriage among Whites in the United States that are similar to the probabilities shown today by African Americans. Moreover, because of high levels of nonmarital child-bearing, cohabitation, and divorce, people will spend a smaller proportion of their adult lives in intact marriages than in the past. Still, marriage would retain its special and highly valued place in the family system.

But I admit to some doubts about whether this alternative will prevail for long in the United States. The privileges and material advantages of marriage, relative to cohabitation, have been declining. The commitment of partners to be trustworthy has been undermined by frequent divorce. If marriage was once a form of cultural capital—one needed to be married to advance one's career, say—that capital has decreased too. What is left, I have argued, is a display of prestige and achievement. But it could be that marriage retains its symbolic aura largely because of its dominant position in social norms until just a half century ago. It could be that this aura is diminishing, like an echo in a can-yon. It could be that, despite the efforts of the wedding industry, the need for a highly ritualized ceremony and legalized status will fade. And there is not much else supporting marriage in the early 21st century.

That leads to a third alternative, the fading away of marriage. Here, the argument is that people are still marrying in large numbers because of institu-tional lag; they have yet to realize that marriage is no longer important. A non-marital pure relationship, to use Giddens's ideal type, can provide much intimacy and love, can place both partners on an equal footing, and can allow them to develop their independent senses of self. These characteristics are highly valued in late modern societies. However, this alternative also suggests the predominance of fragile relationships that are continually at risk of break-ing up because they are held together entirely by the voluntary commitment of each partner. People may still commit morally to a relationship, but they increasingly prefer to commit voluntarily rather than to be obligated to com-mit by law or social norms. And partners feel free to revoke their commit-ments at any time.

Therefore, the pure relationship seems most characteristic of a world where commitment does not matter. Consequently, it seems to best fit middle-class, well-educated, childless adults. They have the resources to be independent actors by themselves or in a democratic partnership, and without childbearing responsibilities, they can be free-floating. The pure relationship seems less applicable to couples who face material constraints (Jamieson, 1999). In particular, when children are present—or when they are anticipated anytime soon—issues of commitment and support come into consideration. Giddens (1992) says very little about children in his book on intimacy, and his brief attempts to incorporate children into the pure relationship are unconvincing. Individuals who are, or think they will be, the primary caregivers of children will prefer commitment and will seek material support from their partners. They may be willing to have children and begin cohabiting without commitment, but the relationship probably will not last without it. They will be wary of purely voluntary commitment if they think they can do better. So only if the advantage of marriage in providing trust and commitment disappears relative to cohabitation—and I must admit that this could happen—might we see cohabitation and marriage on an equal footing.

In sum, I see the current state of marriage and its likely future in these terms: At present, marriage is no longer as dominant as it once was, but it remains important on a symbolic level. It has been transformed from a familial and community institution to an individualized, choice-based achievement. It is a marker of prestige and is still somewhat useful in creating enforceable trust. As for the future, I have sketched three alternatives. The first, a return to a more dominant, institutionalized form of marriage, seems unlikely. In the second, the current situation continues; marriage remains important, but not as dominant, and retains its high symbolic status. In the third, marriage fades into just one of many kinds of interpersonal romantic relationships. I think that Giddens's (1992) statement that marriage has already become merely one of many relationships is not true in the United States so far, but it could become true in the future. It is possible that we are living in a transitional phase in which marriage is gradually losing its uniqueness. If Giddens and other modernity theorists are correct, the third alternative will triumph, and marriage will lose its special place in the family system of the United States. If they are not, the second alternative will continue to hold, and marriage—transformed and deinstitutionalized, but recognizable nevertheless—will remain distinctive.

Note

1. I thank Frank Furstenberg, Joshua Goldstein, Kathleen Kiernan, and Céline Le Bourdais for comments on a previous version, and Linda Burton for her collaborative work on the Three-City Study ethnography.

References

Baehr v. Lewin (74 Haw. 530, 74 Haw. 645, 852 P.2d 44 1993).

Beck, U., & Beck-Gernsheim, E. (1995). *The normal chaos of love.* Cambridge, England: Polity Press.

Beck, U., & Beck-Gernsheim, E. (2002). *Individualization: Institutionalized individualism and its social and political consequences.* London: Sage.

Bellah, R., Marsden, R., Sullivan, W. M., Swidler, A., & Tipton, S. M. (1985). *Habits of the heart: Individualism and commitment in America.* Berkeley: University of California Press.

Boden, S. (2003). *Consumerism, romance and the wedding experience.* Hampshire, England: Palgrave Macmillan.

Bumpass, L. L., & Lu, H.-H. (2000). Trends in cohabitation and implications for children's family contexts in the United States. *Population Studies, 54,* 19–41.

Bumpass, L. L., Raley, K., & Sweet, J. A. (1995). The changing character of stepfamilies: Implications of cohabitation and nonmarital childbearing. *Demography, 32,* 1–12.

Burgess, E. W., & Locke, H. J. (1945). *The family: From institution to companionship.* New York: American Book.

Carrington, C. (1999). *No place like home: Relationships and family life among lesbians and gay men.* Chicago: University of Chicago Press.

Cherlin, A. (1978). Remarriage as an incomplete institution. *American Journal of Sociology, 84,* 634–650.

Cherlin, A. J. (2000). Toward a new home socioeconomics of union formation. In L. Waite, C. Bachrach, M. Hindin, E. Thomson, & A. Thornton (Eds.), *Ties that bind: Perspectives on marriage and cohabitation* (pp. 126–144). Hawthorne, NY: Aldine de Gruyter.

Daley, S. (2000, April 18). French couples take plunge that falls short of marriage. *The New York Times,* pp. A1, A4.

Davis, J. A., Smith, T. W., & Marsden, P. (2003). *General social surveys, 1972-2002 cumulative codebook.* Chicago: National Opinion Research Center, University of Chicago.

Davis, K. (1937). Reproductive institutions and the pressure for population. *Sociological Review, 29,* 289–306.

England, P., & Farkas, G. (1986). *Households, employment, and gender: A social, economic, and demographic view.* New York: Aldine.

Ermisch, J. (2001). Cohabitation and childbearing outside marriage in Britain. In L. L. Wu & B. Wolfe (Eds.), *Out of wedlock: Causes and consequences of nonmarital fertility* (pp. 109–139). New York: Russell Sage Foundation.

Giddens, A. (1991). *Modernity and self-identity.* Stanford, CA: Stanford University Press.

Giddens, A. (1992). *The transformation of intimacy.* Stanford, CA: Stanford University Press.

Goldstein, J. R., & Kenney, C. T. (2001). Marriage delayed or marriage forgone? New cohort forecasts of first marriage for U.S. women. *American Sociological Review, 66,* 506–519.

Hochschild, A. (1989). *The second shift: Working parents and the revolution at home.* New York: Viking.

Jamieson, L. (1999). Intimacy transformed? A critical look at the "pure relationship." *Sociology, 33,* 477–494.

Juby, H., Marcil-Gratton, N., & Le Bourdais, C. (in press). *When parents separate: Further findings from the National Longitudinal Survey of Children and Youth.* Phase 2 research report of the project, "The Impact of Parents' Family Transitions on Children's Family Environment and Economic Well-Being: A Longitudinal Assessment." Ottawa, Ontario: Department of Justice Canada, Child Support Team.

Kiernan, K. (2002). Cohabitation in Western Europe: Trends, issues, and implications. In A. Booth & A. C. Crouter (Eds.), *Just living together: Implication of cohabitation on families, children, and social policy* (pp. 3–31). Mahwah, NJ: Erlbaum.

Le Bourdais, C., & Juby, H. (2002). The impact of cohabitation on the family life course in contemporary North America: Insights from across the border. In A. Booth & A. C. Crouter (Eds.), *Just living together: Implications of cohabitation on families, children, and social policy* (pp. 107–118). Mahwah, NJ: Erlbaum.

Le Bourdais, C., & Marcil-Gratton, N. (1996). Family transformations across the Canadian/American border: When the laggard becomes the leader. *Journal of Comparative Family Studies, 27,* 415–436.

Lyall, S. (2004, February 15). In Europe, lovers now propose: Marry me a little. *The New York Times*, p. A3.

Mair, L. (1971). *Marriage.* Middlesex, England: Penguin Books.

Nova Scotia (Attorney General) v. Walsh. (2002). SCC 83.

Pollak, R. A. (1985). A transaction costs approach to families and households. *Journal of Economic Literature, 23*, 581–608.

Portes, A., & Sensenbrenner, J. (1993). Embedded-ness and immigration: Notes on the social determinants of economic action. *American Journal of Sociology, 98*, 1320–1350.

Smock, P. J., & Gupta, S. (2002). Cohabitation in contemporary North America. In A. Booth & A. C. Crouter (Eds.), *Just living together: Implications of cohabitation on families, children, and social policy* (pp. 53–84). Mahwah, NJ: Erlbaum.

Statistics Canada. (1997). *Report on the demographic situation in Canada 1996* (No. 91-209-XPE). Ottawa, Ontario: Statistical Reference Centre.

Statistics Canada. (2002). *Changing conjugal life in Canada* (No. 89-576-XIE). Ottawa, Ontario: Statistical Reference Centre.

Statistics Canada. (2003). *Annual Demographic Statistics, 2002* (No. 91-213-XIB). Ottawa, Ontario: Statistical Reference Centre.

Thornton, A., & Young-DeMarco, L. (2001). Four decades of trends in attitudes toward family issues in the United States: The 1960s through the 1990s. *Journal of Marriage and Family, 63*, 1009–1037.

U.S. Census Bureau. (2003b). *Married-couple and unmarried-partner households: 2000* (Census 2000 Special Reports, CENSR-5). Washington, DC: U.S. Government Printing Office.

U.S. National Center for Health Statistics. (1982). *Vital statistics of the United States, 1978* (Volume I – Natality). Washington, DC: U.S. Government Printing Office.

U.S. National Center for Health Statistics. (2003). *Births: Preliminary data for 2002.* Retrieved December 15, 2003, from . . .

Weeks, J., Heaphy, B., & Donovan, C. (2001). *Same sex intimacies: Families of choice and other life experiments.* London: Routledge.

Weston, K. (1991). *Families we choose: Lesbians, gays, kinship.* New York: Columbia University Press.

Whitehead, B. D., & Popenoe, D. (2001). Who wants to marry a soul mate? In *The state of our unions, 2001* (National Marriage Project, pp. 6–16). Retrieved February 12, 2004, from . . .

Frank Furstenberg

Can Marriage Be Saved?

A growing number of social scientists fear that marriage may be on the rocks and few doubt that matrimony, as we have known it, has undergone a wrenching period of change in the past several decades. Andrew Cherlin, a leading sociologist of the family, speaks of "the de-institutionalization of marriage," conceding a point to conservative commentators who have argued that marriage and the family have been in a state of free-fall since the 1960s.

Western Europe has experienced many of the same trends—declining rates of marriage, widespread cohabitation, and rising levels of nonmarital childbearing—but has largely shrugged them off. By contrast, concern about the state of marriage in the United States has touched a raw, political nerve. What ails marriage and what, if anything, can be done to restore this time-honored social arrangement to its former status as a cultural invention for assigning the rights and responsibilities of reproduction, including sponsorship and inheritance?

On the left side of the political spectrum, observers believe that the institutional breakdown of marriage has its roots in economic and social changes brought about by shifts in home-based production, structural changes in the economy, and the breakdown of the gender-based division of labor—trends unlikely to be reversed. The other position, championed by most conservatives, is that people have lost faith in marriage because of changes in cultural values that could be reversed or restored through shifts in the law, changes in administrative policies and practices, and public rhetoric to alter beliefs and expectations.

The Bush administration is trying to put into place a set of policies aimed at reversing the symptoms of retreat from marriage: high rates of premarital sex, nonmarital childbearing, cohabitation, and divorce. Do their policies make sense and do they have a reasonable prospect of success? To answer this question, I want to begin with the trends that Americans, including many social scientists, have found so alarming and then turn to the question of how much public policy and what kinds of policies could help to strengthen marriage.

Demographic Changes and Political Interpretations

When compared to the 1950s, the institution of marriage seems to be profoundly changed, but is the middle of the twentieth century an appropriate

Originally published in *Dissent Magazine*, Summer 2005, pp. 76–80. Copyright © 2005 by Foundation for Study of Independent Ideas, Inc. Reprinted by permission. www.dissentmagazine.org

point of comparison? It has been widely known since the baby boom era that the period after the Second World War was unusual demographically: the very early onset of adult transitions; unprecedented rates of marriage; high fertility; an economy that permitted a single wage earner to support a family reasonably well; and the flow of federal funding for education, housing, and jobs distinguished the 1950s and early 1960s as a particular historical moment different from any previous period and certainly different from the decades after the Vietnam War era. For a brief time, the nuclear family in the United States and throughout much of Europe reigned supreme.

If we use the middle of the twentieth century as a comparison point, it might appear that we have been witnessing a deconstruction of the two-parent biological family en masse. But such a view is historically shortsighted and simplistic. The nuclear family, though long the bourgeois ideal, had never been universally practiced, at least as it was in the middle of the last century. Only in the 1950s—and then for a very brief time—did it become the gold standard for what constitutes a healthy family. Indeed, sociologists at that time fiercely debated whether this family model represented a decline from the "traditional" extended family. Even those who argued against this proposition could not agree whether this family form was desirable ("functional" in the language of the day) or contained fatal flaws that would be its undoing.

During the 1960s and 1970s, anthropological evidence indicated that family diversity is universal, and findings from the new field of historical demography revealed that families in both the East and the West had always been changing in response to economic, political, demographic, and social conditions. In short, the nuclear family was cross-culturally and historically not "the natural unit," that many wrongly presume today.

Although it was widely known that the family had undergone considerable changes from ancient times and during the industrial revolution, that family systems varied across culture, and that social-class differences created varied forms of the family within the same society, it was not until the 1960s, when historians began to use computers to analyze census data, that the extent of this variation came into clearer focus. For the first time, family scholars from several disciplines could see the broad outlines of a new picture of how family forms and functions are intimately related to the social, cultural, and perhaps especially the economic contexts in which household and kinship systems are embedded.

From this evidence, students of the family can assert three points. First, no universal form of the family constitutes the appropriate or normative arrangement for reproduction, nurturance, socialization, and economic support. Both across and within societies, family forms, patterns, and practices vary enormously. Second, change is endemic to all family systems, and at least in the West, where we have the best evidence to date, family systems have always been in flux. Typically, these changes create tensions and often ignite public concern. Since colonial times, the family has been changing and provoking public reaction from moralists, scientists, and, of course, public authorities. Finally, family systems do not evolve in a linear fashion but become more or less complex and more elemental in different eras or among different strata of society depending on the economic and social conditions to which families must adapt.

Does this mean that we are seeing a continuation of what has always been or something different than has ever occurred in human history—the withering of kinship as an organizing feature of human society? The decline of marriage suggests to some that this round of change is unique in human history or that its consequences for children will be uniquely unsettling to society.

Many scholars weighed in on these questions. It is fair to say that there are two main camps: (1) those who have decided that the family is imperiled as a result of changes in the marriage system, a position held by such respectable social scientists as Linda Waite, Norvel Glenn, and Judith Wallerstein; and (2) those who remain skeptical and critical of those sounding the alarm, a position held by the majority of social scientists. Many in this second camp take seriously the concerns of the "alarmists" that children's welfare may be at risk if the current family regime continues. Still, they doubt that the family can be coaxed back into its 1950s form and favor adaptations in government policy to assist new forms of the family—an approach followed by most European nations.

·❦·

Some portion of those skeptics are not so alarmed by changes in the family, believing that children's circumstances have not been seriously compromised by family change. They contend that children's well-being has less to do with the family form in which they reside than the resources possessed to form viable family arrangements. Lacking these resources (material and cultural), it matters little whether the children are born into a marriage, cohabitation, or a single-parent household, because they are likely not to fare as well as those whose parents possess the capacity to realize their goals.

I place myself in this latter group. Of course, children will fare better when they have two well-functioning, collaborative parents than one on average, but one well-functioning parent with resources is better than two married parents who lack the resources or skills to manage parenthood. Moreover, parents with limited cultural and material resources are unlikely to remain together in a stable marriage. Because the possession of such psychological, human, and material capital is highly related to marital stability, it is easy to confuse the effects of stable marriage with the effects of competent parenting. Finally, I believe that the best way to foster marriage stability is to support children with an array of services that assist parents and children, regardless of the family form in which they reside.

Marriage and Good Outcomes for Children

A huge number of studies have shown that children fare better in two-biological-parent families than they do in single-biological-parent families, leading most family researchers to conclude that the nuclear family is a more effective unit for reproduction and socialization. Yet this literature reveals some troubling features that have not been adequately examined by social scientists. The most obvious of these is that such findings rule out social selection.

If parents with limited resources and low skills are less likely to enter marriage with a biological parent and remain wed when they do (which we know to be true), then it follows that children will do worse in such single-parent households than in stable marriages. We have known about this problem for decades, but researchers have not been equipped adequately to rule out selection. The standard method for doing so is by statistically controlling for prior differences, but this method is inadequate for ruling out differences because it leaves so many sources of selection unmeasured, such as sexual compatibility, substance abuse, and so on. Newer statistical methods have been employed to correct for unmeasured differences, but strong evidence exists that none of these techniques is up to the challenge. Nevertheless, it is *theoretically* possible to examine social experiments such as those being mounted in the marriage-promotion campaign and assess their long-term effects on children.

Another useful approach is to examine macro-level differences at the state or national level that would be less correlated with social selection and hence more revealing of the impact of marriage arrangements on children's well-being. To date, there is little evidence supporting a correlation between family form and children's welfare at the national level. Consider first the historical data showing that children who grew up in the 1950s (baby boomers) were not notably free of problem behavior. After all, they were the cohort who raised such hell in the 1960s and 1970s. From 1955 to 1975, indicators of social problems among children (test scores, suicide, homicide, controlled-substance use, crime) that can be tracked by vital statistics all rose. These indicators accompanied, and in some cases preceded rather than followed, change in the rates of divorce, the decline of marriage, and the rise of nonmarital childbearing during this period. Conversely, there is no evidence that the cohort of children who came of age in the 1990s and early part of this century is doing worse than previous cohorts because these children are more likely to have grown up in single-parent families. Of course, compensatory public policies or other demographic changes such as small family size, higher parental education, or lower rates of poverty may have offset the deleterious effects of family form, but such an explanation concedes that family form is not as potent a source of children's well-being as many observers seem to believe.

We might also gain some purchase on this issue by comparing the success of children under different family regimes. Do the countries with high rates of cohabitation, low marriage, high divorce, and high nonmarital fertility have the worst outcomes for children? We don't know the answer to this question, but we do know that various indicators of child well-being—health, mental health, educational attainment—do show higher scores in Northern than in Southern Europe. They appear to be linked to the level of investment in children, not the family form (which is certainly more intact in Southern Europe). Still, this question deserves more attention than it has received.

Significantly, many of the countries that continue to adhere to the nuclear model have some of the world's lowest rates of fertility—a problem that seems worse in countries with very low rates of nonmarital childbearing. I am not claiming that nonmarital childbearing is necessarily desirable as a social arrangement for propping up fertility, but it is a plausible hypothesis that nonmarital childbearing helps to keep the birth rate up in countries that would otherwise be experiencing a dangerously low level of reproduction.

Finally, it is important to recognize that family change in the United States (and in most Western countries, it appears) has not occurred evenly among all educational groups. In this country, marriage, divorce, and nonmarital childbearing have jumped since the 1960s among the bottom two-thirds of the educational distribution but have not changed much at all among the top third, consisting, today, of college graduates and postgraduates. Though marriage comes later to this group, they are barely more likely to have children out of wedlock, have high levels of marriage, and, if anything, lower levels of divorce than were experienced several decades ago. In other words, almost all the change has occurred among the segment of the population that has either not gained economically or has lost ground over the past several decades. Among the most socially disadvantaged and most marginalized segments of American society, marriage has become imperiled and family conditions have generally deteriorated, resulting in extremely high rates of union instability. The growing inequality in the United States may provide some clues for why the family, and marriage in particular, is not faring well and what to do about it.

Marriage and Public Policy

The logic of the Bush administration's approach to welfare is that by promoting and strengthening marriage, children's well-being, particularly in lower-income families will be enhanced. At first blush, this approach seems to make good sense. Economies of scale are produced when two adults live together. Two parents create healthy redundancies and perhaps help build social capital both within the household and by creating more connections to the community. The prevalence of marriage and marital stability is substantially higher among well-educated and more stably employed individuals than among those with less than a college education and lower incomes. Wouldn't it be reasonable to help the less educated enjoy the benefits of the nuclear family?

There are several reasons to be skeptical of this policy direction. First, we have the experience of the 1950s, when marriages did occur in abundance among low-income families. Divorce rates were extremely high during this era, and many of these families dissolved their unions when they had an opportunity to divorce because of chronic problems of conflict, disenchantment, and scarcity. In my own study of marriages of teen parents in the 1960s, I discovered that four out of every five women who married the father of their children got divorced before the child reached age eighteen; the rate of marital instability among those who married a stepfather was even higher. Certainly, encouraging marriage among young couples facing a choice of nonmarital childbearing or wedlock is not an easy choice when we know the outcome of the union is so precarious. If divorce is a likely outcome, it is not clear whether children are better off if their parents marry and divorce than remain unmarried, knowing as we do that family conflict and flux have adverse effects on children's welfare.

What about offering help to such couples before or after they enter marriage? This is a good idea, but don't expect any miracles from the current policies. Strong opposition exists to funding sustained and intensive premarital and postmarital counseling among many proponents of marriage-promotion programs. Conservative constituencies largely believe that education, especially under the aegis of religious or quasi-religious sponsorship is the best prescription for shoring up marriage. Yet, the evidence overwhelmingly shows that short-term programs that are largely didactic will not be effective in preserving marriages. Instead, many couples need repeated bouts of help both before and during marriage when they run into difficult straits. Most of these couples have little or no access to professional counseling.

The federal government has funded several large-scale experiments combining into a single program marital education or counseling *and* social services including job training or placement. These experiments, being conducted by the Manpower Research Demonstration Corporation, will use random assignment and have the best hope of producing some demonstrable outcomes. Yet, it is not clear at this point that even comprehensive programs with sustained services will be effective in increasing partner collaboration and reducing union instability.

There is another approach that I believe has a better prospect of improving both children's chances and probably at least an equal chance of increasing the viability of marriages or marriage-like arrangements. By directing more resources to low-income children regardless of the family form they live in, through such mechanisms as access to quality child care, health care, schooling, and income in the form of tax credits, it may be possible to increase the level of human, social, and psychological capital that children receive. And, by increasing services, work support, and especially tuition aid for adolescents and young adults to attend higher education, Americans may be able to protect children from the limitations imposed by low parental resources. Lending this type of assistance means that young adults are more likely to move into higher paying jobs and acquire through education the kinds of communication and problem-solving skills that are so useful to making marriage-like relationships last.

When we invest in children, we are not only likely to reap the direct benefits of increasing human capital but also the indirect benefits that will help preserve union stability in the next generation. This approach is more likely to increase the odds of success for children when they grow up. If I am correct, it probably follows that direct investment in children and youth has a better prospect of strengthening marriage and marriage-like relationships in the next generation by improving the skills and providing the resources to make parental relationships more rewarding and enduring.

So it comes down to a choice in strategy: invest in strengthening marriage and hope that children will benefit or invest in children and hope that marriages will benefit. I place my bet on the second approach.

CHALLENGE QUESTIONS

Is the Institution of Marriage at Risk?

- Cherlin finishes by providing three alternatives for the future of marriage, himself tentatively speculating that marriage may lose a special place in the United States. Which of the three alternatives do you see as most likely?
- As a general value, most people consider diversity a good thing. As such, why do some people endorse the idea that one specific type of family structure is best for adults, while others endorse a diversity of family structures?
- Despite a significant and well-intentioned push toward marriage from people promoting family values, a majority of voters in recent elections within the United States have rejected the idea of allowing homosexual couples the right to legal marriage. If marriage is good for adults, should we not allow all adults the opportunity to marry? Or would that change the nature of marriage to such a degree that it would no longer maintain its traditional value?
- If alternatives to marriage, such as cohabitation, became the norm rather than the exception, would it still be considered a negative developmental outcome?

Suggested Readings

K. Boo, "The Marriage Cure," *The New Yorker* (August 18, 2003)

A. Cherlin, "Should the Government Promote Marriage?" *Contexts* (Fall 2003)

P. England, "The Case for Marriage: Why Married People Are Happier, Healthier, and Better Off Financially," *Contemporary Sociology* (November 2001)

M. Gallagher, "The Latest War Against Marriage," *Crisis* (February 2001)

T. Huston and H. Meiz, "The Case of (Promoting) Marriage: The Devil Is in the Details," *Journal of Marriage and the Family* (November 2004)

S. Jeffrey, "The Need to Abolish Marriage," *Feminism & Psychology* (May 2004)

D. Solot and M. Miller, "Marriage-Only Forces Don't Help Today's Families," *Sojourner: The Women's Forum* (October 1999)

L. Waite and M. Gallagher, *The Case for Marriage: Why Married People Are Happier, Healthier, and Better Off Financially* (Doubleday, 2000)

L. Waite, D. Browning, W. Dohert, M. Gallagher, Y. Luo, and S. Stanley, "Does Divorce Make People Happy? Findings from a Study of Unhappy Marriages," *Institute of American Values* (2002)

ISSUE 16

Can Lesbian and Gay Couples Be Appropriate Parents for Children?

YES: American Psychological Association, from APA Policy Statement on Sexual Orientation, Parents, & Children (July 2004)

NO: Timothy J. Dailey, from "State of the States: Update on Homosexual Adoption in the U.S.," *Family Research Council* (no. 243, 2004)

ISSUE SUMMARY

YES: The American Psychological Association's research concluded that all of the evidence suggests that lesbian and gay couples are as equally competent to parent as heterosexual couples.

NO: In contrast, Timothy Dailey asserts that homosexual relationships are less stable than heterosexual marriages and thus are less able to provide a stable two-parent home for children.

One of the primary developmental tasks for most adults involves raising children. Most parents want to be good at that task. However, we all recognize that there is wide variation in how good adults are at parenting. So what does it take for an adult to be a good parent?

Though there is probably not one single set of characteristics that makes for good parents, most people think of good parents as being engaged in committed and healthy relationships. Although relationship norms have been shifting, the most common and familiar type of relationship in contemporary society remains a marriage between a man and a women. But being common and familiar does not necessarily mean committed and healthy. As such, the controversy about whether gay and lesbian couples can be appropriate parents for children is embedded with a wide range of issues important to the study of lifespan developments.

According to the American Psychological Association, most of the research on gay and lesbian parents suggests that there is no reason to think they cannot be appropriate parents. The APA points out that while there is a significant social stigma against homosexuality, there is no evidence that it is a psychological disorder or a sign of poor mental health. Further, there is no evidence that gay and lesbian parents are, on average, any different than heterosexual parents—which likely means that some couples are great parents, many couples are average, and some couples are bad parents. The APA also notes, however, that there is some evidence gay and lesbian parents may be better in certain ways—partially due to the fact that, on average, it takes more motivation for homosexual couples to have children in contrast to heterosexual couples.

Timothy Dailey, on the other hand, is concerned that gay activists are shaping the way the public understands this issue. From his perspective, the fact that several states have legally prohibited gay adoption suggests that public opinion is against the practice. Further, Dailey implies that this question raises larger issues about the nature of marriage and family. He suggests that allowing homosexual couples to marry and have children will change the committed nature of relationships and thus challenge the norms of healthy parenting.

Because this question relates to how we define and understand what it means to be a family, it involves a number of politically loaded issues. As such, one particular challenge in understanding this controversy is to distinguish between assertions based on politics and assertions based on social science—a task that is not always easy. In popular exchanges the issue of gay parenting can be polemical, with people taking strong and emotional positions on either side. At this point, however, the social science research base is less dichotomous. There is not a large body of carefully controlled research on gay and lesbian parenting, and the research that does exist tends to find few consistent effects. As such, the question here is not so much about whether gay and lesbian couples can engage in successful parenting—clearly they can. Instead, the question is about whether gay and lesbian parenting represents a larger threat to understandings of the family and the normal patterns of adult development.

POINT	COUNTERPOINT
• Many gay and lesbian couples are already parents, and there are no consistent negative effects on children.	• Legal decisions suggest that there is a generally unfavorable attitude toward homosexual parenting.
• Being gay or lesbian in and of itself provides no indication of any other psychological problems.	• Homosexual couples may be less likely to maintain a committed relationship and thus provide a stable home.
• Most research finds that gay and lesbian parents are, on average, as fit as heterosexual couples for parenting.	• Estimates of the number of children being raised by homosexual parents may be too high, and it is clear that homosexual families are not the norm.
• Evidence suggests that children raised by homosexual couples do not differ significantly from children with heterosexual parents.	• Allowing homosexual adoption would change the nature of the family and marriage.

YES

APA Policy Statement on Sexual Orientation, Parents, & Children

Research Summary

Lesbian and Gay Parents

Many lesbians and gay men are parents. In the 2000 U.S. Census, 33% of female same-sex couple households and 22% of male same-sex couple households reported at least one child under the age of 18 living in the home. Despite the significant presence of at least 163,879 households headed by lesbian or gay parents in U.S. society, three major concerns about lesbian and gay parents are commonly voiced (Falk, 1994; Patterson, Fulcher & Wainright, 2002). These include concerns that lesbians and gay men are mentally ill, that lesbians are less maternal than heterosexual women, and that lesbians' and gay men's relationships with their sexual partners leave little time for their relationships with their children. In general, research has failed to provide a basis for any of these concerns (Patterson, 2002, 2004a; Perrin, 2002; Tasker, 1999; Tasker & Golombok, 1997). First, homosexuality is not a psychological disorder (Conger, 1975). Although exposure to prejudice and discrimination based on sexual orientation may cause acute distress (Mays & Cochran, 2001; Meyer, 2003), there is no reliable evidence that homosexual orientation per se impairs psychological functioning. Second, beliefs that lesbian and gay adults are not fit parents have no empirical foundation (Patterson, 2000, 2004a; Perrin, 2002). Lesbian and heterosexual women have not been found to differ markedly in their approaches to child rearing (Patterson, 2002; Tasker, 1999). Members of gay and lesbian couples with children have been found to divide the work involved in childcare evenly, and to be satisfied with their relationships with their partners (Patterson, 2000, 2004a). The results of some studies suggest that lesbian mothers' and gay fathers' parenting skills may be superior to those of matched heterosexual parents. There is no scientific basis for concluding that lesbian mothers or gay fathers are unfit parents on the basis of their sexual orientation (Armesto, 2002; Patterson, 2000; Tasker & Golombok, 1997). On the contrary, results of research suggest that lesbian and gay parents are as likely as heterosexual parents to provide supportive and healthy environments for their children.

Paige, R. U. (2005). Proceedings of the American Psychological Association, Incorporated, for the legislative year 2004. Minutes of the meeting of the Council of Representatives July 28 & 30, 2004, Honolulu, HI. Retrieved November 18, 2004, from the World Wide Web http://www.apa.org/governance/.

Children of Lesbian and Gay Parents

As the social visibility and legal status of lesbian and gay parents has increased, three major concerns about the influence of lesbian and gay parents on children have been often voiced (Falk; 1994; Patterson, Fulcher & Wainright, 2002). One is that the children of lesbian and gay parents will experience more difficulties in the area of sexual identity than children of heterosexual parents. For instance, one such concern is that children brought up by lesbian mothers or gay fathers will show disturbances in gender identity and/or in gender role behavior. A second category of concerns involves aspects of children's personal development other than sexual identity. For example, some observers have expressed fears that children in the custody of gay or lesbian parents would be more vulnerable to mental breakdown, would exhibit more adjustment difficulties and behavior problems, or would be less psychologically healthy than other children. A third category of concerns is that children of lesbian and gay parents will experience difficulty in social relationships. For example, some observers have expressed concern that children living with lesbian mothers or gay fathers will be stigmatized, teased, or otherwise victimized by peers. Another common fear is that children living with gay or lesbian parents will be more likely to be sexually abused by the parent or by the parent's friends or acquaintances.

Results of social science research have failed to confirm any of these concerns about children of lesbian and gay parents (Patterson, 2000, 2004a; Perrin, 2002; Tasker, 1999). Research suggests that sexual identities (including gender identity, gender-role behavior, and sexual orientation) develop in much the same ways among children of lesbian mothers as they do among children of heterosexual parents (Patterson, 2004a). Studies of other aspects of personal development (including personality, self-concept, and conduct) similarly reveal few differences between children of lesbian mothers and children of heterosexual parents (Perrin, 2002; Stacey & Biblarz, 2001; Tasker, 1999). However, few data regarding these concerns are available for children of gay fathers (Patterson, 2004b). Evidence also suggests that children of lesbian and gay parents have normal social relationships with peers and adults (Patterson, 2000, 2004a; Perrin, 2002; Stacey & Biblarz, 2001; Tasker, 1999; Tasker & Golombok, 1997). The picture that emerges from research is one of general engagement in social life with peers, parents, family members, and friends. Fears about children of lesbian or gay parents being sexually abused by adults, ostracized by peers, or isolated in single-sex lesbian or gay communities have received no scientific support. Overall, results of research suggest that the development, adjustment, and well-being of children with lesbian and gay parents do not differ markedly from that of children with heterosexual parents.

Resolution

> **WHEREAS** APA supports policy and legislation that promote safe, secure, and nurturing environments for all children (DeLeon, 1993, 1995; Fox, 1991; Levant, 2000);

WHEREAS APA has a long-established policy to deplore "all public and private discrimination against gay men and lesbians" and urges "the repeal of all discriminatory legislation against lesbians and gay men" (Conger, 1975);

WHEREAS the APA adopted the Resolution on Child Custody and Placement in 1976 (Conger, 1977, p. 432);

WHEREAS Discrimination against lesbian and gay parents deprives their children of benefits, rights, and privileges enjoyed by children of heterosexual married couples;

WHEREAS some jurisdictions prohibit gay and lesbian individuals and same-sex couples from adopting children, notwithstanding the great need for adoptive parents (Lofton v. Secretary, 2004);

WHEREAS There is no scientific evidence that parenting effectiveness is related to parental sexual orientation: lesbian and gay parents are as likely as heterosexual parents to provide supportive and healthy environments for their children (Patterson, 2000, 2004; Perrin, 2002; Tasker, 1999);

WHEREAS Research has shown that the adjustment, development, and psychological well-being of children is unrelated to parental sexual orientation and that the children of lesbian and gay parents are as likely as those of heterosexual parents to flourish (Patterson, 2004; Perrin, 2002; Stacey & Biblarz, 2001);

THEREFORE BE IT RESOLVED That the APA opposes any discrimination based on sexual orientation in matters of adoption, child custody and visitation, foster care, and reproductive health services;

THEREFORE BE IT FURTHER RESOLVED That the APA believes that children reared by a same-sex couple benefit from legal ties to each parent;

THEREFORE BE IT FURTHER RESOLVED That the APA supports the protection of parent-child relationships through the legalization of joint adoptions and second parent adoptions of children being reared by same-sex couples;

THEREFORE BE IT FURTHER RESOLVED That APA shall take a leadership role in opposing all discrimination based on sexual orientation in matters of adoption, child custody and visitation, foster care, and reproductive health services;

THEREFORE BE IT FURTHER RESOLVED That APA encourages psychologists to act to eliminate all discrimination based on sexual orientation in matters of adoption, child custody and visitation, foster care, and reproductive health services in their practice, research, education and training ("Ethical Principles," 2002, p. 1063);

THEREFORE BE IT FURTHER RESOLVED That the APA shall provide scientific and educational resources that inform public discussion and public policy development regarding discrimination based on sexual orientation in matters of adoption, child custody and visitation, foster care, and reproductive health services and that assist its members, divisions, and affiliated state, provincial, and territorial psychological associations.

References

Armesto, J. C. (2002). Developmental and contextual factors that influence gay fathers' parental competence: A review of the literature. *Psychology of Men and Masculinity, 3,* 67–78.

Conger, J. J. (1975). Proceedings of the American Psychological Association, Incorporated, for the year 1974: Minutes of the Annual meeting of the Council of Representatives. *American Psychologists, 30,* 620–651.

Conger, J. J. (1977). Proceedings of the American Psychological Association, Incorporated, for the legislative year 1976: Minutes of the Annual Meeting of the Council of Representatives. *American Psychologist, 32,* 408–438.

Fox, R. E. (1991). Proceedings of the American Psychological Association, Incorporated, for the year 1990: Minutes of the annual meeting of the Council of Representatives August 9 and 12, 1990, Boston, MA, and February 8–9, 1991, Washington, DC. *American Psychologist, 45,* 845.

DeLeon, P. H. (1993). Proceedings of the American Psychological Association, Incorporated, for the year 1992: Minutes of the annual meeting of the Council of Representatives August 13 and 16, 1992, and February 26–28, 1993, Washington, DC. *American Psychologist, 48,* 782.

DeLeon, P. H. (1995). Proceedings of the American Psychological Association, Incorporated, for the year 1994: Minutes of the annual meeting of the Council of Representatives August 11 and 14, 1994, Los Angeles, CA, and February 17–19, 1995, Washington, DC. *American Psychologist, 49,* 627–628.

Ethical Principles of Psychologists and Code of Conduct. (2002). *American Psychologists, 57,* 1060–1073.

Levant, R. F. (2000). Proceedings of the American Psychological Association, Incorporated, for the Legislative Year 1999: Minutes of the Annual Meeting of the Council of Representatives February 19–21, 1999, Washington, DC, and August 19 and 22, 1999, Boston, MA, and Minutes of the February, June, August, and December 1999 Meetings of the Board of Directors. *American Psychologist, 55,* 832–890.

Lofton v. Secretary of Department of Children & Family Services, 358 F.3d 804 (11th Cir. 2004).

Mays, V. M. & Cochran, S. D. (2001). Mental health correlates of perceived discrimination among lesbian, gay, and bisexual adults in the United States. *American Journal of Public Health, 91,* 1869–1876.

Meyer, I. H. (2003). Prejudice, social stress, and mental health in lesbian, gay, and bisexual populations: Conceptual issues and research evidence. *Psychological Bulletin, 129,* 674–697.

Patterson, C. J. (2000). Family relationships of lesbians and gay men. *Journal of Marriage and Family, 62,* 1052–1069.

Patterson, C. J. (2004a). Lesbian and gay parents and their children: Summary of research findings. In *Lesbian and gay parenting: A resource for psychologists.* Washington, DC: American Psychological Association.

Patterson, C. J. (2004b). Gay fathers. In M. E. Lamb (Ed.), *The role of the father in child development* (4th Ed.). New York: John Wiley.

Patterson, C. J., Fulcher, M., & Wainright, J. (2002). Children of lesbian and gay parents: Research, law, and policy. In B. L. Bottoms, M. B. Kovera, and B. D. McAuliff (Eds.), *Children, social science and the law* (pp. 176–199). New York: Cambridge University Press.

Perrin, E. C. and the Committee on Psychosocial Aspects of Child and Family Health (2002). Technical Report: Coparent or second-parent adoption by same-sex parents. *Pediatrics, 109,* 341–344.

Stacey, J. & Biblarz, T. J. (2001). (How) Does sexual orientation of parents matter? *American Sociological Review, 65,* 159–183.

Tasker, F. (1999). Children in lesbian-led families—A review. *Clinical Child Psychology and Psychiatry, 4,* 153–166.

Tasker, F. & Golombok, S. (1997). *Growing up in a lesbian family.* New York: Guilford Press.

Timothy J. Dailey  **NO**

State of the States: Update on Homosexual Adoption in the U.S.

The legal status of homosexual adoption varies from state to state, and is constantly changing due to court decisions and new state laws addressing the issue. Further complicating the issue are gay activist organizations that present misleading accounts of court rulings and laws reflecting unfavorably on homosexual parenting.

States That Specifically Prohibit Gay Adoption

Three states, Florida, Mississippi, and Utah, have passed statutes specifically prohibiting homosexual adoption. The advocates of gay adoption downplay the Utah statute, asserting that it was not intended to prevent adoption by homosexuals. Liz Winfeld, writing in the *Denver Post,* discusses claims that the Utah law was aimed squarely at homosexuals: "Not true. Utah disallows any unmarried person from adopting regardless of gender or orientation."[1]

In fact, the Utah law was enacted specifically to close loopholes in Utah adoption laws that were being taken advantage of by homosexual couples seeking to adopt children. The *Salt Lake Tribune* reports that a battle erupted over "an administrative policy enacted by the board of Utah's Division of Child and Family Service that bars same-sex couples and unmarried heterosexual couples from state-sponsored adoptions."[2]

The ensuing fight led to the legislature passing a statute barring homosexual adoptions. According to Brigham Young University law professor Lynn Wardle: "This was a response to the problem of stealth adoptions. There were a number of judges who were sympathetic to gay and lesbian couples."[3]

States That Specifically Permit Gay Adoption

USA Today reports that seven states, including California, Connecticut, Illinois, Massachusetts, New Jersey, New York, Vermont, and the District of Columbia permit homosexuals to adopt.[4] However, at present the inclusion of California on this list is inaccurate. [see below]

States That Permit Second-Parent Adoption

Homosexual couples have adopted children through "second-parent" adoption policies in at least twenty states. There is no evidence that homosexuals in the remaining states are permitted to adopt children, a fact admitted by the gay activist Human Rights Campaign (HRC): "In the remaining 24 states, our research has not revealed any second-parent adoptions."[5]

At least one state has reversed its policy of permitting second-parent adoptions. In November 2000, the Superior Court of Pennsylvania ruled that same-sex couples cannot adopt children.[6] In addition, a court decision in California has reversed that state's policy of permitting homosexuals to adopt children. On October 25, 2001, the 4th District Court of Appeal (San Diego) ruled that there was no legal authority under California law permitting second-parent adoptions.[7]

Attempting to put the best possible spin on what is a significant setback for homosexual adoption, HRC claimed that the 4th District Court issued a modified decision "omitting the suggestion that previously granted second-parent adoptions may be invalid."[8] This misleadingly implies that the court intended to let stand such adoptions. In fact, the court specified that it was not ruling on *either* the validity or the invalidity of previous gay adoptions under California law.[9]

Homosexual Households in the United States

There are widely varying and unsubstantiated claims about the numbers of children being raised in gay and lesbian households. According to a study on homosexual parenting in the *American Sociological Review*, researchers have given figures "of uncertain origin, depicting a range of . . . from 6 to 14 million children of gay or lesbian parents in the United States."[10]

Some of these claims appear to be based on the discredited assertion by Indiana University sex researcher Alfred Kinsey that up to ten percent of the population is homosexual.[11] According to the *American Sociological Review* study, the upper figures are based upon "classifying as a lesbigay parent anyone who reports that even the idea of homoerotic sex is appealing."[12] The authors favor a figure of about one million, which "derives from the narrower . . . definition of a lesbigay parent as one who self-identifies as such."[13]

However, even the lower figure of one million children being raised in gay and lesbian households does not stand up to statistical analysis:

- The U.S. Census Bureau reports that there are 601,209 (304,148 male homosexual and 297,061 lesbian) same-sex unmarried partner households, for a total of 1,202,418 individuals, in the United States.[14] If one million children were living in households headed by homosexual couples, this would mean that, on average, *every* homosexual household has at least one child.
- However, a survey in *Demography* indicates that 95 percent of partnered male homosexual and 78 percent of partnered lesbian households do *not* have children.[15] This would mean that the one million children presumed to be living in homosexual households would be

divided among the 15,000 (five percent of 304,148) male homosexual and 65,000 (22 percent of 297,061) lesbian households that actually have children. This would result in an astounding 12.5 children per gay and lesbian family.

The cases highlighted by the media to generate sympathy for homosexual adoption typically feature "two-parent" homosexual households. Of course, some children are also being raised by a natural parent who identifies himself or herself as homosexual and live alone. Nevertheless, the hypothetical calculations above give some indication of how absurdly inflated most of the estimates are concerning the number of children being raised by homosexuals. Far from being the proven success that some claim, homosexual parenting remains a relatively rare phenomenon.

Implications for Homosexual Parenting

Demands that homosexuals be accorded the right to adopt children fit into the gay agenda by minimizing the differences between homosexual and heterosexual behavior in order to make homosexuality look as normal as possible. However, as already shown, only a small minority of gay and lesbian households have children. Beyond that, the evidence also indicates that comparatively few homosexuals choose to establish households together—the type of setting that is a prerequisite for the rearing of children. Consider the following:

- hrc claims that the U.S. population of gays and lesbians is 10,456,405, or 5 percent of the total U.S. population over 18 years of age.[16] The best available data supports a much lower estimate for those who engage in same-sex sexual relations.[17] However, assuming the higher estimate for the purposes of argument, this would indicate that *only 8.6 percent* of homosexuals (1,202,418 out of 10,456,405) choose to live in a household with a person of the same sex.
- hrc asserts that "30 percent of gay and lesbian people are living in a committed relationship in the same residence."[18] Assuming HRC's own figures, that would mean over three million gays and lesbians are living in such households, which, as shown above, is a wildly inflated estimate over the census figures. It is worth noting that the hrc claim amounts to a tacit admission that 70 percent of gays and lesbians choose not to live in committed relationships and establish households together.
- hrc claims that the numbers of gay and lesbian households were "undercounted" by the census. However, if true, it would represent an unprecedented, massive undercount of 260 percent on the part of the U.S. Census Bureau.

The census figures indicate that only a small minority of gays and lesbians have made the lifestyle choice that is considered a fundamental requisite in any consideration regarding adoption, and only a small percentage of those households actually have children. The evidence thus does not support the claim that significant numbers of homosexuals desire to provide a stable family setting for children.

The Nature of Homosexual "Committed Relationships"

Gay activists admit that the ultimate goal of the drive to legitimize homosexual marriage and adoption is to change the essential character of marriage, removing precisely the aspects of fidelity and chastity that promote stability in the home. They pursue their goal heedless of the fact that such households are unsuitable for the raising of children:

- Paula Ettelbrick, former legal director of the Lambda Legal Defense and Education Fund, has stated, "Being queer is more than setting up house, sleeping with a person of the same gender, and seeking state approval for doing so. . . . Being queer means pushing the parameters of sex, sexuality, and family, and in the process transforming the very fabric of society."[19]
- According to homosexual writer and activist Michelangelo Signorile, the goal of homosexuals is to redefine the term *monogamy*.

For these men the term 'monogamy' simply doesn't necessarily mean sexual exclusivity. . . . The term 'open relationship' has for a great many gay men come to have one specific definition: A relationship in which the partners have sex on the outside often, put away their resentment and jealousy, and discuss their outside sex with each other, or share sex partners.[20]

- The views of Signorile and Ettelbrick regarding marriage are widespread in the homosexual community. According to the *Mendola Report,* a mere 26 percent of homosexuals believe that commitment is most important in a marriage relationship.[21]

Former homosexual William Aaron explains why even homosexuals involved in "committed" relationships do not practice monogamy:

In the gay life, fidelity is almost impossible. Since part of the compulsion of homosexuality seems to be a need on the part of the homophile to 'absorb' masculinity from his sexual partners, he must be constantly on the lookout for [new partners]. Consequently the most successful homophile 'marriages' are those where there is an arrangement between the two to have affairs on the side while maintaining the semblance of permanence in their living arrangement.[22]

Even those who support the concept of homosexual "families" admit to their unsuitability for children:

- In their study in *Family Relations,* L. Koepke et al. observed, "Even individuals who believe that same-sex relationships are a legitimate choice for adults may feel that children will suffer from being reared in such families."[23]
- Pro-homosexual researchers, J. J. Bigner and R. B. Jacobson describe the homosexual father as "socioculturally unique," trying to take on

"two apparently opposing roles: that of a father (with all its usual connotations) and that of a homosexual man." They describe the homosexual father as "both structurally and psychologically at social odds with his interest in keeping one foot in both worlds: parenting and homosexuality."[24]

In truth, the two roles are fundamentally incompatible. The instability, susceptibility to disease, and domestic violence that is disproportionate in homosexual relationships would normally render such households unfit to be granted custody of children. However, in the current social imperative to grant legitimacy to the practice of homosexuality in every conceivable area of life, such considerations are often ignored.

But children are not guinea pigs to be used in social experiments in redefining the institutions of marriage and family. They are vulnerable individuals with vital emotional and developmental needs. The great harm done by denying them both a mother and a father in a committed marriage will not easily be reversed, and society will pay a grievous price for its ill-advised adventurism.

End Notes

1. Liz Winfeld, "In a Family Way," *Denver Post,* November 28, 2001.

2. Greg Burton, "Couples to Challenge Utah Adoption Ban; Statute Allows Single, but not Partnered, Gays to Become Legal Parents," *Salt Lake Tribune,* December 31, 2000.

3. Ibid.

4. Marilyn Elias, "Doctor's Back Gay "Co-Parents," *USA Today,* February 3, 2002.

5. "Chapter 4: Second-Parent Adoption," in *The Family* (Human Rights Campaign, 2002): available at: . . .

6. Ibid.

7. Bob Egelko, "Court Clarifies Decision on Adoptions," *San Francisco Chronicle,* November 22, 2001. The decision is under review by the California Supreme Court.

8. Ibid., "Chapter 4."

9. Bob Egelko, "Court Clarifies Decision," "The issue of the validity of such adoptions is not presented in this case and has not been briefed by the parties and we do not address it here."

10. Judith Stacey and Timothy J. Biblarz, "(How) Does the Sexual Orientation of Parents Matter?" *American Sociological Review* 66 (April, 2001): 167.

11. See "Serious Flaws in the Kinsey Research," *Insight* (Washington: Family Research Council, 1995).

12. Stacey and Biblarz, ibid.

13. Ibid.

14. "PCT 14: Unmarried-Partner Households by Sex of Partners" (U.S. Census Bureau: Census 2000 Summary File 1).

15. Dan Black et al., "Demographics of the Gay and Lesbian Population in the United States: Evidence from Available Systematic Data Sources," *Demography* 37 (May 2000): 150.

16. David M. Smith and Gary J. Gates, "Gay and Lesbian Families in the United States: Same-Sex Unmarried Partner Households," *Human Rights Campaign* (August 22, 2001): 2.

17. Dan Black et al., "Demographics of the Gay and Lesbian Population," "4.7 percent of men in the combined samples have had at least one same-sex experience since age 18, but only 2.5 percent of men have engaged in exclusively same-sex sex over the year preceding the survey. Similarly, 3.5 percent of women have had at least one same-sex sexual experience, but only 1.4 percent have had exclusively same-sex sex over the year preceding the survey." (p. 141.)

18. Ibid.

19. Paula Ettelbrick, quoted in William B. Rubenstein, "Since When Is Marriage a Path to Liberation?" *Lesbians, Gay Men, and the Law,* (New York: The New Press, 1993), pp. 398, 400.

20. Michelangelo Signorile, *Life Outside* (New York: HarperCollins, 1997), p. 213.

21. Mary Mendola, *The Mendola Report* (New York: Crown, 1980), p. 53.

22. William Aaron, *Straight* (New York: Bantam Books, 1972), p. 208, cited by Joseph Nicolosi in *Reparative Therapy of Male Homosexuality*, p. 125, quoted by Robert H. Knight in "How Domestic Partnerships and 'Gay Marriage' Threaten the Family," *Insight* (Washington: Family Research Council, June 1994), p. 9.

23. L. Koepke et al., "Relationship Quality in a Sample of Lesbian Couples with Children and Child-free Lesbian Couples," *Family Relations* 41 (1992): 228.

24. Bigner and Jacobson, "Adult Responses to Child Behavior and Attitudes Toward Fathering," Frederick W. Bozett, ed., *Homosexuality and the Family* (New York: Harrington Park Press, 1989), pp. 174, 175.

CHALLENGE QUESTIONS

Can Lesbian and Gay Couples Be Appropriate Parents for Children?

- Because they have to fight against social stigmas, some people argue that gay and lesbian couples are actually likely to be more motivated toward good parenting. What are other effects of social stigmas on gay and lesbian parents?
- This issue is often very politically charged. How do you think political viewpoints shape the way people on both sides of this issue consider research evidence?
- Much of the controversy surrounding this issue relates to the quality of the available evidence. What types of evidence would be most convincing, and what other research evidence would be useful to have?
- Dailey asserts that a major problem with the research on gay and lesbian parents is that many studies do not use representative samples. What are the implications for the larger controversy if we accept that only some subgroups of homosexual parents have been found to be appropriate?

Suggested Readings

N. Anderssen, C. Amlie, and E. Ytteroy, "Outcomes for Children with Lesbian or Gay Parents: A Review of Studies from 1978 to 2000," *Scandinavian Journal of Psychology* (September 2002)

J. Chrisler, "Two Mommies or Two Daddies Will Do Fine, Thanks," *Time* (December 14, 2006)

J. Dobson, "Two Mommies Is One Too Many," *Time* (December 12, 2006)

C. Patterson, "Lesbian and Gay Parents and Their Children: Summary of Research Findings," in *Lesbian and Gay Parents* (American Psychological Association, 2005)

J. Stacey and T. Biblarz, "(How) Does Sexual Orientation of Parents Matter?" *American Sociological Review* (April 2001)

ISSUE 17

Is Religion a Pure Good in Facilitating Well-Being during Adulthood?

YES: David G. Myers, from "Wanting More in an Age of Plenty," *Christianity Today* (April 2000)

NO: Julie Juola Exline, from "Stumbling Blocks on the Religious Road: Fractured Relationships, Nagging Vices, and the Inner Struggle to Believe," *Psychological Inquiry* (vol. 13, 2002)

ISSUE SUMMARY

YES: Psychologist and author David Myers asserts that religion is an antidote to the discontent many adults feel despite incredible relative material wealth.

NO: Professor of psychology Julia Juola Exline asserts that research suggesting religion to be a pure good for adult development neglects to account for the fact that it can also be a source of significant sadness, stress, and confusion.

The role of religion in lifespan development presents a challenging dilemma for social scientists: religion is clearly a huge influence upon people's lives, yet by nature that influence is difficult to quantify and measure. Further, many people simply prefer to keep their religious and spiritual lives separate from efforts to define and study the specific characteristics of the lifespan. Something about academic study often (though not always) seems to detract from the mystical power of religion. Yet, basic demographic statistics show that over 60% of Americans are active in a faith group, over 70% identify with an organized religion, and more than that consider themselves very interested in spirituality. While there is a popular trend to bemoan the loss of religion in modern society, many scholars would note that only traditionally organized religions are in decline, while American interest in spirituality may be at an all-time high.

Inevitably, despite some avoidance and trepidations, lifespan development scholars have investigated the role of religion in the lifespan. Generally steering clear of abstract spiritual questions, such as those about the nature and role of God, scholars of the lifespan tend to focus on aspects of religion that can be analyzed and measured using the methods of social science. One of those aspects is well-being in adulthood. After negotiating the challenges of childhood and youth, and settling into work and family roles, adults often find themselves addressing larger questions of meaning, purpose, and spirituality.

In the first selection David G. Myers, a prolific psychologist who has written several prominent textbooks and several other scholarly books about topics ranging from happiness to spirituality, asserts that contemporary society is incredibly well-off by structural measures such as income and material well-being. Yet, in what he calls "the American paradox," as our material well-being rises our psychological well-being is, in his reckoning, in decline. The statistics that he cites are powerful, and suggest that at a large scale level it does seem that religion and spirituality correlate with improved well-being in the form of charity, altruistic work, health, morality, and communal endeavor. In Myers's viewpoint the personal experience of religion is an overall good that can develop individuals who will improve society.

In contrast, Exline points out four very specific ways in which religion can provide individual developmental challenges. While Exline is interested in religion partially because of its powerful potential to create meaningful psychological experiences, she is wary of understanding religion as a panacea. She notes, in concordance with Myers, that significant amounts of data suggest religion and spirituality can have significant positive benefits through the lifespan. But she asserts such findings should not be oversimplified. Personal experiences of religion involve interpersonal challenges, asking hard questions about faith in the face of hardship, facing intellectual and emotional inconsistencies, and dealing with the very real potential for disappointment in adulthood.

POINT

- Although material well-being is at an all-time high, many people in contemporary Western societies indicate declining mental health that corresponds to a lack of spiritual engagement.

- Religious people tend to do better in terms of charity, altruistic work, and engaging with communities.

- Religious communities provide a rich forum for the types of social interaction that are essential to well-being.

- While religious groups have historically been associated with dramatic examples of social problems, the individual experience of religion associates with primarily positive outcomes.

COUNTERPOINT

- Many people who are spiritually engaged face hard and emotionally challenging questions about the meaning of life.

- Religion can lead people to disappointment when confronting the harsh realities of the world.

- Being part of a religious community involves facing inconsistencies between religious doctrines and personal beliefs.

- Although religion generally associates with positive characteristics, those associations do not come without significant challenge and struggle.

YES

David G. Myers

Wanting More in an Age of Plenty

The Paradox of Our Time in History is that
we spend more, but have less;
we buy more, but enjoy it less.

We have bigger houses and smaller families;
more conveniences, but less time;
more medicine, but less wellness.

We read too little, watch TV too much, and pray too seldom.

We have multiplied our possessions, but reduced our values.

These are the times of tall men, and short character;
steep profits, and shallow relationships.

These are the days of two incomes, but more divorce;
of fancier houses, but broken homes.

We've learned how to make a living, but not a life;
we've added years to life, not life to years;
we've cleaned up the air, but polluted the soul.

> —*Excerpted from a 1999 Internet chain mailing,*
> *usually attributed to an unknown source.*

The past four decades have produced dramatic cultural changes. Since 1960 we have been soaring economically and, until recently, sinking socially. To paraphrase Ronald Reagan's famous question, "Are we better off than we were 40 years ago?" Our honest answer would be: materially yes, morally no. Therein lies the American paradox.

There is much to celebrate. We now have, as average Americans, doubled real incomes and doubled what money buys. We own twice as many cars per person, eat out two and a half times as often, and pay less than ever before (in real dollars and minutes worked) for our cars, air travel, and hamburgers. We have espresso coffee, the World Wide Web, sport utility vehicles, and caller ID. Democracy is thriving. Military budgets are shrinking. Joblessness and

From *Christianity Today*, vol. 44, no. 5, April 2000, pp. 94–100. Copyright © 2000 by Christianity Today. Reprinted by permission.

welfare rolls have subsided. Inflation is down. The annual national deficit has become a surplus. The rights of women and various minorities are better protected than ever before. New drugs are shrinking our tumors, lengthening our lives, and enlarging our sexual potency. These are the best of times.

Yet by the early 1990s these had also become the worst of times. During most of the post-1960 years, America was sliding into a deepening social, and moral recession that dwarfed the comparatively milder and briefer economic recessions. Had you fallen asleep in 1960 and awakened today (even after the recent uptick in several indicators of societal health) would you feel pleased at the cultural shift? You would be awakening to a:

- Doubled divorce rate.
- Tripled teen suicide rate.
- Quadrupled rate of reported violent crime.
- Quintupled prison population.
- Sextupled (no pun intended) percent of babies born to unmarried parents.
- Sevenfold increase in cohabitation (a predictor of future divorce).
- Soaring rate of depression—to ten times the pre–World War II level by one estimate.

The National Commission on Civic Renewal combined social trends such as these in creating its 1998 "Index of National Civic Health"—which plunged southward from 1960 until the early 1990s. Bertrand Russell once said that the mark of a civilized human is the capacity to read a column of numbers and weep. Can we weep for the social recession's casualties—for the crushed lives behind these numbers?

Spiritual Hunger in an Age of Plenty

It is hard to argue with Al Gore: "The accumulation of material goods is at an all-time high, but so is the number of people who feel an emptiness in their lives." Moreover, he explained in declaring his presidential candidacy, "Most Americans are hungry for a deeper connection between politics and moral values; many would say 'spiritual values.'" There is indeed "a spiritual vacuum at the heart of American society," agreed the late Lee Atwater, George Bush's 1988 campaign manager. Having solved the question of how to make a living, having surrounded ourselves with once unthinkable luxuries—air-conditioned comfort, CD-quality sound, and fresh fruit year round—we are left to wonder why we live. Why run this rat race? What's the point? Why care about anything or anyone beyond myself?

Ronald Inglehart, a University of Michigan social scientist who follows values surveys across the Western world, discerns the beginnings of a subsiding of materialist values. Not only in Eastern Europe, where materialist Marxism is licking its wounds, but in the West one sees signs of a new generation maturing with decreasing concern for economic growth and strong defense, and with increasing concern for personal relationships, the integrity of nature, and the meaning-of life. At the peak of her fortune and fame, with 146 tennis championships behind her and married to John Lloyd, Chris Evert reflected, "We get into a rut. We play tennis, we go to a movie, we watch TV, but I keep saying, 'John, there has to be more.'"

Materialism and individualism still ride strong. For America's entering collegians, "becoming very well off financially" is still the top-rated life goal among 19 goals on an annual UCLA/American Council on Education survey; it is said to be "very important or essential" by 74 percent in 1998—nearly double the 39 percent saying the same in 1970. Yet Inglehart discerns "a renewed concern for spiritual values."

Pollster George Gallup Jr. detects the same: "One of two dominant trends in society today [along with a search for deeper, more meaningful relationships] is the search for spiritual moorings. . . . Surveys document the movement of people who are searching for meaning in life with a new intensity, and want their religious faith to grow." From 1994 to late 1998, reported Gallup, the percent of Americans feeling a need to "experience spiritual growth" rose from 54 to 82 percent. Although people in surveys exaggerate their church attendance, as they do voting, religious interests seem on an upswing. Since hitting its modern low in 1993, Gallup's "Religion in America" index has been heading upward.

This spiritual hunger is manifest all about us: in a million people annually besieging Catholic retreat centers or seeking spiritual formation guided by spiritual directors; in the NFL, where once-rare chapel services have become universal and after-touchdown kneels are almost as common as struts; in the recent surge of movies with spiritual emphases (*Dead Man Walking, The Prince of Egypt, Seven Years in Tibet*) and in television's *Touched By an Angel* reaching ratings heaven; in New Age bookstore sections devoted to angels, near-death experiences, reincarnation, astrology, and other paranormal claims; in the surge of new publications, conferences, and magazine articles on religion and science and health; in the reopening of school curricula to religion's place in history and literature; and on the Internet, where AltaVista finds "God" on 3.6 million Web pages.

The New American Dream

For Christians—people who experience spirituality in biblically-rooted faith communities—some aspects of contemporary do-it-yourself spirituality may seem gaseous, individualistic, and self-focused. Nevertheless, the essential facts are striking: while we have been surging materially and technologically we have paradoxically undergone a social and moral recession and experienced a deepening spiritual hunger. In many ways these are the best of times, yet in other ways these have been the worst of times. While enjoying the benefits of today's economic and social individualism, we are suffering the costs.

To counter radical individualism, an inclusive social renewal movement is emerging—one that affirms liberals' indictment of the demoralizing effects of poverty and conservatives indictment of toxic media models; one that welcomes liberals' support for family-friendly workplaces and conservatives' support for committed relationships; one that agrees with liberals' advocacy for children in all sorts of families and conservatives' support for marriage and coparenting.

Do we not—whether self-described liberals or conservative—share a vision of a better world? As the slumbering public consciousness awakens, something akin to the earlier civil rights, feminist, and environmental movements seems to be germinating. "Anyone who tunes in politics even for background music can tell you how the sound has changed," observes feminist columnist Ellen Goodman. Yesterday's shouting match over family values has become today's choir, she adds. When singing about children growing up without fathers, "Politicians on the right, left and center may not be hitting exactly the same notes, but like sopranos, tenors and baritones, they're pretty much in harmony." We are recognizing that liberals' risk factors (poverty, inequality, hopelessness) and conservatives' risk factors (early sexualization, unwed parenthood, family fragmentation) all come in the same package.

Whatever our differences, most of us wish for a culture that:

- Welcomes children into families with mothers and fathers who love them, and into an environment that nurtures families.
- Rewards initiative and restrains exploitative greed, thus building a strong economy that shrinks the underclass.
- Balances individual liberties with communal well-being.
- Encourages close relationships within extended families and with supportive neighbors and caring friends, people who celebrate when you're born, care about you as you live, and miss you when you're gone.
- Values our diversity while finding unity in shared ideals.
- Develops children's capacities for empathy, self-discipline, and honesty.
- Provides media that offer social scripts of kindness, civility, attachment, and fidelity.
- Regards relationships as covenants and sexuality not as mere recreation but as life-uniting and love-renewing.
- Takes care of the soul by developing a deeper spiritual awareness of a reality greater than self and of life's resulting meaning, purpose, and hope.

Thanks partly to the emerging renewal movement, several indicators of social pathology have recently shown encouraging turns. Although still at historically high levels, teen sex, pregnancy, and violence, for example, have all subsided somewhat from their peaks around 1993.

Further progress toward the new American dream requires more than expanding our social ambulance services at the base of the social cliffs. It also requires that we identify the forces that are pushing people over the cliffs. And it requires our building new guard rails at the top—by making our business and economics more family-friendly, by reforming our media, by renewing character education in our schools, and by better balancing me-thinking with we-thinking.

Are there credible grounds for adding spiritual renewal to this list? Are George W. Bush and Al Gore both right to trumpet the potential of "faith-based" reforms and social services? Or can skeptical Oxford professor Richard Dawkins more easily find evidence for seeing faith as "one of the world's great evils, comparable to the smallpox virus, but harder to eradicate"? Sifting the evidence won't decide the bigger issue of the truth of Christian claims, but it should indicate whether faith more often uplifts or debilitates.

We now have massive evidence that people active in faith communities are happier and healthier than their unchurched peers. (Recent epidemiological studies—tracking thousands of lives through years of time—reveal they even outlive their unchurched peers by several years.) Is an active faith similarly associated with social health?

God and Goodness

Asked by Gallup, "Can a person be a good and ethical person if he or she does not believe in God?," three in four Americans answered yes. Indeed, examples of honorable secularists and greedy, lustful, or bigoted believers come readily to mind. "God's will" has been used—often by those for whom religion is more a mark of group identity than of genuine piety—as justification for apartheid, for limiting women's rights, for ethnic cleansing, for gay bashing, and for war. As Madeleine L'Engle lamented, "Christians have given Christianity a bad name."

But anecdotes aside—"I can counter Jim Bakker's gold-plated bathroom fixtures with Mother Teresa, and Bible-thumping KKK members with Desmond Tutu," responds the believer—how might faith feed character? It might do so by providing a source of values. It might give us a convincing reason to behave morally when no one is looking. Lacking the ground of faith beneath our morality, cultural inertia may enable a lingering selflessness, but eventually the soil that feeds morality becomes depleted. "If there is no God, is not everything permissible?" Ivan asked in *The Brothers Karamazov.*

"The terrible danger of our time consists in the fact that ours is a cut-flower civilization," philosopher Elton Trueblood prophesied a half-century ago. "Beautiful as cut flowers may be, and much as we may use our ingenuity to keep them looking fresh for a while, they will eventually die, and they die because they are severed from their sustaining roots. We are trying to maintain the dignity of the individual apart from the deep faith that every man is made in God's image and is therefore precious in God's eyes."

Even the eighteenth-century French writer Voltaire found the influence of faith useful among the masses, even though he thought Christianity was an "infamy" that deserved crushing. "I want my attorney, my tailor, my servants, even my wife to believe in God," he wrote, because "then I shall be robbed and cuckolded less often." He once silenced a discussion about atheism until he had dismissed the servants, lest in losing their faith they might lose their morality. Although similarly skeptical of religion, biologist E. O. Wilson likewise acknowledges that "religious conviction is largely beneficent. Religion . . . nourishes love, devotion, and, above all, hope."

Faith and Character

Are Voltaire and Wilson right to presume that godliness tethers self-interest and feeds character? Seeking answers, researchers have studied not just what causes crime, but what predicts virtue. Having two committed parents, a stable neighborhood, prosocial media, and schools that teach character—all of these help. So, too, does a spiritual sense, contends Stanford psychologist William Damon. Children are "openly receptive to spiritual ideas and long for transcendent truth that can nourish their sense of purpose and provide them with a moral mission in life," he believes. "Children will not thrive . . . unless they acquire a living sense of what some religious traditions have called transcendence: a faith in and devotion to concerns that are considered larger than the self." Faith, he reports, "has clear benefits for children . . . enabling some children to adapt to stressful and burdensome life events."

The bipartisan National Commission on Children has concurred that religious faith strengthens children. "Through participation in a religious community—in communal worship, religious education, and social-action programs—children learn and assimilate the values of their faith. For many children, religion is a major force in their moral development; for some it is the chief determinant of moral behavior." Studies confirm that religious adolescents (those who say their faith is important or who attend church) differ from those who are irreligious. They are much less likely to become delinquent, to engage in promiscuous sex, and to abuse drugs and alcohol.

After analyzing data from several national studies, Vanderbilt University criminologist Byron Johnson reported that "Most delinquent acts were committed by juveniles who had low levels of religious commitment. Those juveniles whose religiosity levels were in the middle to high levels committed very few delinquent acts." Even when controlling for other factors, such as socioeconomic level, neighborhood, and peer influences, churchgoing kids rarely were delinquent.

The faith-morality relationship extends to adulthood. In their studies of Jews in Israel, Catholics in Spain, Calvinists in the Netherlands, the Orthodox in Greece, and Lutherans and Catholics in West Germany, sociologists Shalom Schwartz and Sipke Huismans consistently found that people of faith tended to be less hedonistic and self-oriented. Consistent with this observation, sociologist Seymour Martin Lipset notes that charitable giving and voluntarism are higher in America than in less religious countries.

In a 1981 U.S. Values Survey, frequent worship attendance predicted lower scores on a dishonesty scale that assessed, for example, self-serving lies, tax cheating, and failing to report damaging a parked car. Moreover, cities with high churchgoing rates tend to be cities with low crime rates. In Provo, Utah, where more than nine in ten people are church members, you can more readily leave your car unlocked than in Seattle, where fewer than a third are. Voltaire, it seems, was on to something.

Many people sense this faith-morality correlation. If your car broke down in a crime-ridden area and some strapping teenage boys approached you, asks Los Angeles Rabbi Dennis Prager, wouldn't "you feel better to know they had just come from a Bible study?"

Faith and Altruism

So, people of faith (mostly Christians in studies to date) are, for whatever reasons, somewhat more traditionally moral—more honest and law-abiding and less hedonistic. But are they more actively compassionate? Do they really walk the love talk? Or are they mostly self-righteous hypocrites?

People often wonder about Christianity, which has a curious history of links with both love and hate. On one side are Bible-thumping slave owners, Ku Klux Klanners, and apartheid defenders. On the other are the religious roots of the antislavery movement, the clergy's leadership of the American and South African civil-rights movements, and the church's establishment of universities and Third World medical care.

A mid-century profusion of studies of religion and prejudice revealed a similarly mixed picture. On the one hand, American church members expressed more racial prejudice than nonmembers, and those with conservative Christian beliefs expressed more than those who were less conservative. For many, religion seemed a cultural habit, a part of their community tradition, which also happened to include racial segregation.

Yet the most faithful church attenders expressed less prejudice than occasional attenders. Clergy expressed more tolerance and civil-rights support than lay people. And those for whom religion was an end ("My religious beliefs are what really lie behind my whole approach to life") were less prejudiced than those for whom religion was a means ("A primary reason for my interest in religion is that my church is a congenial social activity"). Thus among church members, the devout expressed less prejudice than those who gave religion lip service. "We have just enough religion to make us hate," said the English satirist Jonathan Swift, "but not enough to make us love one another."

"Faith-based" compassion becomes even clearer when we look at who gives most generously of time and money. Fortune reports that America's top 25 philanthropists share several characteristics. They are mostly self-made, they have been givers all their lives, and "they're religious: Jewish, Mormon, Protestant, and Catholic. And most attribute their philanthropic urges, at least in part, to their religious backgrounds."

The same appears true of the rest of us. In a 1987 Gallup survey, Americans who said they never attended church or synagogue reported giving away 1.1 percent of their incomes. Weekly attenders were two and a half times as generous. This 24 percent of the population gave 48 percent of all charitable contributions. The other three-quarters of Americans give the remaining half. Followup Gallup surveys in 1990, 1992, 1994, and 1999 replicated this pattern. An estate-planning attorney at one of western Michigan's largest law firms told me that people in her highly churched area of the state are much more likely to assign part of their estate to charity than are people on the state's less religious eastern side. Much of this annual and legacy giving is not to churches. Two thirds of money given to secular charities comes from contributors who also give to religious organizations.

And of the billions given to congregations, nearly half gets donated to other organizations or allocated to nonreligious programming (and that doesn't count donations of food, clothing, and shelter by most congregations).

The faith-generosity effect extends to the giving of time:

- Among the 12 percent of Americans whom Gallup classified as "highly spiritually committed," 46 percent said they were presently working among the poor, the infirm, or the elderly—many more than the 22 percent among those "highly uncommitted."
- In a followup Gallup survey, charitable and social service volunteering was reported by 28 percent of those who rated religion "not very important" in their lives and by 50 percent of those who rated it "very important."
- In the 1992 Gallup survey, those not attending church volunteered 1.4 hours a week while those attending weekly volunteered 3.2 hours. The follow-up survey in 1994 found the same pattern, as have university-based studies.
- In yet another Gallup survey, 37 percent of those rarely if ever attending church, and 76 percent of those attending weekly, reported thinking at least a "fair amount" about "your responsibility to the poor."
- Among one notable self-giving population—adoptive parents—religious commitment is commonplace. Among a national sample, 63 percent reported attending a worship service often.

So, tell me about the generosity of someone's spirit, and you will also give me a clue to the centrality of their faith. Tell me whether their faith is peripheral or pivotal, and I will estimate their generosity.

Religious consciousness, it appears, shapes a larger agenda than advancing one's own private world. It cultivates the idea that my wealth and talents are gifts of which I am the steward. Spirituality promotes a "bond of care for others," notes Boston College sociologist Paul Schervish. Such altruism, research psychologists Dennis Krebs and Frank Van Hesteren contend, is "selfless, stemming from agape, an ethic of responsible universal love, service, and sacrifice that is extended to others without regard for merit." The religious idea of a reality and purpose beyond self would seem foundational to such "universal self-sacrificial love."

Faith-based altruism is at work here in Holland, Michigan, where the Head Start Day Care program was envisioned by a prayer group at the church where it still operates. The thriving Boys and Girls Club was spawned by the Interparish Council. Habitat for Humanity construction is mostly done by church volunteers. Our community's two main nongovernmental agencies for supporting the poor—the Community Action House and the Good Samaritan Center—were begun by churches, which continue to contribute operating funds. The local theological seminary houses the community soup kitchen. Churches fund the community's homeless shelter. Annually, more than 2,000 townspeople, sponsored by thousands more—nearly all from churches—gather for a world hunger relief walk.

If the churches of my community (and likely yours) shut down, along with all the charitable action they foster, we would see a sharp drop in beds for the homeless, food for the hungry, and services to children. Partners for Sacred Places, a nondenominational group dedicated to preserving old religious buildings, reports that nine of ten city congregations with pre-1940 buildings provide space for community programming such as food pantries, clothing closets, soup kitchens, childcare centers, recreation programs, AA meetings, and afterschool activities.

Thus, mountains of data and anecdotes make it hard to dispute Frank Emerson Andrews' conclusion that "religion is the mother of philanthropy."

To be sure, religion is a mixed bag. It has been used to support the Crusades and enslavement. But it was also Christians who built hospitals, helped the mentally ill, staffed orphanages, brought hope to prisoners, established universities, and spread literacy. It was Christians who abolished the slave trade, led civil-rights marches, and challenged totalitarianism. It was 5,000 Christians who in Le Chambon, France, sheltered Jews while French collaborators elsewhere were delivering Jews to the Nazis. The villagers, mostly descendants of a persecuted Protestant group, had been taught by their pastors to "resist whenever our adversaries will demand of us obedience contrary to the orders of the gospel." Ordered to reveal the sheltered Jews, the pastor refused, saying, "I don't know of Jews, I only know of human beings."

As the debate over government support of faith-based social services emerges—fueled by success stories such as the Rev. Eugene Rivers III's work with Boston teens, Prison Fellowship's work with inmates, and Michigan's program of connecting social-service clients with church-support groups—the church will also need to retain its prophetic voice. In Britain, which is entering a parallel national debate over "the moral and spiritual decline of the nation," the Archbishop of Canterbury, Dr. George Carey, opened "an unprecedented debate on morality" in the House of Lords in 1996 by decrying the decline of moral order and spiritual purpose and the tendency to view moral judgments as mere private taste.

Jonathan Sacks, England's Chief Rabbi, supported his compatriot:

> The power of the Judeo-Christian tradition is that it charts a moral reality larger than private inclination. . . . It suggests that not all choices are equal: some lead on to blessing, others to lives of quiet despair.
>
> It may be that religious leaders can no longer endorse, but instead must challenge the prevailing consensus—the role of the prophet through the ages. In which case the scene is set for a genuine debate between two conflicting visions—between those who see the individual as a bundle of impulses to be gratified and those who see humanity in the image of God; between those who see society as a series of private gardens of desire and those who make space for public parts which we do not own but which we jointly maintain for the sake of others and the future. No debate could be more fundamental, and its outcome will shape the social contours of the twenty-first century.

Julie Juola Exline  **NO**

Stumbling Blocks on the Religious Road: Fractured Relationships, Nagging Vices, and the Inner Struggle to Believe

Tossing and turning in bed, Jim finds that his mind keeps drifting to the television segment he saw on the 11:00 news. This is the third news piece that he has seen in the past year suggesting that religious involvement has benefits for health and well-being. Raised nominally Christian, Jim stopped attending church years ago. He is not even sure that he believes in God anymore, but he has been feeling troubled lately, between his arthritis flare-ups and recurring bouts of anxiety. After mulling over the pros and cons, Jim decides to give religion another try. He asks a colleague for a church recommendation and begins attending regularly. He also commits to reading his Bible each night before bed so that he can get a deeper understanding of the Christian faith. Jim does an admirable job on following through with these religious commitments. However, 6 months later, he is overcome with frustration and disappointment regarding his religious involvement. His dissatisfaction is so strong, in fact, that he decides to abandon his religious quest altogether. What could have happened? Why did Jim end up turning away from religion when he had solid reasons to pursue this coping resource? This article addresses these questions by suggesting some psychological and social stumbling blocks associated with religious belief and involvement.

Can Religion Be Good and Still Be a Locus of Strain?

Within the past decade, a wealth of evidence has accumulated to suggest positive associations between religion, physical health, and mental health. Based on these findings, scientists, scholars, and mental health professionals are beginning to take a more positive view of the role that religious belief and involvement can play in personal and social life. It is especially noteworthy that many of these pro-religion findings have emerged within the field of psychology, which has historically taken a negative or disinterested stance toward

From *Psychological Inquiry*, vol. 13, no. 3, 2002, pp. 182–188. Copyright © 2002 by Lawrence Erlbaum Associates. Reprinted by permission.

religion. The boom in pro-religion findings is likely to prove encouraging and exciting for religiously committed psychologists, providing greater freedom to discuss, study, and perhaps even advocate religious involvement.

However, to promote a balanced view of religion and well-being, it seems wise to consider some caveats and cautions. Consider one possible consequence of the current emphasis on religion, coping, and health: Might some individuals come to view religion primarily or exclusively as a personal coping mechanism? Having noted positive links between religiosity and well-being, some people might focus on only the comforting, self-affirming aspects of religious belief or involvement. Others might go a step further, thinking about religion only in terms of how it might personally benefit them or advance their interests. In one (admittedly extreme) metaphor, some people might view God as a sort of placid smiley face in the sky, advancing humanity's ongoing quest to "have a nice day."

Granted, religious belief and involvement can be powerful tools in coping with life's problems; however, religion is not merely a coping mechanism. Religion involves a quest for ultimate truth. It attempts to answer our deepest questions about life, death, and the purpose of existence. Religion also tends to be prescriptive, telling us how we should live our lives. Thus, religion is likely to make demands on us and to challenge our beliefs and actions in ways that are not always comfortable. Religion is likely to contain seeds of both pleasure and pain, as do other vitally important elements of life (e.g., work, romantic relationships, parenting). To acknowledge the problems associated with any of these pursuits does not negate the value of the pursuit, but because negative stimuli typically carry more psychological weight than positive stimuli, it seems imperative to point out some potential pitfalls that people may encounter in their religious lives.

I make a few clarifications before proceeding. Virtually all examples presented in this article emphasize Judeo-Christian religion. Many are based on Protestant Christianity, the tradition with which I identify and am most familiar. Although different religious systems will no doubt pose different dilemmas and solutions, particularly at the level of doctrine, I believe that the basic principles raised here should be common to many religions. I also note that the goal of this article is to present a series of ideas rather than a review of existing literature. Many of the ideas presented here reflect theoretical elaboration of empirical work that my colleagues and I have done. My thinking has also been directly influenced by the work of Pargament and Altemeyer and Hunsberger. The interested reader is directed to these sources and to other reviews of the field.

The goal of this article, then, is to suggest a number of social and psychological stumbling blocks that religious seekers may encounter. Four major types of stumbling blocks will be considered: interpersonal strains, negative attitudes toward God, inner struggles to believe, and problems associated with virtuous striving. Problems in any of these areas could conceivably turn people away from religion, discourage them from increasing their religious commitment, or create sources of strain and discontent regarding religion.

Interpersonal Strains Associated with Religion: Disagreement, Dissonance, and Disgust

In terms of physical and mental health, one of the primary benefits of religious involvement is that it can be a powerful source of social support. The need to belong, to have close connections with other people, is a central human motivation, and being part of a religious community can help to meet this need. Religious involvement may also provide people with the chance to help others, which can be a powerful antidote for feelings of depression and helplessness; however, if we look more closely, we can see potential for problems in the social arena surrounding religion.

Religious Disagreements

Although religious involvement can help to meet a person's need to belong, it may at the same time threaten that same need. When people choose to align themselves closely with a particular religious group or to adopt a specific set of beliefs, they increase their odds for serious disagreement with others. Such differences sometimes play out in a societal context, adding fuel to intergroup hostility and conflict, but disagreements often arise closer to home, in the circle of the believer's close relationships. If one's parents, spouse, or close friends do not share one's religious convictions, painful rifts may result.

Interfaith marriage provides one example. Although interfaith marriage has become increasingly common, up from 9% in 1965 to 52% in the late 1980s, couples in such marriages are more likely to divorce than those who share the same religious faith. Even when both partners are of the same faith, problems might arise because of differences in religious commitment levels. For example, a woman whose top priority is to love God may elicit feelings of jealousy and resentment from her husband, who now views God as an unwanted third party in the relationship. How can people cope with these religious differences in close relationships? Some may simply agree to disagree, but many religiously committed people may not be satisfied with this option. Because relationship maintenance requires sacrifice and compromise, it may seem viable to convert the unbelieving spouse or to compromise by choosing some third, "neutral ground." However, problems arise with these options as well: Many committed believers will be reluctant to shift their ideas or affiliations, and conversions to please one's romantic partner prove superficial in many cases.

Interpersonal strain may also center on specific religious doctrines, such as those regarding afterlife beliefs. Exline and Yali asked college students what percentage of people they believed were destined for heaven versus hell. To the extent that the students believed that many people were destined for hell, they reported greater social strain associated with religion. These strains included being teased about religious beliefs and behaviors, being the target of religious prejudice or discrimination, and feeling sad or anxious because friends or family members did not share their beliefs. Although preliminary, these data suggest that when disturbing beliefs about the afterlife are part of one's religious system, such beliefs may not only be personally troubling, but they may also be a locus for interpersonal strain. When religious persons believe that the high stakes of eternal destiny are involved, they may find it difficult simply to agree to disagree, especially when they care deeply about the other person.

Attempts to communicate about hell with close others will often be fraught with difficulties. Even with the best of intentions, believers are likely to offend others by insinuating that they are destined for eternal punishment. Another potential problem stems from the fact that images of hell are likely to prompt high levels of fear. Studies have suggested that extremely high levels of fear, rather than prompting behavior change, often lead to emotion-focused coping efforts as people try to defend themselves from the psychological threat. Thus, a believer who confronts another person with fiery images of hell might find that the solution backfires, as the would-be convert calms himself by avoiding all thoughts of the threatening subject.

Interpersonal strains should also surround other doctrines that take a dim view of human nature or are otherwise discordant with the climate of the broader culture. For example, modern evangelical Protestantism has often been linked with conservative political views ("the Religious Right") and with intolerance of homosexuality and abortion. In an era in which tolerance is highly valued, it will prove socially divisive to confront behaviors that are gaining social acceptance. How are believers to respond when their beliefs are socially unpopular? As suggested in the literature on outgroup behavior and prejudice in religion, one response may be to derogate and distance the self from those who do not hold the beliefs of one's group. Another option is to be open about one's views and risk offending others. A more socially comfortable option would be to focus only on points of agreement, perhaps even taking the extra step of softening one's position on controversial issues. The risk, of course, is that when people soften their position on issues central to their faith, they may compromise or misrepresent what they believe to be the truth.

Distaste toward Religious Groups or Persons

For nonbelievers or even for persons who are privately religious or spiritual, another type of interpersonal barrier could prevent them from wanting to affiliate with religious groups: They may look at the behavior of religious persons and not like what they see. Such distaste could stem from many sources. Vivid acts of terrorism and violence, ranging from racial discrimination and abortion clinic bombings to wartime atrocities, have been committed in the name of religion. Many people have observed religious hypocrisy, in which religious individuals claim to uphold high moral standards but fail to do so in their everyday lives. When high-profile religious evangelists are caught in sexual affairs, for example, people may turn to such incidents as evidence that religious people are hypocrites and fakes. Individuals who yield to religious authority (e.g., God, scripture, the Pope, other church leaders) may be viewed as ignorant by those who place higher value on other forms of persuasion, such as empirical evidence or private, common-sense philosophies of life. Religious people may also be viewed as judgmental, prudish, intolerant, and unable to have fun in life—particularly, perhaps, by persons who want to continue pleasurable habits that the religious group views as vices (e.g., sexual promiscuity, gambling, heavy alcohol use).

In short, one probable reason that people do not join religious groups is because they hold negative attitudes toward the groups. Some people might even develop stronger responses such as disgust, in which they recoil from any contact with the group. As with a food aversion, disgust might even spread to taint a person's global impressions of religion: "If that's how religious people behave, I don't want any part of it." Because feelings of disgust are often moralized, people could easily translate their disgust toward religious persons into moral disapproval. In other words, they might come to view religious people not only as unlikable but also as wrong—perhaps even as evil. By crossing the line to moral disapproval, people who dislike religious groups have a ready rationale for derogating them.

Summary

Religion, at least in its organized forms, is intimately tied with human relationships. At its best, it can be a major source of social support and a driving force behind prosocial behavior. However, the social aspect of religion can breed problems for believers and nonbelievers alike. Some people may have to overcome feelings of distaste to even consider affiliating with a religious group. Can they separate their religious ideals from the inevitable flaws that they observe among the all-too-human religious persons that they encounter? When they do make religious commitments, people may find themselves at odds with other important people in their social network who do not share their beliefs. For them, one major challenge is to participate meaningfully in their religious community without resorting to either of two extremes: outgroup derogation or watering down their beliefs.

Disappointment, Anger, and Mistrust toward God

Another major benefit of religious commitment is feeling close to God and the comfort that comes with the belief that an omnipotent being is watching over, protecting, and caring for the self. For many believers, the cultivation of an intimate relationship with God is a cornerstone of religious life. Some scholars have taken this idea a step further, conceptualizing religion as an attachment process. However, as in human relationships, a lot can go wrong in people's relationships with God. For example, some studies suggest that if people have conflicted relationships with their own fathers, they often develop negative or ambivalent feelings toward God as well. As another example, well-meaning religious parents sometimes use references to God or the Bible as self-regulation cues. For example, a parent might try to thwart a child's attempt to steal candy at the grocery store by saying "God is watching you" or quoting a Bible verse such as "Thou shalt not steal." If such statements are often used to curb misbehavior and if not tempered with positive statements about God, a child might come to see God as an oppressor primarily responsible for creating rules and policing people.

As alluded to in the previous section, both children and adults might find some aspects of God's behavior or character distasteful as they read religious texts or hear religious stories. For example, those reading the Bible may wonder this: Does God endorse killing? Why would God allow children to suffer for what their parents had done? How could a loving God send people to eternal punishment after death? For other people, the aspects of the Christian God that embody mercy and grace might be unappealing. A person who values toughness, pride, and retributive justice might be repelled by Christ's advocacy of virtues such as mercy and meekness—not to mention His own humiliating and painful death, which He accepted without protest or complaint.

Negative attitudes toward God could also stem from much more personal, intense hurts, and disappointments. In the wake of negative life events such as bereavement, illness, accidents, failures, or natural disasters, one potential response is to blame God. If God is held responsible for the act, intense feelings of mistrust, frustration, and anger can result, any of which can cause the wounded person to turn away or withdraw from God. Such pains might be especially sharp if the individual had placed hope in God, perhaps praying and trusting God for a specific outcome, only to be disappointed. We might think of such situations as parallel to those in which we feel betrayed, let down, or offended by another person, and in this case, the one who allowed our suffering could have prevented it—a thought that could fuel anger, hurt, and deep-seated grudges against God. Feelings of anger toward God have been linked with depression and anxiety and with poor coping outcomes. Some people might even decide to abandon belief altogether as a result of such incidents—a possibility that we are examining in our current research.

On the brighter side, preliminary evidence suggests that people often resolve feelings of anger toward God, and an ability to do so is associated with better mental health. How do people avoid or reduce feelings of anger at God? Although people often forgive perpetrators when they apologize or admit wrongdoing, they cannot expect such responses from God. Instead, they may have to draw on cognitive strategies. Drawing on research on interpersonal forgiveness, we might suggest that people will feel less angry toward God if they do not believe that God caused the event, if they view God's intentions as positive, or if they can see some good outcome from the incident. Also, because commitment increases the motivation to forgive, people who already feel close to God should be less likely to become angry. We are testing these hypotheses in our current research.

Another distinction made in the forgiveness literature may illuminate other problems in people's relationships with God: the distinction between *forgiveness,* which requires turning away from bitter, vengeful feelings, and *reconciliation,* which requires trust. Regardless of whether people feel angry with God, they may find it difficult to trust God. Within evangelical Christianity, for example, there is a heavy emphasis on coming to God through Christ, confessing one's sins, receiving forgiveness, and surrendering one's life to God. For some people, the prospect of admitting one's weakness and dependence on God could be intensely shaming, and regardless of whether they trust God, many individuals are likely to balk at the notion of having to come under the authority of God (and, in some cases, under the authority of religious institutions as well). For the person who takes great pride in self-reliance, personal control, and autonomy—all of which are highly valued in our Western culture—such concerns could be a substantial barrier to deepened religious commitment.

Summary

Individuals sometimes feel angry, mistrustful, or rebellious toward God. When having a close bond with God is the cornerstone of a person's religious commitment, it becomes crucial to resolve negative feelings or attitudes toward God before they undermine the relationship. People may develop negative attitudes or feelings about God in many ways, ranging from negative childhood associations to personal hurts and disappointments. Suffering persons may find it difficult to resolve anger toward God because God will not apologize to them or admit wrongdoing. To avoid holding a grudge against God, suffering persons might need to reframe hurtful events in positive ways or to remind themselves of their prior commitment to God.

The Inner Struggle to Believe: Intellectual Barriers and Dissonance

Religious beliefs help people to make sense of the world and to find a sense of meaning or purpose in existence. In fact, this meaning-making aspect of religion seems to be one of the major mediators of the association between religion and health. However, for some individuals, the answers provided by religion are not satisfactory at an intellectual or emotional level. The result might be to turn a person away from religion or, at the very least, to create cognitive dissonance about perceived inconsistencies.

Problems Faced by Nonbelievers

Studies have suggested that individuals with no childhood foundation in religion are unlikely to embrace it later in life. Young children are likely to trust what their parents tell them, and they can build worldviews consistent with their early religious learning. However, for an adult with no religious background, considering a new religious view of the world may require exceptional cognitive work. Over time, a nonbeliever will build a cognitive model of how the world works without including God in the picture, and all of these ideas may need to be revisited and challenged in order to incorporate new, God-centered ideas. Many people may not want to expend this level of effort.

Nonbelievers may also be reluctant to discard or revise their own ideas because the issues at hand are so fundamental: the purpose of life, what happens after death, who (or what) is in charge of the universe, and whether there is any reality beyond what our senses experience. Religious doctrines on these topics, faithfully accepted by believers, may not seem plausible to the nonbeliever. A religious seeker is likely to encounter many doctrines that do not offer logically consistent, coherent answers to life's difficult questions— something that a critical mind may insist on before being willing to believe.

Because many adults may find it difficult to accept religion through a purely intellectual search, we might predict that emotional pathways could serve as a shortcut to belief. For example, nonbelieving adults might be swayed by a mystical or miraculous experience by reaching a point of desperation in which they seek God's help or by finding a powerful sense of belonging within a religious group. Such emotionally charged events might provide people with a fresh incentive to adopt a particular faith, even if they have not resolved all of the intellectual fine points. Consistent with this reasoning, Altemeyer and Hunsberger found that among people with no childhood background in religion, those who embrace religion as adults often do so by means of potent social and emotional experiences. Although mainstream religions often address emotional needs, other social groups—such as cults—can also tap into emotional pathways. For a person eagerly seeking guidance, relief, or companionship, virtually any social group that promised to meet these needs could become a persuasive influence—particularly for those who are willing to suspend logic and personal judgment in the service of emotional goals.

Problems Faced by Believers

Even for individuals with some commitment to religious belief, logical stumbling points and troubling doctrines within one's religious system could be a source of cognitive dissonance. For example, many people who read the Bible (some of whom would identify themselves as Jews or Christians) are troubled by the seeming harshness and unfairness of the Old Testament world: the wars, sacrifices, punishments, and plagues that were presented as being part of God's plan for His "chosen people." Many individuals, whether Judeo-Christian or not, may find such material disturbing and inconsistent with their personal views of God. Gender-related issues often prompt dissent, as do doctrines about sexual behavior, and as mentioned earlier, our own research has suggested that Christian doctrines about hell can be a source of fear and emotional turmoil for some believers.

When people have some commitment to religion but are disturbed by specific doctrines, what are their options? For someone who already holds strongly to a religious belief system, it may be possible to tolerate some inconsistencies in religious doctrine while retaining the core beliefs of the religion and continuing to identify oneself as part of the religious group. A person within the system may be willing to suspend reasoning to some degree as an exercise of faith. Other responses might involve changing one's beliefs to reduce dissonance while still providing the benefits of religious or spiritual involvement. For example, a conservative Christian might choose to believe in heaven but not in hell. A Catholic woman may decide to go on birth control or to have an abortion, both privately and publicly disagreeing with the church's stand on these issues but still strongly identify herself as a Catholic. Such practices might be aptly described by a term such as *cafeteria-style religion*, as they involve choosing aspects of existing religious systems that seem logical or comfortable for the self and ignoring or disbelieving those that are not. A person engaging in cafeteria-style religion might make all of his or her choices from within one religion or might choose elements from a variety of different religions. For example, a religious seeker might decide to retain a belief in Christ as an important historical figure while incorporating elements of Eastern or Native American religion into his belief system.

Another dissonance-reducing alternative to orthodox religiosity might be termed *do-it-yourself spirituality*, in which people shape spiritual beliefs and practices based on their own preferences, logic, intuition, and experience. As individualized forms of belief, both cafeteria-style religion and do-it-yourself spirituality draw people away from religious orthodoxy. More orthodox believers would thus argue that they constitute forms of self-deception, as they represent an attempt to hide the truth from oneself. However, both cafeteria-style religion and do-it-yourself spirituality would seem to be popular choices within Western culture's current postmodern ethos with its valuing of tolerance, personal freedom, subjectivity, and relativism.

Summary

When people search for answers within religion, some of them will encounter intellectual or emotional strains surrounding the belief systems themselves. Some people may simply move on, looking for another religious system that better suits them. Others will abandon the religious search altogether. Some believers, viewing apparent inconsistencies as tests of faith, learn to tolerate the resulting confusion. Another alternative is to reduce dissonance through subtle shifts of belief, undercutting orthodoxy in an attempt to create a more personally satisfying or sensible theology.

Cultivating Virtue and Confronting One's Imperfections

Another major benefit of religious involvement is that religion often encourages people to behave in virtuous ways. For example, religious beliefs can promote physical health by discouraging smoking, excessive drinking, and use of illegal drugs. Religion often encourages specific prosocial behaviors, such as forgiveness and generosity. It may also foster habits such as patience and perseverance that help people achieve their goals and regulate their emotions. Virtuous strivings are not specific to religious frameworks, of course. Anyone working toward self-improvement or following an abstract moral code could be seen as pursuing virtue. However, religion often does encourage people to reflect on their behavior and to improve it, and it is possible that virtues endorsed by religion might carry additional weight for many people because they have the backing of authority behind them.

Given that virtuous striving is an important part of religious life, what factors block the pursuit of virtue? Some barriers are motivational, in which people may not be certain that they want to cultivate certain characteristics. As evidenced by Christian virtues such as humility, meekness, gentleness, patience, and forgiveness, religious values often go against the grain of the larger culture. Because all of the virtues just listed involve some degree of self-transcendence or self-sacrifice, they may seem foolhardy to many. How are such behaviors going to fit within modern Western culture, with its emphasis on individual rights, immediate gratification, and materialism? Self-transcendent or self-sacrificing behaviors seem to invite abuse by others who are playing by a more self-serving set of rules. The pursuit of virtue may also entail giving up some favorite indulgences, which might range from overeating and sleeping in on Sundays to darker pleasures, such as revenge fantasies and slanderous gossip. Many people would prefer to follow their appetites than to pursue their virtuous counterparts, especially once deeply pleasurable (but now forbidden) habits have been established.

Even for those who earnestly desire to cultivate virtue and to improve their behavior, some degree of failure is inevitable. Virtuous behavior requires self-control, and humans are limited in their capacity for self-control. For example, consider a man who is trying to stop having thoughts of lust toward women. He is likely to face constant temptations in his environment to indulge in lust, whether by seeing scantily clad women on television and on billboards or by hearing his coworkers tell sexual jokes. He may have to fight a long-standing habit of engaging in sexual fantasies during idle moments, and in a cruel twist, research on ironic processes suggests that his very efforts to keep lusty thoughts out of his mind may make those very thoughts more likely to intrude. In a weak moment, this man is likely to give in and indulge in thoughts of lust.

As the prior example illustrates, individuals trying to control their thoughts and behaviors will often fail. Therefore, unless we are very adept at self-enhancement and self-justification, one consequence of trying to cultivate virtue is that we will be continually reminded of our shortcomings. With increased devotion and commitment to a religious system, people are likely to find more and more areas of their lives that are imperfect. Depending on how such failures are attributed, they might prompt negative outcomes such as self-condemnation, hopelessness, or perceptions of God as punitive or unforgiving toward the self. Another possibility is offered by research on abstinence violation effects: Seeing that the standard of perfection has been violated, people who fail to live up to idealistic standards may give up and indulge in more extreme misbehaviors.

Ideally, religious systems will help people to make sense of their imperfections and to use them in a positive way. Within Protestant Christianity, for example, seeing one's sins and limitations is the first step toward seeing a need for God's forgiveness and direction. Salvation is viewed as a free gift based on the God's grace and Christ's atoning sacrifice for sin, not something earned through good behavior. Virtue, rather than being seen as a cause of salvation, is viewed as a result of salvation and a person's subsequent cooperation with The Holy Spirit's ongoing work. All of these doctrines—the reality of human imperfection, the free gift of salvation, and the help of the Holy Spirit in fostering virtue—will ideally provide believers with a sense of safety and security while encouraging the further development of virtue. In reality, however, many Christians continue to dismiss their shortcomings or, at the other extreme, to condemn themselves for their mistakes.

Summary

Religion often encourages the development of virtue, which can benefit both individuals and society. However, both personal and social resistance may accompany the pursuit of virtue. Virtuous striving requires us to overcome immediate impulses to gratify or protect the self, and when people do attempt to live virtuously, failures may quickly become apparent. The ideal goal would seem to be to value virtue and to cultivate it, but without insisting on perfection.

Conclusion

Religious life is not always characterized by sunny skies. As outlined previously here, people may encounter a number of intellectual, emotional, behavioral, and social problems associated with religious commitment In spite of these problems, however, the broader picture is anything but bleak. There remains a wealth of data suggesting that religion can be a substantial positive force in personal and social life. If the problems raised in this article can be anticipated, understood, and addressed, consider some of the potential gains.

Clearly, the social world surrounding religion is far from perfect—but when people are able to unite successfully with others as part of a religious community, the sharing of values and goals may yield a sense of support, direction, and grounding that few other social ties can provide. People do experience rifts in their relationships with God, but if they can resolve their negative feelings and work to restore the relationship, a stronger bond and a more mature faith might result. Intellectual and emotional barriers may create inner conflicts about belief, but the result might be a "thinking person's faith" rather than a more passive, mindless form of devotion. Striving after virtue is difficult, especially when it confronts people with the painful reality of their imperfections, but virtuous striving might yield a more commendable life, coupled with a humble, nondefensive attitude that could serve the person well in personal, social, and spiritual contexts.

From the perspective of research and theory, an important goal for the future will be to develop empirically testable models that can help to explain when and why strain arises in religious life and how various forms of strain can best be overcome. Models of strain in religious life should complement existing frameworks on related topics such as religious coping and conversion. Some of the psychological concepts raised in this article may assist in building such frameworks. For example, future research might examine the role of self-deception in religious belief, the contrast of human relationships with relationships between humans and God, or the study of virtue and vice in a self-regulation context. Ideally, as suggested by Hill, such pursuits will not only inform the psychology of religion. Research on these religious topics may also provide fundamental insights into human nature, insights that will advance general psychological knowledge.

CHALLENGE QUESTIONS

Is Religion a Pure Good in Facilitating Well-Being during Adulthood?

- While both of these selections focus on religion and spirituality primarily in relation to a Christian tradition, the issue of religion in the adult lifespan transcends one particular faith. All of the major religious traditions share a social function of focusing communities of individuals toward mutual goals and a personal function of addressing the spiritual needs of individuals. As such, is there a universal role for religion in adult development?
- Is there something special about religion generally in the lifespan? Is religion best thought of as a broad social practice, similar to school and work, that should be analyzed for its practical contribution to development? Or is religion something more?
- The general argument that religion is good for people underlies the recent popularity of "faith-based initiatives"—public policies specifically facilitated by faith and religious groups. How might the evidence here warrant policy support for religious participation?
- Exline's perspective is based on a more theoretical approach to religious experience. What types of data might best support her position?

Suggested Readings

S. Barkan and S. Greenwood, "Religious Attendance and Subjective Well-Being Among Older Americans," *Review of Religious Research* (December 2003)

M. Hayes and H. Cowie, "Psychology and Religion: Mapping the Relationship," *Mental Health, Religion & Culture* (March 2005)

A. James and A. Wells, "Religion and Mental Health: Towards a Cognitive-Behavioral Framework," *British Journal of Health Psychology* (September 2003)

N. Krause, "God-Medicated Control and Psychological Well-Being in Late Life," *Research on Aging* (March 2005)

D. Myers, *The American Paradox: Spiritual Hunger in the Age of Plenty* (Yale University Press, 2000)

K. Pargament, "The Bitter and the Sweet: An Evaluation of the Costs and Benefits of Religiousness," *Psychological Inquiry* (2002)

L. Waite and E. Lehrer, "The Benefits from Marriage and Religion in the United States: A Comparative Analysis," *Population & Development Review* (June 2003)

Internet References . . .

This is an academic's site with references to information about "social gerontology" or the study of sociological aspects of old age.

http://www.trinity.edu/~mkearl/geron.html

This Web site has links to information about research into mostly biological aspects of aging.

http://www.senescence.info/

The American Geriatric Society Foundation for Health in Aging works to connect aging research and practice.

http://www.healthinaging.org/

This Web site presents health topics, reviews, and articles addressing healthier living in later adulthood.

http://www.healthandage.com/

This Web site promotes and explains brain exercises as part of a commercial endeavor to facilitate healthy aging.

http://happy-neuron.com/

The Web site for professor Timothy Salthouse's cognitive aging lab provides access to numerous research papers about mental functioning in old age.

http://www.faculty.virginia.edu/cogage/index.shtml

This site contains information and links for research on euthanasia, physician-assisted suicide, living wills, and mercy killing.

http://www.euthanasia.com/

This site provides resources and links related to euthanasia and end-of-life decisions focused particularly on ethics.

http://ethics.sandiego.edu/Applied/Euthanasia/

Later Adulthood

The central question for thinking about later adulthood, the period of life after retirement age, is whether it is an inevitable period of decline or merely a period of adaptation? While we often think of old age as a time of general deterioration, research suggests that most people in this stage actually adjust to the challenges of aging reasonably well. Yet there are unquestionable challenges, including the eventual decline of physical and cognitive functioning and the inevitability of death. Two of the issues in this section consider how people most successfully manage these challenges, while the other addresses the challenging question of how to confront the end of life.

- Can We Universally Define "Successful Aging"?

- Are Brain Exercises Unhelpful in Preventing Cognitive Decline in Old Age?

- Should the Terminally Ill Be Able to Have Physicians Help Them Die?

ISSUE 18

Can We Universally Define "Successful Aging"?

YES: John W. Rowe and Robert L. Kahn, from "Successful Aging," *The Gerontologist* (vol. 37, 1997)

NO: Martha B. Holstein and Meredith Minkler, from "Self, Society, and the 'New Gerontology'," *The Gerontologist* (vol. 43, 2003)

ISSUE SUMMARY

YES: With a drastically increasing population of the elderly, professors of medicine John W. Rowe and Robert L. Kahn suggest a unified model of healthy aging is necessary to guide work with the elderly.

NO: Martha B. Holstein and Meredith Minkler, professors of religion and public health respectively, counter that a unified model of successful aging is based on particular values and assumptions that may not be fair to marginalized populations.

The American population and the world population are both aging. People are living longer, and spending more time in the stage generally described as old age. With more people living longer and longer there has been increasing interest in the field of "gerontology" which is defined as "the comprehensive study of aging and the problems of the aged" (according to the Merriam-Webster Dictionary). This definition points out the traditional emphasis in gerontology on problems, deriving from a general assumption that old age is a period of inevitable decline. The notion of "successful aging" is a direct response to this tendency, and a challenge to the idea that aging has to focus on only problems and decreased well-being.

The concept of "successful aging" owes its popularity largely to the authors of the first selection, John W. Rowe and Robert L. Kahn. Rowe and Kahn are researchers who directed an ambitious 10-year study of aging that was aimed at determining lifespan factors that correlated with healthy outcomes in old age. Their basic premise, as they articulate in the article, was that most work in the field of gerontology focused on classifying the elderly as either sick or non-sick. There was no room in these classes for thinking about people who go beyond non-sick to be well—people who have not only avoided problems, but actually aged "successfully." Based on their research and previous writing Rowe and Kahn published a book in 1997 that has been arguably the most influential work in recent gerontology. The shift they helped create was to stop thinking about aging as something that needs to be fixed when it goes wrong, but instead to think about how decisions throughout the lifespan might create a positive experience of aging. In the second selection, Martha B. Holstein and Meredith Minkler term the changes brought to the study of aging by Rowe and Kahn as a major part of the "new gerontology."

While acknowledging that Rowe and Kahn's research provided useful insight into the characteristics most associated with good health in old age, Holstein and Minkler firmly object to the ideas that underpin one simple definition for "successful aging." They take the perspective of "critical gerontology," which they contrast with more "positivist" models for studying the lifespan. By associating the idea of one model for successful aging with a tradition of logical positivism, Holstein and Minkler are suggesting that successful aging is a misguided effort at finding a universal truth.

POINT

- When thinking about old age, scholars need to move beyond classifying people as either sick or not-sick, and instead focus on those who are doing very well.

- It is important to recognize how the environment shapes successful aging above and beyond any genetic destiny.

- By studying successful aging, we've learned about the importance of maintaining good activity levels in old age.

- In order to facilitate a healthy old age it is important to recognize the potential for people to be productive and engaged.

COUNTERPOINT

- Any attempt to define one universal model for successful development unfairly prioritizes certain types of people and experiences as the norm.

- By defining some people as successful in aging and others as unsuccessful we implicitly suggest that aging well is entirely an individual responsibility and ignore social forces.

- Some people do not have the choice of being physically active in old age, and they should not be blamed for their incapacity.

- The model of successful aging promotes a "new ageism" that discriminates against people who have been confronted by significant challenges in their life.

YES

John W. Rowe and
Robert L. Kahn

Successful Aging

In an earlier article, we proposed the distinction between usual and successful aging as nonpathologic states. Our purpose in doing so was to counteract the longstanding tendency of gerontology to emphasize only the distinction between the pathologic and nonpathologic, that is, between older people with diseases or disabilities and those suffering from neither. The implicit assumption of that earlier gerontology was that, in the absence of disease and disability, other age-related alterations in physical function (such as increases in blood pressure and blood glucose) and cognitive function (such as modest memory impairment) were "normal," determined by intrinsic aging processes, primarily genetic, and not associated with risk.

We hoped that the distinction between two groups of nondiseased older persons—usual (nonpathologic but high risk) and successful (low risk and high function)—would help to correct those tendencies, stimulate research on the criteria and determinants of successful aging, and identify proper targets for interventions with "normal" elderly. In recent years, "successful aging" has become a familiar term among gerontologists and a considerable body of research has accumulated on its characteristics. Much of this work was supported by the MacArthur Foundation Research Network on Successful Aging. In this article we summarize the central findings of that work, propose a conceptual framework for successful aging, and consider some pathways or mechanisms that make for successful old age.

Defining Successful Aging

We define successful aging as including three main components: low probability of disease and disease-related disability, high cognitive and physical functional capacity, and active engagement with life. All three terms are relative and the relationship among them is to some extent hierarchical. As the figure indicates, successful aging is more than absence of disease, important though that is, and more than the maintenance of functional capacities, important as it is. Both are important components of successful aging, but it is their combination with active engagement with life that represents the concept of successful aging most fully.

From *The Gerontologist*, vol. 37, no. 4, 1997, pp. 433–440. Copyright © 1997 by Gerontological Society of America. Reprinted by permission.

Each of the three components of successful aging includes subparts. Low probability of disease refers not only to absence or presence of disease itself, but also to absence, presence, or severity of risk factors for disease. High functional level includes both physical and cognitive components. Physical and cognitive capacities are potentials for activity; they tell us what a person can do, not what he or she *does* do. Successful aging goes beyond potential; it involves activity. While active engagement with life takes many forms, we are most concerned with two—interpersonal relations and productive activity. Interpersonal relations involve contacts and transactions with others, exchange of information, emotional support, and direct assistance. An activity is productive if it creates societal value, whether or not it is reimbursed. Thus, a person who cares for a disabled family member or works as a volunteer in a local church or hospital is being productive, although unpaid. . . .

Heritability, Lifestyle, and Age-related Risk

The previously held view that increased risk of diseases and disability with advancing age results from inevitable, intrinsic aging processes, for the most part genetically determined, is inconsistent with a rapidly developing body of information that many usual aging characteristics are due to lifestyle and other factors that may be age-related (i.e., they increase with age) but are not age-dependent (not caused by aging itself).

A major source of such information is the Swedish Adoption/Twin Study of Aging (SATSA), a subset of the Swedish National Twin Registry that includes over 300 pairs of aging Swedish twins, mean age 66 years old, half of whom were reared together and half who were reared apart. About one third are monozygotic, while two thirds are dizygotic. Comparison of usual aging characteristics in twins of differing zygosity and rearing status enables estimation of the relative contributions of heritable and environmental influences.

SATSA-based studies have determined the heritability coefficients (the proportion of total variance attributable to genetic factors) for major risk factors for cardiovascular and cerebrovascular disease in older persons. These are .66–.70 for body mass index, .28–.78 for individual lipids (total cholesterol, low- and high-density lipoprotein cholesterol, apolipoproteins A-1 and B, and triglycerides), .44 for systolic and .34 for diastolic blood pressure.

Heritability trends across decades of advanced age revealed a reduction in the heritability coefficients for apolipoprotein B and triglycerides and for systolic blood pressure (.62 for people under 65 years old and .12 for those over 65). Consistent with these age-related reductions in heritability are mortality data from a 26-year follow-up of the entire Swedish Twin Registry, 21,004 twins born between 1886 and 1925. Among male identical twins, the risk of death from coronary heart disease (CHD) was eightfold greater for those whose twin died before age 55 than for those whose twin did not die before age 55, and among male nonidentical twins the corresponding risk was nearly four times greater. When one female identical twin died before the age of 65, the risk of death for the other twin was 15 times greater than if one's twin did not die before the age of 65, and 2.6 times greater in the case of female nonidentical twins. Overall, the magnitude of the risk associated with one's twin dying of CHD decreased as the age at which the twin died increased, independent of gender and zygosity.

Beyond twin studies, other evidence indicates the importance of lifestyle factors in the emergence of risk in old age. For instance, advancing age is associated with progressive impairment in carbohydrate tolerance, insufficient to meet diagnostic criteria for diabetes mellitus but characterized by increases in basal and post-glucose challenge levels of blood sugar and insulin. The hyperglycemia of aging carries increased risk for coronary heart disease and stroke, with progressive increases in the usual aging range associated with increasing risk. Similarly, the hyperinsulinemia associated with aging is an independent risk factor for coronary heart disease. Several studies have now demonstrated that the dominant determinants of this risk are age-related but potentially avoidable factors, such as the amount and distribution of body fat and reduced physical activity and dietary factors.

Substantial and growing evidence supports the contention that established risk factors for the emergence of diseases in older populations, such as cardiovascular and cerebrovascular disease, can be substantially modified. In a study demonstrating the modifiability of "usual aging," Katzel and colleagues conducted a randomized, controlled, prospective trial comparing the effects of a 9-month diet-induced weight loss (approximately 10% of body weight) to the effects of a constant-weight aerobic exercise program and a control program on a well characterized group of middle-aged and older men at risk for cardiovascular disease. The study participants were nondiabetic and were obese (body mass index 30 kg/m^2), with increased waist-hip ratios and modest increases in blood pressure, blood glucose, insulin, and an atherogenic lipid profile. Compared to controls, the reduced-energy intake diet resulted in statistically significant reductions in weight, waist-hip ratio, fasting and post-prandial glucose and insulin levels, blood pressure and plasma levels of triglycerides, low-density lipoprotein/cholesterol, and increases in high-density lipoprotein/cholesterol. While the older weight loss subjects (over 60 years old) lost less weight than the middle-aged subjects and had more modest improvements in carbohydrate tolerance, they participated fully in the reductions in other risk factors. In general, the weight loss intervention had greater effects than the constant-weight aerobic exercise intervention.

Taken together, these reports reveal three consistent findings. First, intrinsic factors alone, while highly significant, do not dominate the determination of risk in advancing age. Extrinsic environmental factors, including elements of lifestyle, play a very important role in determining risk for disease. Second, with advancing age the relative contribution of genetic factors decreases and the force of nongenetic factors increases. Third, usual aging characteristics are modifiable. These findings underline the importance of environmental and behavioral factors in determining the risk of disease late in life.

Intra-Individual Variability: A Newly Identified Risk Factor in Older Persons

The traditional repertoire of risk factors identified in studies of young and middle-aged populations may not include some additional risk factors unique to, or more easily identified in, elderly populations. In this regard, the MacArthur Foundation's Studies of Successful Aging point to a previously unrecognized risk factor—altered within-individual variability in physiologic functions—which may be important in determining the usual aging syndrome.

Most gerontological research, and indeed research in all age groups, is not geared to the measurement of short-term variations and changes. Study designs generally focus on the absolute level of a variable, perhaps comparing levels at two or more time points that may be separated by months or years. Nesselroade and colleagues, reasoned that short-term variability in a number of physiological or perhaps psychological characteristics might reflect a loss of underlying physiological reserve and represent a risk factor for emergence of disease or disability. To study the impact of short-term variability, they examined between-person differences in similarly aged residents of a retirement community. They assessed various aspects of biomedical, cognitive, and physical functioning every week for 25 weeks in a group of 31 individuals and a matched group of 30 assessed only at the outset and the end of the 25-week period, and they followed the subjects for several years to ascertain the relationship between within-person variability and its risk.

Within-person variability of a joint index of physical performance and physiological measures (gait, balance, and blood pressure) was an excellent predictor of mortality five years later ($R = 0.70$, $R^2 = 0.49$). Variability of the composite measure was a better predictor of mortality than mean level, which did not represent a statistically significant risk factor. A similar pattern of findings held for the psychological attributes of perceived control and efficacy, for which average level was not a significant predictor of mortality but intra-individual variability scores predicted 30% of the variance in mortality.

It should be emphasized that some functions are highly variable under normal conditions and others much less so. The significant aspect of intra-individual variability as a potential measure of decreased capacity and increased risk must be a change from the normal variability, regardless of whether the change is an increase or decrease. For example, a decline in beat-to-beat variability in heart rate has been shown to be a predictor of mortality in patients who have previously suffered a myocardial infarction. While in the physiological measurement used in this study, an increase in variability was associated with increased risk; in other highly regulated systems, a decrease in variability may be detrimental and represent decreased reserve and increased risk.

Maximizing Cognitive and Physical Function in Late Life

A second essential component of successful aging is maximization of functional status. One common concern of older people relates to cognitive function, especially learning and short-term memory. Another functional area of major interest is physical performance. Modest reductions in the capacity to easily perform common physical functions may prevent full participation in productive and recreational activities of daily life.

The MacArthur Foundation Research Network on Successful Aging conducted a longitudinal study of older persons to identify those physical, psychological, social, and biomedical characteristics predictive of the maintenance of high function in late life. The 1,189 subjects in this three-site longitudinal study were 70–79 years old at initial evaluation and were functionally in the upper one third of the general aging population. Smaller age- and sex-matched samples (80 subjects in the medium functioning group and 82 subjects in the low functioning group) were selected to represent the middle and lowest tertiles. Initial data included detailed assessments of physical and cognitive performance, health status, and social and psychological characteristics (the MacArthur battery), as well as the collection of blood and urine samples. After a 2.0–2.5 year interval, 1,115 subjects were re-evaluated, providing a 91% follow-up rate for the study.

Predictors of Cognitive Function

Cognitive ability was assessed with neuropsychological tests of language, non-verbal memory, verbal memory, conceptualization, and visual spatial ability. In the initially high functioning group, four variables—education, strenuous activity in and around the home, peak pulmonary flow rate, and self-efficacy—were found to be direct predictors of change or maintenance of cognitive function, together explaining 40% of the variance in cognitive test performance. Education was the strongest predictor, with greater years of schooling increasing the likelihood of maintaining high cognitive function. This finding is consistent with several cross-sectional studies, which identify education as a major protective factor against reductions in cognitive function. Since all the subjects had high cognitive function at first evaluation, it is unlikely that the observed effect merely reflected ability to perform well on cognitive tests or was the result of individuals with greater innate intelligence having received more education. Instead, the results suggest either or both of two explanatory mechanisms: a direct beneficial effect of education early in life on brain circuitry and function, and the possibility that education is a proxy for life-long intellectual activities (reading, crossword puzzles, etc.) which might serve to maintain cognitive function late in life.

Pulmonary peak expiratory flow rate was the second strongest predictor of maintenance of cognitive function. In previous studies, this function was a predictor of total and cardiovascular mortality and a correlate of cognitive and physical function in elderly populations.

A surprising finding of this study was that the amount of strenuous physical activity at and around the home was an important predictor of maintaining cognitive function. In a follow-up study to evaluate a possible mechanism of this effect, Neeper, Gomez-Pinilla, Choi, and Cotman measured the effect of exercise on central nervous system levels of brain-derived neurotrophic factor (BDNF) in adult rats. These investigators found that increasing exercise was associated with very substantial "dose-related" increases in BDNF in the hippocampus and neocortex, brain areas known to be highly responsive to environmental stimuli. These data provide a potential mechanism whereby exercise might enhance central nervous system function, particularly memory function.

A personality measure, perceived self-efficacy, was also predictive of maintaining cognitive function in old age. The concept of self-efficacy developed by Bandura is defined as "people's beliefs in their capabilities to organize and execute the courses of action required to deal with prospective situations." In students and young adults, self-efficacy influences persistence in solving cognitive problems, heart rate during performance of cognitive tasks, mathematical performance, and mastery of computer software procedures. Lachman and colleagues have proposed a role for self-efficacy beliefs in maintenance of cognitive function among older people.

In addition to these findings of predictors of maintenance of cognitive function, evidence is accumulating to indicate that it can be enhanced in old age. For example, older people who showed a clear age-related pattern of decline in fluid intelligence (inductive reasoning and spatial orientation) showed substantial improvement after five training sessions that stressed ways of approaching such problems and provided practice in solving them. Moreover, repeated measurement indicated that the improvements were maintained. Studies from the Max Planck Institute in Berlin confirm the finding that cognitive losses among healthy older people are reversible by means of training, although they also shows a substantial age-related training effect in favor of younger subjects. There is a double message in these findings: first, and most important, the capacity for positive change, sometimes called plasticity, persists in old age; appropriate interventions can often bring older people back to (or above) some earlier level of function. Second, the same interventions may be still more effective with younger subjects, which suggests an age-related reduction in reserve functional capacity. These demonstrations of plasticity in old age are encouraging in their own right and tell us that positive change is possible.

Predictors of Physical Function

In the MacArthur studies, maintenance of high physical performance, including hand, trunk, and lower extremity movements and integrated movements of balance and gait, was predicted by both socio-demographic and health status characteristics. Being older and having an income of less than $10,000 a year increased the likelihood of a decline in physical performance, as did higher body mass index (greater fat), high blood pressure, and lower initial cognitive performance. Behavioral predictors of maintenance of physical function included moderate and/or strenuous leisure activity and emotional support from family and friends. Moderate levels of exercise activity (e.g., walking leisurely) appeared in these studies to convey similar advantages to more strenuous exercise (e.g., brisk walking).

Continuing Engagement with Life

The third component of successful aging, engagement with life, has two major elements: maintenance of interpersonal relations and of productive activities.

Social Relations

At least since Durkheim's classic study of suicide, isolation and lack of connectedness to others have been recognized as predictors of morbidity and mortality. Five prospective studies of substantial populations have now demonstrated causality throughout the life course in such associations: being part of a social network is a significant determinant of longevity, especially for men.

Research on the health protective aspect of network membership has emphasized two kinds of supportive transactions: socio-emotional (expressions of affection, respect and the like) and instrumental (direct assistance, such as giving physical help, doing chores, providing transportation, or giving money.

The three-community MacArthur study tested both instrumental and emotional support as predictors of neuroendocrine function and physical performance. Neuroendocrine measures were also studied as possible mediators of the effects of support. Over a three-year period, marital status (being married), presumably a source of emotional support, protected against reduction in productive activity. Men with higher emotional support had significantly lower urine excretion of norepinephrine, epinephrine, and cortisol, and for both men and women, emotional support was a positive predictor of physical performance. Instrumental support, on the other hand, had few significant neuroendocrine relations for men, none for women, and was associated with lower physical performance, probably as an effect rather than a cause.

These varying effects of social support are consistent with research relating the effect of support to the specific situation in which it is offered. For example, instrumental support rather than emotional support influenced the promptness with which older people who experienced cancer-suspicious symptoms actually saw a physician. Opposite results came from a nursing home experiment, however: socio-emotional support (verbal encouragement) had positive performance effects, whereas instrumental support (direct assistance) had negative effects on performance.

Several conclusions seem warranted regarding the properties of social relations and their effects:

a. Isolation (lack of social ties), is a risk factor for health.
b. Social support, both emotional and instrumental, can have positive health-relevant effects.
c. No single type of support is uniformly effective; effectiveness depends on the appropriateness of the supportive acts to the requirements of the situation and the person.

Productive Activities

Older people are not considered "old" by their families and friends, nor do they think of themselves as "old," so long as they remain active and productive in some meaningful sense. In legislative policy, Congressional discussion as to whether the nation can "afford" its older people is as much a debate about their productivity as their requirements for service, especially medical care.

Part of the confusion stems from lack of clarity about what constitutes a productive activity. Our national statistics define Gross Domestic Product (GDP) in terms of activities that are paid for, and exclude all unpaid activities, however valuable. Several current studies (ACL, MacArthur, HRS) utilize a broader definition that includes all activities, paid or unpaid, that create goods or services of economic value, and these studies have generated age-related patterns very different from those for paid employment alone.

The nationwide Americans Changing Lives (ACL) study found that, contrary to the stereotype of unproductive old age, most older people make productive contributions of some kind, more as informal help-giving and unpaid volunteer work than paid employment. When all forms of productive activity are combined, the amount of work done by older men and women is substantial. Among those aged 60 or more, 39% reported at least 1500 hours of productive activity during the preceding year; 41% reported 500–1499 hours, and 18% reported 1–499 hours. The relationship between age and productive activity depends on the activity. While hours of paid work drop sharply after age 55, hours of volunteer work in organizations peak in the middle years (ages 35–55), and informal help to friends and relatives peaks still later (ages 55–64) and remains significant to age 75 and beyond.

Both the ACL and MacArthur studies address the question of what factors enable sustained productivity in old age. Both include longitudinal as well as cross-sectional data, and in some respects the studies are complementary—national representativeness over the full adult age range in the ACL survey, biomedical and performance measures as well as self-report in the MacArthur research. Three factors emerge as predictors of productive activity: functional capacity, education, and self-efficacy.

Functional capacity. Men and women high in cognitive and physical function are three times as likely to be doing some paid work and more than twice as likely to be doing volunteer work. Moreover, for all forms of productive work except child care, functional status also predicts the amount of such work. Indicators of functional decrement, such as limitations with vision and number of bed days during the three months preceding the data collection, predict lesser productive activity.

Education. Educational level is a well established predictor of sustained productive behavior, paid and unpaid. The possible mechanisms of this effect include the role of education as a major determinant of occupation and income, both of which are major influences on the life course, the selective process in education that probably includes genetic elements and certainly includes parental socioeconomic status, and the tendency of education to inculcate values and establish habits that express themselves in later life as higher functional status and engagement in productive behavior.

Self-efficacy.   Self-efficacy and the related concepts of mastery and control are consistent predictors of sustained activity in old age. The ACL study, in addition to identifying a positive relationship between self-efficacy and productive activity, found that two other variables, labeled vulnerability and fatalism, essentially inversions of self-efficacy, were negatively related to productivity. Consistent with these findings, in the MacArthur sample only one factor—mastery—emerged as relevant for both increases and decreases in productivity; increases in mastery led to increased productivity; decreases in mastery had the opposite effect.

Response to stress.   If we had continuous rather than occasional measurement of successful aging, we would expect to find that even older people who are aging successfully have not met the criteria at every moment in the past. They have moved "in and out of success," just as healthy people can be said to move in and out of illness. Under the most fortunate circumstances, aging brings with it some repetitive experience of chronic or recurrent stresses, the "daily hassles" of life and their cumulative effects. Most older people have also experienced more acute episodes, the "stressful life events" that have been much-studied. For example, older men and women may have been seriously ill, temporarily disabled by accident or injury, disoriented after a stroke, or depressed by the death of a spouse. Apart from such crises of illness and bereavement, but similarly stressful, are the experiences of forced retirement, sudden reduction in income, mugging, and burglary.

   We propose the concept of *resilience* to describe the rapidity and completeness with which people recover from such episodes and return to meeting the criteria of success. Determination of resilience in dealing with a specific stressful event would require assessment of relevant functions before the stressing challenge is encountered and subsequent monitoring the observe the initial decremental effect, the time required to regain stability of function, and the level of function regained. While no research has yet robustly evaluated resilience, a number of studies are relevant to it. The work by Nesselroade and his colleagues, described earlier, demonstrated the importance of short term variability in physical function and blood pressure as a predictor of mortality among elderly subjects. We may interpret low variability in blood pressure as an indicator of resilience, but the interpretation must be tentative; we do not know the challenges or stressors to which these subjects were responding.

Conclusion.   Recent and projected substantial increases in the relative and absolute number of older persons in our society pose a significant challenge for biology, social and behavioral science, and medicine. Gerontology is broadening its perspective from a prior preoccupation with disease and disability to a more robust view that includes successful aging. As conceptual and empiric research in this area accelerates, successful aging is seen as multi-dimensional, encompassing three distinct domains: avoidance of disease and disability, maintenance of high physical and cognitive function, and sustained engagement in social and productive activities. For each of these domains, an interdisciplinary database is coalescing that relates to both reducing the risk of adverse events and enhancing resilience in their presence. Many of the predictors of risk and of both functional and activity levels appear to be potentially modifiable, either by individuals or by changes in their immediate environments. The stage is thus set for intervention studies to identify effective strategies that enhance the proportion of our older population that ages successfully.

Martha B. Holstein and
Meredith Minkler

Self, Society, and the "New Gerontology"

The primary task of the critic is to analyze the present and to reveal its fractures and instabilities and the ways in which it at once limits us and points to the transgressions of those limits.

One of gerontology's great strengths has been its multidisciplinary perspective. To date, biology and the social sciences have provided the primary filters through which gerontologists have studied aging and old age. These disciplines have deepened our understanding of the processes of aging, contributed to policy and program development, and influenced new generations of gerontologists. In the past several years, a new paradigm has assumed pride of place. Although linguistically similar to (but quite different in content from) earlier work on successful aging, this paradigm, firmly grounded in the 10-year, $10 million MacArthur Foundation Study of Successful Aging, is hailed as the "new gerontology." It is part of a larger movement in gerontology and geriatrics—a vigorous emphasis on the potential for and indeed the likelihood of a healthy and engaged old age. This view seeks to counteract and replace the old "decline and loss" paradigm that views aging as a series of individual decrements or losses to which both elders and society needed to adapt or adjust. In contrast, the new gerontology adopts a prevention model—modify individual behaviors throughout your life and so avoid these decrements and losses.

In addition to publishing in academic journals, Rowe and Kahn presented their model and a wealth of evidence-based health promotion and disease and disability prevention advice in the form of a book geared at a lay audience. In the years since the publication of *Successful Aging,* this volume has attracted an articulate, popular, and professional following. Greeted as a lodestar for moving the field of aging toward a new understanding of what permits effective functioning in old age and drawing on the contributions of many leading scientists in the field of aging, *Successful Aging* is perhaps the single most recognized work in recent gerontology. Intended to stimulate this wide recognition, the major public relations effort that followed the book's publication and the resulting media attention have deepened its cultural resonance while also influencing the nation's research agenda on aging.

Time and popularity have not, however, erased our concerns about this paradigm and the associated use of the implicitly normative phrase "successful

From *The Gerontologist,* vol. 43, no. 6, 2003, pp. 787–789, 791–795. Copyright © 2003 by Gerontological Society of America. Reprinted by permission.

aging." Its very simplicity and apparent clarity mask vital differences and many critical dimensions of what may be described as a liminal state—"the condition of moving from one state to another"—under circumstances marked by change and uncertainty. It is thus timely, we believe, to take another look at the new gerontology. In particular, we want to apply to the successful aging paradigm and its popular manifestations critical and feminist perspectives, whose standpoints can unsettle familiar and conventional ways of thinking by revealing their often-unrecognized underlying values and consequences. To be critical means to engage in "historically and socially situated normative reflection about research methodologies, assumptions and directions." Critical practices reformulate the questions that research asks, insist on broad sources of knowledge generation, and urge asking traditional "subjects" normative questions—what ought to be—as a way of uncovering hidden normative possibilities. As interested in the particular as in the general, in understanding as well as generalizing, a critical approach enlarges our perceptions and so calls attention to what more positivist approaches cannot or do not notice. . . .

Successful Aging and the New Gerontology

Ironically, the new gerontology has much in common with the century-old Victorian view of successful aging in which good health signaled a life lived according to the strict dictates of Victorian convention. Albeit without today's scientific foundation and inclined to view "vices," such as vigorous sexual activity, as the cause of an unhealthy old age, it still distinguished between positive and negative experiences of aging rooted in individual action over a lifetime. Even in the 19th century, America scientists "sought a 'normal' old age that contained an unstated ideal of health or maximum functioning—the 'good' old age of Victorian morality."

For many years, the modern gerontological enterprise similarly has sought to understand what can make old age better—healthier, financially more secure, and a period of fulfillment and even growth. In the classic edited, work, *Problems of Aging,* published in 1937, Edmund Cowdry invited a stellar group of scientists to bring to the multifaceted problem of aging an "understanding of how things worked" from the perspective of several scientific disciplines. In the years since the publication of this first handbook on aging, we have come a long way toward understanding what that early volume called the "problem of senescence." With improved economic conditions, positive changes in physical and often social environments, and improvements in health care and health care access, many more—though certainly not all—older people can have a relatively satisfactory old age. Since the early 1980s, declining poverty and the mitigation of many diseases of old age have facilitated interest in health promotion and wellness and have contributed to richer, more open perceptions about old age.

The new gerontology is in this tradition. It describes, in detail and with carefully documented scientific support, how individuals can contribute to their continued good health. In this way it provides younger people with an important message about making choices (albeit, as we will discuss, without sufficient attention to the contexts and constraints influencing those choices). Commenting on the impressive scientific grounding of the successful aging model, Scheidt, Humphreys, and Yorgason noted that "at least a hundred studies have shown the efficacy of modifications to environmental and life-style factors for increasing the likelihood that older individuals might achieve success under this triarchic definition. So what's not to like?" We will return to that question after briefly reviewing the premises of successful aging.

Rowe and Kahn argued that three conditions or characteristics are necessary preconditions for successful aging: (a) the avoidance of disease and disability; (b) the maintenance of high physical and cognitive functional capacity; and (c) "active engagement in life." They further suggested that these three components are hierarchically ordered:

> The absence of disease and disability makes it easier to maintain mental and physical function. And maintenance of mental and physical function in turn enables (but does not guarantee) active engagement with life. It is the *combination* [emphasis in the original] of all three—avoidance of disease and disability, maintenance of cognitive and physical function and sustained engagement with life—that *represents the concept of successful aging most fully* [italics added].

While Rowe and Kahn have refined their model over the years, reaffirming more strongly, for example, an emphasis on the importance of "active engagement with life," the instrumental or preconditions for successful aging have become transformed, as the aforementioned quote suggests, into the concept itself. In a few short years, this model has become a central theoretical paradigm within the fields of geriatrics and gerontology. Despite its many strengths and contributions, however, the successful aging model and its attendant publicity are problematic. Following a brief review of the critical gerontology framework, we will use these perspectives as lenses through which to more critically examine successful aging and the new gerontology. . . .

Applying These Perspectives to the New Gerontology

The Issue of Normativity

Because critical perspectives are concerned about hidden value premises, we turn to the new gerontology's implicit (and thus unacknowledged) normatively. Understood as an objective, scientific discourse, the new gerontology upholds a certain status, defined primarily in terms of health, and labels those who exemplify these standards as aging successfully. This stance affirms normative value commitments, offering ways to think about—and judge—our choices (now and in the past), actions, and their results.

Historians, literary scholars, sociologists, and philosophers, among others, suggest reasons why cultural norms matter. Cultural images, representations, symbols, and metaphors are important means to withhold or to express social recognition; they offer the cultural imagery from which we construct identities. Central to this understanding are notions of the self. Mediating between individuals and their environment, the self is a "biographically anchored and reflexive project," realized in conversations with others and oneself. Norms matter because we are situated selves, embedded in society and culture and resonating with what is valued in the environment. Although resistance is possible, indeed probable, as situated selves, we can rarely ignore cultural norms in the construction of a self. Nor are we able to easily dissent, as individuals, from culture. The theologian Rosemary Reuther observed, "alternate cultures and communities must be built up to support the dissenting consciousness." To date, alternative perspectives tend to be ghettoized while the dominant culture accepts as the desired norm the tanned, vigorous couple who are bicycle riding on gently rolling hills and dining in the warm glow of candles.

Even if we put aside the publicity the new gerontology has received, and the strong scientific base of the MacArthur Foundation Study, it is not surprising that the new paradigm has gained popular approbation. Success, a valued attribute in American society, is generally visible and measurable, perhaps countable in dollars, degrees, gold medals, and so on. Evidence of success is commendable, to the individual's credit, and therefore praiseworthy. The new gerontology offers another measurable variable to define success, another source of praiseworthy behavior that has currency in a competitive society.

However, normative terms such as successful aging are not neutral; they are laden with comparative, either-or, hierarchically ordered dimensions. Unfortunately, too many people—most often the already marginalized—come up on the wrong side of the hierarchy and the either-or divide. Its reductionist qualities are revealed by a different sort of comparison: How would it seem to describe a particular kind of childhood or midlife—as such—as successful because the person rarely became ill and participate in many social events? Why then is it is desirable to describe this kind of aging (or more accurately, old age) as successful?

Even if we bracket for a moment our reluctance to apply the term "successful" to aging, the specific norms the new gerontology identifies as measures of success are also problematic. As we discuss in more detail in the paragraphs that follow, if how we live determines how we age, and if how we live is shaped by many factors beyond individual choice, then success is far harder to come by for some than for others.

Hence, because normative concepts are important, dominant cultural images can easily make individual efforts to transform themselves as their lives and bodies change more difficult. These concepts tell us what is worthwhile (on different levels of our lives) and give us criteria by which to evaluate our lives. Thus, the power to identify such normative concepts is pivotal. For this reason, in particular, the authority to create cultural views and images about aging can only rest in an interactive research process, and in a critical awareness of how context and particularities influence how we grow old and what we value once we get there. Exchanges between older people and academic researchers, for example, are unlikely to accept uncritically that a disease-resistant 80-year-old man playing golf at Augusta or skiing at Aspen is aging more successfully than a woman in a wheelchair who tutors inner city children or writes poetry or feels a passionate energy that she is too fragile to enact.

Health, as a normative standard, calls for certain virtues—diligence, caution, and perhaps a touch of solipsism. We must be ever wary of how we govern our lives. This view omits the natural lottery imposed by genetics, the general contingencies of human life, and the more specific damages (and often strengths) that marginalization and oppression bequeath to many individuals.

In raising these concerns about normativity, we are not suggesting that Rowe and Kahn intended to launch what can appear to be a coercive standard that affects individuals and groups in different and, in some cases, potentially damaging ways (see the paragraphs that follow). In an interesting irony, had Rowe and Kahn not labeled their landmark work as "successful aging," it may well have remained what it in essence is—a careful, empirically grounded account of how to help individuals stay as healthy as possible for as long as possible. On this foundation, they would be free, within inevitable limits, to construct the kind of life they choose. The use of the term "successful," however, shifts that intention to help people stay as well as possible to something much larger. What was initially affirmed as the preconditions for effective functioning in old age—the *foundation* on which many varieties of life choices may flourish—in an almost imperceptible move became the concept of successful aging. The foundation became the entirety. The concept does not say, These are guidelines to preserve your health and well-being in old age, all things being equal. Although such a statement gives health a high status, it does not equate good health with success. Eating properly, exercising regularly, and not smoking are connected directly to a goal of good health, a goal that, we suspect, most would treasure. However, we suggest throughout this essay, despite its wide appeal, attaining a healthy old age on the individual level should not be universally equated with the attainment of a good or successful old age.

The "Problems" of Feasibility and Disability

Although our discussion raises broad questions about why both the phrase "successful aging," and the model bearing that name are problematic from a normative standpoint, there are other, more specific concerns that challenge its acceptability as an ideal. A major contribution of Rowe and Kahn's paradigm lay in its message that many of the losses associated with "usual aging" are not "normal" aspects of aging at all but are caused primarily by extrinsic factors, such as poor diet and lack of exercise, and therefore are subject to alteration. However, the value of this message from a health promotion perspective is tempered by another, as the authors go on to suggest that "successful aging is dependent upon individual choices and behaviors. *It can be attained through individual choice and effort* [italics added]." The single endpoint is effective physical and mental functioning. In Rowe and Kahn's words: "We were trying to pinpoint the many factors that conspire to put one octogenarian on cross-country skis and another in a wheelchair."

Such a statement is problematic on several counts; key among them is its implication that had the elder who is disabled but tried harder and made different (health-promoting) choices, he or she might also be enjoying a physically vigorous and able-bodied old age. This individualistic analysis doesn't ask if the 80-year-old skier had county club privileges and a winter home in Colorado, or the 80-year-old in the wheelchair had cleaned houses for a living while holding down a second job as a nurses' aide on the graveyard shift in a nursing home. Nor does this analysis inquire about the inner or family life of our 80-year-old in the wheelchair. These contextual features, at a minimum, shape the conditions of possibility for individuals and determine how they choose what to value. If the ideal is not practically feasible for all, or even most, people—even with the best intentions—then it serves to further privilege the already privileged, a danger that a feminist perspective identifies.

The "problem" of disability also looms. Within the successful aging paradigm, and with a few notable exceptions, disability, even visible "oldness," signifies failure or, at best, "usual" aging. "With midlife the universal ideal, older people meet the stringent criteria of successful aging only insofar as they are not 'old.' If the young body is . . . projected into old age as the norm," all will ultimately fail. This end is particularly troubling. When norms consider frailty and disability as reflections of failure, they reinforce "cultural fears of bodily suffering (and thus of people who are 'old') and [promote] inadequate policy responses" at the same time that they blame people whose bodies are proverbially "out of control." As was the case with its Victorian era predecessors, illness, especially because it prevents active engagement with life, becomes a transgression of cultural rules.

This exaggerated emphasis on the degree to which we can control the body contributes to and denies older people with functional limitations, most of whom are women, the dignity of their struggle to accept what they cannot change. On a broader level, it contributes as well to the cultural denial of disability, dependency, and ultimately death. That struggle, social ethicist Frida Furman says, "is a struggle of the soul to affirm what is yet possible, to let go of what is not."

Similarly, the "new ageism" inadvertently promoted though the skis versus wheelchair analogy simply replaces an earlier generalized dread of aging with a more specific fear of aging with a disability. Frequently internalized by older people themselves, this new variant of ageism ironically can mitigate against the very proactive health promotion and healthy maintenance activities advocated by proponents of successful aging by "substantially lowering the bar of dreams and expectations for and by elders with disabilities." Looking old and suffering from disabling conditions become personal failures, thereby compounding the "problem" of aging and contributing to often self-defeating strategies to preserve "youthfulness" and so appear "not old."

Once an individual strategy—staying fit and vigorous—becomes a societal vision, then "whole social groups and areas of life become marginalized." As already noted, such marginalization can elicit damaging and invidious comparisons, particularly if one is disabled, or simply old and "not well preserved." As Blaikie has argued, the "constant quest for youth, in stigmatizing [sic] the old and sick, casts off these people as human failures."

Devaluing of Women's Roles and Acts of Resistance

The cultural scripts that the new gerontology extols particularly affect older women. The greater burden of chronic illness and functional limitations they experience and their far higher poverty rates couple with differential societal norms that continue to assign a higher value to physical appearance and "youthful physical attractiveness" among women. However, many women have lived by the norms of their own more intimate society, being responsible for others and attending to the everyday business of life, whether that meant scrubbing floors or caring for a dying parent or a grandchild. These features that mark many a woman's moral life neither gain approbation from the wider society nor give her the leisure to tend to the specifics of health maintenance that contribute to successful aging by the criterion that Rowe and Kahn set forth. Hence, as life course and political economy perspectives remind us, the burden on older women—especially women who live on limited incomes and have experienced exclusions based on color, ethnicity, or class—is often particularly heavy.

The new gerontology can render invisible important adaptive and other actions that allow people to cope with change. Many people, for example, particularly older women, with their less than perfect bodies and with one or more chronic illnesses, confront cultural narratives of decline on their own terms. Rarely noted and seldom valued even if noticed, their acts of resistance—"going gray," choosing to live a simpler, less busy life, taking the time to give concentrated care to a parent, a spouse, or a grandchild, accepting "old" as a way to describe oneself—are less a bulwark against the loss of self-esteem than they might be if different cultural norms prevailed. Successful aging, for example, only tangentially—through its attention to active engagement with life—attends to aspects of the moral life such as nurturing, caring, friendship, love, and social activism that have been primary in the lives of many women. Such aspects of life that are publicly underestimated and undervalued become vulnerable as sources of self-worth if they lack sustenance and recognition. Instead of creating conditions that lessen important aspects of women's lives, does society not have a responsibility to "examine, evaluate, condemn, and change . . . expectations . . . that harm some, and militate against the well-being of all, women?"

Potential Problems for Policy

In the policy arena, the notion that health and well-being in old age are largely in the hands of individuals can do further damage. Ironically, we are successfully old when we conform to society's needs; placing responsibility on the individual mitigates demands on social resources across our lives. Exceptionalism—"I made it, why can't you"—is, in our minds, a failing strategy. It does nothing to eliminate larger patterns of oppression, in which certain individuals and groups lack the advantages privileged groups possess by virtue of their social location. When the tasks essential to aging successfully are vested in the individual aging person, the young and the middle-aged hear about these splendid people who have aged so well and wonder why all the fuss about old age in America. Policies promoting increased Medicare coverage for home modifications and assistive devices, as well as increased Supplemental Social Security Income payments that would bring elderly and disabled recipients above the poverty line, may well suffer at the hands of a populace and a legislature that has bought the stereotypes of a new breed of successfully aging seniors who no longer need much in the way of government support. Particularly in the current political climate of major government cutbacks in the face of economic downturns and military buildups, overly optimistic images of "successful agers" may make even more vulnerable the position of many older women for whom more, rather than less, government assistance is vital.

The new gerontology can hinder the development of a thoughtful and morally rich account of dependency and interdependency. The often implicit singling out of disabled elderly persons as unsuccessful agers also allows us to evade the inevitable confrontation with sickness and death. In this way, it may further diminish policy attention to the need for greater engagement with these issues in a rapidly aging society. . . .

Conclusion

Growing old in a society that not only valorizes youth but informs people *whoever they are* that successful aging—defined almost exclusively in terms of health status—"can be attained through individual choice and effort" is potentially damaging personally and politically. Such a perspective tends to trivialize the role of gender, race, socioeconomic status, and genetics in influencing both health and broader life chances both throughout life and in old age. At the same time, and precisely through its failure to take into account the unacknowledged role of broader sociostructural and environmental forces, this viewpoint transforms the particular into the universal and absolves social and political institutions of their responsibilities for the health and well-being of residents. By suggesting that the great majority of those elders in wheelchairs could indeed have been on cross-country skis had they but made the right choices and practiced the right behaviors can burden rather than liberate older people. Hence, we emphasize that concepts such as successful aging are marked by important and unacknowledged class, race, and gender concerns that result in further marginalizing the already marginalized. The perpetuation of privilege is not a desirable end.

However, even setting aside these concerns, the new gerontology offers an impoverished view of what a "good" old age can be. As suggested earlier, the MacArthur Foundation Study of Successful Aging led by Rowe and Kahn made a critical contribution in helping to provide a strong empirical base for the utility of a variety of health-promoting practices and behaviors throughout life and in old age. Nevertheless, the equation of good health with successful aging (and by extension, disability and poor health with failure) together with the simplistic popularization of these proscriptive views in the mass and popular culture fail to honor the many ways in which individuals face the physiological, emotional, or contextual changes that accompany aging.

We end with some ideas about how to alter the problematic aspects of the successful aging model's foundational assumptions. Act of resistance, already touched on, are beginning points. The tyranny of youth-preserving technologies and lifestyles that demand more and more time and money hinders a respectful attitude toward old age. How can we respect age if we do everything in our power to deny it? What most assume as a matter of course in youth and middle age—that is, health and activity—cannot be the critical measure of success in old age. At a minimum, it reduces old age to the most basic norms, less than we would accept at other times of our lives. It offers continuity, but old age is also importantly about transformation as we learn to accept what we cannot change, rage when we must, and adopt new ways of life as needed. Writing in her 60s, the late May Sarton, poet, essayist, and novelist, reflecting on the imminence of death, noted that "preparing to die we shed our leaves, without regret, so that the essential person may be alive and well at the end." Biomedicine, as important as it is, does not see the luminous moments that offer promise despite uncertainty and the proximity of death. Its tools cannot diagnose the mischief the very term "successful" can do, particularly in a competitive, youth-driven society.

We might return to the ancient question: What is the good life—for the whole of life—and what does it take to live a good old age? What virtues do we strive for and how do we honor difference? Germain Greer said it well: "Liberation struggles are not about assimilation but about asserting difference, endowing that difference with dignity and prestige, and insisting on it as a condition of self-definition and self-determination."

CHALLENGE QUESTIONS

Can We Universally Define "Successful Aging"?

- This controversy is embedded in a much larger controversy about the philosophy and practice of science: will research and scholarship lead us to one clear "best" model of the human experience (and of lifespan development)?
- Does defining only one version of successful aging deny the diversity that is inherent in lifespan development?
- Rowe and Kahn suggest that active engagement and individual effort are keys to successful aging, but how much control do individuals actually have in determining their own lifespan? Does suggesting that "success" in aging is due to good individual choices deny the impact of social and cultural forces that are beyond individual control?
- Both sides argue that how we conceptualize successful aging has implications for policies geared toward old age. What types of policy implications might derive from taking one side or the other on this issue?
- With a rapidly aging population there is great interest in trying to make old age pleasant. Some of the fastest growing professions and industries cater to geriatric populations. So how should such professionals and industries focus their attention? Should they address individual choices, assuming with Rowe and Kahn that our personal actions craft our later life outcomes? Or should they address societal structures, assuming with Holstein and Minkler that the inequalities of society are reproduced and accentuated by valuing one model of "successful aging" as a universal good?

Suggested Readings

P. Baltes and M. Baltes, "Savoir Vivre in Old Age," *National Forum* (Spring 1998)

P. Baltes and J. Smith, "New Frontiers in the Future of Aging: From Successful Aging of the Young Old to the Dilemmas of the Fourth Age," *Gerontology* (March/April 2003)

J. Birren and K. Schaie, *Handbook of the Psychology of Aging* (San Diego Academic Press, 1990)

R. Kahn, "On 'Successful Aging and Well-Being: Self Rated Compared with Rowe and Kahn'," *Gerontologist* (December 2002)

E. Phelan, L. Anderson, A. LaCroix, and E. Larson, "Older Adults' Views of 'Successful Aging'—How Do They Compare with Researchers'

Definitions?" *Journal of the American Geriatrics Society* (February 2004)

E. Phelan and E. Larson, "'Successful Aging'—Where Next?" *Journal of the American Geriatrics Society* (July 2002)

J. W. Rowe and R. L. Kahn, *Successful Aging* (Pantheon, 1998)

W. Strawbridge, M. Wallhagen, and R. Cohen, "Successful Aging and Well-Being: Self-Rated Compared with Rowe and Kahn," *Gerontologist* (December 2002)

G. E. Vaillant, *Aging Well: Surprising Guideposts to a Happier Life from the Landmark Harvard Study of Adult Development* (Little, Brown, 2002)

ISSUE 19

Are Brain Exercises Unhelpful in Preventing Cognitive Decline in Old Age?

YES: Timothy A. Salthouse, from "Mental Exercise and Mental Aging: Evaluating the Validity of the 'Use It or Lose It' Hypothesis," *Perspectives on Psychological Science* (2006)

NO: Carmi Schooler, from "Use It—and Keep It, Longer, Probably: A Reply to Salthouse," *Perspectives on Psychological Science* (March 2007)

ISSUE SUMMARY

YES: Although mental exercises designed to maintain mental functioning in old age have become quite popular, psychologist Timothy Salthouse asserts that there is little convincing evidence to support that appealing idea.

NO: Carmi Schooler, a researcher at the National Institute of Mental Health, counters that although the loss of mental functioning with age is not fully understood there is good reason to believe that more activity can delay cognitive decline.

Among the sometimes scary aspects of growing old is the prospect of cognitive decline—the gradual loss of intellectual functioning. Studying cognitive and intellectual changes over the lifespan has thus been an important area for researchers learning about old age. Over decades of study a general picture has emerged with some consistency. We know, for example, that dramatic cognitive decline is not an inevitable fact of aging, although in some ways our intellectual functioning does inevitably change with time. We also know that not all cognitive and intellectual functioning reacts to aging in the same way. Overall, with the knowledge that dramatic cognitive decline is not inevitable and that patterns of change vary, many people are optimistic that under the right conditions people may be able to gain control over what happens to their minds in old age.

The idea of being able to control cognitive and intellectual changes with age is so appealing that a cottage industry has emerged, offering "brain gyms" and mental exercise programs for older adults. Just as with the other end of the lifespan, where companies are creating popular brain stimulation media and toys for infants, there is clearly a market for products that might make us smarter. But scholars are less interested in the market than in the claims of these products—ultimately these products are making an empirical claim about the flexibility of the brain, and that claim requires convincing evidence.

In his review of the evidence Timothy Salthouse, finds that the appealing idea of "use it or lose it" is not well supported. He reviews a wide variety of studies investigating cognitive and intellectual functioning in old age and finds them limited by classic challenges of research. Thus, for example, while most research does show that more intellectually engaged older adults function at higher levels it is not clear whether that is a product of mental exercise or a product of a lifetime of high cognitive functioning. This is the ubiquitous question in social science of whether a relationship is causal, or simply correlational, and Salthouse finds many such questions in his thorough review of literature.

Carmi Schooler, on the other hand, asserts that Salthouse is too quick to dismiss the value of the available evidence about mental exercise. Schooler, drawing on his own research and that of other scholars, notes that most findings are at least consistent with the idea of "use it or lose it." In other words, most research finds that more intellectually engaged older adults maintain cognitive and intellectual functioning. While this consistency may not constitute conclusive proof, for Schooler it is not insignificant.

POINT	COUNTERPOINT
• The idea of "use it or lose it" is mostly just intuitively appealing because it suggests individuals can control their destiny.	• In common usage the idea of "use it or lose it" does not mean that people will completely reverse any cognitive decline—just that people who are mentally active do better than people who are not.
• Proponents of mental exercises in old age rarely cite good empirical evidence.	• Salthouse's criteria for supporting "use it or lose it" are too high—there is a good amount of evidence that is at least consistent with the idea that mental activity is important.
• It is quite likely that people who are actively engaged mentally in old age are people who were always more engaged—and thus the relationship between mental exercise and acuity may be a correlation rather than causal.	• Some of the ability to limit cognitive decline may relate to being more engaged intellectually throughout life, but that does not mean staying active does not also matter.
• In studies that compare training in mental tasks during old age most of the results seem limited and domain-specific.	• It is unreasonable to expect that mental activities in one domain will have broad effects on other domains.

YES

Timothy A. Salthouse

Mental Exercise and Mental Aging: Evaluating the Validity of the "Use It or Lose It" Hypothesis

Cross-sectional comparisons of people of different ages have consistently revealed that increased age is associated with lower levels of performance on a wide variety of cognitive measures. Differences of this type have been reported in studies in which relatively small samples of college students were compared with adults in their 60s and 70s on single variables, and in larger projects involving hundreds of adults ranging from 18 to 100 years of age and comparisons of multiple variables.

Typical patterns from past research can be illustrated with results from a number of studies conducted in my laboratory. Similar relations between age and performance have been reported for many variables, and thus the trends can be illustrated with four variables representing episodic memory (paired associates), perceptual reasoning (spatial relations), perceptual speed (Wechsler Adult Intelligence Scale, WAIS, Digit Symbol test), and word knowledge (WAIS Vocabulary test). Figure 1 portrays the means of these four variables as a function of age for samples of between 1,200 and 2,500 individuals each. To facilitate comparisons across variables, the measures from different tasks have been converted to standard deviation units based on the scores from the entire sample. As the figure shows, the cross-sectional age differences on these variables begin when adults are in their 20s or 30s, and the decline that begins at that time possibly accelerates around age 50. The primary exception to this pattern is for variables with a large knowledge component, such as measures of vocabulary. With these variables, the trend is for an increase until about age 50 or 60, followed by a gradual decline. The existence of different age trends for different variables has led to an important distinction between two types of cognition. Many labels have been proposed for the two types, such as fluid and crystallized, but the terms *process* and *product* may be the most descriptive. That is, process measures of intelligence reflect the efficiency of processing at the time of assessment, and product measures of intelligence reflect the cumulative products of processing carried out in the past.

Almost as soon as age-related differences in mean level of performance were found, it was recognized that there is also substantial variability in

From *Perspectives on Psychological Science*, vol. 1, no. 1, 2006, pp. 68–77, 79, 81–82, 84. Copyright © 2006 by Association for Psychological Science (formerly American Psychological Society). Reprinted by permission. Reference omitted.

Figure 1

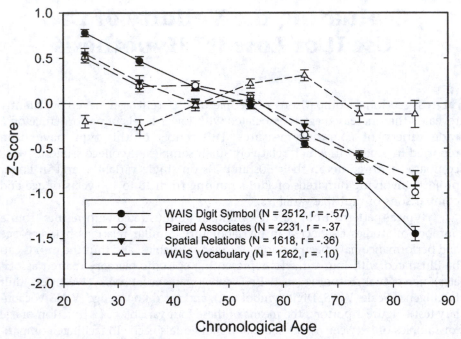

Means (and Standard Errors) of Z Scores for Four Cognitive Variables as a Function of Age

WAIS = Wechsler Adult Intelligence Scale.

cognitive performance among individuals at every age. Figure 2 illustrates this type of variability with data from a paired-associates task in which participants viewed six pairs of unrelated words and later attempted to recall the second member of each pair when presented with the first member. The figure portrays the distribution of paired-associates scores for 358 adults between 60 and 69 years of age. The graph shows considerable variability among people of nearly the same age, with a few individuals recalling all of the pairs and some individuals recalling none of them.

Quantitative estimates of the variability that is unrelated to age can be obtained from the correlation coefficient relating age to test score. That is, the square of a correlation indicates the proportion of variance that is shared between two variables, and thus 1 minus the squared correlation between age and test score indicates the proportion of variance in performance that is not shared with age. For the three variables in Figure 1 with the strongest correlations with age, between 68% and 87% of the total variance in the scores was not related to age. It is therefore clear that although on average increased age is associated with lower levels of performance on many cognitive tests, there is also substantial variation in performance at each age.

Figure 2

Distribution of Scores on a Paired-associates Memory Test for 358 Adults Between 60 and 69 Years of Age

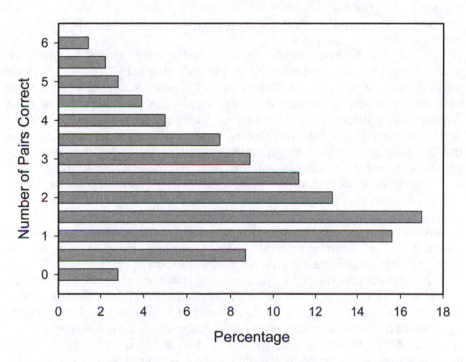

Two key questions in the field of cognitive aging are, what is responsible for this large between-person variation among individuals of nearly the same age, and to what extent does the variability reflect processes related to differential aging? A particularly intriguing possibility is that factors associated with lifestyle, such as the degree of engagement in mentally stimulating activities, contribute to the variation among people at each age, and perhaps also to variation in the rate of mental aging. The idea that lifestyle factors can affect both the level of cognitive functioning and the rate of age-related change in cognitive functioning is obviously very appealing because it implies that individuals can control aspects of their own destiny. Many dimensions of lifestyle have been investigated with respect to their relation to cognitive functioning, but the focus in this article is restricted to mental stimulation, and does not extend to other characteristics, such as diet, physical activity, or amount of social interaction.

The mental-exercise hypothesis was mentioned by the earliest researchers in the field of cognitive aging and it is a prominent theme of many books on aging oriented toward the general public. The view that keeping mentally active will maintain one's level of cognitive functioning, and possibly even prevent cognitive decline and the onset of dementia, is so pervasive in contemporary culture that it is frequently expressed in the "use it or lose it" adage. The wide variety of activities that have been mentioned as offering potential protective benefits includes playing bridge, working on crossword puzzles, learning a foreign language, learning to play a musical instrument, and even shopping. An early proponent of this position went so far as to suggest that to prevent cognitive decline, people should order their lives such that they constantly find themselves in new situations and confronted with novel problems.

A relation between mental exercise and mental fitness is intuitively plausible because it is consistent with the well-established relation between physical exercise and physical fitness, and with neurobiological evidence that new connections may be formed among neurons as a consequence of novel environmental stimulation. The relation also seems to be supported by anecdotal observations that high-functioning older adults often appear to be more intellectually active than lower-functioning older adults. Despite the obvious appeal of the mental-exercise hypothesis, however, the evidence for it has rarely been examined critically, in part because advocates of the hypothesis seldom discuss, or even cite, relevant empirical evidence. A primary goal of this article is to provide such an evaluation of the hypothesis that there is a causal relation between amount of mental activity and rate of mental aging. Because I reviewed much of the early literature relevant to this hypothesis about 15 years ago, the current article emphasizes material not covered in that book.

A fundamental thesis of this review is that the existence of a relation between level of mental activity and level of mental functioning among adults at any given age is, by itself, not very informative about the mental-exercise hypothesis because there are a number of different ways that a relation of this type could be produced. In particular, the relation could occur because, as proposed by the mental-exercise hypothesis, the amount of mental activity throughout one's life contributes to the level of mental ability at later periods in life, but the relation could also originate because the amount of mental activity at any age is at least partially determined by one's prior, and current, level of mental ability. More generally, although it is tempting to attribute some of the variability in cognitive performance apparent at any given age to individual differences in prior rates of age-related change in cognitive abilities, it is important to consider the possibility that much of that variability was present at earlier ages, and may have little or nothing to do with differential aging. (This argument also applies to many discussions of the concept of "successful aging," because before attributing individuals' current status to dynamic processes of aging, it is important to consider their status at earlier ages. Only if there is evidence that people have differed in their rates of aging does it seem appropriate to characterize them as having "aged" successfully, as opposed to having been successful at every stage in their lives.)

One way to distinguish between the two alternatives involves examining the relation between age and mental performance as a function of amount of mental activity. That is, to the extent that mental activity alters the rate of mental aging, amount of mental exercise would be expected to moderate the relations between age and measures of mental functioning. In a longitudinal study, involving comparisons of the same people at different ages, this situation would be manifested in smaller age-related declines (or possibly even larger age-related improvements) among individuals who engage in greater amounts of mental activity. In cross-sectional comparisons, based on people of different ages examined at the same point in time, the differences in mental performance between individuals with different amounts of mentally stimulating activity would be expected to become progressively larger with increased age as the effects of differential mental activity accumulate over time.

This prediction, which can be designated the *differential-preservation* hypothesis because the degree to which performance is preserved across increasing age is postulated to differ according to level of mental activity is portrayed in the left panel of Figure 3. Notice that individuals with greater amounts of mental stimulation are postulated to have less negative (or more positive) relations between age and level of performance on cognitive tasks. However, the right panel of Figure 3 portrays an alternative possibility that needs to be considered, namely, that people who are more mentally active are likely to have had high levels of cognitive functioning throughout their lives. According to this proposal, the differences in performance are preserved across all of adulthood, so it has been termed the *preserved-differentiation* hypothesis.

The key difference between these two perspectives is that the differential-preservation hypothesis views mental activity as a factor that protects against age-related decline in mental ability, whereas the preserved-differentiation hypothesis views an individual's current level of mental activity as at least partly a manifestation of his or her prior level of mental ability. The distinction can be elaborated by considering how each perspective would explain a finding that people who play bridge tend to have somewhat higher levels of cognitive functioning than people who do not play bridge. The differential-preservation

Figure 3

Schematic Representation of Two Interpretations of Variability at a Given Age. The Left Panel Portrays the Differential-preservation Perspective, and the Right Panel Portrays the Preserved-differentiation Perspective. The Ellipses Indicate that the Two Perspectives Cannot be Distinguished on the Basis of a Comparison of Adults within a Narrow Age Range.

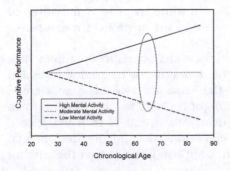 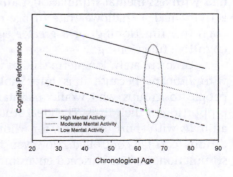

hypothesis would suggest that playing bridge builds mental muscle that prevents atrophy of mental ability, whereas the preserved-differentiation hypothesis would suggest that a minimum level of mental strength is needed for individuals of any age to be capable of playing bridge.

Investigating the Mental-Exercise Hypothesis

It is well recognized that the ideal method of investigating a causal hypothesis is a randomized clinical trial in which one group of individuals is assigned to the experimental treatment (in this case, mental exercise) and another group is assigned to a suitable control activity, and both groups are monitored to determine the effects of the intervention on one or more critical outcome variables. Note that if the outcome of interest is the rate of mental aging, then the individuals must be followed long enough to determine whether the experimental and control groups differ in the relations between age and the relevant measures of mental functioning. Effects immediately after an intervention can be interesting and important, but they are not necessarily informative about age-related changes in mental ability that occur over a period of years or decades. Because large immediate effects could dissipate rapidly, and small immediate effects could accumulate slowly, long-term monitoring is needed to investigate influences on rates of aging.

The ideal study to investigate the mental-exercise hypothesis would therefore possess three critical characteristics. The first is random assignment of individuals to the experimental and control groups to minimize influences associated with preexisting differences such as initial level of cognitive ability and amount of education. The second characteristic is rigorous control of the treatment in terms of the type and amount of mental exercise. And the third critical characteristic is long-term monitoring of the amount of mentally stimulating activity and the level of cognitive functioning to allow influences on the rate of mental aging to be examined. Several aspects of cognition should be monitored during this phase because mental exercise might have different effects on process and product measures of cognitive functioning. (In fact, there have been several suggestions that lifestyle may have greater influences on knowledge-sensitive product measures than on measures of processing efficiency.) A study with these critical characteristics would provide support for the mental-exercise hypothesis if, compared with individuals with less mental stimulation, individuals with more mentally stimulating activity had a shallower rate of age-related decline in process measures of cognitive functioning, or a greater age-related gain in product measures of cognitive functioning.

Unfortunately, long-term studies with these characteristics are impractical with humans because it is impossible (and unethical) to randomly assign people to groups who would maintain the same lifestyle for a substantial proportion of their lives. The ideal study might be more feasible in nonhuman animals with short life spans, for whom nearly all aspects of their living conditions can be controlled. However, interventions that might affect mental stimulation, such as enriched environments, are also likely to alter the amount or variety of social interaction and physical activity, which makes it difficult to isolate the role of mental stimulation on any effects that might be found.

Another major barrier to implementing the ideal study is that no methods are currently available to accurately evaluate an individual's level of mental stimulation. Amount of physical exercise can be quantified with measures such as metabolic expenditure units, but there is no comparable measure of mental exertion. Subjective ratings of mental workload could be obtained, but they are difficult to compare across people, and at the current time, neurobiological assessments, such as rate of glucose metabolism, are available only with activities that can be performed while the individual is in a neuroimaging scanner. A detailed inventory of all of the activities performed by an individual and the cognitive demands of each activity would be extremely valuable, but, unfortunately, very little information on the range of activities in which people engage is currently available, and even less information on the mental demands of those activities is available.

For the reasons just mentioned, all research relevant to the mental-exercise hypothesis has been based on approximations to the ideal, with each category of research lacking one or more of the critical characteristics. Nevertheless, the various approaches differ in their respective strengths and weaknesses, and thus it is informative to examine the findings from all the approaches to determine whether they converge on a similar conclusion.

Training Interventions

One category of research considered relevant to the mental-exercise hypothesis consists of training studies in which the researcher provides the participant with the relevant mentally stimulating experience. Training studies have the advantage of controlling the amount and type of experience the individual receives, but they have the disadvantage that the amount of experience is greatly limited in breadth and depth relative to the experience typically acquired in an individual's lifetime.

Many of the training studies involving only older adults were apparently motivated to challenge the cliché that old dogs cannot learn new tricks. This view was worth challenging because it was expressed by no less an authority than William James, arguably the most influential American psychologist, in his classic *Principles of Psychology*, in which he stated that

> outside of their own business, the ideas gained by men before they are twenty-five are practically the only ideas they shall have in their lives. They cannot get anything new. Disinterested curiosity is past, the mental grooves and channels set, the power of assimilation gone.

A great deal of research has clearly established that in this respect James was wrong, because there are now many studies indicating that adults of all ages can benefit from experience.

One very impressive training project was conducted in the context of the Seattle Longitudinal Study. The study involved older adults who received 5 hr of training on either series-completion or spatial rotation problems and then took tests on both types of problems immediately after training and again 7 years later. Because the training benefits were ability-specific (e.g., series-completion training led to gains only on series-completion problems and not on spatial rotation problems), the group receiving each type of training can be considered the control group in the comparison testing the effects of the other type of training. For the current purposes, the most relevant results of this project were that the slopes from the immediate posttest to the 7-year follow-up test were very similar for the training and control groups. Although the training altered the level of performance on the trained tasks, and although at least some of the training-induced gains appeared to persist over 7 years, the training intervention apparently had little or no effect on the rate of age-related decline on either the reasoning or the spatial variable.

What is almost certainly the largest cognitive training study conducted with older adults is the ACTIVE (Advanced Cognitive Training for Independent and Vital Elderly) clinical trial. This project involved a total of 2,832 adults between 65 and 94 years of age who were randomly assigned to one of four groups: a no-contact control group and groups receiving 10 sessions of training on memory, reasoning, or speed abilities. All of the participants received the same cognitive assessment at baseline, immediately after the intervention, and again on two annual posttests. The assessment included measures of the trained and untrained cognitive abilities and of outcomes assumed to be relevant to the ability to live independently. . . .

Because of its scope, the ACTIVE project has received considerable attention, but some of the interpretations of the findings have been somewhat misleading. For example, one recent report described the results as demonstrating "reduced cognitive declines after cognitive training", even though the pattern apparent . . . is actually more consistent with the training groups experiencing accelerated declines relative to the control groups. Because the data were collected over a relatively short interval, this pattern likely reflects a loss of the training benefits rather than a faster rate of mental aging, but it is nevertheless inaccurate to claim on the basis of the available results that the training reduced the rate of age-related cognitive decline. . . .

These studies seem to suggest, therefore, that rather than slowing the rate of aging, exercise might actually accelerate the rate of physical aging.

The critical question in the current context is therefore not the magnitude, nor the durability, of training effects, but rather the influence of the relevant experience on the rate of change in measures of cognitive functioning over time. The mental-exercise hypothesis would be supported only if there was a smaller age-related decline in the relevant measure of cognitive performance over time in the training group than in the control group, such that differences between the groups increased as a function of age. Failure to appreciate this point has led to confusion regarding the relation between the finding of immediate benefits of an intervention and causes of age-related cognitive decline. For example, Kramer and Willis claimed that "age-related decline in cognition can sometimes be reduced through experience, cognitive training, and other interventions such as fitness training". However, this assertion of a connection between the short-term intervention findings and age-related decline in cognition may be too strong because Kramer and Willis did not mention any studies that monitored the relation of age to cognition over a period of decades to determine whether there were any effects on rate of decline.

Comparisons of Preexisting Groups

Most of the remaining research relevant to the mental-exercise hypothesis has involved comparisons of people of different ages who are assumed to vary in their amount of cognitively stimulating activity. Research of this type has the advantage that relations between age and measures of mental functioning can be examined across a wide age range in individuals with different levels of mental activity. However, the lack of control over the "treatment" means that there could be variation in the nature and amount of relevant activity, and may differ in characteristics other than level of mental activity. Nevertheless, this type of research can still be used to examine the critical prediction of the mental exercise hypothesis, namely, differential aging in the form of an interactive effect of age and amount of mental activity on measures of cognitive performance.

There are two categories of nonexperimental research relevant to the mental-exercise hypothesis. One category consists of studies of people from special groups who are assumed to differ from other people in the amount and type of mental activity they engage in. The other major category consists of studies in which people are administered questionnaires to evaluate their level of mental activity.

Special Groups

Experts
A particularly interesting special group consists of experts in domains such as chess, music, or Go. By definition, experts have a very high level of performance in a particular domain, and that level of performance is assumed to be largely achieved by extensive practice and not simply innate talent. Because of experts' extensive experience, it is natural to ask whether they differ from nonexperts with respect to the effects of aging on performance within their domain.

Before attempting to address this question, it is important to distinguish between experts, who are defined on the basis of their very high level of performance in a specific domain, and people who merely have considerable experience with an activity. From the current perspective, only a small number of people should be considered experts, and thus research based on people categorized according to their amount of experience, regardless of their level of skill in a domain, is examined in a later section.

Chess is the most frequently studied domain of expertise because of the availability of an objective measure of skill based on performance in competitions. The most commonly used measure of chess proficiency is the Elo score, which takes into consideration the quality of a player's opponents, as well as the player's success rate in competitions. A plausible prediction from the mental-exercise hypothesis is that the relation between age and chess performance among highly skilled chess players would not exhibit the same type of age-related declines found with other measures of cognitive functioning because these players continue to engage in mentally stimulating activity.

Figure 4 portrays results from two types of comparisons relevant to this prediction. The cross-sectional data are based on 46,888 rated players whose birth dates were included in the International Chess Association (FIDE) file as of January 2005, and the longitudinal data are based on 14 masters whose ratings between the ages of 21 and 60 were reported by Elo. The vertical scales for the two comparisons are different, and thus it is not possible to compare the absolute level of performance across the two functions. Nevertheless, it is clear that the relation between age and performance is qualitatively similar in the cross-sectional data of competitive players and in the longitudinal data of very elite players. At least in the field of chess, therefore, it appears that relevant measures of cognitive functioning decline with increased age even among experts in the domain. . . .

The little information that is available about the relations between age and expert performance in the domain of chess suggests that age-related

Figure 4

Chess Performance as a Function of Age in a Large Cross-sectional Sample of Rated Players and in a Small Longitudinal Sample of Chess Masters. Note that the Cross-sectional Relations (Filled Circles) Refer to the Left Vertical Axis, and the Longitudinal Age Relations (Open Circles) Refer to the Right Vertical Axis.

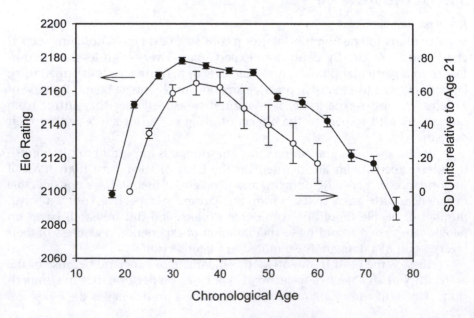

declines are often found among experts even in their specialized domains. In a discussion of age and expertise, Ericsson claimed, "Much of the decline in performance attributed to aging results from reduced levels of deliberate practice among older individuals". The evidence relevant to this speculation is still quite limited, but if it does turn out to be true, it would then raise the question of why so many people reduce their level of activity as they get older. Are the incentives to excel no longer as attractive, or is the activity more demanding because of age-related declines in relevant cognitive abilities? It is not very satisfying to attribute the phenomenon of age-related cognitive decline to a reduction in level of activity without explaining what is responsible for that reduction.

Occupational Groups

Another special group relevant to the mental-exercise hypothesis consists of people in particular occupations, because members of different occupations are assumed to vary in the amount of specific types of mental activity they engage in. There has been considerable interest in the age-cognition relations among academics, because professors like to believe that they live in a constant state of mental stimulation, and therefore if the mental-exercise hypothesis is correct, they might be able to look forward to less pronounced age-related declines in cognitive functioning than people in less stimulating occupations. Unfortunately, most of the empirical evidence has not been consistent with this optimistic expectation.

One of the earliest, and still among the most impressive, studies involving college professors was reported by Sward. Not only did he match young and old professors on many characteristics, but he administered a broad variety of cognitive tasks of which only a few had time limits. In this sample of college professors, Sward found age differences in reasoning, memory, and speed that were very similar to those reported in other types of samples. Numerous studies since Sward's have also found typical patterns of age-related differences in samples of college professors. The project by Christensen and her colleagues is particularly noteworthy because although many of the older academics in this project were officially retired, a substantial proportion reported that they were still engaged in scholarly work for 60 hr a week or more. Nevertheless, significant age-related differences in measures of cognitive functioning were reported among the academics in both cross-sectional and longitudinal comparisons. . . .

Change in Work and Leisure Activities

Schooler and his colleagues have published a number of reports on a unique project in which the same individuals were interviewed about work and leisure activities, and assessed for "intellectual flexibility," in 1964, 1974, and 1994. The availability of longitudinal data allowed simultaneous estimates of the influence of mentally demanding activity on intellectual flexibility and of the influence of intellectual flexibility on activity. The major finding in each study was that the relations are reciprocal, such that higher intellectual flexibility appears to contribute to higher levels of mentally stimulating activity, and greater amounts of mentally stimulating activity appear to contribute to higher levels of intellectual flexibility.

These results have been interpreted as supporting the mental-exercise hypothesis because engaging in intellectually demanding activities seems to have an effect on level of cognitive functioning. However, although these results clearly could be relevant to the hypothesis, interpreting them is complicated by the unusual measure of cognitive functioning used in this project. The measure of intellectual flexibility was based on five variables, three measurements derived from ratings by the examiner and two objective measurements. However, unlike most measures of process cognition, the intellectual-flexibility measure was not significantly related to age in 1964 ($r = .00$), 1974 ($r = -.01$), or 1994 ($r = .04$), and therefore it may not reflect the same phenomenon of mental aging apparent with more traditional cognitive measures. Another complication is that the patterns of longitudinal change from 1964 to 1994 differed across the individual variables used to form the intellectual-flexibility factor, as there were large declines in the two objectively measured variables, but substantial increases in the three rating variables. This overall pattern raises the possibility that the meaning of the composite intellectual-flexibility variable formed by combining the individual variables may have changed from one measurement occasion to the next, and that some of what was interpreted as a change in intellectual flexibility may have actually reflected a change in what was being assessed.

Schooler and his colleagues were sensitive to some of these measurement concerns, and they reported a moderately high correlation between the intellectual-flexibility measure and a composite measure based on a combination of more traditional cognitive measures. However, the correlations between the variables belonging to the intellectual-flexibility factor and the correlations between the variables belonging to the general cognitive factor were relatively weak, and thus it is difficult to determine exactly what each factor represents.

For the reasons just mentioned, it is probably premature to summarize the findings of this project, as Fillit et al. did, by stating that "complex intellectual work increases the cognitive functioning of older workers". Schooler's project is extremely intriguing, but the available results are quite complex, and the extent to which they should be considered as providing support for the mental-exercise hypothesis is not yet clear. . . .

General Activity Questionnaires

The most frequently used approach to investigate the mental-exercise hypothesis has consisted of asking people questions about their amount of engagement in different types of activities assumed to be mentally stimulating, and then examining relations between each individual's inferred level of mental activity and his or her performance on a variety of measures of cognitive functioning. Although many questionnaires have been designed to assess level of mental activity, this category of research has shown little consistency in assessment, or in the outcome variables and analytical methods used. Because each of these factors could influence results, they need to be considered when evaluating these studies. . . .

To the extent that self-reports of activities provide valid assessments of an individual's lifestyle, the results suggest that people who engage in high amounts of cognitively stimulating activities exhibit the same relation between age and performance on a variety of cognitive tasks as do people who engage in low amounts of cognitively stimulating activities. Only with the knowledge measure of vocabulary is there any evidence for the mental-exercise hypothesis, and that may simply reflect differential opportunities to acquire relevant information rather than differential preservation of mental ability.

Although studies based on self-reports of activity constitute the largest category of research considered relevant to the mental-exercise hypothesis, the results of these studies may be distorted because of positive self-presentation or desirability bias, or because the relevant information cannot be retrieved from memory or is inaccessible for other reasons. One indication that the self-report estimates are not always accurate is that when asked to estimate the durations of the 22 activities in the new self-report activity questionnaire several individuals reported a total of more than 168 hr per week. Even if one allows for the possibility that some activities might be performed concurrently, it is unlikely that all of the time estimates were realistic.

Because many of the studies with self-report questionnaires involved only older adults, they were limited to examining relations between mental activity and mental performance over a restricted age range. These studies may therefore have had low power to test the primary prediction of the mental-exercise hypothesis—that the rate of age-related cognitive change varies according to the individual's level of mental activity.

Another major limitation of this category of research is that there has been little consistency in the methods used to assess either mental activity or mental performance, or in the analytical procedures used to examine the relationship. As a consequence, few true replications have been reported, and there is a risk that some of the published findings are a positively selected subset of the results from studies with mixed outcomes. . . .

Conclusion

There have been many reports of a significant positive association between engagement in mentally stimulating activity and level of cognitive performance. There is also convincing evidence that cognitive training and other interventions can have an immediate beneficial effect on the level of performance in the trained tasks in adults of all ages. Results such as these have led to widespread acceptance of the view that continued engagement in mentally stimulating activities will maintain one's cognitive abilities, and may also prevent age-related cognitive decline.

Unfortunately, the research reviewed here is not very consistent with this optimistic interpretation. A variety of different types of findings have been interpreted as supporting the mental-exercise hypothesis, but there are very few examples of what I have argued is the most convincing type of evidence—demonstration that the differences in mental performance associated with varying levels of mental exercise increase with increased age. . . .

Given what appears to be a general lack of empirical support, it is worth considering why the mental-exercise hypothesis seems to be so well accepted. Among the likely reasons are a plethora of anecdotal observations, what seems to be a compelling analogy to the effects of physical exercise on physical functioning, and a commitment to the assumption that humans can exert control over their own destiny by choice of lifestyle. Still another reason for an optimistic perspective on the role of mental exercise may be related to a particular conceptualization of mental functioning in which there is some absolute threshold for functioning, perhaps related to a diagnosis of dementia or ability to live independently. If a threshold of this type exists, then anything, perhaps including increased mental activity, that will increase the distance of one's level of functioning from that threshold will likely prolong the interval until the critical level of performance is reached. For example, if an individual is 6 units away from the threshold and is declining at a rate of 3 units per year, then he or she will reach the threshold in 2 years. However, if the individual's level of functioning could be increased by 3 points, then even without affecting the rate of age-related decline, the time until the threshold is reached will be increased from 2 to 3 years. Under these circumstances, therefore, an increase in the individual's level of functioning would have the effect of slowing the progression to the critical level of functioning. Although an outcome of this type would not be considered evidence for the mental-exercise hypothesis according to the argument developed here, the practical benefits of this kind of finding could be enormous and might lead to an understandable lack of concern about the theoretical issue of whether there is an effect on the rate of age-related change.

Despite frequent assertions of the mental-exercise hypothesis, its intuitive plausibility, and an understandably strong desire to believe that it is true, the results and interpretations discussed here suggest that there is currently little scientific evidence that differential engagement in mentally stimulating activities alters the rate of mental aging. All of the available research has limitations, and thus it is conceivable that future studies that overcome some of the weaknesses will yield more positive results. Although my professional opinion is that at the present time the mental-exercise hypothesis is more of an optimistic hope than an empirical reality, my personal recommendation is that people should behave as though it were true. That is, people should continue to engage in mentally stimulating activities because even if there is not yet evidence that it has benefi-cial effects in slowing the rate of age-related decline in cognitive functioning, there is no evidence that it has any harmful effects, the activities are often enjoyable and thus may contribute to a higher quality of life, and engagement in cognitively demanding activities serves as an existence proof—if you can still do it, then you know that you have not yet lost it.

Carmi Schooler

 **NO**

Use It—and Keep It, Longer, Probably: A Reply to Salthouse (2006)

In his review article, Salthouse argued that there "appears to be a general lack of empirical support" for the *use-it-or-lose-it* hypothesis regarding mental exercise and mental aging. Here, I argue against his conclusion in three ways. First, citing both already published and currently in-press findings, I show that the long-term longitudinal study with which I have been involved provides more substantial proof of, and corroborating evidence for, the use-it-or-lose-it hypothesis than Salthouse admitted. Second, I review other relevant experimental and nonexperimental studies and conclude that their findings are not as antithetical to the use-it-or-lose-it hypothesis as Salthouse maintained. Third, I argue that Salthouse set the bar of proof too high by postulating that for a study to provide proof of the use-it-or-lose-it hypothesis, its findings must contain a significant interaction indicating that doing some form of "mental exercise" decreases the rate of decline more for older than for younger individuals. A more appropriate criterion would be whether doing such mental exercise increases the likelihood that a given individual's level of cognitive functioning will be better than if he or she had not done such exercise and will continue to be better for a consequential period of time.

In what follows, I critique Salthouse's criticisms and concerns about (a) the National Institute of Mental Health's Section on Socio-Environmental Studies' (SSES) long-term longitudinal survey research program, (b) other relevant nonexperimental research, and (c) experimental-design-based studies. I conclude by summarizing the arguments against Salthouse's rejection of the use-it-or-lose-it hypothesis.

Salthouse's Criticisms of the SSES Longitudinal Survey Research Program

A major goal of the SSES longitudinal research program has been to disentangle the effects of cognitively demanding environments on psychological functioning from the selection effects of psychological variables on individuals' environments. To do this, we have used reciprocal-effects structural equation

From *Perspectives on Psychological Science*, vol. 2, no. 1, 2007, pp. 24–28. Copyright © 2007 by Association for Psychological Science (formerly American Psychological Society). Reprinted by permission. References omitted.

modeling (SEM) to simultaneously estimate the psychological effects of the environmental conditions in question on the person and of the person's characteristics on the likelihood that he or she will be subjected to these environmental conditions. Our findings indicate that although individuals with relatively high levels of cognitive functioning are more likely than others to be selected into cognitively demanding environments, the reciprocal effect also holds: Exposure to such environments, regardless of age, leads to better cognitive functioning. Using longitudinal data and SEM, we have shown that these findings hold true for paid work and leisure-time activities and have recently extended these longitudinal findings to women's and men's housework. If anything, positive effects of complex environments are greater for older than for younger people.

Salthouse expressed several significant reservations about our findings. His primary reservation was that our measure of intellectual functioning is apparently not negatively related to age and that, consequently, we may not be measuring a type of intellectual functioning relevant to the mental-exercise-and-aging hypothesis.

Salthouse was correct that our correlations between age and intellectual functioning in 1964, 1974, and 1994–1995 were very low. It should be noted, however, that these correlations were for a select subsample—men who were working at all three time points ($n = 166$). It should also be noted that the tables in that article were based on regression factor scores, which, because they do not fully account for measurement error, tend to underestimate true correlations.

Elsewhere we have provided SEM-based estimated correlations (i.e., correlations that do take measurement error into account) separately for those respondents (men and women combined) who were and were and not working in 1974. Among those who were not working in 1974 ($n = 190$), the correlation between age and 1994–1995 intellectual flexibility (IF) was $-.27$ ($p < .001$); the correlation between age and 1974 IF was $-.16$ ($p < .03$). Among those who were working in 1974 ($n = 516$), the parallel correlations were $-.20$ ($p < .0001$) and .01 (not significant).

The correlations between IF and age for all of the men ($n = 351$) and all of the women ($n = 355$) in the 1994–1995 sample were as follows. For men, the correlation was $-.33$ ($p < .0001$) in 1994–1995 and $-.25$ ($p < .0001$) in 1974. The parallel correlations for women were $-.38$ ($p < .0001$) and $-.22$ ($p < .0001$). Other analyses revealed that in the total population, the correlation between IF and age was $-.34$ ($p < .0001$) in 1994–1995 and $-.22$ ($p < .0001$) in 1974. Thus, in the total sample, as well as among men and women considered separately, there was a clear and significant negative correlation between age and our IF measure.

Taken across all of the various analyses, the correlation between age and IF is reduced to the degree that there is evidence of a relatively continuous work history in the particular subsample being examined. As noted, the correlation between age and IF was very low among the subsample of men selected as working in 1964, 1974, and 1994–1995. It was higher among the subsample of men and women who were not working in 1994–1995 than among the subsample that was. The negative correlations between age and intellectual functioning were distinctly higher when the total sample and the full samples of men and women were considered. It is plausible that these differences may have been due to some combination of the characteristics of those older individuals who stay in the workforce and of the way the cognitive demands of their work affect them. Nevertheless, even if the correlation between age and IF appears to be affected by how subsamples are selected in terms of work history, the negative correlation between age and IF seems to generally hold true. Not only was the negative correlation between age and IF relatively high in the full sample, but the correlations between age and IF tended to be higher the older the sample was at the time IF was measured (e.g., the correlation between age and 1994–1995 IF was higher than that between age and 1974 IF).

In addition, as we have noted, the correlation between our IF measure and a latent factor based on more standard cognitive measures (immediate recall, category fluency, different uses, number series, verbal meaning, identical pictures) is very high ($r = .87$). It is also worth noting, given Salthouse's concerns with age-based interactions, that in Schooler et al., we reported and discussed a difference between the older and younger workers in the effect of substantively complex work on IF—the effect actually being greater for the older than for the younger workers.

Salthouse raised several other concerns about our research methods that are not justified. He stated that "the measure of intellectual flexibility was based on five variables, three measurements derived from ratings by the examiner and two objective measurements." Actually, only one of the indices of the latent IF factor (i.e., interviewer's rating of the respondent's alertness and estimated intelligence) was based on a subjective rating. The answers to the two other questions that Salthouse seems to be referring to as "subjective"—"What are all of the arguments you can think of for or against allowing cigarette commercials on TV?" and "What questions would you consider in deciding which of two locations offers a better business opportunity for opening a hamburger stand?"—were coded by trained coders using relatively objective ratings. For the cigarette-commercial question, the answers were coded in terms of whether the respondent could provide no argument, an argument for or against such cigarette commercials, or arguments for both sides (scores of 1, 2, and 3, respectively). Adequacy of response to the hamburger-stand question was scored according to whether the respondent's answer did not deal with the question, reflected a concern for either potential costs or potential sales, reflected a concern for both costs and sales, or reflected an explicit understanding that profits result from the difference between the two (scores of 1, 2, 3, and 4, respectively). The coding of neither the cigarette-commercial question nor the hamburger-stand question was more subjective or difficult than that used in many standard IQ subtests (e.g., Similarities subtest of the Wechsler Adult Intelligence Scale-Revised).

Salthouse combined all of his doubts to raise

the possibility that the meaning of the composite intellectual-flexibility variable formed by combining the individual variables may have changed from one measurement occasion to the next, and that some of what was interpreted as a change in intellectual flexibility may have actually reflected a change in what was being assessed.

The points discussed earlier address this concern. In addition, it is the case that the analyses reported in Schooler and Mulatu, Schooler et al., and Caplan and Schooler were all based on models in which the factor loadings of the IF indicators were constrained to be equal over time, so that the relative contribution of each indicator to determining the latent factor remained the same across time points. Even when these equality constraints were included in the statistically more conservative full-information SEM approach in which the measurement and causal aspects of the model are estimated simultaneously, we demonstrated a significant and substantial effect ($\beta = .26$) of complex, cognitively demanding work conditions on intellectual functioning.

Salthouse concluded his discussion of the SSES's longitudinal research program's findings by stating that it is "probably premature to summarize the findings of this project . . . by stating that 'complex intellectual work increases the cognitive functioning of older workers' . . . the available results are quite complex, and the extent to which they should be considered as providing support for the mental-exercise hypothesis is not yet clear". I would argue that although many questions remain about who can be helped how, how much, and under which conditions, our findings provide quite strong nonexperimental support for the use-it-or-lose-it mental-exercise hypothesis and its applicability to older people.

Salthouse's Critique of Other Relevant Nonexperimental Research

Although the SSES findings provide the strongest nonexperimental support for the use-it-or-lose-it hypothesis, there have been numerous studies including examples cited by Salthouse, that have shown that people who do, or have a history of having done, more cognitively demanding paid work tend to have higher levels of intellectual functioning than those who do, or have a history of having done, less cognitively demanding work. In addition, numerous studies have shown parallel findings for leisure-time activities. These relationships tend to hold whether one focuses on "normal" cognitive functioning or dementia. These studies should be credited as at least being congruent with the use-it-or-lose-it hypothesis. Nevertheless, Salthouse was correct that these studies provide no fully convincing proof of the hypothesis. This is so because they do not allow one to assess the relative importance of the two potential sources of covariance between the cognitive demands of the activities in question and the intellectual functioning of the people carrying them out: (a) the effects of these activities on the intellectual functioning of the people who carry them out and (b) the likelihood that people having a given level of intellectual functioning are in a position to, or are predisposed to, carry out such cognitively demanding activities.

A further argument that Salthouse used against the applicability of general activity questionnaires is more questionable. Arguing for an essentially subjective measure of cognitive difficulty, he noted, "Some researchers have relied on judges' ratings of cognitive demands. . . . However, because most of these judges were likely of high cognitive ability, they may not have an accurate perception of the difficulty of the activities for lower-ability individuals". Leaving aside the issue that, contrary to Salthouse's implications, it is possible to develop relatively objective coding schemes to rate the cognitive difficulty of various environmental demands (e.g., the U.S. Department of Labor's, 1965, 1977, *Dictionary of Occupational Titles* codes for "complexity" of work with things, data, and people), there is no reason to necessarily define the intellectual demands of the task in question in terms of how complex it seems to the person carrying it out. In fact, the argument can be made that individuals' subjective judgments about how intellectually demanding their environments are do not necessarily represent a reasonably valid estimate of how cognitively complex and demanding their environments actually are. For example, in the SSES sample, someone whose job it was to sort potatoes into grades A, B, C, and so forth, saw this task as intellectually demanding because of the number of decisions required, but this does not mean that the cognitive demand posed by these relatively simple decisions represents the level of cognitive challenge (i.e., proximal developmental scaffold) that could lead that individual to better cognitive functioning.

Salthouse's Empirical and Theoretical Critique of Experimental-Design-Based Studies

Salthouse's strong doubts about the existence of studies supporting the use-it-or-lose-it hypothesis extend beyond those based on nonexperimental surveys or comparisons of preexisting groups to include those that follow essentially experimental designs. His doubts that experimental studies support the use-it-or-lose-it hypothesis rest on two bases: empirical and theoritical. His empirical concerns stem from what he sees as the lack of generalizability from trained to untrained skills. However, given that psychologists have spent a fair amount of time and effort attempting to isolate theoretically and empirically independent psychological processes, it should not be too great a surprise that research designs that tend to focus on improving a carefully delimited cognitive function do not necessarily show much transfer or generalization to other functions. Nor is improvement in an even relatively delimited area of functioning either a useless functional gain or a clinching disproof of the use-it-or-lose-it hypothesis. Nevertheless, one could argue that cognitive interventions should include training in transferring the skills learned to a variety of tasks. Furthermore, given that many daily activities involve the functional integration of relatively independent psychological processes it would seem desirable for cognitive-intervention protocols to include training in selecting from the armamentarium of cognitive processes those processes that can be most effectively integrated and brought to bear to deal with the problem at hand.

Interestingly, recent experimental studies that have provided evidence of generalization in older adults have focused on providing training applicable to a variety of tasks. They have done so either by promoting a particular strategy that is applicable in diverse tasks or by training people in a particular skill over a multiplicity of activities. Following the former approach, in an experiment using word-series, letter-series, and letter–sets tasks, Saczynaski, Margrett, and Willis found that training older individuals in inductive reasoning led them to use effective strategies (e.g., underlining repeated letters or words in a series) that, in turn, significantly improved performance on all three tasks. The improvement on the letter-series and letter-sets tasks remained significant when assessed in a 3-month posttest. In another experiment with older adults, Dunlosky, Kubat-Silman, and Hertzog found that "training a monitoring skill— self-testing—can improve older adults' learning".

Following the approach of directly training people in a particular skill— speed of processing—through training sessions involving different types of tasks with different demands, Edwards et al. found that, although their speed-of-processing training did not generalize to psychometric measures of other cognitive domains, the training improved the performance of older adults not only on the Useful Field of View measure, which tests rapidity of processing multiple stimuli across the visual field, but also on the Timed Instrumental Activities of Daily Living test, which involves laboratory measurement of timed tasks that emulate instrumental activities of daily living. The gains appear to be particularly reliable for individuals with initial processing-speed or processing difficulties. Roenker, Cissell, Ball, Wadley, and Edwards reported generally similar findings for the effect of the computerized speed-of-processing training protocol on driving. They found that although speed-of-processing training did not affect performance on a variety of generally used cognitive tests (e.g., Trails A and B or Stroop), such training not only positively affected function on a laboratory test constructed to mimic performance in real-life situations (i.e., the Road Sign Test administered in a driving simulator, but also improved actual driving).

Evidence for the potentially relatively long-lasting effects of cognitive training is provided by a study conducted by the ACTIVE (Advanced Cognitive Training for Independent and Vital Elderly) Study Group. Participants were randomly assigned to one of four groups: a control group and three experimental groups. Each of the experimental groups received 10 sessions of group training in one area of cognitive functioning (i.e., memory, reasoning, or speed of processing). Although the significant training effects were limited to the cognitive function trained and did not seem to carry over to the measures of everyday function used, they endured through the 2-year follow-up—the effects being stronger among participants who received four-session booster training after 11 months than among those who received no booster training. The training effects were equal in magnitude to the amount of decline expected over 7- to 14-year intervals in elderly persons without dementia. As the authors observed, the notable ceiling effects due to the relatively high initial level of functioning of the experimental and control participants, taken together with the powerful practice effects resulting from the control subjects' 5 hr of practice on cognitive testing, may explain why there were no significant differences between the experimental and control groups in generalization to the daily-functioning measures.

The likelihood of finding further experimental evidence of some forms of learning generalization in older adults is increased by the findings of the SSES survey research program. As Ceci noted, the program's findings based on its 1964 and 1974 survey waves provided as strong evidence as then existed that a range of cognitive skills and lessons learned in meeting the cognitive demands of one's environment can be transferred to meeting the cognitive demands of other environments. As described earlier, further findings, based on analyses including the data from the1994–1995 survey wave, indicate that such transfer occurs at least as much in older as in younger adults.

Salthouse's strongest doubts about whether the experimental studies provide acceptable evidence for the use-it-or-lose-it hypothesis were essentially based on the same theoretical concerns as were his doubts about almost all of the other types of studies he discussed—the lack of a significant interaction indicating that the given intervention or experience reduces the rate of decline more for older than younger individuals. It is not as though Salthouse did not see the potential benefits of mental (or physical) exercise very clearly. As he stated:

> Still another reason for an optimistic perspective on the role of mental exercise may be related to a particular conceptualization of mental functioning in which there is some absolute threshold for functioning. . . . If a threshold of this type exists, then anything, perhaps including increased mental activity, that will increase the distance of one's level of functioning from that threshold will likely prolong the interval until the critical level of performance is reached. For example, if an individual is 6 units away from the threshold and is declining at a rate of 3 units per year, then he or she will reach the threshold in 2 years. However, if the individual's level of functioning could be increased by 3 points, then even without affecting the rate of age-related decline, the time until the threshold is reached will be increased from 2 to 3 years. Under these circumstances, therefore, an increase in the individual's level of functioning would have the effect of slowing the progression to the critical level of functioning. Although an out-come of this type would not be considered evidence for the mental-exercise hypothesis according to the argument developed here, the practical benefits of this kind of finding could be enormous and might lead to an understandable lack of concern about the theoretical issue of whether there is an effect on the rate of age-related change.

More generally, it seems that if one spate of exercise increases an older person's level of intellectual functioning so that it would take that individual longer to decline to a given lower level of intellectual functioning, then, assuming that the asymptote of possible exercise-based improvement has not been reached, two exercise spates would mean it would take that individual even longer to reach that lower level than if he or she had engaged in only one spate of exercise.

The same logic that suggests that two spates of exercise would be better than one spate also suggests that three spates would be better than two spates. One must again bear in mind the possibility of reaching an asymptote where further exercise does not result in an improvement of function. Nevertheless, it seems reasonable to ask whether continuous exercise, with its possibly continuous bumping up of the individual's level if cognitive functioning, would eventually lead to a slowing of that individual's rate of decline compared with what it would have been had that individual not done the exercise. Long-term experimental studies testing this possibility have not been carried out. The findings of the longitudinal SSES studies on the cognitive effects of carrying out cognitively demanding paid work, housework, and leisure-time activities suggest that mental exercise does improve cognitive functioning. Salthouse's own data also suggest that carrying out relatively complex tasks may reduce the slope of cognitive decline. In the analysis of crossword-puzzle experience that he reported, at the youngest age (around 25 years), the reasoning ability of individuals in the lowest quartile of crossword-puzzle experience. At the oldest age (around 75 years), individuals in the highest quartile if crossword-puzzle experience showed significantly greater levels of reasoning ability than those in the lowest quartile, and, in fact, the relative advantage of being in the highest quartile did seem to increase with age. Of course, older individuals with higher reasoning ability may be more likely to do crossword puzzles than those with lower reasoning ability, and one cannot specify how much such self-selection may have affected the results. Nevertheless, Salthouse's findings are congruent with the possibility that mental exercise can slow the rate of mental decline.

Conclusions

In common usage, the saying "use it or lose it" does not necessarily imply a change in rate of decline. All it implies is that people are more likely to "lose it" if they do not "use it." Given that everyone will "lose it" in the end, at issue is whether a given person is likely to function at a higher cognitive level for a longer period of time if he or she exercises mentally (or physically). One cannot say that this is always the case, and most likely it is not. Nor can one confidently specify the extent to which the benefits of various particular types of mental exercise generalize across different types of cognitive functions. Nevertheless, the weight of the experimental and nonexperimental evidence strongly suggests that the hypothesis is generally correct—if a given person exercises mentally, that person is likely to function to some degree better for longer than if he or she had not done that exercise. Furthermore, taken together with all of the other evidence discussed here, even Salthouse's crossword-puzzle findings suggest that it is at the very least premature, and most probably wrong, to rule out, as Salthouse did, "the idea that the rate of mental aging is moderated by amount of mental activity."

Salthouse did recommend that "people should continue to engage in mentally stimulating activities because . . . there is no evidence that it has any harmful effects, . . . and [it] may contribute to a higher quality of life". In this he was correct, but the reasons for engaging in such activities go further. The available evidence distinctly points to the probability that for older individuals, mental exercise has a positive effect both on the level of cognitive functioning and on the probable rate of decline. It remains for further research to determine how much of an effect there is, who can benefit from it, and exactly which kinds of activities have specific kinds of effects. Even if the whole story is not yet known, in regard to cognitive function, at some level and to some degree, "using" it often delays the eventuality of "losing" it.

Acknowledgments. This article is dedicated to my mother, Eva Schooler (1908–), still an intrepid reader of the *New York Times*. I would like to thank Leslie J. Caplan for her critical readings of earlier versions of and editorial contributions to this article.

CHALLENGE QUESTIONS

Are Brain Exercises Unhelpful in Preventing Cognitive Decline in Old Age?

- Both sides of this controversy point out the difficulty in conclusively knowing that mental exercises make a difference beyond normal life experiences. Why is this such a difficult area to research, and what kind of evidence would be most convincing to you?
- Both authors acknowledge that the "use it or lose it" hypothesis has an intuitive appeal. Why is it so appealing to us, and what are the implications for our broader understanding of lifespan development?
- Salthouse points out that much of the research supporting the value of mental exercise does not clearly establish causality. Why not? What is the problem with simply finding that being more intellectually active is correlated with better cognitive functioning?
- Schooler thinks "use it or lose it" is an important principle, even if it does not mean that older adults can completely eliminate cognitive decline in old age. Does that mean that the loss of intellectual functioning is an inevitable part of old age?

Suggested Readings

H. Christensen, A. Henderson, K. Griffiths, and C. Levings, "Does Ageing Inevitably Lead to Declines in Cognitive Performance? A Longitudinal Study of Elite Academics," *Personality and Individual Differences* (July 1997)

D. Hultsch, C. Hertzog, B. Small, and R. Dixon, "Use It or Lose It: Engaged Lifestyle as a Buffer of Cognitive Decline in Aging?" *Psychology and Aging* (June 1999)

A. Kramer and S. Willis, "Enhancing the Cognitive Vitality of Older Adults," *Current Directions in Psychological Science* (October 2002)

T. Salthouse, "Reply to Schooler: Consistent Is Not Conclusive," *Perspectives on Psychological Science* (March 2007)

K. Schaie, Developmental Influences on Adult Intelligence: The Seattle Longitudinal Study (Oxford University Press, 2005)

C. Schooler and M. Mulatu, "The Reciprocal Effects of Leisure Time Activities and Intellectual Functioning in Older People: A Longitudinal Analysis," *Psychology and Aging* (September 2001)

E. Singer, "Exercising the Brain," *Technology Review* (November 2005)

ISSUE 20

Should the Terminally Ill Be Able to Have Physicians Help Them Die?

YES: Richard T. Hull, from "The Case for Physician-Assisted Suicide," *Free Inquiry* (Spring 2003)

NO: Margaret A. Somerville, from "The Case against Euthanasia and Physician-Assisted Suicide," *Free Inquiry* (Spring 2003)

ISSUE SUMMARY

YES: Philosopher Richard T. Hull claims that allowing physician-assisted suicide will appropriately give control over dying to patients and families rather than medical professionals.

NO: Ethicist Margaret Somerville instead asserts that allowing euthanasia oversimplifies the complex issues at the end of life, and allows people to ignore the imperative of providing appropriate care.

Although the end of life is inevitable, it is rarely simple. For those concerned with lifespan development the end of life is embedded with complicated meanings and values that reflect broader attitudes toward human life. These meanings and values are starkly evident in the debate about physician-assisted suicide, which has been intermittently sparked by maneuvering about the legality of allowing doctors to help end a life. The most prominent example is the state of Oregon's "death with dignity" law, which was first passed in 1994 but has been a source of long-running controversy.

While there are important and complicated legal issues surrounding laws such as Oregon's "death with dignity," such laws also raise important questions for scholars interested in lifespan development. The end of life has always had important symbolic meaning, but has become more contentious with advanced technology that allows for prolonged life in ways distinct through human history. For much of the twentieth century, scholars focused primarily about how to prolong life, rather than focusing on what the possibility of technologically prolonging life meant to individuals. In her famous 1969 book *On Death and Dying*, however, Elisabeth Kübler-Ross brought widespread attention to death as a meaningful psychological process. Though Kübler-Ross's specific ideas have since proved controversial in their own right, they have led to important thinking about what qualifies as a "good death."

Many scholars consider a central element for a "good death" to be a situation where an individual is able to die with a sense of the dignity that comes from having some control. In his article, philosopher Richard T. Hull argues that such dignity is best accommodated by making physician-assisted suicide a legal option. As he has watched the debate about physician-assisted suicide, Hull has seen medical professionals becoming more attuned to the needs of those who are dying. He feels that people at the end of life deserve to have their needs met, and that giving them the power to choose the way they will die is the best method toward that end.

Ethicist Margaret A. Somerville, on the other hand, asserts that physician-assisted suicide is profoundly disrespectful to the meaning of death. She asserts that allowing physicians to actively assist people in death goes against any version of civilized morality, and holds dangerous implications for a just society. Rather than giving power to dying patients, Somerville argues that physician-assisted suicide takes away the moral authority that comes with being responsible for ethical care. Her perspective provides an intriguing endpoint for this book because it points out the interesting ways in which our attitudes toward death reflect our broader perspectives on the meaning of life.

POINT	COUNTERPOINT
• Allowing physician-assisted suicide forces the medical community to attend appropriately to pain management at the end of life.	• It is wrong to kill someone no matter the circumstances.
• Without choices about how to die, people at the end of life are left without any power for self-determination and humanity.	• Legalizing physician-assisted suicide has broad and dangerous social implications.
• There has been inadequate management of suffering for years.	• Decisions surrounding death are symbolic of how we think about the importance of human life, and as such must be cautious and respectful rather than technologically efficient.
• There are many cases of people choosing to die with honor, such as soldiers in battle, yet we do not condemn that choice.	• Allowing physician-assisted suicide will invite abuse of end of life regulations.
• The fact that physicians can withdraw life support means that we already condone medical professionals being involved with the end of life.	• Prohibiting physician-assisted suicide will erode public trust in doctors.

YES

Richard T. Hull

The Case for Physician-Assisted Suicide

In early 1997, the medical community awaited the U.S. Supreme Court's decision in *Vacco* v. *Quill*. Ultimately the high court would overturn this suit, in which doctors and patients had sought to overturn New York's law prohibiting physician-assisted suicide. But it was fascinating to see how much attention physicians suddenly paid to the question of pain management while they were waiting.

Politicians and physicians alike felt shaken by the fact that the suit had made it as far as the Supreme Court. Medical schools scrutinized their curricula to see how, if at all, effective pain management was taught. The possibility that physician-assisted suicide would be declared as much a patient's right as the withdrawal of life-sustaining technology was a clarion call that medicine needed to "houseclean" its attitudes toward providing adequate narcotics for managing pain.

The ability to demand physician aid in dying is the only resource dying patients have with which to "send a message" (as our public rhetoric is so fond of putting it) to physicians, insurers, and politicians that end-of-life care is inadequate. Far too many patients spend their last days without adequate palliation of pain. Physicians sensitive to their cries hesitate to order adequate narcotics, for fear of scrutiny by state health departments and federal drug agents. Further, many physicians view imminent death as a sign of failure in the eyes of their colleagues, or just refuse to recognize that the seemingly endless variety of tests and procedures available to them can simply translate into a seemingly endless period of dying badly. Faced with all this, the ability to demand—and receive—physician aid in dying may be severely compromised patients' only way to tell caregivers that something inhumane stalks them: the inhumanity of neglect and despair.

Many physicians tell me that they feel it is an affront to suppose that their duty to care extends to a duty to kill or assist in suicide. If so, is it not even more an affront, as dying patients and their families tell me, to have to beg for increases in pain medication, only to be told that "We don't want to make you an addict, do we?" or that "Doctor's orders are being followed, and Doctor can't be reached to revise them." If apologists for the status quo fear that a slippery slope will lead to voluntary euthanasia, then nonvoluntary euthanasia, the proponents of change already know that we've been on a slippery slope of inadequate management of suffering for decades.

Let's examine some of the stronger arguments against physician-assisted suicide—while keeping in mind that these arguments may not be the deepest reasons some people oppose it. My lingering sense is that the unspoken problem with physician-assisted suicide is that it puts power where opponents don't want it: in the hands of patients and their loved ones. I want to see if there are ways of sorting out who holds the power to choose the time and manner of dying that make sense.

1. Many severely compromised individuals, in their depression, loneliness, loss of normal life, and despair, have asked their physicians to assist them in dying. Yet later (after physicians resisted their requests and others awakened them to alternative opportunities) they have returned to meaningful lives.

No sane advocate of physician-assisted suicide would deny the importance of meeting the demand to die with reluctance and a reflective, thorough examination of alternative options. The likelihood of profound mood swings during therapy makes it imperative to distinguish between a patient's acute anguish of loss and his or her rational dismay at the prospect of long-term descent into the tubes and machines of intensive care.

But note that, in stories like the above, it is the very possibility of legal physician-assisted suicide that empowers patients to draw attention to their suffering and command the resources they need to live on. Patients who cannot demand to die can find their complaints more easily dismissed as "the disease talking" or as weakness of character.

2. Medicine would be transformed for the worse if doctors could legally help patients end their lives. The public would become distrustful, wondering whether physicians were truly committed to saving lives, or if they would stop striving as soon as it became inconvenient.

Doubtless there are physicians who, by want of training or some psychological or moral defect, lack the compassionate sensitivity to hear a demand for aid in dying and act on it with reluctance, only after thorough investigation of the patient's situation. Such physicians should not be empowered to assist patients to die. I would propose that this power be restricted to physicians whose primary training and profession is in pain management and palliation: they are best equipped to ensure that reasonable alternatives to euthanasia and suicide are exhausted. Further, patients' appeals for assisted suicide should be scrutinized by the same institutional ethics committees that already review requests for the suspension of life-sustaining technology as a protection against patient confusion and relatives' greed.

3. Euthanasia and physician-assisted suicide are incompatible with our obligations to respect the human spirit and human life.

When I hear *all* motives for euthanasia and physician-assisted suicide swept so cavalierly into the dustbin labeled Failure to Respect Human Life, I'm prompted to say, "Really? *Always?*" Those same opponents who find physician-assisted suicide appalling will typically excuse, even acclaim, self-sacrifice on behalf of others. A soldier throws himself on a grenade to save his fellows. A pedestrian leaps into the path of a truck to save a child. Firefighters remain in a collapsing building rather than abandon trapped victims. These, too, are decisions to embrace death, yet we leave them to the conscience of the agent. Why tar all examples of euthanasia and physician-assisted suicide with a common brush? Given that we do not have the power to ameliorate every disease and never will, why withhold from individuals who clearly perceive the financial and emotional burdens their dying imposes on loved ones the power to lessen the duration and extent of those burdens, in pursuit of the values they have worked to support throughout their lives?

Consider also that some suffering cannot be relieved by any means while maintaining consciousness. There are individuals, like myself, who regard conscious life as essential to personal identity. I find it nonsensical to maintain that it is profoundly morally *preferable* to be rendered comatose by drugs while awaiting life's "natural end," than to hasten death's arrival while still consciously able to embrace and welcome one's release. If I am irreversibly comatose, "I" am dead; prolongation of "my life" at that point is ghoulish, and I should not be required to undergo such indignity.

Finally the question, "What kind of life is worth living?" is highly personal. There are good reasons patients diagnosed with a wide range of conditions might not wish to live to the natural end of their diseases. How dare politicians and moralists presume to make these final judgments if they don't have to live with the results? Of course, every demand for physician-assisted suicide must be scrutinized, and determined to be fully informed. To withhold aid in dying beyond that point is, first, barbarically cruel. Second, it only increases the risk that individuals determined to end their lives will attempt to do so by nonmedical means, possibly endangering others or further magnifying their own suffering.

4. The time-honored doctrine of double effect permits administering pain-relieving drugs that have the effect of shortening life, provided the intent of the physician is the relief of the pain and not the (foreseen) death of the patient. Isn't that sufficient?

Others may find comfort in the notion that the intention of the agent, not the consequences of his or her action, is the measure of morality. I do not. In any case, preferences among ethical theories are like preferences among religious persuasions: no such preference should be legislated for all citizens. For the thinker who focuses on consequences rather than intentions, the fact that we permit terminal care regimens to shorten life *in any context* shows that the line has already been crossed. The fact that physicians must, at the insistence of the competent patient or the incompetent patient's duly appointed surrogate, withdraw life-sustaining technology shows that physicians *can* assist patient suicides and can perform euthanasia on those fortunate enough to be dependent on machines. It becomes a matter of simple justice—equal protection before the law—to permit the same privileges to other terminal patients. That the U.S. Supreme Court has ruled against this argument did not dissuade the citizens of the State of Oregon from embracing it. States like New York that have turned back such initiatives must bear the shame of having imposed religious majorities' philosophies on all who suffer.

Margaret Somerville

 **NO**

The Case against Euthanasia and Physician-Assisted Suicide

There are two major reasons to oppose euthanasia. One is based on principle: it is wrong for one human to intentionally kill another (except in justified self-defense, or in the defense of others). The other reason is utilitarian: the harms and risks of legalizing euthanasia, to individuals in general and to society, far outweigh any benefits.

When personal and societal values were largely consistent with each other, and widely shared because they were based on a shared religion, the case against euthanasia was simple: God or the gods (and, therefore, the religion) commanded "Thou shalt not kill." In a secular society, especially one that gives priority to intense individualism, the case for euthanasia is simple: Individuals have the right to choose the manner, time, and place of their death. In contrast, in such societies the case against euthanasia is complex.

Definitions

Definitions are a source of confusion in the euthanasia debate—some of it deliberately engendered by euthanasia advocates to promote their case.[1] Euthanasia is "a deliberate act that causes death undertaken by one person with the primary intention of ending the life of another person, in order to relieve that person's suffering."[2] Euthanasia is not the justified withdrawing or withholding of treatment that results in death. And it is not the provision of pain relief, even if it could or would shorten life, provided the treatment is necessary to relieve the patient's pain or other serious symptoms of physical distress and is given with a primary intention of relieving pain and not of killing the patient.

Secular Arguments against Euthanasia

1. *Impact on society.* To legalize euthanasia would damage important, foundational societal values and symbols that uphold respect for human life. With euthanasia, how we die cannot be just a private matter of self-determination and personal beliefs, because euthanasia "is an act that requires two people to make it possible and a complicit society to make it acceptable."[3] The prohibition on intentional

killing is the cornerstone of law and human relationships, emphasizing our basic equality.[4]

Medicine and the law are the principal institutions that maintain respect for human life in a secular, pluralistic society. Legalizing euthanasia would involve—and harm—both of them. In particular, changing the norm that we must not kill each other would seriously damage both institutions' capacity to carry the value of respect for human life.

To legalize euthanasia would be to change the way we understand ourselves, human life, and its meaning. To explain this last point requires painting a much larger picture. We create our values and find meaning in life by buying into a "shared story"—a societal-cultural paradigm. Humans have always focused that story on the two great events of each life, birth and death. Even in a secular society—indeed, more than in a religious one—that story must encompass, create space for, and protect the "human spirit." By the human spirit, I do not mean anything religious (although this concept can accommodate the religious beliefs of those who have them). Rather, I mean the intangible, invisible, immeasurable reality that we need to find meaning in life and to make life worth living—that deeply intuitive sense of relatedness or connectedness to others, the world, and the universe in which we live.

There are two views of human life and, as a consequence, death. One is that we are simply "gene machines." In the words of an Australian politician, when we are past our "best before" or "use by" date, we should be checked out as quickly, cheaply, and efficiently as possible. That view favors euthanasia. The other view sees a mystery in human death, because it sees a mystery in human life, a view that does not require any belief in the supernatural.

Euthanasia is a "gene machine" response. It converts the mystery of death to the problem of death, to which we then seek a technological solution. A lethal injection is a very efficient, fast solution to the problem of death—but it is antithetical to the mystery of death. People in postmodern societies are uncomfortable with mysteries, especially mysteries that generate intense, free-floating anxiety and fear, as death does. We seek control over the event that elicits that fear; we look for a terror-management or terror-reduction mechanism. Euthanasia is such a mechanism: While it does not allow us to avoid the cause of our fear—death—it does allow us to control its manner, time, and place—we can feel that we have death under control.

Research has shown that the marker for people wanting euthanasia is a state that psychiatrists call "hopelessness," which they differentiate from depressions[5]—these people have nothing to look forward to. Hope is our sense of connection to the future; hope is the oxygen of the human spirit.[6] Hope can be elicited by a sense of connection to a very immediate future, for instance, looking forward to a visit from a loved person, seeing the sun come up, or hearing the dawn chorus. When we are dying, our horizon comes closer and closer, but it still exists until we finally cross over. People need hope if they are to experience dying as the final great act of life, as it should be. Euthanasia converts that act to an act of death.

A more pragmatic, but nevertheless very important, objection to legalizing euthanasia is that its abuse cannot be prevented, as recent reports on euthanasia in the Netherlands have documented.[7] Indeed, as a result of this evidence some former advocates now believe that euthanasia cannot be safely legalized and have recently spoken against doing so.[8]

To assess the impact that legalizing euthanasia might have, in practice, on society, we must look at it in the context in which it would operate: the combination of an aging population, scarce health-care resources, and euthanasia would be a lethal one.

2. *Impact on medicine.*[9] Advocates often argue that euthanasia should be legalized because physicians are secretly carrying it out anyway. Studies[10] purporting to establish that fact have recently been severely criticized on the grounds that the respondents replied to questions that did not distinguish between actions primarily intended to shorten life—euthanasia—and other acts or omissions in which no such intention was present—pain-relief treatment or refusals of treatment—that are not euthanasia.[11] But even if the studies were accurate, the fact that physicians are secretly carrying out euthanasia does not mean that it is right. Further, if physicians were presently ignoring the law against murder, why would they obey guidelines for voluntary euthanasia?

Euthanasia "places the very soul of medicine on trial."[12] Physicians' absolute repugnance to killing people is necessary if society's trust in them is to be maintained. This is true, in part, because physicians have opportunities to kill not open to other people, as the horrific story of Dr. Harold Shipman, the British physician–serial killer, shows.

How would legalizing euthanasia affect medical education? What impact would physician role models carrying out euthanasia have on medical students and young physicians? Would we devote time to teaching students how to administer death through lethal injection? Would they be brutalized or ethically desensitized? (Do we adequately teach pain-relief treatment at present?) It would be very difficult to communicate to future physicians a repugnance to killing in a context of legalized euthanasia.

Physicians need a clear line that powerfully manifests to them, their patients, and society that they do not inflict death; both their patients and the public need to know with absolute certainty—and to be able to trust—that this is the case. Anything that would blur the line, damage that trust, or make physicians less sensitive to their primary obligations to protect life is unacceptable. Legalizing euthanasia would do all of these things.

Conclusion

Euthanasia is a simplistic, wrong, and dangerous response to the complex reality of human death. Physician-assisted suicide and euthanasia involve taking people who are at their weakest and most vulnerable, who fear loss of control or isolation and abandonment—who are in a state of intense "pre-mortem loneliness"[13]—and placing them in a situation where they believe their only alternative is to be killed or kill themselves.

Nancy Crick, a sixty-nine-year-old Australian grandmother, recently committed suicide in the presence of over twenty people, eight of whom were members of the Australian Voluntary Euthanasia Society. She explained: "I don't want to die alone." Another option for Mrs. Crick (if she had been terminally ill—an autopsy showed Mrs. Crick's colon cancer had not recurred) should have been to die naturally with people who cared for her present and good palliative care.

Of people who requested assisted suicide under Oregon's Death with Dignity Act, which allows physicians to prescribe lethal medication, 46 percent changed their minds after significant palliative-care interventions (relief of pain and other symptoms), but only 15 percent of those who did not receive such interventions did so.[14]

How a society treats its weakest, most in need, most vulnerable members best tests its moral and ethical tone. To set a present and future moral tone that protects individuals in general and society, upholds the fundamental value of respect for life, and promotes rather than destroys our capacities and opportunities to search for meaning in life, we must reject euthanasia.

Notes

1. Margaret Somerville, "Death Talk: The Case Against Euthanasia and Physician-Assisted Suicide" (Montreal: McGill Queen's University Press, 2001), p. xiii.

2. Ibid.

3. D. Callahan, "When Self-Determination Runs Amok," *Hastings Center Report* 1992, 22(2): 52–55.

4. House of Lords. Report of the Select Committee on Medical Ethics (London: HMSO, 1994).

5. H.M. Chochinov, K.G. Wilson, M. Enns, et al. "Depression, Hopelessness, and Suicidal Ideation in the Terminally Ill," *Psychosomatics* 39 (1998): 366–70, "Desire for Death in the Terminally Ill," *American Journal of Psychiatry* 152 (1995): 1185–1191.

6. Margaret Somerville, *The Ethical Canary: Science, Society and the Human Spirit* (Toronto: Viking/Penguin, 2000).

7. K. Foley and H. Hendin, editors, *The Case Against Assisted Suicide: For the Right to End-of-Life Care* (Baltimore: The Johns Hopkins University Press, 2002).

8. S.B. Nuland, "The Principle of Hope," *The New Republic* OnLine 2002: May 22.

9. This section is based on Margaret Somerville, " 'Death Talk': Debating Euthanasia and Physician-Assisted Suicide in Australia," *AMAJ* February 17, 2003.

10. H. Kuhse, P. Singer, P. Baume, et al. "End-of-Life Decisions in Australian Medical Practice," *Med J Aust* 166 (1997): 191–96.

11. D.W. Kissane, "Deadly Days in Darwin," K. Foley, H. Hendin, editors, *The Case Against Assisted Suicide: For the Right to End-of-Life Care,* pp. 192–209.

12. W. Gaylin, L. Kass, E.D. Pellegrino, and M. Siegler, "Doctors Must Not Kill," *JAMA* 1988; 259:2139–2140.

13. J. Katz, *The Silent World of Doctor and Patient* (New York: Free Press, 1984).

14. K. Foley and H. Hendin. "The Oregon Experiment," in K. Foley, H. Hendin, editors, *The Case Against Assisted Suicide: For the Right to End-of-Life Care,* p. 269.

CHALLENGE QUESTIONS

Should the Terminally Ill Be Able to Have Physicians Help Them Die?

- Both sides agree that improved palliative care and pain management are essential for end of life care. Why do you think the medical system is not effective with such types of care?
- Both sides imply that our attitudes toward the process of death reflect broader attitudes toward the lifespan. What are some attitudes about lifespan development embedded in this issue, and why do they matter?
- Hull argues that allowing physician-assisted suicide has the somewhat paradoxical effect of improving the amount of attention we pay to the dying process. Why is the dying process so hard for people to acknowledge as important and complex?
- Sommerville argues that it is wrong to kill no matter the circumstances. Have social changes and technological possibilities changed the meaning of similar moral codes?
- Lifespan development scholars often refer to the idea that society has a responsibility to ensure people experience a "good death." What do you think a "good death" might look like?

Suggested Readings

I. Dowbiggin, *A Merciful End: The Euthanasia Movement in Modern America* (Oxford University Press, 2002)

R. Henig, "Will We Ever Arrive at the Good Death?" from *The New York Times Magazine* (August 7, 2005)

S. Kaufman, *And a Time to Die: How American Hospitals Shape the End of Life* (University of Chicago Press, 2006)

D. Kuhl, *What Dying People Want: Practical Wisdom for the End of Life* (Public Affairs, 2003)

S. Nuland, *How We Die: Reflections on Life's Final Chapter* (Knopf, 1994)

M. Webb, *The Good Death: The New American Search to Reshape the End of Life* (Bantam, 1997)

Contributors to This Volume

EDITOR

ANDREW M. GUEST is a developmental psychologist and faculty member in the department of social and behavioral sciences at the University of Portland. He has research experience investigating development in impoverished communities, studying culture in relation to social development during middle childhood, and evaluating the influence of extracurricular activities during adolescence. He also has experience working with programs focused on enhancing lifespan development for disadvantaged populations in the United States, Malawi, Mexico, and Angola. He received a B.A. from Kenyon College in psychology, an M.S. from Miami University in sports studies, and a M.A. and Ph.D. from the University of Chicago's Committee on Human Development.

AUTHORS

THE AMERICAN PSYCHOLOGICAL ASSOCIATION represents psychology researchers and professionals in the United States. It is the largest association of psychologists in the world.

DANIEL R. ANDERSON is a professor of psychology at the University of Massachusetts–Amherst. He does research on television, children, and cognitive development, while also serving as an advisor to television shows including *Sesame Street* and *Dora the Explorer.*

JEFFREY JENSEN ARNETT is a research professor in the Department of Psychology at Clark University. He has done extensive scholarly work on the concept of "emerging adulthood" as a lifespan stage between adolescence and adulthood, including publishing a book titled *Emerging Adulthood: The Winding Road from the Late Teens Through the Twenties.*

ROY F. BAUMEISTER is the Francis Eppes Eminent Scholar and a member of the social psychology faculty at Florida State University. A Ph.D. from Princeton University, Baumeister is an expert in self and identity and the author of several books.

MARIAH BLAKE is a journalist, and a former assistant editor at the Columbia Journalism Review.

GWEN J. BROUDE teaches developmental psychology and cognitive science at Vassar College and is the director of the college's Cognitive Science Program. She is the editor of cross-cultural encyclopedias on growing up and marriage, family, and relationships.

JENNIFER D. CAMPBELL is an emeritus professor of psychology at the University of British Columbia. Her research has focused on self-concept, perfectionism, and adjustment.

CHRISTINE CHANG-SCHNEIDER is a doctoral student in clinical, social, and personality psychology at the University of Texas.

ANDREW J. CHERLIN is the Benjamin H. Griswold, III, Professor of Public Policy in the Department of Sociology at the Johns Hopkins University. He is an expert on the sociology of the family, and is the author of the text *Public and Private Families: An Introduction.*

TIMOTHY J. DAILEY is a research fellow at the Center for Marriage and Family Studies of Family Research Council. He has a Ph.D. in Religion from Marquette University.

JACQUELYNNE S. ECCLES is a professor of psychology and education at the University of Michigan. She is a national expert on adolescent development, and a past president of the Society for Research on Adolescence.

PAUL EHRLICH is the Bing Professor of Population Studies in the Department of Biological Sciences at Stanford University. He is an expert in population and natural resource issues, and is a prominent voice in concerns about global overpopulation.

JULIE JUOLA EXLINE is a member of the Department of Psychology at Case Western Reserve University. Dr. Exline specializes in research about religious and spiritual struggles as they relate to morality and humanity's relationship with God.

THE FEDERAL TRADE COMMISSION BUREAU OF ECONOMICS STAFF is part of the United States Government agency responsible for ensuring consumer protection and competitive business practices. The Bureau of Economics is specifically charged with analyzing the impact of regulations on consumers and competition.

MARCUS FELDMAN is a professor of biological sciences at Stanford University, with primary research focusing on the interaction of biological and cultural evolution.

JONATHAN L. FREEDMAN is a professor emeritus of psychology at the University of Toronto and has focused a great deal of his work on the effects of media violence on aggression.

MICHAEL FUMENTO is an author, journalist, and attorney specializing in science and health issues. He has written for numerous newspapers and magazines and his work has been nominated for the National Magazine Award.

FRANK F. FURSTENBERG, JR. is a professor of sociology and a research associate in the Population Studies Center at the University of Pennsylvania. He has been chair of the MacArthur Foundation Research Network on the Transition to Adulthood and co-editor of *On the Frontiers of Adulthood: Theory, Research, and Public Policy.*

HOWARD GARDNER is professor of cognition and education at the Harvard Graduate School of Education and founder of *Project Zero,* a research group to aid development of personalized curriculum designed for multiple intelligences (the theory Gardner is most known for). Winner of numerous honors in the fields of education and psychology, Garner is also author of more than twenty books.

ELIZABETH HAMEL is a senior research associate in Public Opinion and Media Research for the Kaiser Family Foundation.

ANGEL L. HARRIS is on the faculty of Princeton University in the Department of Sociology. His research focuses on academic inequality.

JUDITH RICH HARRIS has psychology degrees from Brandeis and Harvard Universities and has authored several textbooks in developmental psychology, most notably *The Child* and *Infant and Child.* She is an expert in child environments, parenting, and the nature-vs.-nurture question.

MARTHA B. HOLSTEIN has taught at DePaul University and has a Ph.D. in medical ethics from the University of Texas Medical Branch.

RICHARD T. HULL is professor emeritus of philosophy at the State University of New York at Buffalo and an expert on biomedical ethics.

ROBERT L. KAHN is a professor emeritus in psychology and public health at the University of Michigan, where he also founded the Institute for Social Research. A former fellow at the Center for Advanced Study in the Behavioral Sciences at Stanford University, Dr. Kahn's research has concentrated on organizational behavior and aging.

THE KAISER FAMILY FOUNDATION describes itself as "a non-profit, private operating foundation dedicated to providing information and analysis on health care issues to policymakers, the media, the health care community, and the general public."

JOACHIM I. KRUEGER is on faculty in the Department of Psychology at Brown University and specializes in self-perception, particularly as it relates to the egocentric processes of self-enhancement and social projection.

KATIE LARSEN McCLARTY received a Ph.D. in social psychology from the University of Texas and works as a research scientist with Pearson Educational Measurement.

MEL LEVINE is founder of All Kinds of Minds, an institute for understanding different types of learning. Dr. Levine is a professor of pediatrics at the University of North Carolina School of Medicine.

JOSEPH L. MAHONEY is a developmental psychologist and associate professor in the Department of Education at the University of California, Irvine. He was formerly on the psychology faculty at Yale, and recently edited the book *Organized Activities as Contexts of Development*.

GARY MARCUS is the director of the NYU Infant Language Learning Center, and a professor of psychology at New York University. His books include *The Birth of the Mind*, *The Algebraic Mind*, and *The Norton Psychology Reader*.

SHERRI McCARTHY is professor of educational psychology at Northern Arizona University and a former Fulbright scholar.

MEREDITH MINKLER is a faculty member in the School of Public Health at the University of California, Berkeley with a specialty in health and social behavior.

DAVID G. MYERS is a social psychologist with research interests in happiness and spiritual well-being. A professor of psychology at Hope College, Meyers has written several popular psychology textbooks and multiple other scholarly books.

TIFFANY A. PEMPEK completed her doctoral work at the University of Massachusetts–Amherst and is now a post-doctoral research fellow at the Georgetown University Children's Digital Media Center.

STEVEN PINKER is a specialist in language and cognition and professor of psychology at Harvard University. His books include *How the Mind Works* and *The Blank Slate*.

C. CYBELE RAVER is a faculty member in applied psychology at New York University and the director of NYU's Institute of Human Development and Social Change. She previously held faculty positions at the University of Chicago and Cornell University, with research focusing primarily on the well-being of children and families.

VICTORIA RIDEOUT is a vice president for media and public education at the Kaiser Family Foundation, where she directs the Program for the Study of Entertainment Media and Health.

ALVIN ROSENFELD graduated from Harvard Medical School and works in private practice doing child and adult psychiatry. He is also an associate psychiatrist at Massachusetts General Hospital and serves on the Board of Governors for Harvard Medical School's Center for Mental Health and Media.

JOHN W. ROWE, M.D. is currently on the faculty of Columbia University Mailman School of Public Health, after retiring as Chairman and CEO of Aetna, Inc., one of the nation's leading healthcare organizations. Formerly a professor of medicine and founding director of the Division on Aging at Harvard Medical School, he leads the MacArthur Foundation's Initiative on An Aging Society.

TIMOTHY A. SALTHOUSE is the Brown-Forman Professor of Psychology in the Department of Psychology at the University of Virginia, and an expert on cognition and aging.

CARMI SCHOOLER is the Chief of the Section on Socio-Environmental Studies at the National Institute of Mental Health. He has done extensive research on how environmental conditions influence psychological functioning as people age.

NANCY SIGNORIELLI is a professor in the department of communication at the University of Delaware. She does research on the effects of mass media images.

MARGARET SOMERVILLE is a professor on the Faculty of Medicine at McGill University in Montreal, Quebec, Canada. She is also the founding director of the McGill Centre for Medicine, Ethics and Law.

ELIZABETH S. SPELKE is the Marshall L. Berkman Professor of Psychology at Harvard University, and is an award winning scholar with particular expertise in infant cognitive development.

WILLIAM B. SWANN is professor in the Department of Psychology at the University of Texas. He is an expert on the social psychology of self and identity.

JEAN TWENGE is a faculty member in the department of psychology at San Diego State University. Her recent book is titled *Generation Me: Why Today's Young Americans Are More Confident, Assertive, Entitled—and More Miserable Than Ever Before.*

THE U.S. DEPARTMENT OF HEALTH AND HUMAN SERVICES is the United States government agency responsible for public health and social services. The department oversees several hundred programs, many of which serve disadvantaged populations.

KATHLEEN D. VOHS is a social psychologist, McKnight Land-Grant Professor in Marketing at the University of Minnesota, and former faculty member at the University of British Columbia.

THOMAS F. WATERS is a faculty member teaching criminal justice at Northern Arizona University.

ROGERS H. WRIGHT is a clinical psychologist and a fellow of the American Psychological Association.

ZERO TO THREE is a not-for-profit organization working to promote the healthy development of infants and toddlers.

EDWARD F. ZIGLER is emeritus director of the Zigler Center in Child Development and Social Policy at Yale University. Zigler is the author of several books, including *Children's Play* and *The First Three Years and Beyond*, and was closely involved with developing the federal Head Start preschool program.